A DRAMATIC
CENTER-OF-INTEREST
CORNER

Unusual interest and effectiveness is given to this corner by carefully thought-out grouping and color-contrast. The divan, with the large mirror above it, provides informal balance for the group formed by the tall window, together with the early 19th Century portrait and the tripod-stand. Formal balance is used in the arrangement of the coffee table and Directoire armchairs, also the two green chairs glimpsed in the foreground. The plain dark wall, popular in Directoire and Empire interiors, is a perfect foil for the richly brilliant fabric of drapery and upholstery material, in a striped pattern characteristic of those periods. Note how the quiet cloud-gray carpet softens the whole effect, making the vivid colors seem striking but not restless. The sculptured pile of the carpet is a popular modern device used to achieve a light-and-shadow effect without too-obvious pattern — especially desirable in a room like this with plain walls and bold stripes in upholstery and hangings.

CONVENIENT CORNER
FOR HOME OFFICE
OR STUDY

The picture above shows how a small unused maid's room can be converted into a home office. A similar arrangement could be used in any living room to make a corner into a center-of-interest nook for reading, study, or "home work." The simple but effective design of the space-saving wall shelves could be easily copied by the home craftsman. The sturdy desk has drawers for storage, and the chair is comfortable as well as colorful.

The Complete Book of

INTERIOR DECORATING

The Complete Book of

INTERIOR DECORATING

by

Mary Derieux

and

Isabelle Stevenson

New York • GREYSTONE PRESS • *1951*

PRINTED IN THE UNITED STATES OF AMERICA BY
KINGSPORT PRESS, INC., KINGSPORT, TENNESSEE

IN GRATEFUL ACKNOWLEDGMENT AND APPRECIATION . . .

To all those whose sincere interest and cooperation have been of inestimable value in gathering and preparing material for this book, may we extend our thanks.

For many of the illustrations which enrich its pages, we take this opportunity to thank the following organizations and persons:

Abraham & Straus; B. Altman & Company; Aluminum Company of America; illustrations on pages 172, 175, by courtesy of Aluminum Window Corporation; American Gas Association; American Walnut Manufacturers' Association; photographs on pages 26, 27, 96, 149, 194, 203, 296, 318, 331, 348, by courtesy of Amsterdam Textiles; *Architectural Forum*, and Architects Kem Weber, Victor Civkin; *Architectural Record*, and Architect Gardner Dailey; photographs on page 377 by courtesy of the makers of Armstrong's Asphalt Tile, those on pages 6, 42–43, 71, 356, 384–385, by courtesy of the makers of Armstrong's Linoleum; Artek-Pascoe, Furniture; Baker Furniture, Inc., and Manor House; Barker Brothers; photographs on pages 44, 52, 107, 184, 309, by courtesy of *Better Homes & Gardens* Magazine; Bigelow-Sanford Carpet Company, Inc.; Bloomingdale's; Blue Ridge Glass Corporation; Cabin Crafts (Bed Spreads); Callaway Mills; Carson Pirie Scott & Company; Charm Magazine; Cyrus Clark Company, Inc., Drapery Fabrics; Cotton Textile Institute, Inc.; Plumbing and Heating Supplies; Deltox Rug Company; F. M. Demarest, Photographer; Detroit Steel Products Company, Manufacturers of Fenestra Windows; Donley Brothers Company, Fireplaces; E. I. du Pont de Nemours & Company; Drix Duryea, Photographer; Fred Eldean, Photographer; Fir-Tex Insulating Board Company; General Electric Company; Georg Jensen, Inc.; Gimbels; Glidden Company, Paints; Gold Seal Congoleum, Kearny, N. J.; H. Leo Gould, Inc., Chinese Importers; Gribbon Company, Inc., Linens; Hammacher Schlemmer & Company, Inc.; Hedrich-Blessing Studio, Photographers; Mattie Edwards Hewitt, Photographer; Louis Hoeberman, Photographer; Imperial Glass Corporation; International Pictures, Inc.; International Silver Company; The Irish Linen Guild; Jiffy Join, Inc., Fasteners; Johns-Manville Corp., H. L. Judd Company, Inc., Drapery Fixtures; Kalamazoo Stove & Furnace Company; Katzenbach & Warren, Inc., Wallpaper; Kirsch Company, Drapery Fixtures; Klearflax Rug Company; *Ladies' Home Journal*; Lewis & Conger; Libbey Glass; Loeser's; Raymond Loewy Associates, Architects; Lord & Taylor; R. H. Macy & Company; *Mademoiselle* Magazine; Mahogany Association, Inc.; Mayer & Whittlesey, Architects; James McCreery & Company; Dana Merrill, Photographer; Jacques Mersereau; The Metropolitan Museum of Art; Modernage, Furniture; Modernfold Doors by Newcastle Products, floors by Armstrong Cork Company; *My Baby* Magazine; Nahigian Brothers, Inc., Rugs; photographs on pages 53, 121, 141, 143, 168, 234, 296, 342–343, 344–345, 350–351, 376, 394, 417, by courtesy of Nairn Linoleum, Kearny, N. J.; The Namm Store; *The New York Times*; Old Hickory Furniture Company; Owens-Illinois Glass Company; Paulsen Studios, Photographer Charles Kanarian; Pittsburgh Plate Glass Company; Plan-Tech Associates, Architects Joseph P. Richardson and H. Jackson, and Photographer Paul Davis; *Popular Home*, and De-Je Studios; RKO Radio Pictures, Inc.; Gilbert Rohde, Peggy Ann Rohde, Designers; Rohm & Haas Company, for photographs of Plexiglas Products; David O. Selznick's "Since You Went Away"; Julius Shulman, Photographer; Singer Sewing Machine Company; W. and J. Sloane; Sohmer & Company, Inc., Pianos; Raphael S. Soriano, Designer; Standard Coated Fabrics—Courtesy of Sanforized; Stern Brothers; Roger Sturtevant, Photographer; Styne & Ballard, Inc.—interiors and furniture designed by Alexander F. Styne; Textron, Inc.; L. Bamberger & Company; Richard E. Thibaut, Inc., Wallpaper; The Upson Company, Upson Panels; United Wallpaper, Inc.; United States Gypsum Company; United States Plywood Corporation—Weldwood; Hans Van Ness, Photographer; Arthur S. Vernay, Inc., Antiques; Sherle Wagner, Closet Engineer; Wallpaper Guild; Weathervane Co., Inc., Furniture; Western Pine Association; Westinghouse Electric Corporation; Whitehead Monel Kitchens; photographs on pages 420–421 by courtesy of *Woman's Day*—picture on page 422 photographed by Robert Coates; Woodhall Fabrics; photographs on pages 246, 259, 269, by courtesy of The Art Institute of Chicago—European and American Rooms in Miniature, by Mrs. James Ward Thorne; illustrative material for Period Charts, *Decorating Bulletin—The Principal Periods of Furniture Design Since the Twelfth Century*—prepared by Meyric R. Rogers, Curator of Decorative Arts at the Art Institute of Chicago, for the Good Housekeeping Studio of Architecture, Building and Furnishing.

Full color illustrations courtesy of Bigelow-Sanford Carpet Company, Inc.—Serenade rug, page 86 (upper picture), Beauvais and Cassandra rug, page 150; Drexel Furniture Company—from the Precedent Collection, pages 70, 167, 182, 198, 354, 371 (lower picture), 387; E. I. du Pont de Nemours & Company—Peter Hunt Designs, page 151; Flexalum, page 116; Glidden Company, Manufacturers of Paint Products—pages 370, 403; Gold Seal Congoleum, Kearny, N. J.—page 183; B. F. Goodrich Company—Karoseal Upholstery, jacket picture; David E. Kennedy, Inc.—pages 7 (upper picture), 386; A. M. Karagheusian, Inc.—Gulistan Renaissance Carpets, pages 6 (upper picture), 22; *Popular Home*, U. S. Gypsum Company—pages 23, 71, 199, 355, 402; Rich's, Inc.—page 86 (lower picture); *Woman's Home Companion*—page 87; Nairn Linoleum, Kearny, N. J.—page 7 (lower picture).

WITH EQUALLY GRATEFUL APPRECIATION . . .

to Karen Hollis, Myrtle Fahsbender, Irma Hopper, and Clara Bjorkman, for assistance, criticism, and advice; and to Charlotte D. Adams, who wrote the chapter "Remodeling Furniture."

Contents

The Complete Book of
INTERIOR DECORATING

The living room pictured is cool and spacious in soft background tones of green; the fabric patterns and accessories are of warm geranium pink. Twin love seats, tables and reading lamps provide comfort and proper lighting for a fireplace grouping. The large painting over the mantel adds importance to the central wall flanked by two tall windows, while the table-and-picture grouping at the right provides a second center of interest which balances the fireplace wall.

The room is an interesting example of the charm which may result from harmonizing traditional with modern furnishings. 18th Century French influence is shown in the curves of the mantel, the picture frame above it, and the large table at the right. A colorful print from India furnished the design used here for draperies and slip covers in beige, green and pink. The traditional table is finished in modern style with natural bleached wood tones and fitted with sliding sections which

CHAPTER ONE

How to Begin

INTERIOR DECORATING as applied to the home is probably the oldest of all arts. When properly understood, it turns out to be also the most friendly and approachable. This is partly because it is based upon an essentially simple formula—beauty plus utility, worked out within the framework of each family's requirements.

To decorate your own home successfully you have only to apply the formula, adapted to your budget. This has never before been so easy, so interesting, so richly rewarding as it is today. Designers, inventors and manufacturers have combined to open up a fascinating new world of styles and materials while still utilizing the best of the old.

It is not necessary to delve deeply into historical backgrounds, to master intricacies of periods and styles, in order to get the most fun and the most profit out of decorating your own home. It is only necessary to find out what you want, then follow a few basic rules and be alert to new developments in the field. The essence of contemporary "style" is to mingle freely any good, time-tested features from the past with the latest innovations of modern designers. Half a dozen easily understood principles will enable you to work out combinations and arrangements which will be appropriate and therefore satisfying, no matter what type of room you are planning.

DECORATING MADE EASY

Decorating a room, or a whole house, is simplified if you make a careful analysis of yourself and your family before you begin—what you like, what you want, what you do, what you hope to do someday. Put the whole thing down on paper. Be guided by this analysis in your choice of furniture, accessories, color schemes, arrangements. Don't be afraid to give expression to your own taste in making your selections. It is *your* home. With a little guidance you can decorate it more successfully than any outsider because you know better than anyone else what will appeal to your family and take care of their various needs. Don't be afraid to experiment. There are so

MODERN MANNER

pull out to seat a number of guests. Early 19th Century chairs have seats in green and white stripes matching the modern arm chair in light bleached wood drawn up to the table—which doubles as a desk when not in use for dining. The old painting over the mantel and the well-arranged group of old prints on the wall seem quite at home with the modern cotton rug in large squares of dark green, chartreuse and geranium pink. Modern shades top quaint old lamp bases.

3

many clever camouflage, conversion and cover-up tricks to be learned that a mistaken purchase seldom needs to be written off as a loss. The salvaged article may prove even more attractive when you get through with it than if it had been right in the first place. You will have made it really yours by application of your own imagination and your own ingenuity.

PROBLEMS ANSWERED AT A GLANCE

It may be helpful to visualize each room in your home as a stage which you can furnish and decorate to provide a comfortable, pleasant setting for the personalities and activities of the people who will use it. Into a certain fixed space must be fitted equipment for whatever special purpose a room is designed to fulfill, arranged to combine comfort and convenience with an attractive appearance. There is nothing difficult about this combination. A high degree of usefulness in furniture for any room in the house implies sturdiness of construction, simplicity of line, excellence of finish—all qualities which have a certain beauty in their own right and at the same time provide the best possible foundation for decorating a really livable home.

Probably the most universal of all decorating problems is how to relieve the monotony of sameness. If you live in a house or apartment which differs very little from all the others around you, consider this as a challenge—a challenge to create a distinctive and individual atmosphere even in surroundings which may seem at first hopelessly drab and uninteresting. You can do it. In the chapters which follow, with their hundreds of photographs and illustrations, you will find useful knowledge, helpful suggestions, hours of delight and interest.

Because it is easier to understand and remember what is seen with the eye rather than pictured in words, you will find every important phase of home decorating illustrated by photographs and sketches. These serve a double purpose. Most of them have been selected so that each room picture not only

EFFECTIVE CONTRAST

This corner of the room which is shown on the preceding page adds another note to the happy blending between traditional and modern. Here the very useful modern chest of drawers, enameled pale green and decorated with a design of trailing ivy leaves in darker green, contrasts pleasantly with the rather elaborate traditional coffee table and lamp base. An equally attractive streamlined chest could be made by cutting down a small bureau to its foundation framework and drawers, refinishing, decorating with stencils or cutouts, and adding modern-style drawer pulls. The shadow box is another thing which can be made by using a large outmoded picture frame.

throws light upon the topic under discussion but also covers as many other points as possible. By means of careful analysis in descriptions which accompany the pictures these points are explained so that each picture tells the story of one successfully decorated room, together with the reasons underlying that success. There is such a wealth of illustrations that somewhere among them you will surely find a solution for any special problem you may have, or at least a suggestion which you can adapt to your needs.

As you look at the pictures and check them with the descriptions you will *see* what is meant by many decorators' terms. They will no longer seem abstract or confusing and you will soon be able to recognize all the basic principles you need for guidance. After that, success in applying them to your own rooms is only a short step ahead—a step which will lead you into many delightful decorating adventures while it opens new vistas into variety, usefulness, economy and beauty for your home.

IMPORTANCE OF A DECORATING PLAN

You don't have to be a draftsman and turn out a complicated blueprint or sketch of the room you are planning, as a professional decorator would do, but there is much to be learned from his approach. Most important is the simple matter of knowing where you are going before you start. You will find that formulating a plan—even the sketchiest outline—will clarify your ideas and help get you off on the right track. The more details you can fill in, the easier it will be to carry your decorating through to a successful conclusion and the fewer mistakes you will have to correct.

The first point to settle in working out a plan is purely practical—what is the room to be used for? An answer to this is comparatively easy because the chief function of a room is usually determined in advance by the architect or the builder. However, unless your home has been recently built to your own specifications, you may want to alter or add to the original functions of your room. In either case it is helpful to set down in detail every activity which is likely to be carried on there. Only in this way can all the important ones be provided for without crowding, confusion, or disturbance of the decorating effects you are trying to achieve.

From the artistic standpoint, a plan is as essential in decorating a room as a design would be if you were making a dress. To have charm a room must express the personality of the people who will live in it, just as a dress must be keyed to the individuality of the woman who will wear it. Before you take the first

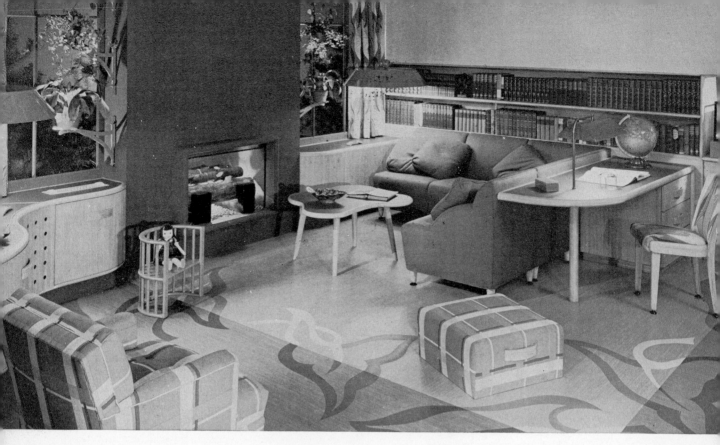

A ROOM PLANNED FOR ALL THE FAMILY

The living rooms facing each other on these pages illustrate two interpretations of comfort, convenience, and charm in contemporary living. The room above expresses "family life" in modern terms, relying for decoration upon color, texture, and large bold design rather than upon detail. Planned for active use, it is so compact that there is no feeling of clutter or confusion, thus demonstrating many points at which modern design comes to the assistance of today's busy homemakers. Every detail is engineered to combine comfort and safety for the children with ease of upkeep. There are no sharp corners. Even drawer and cabinet handles are curved. Lamps cannot be upset; they are anchored at just the right points for efficient lighting. Novel brackets lift flowerpots out of children's reach. Built-in book shelves and lighted aquarium are safely high, allowing for a convenient toy-storage cabinet below the aquarium. A radio-phonograph, sunk into the curved cabinet beneath the window, is protected from childish meddling. The coffee

steps in even a minor decorating adventure, analyze your own and your family's tastes and temperaments to make sure the new environment is harmonious.

Many people find it helpful to work out a greatly simplified version of the professional decorator's blueprint by cutting out tiny bits of cardboard in scale with the pieces of furniture in the room—or planned for it—and moving them about on a sheet of paper cut to the shape and scale of the floor. Others rely entirely upon charts and outlines. Your whole plan may be carefully worked out in detail, or it may be only a collection of rough notes. It depends upon your temperament. The important thing is to have it all down on paper, in some form, arranged so that you can refer to it easily and quickly.

If you have never tried it, you will be astonished to find out how much fun it is to keep a record of the things you need to make your home more efficient and the things you want to make it more charming. Best of all, when the time comes for redecorating

you will find the foundation for your plan already laid.

Once you become decoration-conscious you will discover helpful suggestions on every hand. Start an indexed scrapbook in which you can collect magazine articles, advertisements of new types of equipment and furnishings, room pictures and color schemes which appeal to you. Have a section where you can pin actual samples of colors and fabrics into your book, or provide convenient labeled pockets for keeping them. In another section, or in a card file, or in your reminder notebook, jot down carefully details you see and like in stores or in other people's houses.

Make the scrapbook a family affair, so that everyone's tastes and needs will be represented, or encourage each member of the family to keep one for himself. Set aside an evening every now and then for comparing notes, throwing out duplicate clippings and samples, bringing all the files and records up to

TRADITIONAL BEAUTY
KEYED TO COMFORT

The Georgian-American living room-library above is a faithful reproduction of the type of room popular in America shortly before the Revolution. Pine walls, in natural finish, are examples of the simple classical style in architectural details. The rich tapestry-like effect of many book bindings provides warmth and color against soft brown walls. An 18th Century desk, with traditional fittings, and the drop-leaf Pembroke table illustrate how well rich mahogany tones may blend with a semi-formal pine background. An American Chippendale armchair is upholstered in a textured fabric, of the same creamy color used for the satin brocade of a roomy sofa— traditional in feeling but modern in deep-seated comfort. The sculptured pile carpet, in soft green, provides a unifying color foundation for the room, while its carved pattern creates a pleasant light-and-shadow effect. In the traditional furniture group at lower right, a very modern note is struck in the upholstery material used for the 18th Century high-backed wing chair. Soft and lovely in appearance, this is one of the synthetic fabrics which make light colors practical even in the smokiest city. It sheds soot, grease, acid, water, and needs only soap and water to keep it permanently clean and new-looking.

LINOLEUM FOR A NEW HOME— OR REMODELING AN OLD ONE

A fireplace, books, comfortable chairs — these form the traditional nucleus of a home. In room above, asphalt tile makes an interesting floor, with the rich red of the squares repeated in wall linoleum used as a facing on the chimney breast. White against red is a very striking color arrangement, but here the simplicity of line keeps it from being flamboyant, and the use of black for accent also has a softening effect. Note how well the mahogany tones of the drum-shaped combination lamp-table-bookcase blend with the deep red of the asphalt tile, and how the chintz of the armchair at left of the fireplace repeats the white, red and black of the color scheme. The hallway and powder room at right illustrate how attractive a small entrance hall can be, with only the simplest of decorative treatment. The soft purplish gray of the linoleum blends charmingly with pastel lavender striped wallpaper and lavender woodwork. An inlaid border in the same pastel tone dresses up the floor so that no rug is necessary. A bit of rose-colored swag drapery, a wall clock reflected in a long mirror, a closet converted into a tiny powder room — these add up to a hall expressive of hospitality and charm. In both of these interiors, linoleum takes the place of carpeting or rugs, providing a much less expensive floor covering which will be excellent later on as a foundation if rugs are added. In many homes decorative linoleum is left uncovered for summer coolness, while rugs are placed over it for winter.

date. A game like this may uncover hidden decorating talents in some member of your family. This happens surprisingly often; it almost always results in a more lively interest in home affairs, with increased willingness to help in home upkeep and repairs.

Don't throw away manufacturers' labels from furniture, upholstery or fabrics. Learn to understand them. Keep them also in an easily accessible file. You will find them a mine of information which may prove very helpful when you are ready to buy.

In discussion of the easiest way to work out a complete and helpful plan it may be necessary to include some points which seem to have no application to your particular case—but consider carefully all those mentioned in this chapter before you decide that they should not be included in your calculations. Better put down all the headings which follow even if some of the spaces under them are left blank. As your plan grows you may find there are notations which should go there after all.

The preliminary analysis of your own special decorating problem should include answers to several definite questions listed below in the order of their importance. These answers will have—or should

have—a deciding influence upon various phases of your plan. Thinking them through in advance may save time and money. It may also prevent possible disappointment with your results. Write down the questions. Make written answers as complete and as honest as you can. Do not be afraid they will complicate your plan-making. On the contrary, they will simplify it for you and clarify it by automatically ruling out certain styles and types of decorating or furniture which you will see at once are not in harmony with answers you have made to various questions.

What Do You Need? A house may be a decorator's dream—or your own dream come true—but if it is not suited to the activities of your family they will never feel at home there. If they do not feel at home, then regardless of everything else, the house is a failure. So, in constructing your plan, first check your family's interests by listing all the things they must do, or would like to do, in the house, then tailor your furnishings and decorations to fit. This will mean a good deal of eliminating. If you have growing youngsters, for example, you will have to forego fragile furniture and delicate fabrics no mat-

BEAUTY AND COMFORT IN A COLONIAL SETTING

table is just the right height for a play table. Every table or cabinet surface is playproofed by a linoleum sheet, ending worry about spots and spills. The color scheme is as modern as the design. A light gray wall behind the book shelves sets off the rich colors of bindings, tones into the light natural finish of the wood in the room. This soft beige-gray is repeated in the off-center panel, set into a blue jaspé linoleum floor with inlaid elephant-ear motifs. The room below, with Early American decorations and furnishings, is as traditional

as the other one is modern. With its quaint figured wallpaper and frilled window draperies, it has a woven cotton wall-to-wall rug modern in size and weave but Colonial in feeling. The furniture is in soft dark natural finish pine, with all accessories in harmonizing style. The simple appeal of many Early American rooms is exemplified here in the fireplace treatment, with its narrow, graceful mantel shelf—note the ingenious device for parking baby built into the old fireplace bench—occupied here by a child's doll.

ter how much they may appeal to you. Children are always happiest in a home which will take a little hard usage.

Make a list of questions such as these to ask yourself: Is my family informal, fond of games, sports and hobbies? Or are they quiet, studious, artistic? Does my husband want a home primarily to relax in, or must it also be a business asset which will create a certain impression upon outsiders? Will we need facilities for formal entertaining? For overnight guests? For frequent children's parties? Questions like these should be answered frankly, with a complete list of all important family activities. This will have much to do with the success of your final plan.

ASK THESE QUESTIONS BEFORE YOU BUY

In deciding the type of furnishings you need, don't forget the question of how much care they will require. Figure out roughly the amount of time you want to spend in cleaning and caring for your home, also how much you can afford to pay for various types of professional services. Then adjust your decorating program accordingly. If you have to handle a house with one hand and a job with the other, if you like to have time for outside activities, if for any reason your time and strength are limited, you should make simplicity and ease of care major factors in your choice of furniture and decoration.

What Do You Like? No home can be successfully decorated merely by applying a set of rules. If it is to have warmth and charm it must reflect the tastes and interests of the people who live in it by means of a decorating program built around them and for them. It must express their personality. Analyzing this element of individual taste, to decide what you like and do not like, often does away with more decorating complications than any of the other points mentioned in this chapter. And it should. Never let yourself be sold on a plan, a style, or even a single article you do not like. If it does not appeal to you, it is not right for you no matter how "correct" or how "smart" it may be. Guard against fads. A decorating fad often proves very expensive.

Rely upon your own taste—but begin at the same time to educate it in every possible way. This is not hard to do, but you must keep an open mind. It is just as much a mistake to close your mind to all decorating ideas which happen to be new to you as it is to be swayed too easily by other people's opinions. You will find that in decorating, as in any art, good taste is usually only a matter of having some knowledge of the basic principles underlying the art. These provide a handy yardstick for measuring your own likes and dislikes. You may be one of the people who

seem able to decorate by instinct, just as others can play the piano or paint a picture without instruction, but you will still find it useful to understand certain rules of the craft. This knowledge will broaden your taste and at the same time provide a tool to help you get the results you want more easily and more quickly.

What Can You Afford? Your home should be as beautiful and as comfortable as you can make it; it should furnish a background for living which is both stimulating and quietly satisfying. But don't overload yourself with debt in order to achieve it. You cannot relax in a room, or enjoy it, if you are worried about paying for it. Counting the cost before you buy, not after, will keep you from getting beyond your financial depth. Here a carefully budgeted plan is just about your only protection. Obviously it will simplify your program by eliminating many things you do not really want or need as well as those you cannot afford. If it also rules out a few articles which would be very desirable, write them into your plan as future developments. They are worth waiting for.

What Are Your Plans for the Future? Are you settled down in your own home for a long stay, or are you starting out in more or less temporary quarters expecting to move soon? Is the size of your family fixed, or is it likely to increase? Many practical considerations such as these will influence your choice of a decorating scheme. The "five-year plan" which is wonderful for a family building or buying their own home would be meaningless for a young couple marking time in a tiny flat while waiting for promotion. But with a modest outlay—and a little "know how"—even the tiny flat can be made "home."

What Climate Do You Live In? This item is often a great simplifier. If your home or apartment building has been properly designed it will be built for comfort in the prevailing climate of the region. Well-planned furnishings in such a home will be in general harmony with the house and therefore with the climate. On the other hand, if your home is not adapted architecturally to its climatic background you can at least make up for it by the way you furnish and decorate the interior. In either case your choice is limited by suitability. If you live in a hot climate you will want to use cool, soft colors and create a feeling of space by opening up vistas between rooms. Where winters are long and cold you can create an atmosphere of warmth and comfort by use of deep, warm colors and heavy draperies, but you will have to rule out unnecessary openings, bare floors, plain airy backgrounds. If your weather year is fairly evenly divided between cold winters and hot summers, any decorating plan should supplement the warm furnishings planned for cold weather with cooling slip covers, rugs, and various hot weather replacements.

What Is the Architectural Style of the Building? If possible there should be a pleasing harmony between the general architectural style of a building and the furnishings planned for its interior. Your field of choice will be narrowed again if you take this into consideration. Early American, Colonial, Tudor, French Provincial, Pennsylvania Dutch, Mexican, American Southwest—these are only a few of the influences we trace in our house designs. In most cases what we call regional styles and period styles in furnishings grew up with certain types of architecture. Therefore, if the design of your home belongs to any well-defined type your most effective decorating formula will be to key your furnishings in some way to the house. If the house suggests

AVOID MISTAKES BY TRYING OUT SAMPLES

After you have worked out a decorating plan on paper, it must be translated into action. Look at the colors, designs in the place where they are to be used and under the lights there, both natural and artificial. Never guess how textures, colors, designs, or weaves go with each other. Put them side by side and be sure. In this picture you will see the advantage of taking home large samples of all materials to show the complete design and give the whole color picture. By placing one over the other, and shifting them around, you can really form an idea about how they will look in the room. Notice the useful nest of tables. The large table is twice the size of the small ones which slide under side by side instead of in the conventional manner, leaving enough space between the table tops to serve as a small shelf. The other table would make a convenient end table, with room for a lamp and accessories on top, magazines or books below.

a style of decorating you do not care for, try using a little imagination and ingenuity. Work out a plan in which a modified form of that background style provides a unifying flavor, then combine it with details which more nearly express your own taste. If your house is not regional or period, but just bad architecture, you may be able to offset some of the defects through your decorating. Aside from this, go ahead with any style which fits the rest of your program.

WHEN YOUR PLAN MUST COMBINE NEW FURNITURE WITH OLD

Even a bride seldom starts decorating with a clear field of choice before her. Usually she has gifts, possibly heirlooms, or just hand-me-downs, which have to be incorporated in her brand-new home. For many people the decorating problem is almost entirely one of refreshing, renovating or supplementing furniture and hangings already in use. If this is your case, intelligent planning is even more important than it would be if you were making a fresh start. Before you do anything else check all old furniture, hangings, floor coverings and accessories. Separate them into the following three groups, jotting down a little description of each piece you think you may be able to work into your decorating plan:

1. Articles which can be used as they are will include furniture, hangings, etc., in good condition and adaptable to the various color schemes and plans of decoration you work out.

2. Articles which need a certain amount of renovation will include wood furniture which can be restyled with hammer and saw, refinished, or decorated with paint and stencils; worn upholstery which can be replaced or concealed under slip covers; draperies which can be dyed, or remade by combining with new material; accessories which can be converted to usefulness or given more beauty—as when the meaningless "ornament" becomes a lamp base, or a lamp is transformed by a new shade.

3. Articles which must be entirely done over or discarded will include everything which is badly worn or damaged—as well as those fundamentally unsuitable. When you come to this third group be ruthless. Discard any article which does not, or cannot be made to, contribute some degree of beauty or comfort or both to the room you are planning. If a use for it can be found in some other room, transfer it there. If not, get rid of it. But consult the index for reclamation ideas before you throw anything away and be sure there really is no constructive use to which it can be adapted.

PLANS THAT GROW

Don't decorate in haste and repent at leisure. Even if you have the money to carry out your whole decorating program at once, don't be rushed into buying anything which will compromise the effect you want. After you have the few actual necessities for your room you can afford to give yourself the fun of searching out really distinctive pieces to complete it, accessories that are exactly right.

The ensemble idea is just as important in decorating a room as in assembling a woman's costume. Individually beautiful items, carelessly chosen and inharmonious with each other, will fail to create a charming and livable room. On the other hand, the simplest elements of decoration, combined with taste and care, may succeed in doing just that. Such a room will be pleasing at first sight to strangers. Also, it will "grow" on those who live with it.

Don't be discouraged if you have to operate on a budget. Decide what you can comfortably spend in the beginning and put most of it into basic pieces which will be a permanent investment in satisfaction and comfort. Then spread the rest of it out over makeshifts which will do until they can be replaced. These substitutes may be only stop-gaps until you can afford something better; or they may turn out so charming or so useful that you will not want to give them up.

Having worked over your plan until you are satisfied with it—and put it in writing—stick to it. Parts of it may need altering as you go along because you have found they can be improved, but make sure the improvements will fit into the original picture. Don't be tempted for the sake of a bargain, or for any other reason, to spend time or money on a single article which will not add to the effectiveness of your decorative scheme as you have outlined it.

The thing to remember is that you can spend a great deal of money, or a comparatively small sum, on the average room and get equally pleasing results. Decorating materials, for example, with lovely cheerful designs and colors are to be found in every price range. A charming and suitable piece of furniture may be a costly antique or it may be something you have picked up for a few dollars in a second-hand store and renovated yourself.

There are a thousand and one ways you have probably never thought of in which you may substitute time for money in furnishing your home. It is largely a matter of planning, of knowing what to buy, of doing things step by step if you can't manage them all at once. You will find that a little decorating knowledge pays dividends in better values as well as in satisfaction, comfort and pride in your home.

A ROOM THAT GREW WITH A PLAN

The three views shown here dramatize what may be done by working from, and with, a decorating plan carried out over a period of time. In the first sketch you will see the beginning of a room well planned for growth. There are two comfortable chairs with muslin covers, and Venetian blinds at the windows with a plain shaped valance to soften them a little. The background colors are green and beige, two of the most adaptable shades and therefore useful in a growing and changing room. The two inexpensive prints on the wall, the painted chair, the card table used for desk or refreshments, may look a bit sketchy but are adequate for actual needs. In the second picture another step has been taken to bring more color and life into the room. The chairs have been upholstered and a really fine mirror hung on the wall, surrounded by more of the inexpensive but quaintly Victorian framed prints. The card table has been put away for use as a card table, a small Duncan Phyfe drum table and a convenient magazine rack contribute new notes of convenience. In the third sketch the room has come of age. The edge of a couch can be made

out behind the useful combination tray and coffee table in the foreground. The addition of the couch allows for center-of-interest grouping of easy chairs near the window, which has now been dressed up with floor-length draw-curtains headed by the original valance. By waiting and saving up it was possible in this case to invest in a faithful reproduction of an old English table-desk which fits perfectly under the 18th Century-style mahogany and gilt mirror. A pair of fine antique wall sconces painted white dramatize the window and contrast with the modern mirror-frame of the picture at the left. The conversation group of couch and chairs is tied together by a colorful Oriental-style rug on the floor, which has been bare up to this point. If a room like this one had been furnished on a budget, all at once, these fine occasional pieces and accessories which give it real tone and atmosphere would have been out of the question. By making the compromise and using the transition plan of decorating, no money was wasted on useless or temporary furniture and the fine things were fitted into the budget with no strain at any time.

11

The comfortable living room above exemplifies many of the elements of room decoration mentioned in this chapter. A mood of serene dignity has been established by use of plain dark backgrounds and predominance of straight lines. Graciousness and charm are added by curving lines in accessories and light colors in slip covers. There is a touch of gaiety in the bright flowers. Note the high flower-stands flanking a

fern-filled fireplace, and the white wall-basket for flowers. An appearance of space provided by a mirrored panel above the fireplace is increased even more by mirrored folding screens at each side which open vistas by reflecting from different angles an oval mirror on the opposite wall. Optical balance is used in the grouping of the couch and end table facing two chairs with a lamp table between them. This is

CHAPTER TWO

How to Arrange Furniture

A HAPPY mingling of beauty, convenience and comfort is the objective of all home decorating. To insure this result in any room, planned furniture arrangement is just as important as planned buying. In both cases you need to know beforehand the effect you want, then find out the best and easiest ways to go about creating it. These "best and easiest ways" have all been worked out, tested, and written about by professional decorators. There is nothing to keep you from profiting by their experience, and getting their kind of results—rooms combining fundamental charm with professional trimness in finishing details.

MAKE DECORATING KNOWLEDGE WORK FOR YOU

Decorating standards are based upon a few general principles of what artists call "composition," none of them difficult to understand in connection with furnishing and decorating a room. A speaking acquaintance with them, also with some of the professional decorating terms most often used, will prove helpful as you study pictures of rooms which appeal to you.

Familiarity with a mere handful of decorators' rules, including methods and devices they have worked out to get their results, will give you confidence. This knowledge will make it easier for you both to recognize good ideas when you see them and adapt them to your own use—which is really all that is meant by *technique*. This is nothing more than the use of methods in any art or craft which have been proved by experience of skilled workers to be the best for producing a desired effect. In your decorating you will find this knowledge a handy

TO BE EXPENSIVE

one of the most satisfactory types of fireside groupings, providing for comfortable conversation, with space for one or more additional chairs to be brought up facing the fire. An arrangement such as this has dignity and balance, without stiffness. The trick of using mirrors effectively is worth learning, if you have a room which seems crowded or dark —just simple unframed panels are often the most effective.

CENTER-OF-INTEREST IN A CONVERSATION GROUPING

tool which you can use to save time and money as well as to avoid mistakes. You will see in the course of this chapter—and wherever it is mentioned in other parts of the book—how understandable a simple home-decorating technique can be and how easily you can take advantage of its friendly helpfulness in your own decorating adventures.

MOOD IS THE KEYNOTE IN ROOM DECORATION

The very first step to take in planning to furnish or do over a room is to determine the kind of mood you want it to express. Mood is a word we all know. In decorating it means exactly the same thing it

The early 19th Century dignity of the room above is given a feeling of formality by preponderance of tall up-and-down lines, offset by long low comfort-lines in the modern sofa and easy chairs, also in the huge low table in the center. Note the feminine touch in graceful curves of the draperies, in soft glass curtains. The mood of quiet dignity and restfulness in the studio-library-living room combination at the right would appeal to almost any man with a love of comfort and books. Paneled wood walls and soft dark horizontal lines combine to create a dignified feeling despite the small scale of the room. Dueling pistols, old maps, clipper ship pictures, shaggy rug texture and raised fireplace add interest to the room with its plain backgrounds and upholstery. Round table and lamps, with the arched fireplace and graceful winged chair, provide curved-line contrast and increase the feeling of ease. The chair-and-table grouping at the left, opposite the large sofa, is an example of successful optical balance.

means to you in your daily life. People speak of the atmosphere of a room, its tone, or the feeling it gives them. By these words they usually mean *mood* as expressed through choice of furnishings and decorations—as when an impression of cheerfulness is achieved, even in a dark cold room, through use of sunlight background colors and bright hangings. A little knowledge of how to use such factors as color, texture and arrangement will enable you to counteract undesirable features and to create almost any mood which appeals to you in almost any room.

You will find there are as many shades of mood to choose from as there are different types of dispositions, but most of them can be grouped under three general headings—gaiety, dignity, stimulation. Qualities such as restfulness, graciousness, charm, utility are independent of mood. Their presence, in some degree, adds attractiveness to any type of room or style of decoration. Having selected the mood to be established in your room, make sure it is reflected in each phase of your decorating program—style, color and arrangement.

Color is the decorator's handyman, called in to help solve almost any kind of problem. In establishing or changing the mood of a room it is particularly useful. It has been demonstrated in scientific tests that the colors surrounding you react upon you in certain definite ways—physically as well as mentally—according to the wave-lengths of their vibrations. You can bring the healing or disturbing, the relaxing or stimulating qualities of color into any room in your home. Knowing this, it is easy to see the connection between *mood* and *color*. In the suggestions given below to help you select the mood you want for your room you will notice the part often played by color.

Gay Rooms: Gaiety gives a lift to the spirits. You can create it by choosing bright, cheerful, light-reflecting colors, designs with a feeling of animation, lively patterns rather small in scale. It is best used in a cozy room where informality is desired, with a sense of intimacy and friendly welcome. Gay decorating is usually simple, often feminine in feeling, and almost always has a suggestion of youthfulness about it. These qualities make it especially appropri-

KEYED TO MASCULINE COMFORT

DINING ROOMS CAN BE DARING AND DIFFERENT

The rooms shown on these pages—approximately the same in size, proportions and purpose—dramatize the widely different moods which can be created by the type of decorating in an ordinary room. Both these rooms are dining rooms, but the one at the right is keyed primarily to family living, the one shown above to entertaining or formal home dining. The dramatic dining room in modern, exotic style exemplifies a stimulating mood, as well as novelty in theme. Here the theme is drawn from the boldly patterned textured fabric chosen for chair upholstery. Curved lines give comfortable ease to arm chairs used for dining, and increase the feeling of luxury in the room. These curves contrast interestingly with straight modern lines and classic floor border. The unusual background of black walls, with white ceiling and over-

mantel, is emphasized even more by black linoleum flooring, white inset border, and the cornice treatment which tops rich over-draperies used to frame both the wide window and the fireplace. Good wall-balance is illustrated here by a distinctive treatment which enlarges the area around the mirrored fireplace-facing to balance the wide window. Only sheer glass draw-curtains are used over this window—a necessary provision in a room where there are so many dark surfaces to absorb light. Against the dark wall the novel lines of a tall white lamp stand out in dramatic contrast, pouring light against a highly reflective ceiling. Glass and plastics used for small table, chandelier and fireplace fittings sparkle against the dark setting. The deep green of draperies is picked up from the flower picture above the mantel.

ate for nurseries, breakfast rooms, kitchens and small, home-like living rooms. A gay room may have a note of frivolity somewhere in its decoration, but the charm of gaiety is increased by a certain amount of reserve. It loses its meaning when it loses freshness and simplicity.

Dignified Rooms: Dignity is inherent in large, well-proportioned, high-ceilinged rooms. You can establish it by use of heavier furniture, darker color tones, more conservative designs. There is always a feeling of solidity associated with dignity, often of formality. Dining rooms, halls and libraries are especially adapted to dignified furnishings and decorations, also rooms where formal entertaining is to be done. It is a mature mood, more or less masculine, rather reserved, and often traditional in the English or the later Colonial manner. Try to introduce a touch of this dignity and masculine reserve into any room shared by the men of the family. At its best, dignity gives a feeling of restfulness and serenity to a room. Carried too far it becomes stiffness, severity, even austerity or somberness.

Stimulating Rooms: Stimulation in decorating is like the same quality in other phases of life—very desirable in moderation and in the right place. A stimulating room is arresting and dramatic. You can produce this mood by using strong, clear color tones with sharp contrasts, unusual and distinctive designs, bold patterns, all sorts of novel and striking effects. In its more extreme expression you will find the quality of stimulation most satisfactory if you confine it to the semi-public rooms of the house where restfulness is not needed—halls, dining rooms, game rooms, bars. However, a touch of it may provide a refreshing note in almost any room. Stimulation and sophis-

tication are often linked in modern decorating, sometimes merging in a luxurious or exotic type of furnishing rich with color, brilliance and lushness of the tropics. Strong values such as these should be used with great restraint in family living quarters.

BUILDING YOUR PLAN AROUND A THEME

Theme, as used in decorating, is any definite idea or motif which is employed as a device to introduce unity into a room by tying together the various elements of decoration. This obviously makes for harmony. One advantage of having such a theme is that it often suggests interesting details or color combinations which make your decorating selections easier, and give your room more individuality and distinction. Inspiration for a theme may be found almost anywhere, and may provide a very good method for keying your room to the tastes and interests of its occupants.

If some particular period or regional style—Georgian English or Pennsylvania Dutch, for example—has a special appeal for you, it will simplify your

GAY INFORMALITY FOR FAMILY DINING

In this sunlit, Colonial-style room the mood is cheerful and friendly. A gay, informal period flower theme is expressed through garden flowers in old vases on the tables as well as in the Colonial floral design in wallpaper. Soft tones in a woven cotton rug, predominantly straight lines in small-

scale furniture harmonize with the mood and proportions of the simple room. Monotony is avoided by introduction of curves in softly draped white glass curtains, rounded chair backs and circular flower containers, also by the interesting carved design of table and buffet legs.

INSPIRATION FROM AN EARLY NEW ENGLAND COTTAGE

The usefulness of theme for introducing unity into a room-picture is demonstrated in the photographs shown here. Both with regional motifs, they are widely different. Each theme results in a distinctive room treatment and in each room the mood harmonizes with the theme. In the small living room on this page, a Colonial-American background with scenic-type wallpaper is combined with simple maple furniture in natural finish and checked gingham slip covers. This establishes a cheerful, friendly mood—informal, with a note of rustic quaintness appropriate to the period which supplies the theme. A pleasant mingling of straight lines with curves softens the plainness of natural wood finishes and the simplicity of the painted wood chimney breast. Notice how the Early American theme is repeated in all the accessories. The one modern note—the rush rug made from woven squares—harmonizes perfectly with the atmosphere of country living suggested by the Colonial theme. Notice the small scale of the comfortable chairs, love seat,

tables and cabinet. It does not lessen their comfort but helps them fit into the scale of the room without crowding. The wall mirror at the left helps make the small, cozy room seem larger. The blue-green used for woodwork and repeated in the design color of the wallpaper is cool, restful, suggestive of space. A note of cheer and warmth is introduced by the wine-red upholstery plaid. The room opposite (right) is as distinctly a product of its theme as the other one. In this case everything speaks of the American Southwest from which the theme is taken, expressed in a modern adaptation which stresses comfort and harmonizes with colorful Mexican and Indian decorations. Straight draperies and structural lines, contrasted with curves in the fireplace area, coffee table and couches, complete a fireplace grouping with identical balance. Interesting texture in the rug of nubby cotton harmonizes with the weave, design and texture of drapery and upholstery fabrics inspired by primitive weaves and patterns found in that part of the country.

problem. Tradition will help by providing many decorating examples for you to follow, and historical or regional themes will be automatically suggested. In such a case the theme often runs through a number of rooms, giving an impression of unity to the entire house. The theme-sources noted below have

been drawn upon by many people as inspiration for successful rooms, but no list could be complete. Use these suggestions to stimulate your imagination, then develop some ideas of your own.

Special Interests and Occupations are fruitful sources of inspiration for themes. A room may be

18

designed around music, books, trophies, hobbies or sports.

Collections of Decorative Objects, appropriately displayed, provide interesting and highly personalized themes. They are at their best in surroundings more or less keyed to them in historical or regional feeling. For instance, a collection of Early American glass may be doubly attractive against the background of a simple Colonial room.

Any Article of Furniture or Any Accessory which has some special beauty or interest may well be used to suggest a theme. A Chinese vase may inspire a whole room worked out in traditional Chinese Chippendale style or in dramatic Chinese Modern.

Pictures are probably the most satisfactory of all theme-providers because of their definite idea value and their wide variety of subject matter. Obviously a set of quaint Currier and Ives prints would call for an atmosphere of 19th Century American furnishings, adapted and modified to provide present-day comfort and simplicity of line. A fine old portrait in oil would suggest the more formal decorative style of the Colonial Federal period or 18th Century English. The characteristics of what we call the modern school of painters—such as Matisse, Degas,

Picasso and many others—adapt themselves perfectly to rooms developed in the modern functional manner with simple architectural lines and bold use of color. Flower prints, bird prints, sporting prints often furnish themes easily carried through the furnishing details of a room.

FURNITURE ARRANGEMENT

Having selected the mood your room is to express, and perhaps a theme also, you are ready to concentrate upon the furnishings you need and how to arrange them. Your color scheme is just as important, but the entire subject of color is so packed with interest that it must be handled in a chapter of its own (Chapter 4). Many of the decorating principles mentioned in the present chapter apply not only to furnishings but equally to room backgrounds—floors, walls, ceilings. Furniture and furniture arrangement is taken up here, ahead of the chapters on backgrounds, because so often in redecorating backgrounds must be left as they are, with changes confined to movable features of the room.

Special-duty rooms such as bedrooms, dining rooms, kitchens, etc., have certain fixed requirements

THEMES FROM MEXICO AND OUR OWN SOUTHWEST

for comfort and convenience. Each of these has its own types of furniture and its own way of applying rules for arrangements, all covered in later chapters on special rooms. Living-room plans are used here to illustrate the broad underlying principles of arrangement because all the general rules apply, while at the same time the decorating problem is complicated by the varied activities which must be provided for in a room shared by all the family.

Making a Floor Plan: Before you attempt to plot your floor space be sure you have a list of every possible activity which must be carried on in the room, with notes covering all the special furniture and equipment needed. List all major pieces of furniture, both those you already have and those you are planning to buy. Take the over-all measurement of your room, noting the width and location of doors and windows, also any special features such as fireplace, alcove, bay window, built-in book shelves or other stationary furniture. Now you are ready to do what the professional decorator does—work out a floor plan on paper.

First draw an outline of your room marking the positions of all fixed features. In this way you can see

ARRANGED FOR COMFORT WITHOUT CROWDING

The living room above illustrates a good conversation grouping. The couch is placed against the wall but two small comfortable arm chairs balance each other by the fire. Notice that side chairs which can be easily moved have been brought up here to round out a temporary grouping for more than two people. In a room which would be crowded by ordinary furniture this type of arrangement may prove very useful. Notice also the small scale of the sofa, which is made into a wall composition by the tables and lamps at each end and the large painting above on the wall. Notice also the mirror hung over a mirror-paneled wall which frames the fireplace. This is another device which would be very helpful in a small room. It keeps the room from seeming crowded by doubling the appearance of space.

20

MODERN SPACE-SAVING WITH SECTIONAL SOFAS

If you have a fireplace in any type of living room it will almost automatically become the primary center of interest. In the room above, the sectional couches arranged to form a corner grouping provide seating space for a number of people, forming a nook or alcove effect in the fireplace section of the room. The fireplace arrangement shown below illustrates formal balance in a traditional room with twin period love seats arranged to face each other in a fireplace grouping. Note the small rug placed over the carpet to tie the fireplace group together. Use of love seats is often a solution to fireplace grouping in a small room where even one full-sized couch would be out of scale.

TRADITIONAL SPACE-SAVING, WITH TWIN LOVE SEATS

PIANO CENTER-OF-INTEREST GROUP FITTED INTO A CORNER

In the room above a small baby grand piano is the focal point in a center-of-interest grouping. Such a group often includes, as it does here, only a piano correctly placed with its straight side in line with the wall and a small chair and table arranged in the curve. Other pictures and suggestions for piano arrangements will be found in Chapter 22.

exactly where your wall spaces are in relation to doors and windows or any other fixtures, also where the most convenient locations for grouping furniture seem to be.

You may find it easier to visualize your room plan if you can try out the effect of various arrangements without having to draw them in on your "blueprint," then erase them. To avoid this, cut out pieces of paper which roughly correspond to the size and shape of your furniture. Label these for identification and place them on your floor plan in groups where you think they should go, as shown in the sketches on page 36.

Center of Interest: A feeling of warmth and friendliness in your living room can be achieved partly by means of furniture assembled in small intimate groups which suggest friendly conversation or some interest shared. The most important group will naturally be placed where you can take advantage of the best feature in the room, architecturally or decoratively speaking. If there is a fireplace it usually suggests itself at once for this purpose and becomes what is called a primary center of interest for the room. A picture window, or any group of windows with a lovely view, would be another possibility for such a center. A grand piano might serve as focus for the room, or shelves filled with books. If you have two or more of these features in the same room you can make one of them the main center of interest and treat the others as secondary group centers. Unless your room is very small it will have at least one secondary center of interest, and most well-arranged rooms have also one or more additional groupings usually spoken of as "subordinate."

Concentrate first upon the primary center-of-interest grouping and work that out before you decide about others. Naturally the largest pieces of furniture must receive first consideration when you are planning how to make the best use of your floor and wall spaces. Having decided upon your chief center of interest you can arrange other groups with relation to it, in order to take care of as many different interests and activities as possible. There might be a radio grouping, two or more conversational groupings, a game table grouping, or other similar centers. With each group there must be chairs, occasional tables, lamps, useful accessories—whatever is required for comfort. Most groups in a living room should be arranged for smoking and reading convenience whatever their primary purpose may be.

When a room has no natural pivotal point architecturally—as so often happens—study your plan carefully to see where you can best establish a substitute. This can be done very successfully by arranging an attractive furniture group against an unbroken wall space which may be decorated if necessary to serve as a frame for the grouping. Pictures may be used to build up this wall interest, also mirrors, fabrics, wallpaper, draperies, screens, panels or decorative borders. The groupings in these cases will probably be centered about your largest or most interesting piece of furniture. It may be a couch, a handsome table or chest, a desk, or a unit grouping of twin chests with a large mirror above. If your

A PICTURE WINDOW IS A NATURAL CENTER OF INTEREST

In the room below the large picture window is the logical choice for a center-of-interest grouping. The conversation group of couch, tables and chairs is framed on each side by the draperies and above by the window cornice of bamboo matching the informal furniture of the room. The textured rug with its diagonal design harmonizes with the summery type of furniture and with the outdoor effect created by the window filling the greater part of the wall. With a window

like this, or any large window with a view, a group of chairs or a couch-and-chair combination can all be faced partly toward the window to take full advantage of the view. Other groupings will suggest themselves to you. The thing to remember is that a group should be centered either directly in front of a wide window or a group of windows, or between two separated windows where the drapery will form a frame outside the group.

PICTURES GROUPED FOR WALL INTEREST

The above picture and the sketch on this page may suggest to you various ways in which you can create a center of interest against a blank wall by means of furniture, pictures, hanging book shelves, applied wall decorations, etc.

room has a theme this will often coincide with your chief center-of-interest grouping—as when a picture which has inspired the theme is placed above a fireplace or a large piece of furniture and becomes the dominant decorating feature of the room.

Practical Aspects of Your Floor Plan: Comfort, convenience and safety must never be forgotten in laying out floor plans. Don't allow furniture to interfere with door or window openings, with easy passage between rooms, with access to closets or cupboards. One group must not block free use of some other group. If your home is properly arranged, lights will be close to electric outlets, or extension cords will be protected and placed along the walls. Adequate lighting will be provided everywhere. Small rugs will not be used where traffic is heavy,

and in any case they will be anchored in place by non-skid pads. Occasional furniture, ash trays and all other usable accessories will be large enough and substantial enough to serve the purpose for which they were intended.

BALANCE

In every phase of decorating balance is simple and easy to achieve, but none the less important. A well-balanced arrangement may make a room with rather ordinary furnishings more attractive than one filled with lovely pieces badly placed. The psychological value of balance in decorating is just what the word implies in other connections—poise, equilibrium, a sense of restfulness.

Balance is order and creates a definite feeling of repose, therefore of comfort. A room or a grouping of objects is in balance when it appears to be at rest—that is, when the pieces of heavy furniture are placed so that they are not all on one side or one end of a room, or a group. The same principle applies to high pieces. If a tall cabinet or bookcase is placed on the same wall with tall windows, facing a low couch-and-table group there will be no balance and no feeling of restfulness. The effect will be more like the sensation experienced on the deck of a listing ship.

Height should be distributed so that a tall secretary will balance a tall window on the opposite side of the room. If a low piece must be opposite, it should be carried up in effect by decorations arranged above it in such a way as to link the furniture with the wall. The groupings on opposite walls should have a general similarity of outline if possible. If you cannot manage this, at least try for an appearance of balance through quantity, size and arrangement of available pieces. In an ideal room each wall would have an object of central interest, with other furniture and accessories grouped about it to create a pleasing composition, and each wall would provide balance for the wall facing it.

Looking at many of the photographs in this book you will observe that the principle of balance is

A WALL SCREEN PANEL ADDS IMPORTANCE

A

B

Balance is especially important in paneling used on walls and in relation to furniture. Sketch A shows wrong arrangement of furniture against a paneled wall. A group should always be placed where there will be balance between panels, and the furniture will be centered so that the panel outlines will frame it in some way, as in sketch B.

deeply respected by experienced decorators. You will also see how they avoid monotony by using two different types of balance in most of the rooms shown. Contemporary design places great stress upon this point as a means for adding variety and interest in a room.

Identical Balance: As the name indicates, identical balance is like holding the two arms of a scales at an

THE HANGING BOOK SHELF HELPS CREATE A CENTER OF INTEREST

THE COUCH COVER FABRIC, CARRIED UP ON THE WALL, PROVIDES
BALANCE FOR THE WINDOW END OF THE ROOM

exact level by placing weights identical in size and number in the two balance pans. Apply this principle to arrangement of decorations or furnishings in a room. Take a grouping of objects—say a center-of-interest fireplace group with mantel ornaments, a picture above the mantel, also tables, lamps and couches at each side of the fireplace. Draw an imaginary line straight down the middle of the fireplace from ceiling to floor. If the line divides the group into two equal parts, with each side exactly like the other side in every detail, then the grouping is said to have identical balance. Several other names are given to it, but they all mean the same thing. It is often called *"symmetrical" balance;* also *"formal" balance* because the exactness of the division into imaginary identical halves creates a feeling of formality. "Twin" pieces in accessories and furniture are necessary for this grouping.

26

| A—FORMAL BALANCE | B—INFORMAL BALANCE |

The difference between the two types of balance—identical (or formal), and optical (or informal)—is illustrated by furniture arrangement in the sketches above. Sketch A shows a group in which a line drawn down the middle would divide the group into two parts identical in size, shape and position. In sketch B an "optical illusion" of likeness between the parts on each side of the line is pro-duced by objects which are not identical but are arranged so that both groups *appear* to have the same value. That is to say, the size and weight of a large piece of furniture such as a couch may be "balanced" by two chairs and a table placed in an opposite position where they will oc-cupy approximately the same amount of floor space. (See text for further explanation.)

GROUPED FOR COMFORT

An attractive subordinate grouping may be built around a reading table with a picture above it, and two really com-fortable chairs placed where they will be most convenient for conversation—or knitting and a quiet game.

Traditional decorating in the Western World has always leaned heavily upon identical balance because it is easy to work out and makes for stability, dignity and restfulness in a room. Too much of it may result in monotony and stiffness, but too little may create an atmosphere vaguely disturbing, unrestful, even unpleasant. Every room has both vertical and horizontal lines in its decoration and this type of balance provides a pleasant way to combine them—as when a tall vertical object is flanked by twin horizontal objects, or the reverse. Identical balance can seldom be applied to relationships between all four walls of a room because of architectural variations such as doors and windows. Besides, it would be monotonous. It is applied most often to individual groupings of furniture and decorations, or to one entire wall of a room.

Optical Balance: Again we find a clue in the name. The second type of balance is really a kind of optical delusion. It consists of an arrangement of objects which are similar but not identical in such a way that they create an impression of symmetry and balance within the grouping, or in relation to another group facing them. Optical balance is more complicated to handle than identical balance, but it is more interesting to work out because so many variations are possible. A grouping of several small objects on one side of a fireplace may balance one large object on the other side. A tall secretary desk is often used to balance a window. Book shelves on one side of a room may provide a good balance for a fireplace and mantel on the opposite side. And so on, in as many combinations as you can think out.

MODERN USE OF BALANCE

Oriental decoration makes extensive use of this more subtle and difficult Occult balance. So does our own modern school, which feels that it gives wider range to the individual imagination and sometimes frowns upon the traditional custom of buying furniture and accessories in pairs for the sake of identical balance. Alternative names often applied to the principles of optical balance carry their own explanation. *"Informal" balance* goes naturally with the more fluid lines of this arrangement. *"Occult" balance* refers to the fact that this type of balance must be governed partly by an instinctive feeling for it, rather than by exact measurements.

Optical balance is affected by color and texture and this must not be overlooked when you are assembling your groups. Dark colors and rough finishes make pieces of furniture appear heavier than they are, while light colors and smooth surfaces make them look larger. An extended area of soft

GAY COLORS—RESTFUL LINES

The two views of the room shown here include almost every element of good furniture arrangement necessary in a room used for living and entertainment purposes. Everything about the room speaks of friendliness and ordered comfort. It shows clearly the value of balance (both formal and informal) in furniture arrangement. Notice the interesting wall composition and centers of interest. You will find one primary grouping, one secondary, and two subordinate. The fireplace with its copper hood provides the focal point for a grouping in formal (or identical) balance. Twin couches, end tables and lamps are arranged facing each other in exactly the same relation to the fireplace. The entire wall is also an example of identical balance, with window draperies at each end of the room framing the fireplace group in something like an alcove effect.

Facing the fireplace, the secondary interest group at the right has for its focal point a couch-chair-and-wall grouping making up an entire wall composition which balances the fireplace wall on the other side of the room by optical balance. If you study the pictures you will see how details are also worked out according to the principles of optical or informal balance. The framed fabric panel balances the fireplace hood in size and position. The couch-and-table group balances the fireplace and the furniture group around it. There is no repetition of identical objects in the two groups, but the general similarity in size, weight and effect creates a restful feeling of balance between the two sides of the room. The ends of the room provide subordinate centers of interest—at one end the game table, with the reading table close by, at the other a small service bar with a tiny piano at the side. This room is a charming example of traditional and modern successfully combined.

neutral color will often balance a much smaller spot of bright intense color, just as a wide expanse of dull surface may balance a smaller brightly burnished area.

HOW TO MAKE USE OF LINE

Most women have already discovered the power of line in relation to their clothes. You know, of course, that up-and-down pleats or trimming make you look taller, that stripes running around make you look shorter and broader, that straight lines tend toward a trim tailored effect while curves emphasize femininity. Apply the same principles to dressing your room. It will work the same way. A little knowledge of line is one of the most useful decorating tools you can have. Understanding the connection between line and psychological effect, you will be able to do fascinating things to a room.

Lines stand out clearly in a room in details such as door and window trim, stripes in decoration, edges of furniture. Less definite lines are created when two

TWO KEYNOTES—RELAXATION AND COMFORT

SPACE-SAVING COUCH AND BOOK-SHELF ARRANGEMENT IN A

The modern room illustrates the long low lines of comfort and repose in its couch and book-shelf combination filling one entire wall. Three small sectional love seats are lined up to make the couch. Notice that the back cushions are placed against a convenient narrow shelf with fluorescent lighting. The sketches at right have dotted lines which indicate how you can apply the test of imaginary lines to a grouping. In sketch A the lines leading the eye from one object to another emphasize the restless effect of bad grouping, which creates confusion, instability, disorder. Note the restful impression created when related lines lead the eye from one piece to another in a symmetrical and orderly pattern. The same large pieces of furniture are grouped here according to principles of correct scale and identical balance. To achieve this, a second lamp table had to be added. The lamp shade and pictures had to be changed entirely as they were not different color areas or two contrasting textures are placed side by side. They are equally important. If you know your lines—and what they mean—you will be able to select furnishings which complement each other and suit the background of the room. You will be able to arrange groups with the right mingling of stability and grace. You will avoid monotony and many other decorating mistakes. Your room will say what you want it to say.

TYPES OF LINES

There are actually only two basic lines—straight and curved. But many interesting combinations of the two are possible and each combination has its own helpful meaning for you no matter what kind of room you may be decorating. Any successful room must have a pleasing combination of straight lines and curves, both in background and furnishings. One or the other should always predominate, but remember that any one type of line used to excess in a room will result in monotony.

OBJECT LESSONS IN GROUPING
A—WRONG

B—RIGHT

RESTFUL MODERN ROOM

only out of scale but also inharmonious in feeling. Three small pictures over a large couch would look completely lost even if they were correctly grouped and hung. The large picture provides balance because it is in scale with the grouping of which it is a part. It forms the climax of a small, well-balanced wall composition which will be a harmonious element in the room picture as a whole, as well as pleasing in itself.

MAKING GOOD USE OF A LIVING-ROOM CORNER

In the room above a pleasing balance of various types of lines creates an impression of dignified charm. Traditional furniture is combined with a modern wall and door treatment at the left. The prevailing lines are vertical in feeling, as shown in the tall narrow bookcases, the tall twin cabinets topped by globes, the desk with its two side-drawer compartments, and the panel of pictures above it reaching almost to the ceiling. So much for dignity. The horizontal top of the long desk, the decorative border at the ceiling line, the stripes in the stool upholstery—all these contribute to an impression of stability. Charm and grace are added to the picture by the circular wallpaper patterns, curves in lamps, globes, and other accessories, the round chandelier, also the curving sides of the bookcases. A nice balance is shown (optical) between the desk-and-picture grouping and the tall door and bookcase group. Twin lamps, globes, and cabinets are identically balanced at each side of the desk and picture-panel. A desk grouping like this would furnish an attractive office corner in a living room where work had to be done at home.

In the sketch shown below note how the predominance of curves in drapery, pictures, and sofa design is kept from monotony by introduction of long straight lines in the glass curtains, stripes in the sofa upholstery, and the diagonal stripes of the wallpaper pattern.

32

The combination which will prove most attractive in any particular room depends upon what you like, the mood you want to express, the style of the room and the purpose for which it will be used.

CHECK LIST ON WHAT LINES MEAN

1. Vertical Lines in furniture, wall decoration, or hangings make objects or rooms seem taller and narrower. They tend toward formality, dignity, stiffness. Psychologically they are stimulating.

2. Horizontal Lines are most often associated with long, low objects such as couches, beds, and dining tables. For this reason they suggest relaxation and comfort. Horizontal lines make things seem longer, lower and less formal. They are restful in feeling.

3. Straight Lines Parallel to Each Other suggest harmony and peacefulness, a desirable attribute for any room meant to be lived in.

4. Straight Lines in a Combination of Vertical and Horizontal are essential in decorating. When properly balanced they support the room by giving it a feeling of solidity and permanence. In fabrics they give strength to the weave, boldness to the design, as in checks and plaids.

5. Slanting Lines organized with balance between backward and forward slant as in the herringbone design, produce an agreeably strong and substantial effect. But nothing is more disturbing than when disorganized, unnecessary lines slant at acute angles. The only impression they can create is one of confusion and fatigue.

6. Rectangles are more interesting than squares or cubes because the eye naturally follows the line of length.

7. Curved Lines in the Form of Regularly Repeated Scallops or small curves in a design are informal yet restrained, sometimes even prim. When they are small and neat they fit best into a cottage-type background or a small cozy room.

8. Curved Lines Repeated Irregularly are entirely different from scallops in feeling. As used in France in the period of Louis XV, they symbolized the gaiety of court life, its luxury, irresponsibility, and care-free charm. Lavish and graceful, they appeared in the form of garlands, painted and carved, in fabric designs, in billowy draperies. Applied to modern decoration, this type of curve is often used, with much more restraint, to introduce a note of vivacity and careless grace even into a slightly formal background.

9. The Oval has more appeal than the circle and can be used more freely, for the same reason that the rectangle is more attractive than the square.

10. The Free, Sweeping Curves of Nature—as in clouds, rivers, hills—are the loveliest of all possible lines. They express movement, ease, comfort, peace. Always used in some degree—notably in Oriental rather than in Western designs—they are now a major source of inspiration for many contemporary streamlined designs keyed to simplified but gracious living.

Analyzing these classifications you will see that certain general characteristics stand out. Straight lines contribute simplicity, strength and control to a room or a design. Curved lines add grace, softness, vivacity. A predominance of straight, squared lines creates an impression of masculine strength which may easily become stiffness if it is overdone. A predominance of curves, suggesting feminine charm, may be carried too far and degenerate into fussiness.

If you are not sure of yourself on this subject of line, start educating your eye to recognize the various types. Make a game of it. In pictures of rooms you like, see how clever decorators have combined straight lines and curves to produce certain impressions. You will find almost at once that you can trace the connection between the way they have used line and the effects they have created. The more you practise it, the more interesting and rewarding the game will become. Try it out on rooms in other people's houses. You will soon be able to tell at a glance why one room gives you a pleasant feeling of ease and harmony, while another creates an impression of tension, confusion, fatigue.

NOTES ON GROUPING

In any effective stage setting, or picture of a pleasing room, you will notice that each grouping is carefully related to its background and to other groups in the room. Arrangement of individual items in the group—its "composition"—will be just as carefully worked out. Unless each separate grouping of furniture, accessories and background features in your room is well thought out and placed according to principles outlined in this chapter it may strike a discordant note which will disturb your whole effect.

In addition to the fundamental principles included under balance and line, there are a few others which also apply to all phases of room decorating.

Scale: We often see a small insignificant lampshade perched above a large heavy base. This means that the importance of scale has been overlooked or ignored. There is not much excuse for this particular type of mistake. Most of us are used to thinking of people and things in terms of sizes and relations between them. We know that standing a pony beside an elephant will make the pony look smaller and the elephant look larger—yet we continue in our

RESTFUL EFFECT OF GOOD GROUPING FOR SCALE

The individual objects in the reading-writing furniture group pictured on this page are examples of correct scale in their relation to each other. The rather small desk-and-chair group is balanced by an upholstered chair and lamp table which are also small and rather light in effect. The large bookcase provides a background for a lamp big enough to be in scale with it, but not too big for the table on which it stands. The picture over the desk carries interest up onto the wall and keeps the desk from looking too small beside the built-in bookcase. Notice the conversation possibilities in the facing arrangement of the two chairs.

homes to do such things as placing delicate little tables next to massive over-stuffed sofas. Then we wonder what is wrong with our room.

Correct scale depends upon nothing more difficult than a pleasing and harmonious relationship between sizes of objects used near together, or between those objects and their background. A large stately room is at its best when it is fitted out with large stately furnishings. A small intimate room calls for smaller pieces, lighter in weight and design. The principle applies in the same way to individual furniture groupings in the room, to patterns in wallpaper or fabrics, to accessories, to background designs, to any other kind of decorations.

A helpful clue to success in combining furniture of different types or from different periods is to be found in correct use of scale. Looking over photographs and charts in the period chapter you will notice that each period has a characteristic scale which runs through all its various types of furnishings. If you want to combine furniture in several period styles, as is so often done today, choose all the important pieces from periods which are similar in scale.

If you are buying new things, you can always take scale into your calculations and make sure what you buy is right in size for its surroundings. However, if you are faced with the usual problems of bringing

A   DETERMINING CORRECT SCALE   B

The two sketches on this page (above) illustrate graphically the difference between a grouping which is right in scale and one which is not. In sketch A the size of the dark chest looming up against the light wall appears even greater than it is because of the small scale of the lamp, picture, chair and rug around it. Sketch B shows how easily bad scale in this grouping was corrected. Replacements with a large mirror, a larger lamp and a substantial-looking chair were the first steps. The small

picture, in a light frame, was hung above the chair for the sake of balance. This would have been still further improved if the cabinet had been placed in the center of the wall with a chair on each side. In order to lessen the apparent size of the cabinet, color was called into play. Painted the same color as the wall, the cabinet seems to "retire" into its background and to look considerably smaller. This effect is helped along by an over-all floor covering in place of the rug in sketch A.

FURNISHINGS, IN SCALE WITH A LARGE ROOM

In the dignified traditional room below, a center-of-interest grouping has been arranged against a blank wall by use of a massive bookcase which dominates the wall. The substantial lamp table and tall lamp are in scale, as are also the heavy upholstered pieces, the large French arm chair, the coffee table and the bold, open design of the Aubusson rug. Naturally, the room suited to these furnishings must be spacious and dignified in line. Here the height of the bookcase and its vertical panel lines are balanced by the long straight draperies from ceiling to floor. A possible feeling of heaviness in this grouping is relieved by the graceful draping of the window valance, the gay floral pattern of the rug with its oval center, the round table and lamp, the curving lines in arm chair and table. In this room the rosy beige tones of the rug are matched exactly in the color of walls and draperies.

into focus furnishings which you already have and must use, there are numerous helpful devices you can try out. Sometimes all that is needed is a careful rearrangement, or a change in the color of certain pieces. Sometimes a few new accessories at strategic points will cure the trouble by building up scale or providing balance. A group of pictures, for example, might be placed above a couch to make it seem more important and increase its appearance of size, or to make the couch balance a large picture-and-table group on the opposite wall. You will find answers to many special problems by consulting the index.

ARRANGING AND PLACING A FURNITURE GROUP

Each center-of-interest group, even each grouping of small decorative accessories, should be a complete picture in itself as well as a harmonious unit in the picture presented by the whole room. You will find it easy to do this. Balance one side of the group against the other side, using whichever type of balance is most appropriate. See that no object in the group is out of scale with the others. Unify them by means of a theme; by color or texture. In all your groupings remember that uneven numbers make for grace. Even numbers in a group are difficult to handle without an effect of stiffness. You will find that a furniture grouping will be more pleasing if a little of the same color appears in all the pieces and textures are not too different in character. If one inharmonious piece must remain in a certain group bring it into line by a slip cover or a new finish.

In laying out your floor plan remember that a dark, dull-surfaced group will be partly lost in a shadowy corner; a light group may be too conspicuous in full light from a window. Brighten up the dark corner by a group with light colors and smooth surfaces, and bring out the values of a dark group by placing it near the light.

Remember also that dark objects against a light wall stand out very clearly and dark pieces of furniture should not be arranged against white or very clear light walls unless they are very good both in outline and finish. Either arrange less attractive pieces against a soft neutral wall, not too light, or alter them with paint or slip covers so that they will merge with the light wall behind them. On the other hand, if a piece of furniture is particularly graceful you should place it where a contrasting background will show it off. If your wall is not right for this you can always plan to have a plain panel or screen, in the right color, behind the piece you want to display.

Tying Parts of Your Room Together: You can increase the harmonious appearance of your room by repeating certain motifs, notes of colors, patterns, textures, or identical objects such as small chairs or lamps in several places. This device—sometimes known as *rhythm* in decorating—carries the eye naturally from one object or spot to another, creating a pleasant sense of order and pattern. It is this same feeling of rhythm which makes a grouping more attractive when the objects are not all the same size or height. They must be in scale with each other, but planned so that larger pieces are flanked by smaller ones, or the reverse. The exception to this is when a panel or border effect is created by use of pictures or other small accessories. Don't overdo repetition. Too much of it may become monotony. A successful room must have variety and contrast— a touch of drama now and then.

The touch of drama is often furnished by a spot of bright color or some highly burnished object used to place emphasis at the right point or provide a climax for some important grouping. If you look for them in the pictures of your favorite rooms, you will discover many clever little tricks for this placing of emphasis at strategic spots—sometimes merely by use of contrast color in accessories or small furniture, or by locating a mirror where emphasis or a vista is needed, sometimes by more unusual devices.

HOW TO WORK OUT A FLOOR PLAN

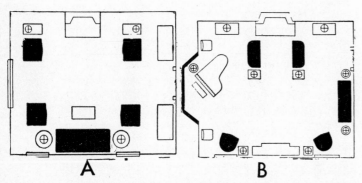

A   B

In drawing the floor plan of your room reduce your measurements from feet to inches. You may prefer to use a large sheet, with each foot represented by one inch on the plan, or a smaller sheet with ½ inch or ¼ inch representing one foot. Keep to the same scale in marking the wall features and drawing the base of each piece of furniture. These you can cut out of scraps of light cardboard. In this way you can shift pieces about in various groupings until you have found what seems to be the best possible arrangement of all the large objects. This will save you much back-breaking labor, and also show the proportionate space available for any new pieces you are planning to buy. These floor plans are intended merely as examples of how to go about using a plan, but they also illustrate the two types of balance. In sketch A on this page the fireplace wall (1) is arranged in identical balance. The center-of-interest couch-chair-and-table group (2) facing it follows the same principle. This conversation group is placed between two windows where the draperies will frame the grouping. The relationship between these two walls is one of general balance in feeling, that is, of optical balance with no duplication of individual objects. The end-wall composition, with the doorway (3), is balanced by the placing of identical pieces of furniture at each side of the entrance door. The fourth wall is not balanced within itself, nor against any other part of the room. This type of arrangement with identically balanced groups on three walls is less interesting and attractive than one with more fluidity resulting from a free use of optical (or informal) balance, but it is often necessary in a small room where only this even arrangement will keep the effect from being cluttered and unrestful. Sketch B illustrates the use of identical balance on each side of the longer walls, with optical (or informal) balance in the weight and arrangement of these walls with relation to each other. The large breakfront cabinet between the windows on one side balances the fireplace on the other. The two end walls are arranged with less reference to balance but are planned to take the best possible advantage of available space. The alcove, or bay window, provides a space-saving location for the piano. If you have both a piano and an alcove this arrangement is usually the best solution. Sketches C, D and E suggest several other good piano and furniture groupings.

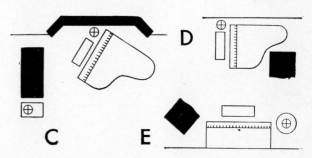

D

C   E

RESTFUL LINES ALLOW THREE CENTERS OF INTEREST WITHOUT CROWDING

The room above combines modern sectional couch units, in a space-saving corner arrangement, with traditional furniture. This section of the room shows three centers of interest—the corner referred to, with the coffee table for hospitality, the wide window at the right with a reading lamp and two easy chairs for pleasant conversation, and the game table which is kept in readiness in front of the bay window. A kind of picture-window grouping is framed by wide draperies with a background of growing plants arranged on glass shelves in the window. The effective use which can be made of window treatment is evident here. These steel casement windows can be installed in any room where a center of interest is lacking and more light is needed. Notice the mirror above the couches. It is carried around the corner to provide a sense of balance for the windows at each side of the opposite corner. Notice also the modern "cove" lighting at the ceiling line, the solid feeling produced by straight squared lines, and the appearance of spaciousness resulting from restful lines and plain backgrounds.

To test the effectiveness of your room arrangement try to look at it with a sense of perspective—as you might look at a stage setting or as an artist would look at his painting. Examine it from different angles. Stand back from the doorway and try to see it as a stranger entering would see it. If the large pieces of furniture are satisfactorily arranged, in comfortable, attractive groupings, don't worry about the finishing touches. You can keep trying out different effects with those until you find just what you want.

SOME SPECIAL PROBLEMS IN ARRANGEMENT

There are a good many special problems in connection with arranging furniture, but most of them can be solved by applying common sense and a little knowledge to the situation.

1. Conversation groupings require comfortable seats, accessories near at hand, light for reading if desired, provision for serving refreshments. Chairs should be not more than six or eight feet apart, lamp tables the height of the couch arms, coffee tables low and sturdy and at least a foot away from the edge of the couch. Too many small occasional tables may look cluttered, yet for comfort everyone must have a table handy. One solution is to group the chairs so that one larger table will serve two or more chairs. Another possibility is to have several nests of tables which can be separated when needed, or a supply of light folding tables.

2. If it is going to be used often, a game grouping is always more satisfactory when an attractive table can be made a real part of the room furnishings, with its chairs left in place, instead of having only a folding card table which must be dragged out and put back every time it is used. With a little thoughtful planning a spot can usually be found for this arrangement, and many cleverly worked out tables available in the shops are adaptable to several games.

COMFORT IN A CORNER GROUPING

3. Novelty designs in furniture, such as modern curved couches, bookcases, and special groupings of unit pieces, often require different arrangement from those customary with traditional furniture. The essence of modern design is to save space, and every foot of floor space around the wall in a modern room may be filled with streamlined shelves, cabinets, drawers, etc. Even seating units are often built-in; when they are not they may be designed in sections to be set out into the room. Curving couches are very effective facing a fireplace or picture window. Their lines also show to advantage when they are located in a corner of the room. This modern, planned space-saving has influenced our arrangement of traditional pieces. By purchasing these in pairs you can often make up your own "unit" furniture and still use period designs.

4. Corners, alcoves and bay windows are often overlooked in arranging furniture. They provide a wonderful opportunity to save floor space in your room and at the same time create a charming nook for some special interest. In Chapter 14 you will find many suggestions for making the most of alcoves and bay windows. The use of corners is illustrated by pictures and sketches in this chapter. There is one rule for corners which should never be broken—don't put anything cater-cornered across them. It wastes space and the slanting lines create a sense of confusion. If the corner is small you can always find a small corner cabinet or corner shelves which will fit into it. If you feel you must have a chair there, make it one with a tall rounded back. Better still, group two smaller chairs with a table suitable for a corner.

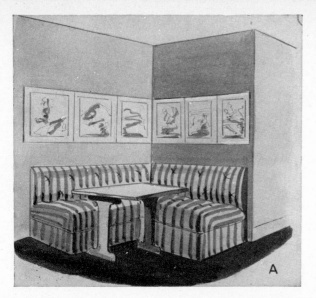

HOW TO MAKE CORNERS USEFUL

Modern emphasis upon space-saving in furniture design and arrangement has brought out a great variety of plans for making use of hitherto wasted corners. The photographs on these pages illustrate attractive solutions of the corner problem through the use of unit furniture and special designs. The square corner (left) is filled in with a triangular table and the couches are fitted against it to make a comfortable conversation group. In this case the center-of-interest wall-emphasis is provided by book shelves reflected in the mirror around the corner. The sectional pieces are in brown and beige ribbed chenille trimmed in beige leather with the table in natural walnut. The lamp is in white bamboo with brass trimming, the coffee table in chromium with plate-glass top

and mirror shelf. With walls in egg-shell pink, beige pebble-twist carpet on the floor, and accent colors of henna and yellow, the room is a charming example of modern color scheme and decoration. In the picture below a corner window is made dramatic by draw-curtains under a curving cornice behind curving unit seats. Notice the interesting lines of the circular bookcase-table-and-desk combination with a small chair just outside the window picture. The shaggy rug texture provides dramatic contrast with satiny wood finish, smooth leather upholstery and boldly figured fabric. The group of sketches may suggest ways in which you can turn to account some wasted corner in living room, hallway or game room.

STRAIGHT LINES IN DRAPERIES BALANCE CURVES

CORNER ARRANGEMENT FOR DOUBLE-DUTY ROOM

The corner above illustrates a very popular modern arrangement in rooms which must be used for sleeping as well as for general living purposes. Valuable corner space is utilized, and each of the couch-beds has bedside table space, also a reading light. Pillows can be stored away during the day in the round bolsters. In this group, the window draperies and the paintings on the wall help to build up the picture and also to balance the size and weight of the large comfortable couches and the oversize coffee table. Notice the convenient radio shelf, easily accessible from both of the couches.

5. Large pieces of furniture are usually most orderly and restful in arrangement when they are placed against the wall, except in a large room with plenty of floor space where you can work out one or more subdivisions of the room with groups of furniture. This is often done in a room with a dining, library or study end. In this case a couch, bookcases, or other piece of furniture may be placed across part of the floor to give the effect of a semi-partition. Of course, smaller groupings of chairs and tables must be out in the room, but keep them close enough to walls so that they will not interfere with passage through the room.

6. Large rooms often have too little furniture and too much space, particularly if you are furnishing by a plan of gradual development. In this case you still follow the rules of convenience. Don't try to spread your furniture out over the whole room, with the result that all the chairs are far apart and there is no real center of interest. Select the most suitable section of the room, establish a center of interest there, and arrange your furniture groupings in comfortable relation to that point. You can expand later into the far corners of the room. If you are buying furniture for a large room like this, remember not to choose it too small in scale.

EARLY AMERICAN ROOM MADE WIDER BY CLEVER GROUPING

FURNITURE USED IN THE MODERN STYLE TO DIVIDE A ROOM INTO SEVERAL UNITS

The rooms shown here illustrate two entirely different types of furniture arrangement for a long narrow room, also many typical points of difference between a completely traditional and a completely modern room. In the quaint old living room (left), with its wide yawning fireplace in the center of a very long wall, all the furniture is arranged to keep a clear passage open down the middle of the room. The couch opposite the fireplace, with its table and reading lamp, provides a center of interest and opposite-wall balance which is really part of the chair-bench-and-table grouping against the fireplace. A secondary center of interest at the end of the room includes book shelves, reading table in front of the window, and two chairs. A subordinate group on the left wall, made by a couch between two tables, balances the long table opposite. The dominance of horizontal lines helps make the room informal and very restful. Notice the way in which old fireplace fittings and all accessories are in harmony with the Early American feeling of the room and its interesting authentic hooked rugs. The room above expresses the modern idea, emphasizing the most effective use of every foot of floor space. The fireplace, at the end of the room this time, is made a center of interest by the backs of book shelves which form a nook for the couch facing the fire. The books themselves and the mirror panel form a secondary group, the mirror reflecting a picture window on the other side of the room—a third center of interest. The mirror placed at this point widens the room and doubles the effectiveness of the window. Notice the interesting upholstery of the arm chairs, with outside finish in a light smooth fabric which contrasts with the nubby dark material used for the rest of the upholstery. Judicious use of curves in furniture combines with the freely flowing natural curves of plants inside, and branches outside the window, to soften the severity of long straight lines and squared angles. The sketch below offers another suggestion for breaking up floor space in a very long room by means of furniture arrangement. Placing twin chests at the back of a couch provides lamp tables for reading, a substantial division between living and dining sections, and also a storage place for table equipment.

SEPARATION FOR DINING AND LIVING SPACE

This airy, attractively furnished living room illustrates a cardinal principle of modern design—eliminate walls you don't need and get double service out of the ones you keep. In this room there is only a suggestion of partition to indicate the break between the living room proper and its library-studio-den companion. This gives an unbroken sweep of light and air through both rooms from tall picture windows which slide back into the wall if desired. Notice the planting inside the window which brings the flower bed outside straight into the room. Starting at the left observe built-in book shelves, magazine rack, writing desk, storage cupboards, and serving shelf which sweeps around the partition to the built-in couch. Above the couch a built-in cabinet takes care of the radio-phonograph. Between the couch and the wall by the window a table fits into a cozy dining nook—its own illumination sunk into the top of the table

—HALLMARKS OF MODERN DESIGN

and diffusing a soft glow over the corner. All illumination is concealed. All surfaces are smooth, uncluttered, easy to take care of. The color scheme is striking—beige woodwork; floor in jaspé linoleum with beige ground; living room walls and ceiling all in hunter's green; couch in henna and brown; chintz upholstery and flower border around the dining nook in beige fabric with bold design in green, yellow, red and henna, all repeating the garden colors outside.

CHAPTER THREE

How to Put Walls to Work

WALLS form such a large part of the background in any room, that the treatment given them can make or break the success of your decorating program. Before you take any other decorating steps study your walls. If they are drab or depressing do something to revitalize them. If they are inharmonious with the furnishings you already have or are planning to buy, do them over even if the new couch or new rug has to be postponed for a little while. If the background of your room is right you can take your time about decorating the foreground. If the background is wrong even the loveliest furnishings will lose much of their effectiveness.

If you decide to refinish your walls be sure to select a treatment which will harmonize with the mood and theme you want for the room. According to color and design, walls can be neutral or assertive, serene and restful, or gay and stimulating. Traditional walls are dignified with panelings and moldings, modern walls are severely streamlined and functional.

There is so much variety in finishes for walls that if your room is normal in size, pleasing in proportions, adequately lighted, free from structural flaws, there is nothing to prevent your working out practically any wall treatment and any decorating scheme you select. But if there is something wrong structurally, architecturally or esthetically, you must either correct it or adapt your decorating plans to it.

Colors in paint, wallpaper and fabrics perform miracles in transforming the apparent size and shape of rooms. (See Chapter 4.) Floors, window treatment and furniture arrangement all contribute to correction of defects. (See Chapters 2, 10, 14.) But for the moment we are concerned with minor struc-

REMODELING PROVIDES OPPORTUNITIES TO MAKE WALLS USEFUL

The photograph at the left shows what can be done in an old interior to carry out the same space-saving principles emphasized by modern design. Notice the open door which reveals a tiny kitchenette and serving-pantry arrangement completely hidden when the door is closed. Another door at the right leads into a storage cupboard. Shallow units like this can be easily built into the wall of any average-sized room in the course of remodeling by merely installing a new wallboard or plywood wall a foot or more in from the old wall, instead of using it for a direct facing. At the end of the room notice the fireplace with its over-large brick front, brought completely into scale with the room by filling the space all around it with book shelves and cupboards. Notice also that the book shelves continue to the wall, forming a wide ledge under the window. This furnishes a foundation which gives the fireplace end of the room a new importance and makes it harmonize with the rest of the room. A treatment like this could be applied to almost any room, and to any over-large or too ornate fireplace and chimney breast. Painting the bricks in the same white used for surrounding woodwork merges them with it and makes them less conspicuous. If an alteration like this were undertaken in a more formal room, a facing of mirror, wood, plastic or some other decorative material could be used to conceal the bricks.

INEXPENSIVE WALL AND WOODWORK ALTERATIONS FOR A NEW ROOM

These before-and-after pictures clearly indicate how completely you can transform a room by changing its background. In the photograph at left, the paper and plaster are obviously in very bad condition and the dark oak sliding door looms up as big as a garage door. The fireplace—with its ugly tall mantel and closed-grate arrangement—emphasizes its inconvenient location in a corner. A simple, inexpensive operation on this room made it into the trim, cheerful-looking spot you see in the other picture. Instead of trying to do expensive repairs on bad plaster, a brand new face was given the room by the use of wallboard for dado and wall covering plus a composition board ceiling. Because the ceiling was too high for the small room, a wide cornice was used around the top, and the ceiling, cornice and dado were all painted a darker tone than the walls. The wallboard was put on in panels of two different widths with beveled edges, and strips of wallpaper border were applied in stagger fashion along the edges to outline the panels. New doors and mantel—stock models—were installed. The old grate was torn out, the new mantel (much lower than the old one) was put in with a new facing of marbleized composition material. The new color scheme was made up of soft blue-gray in several shades for background with white and gold, and soft rose accents.

TWO SOLUTIONS FOR THE PROJECTING RADIATOR PROBLEM

The all too frequent problem of the projecting radiator beneath one window, or a group of windows, can be taken care of by enclosing the radiator in a grill which will not obstruct heat, then building in whatever features you need or would like over it and around it. The photograph below shows how a charming room could be made from a very ordinary one by using softly finished natural wood for a dado, then adding an inexpensive small bay window and a corner cupboard at each side of the window. Windows, cupboards, and woodwork like this can all be had ready to install at a very reasonable price. The sketch shows the same difficulty differently remedied by filling in the whole end of a room with book shelves as a frame for the windows, then building a comfortable padded window-seat couch across the whole wall, with storage cupboards at the ends between wall and radiator. Notice the provision made on the two lower shelves for radio and reading lamp. There are many variations of this scheme which can be used to turn an ugly window-and-radiator combination into a beauty spot in a room—perhaps even a center of interest for furniture grouping. You will notice other sketches and pictures in this chapter which might easily be adapted to the radiator problem.

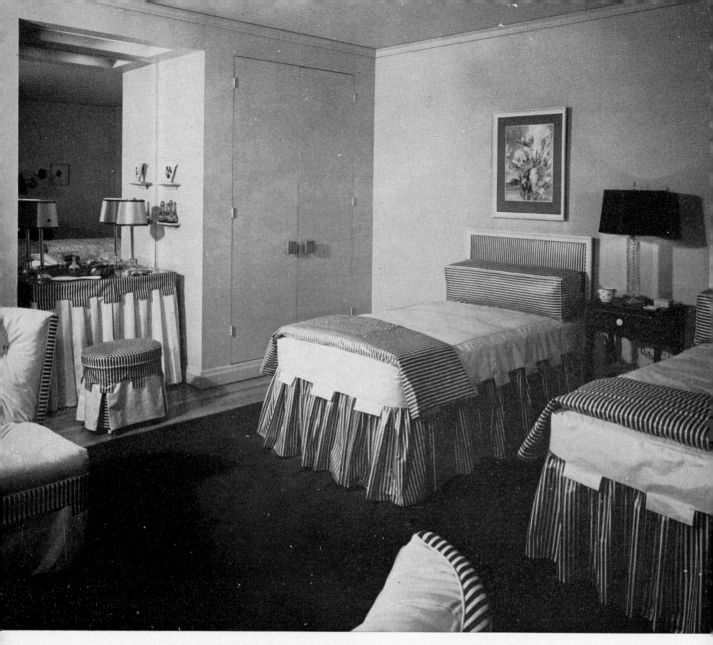

USEFUL BUILT-IN CLOSETS IMPROVE PROPORTIONS

Beams or structural supports which fill up corners may often be turned into decorative features by building around them, against them or between them. In the room above one very effective method is shown. Here the entire wall space is filled in with closets, except for the opening in the middle wide enough for a dressing table and mirror to be installed. A closet like this need not cut down the size of the room appreciably as the built-in feature need be no deeper than just enough to cover the beam. Notice the attractive, plain composition board used for the cupboards, also the overhead light conveniently installed above the dressing table. The tailored style of the room is attractively carried through all the decorations. The color scheme calls for a carpet of royal blue, striped chintz in white and flamingo red against white areas to soften its boldness. The background is in soft gray-blue.

tural or architectural changes, or substitutes for such changes. Ready-made units of unfinished furniture can be fitted to spaces in such a way that they look built in and so become part of the background, but are removable and can be taken into a new home. Whenever built-in features are mentioned the suggestions include these substitutes, designed for those who are not carpenter-minded to the extent of building their own. (See Chapter 17.)

Study your walls not only for defects to be corrected but also for possibilities of using them to add features of comfort, convenience or beauty overlooked by the original builder. In many cases the same methods may be used to accomplish both purposes.

46

STRUCTURAL ALTERATIONS

Really fundamental changes in the background of a room are usually made only when the house or apartment is not a rented one. If you own the place in which you live do not overlook the present-day stock remodeling units which you can get in a very wide variety of materials, styles and designs. There are almost no alterations for which you cannot obtain these custom-made units at a reasonable price and with all necessary directions for use. They will include door and window installations, every type of woodwork, even what you need for such major operations as turning a box-like living room into one of gracious lines and real charm by merging it with whatever room adjoins it. Many a house has been redeemed from the commonplace by this operation. Often the adjoining room is a small dining room which under modern living conditions is squandered space, put to much better use as part of the living room. If you decide upon this, keep the dining-room end of the combination for attractive treatment as a dining-alcove arrangement, perhaps with corner cupboards as illustrated on page 56.

The principle to be followed in making a square room look longer is to choose which two opposite sides you want to have carry the length, then plan everything you do with that in mind. The choice of walls for this lengthening operation will be affected by strategic placing of doors and windows, traffic lanes, and practical grouping of furniture.

ALTERATION BY DECORATING

If you like dadoes or moldings or panels, the square room is where you can use them to create long horizontal lines along your chosen walls. The end walls are left for contrast color, or different decoration and style of finish. For instance, you may have plain painted walls with your horizontal wood trim, but use wallpaper or fabric for the end walls. You will find many suggestions in Chapters 5, 6 and 7 for treatments which will help you solve this problem. The low streamlined, built-in type of furniture created by the modern decorative school can be used instead of wall trimmings to help create the illusion of length. All these methods involving horizontal lines will also seem to lower your ceilings if they are too high. If you use panels they must be in scale with the wall—and horizontal, not vertical, in design.

For shortening rooms you must reverse the processes described above. Break up the long walls by vertical panels or other trimming. Make the end walls striking and dramatic by using dark colors and bold designs which will seem to bring them in toward each other. Always balance what you do at one end by appropriate treatment at the other, using formal or informal balance, whichever is best suited to your problem. (See Chapter 2.) If the room is long enough you will probably want to set off one end for special treatment which will make it seem like a partially separated room. Illustrations on pages 56 and 57 will suggest methods to you for doing this easily.

EVER-USEFUL BUILT-IN CHINA CLOSET—COLONIAL STYLE

WIDE PICTURE WINDOW AND BUILT-IN CUPBOARD ADD TO DINING-ROOM CHARM

Installing a new wide window in the place of a small one, or putting in a window where there was only blank wall may transform a dark, cheerless room into a center of cheerful family life. Attractive, easy-to-put-in units in wood or metal—like the aluminum casement window shown above may be obtained at very reasonable prices. They come in many shapes, styles and sizes—bay windows as well as regulation models. In the room shown here the new aluminum window is combined with a stock unit corner cupboard and a wood cornice to create a charming Colonial dining room with quaint hooked rug and appropriate furniture. Notice the unusual curtain treatment designed to frame the view from the window without cutting it off. Over-draperies are hung on the wall beyond the window at each side and sheer glass curtains are made to draw across it beneath a valance of sheer fabric. For other suggestions see the chapters on windows and draperies. If you cannot achieve new windows there are many ways in which you can improve the ones you have and make them contribute to the success of your background treatment.

USE CAMOUFLAGE TO IMPROVE APPEARANCE OF A SMALL, HIGH WINDOW

One of the two sketches above shows a small window which seems lost in the wide wall space. The small window is sketched again after it had received treatment to make it appear larger and bring it into scale with the wall. It was widened by draperies hung over the walls and the trim at the edges of the window instead of over the panes. It was lengthened by having the long valance board lifted above the window top, and a false sill built below in the form of a small shelf for plants or books which would hide the wall. The apparent height was increased still more by using straight floor-length draperies. The chest placed below the false sill adds weight to the whole picture. If there are several windows close together, unite them by a long cornice or valance and drape them as if you have one very long window instead of several small ones. If their height is uneven, or they are too short, put the valance board wherever it is most effective and make the valance long enough to cover any wall which shows above them. If there is a radiator under one of the windows build a long window seat which will include the radiator.

DRAMATIZED DOORWAYS
MAY BE
SPACE-SAVING,
USEFUL,
AND ATTRACTIVE

The problem of doors which are unnecessary or even in the way is one easily solved if the opening is not needed for light or ventilation. Remove the door and cover one side of the opening with wallboard. This can be treated as a decorative panel on one side, camouflaged to seem part of the wall, or concealed by fabric hangings. On the other side you can fill in the space, as shown in the sketches above with built-in shelves, or you can have a tall bookcase made to fit into the space. Doorways filled in like this are attractive when the background and shelves are painted in the accent color of the room; when the opening is faced with mirror glass and glass shelves are used; or when they are finished entirely in the same color as the wall. The picture below illustrates a ready-to-install stock unit which can be used to replace an ugly wide arched doorway or any other unattractive

opening. Shelves and storage cupboards like these—with the simply paneled door between them and the shaped wood valance linking all three in one unit treatment—would give distinction to the most prosaic dining room. Notice how effectively the plain-paneled cupboard doors display the interesting Colonial-type hinges and latches, and how the dark shelf background color plays up the charm of old china. "Vista" type of Colonial paper on side walls widens the room by giving it a feeling of "openness" (see Chapter 6). It combines with painted woodwork and color on the end wall to make this treatment an excellent remedy for a badly proportioned room, too long and too narrow. Here the period paper is used without its customary dado because the ceiling of the room is low and the wall should not be cut up by horizontal lines.

SETTING OFF ONE END OF A LONG ROOM

Variety and interest are given to a floor plan by a slightly
raised floor level in a section of the same room or in an
adjoining room. If the ceiling is not too low you could work
out an arrangement, like the one shown above, at the end
of a long narrow room and add greatly to its beauty as well
as its usefulness. The archway could be merely suggested by
a decorative molding or border instead of being framed by
a structural feature as it is here. Notice the effective dark
background for built-in dish shelves and the modern-style
light with a mirror placed where it will double the light by
reflection. The end of a room can be made into a den,
library, game or music center, just as easily as into a dining
nook like this. The floor plan shows another way of producing an effect of separation by means of shelves.

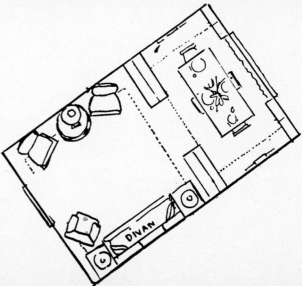

50

BOOK SHELVES TURN A LIVING ROOM INTO A CONVENIENT LIBRARY

In the room below it was easy to take advantage of an ell-shaped extension to create a comfortable, friendly library and writing nook. Notice the built-in shelves in various heights to accommodate books of different sizes. The old-fashioned "center table" has been painted to match the summery effect of light terrace curtains, gayly flowered slip covers and bare flagstone floor. A quaint Victorian lamp and other accessories contribute an amusing note to the serious atmosphere of books and writing desk. Note the arrange-

ment of the book shelves—the lowest one high enough to make stooping unnecessary, and floor cleaning easy. In almost any fairly large room a corner arrangement like this could be worked out. A large secretary-desk, a set of shelves, a cabinet, even a decorative screen, could be placed at a right angle with the wall to create an alcove effect. Book shelves have the advantage of requiring very little depth—just the width of the books. When space is at a premium, the narrow shelves can be carried to the ceiling, as here.

FRIENDLINESS AND WARMTH IN SHELVES FILLED WITH BOOKS

Books are equally at home in traditional or modern rooms—but they must have an appropriate setting. In the modern library-desk corner below, the colorful bindings of the books, which solidly fill shallow recessed shelves, serve to help soften the austerity of plain modern surfaces and simple lines. An interesting feature of this room is the use of linoleum for a smart finish on walls and desk top as well as on the floor. Notice the comfortable working space provided by the desk-shelf which sweeps about a curving wall, also the fluorescent light fixture at exactly the right spot above the writing pad. The book shelves at the left, built in to fill up a large opening between a hall and living room, are as traditional in feeling as the others are modern. In simple painted wood, like the Early American walls of the living room, they are attractively arranged with open spaces in which period ornaments alternate with books. Any home carpenter should be able to manage simple shelves like these, with storage space below. They could be installed—for books, dishes, or any other use—wherever an extra partition would be useful, in an unused doorway, between windows, on the wall going up a straight stairway, at the end of a hall, on almost any wall which needs building up to greater importance or usefulness. If you have plenty of furniture in a room, shelves of books can always be used as a colorful background. If your larger pieces are still in the future, the shelves will go a long way toward making the place seem furnished and the atmosphere friendly and homelike. If you haven't enough books, fill in with plants or ornaments.

The charming bedroom in the picture below shows how several difficult problems were solved. The arrangement of furniture in a long narrow bedroom naturally falls into the pattern used here. The special problem lay in the beamed ceiling with its high center section and the two small windows in the end wall which were out of proportion with the room. The shallow framework built around the window space provides a dramatic center of interest, and a climax to the wall grouping. The narrow shelves with cupboard base fill in the space between window and wall to complete the wall composition and offset the awkward lines of the ceiling beams. To cover the wall space above the windows very full ruffled draperies were used in criss-cross style with a valance at the top framing the dressing table. Graceful lines of traditional mahogany furniture harmonize with the waxed wood floor, graceful accessories, and the charming pattern of the chintz draperies in soft pink with rose, green and shades of blue. Soft green walls provide an appropriate background. The bed covers of heavy-textured off-white material

match shaggy white modern rugs on the floor. Note the arrangement of small rugs on a large floor—placed where they will tie groups of furniture together and lie parallel with lines of the room. In spite of its dramatic end wall, this room is very restful. One secret of this is in the balance between straight lines and curves. Another is in the use of plain backgrounds for flowered fabrics and frills. Still another is carefully balanced arrangement of furniture and accessories. The window wall itself is worked out in symmetrical balance, while the two small furniture groupings at right and left are balanced in feeling only (optical). This is true also of the twin-bed-group which faces a chest-of-drawers-and-mirror arrangement. The wall brackets above the low headboards of the beds serve to carry the effect of the group-picture up on the wall, to balance the wall treatment facing it. It is important in a case like this to have the side walls decorated high enough so that there will not be too much contrast with a tall object such as the overlarge window which dominates the end of this room.

EASILY INSTALLED WOOD PANELING MAY SOLVE YOUR SPACE PROBLEM

The delightful small dining center below shows a treatment which can often be worked out to give new life to a commonplace wall. Woodwork like this in soft natural pine finish can be obtained in stock sizes to fit almost any measurements. Inexpensive and easily installed it is a special boon if you have a badly proportioned room. In this case it provides needed storage, takes the place of furniture for which there is no space, and makes the wall so attractive that it helps to offset too great length. If you have a dining nook at the end of your living room this would be an excellent way to set it off from the rest of the room. If the room is very long you might use balancing panels and bookcases at the other end and convert that end into a small library nook.

In the picture above, a compact arrangement for a bedroom is worked out in knotty pine which is specially well suited to the kind of sturdy room a boy loves. Closets and storage cupboards completely surround the bed-bunk, with desk and book shelves at the right adding a special note of convenience. Many variations of the basic idea are possible. The wood may be painted, or wallboard may be used instead of wood. Closets could be combined with more desk and book space and the bed eliminated, or the recess could be turned into a decorative frame for the head of the bed, or a dressing table alcove. The bunk-and-closet unit is shown here combined with paper on the other three walls, but almost any combination of finishes would be possible.

ANSWERS TO
SEVERAL DIFFICULT
WALL AND WINDOW PROBLEMS

These before-and-after views of two types of corner beams, present different solutions to the same problem. At lower right, two single beams were enclosed with book shelves and storage cabinets built out (lower left) to allow for a comfortable bed-couch between them. The window picture was enlarged by carrying the draperies from the window to the book shelves and hiding the wall above by a shaped fabric valance. The result is a dramatic and pleasing picture which could be copied in any room, with some slight modifications perhaps. This particular arrangement would work out very well in a narrow room, but is not confined to that. In a wider room the book shelves could be made wider

across the front. In the upper sketches (left and right) a structural defect is shown which is often considered hopeless; as a matter of fact, it could easily be taken care of by any of the methods suggested here. Even corner cupboards could be used to cover up beams by making them wide enough and using closed wooden doors which would conceal the irregularities within. A device like this would be excellently adapted to setting off the end of a narrow room as a small dining nook, game corner or library. The shelves could be used for books, hobby collections or anything else needed for the "activity center" in the tiny alcove formed by the shelves.

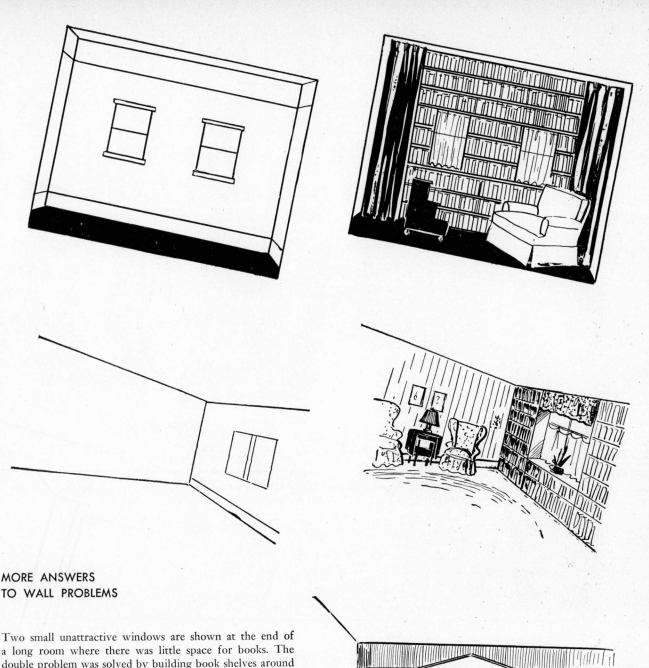

MORE ANSWERS
TO WALL PROBLEMS

Two small unattractive windows are shown at the end of a long room where there was little space for books. The double problem was solved by building book shelves around the windows from ceiling to floor, with draperies at the side walls and only sheer glass curtains over the windows. Library steps are provided for reaching the upper shelves. This arrangement allows plenty of light for reading from uncluttered windows, and the rich coloring of books on the wall seems to draw the end of the long room closer. By installing the draperies as draw-curtains on a traverse track across the ceiling a short distance from the windows, you could have privacy whenever desired in a cozy reading alcove. The center sketches illustrate one thing which may be done when the windows are close together instead of being separated. Here they are curtained as one window, with a valance above to cover the wall and thus make the window appear taller. Book shelves are built below and up both sides, again with the effect of shortening the long room. The shelves in the sketch at lower right are traditional in feeling, dignified and attractive, yet simple enough to be built by anyone handy with tools. They could be widened to fill an end wall.

The soft dark tones of the painting on the wall are repeated in the olive green used for walls and floor in this attractive living room. Off-white draperies, rug, and love-seat upholstery, with glass lamps and white shades, bring the room to life. Antique satin in white and green is used for the benches and the two Sheraton-style arm chairs, while the two love seats placed together for a sofa are covered with a rich green and white printed fabric in a heavy modern textured weave. Green and white striped satin on the traditional side chairs carries out the basic harmony. The antique

INTEREST AND DRAMA

gold of the picture frame sets the accessory accent colors—gold-flecked tortoise-shell of the coffee table, polychrome shades in the ornamental clock above the mantel, and the brass candlestick. Traditional and modern furnishings are skillfully mingled here against the plain dark background.

CHAPTER FOUR

How to Use Color

COLOR is your most effective decorating aid. Make it work *for* you. You will find in its use the easiest and least expensive way to bring light into dark rooms, warmth into coldness, sparkle into dullness, and variety into monotony. There is power in color, but you need not be afraid to use it. Behind almost every drab, depressing room you will find someone who was afraid to take a chance with color merely because its simple principles were not understood.

The use of color is easy to understand because its every aspect takes us back to nature. The rainbow provides our color spectrum from which all color variations are derived. The meanings we associate with the "language of color" are those nature has made familiar to us. The "warm" colors, in the red and orange family, are merely those which remind us of fire and the brilliant hues of tropical blossoms in hot climates. Passing through orange in the spectrum we come to yellow, the warm comforting color of distilled sunshine, or spring daffodils and autumn goldenrod. Green, in the center, is nature's rest-cure, the soothing background color of summer fields and woods, indispensable modifier for the intensity of bolder and more aggressive hues. Emerging from green into blue we still have a color restful in nature, "cool" and serene, tending to coldness as it melts into violet.

All these meanings are subject to endless modification as we mix the three primary colors—pure red, blue and yellow—to get the hundreds of shades and tones derived from that source. In general, the warm fire colors are cheerful, dramatic, and interesting—but over-stimulating if used without discretion and restraint. The warm sunlight colors are gay, cheerful and generally useful. Green is an invaluable bridge

59

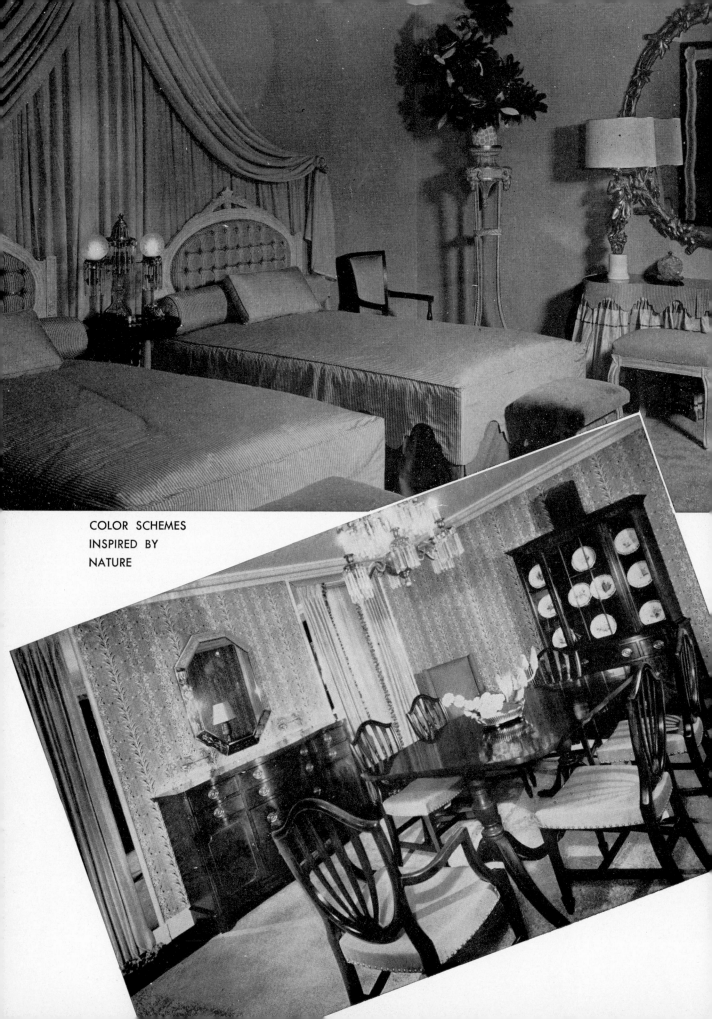

COLOR SCHEMES
INSPIRED BY
NATURE

THREE INTERESTING COLOR HARMONIES

Furniture in antique French style gives to the bedroom at left an air of period elegance which is interestingly modernized by tailored bed covers and a color scheme based upon the hot colors of our own Grand Canyon. Walls and rug are of mountain smoke tone, with orange draperies. Bed coverings are in orange and white stripes, chair upholstery is chartreuse. "November Sunshine" is the appropriately symbolic name given to the traditional dining room by its designer. Harvest gold carpet, pale sunshine-yellow-and-gray patterned wallpaper, make a softly bright background for mahogany furniture with chair seats covered in rust-colored shot silk like the upholstery of the wing chair in the corner. Oyster-white silk draperies are trimmed with dark multicolored fringe for accent. This use of a monochromatic color scheme shows that it need not lack variety nor interest. Note the "sunny" sparkle introduced by mirror frames around the windows, and also by the crystal chandelier above the table. Restfulness in the living room below is achieved by use of soft neutral background colors, plain surfaces, and balanced arrangement. These same factors help create the impression of space in this room of average size. The couch and chairs suggest comfort in every line, the center-of-interest window group balances the large center-of-interest desk and chair group, the pictures are arranged to balance wall spaces above furniture. Notice the window draperies, lifted to the ceiling line for height and extended beyond the windows to couch width in order to make a frame for the couch—a useful device wherever windows are small in relation to wall space or furniture. Absence of other design in the room—except for a little striped fabric used for chair seats—allows the choice of large bold pattern in the draperies which set the color scheme for the room. Made to be drawn across the windows at night under the shaped valance, they give the needed touch of drama to the quiet room. Two shades of gray in the mohair and rayon drapery fabric are worked into the design which is highlighted by large "Victory Wreaths" in gold. Walls and carpet are in tones of gray with lighter ceiling. The couch is upholstered in rough-textured gold fabric, the arm chairs in fog-blue. Accents, in couch pillows and accessories, are white and red. The primary blue, yellow and red color combination is translated here into a restful harmony of softly grayed shades against a neutral background with only the red accents left in bright tones. Traditional furniture is combined with modern plainness of surface and modern texture roughness to create a room which is at the same time restful and interesting.

SOFT BACKGROUND COLORS FOR RESTFULNESS AND A FEELING OF SPACE

between colors, a perfect background for a "restful" room. However, as in nature, it must be enlivened with brighter hues such as the deep blue of a summer sky, the brilliance of flowers, the sparkle of sunlight on water. Blue—the tranquil, quiet, relaxing color—is one of nature's favorites and the favorite color of many people, but it is a light-absorber. Used to excess in its duller shades it easily creates the depressing atmosphere we associate with "being blue." Blue tones of violet are so cold and impersonal that they are not often used in home decoration except in modified tones or in small amounts for accent or contrast. Because of this very coldness and impersonality they have long been associated with the background and trappings of royalty.

TYPES OF COLOR

Colors fall naturally into the two groups suggested above—*warm* and *cool*—with transitional groups between. There are also the colors called "neutral," including black and white which are treated as neutrals. Each group has certain general characteristics and a knowledge of these will not only help you use colors artistically but will enable you to solve many decorating problems.

Warm, Advancing Colors: Red and yellow are always warm colors, also orange which comes between them in the color circle. When you look at these colors they appear to be closer to you than they actually are. For this reason they are known also as *near* or *advancing* colors. Any mixed hue in which red, yellow or orange predominates becomes automatically a warm, advancing color even in its paler shades. All dark *rich* colors will prove to have a mixture of one of the warm colors, and to some degree will have the quality of advancing. For example: One color series ranges from ivory and cream through tan, buff, peach, pink, rose, coral, to deep colors such as rust or burgundy, and each one of these would be classified as a warm, advancing color.

Cool, Receding Colors: Blue is the center of the cool color group. The feeling of coolness it creates is reminiscent of water, ice, and skies far overhead. When you look at a blue object it takes on this quality of distance—it appears farther away from you than it actually is. So the cool color group is known also as the *distant* or *receding* group. It includes all mixed colors in which blue predominates; also white, and the very light tints of most other colors resulting from mixtures with a large proportion of white.

Transitional Colors: Green is a transitional color because it is made by combining a warm with a cool primary color—yellow with blue. If there is more yellow the green swings toward the warm group; the more blue predominates the cooler the green is. Violet, in the same way, is the link between blue and red. Lavender tones in which violet is mixed with blue are cool; but they take on warmth as the violet is mixed with red to make mulberry.

Neutral Colors: Pure gray is the 100% "neutral" color made by mixing in equal proportions either black and white, or the three primaries (blue, red and yellow) from which all other colors are made. This makes gray a great harmonizer between other colors because it has something of all of them in it. Various tones of gray are made by varying the proportions of colors used. Gray is usually considered a cool color, and "graying" a warm color is said to "cool it down." However, like green, gray swings from cool to warm according to the proportions in which the colors are mixed. Shading from light to dark, pure gray ranges from pale silver to deep slate-gray—all cool tones. But when more color from the warm group is used in mixing, or is added to it, the gray takes on the warm pinkish glow of beige, or a yellowish cast which brings it closer to tan.

BOLD USE OF BLACK IN A DINING ROOM GIVES DRAMATIC CONTRAST

A dramatic version of modern color harmony is expressed in the dining room below with its various interesting features. Blue and green provide the basis for an analogous color scheme, motivated by the design pattern in the draperies which stand out in bold relief against severely plain room surfaces. This striking effect is intensified by the broad "frame" around the window-picture in the shape of a cornice extended down both sides and painted in a darker shade of the soft pale green used for walls. Blue upholstery, blue and silver accessories, with cotton rug in off-white like the drapery background, make up the blue-green and neutral harmony. Black is usually considered neutral, but it is so dramatized here that it really plays the featured role. The chair legs are black, also the floor, but the focal point of room interest is the black carrara glass used for table and console tops, laid across cylindrical supports of seafoam glass which can be arranged in a variety of ways. These glass tops are treated so that neither temperature nor scratches affect them, and they can be turned over for use on either side.

COLOR INSPIRATIONS DRAWN FROM FABRIC DESIGNS

SOFT TONES IN A BEDROOM

The popularity of nature as an inspiration for color schemes is shown once more in the delightful flower-decked bedroom (left). Off-white woodwork is a foil for the matching wallpaper and chintz covered with purple pansies shading to blue and mingled with occasional petals of purple-red and light golden yellow. The rich tracery of green ferns carries a continuous background pattern over paper and chintz. Chintz used for drapery flounces, quilted valance and upholstery is in gold. Glass curtains and dressing-table skirts are off-white to match the woodwork, while red ribbon bows and bed-spread border pick up red tones in the flowers. The carpet is soft grayed-blue. This color arrangement is an interesting example of the three primary colors greatly softened and combined with adjacent colors to form almost a rainbow symphony. The effect of the whole room, in spite of the rich use of color, is restful because of the neutral gray used for softening and the plain color areas in floor, ceiling, woodwork and upholstery. Notice the interesting way in which a small bay window has been set off by valance and draperies as a tiny white-curtained dressing room.

WARM
WINTER DRESS

COLOR-AIDS IN SEASONAL DECORATING

Adapting a room to its environment or to a change in season is one of the most valuable functions of color. This is graphically shown in the two pictures here. In the one below, a living room appears in its winter dress, above as it has been prepared for summer. An interesting point to notice here is the use which has been made of pictures to establish color schemes. The portrait reproduction over the mantel has a background color too dark for this room background, so the lady's gown is used as inspiration for old-ivory wall color. Her scarf sets the tone for rich amethyst and wine shades in carpet, hangings and lounge chair by the fire. The background of the picture is carried into the room by the sapphire blue of couch and other pieces not shown here. The fireplace rug and lamp shades are ivory with the two comfortable chairs upholstered in ivory and wine. The furniture wood is mahogany, traditional in design. Accessories in wine, blue and white complete a warm, rich color scheme. The rule for using primary colors together in softened tones is followed. The yellow is found in the very light tints of old ivory; the red is grayed to deep, soft shades; the blue has a slightly green cast which means there is a touch of yellow in its make-up and that helps tie the room and the ivory walls together. Notice the arrangement of the furniture which allows the fireplace group to share interests centering about the couch-and-chair-conversation group at the left.

The summery atmosphere in the transformation above is keyed to the rose and blue of the flower print which replaces the portrait over the mantel. A glimpse of ivory background between blue-green draperies in the picture keys it to the ivory walls of the room. The drapery color in the picture is repeated in a blue-green slip cover (with ivory fringe) on the wing chair, while the flowers in the bowl are inspiration for flowered chintz draperies and slip cover. Notice the less formal lines of the summer drapery. The deep window is not changed because the metal trellis with growing vines is equally attractive for winter or summer. Framed in wine color (like the drapery cornices) it is designed to balance the book shelves on the other side of the fireplace. The problem of hard-to-take-up carpeting is here solved by placing a large beige summer rug with design in blue-green and wine over the center of the carpet. The reproduction of an old metal folding fireplace screen is so charming that it is left in the "summer" room, though growing plants or flowers might be used to give the fireplace a summer dress too.

VALUE OF NEUTRAL COLORS

The gray tones are valuable in decorating, both as background colors in their own right and to tone down colors which are too bright. You can neutralize or "gray" a bright paint or dye by adding a little of the color opposite it in a color circle, but it is usually simpler to add pure gray. The most aggressive color can be neutralized with gray and made a softly pleasant background color. The drab, muddy tones people mistakenly call neutral come from too much gray in the mixture. Such charming shades as bois de rose, sage green, old gold, eggplant, resada green, gray-blue, rose-beige, etc., are all neutralized colors.

Neutral brown has much the same useful harmonizing quality as gray, since it too results from a mixing of all colors. But in pure gray there is an equal mixture, while there is no brown shade without some preponderance of warm colors over cool. This makes the lighter tints—tan, beige, etc.—excellent background colors where a warm tone is needed, with the deep, strong brown shades as foundation colors for floors and furniture. Like the sturdy bark of the tree trunk, or the velvety richness of plowed earth, the brown and reddish earth colors suggest strength, vigor and dignity—qualities a man likes in his study or library.

Relating a Room to Its Occupants: Color is a useful agent in personalizing a room through expression of individual tastes. Almost everyone has certain favorite colors—but it is well to remember that in general men prefer a background of darker and stronger color tones than those which appeal to women, and young people usually like brighter, gayer colors than their parents. As in all generalizations, these statements are based upon average reactions. Don't be limited by rules or averages. Analyze your own color likes and dislikes, and compare them with the suggestions in this chapter. You may discover you have been using the colors you like in the wrong combinations and getting unsatisfactory results which a little knowledge will help you correct. Or you may find there are delightful color harmonies you have never thought about before which are much more satisfying.

FINDING INSPIRATIONS FOR COLOR SCHEMES

Both the world of nature and the world of art are filled with answers to your color problems, but combinations found in art are more easily adapted to your needs. If you base your color scheme upon a painting, a fabric pattern or a wallpaper design you have the advantage of seeing how the colors actually look together. Also, you know that the proportions in which they are used have been worked out by an artist or a designer who understands the fine points of harmonizing colors. He has already mixed the pigments on his palette, experimented, and achieved a harmony. If you like his results you can apply the same scheme of color to decorating your room, as in the following examples.

Pictures or Paintings: Analyze your picture and figure out roughly the proportions in which the artist has used the different colors. Select the dominant color in the painting for the largest areas in your room unless it is such a strong tone that you must follow a different plan. Distribute the others in the same general proportions the artist has used for the elements of his composition. For you that will usually mean using (1) the dominant or controlling color on walls, (2) the secondary color on the next largest area which will probably include floor and draperies, (3) a subordinate color for large pieces of furniture, (4) bright clear accent color for the smallest areas such as occasional furniture, accessories, trimming, fabric or wallpaper designs.

It is not necessary to match the exact shades the artist has used. Select fabric or paint colors which tone in harmoniously with the tints and shades in the picture. If needed, a touch of gray, the harmonizer, added to one or more of the colors will bring all your colors into line.

Fabric or Wallpaper Designs: In a floral pattern the color of the leaves would probably be a good choice for your floor covering with one of the deeper flower tones for upholstery. A lighter flower color could be used for one of the stripes in the drapery. The walls might be either a light tint from a smaller flower (or petal) or the background color of the figured material. Take your accent cue from an accent color in the design, or select it by finding the complementary contrast for your dominant color. This method can be followed whether the figured material is actually to be used in your room or is merely serving as a color inspiration—only be sure you have a large enough piece so that you can get a clear idea of the color tones.

DINING ROOM COLORS DRAWN FROM A DELLA ROBBIA PLAQUE

The tiny Della Robbia plaque above the doorway sets the entire color scheme for the charming dining room below. The background of the plaque is soft blue, the border is a wreath of foliage and sun-ripened fruits with a predominance of dusty violet and yellow accented by warm red. The figure in the center is characteristically snow white. The color scheme for the room is worked out in soft yellow for walls, reddish-violet for rug, shelf background and wall decorations, blue for draperies. The drapery pattern is in wine and white. The ceiling is azure blue and there are snow-white glass curtains at the large picture window. This will be recognized as the primary red, blue and yellow triangle with all the colors muted in a soft harmony which still suggests the gaiety of spring sunshine, flowers and fruit under a Mediterranean sky. Note the useful and decorative shelf-and-cupboard arrangement which was built in at very slight expense. The furniture is in soft natural finish with light wood tones; accessories carry out the colors of the plaque.

WHITE ACCENTS FOR COOLNESS IN TWO VIEWS OF A
LIVING ROOM READY FOR SUMMER

A practical and unusual color scheme is illustrated in the living room above which combines traditional furniture with modern touches in rug and pictures. Chocolate brown walls are made possible here because of the abundance of light, and they provide an effective foil for pink valances, pale pink polka dot curtains and dramatic cretonne draperies which pick up all the colors of the room. The fiber rug in tones of rose, the fresh green growing plants, flowers and drapery-foliage complete the modified complementary color scheme of red and green worked out against a neutral background of brown. White accents add to the summery feeling of rug and draperies. Notice the combination of plain surfaces with boldly flowered fabric and geometric designs. The small picture below shows another corner of the room with the pink of the window valance carried into it by means of slip covers. Cretonne flounces and white accessories relieve bareness of plain dark walls. Notice the pleasant grouping of love seats and table for conversation.

Art Objects: You may find your inspiration in almost anything you see which happens to appeal to you in the way of a figured bowl, vase, mosaic tiling, stained glass, pottery, plaque, rug. A tiny Della Robbia plaque may set a charming color scheme for a whole room (see illustration, page 66), and many a lovely plan has been worked out from the delicate harmonies of an Aubusson rug or the rich colors found in Orientals. For unusual inspiration go into a Chinese shop and study the marvelous color harmonies in the porcelain vessels there. No matter what your color preference may be you will find some bowl or vase created by these master craftsmen which will show it worked out in a beautifully satisfying harmony.

Nature: No artist has ever surpassed nature's color harmonies, but when natural colors are transplanted into the different lighting and perspective of a room indoors a little artistry must be used. The original shades in nature often need to be toned down somewhat, except for small flashes of your accent tones. Many people have a favorite season which they like to express in decoration. A color scheme inspired by spring would be gay with soft pastel tones and misty harmonies. Summer would be rich and alive, with full, deep shades of flowers in full bloom. Autumn's display of red, gold and brown would bring mellow charm into a living room or library. The cool, serene white and blue of winter with violet shadows provides a scheme entirely different in mood and effect. Other suggestions for drawing inspirations from nature will be found in this chapter.

HOW TO SUIT YOUR COLOR SCHEME TO YOURSELF

Many women like to decorate a room in tones which provide a harmonious background for their own special types of coloring. In this case you simply pick out the color scheme you have found most flattering in selecting your clothes and transfer it to the room you are decorating, with whatever modifications that requires. However, don't forget that in a living room other people must share the room too. The background should not be done in colors which will become you, but be unflattering to some member of your family or a probable guest. For instance, if you are the dramatic, vivid, dark-haired type, you might be made even more dramatic and vivid by a room in colors so intense that the average woman would be extinguished by them. So use discretion in fitting your background to yourself.

There is one thing every woman should remember in this matter of relationship between herself and her background. Application of this principle need not react against anyone else, and it will help her to appear at her best. Avoid all colors or decorations which are definitely *not* becoming to you, or which emphasize any defect in your appearance. If your coloring is on the pale side, don't make it paler by too-delicate pastels, or overshadow it by too-vivid

EFFECTIVE COLOR SCHEME

Built around a color scheme which is practically monochromatic, this living room draws its color theme from an interesting stylized picture in turquoise and brick red. With this complementary combination of blue-green and softened red, the blue was obviously best suited for the dominant color with red reserved for accent. Notice the interesting texture variety achieved here by combinations of rough and smooth fabrics in several weaves; different types of fringe on the couch, chair and draperies; also the geometrical pattern of the sculptured carpet in self-color. Furniture and draperies shades. If you have any figure defect, put a becoming color on your walls and furniture and then wear dresses in matching or harmonizing tones of the same color. This merges your figure into the background and directs attention from it, at the same time bringing out best features of your complexion and hair.

BASED UPON A PICTURE

are traditional in design, harmonizing with the classic feeling of the urn in the picture. Tall white lamps and shades combine with small red pillows and a few other accessories to relieve possible monotony of color. The three-cornered game table in the foreground creates a subordinate-interest grouping. Notice the well-balanced conversation arrangement of the furniture grouped against the plain wall in the background. The draperies are carried to the ceiling in a dignified line giving height to the room and balancing the size of the picture above the couch.

TYPES OF COLOR SCHEMES

Endless variations in color combinations can be developed in any room, under any given set of conditions, but they will all belong to one of four general types of color schemes. White, black, or one soft neutral tone may be added to any of these combinations without essentially changing the color plan. Here is a note of caution—don't try to handle too many colors in one room. Too few are always better than too many. Remember that you are free to use various shades and tints in each color as well as bright and soft tones. This will prevent monotony even if you do not go outside one or two basic colors.

Monochromatic Color Scheme: To work out what is called a "monochromatic" scheme, select your color, then use that color alone in various shadings, throughout every detail of your decorating. This may *sound* monotonous, but some really exciting and dramatic modern rooms have been done without even color shading—with no variety at all except that in weaves, wood grains, and textures. In using such a one-color scheme there are two secrets of success. One is a pleasing variety in shading and intensity of your single color. The other is a striking difference in textures of materials used in the room.

In these rooms—and even more where only one tone of the one color is used—textures and wood grains move into the most important spot in the decorating picture. When the one-color scheme is well done it results in a subtle, sophisticated style of room in spite of its apparent simplicity. Line, finish and detail must be very nearly perfect—there are no frills to camouflage defects in this type of decorating.

One of the most interesting color-studies in nature is the use of these monochromatic schemes with no resulting monotony. With nature as a guide you can build a cool restful room entirely around the one-color theme found in a bit of garden woodland in early spring. Green tones range from the subtle gray-green or yellow-green of buds and opening leaves, through fresh pale green of new foliage, to deeper tones of evergreens in ornamental clumps or hedges. New grass or dark green moss is like a green overlay on a carpet. From a little distance even twigs and branches seem to take on a cast of muted green, bringing them into the one-color harmony too. If you want an exquisite blending of pink tones in a rose bedroom, examine the petals of a freshly opened rose. A bouquet of delphiniums will suggest an equally charming scheme in blue specially well adapted to a young girl's bedroom.

Analogous (Related, or Adjacent) Color Schemes: In using consecutive colors, with transition shades between, the color series never goes far enough in either direction to include any contrast color in the harmony. If contrast is used it is only a dash of complementary color in the form of accent. Textures play a part here, in preventing a feeling of monotony as they do in the monochromatic, but the scheme is easier to handle successfully than one limited to a single color. The shades and tints used are often drawn from the subtle inbetween steps on the scale, and the feeling is modern but rather feminine.

To illustrate how this scheme might work out in a room where green was to strike the dominant note, you could use tones ranging through various blue-green intensities, with yellow or chartreuse for accent colors. Green, blue-green, blue, blue-violet, and violet would be another series, stopping short of mulberry which has more or less red in its composition and would introduce contrast. Examples of how to visualize these colors are shown in color wheel number 4 on page 405.

This color scheme is another favorite with nature, and here are some of the possibilities suggested by familiar scenes. A vista through a picture window showing a symphony with gray-green sea, gray rocks, blue or blue-gray sky, takes in only a group of analogous colors. Colors of the pine forest in a series of browns and ochres in trunks, branches and needle-piled earth would combine with the deep or yellowish greens of live needles to decorate a sturdy, restful room for reading or study. This combination is made up of greens and adjacent yellows, more or less deeply grayed. Yellow or red or clear bright green could be used for accent brightness. A life-giving harmony for a gloomy room could be based on a bouquet of marigolds and zinnias in the series ranging through yellow, orange, and deep red. Another series akin to this would include the red, orange, and brown of oaks and maples in the fall. A clear blue sky over a group of silver birch trees with gray-white trunks and soft green leaves might inspire a cool and restful summer bedroom.

Complementary Color Schemes: This is the type of decorating scheme most widely used both in traditional and contemporary designs because it has the greatest natural variety and interest. To apply it, select a color you want to make important in your room, then use with it the complementary color shown in color wheel 2. There are more colors involved in this scheme than in the other two but it is easier to handle successfully. It has a tendency to be vigorous and masculine in feeling when the dominant color is strong and clear.

The complement of each warm color is a cool color—which means that every color scheme in that group will have an automatic balance between warm and cool, and the resulting harmony will be of a highly satisfactory quality. By choosing a warm dominant color for a room where cheerfulness is needed, and making its cool complement the secondary or the subordinate color, you will have a stimulating atmosphere relieved by the restfulness of the cool color. On the other hand, if you want to create a feeling of cool serenity, make the cool color dominant, with only enough of its warm complement to keep the atmosphere from seeming cold or unfriendly.

HOW TO WORK OUT A COMPLEMENTARY SCHEME

Be sure your dominant color *dominates*. If a softened ("grayed") tone of the color, it will not dominate unless it is spread out over the largest area. If it is in a bright, clear tone, it will dominate by its strength, even though its area is smaller than that of a soft neutral. Complementaries are contrasts—competitors. If you use them both in the same room, in strong tones and approximately equal amounts, they will clash. The subordinate one must be either materially softened in tone, or used in much smaller amounts. Never try to make a fifty-fifty division of importance between these contrast colors.

For additional hues to give greater variety and interest you can consult the color wheels and use any color indicated there as harmonious with one of your colors. For example, if you are using a dominant green, softened and combined with softened tones of complementary red, you will find that orange or violet may be used for accent. Charts on the color page will suggest many possibilities.

The complementary color scheme is easy to adapt to a room already partly furnished as it allows several colors to be shuffled about and combined with others in many different ways. For example, if you have a couch upholstered in a clear blue with a deeper blue rug, you will select orange for the subordinate color, using soft orange and soft blue in draperies or on other furniture, with pale gray-blue or soft ivory walls, depending on whether there is much or little light in the room. Select other colors for accent according to suggestions in the paragraph above.

In most of the complementary color schemes which are taken from nature green plays some part, but it is interesting to note how this color is "keyed" to the type of plant and the color of its flowers. It will change by many tones, even in a single branch, so that the flower cup will be continuously in perfect tune with the pale bud and the more deeply colored blossom. A lovely complementary color theme for a bedroom or a gay informal living room is found in the blooming of an orchard in the spring. Delicate

COLOR DRAMA
IN THE
DINING ROOM

The greatest charm of this room lies in a subtle blending of modern and traditional decorating colors and themes. Modern furniture and mirrors, with their clear, simple lines, are reminiscent of the French Directoire period, when plain walls in strong, dark colors were as popular as they are in modern interiors. Dark, rich background colors provide an effective setting for light wood and accents in white. Against an off-white ground, the floral pattern of formal window draperies picks up the red, green and blue of the bold complementary color scheme. Early 19th Century preference for marble floors, without carpeting, is translated here into a striking design of huge blocks in softly waxed composition flooring.

COLOR-SUBSTITUTE FOR ARCHITECTURAL CHANGES

In this long, narrow room, the use of one color — for walls, woodwork, carpeting and draperies — widens and shortens the appearance of the room by making the observer unaware of breaks between walls, floor and the many windows at one end (below). Contrast to the rose background is furnished by complementary green tones in chintz and accessories. Large contrast areas on the fireplace wall (top) bring it forward, to lessen apparent length.

DISTINCTIVE USE OF BACKGROUND COLOR FOR AN ATTRACTIVELY INDIVIDUALIZED BEDROOM

The room above is proof that all bedrooms do not have to look alike. As shown here, it is the result of imagination applied to a perfectly conventional bedroom. In this case the well-made mahogany furniture was retained in its original state. It was merely surrounded with a new atmosphere and placed against an entirely different background created in the same room. No structural changes were made, except for the corner closets with full-length mirrors. These were built in to make an alcove setting for the bed, break up the square boxlike lines of the room, and incidentally provide much-needed closet and mirror space. A rather unusual decorating idea was used to turn the room into a shell of color to frame the interesting picture made by the new bed-group. The former carpet was removed and jaspé linoleum in soft green was substituted. The same shade was carried up onto walls and ceiling, creating a cool and appropriate foliage-colored background for the riot of flowers on the chintz

used for bedcovers, slip covers and lamp shades. Against this green the complementary shades of reddish violet and rose combine to create a light color symphony in which all the tones are softened enough to keep the effect from being garish. Yellow flowers mingle with rose in the chintz to add a gay accent color. There are several interesting points to observe in this room. One is in the cotton string rug made up in an unusual shape by sewing small rugs together. Placing the two gold upholstered chairs and the game table at the foot of the bed provides balance for the overhanging canopy above the bed. This canopy was made by installing a molding frame for draperies hung from the ceiling, and using the same material as the bedcover for curtains and valance. The original mahogany headboard was retained, but completely covered up by frilled pillow covers. Plain draperies in the same color as the wall can be drawn across the window to make the soft green shell effect complete.

71

pink blossoms and tender green branches, with the blue of the sky, fit into a favorite complementary color scheme. Another complementary theme is found in an old-fashioned flower garden with its combinations of warm and cool colors, and contrasting hues side-by-side. A complementary contrast theme is strikingly effective when a brilliant patch of vermilion blossoms lights up a soft, quiet background of deep green moss or lichens.

The split complementary scheme is a variation of the complementary which is often helpful. When a warm dominant color in a strong tone is used it may take two cool colors to balance it. In wheel number 3 you will see how this works out for you. The three combinations sketched illustrate the principle. Place the sharp point of the triangle on any color and draw your lines as shown.

The Primary Triangle Color Scheme: Called a "triad" grouping, this scheme brings together the three primary colors, or the three secondaries, or the three tertiaries, or any corresponding group of transition shades between them, as shown in color wheel number 1. The tertiaries are sufficiently grayed (see page 405) so that it is possible to use them in

GAY STRAWBERRY-PATTERNED CHINTZ SETS A COLOR SCHEME

Remodeling possibilities in a house with small rooms are delightfully illustrated in the combination living-dining-and-game room above. Made by tearing out partitions in a small Colonial farmhouse, the effect of cool, airy spaciousness is achieved despite low ceiling and small windows. A soft green-and-white background helps, also the carefully balanced furniture grouping. The color scheme is drawn from the chintz design, with a stylized strawberry pattern showing both the red of the fruit and the deep green of the leaves. The floor is painted dark green and softly waxed. Lamp shades in dark green textured material match the floor color. The draw-curtains in the windows are strawberry red sailcloth, also the cushions on black chairs. Pine and maple furniture and hand-braided rag rugs carry out the Early American atmosphere. Notice the restful formal balance in the arrangement of seats, lamps and tables at the fireplace; also the way in which the plant-covered commode at the right balances the small dining group at the left. This time the balance is informal—a matter of feeling, rather than identity. Draperies attached to the original house beams suggest where a partition once stood, and break up any possible impression of bareness in the sweep of floor space.

fairly equal proportions in this grouping. A better plan, however, is to make one of them strongly dominant, with at least one of the other two definitely subordinate. In order to use the secondaries, and above all the primaries, in a triad combination, you must bring them into harmony by graying them— or select slightly grayed tones in paint or fabric you buy. For instance, pure primary red, yellow, and blue are harsh and glaring together. But when each is mixed with gray to produce rose, tan, and soft blue, they become a highly effective decorating trio.

NOTES ON COMBINING COLORS

No matter what color scheme you prefer there are a few general principles which will help you select your colors and combine them most effectively. Proper use of samples is very important in matching your colors, and you need also to know the effect of daylight and artificial light on colors.

The general rule for combining colors in a room is to follow one of the three types of color schemes, adapting it if necessary to any furniture or background you must keep as it is. Sometimes introduction of only small areas of contrast color will give a new tone to the whole decorating scheme. Whenever you use a bright accent color repeat it in more than one place in the room, even if it is in very small spots such as touches of trimming or piping on a sofa cushion.

Avoid using all cool colors or all warm colors, all light colors or all dark colors in a room. You must have a certain amount of contrast in order to make each color effective, also for the sake of interest and variety. The one exception to this would be a monochromatic color scheme where texture provides the contrast. Warm colors and bright colors are more aggressive than cool, soft shades. Always balance an area of warm, dark or bright colors against a larger area of cool, light, or soft color. Use bright primary hues sparingly. A little of some warm vibrant color may be safely placed against a neutral background, while fairly equal amounts of strong and neutral colors lack color balance and interest.

HOW TO HARMONIZE ROOMS THROUGH COLOR

Wherever you have rooms which open into each other, into a common hallway, or into small alcove-type rooms, you must include them all in your color harmony. Try to select a color scheme for the most important of the rooms which will allow you to carry the same basic color, or your key color, into the other rooms in some way. If the rooms are small the best method is to use the same color for background in all of them, but not necessarily the same shade. This increases the effect of spaciousness by carrying the eye along a continuing vista from one room to the next.

CORRECTIVE USE OF COLOR

When a room is too small you can do two things to remedy the trouble—eliminate all superfluous or out-of-scale furniture and use color correctly to gain an effect of more space. In the sketch above a room is decorated entirely in shades of one color (monochromatic) in a light receding tone. Furniture is planned to save floor space and seem inconspicuous because it merges with the color of its background. The same thing applies to draperies. Wall-to-wall floor covering in the deepest shade of the color chosen is helped out by grouping furniture against walls and utilizing corners. Draperies are a little lighter than floor, furniture upholstery is as light as the walls and the ceiling lighter still. (See suggestions in this chapter for working out this type of monochromatic color scheme.)

In this sketch, a barnlike room is given the reverse treatment. Two large rugs break up floor space. Panels and hangings make walls seem smaller and help "fill" the room. It is possible to cut the appearance of many square feet from your walls by making them the right color, then putting the right things in front of them. A room like this is where you can indulge any fondness you may have for woodwork and wall trimmings which contrast with their background.

ALTERING APPARENT PROPORTIONS OF A ROOM BY MEANS OF COLOR

In the living room sketched here (at the left) the too-long narrow effect was lessened by the correct use of color alone. The side walls were treated with paint in a light receding color to make them seem farther away and widen the room. The end wall was painted in a warm, dark advancing color which seemed to bring it in toward the center of the room. If you cannot repaint your wall you can get something of the same effect by placing dark masses against it in the form of book shelves, panels or draperies. Horizontal color lines are used to bring down the ceiling and lengthen the walls. Using a dark color on the ceiling helps further to make it seem closer—that is, lower. Long low book shelves or other furniture used along the wall will have something of the same effect when the color is in contrast

to wall color. The photograph above shows a corner in a modern living room in which one wall has been dramatized by decoration in contrast to plain walls in a receding neutral color. Stripes chosen for the decorated wall help to make the ceiling higher as well as to emphasize the wall. If your ceiling is too high, you can still use stripes by reversing them and using them in the horizontal style favored in some modern designs. Notice here the cozy conversation corner created by the unusual arrangement of twin love seats and a matching couch. The boldly figured upholstery fabric is used with plain surfaces and stripes in correct combination for effectiveness. Various ways in which color can be used to correct unattractive proportions in a room are suggested on page 76, also other remedial uses. The camouflage value of color is as important as its effect on size and proportion. An ugly radiator, for example, or an eyesore such as a projecting pipe, can be retired into the background and made much less noticeable by painting it the shade of the wall.

If spaciousness is not an object, you still need to carry a feeling of harmony through all the rooms. This can be done by repeating in the other rooms some element of the central color scheme by making it a base for a different but synchronized decorating plan. If you are using wallpaper in all or some of the rooms you can find harmonizing sets of paper and fabrics worked out by manufacturers for this purpose. With these sets you can easily harmonize paint for one or two of the rooms with wallpaper in the others by picking up your paint color from one of the design colors in the paper.

COLOR FOR MODERN ROOMS

Traditional color schemes lean heavily toward the harmonizing qualities of the softened, or grayed, tones, while the modern idea emphasizes the dramatic use of clear, vibrant tones for walls, ceilings, and floors as well as for furniture and draperies. With the large areas of plain surfaces and the uncluttered effect of modern furnishings, color plays a major part in styling a room.

The monochromatic scheme in a neutral tone is a modern favorite. On the other hand, against a light, plain background, masses of clear fresh colors such as emerald green, coral, pale azure blue, gold and platinum glow with a jewel-like quality which is also a distinctly modern touch. With these strong tones a little knowledge of fundamental color principles becomes more important than ever.

The stimulus of modern decorating interest in color is partly responsible for a greatly increased variety in manufactured prepared paints, dyes, and wood finishes which eliminate the necessity for dabbling in paint mixing. Side by side with the chemical improvements which make paints quick-drying and easy to apply go excitingly clear and beautiful colors in such a wide range of shades and tints that you can easily carry out any decorating

BLACK ACCENTS IN A COOL NEUTRAL COLOR SCHEME

In the serenely gracious living room below a large room has been furnished so that it retains its dignity and its cool spacious atmosphere, yet breaks up any feeling of oversize by wall decoration. A plain carpet was used for the sake of restfulness, walls were kept plain to serve as background for draperies and woodwork. Beautifully spaced door panels are outlined, like the door itself, with trimming bands permissible because it was desirable to break up wall spaces. Set-in book shelves and decorated window valances, black marble mantel and green ivy-leaf design on slip covers and draperies —all help complete the color scheme of green and black against a pearl-gray background.

scheme you choose. By merely adding white pigment to make these new tones lighter, or black to make them darker, you will have a whole gamut of fascinating colors at your disposal. They come in clear, light pastels for backgrounds, and in deep, bright shades for furniture, floors, and accessories, all specially keyed to contemporary decorating needs.

Exactly the same shades and tints are also being used by the manufacturers of furniture, floor coverings, novelties, and accessories. This means that you will be able to match samples of paint, paper, and fabric with a quickness and ease which has never before been possible.

TRICKS YOU CAN DO WITH COLOR

Since warm color on a wall makes it seem to advance toward you it will naturally create an impression of narrowing space; while a cool color which seems to recede from you will create an impression of greater roominess. This is the key to your color sleight-of-hand. You will never realize until you try it yourself how many changes color can make in your room. If the proportions are bad you can do a great deal toward adjusting them, at least in appearance, by nothing more than a clever use of dark and advancing, or light and receding colors.

Color is also useful in bringing the furniture of a room into focus by making it stand out and seem larger through contrast, or by merging it with the background color to make it seem smaller. The apparent size of individual pieces of furniture can be changed by covering them in advancing or receding colors. For example, a sofa in rose or coral against a white wall would seem much larger than one in soft gray-blue against a gray wall.

Room Too Long and Narrow: The narrow room is always a problem and has already been treated from several different angles in other chapters. Whatever measures you take to make it look shorter, color will increase their effectiveness. If you do not want to make structural readjustments, color alone may be sufficient to create pleasing balance between the long and the short walls. You will find several suggestions in the illustrations in this chapter.

Room Too Square: Decide first which way you prefer to have the room's length increased, then treat two opposite walls with advancing colors to bring them in toward you. For the other two walls which are to be pushed back select a light receding color. This will immediately create an illusion of rectangular rather than square shape. If one of your walls is particularly interesting you can vary this treatment by using a neutral color on three walls and making

the interesting wall very striking by bold design or dark color. You can also break up the "long" walls by horizontal lines of color in the form of dadoes, cornices and moldings—unless your ceiling is too low for this treatment.

Ceilings Too Low or Too High: There are many tricks which color can perform in these situations—the remedy in each case being the exact reverse of that used in the other case. In addition to using continuous horizontal or vertical lines of color (see sketches pages 73, 74), you can use panels of various kinds in different color from the background wall. For a too-high ceiling keep the shape and line of the panels horizontal, for a too-low ceiling make them vertical.

Room Too Large: Combined with liberal use of warm colors, contrast is the key to making the large room seem smaller. Select colors for draperies, woodwork, wall trimmings and furniture which will be in contrast with their background. Bring in the walls and bring down the ceilings by finishing them in a harmonizing scheme of dark, rich, warm colors—advancing colors. Dress up your furniture in bright tones and large patterns to make the pieces seem larger. Remember, the same warm tones which make your walls come closer also make a piece of furniture seem nearer to you and therefore larger. In a large room you can indulge your taste for brightness in color and pattern as that helps to fill the room and make it seem smaller.

Room Too Small: You can push the walls back in several interesting ways which are in general just the reverse of those mentioned for an over-large room. Everything about the small room must be planned to eliminate contrast and lines of division. This is an excellent place to use either monochromatic or analogous color schemes—always in a soft, light receding color. (See sketches.)

Room Too Dark: White reflects more light than any other color—but it is cold, and a dark room is usually one without sun, either because of too few windows or because of exposure only on the side of a cold north light. The problem is to combine warm colors needed for light and brightness with cool tones so often desired to make the room look larger. If the room is large, you will want to use warm advancing colors anyway to make it look more friendly. In general, the color scheme in a dark room should be light and bright. Learn to use so-called "luminous" colors. Remember that all colors need *less* toning down—less graying—in a room on the dark side. If one wall is in shadow which makes it even darker than the others paint the one wall in a luminous tone or in a tint even lighter than the other walls. Always avoid rough textures in a dark room.

Room Too Light: It is much easier to cut out an excess of light or to soften it than to lighten up a dark room. If there is a glare on one wall alone you can paint that one a little darker than the others. If the ceiling is the offending light-reflector, paint that in a darker color than the walls. By controlling the windows you can usually adapt a bright room to any color scheme you desire, but remember that even a very light, bright room can be drab and dismal if it is completely filled with dark, muddy colors and dull textures which soak up the light. On the other hand, if you want to use strong bright tones you must temper the light accordingly or you will have a room which sooner or later will get on your nerves. If you have a taste for dark colors a room like this offers great opportunity to use many of the rich, dark tones which are impractical when there is only average light, and impossible where there is less than average.

HOW TO BALANCE A ROOM WITH COLOR

One of the important uses of color as a corrective agent lies in the fact that it has *weight*. Place a chair in dark upholstery opposite one which is exactly the same size and shape but done in light tones. The dark chair will appear definitely heavier than the light one. The appearance of weight is the psychological reason for the general use of darker colors on the floor, with lighter tones on the walls, and still lighter tints on the ceiling. (See page 76.) When the general practice is varied by using light carpets or rugs with a dark ceiling, it is done deliberately either for sheer unusualness or to offset some defect such as a too-high ceiling.

If your room is one of those with all the architectural interest on one wall, try balancing that wall by color-weight on the opposite side of the room. For example, if you have a fireplace and book shelves facing a blank wall, place a color panel in rich, dark tones opposite the fireplace, behind a couch upholstered in one of the warm, dark shades. If three walls of a room have interest and only one is blank, bring that one into balance by finishing it with color differing from that of the other walls. You will find many ways in which this principle of weight in color can be turned to good use on your walls.

STRIKING COLOR SCHEME FROM DRAPERY PATTERN

The dashing design of the hunting print in this room, with its bold motifs and suggested action, provides a color scheme as well as a theme. The old English print over the mantel serves both to repeat the theme and to pick up the colors. The mood of simple dignity suggested here is very appropriate for such a definitely masculine atmosphere, with emphasis on solid comfort. Note how well the traditional English fireplace fittings and lamp table harmonize with the modern comfort of deep chairs, the tweedlike texture of the upholstery, and the nubby carpet. The plain dark wall helps to set off both the dramatic pattern of the draperies and the bright colors which stand out against the light fabric background.

FRENCH PROVINCIAL FEELING—MODERN

Painted wood provides a charming background for this contemporary living room in 18th Century feeling. Grooved acoustic wallboards give the effect of a wood-paneled ceiling. The old-fashioned folding shutters and the graceful cornices which frame both window alcove and fireplace are decorated with curves and stencils which create an atmosphere of French Provincial peasant gaiety in the room. The window valance ruffle is repeated above the fireplace plate rail, softening the large opening. The interesting fireplace itself is reminiscent in design of a much earlier period in fireplace history. Early American settlers brought this "ingle nook" idea from drafty old English cottages and found its coziness useful in the cold New England climate. Ingle nooks were worked out in various ways but they always provided warm corners by having the fireplace recessed in the center of a huge chimney with a raised hearth in front

IN LIVABILITY

of it, and seats or benches built into the corners at each side of the fireplace. The room is arranged around this center-of-interest hearth, with comfortable twin sofas traditional in style and a quaint old cradle converted into a combination coffee table and magazine rack. A modern note is introduced by the deep shaggy room-size rug. Note the table and chairs placed in a bay window alcove which provides comfortable space for dining or games.

CHAPTER FIVE

How to Use Painted Walls

BEFORE you select a finish for your walls decide what you want them to do for your room. They may serve merely as a pleasing but unobtrusive background to set off beautiful furnishings, or they may be important in their own right because of dramatic treatment in design, color or decorations. In the latter case they more or less dominate the scene and the whole room must be carefully planned with that in mind. Many types of finish and many novelty materials are available for these unusual wall treatments. But when the decorative effect is to depend largely upon furniture, lamps, hangings, pictures, mirrors, and other accessories, with the walls themselves treated as pure background, paint is the most generally satisfactory finish.

There are paints for careful, long-lasting thorough work, others specially prepared for the quick cover-up job when only a short-term refurbishing is needed. Many of these paints and enamels stand up under repeated cleaning, show no brush marks, have no odor, and dry with incredible speed. You will be surprised to discover also the beautiful textures and colors available in quick-drying wall finishes—all the way from a washable super-calcimine to gloss enamels.

The quality of paint is important, and it is wise to buy only reputable brands since the cheaper kinds are not fully satisfactory and do not stand up under wear and cleaning. You will find an extraordinarily wide range to choose from at modest prices. These include familiar tested brands in the well-known lead paints as well as many new finishes. Some of them are designed for use on practically all surfaces, others are definitely limited to special purposes. Having the home decorator in mind, the manufacturers usually include mixing directions with their products and these should be carefully followed.

The general rule for painting woodwork is to make it the same color as the wall unless you have a large room which needs to have the walls broken up, or the woodwork is particularly handsome and you want to call attention to it. This is naturally a rule which is often broken. If there is much woodwork, it is part of your decorating plan and may need to be in a different color from the wall. However, if the woodwork consists of trim around doors and windows it is very seldom emphasized by being finished in a color which would make it stand out from the walls. When you combine wallpaper with painted woodwork either select the background color of the paper for the woodwork or one of the lighter tones in the design.

SPECIAL PAINT FINISHES FOR SMOOTH PLASTER

In painting smooth-plastered walls there are several different techniques which create slight variations in effect. These add wall interest without detracting from the simplicity of the painted background. When oil paints—even the flat types—are applied with the "brush" finish resulting from the customary up-and-down motions of the paint brush, a slight sheen is left on a non-absorbent surface. In using dark colors on a plaster wall this is often desirable as dark colors absorb light and the suggestion of glaze gives them more life through better reflection. On plain light walls, however, a soft mat effect is usually preferred because in paler, more light-reflecting tints a gloss may give a suggestion of glare. This is especially true in a large and well-lighted room.

Stippling: Stippling is done by pounding the freshly painted surface with a stipple brush, which obliterates all brush marks and gives a soft mat finish to oil-based paints. It may be done on the final coat, or, if you wish a particularly fine job, use it on both coats. If you can get someone to help you with your stippling the easiest way is to have your "assistant" follow you almost immediately, going over the freshly painted surface with short, quick blows from the flat side of the brush. In place of the special brush which is best for this purpose a sponge may be used, a piece of burlap or cheesecloth, or even crumpled paper. Here is a note of warning, whether you are doing the work yourself or employing someone else to do it: If the paint is good quality, and not too thick when it is put on, the stipple marks will not show, but if you are trying to save time, labor or money by using thick paint the marks of the brush may be

noticeable and the effects disappointing. Always clean your stipple brush thoroughly after each using by washing it in turpentine and rinsing it in benzene.

Scumbling: This process is designed to produce a slightly mottled effect on your plain wall. It is the same process used on floors and you will find directions in Chapter 10. It will be more effective if the ground coat is in a slightly lighter tone than the final coat.

PATTERNS IN PAINT

If you want the simplicity and cleanliness of paint but have a longing for more dramatic patterned backgrounds you do not have to be an artist who can produce beautiful murals (nor have the money to hire one). A whole new industry has developed around the decorating of home interiors through the use of stencils and other trimmings in paint applied to walls, woodwork, furniture and textiles. Many attractive methods and designs for wall treatments have been simplified and adapted to non-professional use. If the size, purpose, and mood of your room permit this kind of wall treatment, make sure the method you choose is suitable to the type of furniture and other decorations you are using or planning to use.

Painted Panelings, Moldings, and Molded Plaster: These are the most familiar ways to dress up a smooth wall. They are particularly useful when you want to tie several styles of period furnishings together in a harmonious effect in one room. Often just a suggestion of very simple, painted paneling or molded plaster will give a definite "period feeling" to such a room. There are many types of plain plaster panels, framed with wooden moldings (or with molded plaster), varying in style from those suited to the simple apartment living room to those at home in a formal period drawing room.

There is also the possibility of using colored panels against a wall painted in a different shade or color. This treatment is not advisable in the average room but may be used to advantage to break up over-long wall spaces in large rooms. Molded ornamental plaster and mural designs built up in the plaster in low relief (intaglio murals) are among the more elaborate types of painted plaster used for formal rooms. Even in a simple room of contemporary design molded motifs may sometimes be used to highlight points of special importance.

Stripes in Paint: Wide vertical or horizontal stripes may be painted on your walls usually in closely similar color tones but two values, one slightly deeper than the other so that the stripes in the design are apparent but there is no strong contrast between

SIMPLE
PAINTED
BACKGROUND
FOR A
MODERN
ROOM

TRADITIONAL
WALL
PANELING
IS
HARMONIOUS
WITH
CHINESE
DECORATING
MOTIFS

The rooms grouped on this page tell a story of backgrounds which express two completely different moods and themes, with wall treatments which harmonize with the atmosphere of each room. The upper room makes use of plain painted wall surfaces and bold color contrast. The austerity sometimes resulting from this combination is softened by the flower theme drawn from the deep border pattern on soft rose draperies. This is carried through the room and dramatically repeated by use of a hedge of growing plants and vines to top a semi-partition between the living room and a small stepped-up dining nook where the entire window wall is draped with the flower-bordered fabric. The rose and green color theme inspired by the drapery design is worked out against a background of white painted walls, with a soft shaggy rug in deep rose on the floor. One couch, upholstered in nubby-textured white, contrasts with furniture upholstered in dark green like that of the laurel leaves

in the fireplace and other foliage in the room. A traditional note is introduced by coffee table and mirror frame with light graceful curves. Note the unusual sofa design, the amusing ashtray in the form of an over-sized wine glass. Equally interesting in its own way is the lower room with a Chinese theme. This is carried out in pictures, lamp bases and other accessories in a setting which mingles traditional style and modern comfort. Painted plaster walls are paneled to frame and emphasize the rich color of books on built-in shelves, also the Chinese print above a well-arranged mantel group. Notice the beautifully balanced fireplace and furniture arrangement between the tall windows, also the effectiveness of large-patterned fabric, used in combination with plain color for walls and floor and stripe in the upholstery fabric. The mantel is unusually graceful and simple, with a shaggy modern rug in front of it to tie the center-of-interest furniture grouping together.

PANELS IN TWO-TONE EFFECT

The wall in the picture above shows the effectiveness of two tones in paint of the same color. In this case wallboard panels are used in alternating widths, the narrow panels painted in the darker tint. The same effect is possible on a solid surface of plaster or wallboard. The panels may be emphasized, if desired, with a very narrow molding covering the joinings. Note how much at home the old portraits and the Colonial type of furniture seem to be with this simple panel effect as a background.

them. In painting stripes, apply painters' tape as a guide line for the edges. You can pull it off easily when you are through, and have no uneven edges where your stripes meet.

Spattering: This amusing and sometimes very effective decoration must be used with care and always with harmonizing colors to keep it from becoming merely sensational instead of beautiful. When it is correctly done, the colors will appear to blend when you get a few feet away from them, giving the wall an appearance of being finished in one pleasantly shaded color. The process is simple, but it is well to practise on a surface you don't care about before you try it in your house. Ordinarily a dark or dull color is used for the foundation of the treatment, and the spattering is applied with bright colors. You may use only one bright color, in which case the spattering will stand out more, but it is customary to mingle spots in different harmonious colors. It is safer not to try more than three colors. For a hall or game room a deep blue background might be attractive, with the spattering done in gold and bronze like a midnight sky filled with stars. This spatter-dash treatment can be applied as a dado by tacking a row of papers just above the top of the dado to catch the overflow of spatters while you work.

For this spattering process you need only an old bristle brush, and oil paint in a little heavier mixture than you used for your foundation coat. After this first coat is dry, dip your bristle brush in one of the

bright colors you have chosen and bang it against a stick of wood held in your left hand six to ten inches from the wall. The paint that flies from the brush will cover the wall with innumerable dots, ranging from tiny pinpoints to fairly large spots. Another method is to scrape the bristles of the brush with a table knife. (See Chapter 10.)

Repeat this process along a strip of wall, then go back and do the same thing over with one of your other colors. Cover the wall in this way, finishing one strip at a time.

Misting: Misting is similar to spattering, except that the paint is sprayed on the wall with a specially designed gun. It is usually better to leave this to a professional painter. It is a decorating device occasionally employed in modern rooms to procure gradations in color, darker spray being used near the floor, shading into lighter tones toward the ceiling.

Murals: Murals include frescoes, painting done on canvas panels and applied to the wall, stencils, and

HAND WORK ON WALLS

STENCILED BORDER FOR A DRAMATIC TOUCH

The photographs on these pages and the sketch indicate some of the possibilities for home decoration by means of paint. In the room at lower left several free-hand mural-type paintings are used to dramatize a child's room. Note the attractive built-in book shelves with cabinet bases and the storage cupboard space between them. Using the large flat cupboard doors and the area about them for the design partly camouflages the fact that they are doors and makes them seem part of the wall. Two of the rooms and the sketch show how stencils can be made to outline structural features and provide a simple decorative note, particularly suitable for bedrooms, sunrooms, dinettes, and other informal types of rooms. An interesting angle is the way in which stenciling is equally at home in the traditional bedroom with its charming reproductions of Early American furniture, and the modern sunroom with unit-type reed furniture.

other types of painted wall decorations. Many a Colonial farmhouse owes its charm to the free-hand pictures left on its wall by some journeyman painter of the day. In our modern houses stenciling and other substitutes are more often used.

However, if you feel equal to trying your hand at mural painting you can get easy-to-follow directions and designs for use on walls or other surfaces. The safest practice with free-hand frescoes is to paint them on a canvas panel exactly the size of the wall space and apply them so that they look as though they had been painted directly on the wall. When large murals are used they should be placed above a dado of wood or other plain finish so that none of the picture will be hidden by furniture.

No matter what the type or subject of a mural decoration in a home the picture should not be too strong in its color values. Vivid effects or too great contrast of light and shade will make the picture stand out too strongly against the wall. Extremely realistic or lifelike presentations will also have this effect. Remember, this kind of painting is usually on a fairly large area which, after all, is background. Your murals will be much more successful if you keep them simple, using comparatively few colors in the flatter tones.

Stenciling: Stenciling, widely used in Early American houses, has the advantage of being one kind of mural painting which everyone can do. The mechanical process is simply applying a design to any surface by brushing paint, stain or dye through the cutout openings of a stencil pattern. Charming patterns may be purchased or you can use small pointed scissors to cut out your own. In any case be sure to choose designs in harmony with the style, color and mood of your room, also in scale with the wall surfaces to be decorated.

Before you are ready to use your pattern mark the points at which you will apply your decorations in order to be sure of proper spacing. A good way is to snap a chalked string against the wall to mark it in squares. This makes it easy to regulate exactly repetitions or groupings of parts of the design. Now take your pattern and thumbtack it to the wall. It is best to use a special paint for stenciling, usually more opaque than regular paint. You must also have a special brush for this work. Before you begin to paint, test your colors in an old dish or on a piece of glass, mixing them as an artist mixes pigments on his palette. Be careful not to use too much turpentine in mixing your paint. If it is too thin it will run down on the wrong side of the pattern. Be sure also to wipe off excess paint on the glass.

The correct way to apply the paint through the cutouts in the stencil is with a circular hammering motion of the brush. Work from the edges toward the center, holding the brush out from the wall at a right angle to keep paint from running underneath the pattern. You must have a different stencil for each color in your design, and the paint must dry before each application of color. If you have five colors you must use five different stencils and make five separate applications—one for each color in your spot motif. After each application clean off your pattern. Use turpentine for this if your paints are oil; water, if they are water colors.

SPECIAL TYPES OF PAINT

In addition to the familiar oil paints there are several wall-covering materials made from various bases and mixed with water. All of these produce a flat finish, but they are not handled in quite the same way. Calcimine is a powder, while most casein paints and the new oil-resin-water finishes come in paste form with directions for thinning and applying. These synthetic, or "plastic," paints are heavy in body, washable, easily applied and odorless. They dry at super-quick tempo. There are a number of different varieties with many interesting special uses aside from the smooth-wall treatment we are considering here. Ordinarily they require only one coat and are easy to use by following directions on the container.

TEXTURED WALL FINISHES

If you are painting rough plaster walls make sure the paint is recommended for that purpose and choose it several tones lighter in color than you want your finished walls to be. Rough textures absorb light and make colors appear darker than they are. If for any reason your room is not well lighted you can brighten it up by using light paint on the rough plaster and following that with a transparent glaze which will help reflect light. Sometimes merely washing down rough plaster walls, without repainting, and following with a tinted glaze will freshen or lighten them sufficiently.

When a coat of old plaster is a little too rough to suit the type or style of the room you are planning, you may find this glazing will also tone down the texture enough to bring it into harmony. But if the roughness is exaggerated and hopelessly out of place in your picture you will have to change the texture. This you can do by applying a thin coat of plaster as a base for paint, or using plastic paint. However, if you find that more drastic measures are necessary you can conceal the old plaster under inexpensive wallboard which may be pre-finished or decorated

DARK PAINTED WALLS CONTRAST GLOWING COLORS IN AN ORIENTAL RUG

Both rug and furniture in this lovely living room are traditional in theme, yet the decorative scheme of the room is definitely contemporary. The allover design of the figured Persian Oriental rug blends equally well with the traditional furniture and the modern setting, tying them together in complete harmony. Notice the dramatic drapery with its heavy dark fringe. Flanked by formally balanced table-lamp-and-chair groups, the window helps make a corner into a center-of-interest grouping. The color scheme of the room is drawn from the rich shades of the rug with its dark blue field and various colors, mellow and reserved but made distinct through contrast. The border is in pale green with secondary margins of light blue. Furniture arrangement leaves a clear space to display the beauty of the rug.

with paint or paper after it is installed. You can also use fabric to conceal the rough walls. Plain muslin may be stretched over frames and used as a smooth base for paint or paper, or decorative fabrics may be stretched or hung as a finish.

SIMULATED TEXTURES FOR WALLS

If your walls are smooth plaster, wood or wallboard and you like the warmth, period feeling, or rustic simplicity of one of the many types of textured surfaces, you can have it through an operation about as simple as putting on an ordinary coat of paint. The so-called "plastic" finishes perfected in recent years may be applied directly over wood or wallboard, old or new plaster. Only when old plaster is badly cracked or marred is it necessary to do the extensive repairing required before the application of ordinary paint or paper. Most plastic paints cover up the minor imperfections. These finishes are soft in texture and appearance, but hard in fact. Practically permanent, they are highly resistant to injury and wear.

The plastic finishes come in various types, with slightly different surface effects, but most of them may be used to reproduce structural rough plaster. While it is not necessary to repair small breaks in the foundation surface before applying them you do have to remove grease or wax spots with cleaning fluid or benzene. The best way to prepare the old wall is to size it with glue preparation after it has been cleaned.

85

Powder-Type Plastics: There are several plastic finishes sold in powder form with full directions for applying. One of the most inexpensive finishes, also satisfactory and easy to handle, is a powder made from English chalk, casein, and other ingredients thoroughly stirred to a paste in hot water. If a heavy texture is desired you may put this paste on the wall with a trowel as you would any rough plaster. For a less rugged texture a stiff wall brush will do.

PAINTED WOODWORK IN A SIMPLE COLONIAL INTERIOR

Two views of this charming Colonial dining room show how effective painted woodwork may be as a room background. Combined here with quaint figured wallpaper on the small areas not taken up by wood finishes it has a fresh charm very suitable to the type of dining room in which it is used. The paneling is particularly good with its careful spacing to the wall area and its combination of straight lines with graceful curves. An excellent feature here is the recessed window, with broad ledge provided by a built-in cupboard below. Notice the traditional shining brass fender; also the oval sculptured rug which makes a foundation for the dining-table group in the center of the room. Colonial ruffled curtains and valance used with plain sash curtains on the lower half of the window are in keeping with the room. Ordinarily such short windows are treated to make them look taller, but in this case the quaintness of size and shape is an attractive feature and is appropriately emphasized by the curtain. The lower picture shows a view of the room from the living room across the hall where harmonizing wood paneling is also used to create unity between rooms.

GREEN FOR RESTFULNESS WHITE FOR CHARM

In the living room at right, wide plank paneling in early American tradition is painted a soft green, with white fireplace molding and accessories for contrast accents. Tones of orange-red in fireplace bricks, lampshades and upholstery are effective against the green background. Traditional accessories, and small tables, are in correct scale to combine well with the modern easy chairs. Yellow flowers and slip cover repeat the color of shining brass andirons and fender. In this small room, a soft beige carpet, covering the entire floor, gives a sense of spaciousness. The textured weave provides pattern interest without breaking up floor space.

GREEN FOR RESTFULNESS WHITE FOR CHARM

The room at left is a carefully thought-out reproduction of an American-Georgian living room. The classic simplicity of mantel and molded plaster wall paneling calls for a traditional painted finish. Here the off-white color provides an effective background for a dark portrait in a heavy gold frame, and rich tones of mahogany in chairs and tables. Note how carefully accessories are harmonized with the period—crystal candelabra, mirror, wall sconces, figurine lamp-base, andirons, ornaments. French influence, characteristic of the period, is evident in the graceful curves of the coffee table and the formal cornice topping long draw-curtain draperies over ceiling-tall French windows, also in the lines of white-upholstered twin armchairs.

WALLPAPER PROVIDES BACKGROUND INTEREST AS WELL AS COLOR

Illustrations on this page show the importance of close harmony between wallpaper and the decorative scheme of a room. In the center-of-interest grouping above, this is done by repeating the colors of the paper in wood-tones, fabrics, and accessories. The gray-blue checked paper at lower left, with its simple pattern, calls for simple furnishings such as the blue-painted desk and shelves shown. At lower right, wallpaper colors repeat in the drapery.

PAINTED PANELS GIVE SPECIAL INTEREST TO A FIREPLACE WALL

This picture shows the simple restful charm of painted wood paneling on a fireplace wall. Notice the projecting moldings which frame the panels, and the beautifully proportioned traditional panel design. Above the fireplace the old oil painting is framed in the large center panel. The walls are light turquoise against which the soft white of the classic mantel is striking. Upholstery of turquoise textured fabric adds a modern note, as does the string rug over the carpet.

Whichever you want do not try to apply it too evenly. While the plastic is setting it may be stippled with a steel brush or whisk broom, then patted with your hand—just as the old builders patted their plaster against stone walls of early English houses. A slightly different texture results when you press the surface down with a sponge, then smooth it over with a soft wet brush. For certain interiors you may like to try giving the plastic a design. You can do this by passing a whisk broom over it in circles, smoothing it down in other spots with a damp brush.

Allow the surface to harden thoroughly, then sandpaper it and cover it with a thin, white shellac. There is also a special lacquer sizing which you may like better. With textural finishes it is often desirable to create a feeling of age and this may be done by glazing the wall with raw umber.

Cement-Type Plastics: An excellent plastic finish of the cement type is an emulsion of white cement, oils, and driers. It is more expensive than some of the other finishes but a real economy if you include upkeep and replacement costs in your calculations. It requires only washing and is highly damage-proof.

Cement-type plastic may be applied in its original creamy white color; or small quantities of tinting color thinned with turpentine may be added after the paste mixture has been thinned with 1 part of boiled linseed oil to 4 parts of turpentine. It works better if you mix it in large batches. The finish has a sandy quality, fine or rough according to the way you apply it to the wall. A stiff brush, or a trowel, is used for rougher effects. Experiment on a storeroom or attic wall until you discover just the way to get the textured effect you want.

The dining room above illustrates the suitability of pictorial wallpaper to rooms decorated in period style. With the formal English 18th Century atmosphere of the room, the blue and white paper is in an appropriate classical pattern, with large pictorial motifs in an "allover conventional" design (see Wallpaper Chart). Notice the classic urns—both in the alcove scene and on the table—which harmonize with the wallpaper design and with the classic lines of graceful valances over dignified draperies, in off-white moiré with blue ball-fringe. The tiny alcove has been treated in such a way that it not only provides a charming nook for breakfast or tea, but seems to add size and vista to the room. Above the semi-circular seat, upholstered in red self-stripe material, a scenic wallpaper panel is applied to the curved wall. The

DINING ROOM DISTINCTION

road leading into the horizon, the expanse of sky, the perspective of trees growing smaller as the eye follows the road, all help to create an illusion of distance and space. The soft blue of the sky is repeated in the blue of the wallpaper. Pale blue upholstery and dark blue carpet, with woodwork, wall and ceiling in off-white like the draperies, complete the color scheme, with red for accent.

CHAPTER SIX

How to Use Wallpaper

MODERN PROCESSES and designs have added greatly to the wearability and versatility of paper as a wall covering. No matter what your decorating need may be you will find there is a paper which meets your requirements, in a wide range of prices.

If you are doing a room over entirely the choice of wall covering is largely a matter of taste, but if you have old furniture to incorporate in a new setting you may find that paper is the most adaptable. In working with fixed quantities in furniture, draperies, rugs and upholstery, the wide variety of wallpaper styles and designs often makes it possible to find a combination which ties any discordant elements of a room together. Addition of wallpaper design and texture to color gives you new tools for working out a harmonious decorating plan.

Wallpaper may be used to bridge the gaps between periods—even to make traditional furniture look at home in modern surroundings. If you are just beginning to furnish your room, wallpaper may have another special contribution to make. Where there is not quite enough furniture the use of pattern on the wall often helps to "fill" the room so that it looks less empty.

In choosing between plain or patterned paper you must decide whether you want your walls to be exclusively background or to help carry the decorative burden. There are many types of paper which can be utilized for making a wall the most important feature in the room, specially the very fine qualities in patterned or scenic papers. When the paper is to be in a figured design you must be sure it is harmonious in color, appropriate architecturally, suitable to the use you make of the room, and keyed to room psychology. Paper which would be striking, interest-

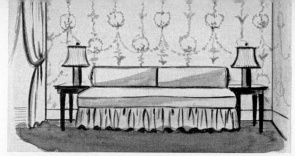

ing and pleasing in hallways or dining rooms not in constant use might become annoying in a living room where the occupants expected to find long periods of restfulness.

With perfectly plain paper you need to consider only color, texture and price. In studying color we found that graying a shade by mixing with gray or a complementary hue gave a softer, more receding appearance. In plain wallpapers this "softening" is often accomplished by printing fine threadlike lines of another color over the base color—an "overprint." This creates a subtle, two-toned effect which softens both color and texture and is seen particularly often in tapestry-type papers. Its soft quality makes it a very kind background for furniture which might look a bit tired and shabby outlined against a clear light-painted wall. Pattern may play a part here too, by drawing attention away from the furniture— which explains the desirability of using a plain paint or paper background instead of a dramatic pictorial type if you want your furniture to be on display.

BASIC WALLPAPER DESIGNS

When you are shopping for wallpaper be guided as far as color is concerned by the same principles discussed in Chapter 4. With reference to design remember that (1) all patterns look smaller on the wall than they do in samples; (2) all colors look darker on the wall than in samples; (3) all design and pattern figures must harmonize with the room in scale as well as in style and color; (4) brightly colored floral or

WALLPAPER PATTERNS KEYED TO ROOM SIZES

When rooms are too large or too small wallpaper may help bring them into scale—but it must be used in the right way. For the large room select a spreading design such as you will find in many large allover patterns (see top sketch), or one with detached motifs and large-scale figures, without perspective or vista and in warm tones. In a small room (lower sketch), the suggestions are applied in reverse. Use paper with small widely scattered motifs and plenty of light background color showing, or plain paper in light cool receding color values, or small-scale scenic patterns with perspectives which create depth. Shadow effects in the background of the paper or patterns with a distinct horizon are particularly useful.

Four popular types of paper are shown on these pages—two floral and two geometrical patterns. The bedroom above illustrates the harmony between an "allover natural" rose design and American Colonial furniture. The paper is in shades of rose-red, blue, purple and yellow. The "detached motif" paper in the room at upper right with groups of flowers is equally at home with traditional painted beds and ruffled tie-backs. Note the correct draping of glass curtains at the same point as the over-draperies at the side. Plaid papers are often very appropriate with simple Colonial-style furniture in natural wood finish, as in the room shown at right. The fiber rug used here, with a suggestion of plaid in the design, is an attractive note. The room at left illustrates the effectiveness of stripes as a background for plain drapery, upholstery and floor fabrics. Blue and red stripes on a white ground, draperies in soft red sailcloth, red and blue pillows, blue rug and eggshell spreads make up a gay and lively color scheme, specially good in a studio bedroom.

STRIPES ARE MODERN FAVORITES

The dining room and the bedroom above both show the modern trend toward stripes in wallpaper—across as well as up and down. The simple straight lines of furniture and draperies are characteristic, as well as the use of contrasting textures to give variety. Notice the effectiveness of blond wood against dark tones in paper, carpet and fabrics.

ribbon patterns are informal while tapestries, toiles, brocades, conventional diagonal or rectangular patterns are more formal and dignified.

Never trust a small sample. Get as large a piece as possible to try out *in the room*, with other colors, fabrics, etc. Insist upon seeing two *lengths* of patterned paper, matched, in order to visualize the design.

Period or Regional Styles: In contemporary decorating many clever schemes have been worked out for harmonizing colors, periods, styles and moods which would once have been considered hopelessly discordant—but merely jumbling them together

doesn't do it. There must be a unifying element, a fundamental harmony, and use of wallpaper affords one of the best opportunities for achieving this.

SCENIC PAPERS

The special value of scenic paper lies in its contribution to the furnished look of a room and to the solving of various decorative problems. Be careful not to use it except where the wall is to be made a feature. As a class, scenic papers are more expensive than many other types. This is offset, if you are on a budget but like scenic paper or need its corrective qualities, by the fact that you can use a small amount of it to great advantage. You can apply it to one wall in a room in combination with paint or less expensive paper on the other three walls, or use it in various types of panels, or make charming screens.

The original designs for many scenic papers were painted by excellent artists and are safe guides to follow when you are choosing a color scheme. Their motifs all consist of definite pictures. These may be repeated over and over; they may be small or large; they may reproduce complete paintings designed to serve as murals or panels. Their subject matter ranges from simple vistas in nature through historical, romantic, or stylized scenes from many lands and periods. Whatever the theme, natural objects are almost always woven in, either as part of the background or as frames for the motifs.

How to Use Pictorial Scenics: Scenic patterns come in (1) long, horizontal designs made to be used in a frieze or border, (2) tall designs, wide or narrow, repeated all the way around the room, (3) those which are worked out specially for panels in various dimensions, (4) designs intended to carry one picture over one whole side of a room.

All-over scenics may be hung in several ways, although they are practically always placed above a dado which reaches high enough to protect the paper and to prevent furniture from cutting into its design.

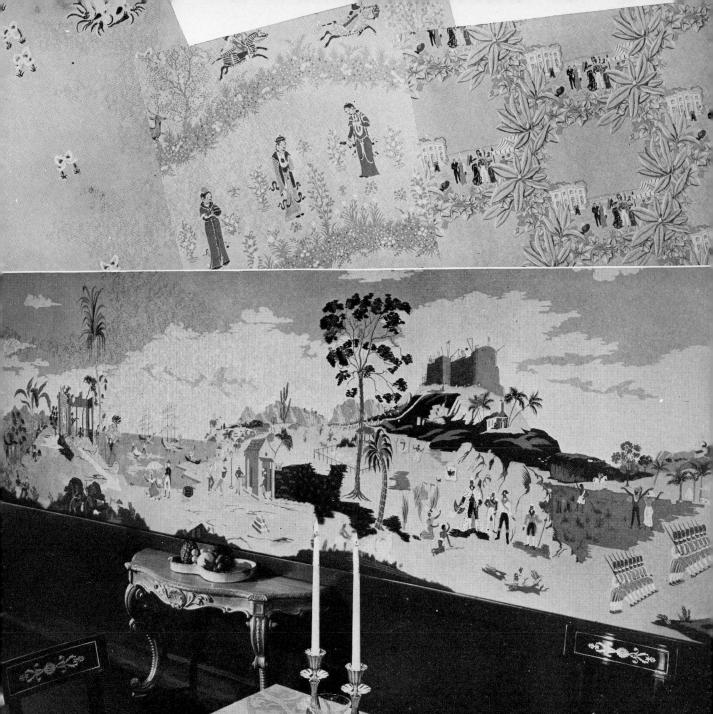

PICTORIAL SCENICS FOR AUTHENTIC TRADITIONAL ATMOSPHERE

The wallpaper designs in this group include several typical scenes and motifs. The "costume-party" papers at the top of the page belong to a popular type which comes in a great variety of designs and covers a very wide range of periods and background themes. Naturally, they are particularly harmonious with furnishings in a corresponding period style. The pattern in the center of the top row illustrates an Oriental contribution to pictorial design. The one shown here happens to be a Persian landscape, which is encountered less often than the Chinese patterns popular ever since the early masters of period design introduced them into Europe. Originally hand painted on rice paper, many quaint authentic Chinese designs are now reproduced in charming patterns—without perspective—which are equally at home in period rooms or modern. The classic emphasis in the diagonal design (left), and the large size of the laurel-framed diamonds, makes this type of paper suitable only for spacious formal rooms, hallways, or traditional dining rooms. As in this design, these papers often picture romantic ruins of classical buildings. The scenic panel in the dining room (large photograph) illustrates a type of pictorial paper appropriate for use only where a good view of it is assured.

1. They may be hung in continuous strips around the room, like ordinary wallpaper.

2. They may be applied in panel effect with the pictures separated by actual moldings or by dividing lines suggesting a border or frame around each complete scene.

3. They may be made so that the strips match themselves, or match each other, which allows any special scene to be placed in the space most desirable for it. This interchangeable plan also provides relief from repetition.

Scenic papers come in sets or individual sections, with numbers or directions for assembling them. Suggestions given here will guide you in analyzing your room to see if there is not some way in which a comparatively small amount of this lovely paper may solve a problem for you or bring a new lift into your background.

But remember: (1) *Don't* crowd a small room with large scenic wall-pictures. (2) *Don't* forget about scale—select pictures in harmony with the proportions of your room. (3) *Don't* use these papers if you want to emphasize the furnishings in the room. (4) *Don't* hang pictures and wall decorations over them —except occasionally a mirror or a picture large enough to balance the design in the paper, and then only if that design is "open," without too much detail.

BORDERS, CUTOUTS AND PANELS

To use in combination with plain paper, wood trim, or painted plaster, various special trimming designs have been created in wallpaper—all the way from simple decorative borders to almost three-dimensional columns simulating architectural features.

Borders: Wallpaper borders may include plain or figured trimming bands in various widths, also bands which simulate moldings, plate rails, chair rails, dado caps, cornices, friezes and dadoes, in wood or wallpaper reproductions of wood. Used with discretion on large walls in contrast color values the various types of borders may be very helpful.

Wallpaper Dadoes: These dadoes are wallpaper panels running lengthwise around the base of the wall to a height of three feet, or perhaps a little less, the same as wood dadoes. They may be in plain paper contrasted with figured paper above; they may be in dark paper contrasted with light; or they may be in one of many specially processed papers. In very large, formal rooms, with high ceilings, a dado of figured paper is sometimes used with a different figured paper above. If you attempt a combination like this, better get expert advice from your paper dealer in making your selection. Wallpaper dadoes are very

MODERN VERSIONS OF PICTORIAL WALLPAPERS

Pictorial motifs have been adopted by many modern wallpaper designers who have created a variety of new scenic effects with a wide range of subjects. These papers are often gay, sometimes with a flavor of whimsy or humor suitable to special rooms, almost always more or less dramatic in feeling and design. In the bedroom and dining room above two striking modern patterns in wallpaper are shown. In the dining room green tropical foliage stands out boldly against a white background. White celanese draperies with deep green fringe provide corresponding drama at the windows. Bleached oak furniture in simple lines is dominated by an oval mirror, with antique glass border, and a tall pedestaled china dish filled with fruit. The bedroom illustrates a most unusual silver wallpaper on which plants with pastel flowers in pale peach and green seem to grow from the baseboard around the room. Glass bedside table and mirrored bed—both headboard and footboard—intensify the softly luminous effect created by the walls. The textured peach bed spread and the pale green rug complete a distinctive color scheme and treatment. The middle picture in the group dramatizes a modern stylized version of the small pictorial motif. Oriental in feeling and coloring against a dark background, the motifs accent attractive modern design in the game table and group of chairs. Notice removable ashtrays built into the corners of the table with its inlaid checkerboard, also comfortable chairs upholstered in rough-textured rose-colored fabric. The paper illustrated at lower right is an example of a modern design in which the subject is highly stylized as in the "cornfield" pattern shown. Note the interesting combination of this paper with period mantel and accessories.

94

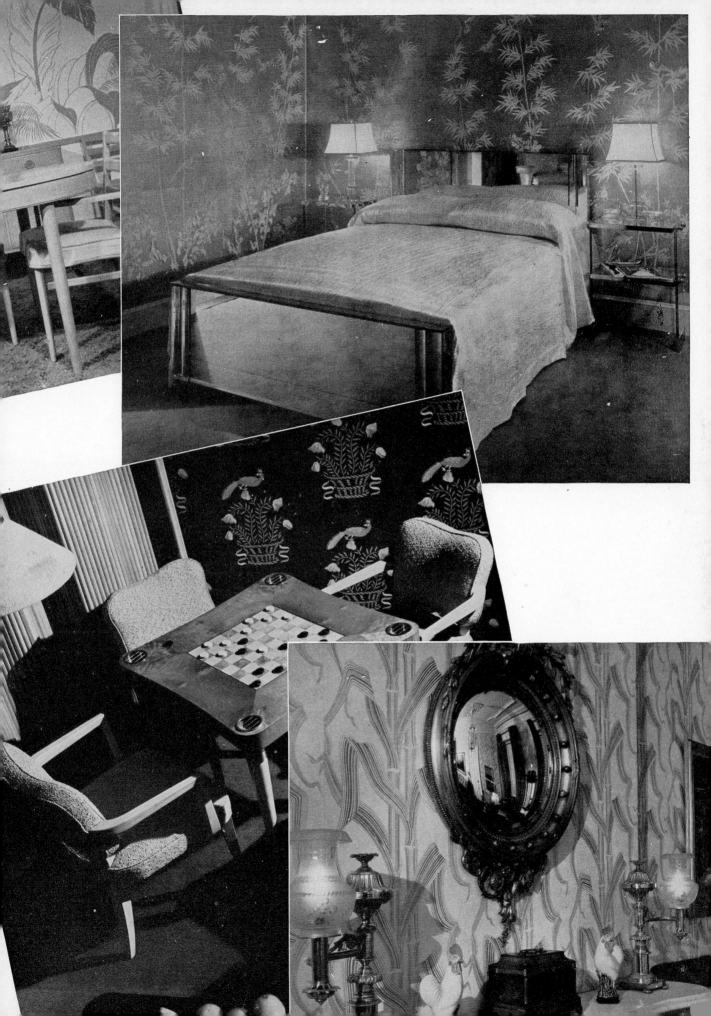

useful in solving hallway problems—following up the stair wall, etc.

Frieze: A frieze is a very wide border or a narrow mural, usually reproducing classic designs in low relief or other traditional effects. Friezes are dramatic and interesting but must be used only in rooms keyed entirely to classic or traditional themes—unless the frieze has been specially designed in the modern manner to fit a modern room.

Architectural Papers: Architectural designs in paper have limited use, but can sometimes be helpful in correcting an architectural defect or emphasizing some particularly good line. They are better in period rooms, classic rooms, or entrance hallways. These architectural papers are really mammoth cutouts which reproduce, more or less realistically, balustrades, marble or stone columns, capitals, bases, cornices, pilasters, ornamental door frames, panels, etc. Usually in classic design, they come in sets ready to apply over plain colored background papers. Again, it is better not to attempt their use without expert advice. If they are not applied in exactly the right places they will create architectural defects instead of curing them.

HOW TO USE CUTOUTS FOR WALLS

Decorating a plain wall with various cutout applications is an easy way to bring color and design into a drab room or to cover up damaged spots on walls. You can also use them to tie a room together by repeating on the wall colors or designs from draperies or furniture. If you are using wallpaper cutouts on a dinette wall, for example, you might cut a large piece to be glued on the dinette table, shellac it, and have an attractive, washable, laundry-saving tabletop. You could adapt the same idea to a dressing table in a bedroom, or to tables in children's rooms. There are several different methods for creating charming, interesting or amusing effects with cutouts, depending on the type of room and the mood you want to establish in it. If you do the whole thing yourself you will need a little patience. Aside from that only a few simple tools are required. If you buy some of the ready-made products you won't need any tools at all.

To cut your own wall trimmings you will need very sharp, small scissors so that you can go into all the corners of your design. Paste the cutouts on the wall with wallpaper paste. After they are dry, brush them over—just beyond the edges—with a thin coat of wallpaper lacquer or white shellac. Be sure to try out the spacing of your motifs before pasting.

Decalcomania or Ready-Made Cutouts: There are several kinds of ready-made cutouts so be sure to

DECORATING WITH WALLPAPER BORDERS AND CUTOUTS

In the room at left center, with average-height ceiling, a border was used to neutralize the effect of up-and-down stripes which would have made the ceiling seem higher. These borders may be used with a plain paper to give a desired color contrast, or printed to match the paper. You can make up a border yourself by choosing a straight band like the one shown and cutting out the design at the lower edge. Or you can trim both edges and apply it anywhere you like as a cutout design. Notice the combination of floral pattern and plain fabric with the geometrical striped design used for the wallpaper and the attractive woven cotton carpeting on the floor. On the plain composition-board wall at lower left a border is used to simulate a dado cap and give the impression of a dado. Notice here the use of tiny wallpaper cutouts as decorative concealment for nailheads used in applying the wallboard. Borders like this are often useful to increase the apparent length of a room, when end walls are left plain, taking away some of the square effect. Various types of narrow border strips come in a great variety of designs making it possible to fit them into almost any decorating plan. They may be used to furnish a sharp accent along the edge of a baseboard, around door and window trim, at the top of a dado, up the corners of a room, to outline panels, to highlight a cornice. They have much the feeling of the Early American stenciling described in Chapter 5 and can be used in the same manner. One attractive design outlines a chimney breast, another carries the border up a stairway wall to balance the handrail. In the bedrooms above cutouts were arranged on the bed wall to create a center of interest there. This is emphasized even further in the room at left by painting the wall white as a background for the rose, red and green of the border, while the other three walls are apple green with a chair rail painted white, like all the woodwork. In the other room the cutouts were made from chintz used for draperies and applied as garlands over the bed to offset the lack of headboard. Notice that the same cutouts are appliquéd on the quilted top of the bed covering to tie the wall and decorations together.

97

COMBINING PATTERNED WALLPAPER WITH PLAIN PAINTED WALLS

Wallpaper panels have many corrective uses in addition to being highly decorative. Framed with molding or some other border they may be used on paneled walls or in combination with a different type of paper. Narrow panels with vertical lines add height to a room, long horizontal panels lengthen walls and lower ceilings. Panels repeated around the wall help break up the space and make a large room seem smaller, while panels like vistas often seemingly enlarge the room. In the bedroom above a wallpaper panel with a large open design was used to frame the bed group. This type of panel would be particularly good to lengthen a too-square room. The same effect is produced in the bedroom below by side walls which are a warm peach pink (advancing color) while the paper on the bed wall is a pastel print in pale green, pale pink and other light tints (receding). The striking bedcover is green- and white-striped chintz with box-pleated white net flounces. For seeming to shorten a too-long-and-narrow room reverse the treatment and bring one end forward by using a warm, dark, or strongly designed paper on an end wall while keeping the others in soft light receding tones, thus "fading out" the walls which are too close together.

read the instructions and follow them carefully, though with all of them you follow the same general process. The "decal," or picture, is simply transferred from the card, paper, or fabric on which you buy it to any washable surface you want to decorate. You can cut the elements of several designs apart and rearrange them in any grouping or combination you like. Then proceed as follows:

1. Before you separate the designs from their backing, pin them up against the wall to be sure you have them where you want them, then mark the spot where they will go.

2. Soak the design in warm water for a few seconds.

3. Wet the wall where it is to be applied and slide the transfer from its backing onto the desired location, face up.

4. Smooth it with a soft cloth by wiping from the center toward the edges to get out any air or water bubbles.

5. Allow it to dry thoroughly for eight or ten hours before you touch it. There are slight variations in this process when using different products, so don't neglect directions.

Decorating with Maps: Maps are an interesting variation of pasted-on decorations, particularly for a den, a study, or a boy's room. Apply the maps with wallpaper paste, then shellac or lacquer over them as directed for the wallpaper cutouts. Let the paste dry for several days before you apply the shellac.

Wallpaper Panels: Any figured paper with a definite design, not too small, may be put on the wall in panels, combined with plain paper or wood trim or painted walls. The panels may extend all the way from floor to ceiling, set off by strips (called stiles) made of wood molding, narrow paper borders, or one of many novelty materials. Panels may also be formed in oblong rectangles, up and down, or lengthwise along the wall, framed as described above or in elaborate curved moldings in various period styles.

HOW TO SOLVE WALL PROBLEMS WITH PAPER

Paper is more than something with which you decorate your walls. To the corrective qualities of color wallpaper adds new possibilities through line and pattern. It is an invaluable ally if you want to adjust or offset a structural defect without making extensive alterations. If the architectural aspects of your room are good you can use plain paper to bring them out. If your room has bad lines which need hiding, paper will do a wonderful job of camouflage.

In this chapter a number of sketches and photographs illustrate the application of wallpaper to special problems, but they are only a few of the ways in which it can be used. A few more are suggested below.

1. If your walls are over-trimmed you can streamline them by stripping off the superfluous wood trim. For refinishing purposes paper is excellent because less careful plaster repairs are necessary than for painting. If you must leave some of the wood trim on, you can paint it the same color as the background of your paper—which should be plain, or at least inconspicuous in design.

2. When a room is too small the walls must be simplified and pushed out as much as possible. Eliminate wood trim as suggested above, avoid all contrasts in backgrounds, use paper in soft receding colors and in small design or with much vista. If there are many doors which break into the wall space and make it seem smaller you can panel some of them with inexpensive wallboard, then paper them like the wall. Use scenic paper for a large panel on one wall.

3. When a room is too large you can use decorative panels, borders, dadoes, friezes—all in designs which break up wall space. Figured borders framing doors and windows increase their apparent size. If the wall is very high, concentrate on the horizontal trimmings and choose wallpaper in a large pattern with horizontal feeling. If the room is large and the ceiling low, the most effective treatment is in use of wide vertical stripes or long, narrow panels in unbroken lines from floor to ceiling.

4. If room proportions are not pleasing you will find that wallpaper seems actually to alter dimensions. If the room is too long and narrow and you are setting off one end of it for some special purpose (see page 50) you can use paper on that end in a harmonious but different color and design from that of the rest of the room. For example, if the room is papered in a large detached motif design, select paper for the "nook" in a plain color taken from one of the darker tones of the living room paper, or a striped pattern picking up two of the colors. If you are using panels on the walls select fabric effects in wallpaper, in contrast colors, framed with moldings to give them importance. Another device is to use scenic paper with vistas on the long walls, combined with plain dark paper or simulated wood paneling on one or both of the end walls. For a too-square room use vista design in receding colors on opposite walls to extend them, with advancing colors on the two remaining walls to draw them in. Make use of horizontal lines in wallpaper design, borders, wood trim, dadoes, etc.; or if the room is small use receding effects in design and color on three walls, advancing effects on the fourth. If the room is large reverse this arrangement.

5. If ceilings are too low or too high there are a number of things you can do with your walls in addition to special ceiling treatment described in Chapter 9. If the ceiling is low, confine all wall trimmings to vertical lines. Architectural paper in the form of simulated columns creates an effect of height, if the room is formal enough and large enough for this treatment. With low ceilings eliminate all horizontal lines on the wall and add vertical lines in any way you can. Patterns in the paper must always be chosen either in real or shadow stripes, or with definite vertical feeling in the design.

You will find papers with long, upward stems of flowers, plants, and trees running from baseboard to ceiling without interruption. Such designs will give an illusion of height to your room almost as effectively as actual stripes. Reverse this treatment for ceilings too high, use wide cornices at the ceiling line in wood or plaster instead of moldings. Carry the ceiling paper or color down onto the wall, use dadoes and cornices together if the ceiling is very high. If you are using scenic murals, a frieze effect above them and a dado below will do a great deal to bring the ceiling down.

SMALL, OPEN PATTERN IN A SMALL ROOM

Alcoves and gables present a special problem in the use of wallpaper. The paper shown in this charming small Early American attic bedroom has a soft white background with tiny pink roses as figures in a spot motif design. A tiny dormer like the one here should always be papered the same as the wall around it, but an alcove-size dormer in a large room may be made a feature by using contrast paper. If the ceiling is too high, bring it down by using darker paper than the walls. Avoid large set figures or stripes as it is very difficult to match them around the broken-up areas where windows are set in. In a small room it is best to use the same paper from the floor straight over the ceiling.

SIMULATED WOOD PAPER FOR A MODERN BEDROOM

An effective use for wood paper is shown in the bedroom above. Combined with the plain, modern furniture it makes a striking background for the bed-and-table group. Note the interesting harmony between the square inlay pattern of the paper and the plaid design of the draperies, also between the blond wood finish of the paper and the blond furniture wood. Using a wall like this at one end of the room with the other wall plain is effective for altering proportions.

SPECIAL PAPER FINISHES

Modern inventiveness applied to wallpaper has resulted in a number of paper-backed wall coverings applied like wallpaper ranging all the way from washable sanitary finishes to actual veneers of fine wood.

The velour effects in wallpaper come in two groups—flock paper and velvet paper. These are finished to look like deep-piled fabrics, plain or with self patterns sculptured on the surface. They are expensive and perishable, but make beautiful panels even for those who must furnish on a budget. Many fabric reproductions are available in every type of weave and pattern from gingham and calico to heavily embossed brocades and watered moirés. Many of these are washable.

Another type of finish uses paint and enamel on strong muslin, plain or patterned, in gloss or flat finish. Gold and silver are among the colors used for this washable wall covering. Another metallic wall material produces various effects so realistic that they are used in the most elaborate interiors. These metal finishes are favored in modern designing.

Masonry paper simulating tiles, marble and other stone facings are durable and useful for foyer walls, and dadoes in hallways, game rooms, etc. A very interesting innovation in the way of wall covering can be used to make scenics, art-tile papers, tapestry effects, pictorial friezes, mosaics, panels, and all kinds of murals. Leather papers are also available which are perfect reproductions of all types of real leather.

Wood veneer papers are not only imitation wood; they are also made by applying a very thin veneer of real wood to a paper backing. One advantage of these is that they are flexible and can be used on curved surfaces.

TWO WAYS FOR USING FABRICS ON WALLS

Some of the attractive possibilities of fabric on walls are shown in the two rooms here. The small informal living room above has a valance built out over the couch to head plain draperies like those used at the windows, making it possible to conceal the bed if desired. When the draperies are pulled back (as here) they reveal a charming niche with walls covered in the same material used for the smart tailored couch cover and bolster roll. Combined with a simple rustic carpet and plain walls elsewhere in the room, this little living corner has definite appeal. In the living room below, heavy drapery fabric is used to dramatize the wall. In green with white flowers it hangs in full graceful folds from the ceiling. Draperies like this may be used in front of windows or solely as decoration for a plain wall. In the latter case the pleats may be caught at the bottom as well as at the top.

UTILITY IN WALLPAPER

Wallpaper once was divided into two groups—attractive paper and washable paper. But now washable papers come in designs suitable for any room in the house. Some of them are guaranteed to be actually "scrubbable," but most of them should be gently wiped off rather than scrubbed, and they should not be left wet.

Almost all papers are now relatively fade-proof, many of them guaranteed by the manufacturers to be completely so. The spot where the sun shines most brightly will retain the same shades as the shadowy corner where its rays never reach; pictures and furniture can be moved without leaving dark, unfaded spots surrounded by lighter areas. The non-fade process is used even in many inexpensive papers, but the washable papers are not always obtainable in the lower price range. If you cannot find a washable paper within your budget, or in a design you like, or if you already have paper on your walls which you cannot change, you can treat the surface in one of the following ways.

Wax Coating for Paper: A colorless wax, specially prepared for wallpaper, gives a finish which can be wiped clean with a damp cloth. This wax is applied with a cheesecloth pad and can be polished so that the paper has a slight gloss, or left without polishing. This protective coat lasts a long time, unless there is a great deal of dampness, and another coat can always be applied over it.

Lacquering and Glazing Papers: Lacquer is applied to papers both for protection and during the process of treating it for the mellowness of age. If you want to make the surface durable and washable, but keep the colors undimmed, use a clear white shellac or wallpaper lacquer. If you want the surface to look antique, or if you want to tone down a too-brilliant pattern, use a special lacquer and follow with a glaze for this purpose. Lacquer, with or without glaze, is applied to scenic papers to soften the printing effect and to marbleized papers in order to deepen the marble-like appearance. Wallpaper screens should always be lacquered, and all very delicate or expensive papers. If you are lacquering over old paper, clean the paper first.

FABRIC WALL COVERINGS

All sorts of fabrics from chintz, cretonne, linen, canvas, burlap, gingham, calico, percale, down to plain denims and striped ticking are used on walls. They may cover all four walls or be used to camouflage, decorate, or emphasize a section of one wall, or as panels. In the two latter cases they are usually made of the same material as the window draperies. The cotton prints in bright colors give gaiety to a room, plain denims furnish contrast with figured wallpaper, and plaids and stripes are used most effectively. Rich fabrics such as brocades and damask are confined to formal or period rooms.

How to Use Fabrics on Walls: Fabrics can be treated with paste and put on like wallpaper. They may also be stretched or draped over a whole or part of a wall. You can do this by sewing the lengths of the material together and tacking a thin wooden lath to the wall at the top of the space you wish to cover, another lath at the bottom. Stretch your fabric plain from one lath to the other or pleat it top and bottom with small tacks, or tack it at the top only and allow it to fall in folds. When it needs to be cleaned you can remove it from the frame, wash it or have it dry-cleaned, and replace it.

Burlap and Decorated Canvas: Burlap comes in widths all the way from 36 inches to 108 inches, so it is easily adapted to any use, from dadoes to entire wall coverings with few seams. It is sized on the back which makes it easy to hang, like paper, and straight trimming makes absolutely invisible seams possible. It takes paint well, but the paint must be flat and thin or it will hide the woven texture. This useful fabric can be fitted into many decorating schemes, from those which are frankly rustic to almost any of a not-too-formal nature. Its durability makes it excellent for hard-wear purposes. Canvas is very decorative, less coarse in texture than burlap, with lovely soft colorings and attractive designs.

Grass Cloth: This cross between paper and fabric has long been a favorite for many types of rooms. It is woven like fabric, with a warp of shredded fibers taken from the bark of various vines and a woof of strong thread. It is backed by thin, tough paper strips, rolled, and sold in lengths of 24 feet by 4 feet wide. It comes in a wide range of colors and its uneven hand-woven texture makes it a very interesting wall finish adaptable to many types of rooms—specially those in the modern, handcraft styles. It must always be examined from several angles to check color values. These are sometimes deceptive, as the weavers use one color for dyeing the fiber and a different color for the threads. Grass cloth comes in gold, in silver, and in designs as well as plain styles. To prevent stretching it should be mounted over a lining paper.

Leather: Modern artists have produced some striking effects with leather by finishing it in light tones and using it on entire walls. In its various finishes—both real and imitation—it is lovely used as panels on library walls. It will undoubtedly become more and more popular as synthetic products are perfected.

For a room of mellow charm and gracious dignity fine wood paneling has never been excelled. The room photographed here shows excellent furniture arrangement, having two distinct centers of interest—fireplace and bay window. The paneling in this room is keyed to 18th Century France. Curving lines of furniture follow those of the marble fireplace and the beautifully proportioned wall panels in large veneer sheets. The window cornice is designed in the same graceful curved pattern. Notice here how built-in book shelves fill the space between chimney breast and wall, also the storage cupboards provided below. In this room, with plain carpet and ceiling and only geometrical designs used in upholstery, the mottled marble of the fireplace, the rich colorings of painting and books, combine with boldly patterned drapery fabric at the windows to provide needed notes of drama and color. Notice the distinctive framing of the painting over the mantel in a panel-molding following the lines of the regular panel. The comfortable dignity, without formality, in this

SOFTLY WAXED WOOD

living room illustrates how elaborate Louis XV curves may be modified and simplified by translating them into French Provincial adaptations. Simple paneling like this would be attractive in walnut, in knotty pine, in one of the light woods preferred by moderns; also in some inexpensive wood painted in a color characteristic of the period. The design could even be worked out in wallboard, with panels outlined by applied wood moldings. Notice how the width of each panel is proportioned to the space it fills.

CHAPTER SEVEN

Wood on Walls

EXCEPT for stone, wood is probably the oldest finish for walls. Over a long period of time its use crystallized into certain definite forms, some serving utilitarian purposes, others becoming largely decorative. In contemporary houses the first group includes doors, wood framework for doors and windows, baseboards, picture moldings and mantels. The second group includes dadoes and wainscots, chair rails and dado caps, cornices and coves, and all-over paneling. Built-in features are usually utilitarian but may be made important decorative features by clever planning. There is a right and wrong treatment for every type of woodwork in both groups, depending largely upon the size and style of the room, partly upon the use which is made of it.

TYPES OF WOODWORK

Doors and Windows: In decorating you may regard the doors and windows of your room as primarily utilitarian and retire them into the background by making them the same color as the walls, even to draperies. On the other hand you may employ contrast to make them an important part of your room composition. (See Chapter 12.) In either case the framework which surrounds door and window openings is definitely structural and the trim used for facings around openings shares that quality. In width this trim should be in scale with the room. For an average opening in the average room this is normally about 4½ to 5 inches. Less than this will look skimped; more may look heavy. If the trim is out of scale your best remedy is to paint it in a flat finish using the same color as the wall background. It will merge with the wall and bad proportions will be less noticeable. If the openings themselves are out of scale or badly placed you can correct the defects by devices described in the chapters on doors, windows and window treatments.

Baseboards: A baseboard is the plain or decorated board anywhere from 6 to 12 inches wide placed around the bottom of the wall to cover and protect the joining between wall finish and floor, also to act as a buffer against wall damage from furniture. It is usually topped by some type of decorative molding and painted or finished in the color of the wall immediately above it or to match other woodwork in the room. Sometimes the baseboard is made from several boards, overlapping or joined by moldings. A narrow strip called a "shoe molding" may be fitted in the angle between the floor and the board.

Wood Picture Moldings: Contemporary decoration has more or less dispensed with visible wires for hanging pictures in favor of invisible hooks behind them, but picture molding still serves a useful purpose as a ceiling-line finish where there is no cornice. Molding at the ceiling line should be ¼ inch below the ceiling and is usually painted the same color. It should not be placed at a lower point on the wall except to correct a too-high ceiling when a cornice is not used. In that case the ceiling may be "dropped" by bringing its finish down onto the wall anywhere from 3 inches to 18 or more and using molding to conceal the joining between wall and ceiling finish. In some modern rooms woodwork is kept to the minimum, and the line of joining, whether at the ceiling line or below, is marked by a band of paint, metal, glass, or plastic.

Other Uses for Moldings: Wood moldings have innumerable uses in addition to those mentioned in connection with the ceiling line. (1) They give a finish to other woodwork, in which case they are treated as part of the wood they are used with. (2) They are indispensable as finish for built-in features such as bookcases, closets, etc., also in remodeling walls and furniture. (3) They frame panels of all sorts—wood, plaster, cloth, wallpaper—and are then finished to harmonize with the background or the panel, or in a contrast finish if there is a reason for making the panel stand out against the background. (4) They may be used in place of a dado cap or chair rail. (5) They frame fireplace openings when a mantel is dispensed with or is used without side supports. In this case they are usually "bolection" moldings, a series of moldings joined to each other and projecting from the surface to which they are applied.

Types of Moldings: There are moldings in other materials than wood—plaster, metal, composition, plastics, various novelties—but they are all used in the same way and for the same purpose as the wood moldings, and nothing else has yet equalled wood for versatility and usefulness. Wood moldings may be bought in many varieties, designs, and finishes; in sizes for every possible use, from 1 to 3 inches wide, cut in any necessary lengths. The present-day styles are usually not carved, but carving may be had if needed for authentic wall trim in a period room.

Even a little molding, in correct period "feeling" and cleverly applied, may go far toward creating some special atmosphere desired.

Cornices: Cornices are closely associated with style periods and play an important part in period designs. They are extremely useful in any large room with a high ceiling but should not be used in small, informal rooms or those with too-low ceilings. The cornice is an ornamental strip which takes the place of a molding at the ceiling line and is usually made of wood or simulated wood, though various other materials are sometimes used.

An adaptation of the ceiling-line cornice is a popular device for covering the tops of draperies, shades or blinds used at windows. A wood cornice may be a very simple combination of plain flat surfaces and moldings, or elaborately decorated. It may be only a few inches wide or extended some distance down the wall. In a well-proportioned room the average depth of the ceiling line cornice is about $\frac{1}{14}$th the height of the room. For an over-high ceiling it may be as much as $\frac{1}{10}$th. Cornices may be purchased complete, or easily assembled by combining various moldings; also by applying molding to plain strips of wood or wood substitutes. They are a valuable aid in correcting bad room proportions.

Cornices often have a "cove" section—a concave surface which gives the impression of a ceiling rounded down onto the wall. This cove treatment of the ceiling line is often used without a cornice, plain or bordered by narrow moldings. In this case it is usually made of plaster rather than wood. The color and finish of cornices and coves depend entirely upon the question of height. When they carry the ceiling color down they make the room seem lower; when they carry the wall color up they make it seem higher.

Wood Mantels: Wood has always been a favorite material for mantels and must be treated to harmonize with the rest of the architectural wood in the room. Mantel and fireplace treatments are so important that they have been taken up in detail in a later chapter. You will find wood mantels discussed there in greater detail (Chapter 24).

Wainscots: Technically "wainscot" means paneling carried all the way up to the ceiling but in ordinary usage it applies to paneling which stops at the height of a plate rail or frieze. Except in a too-high room where a frieze treatment is used to lower the ceiling, paneling is much more effective when it goes all the way up. Otherwise it divides the wall space in awkward proportions.

Wood Dadoes: Like baseboards, wood dadoes were once purely functional and may still combine functional with decorative qualities. A dado is simply

WOODWORK
WAS AN
IMPORTANT
FEATURE
OF
EARLY
AMERICAN
HOMES

The pioneer-type of fireplace, broad-paneled floor and beamed ceiling in the photograph above are characteristic of many country homes of early Colonial days. Note the grooved painted wood dado carried up to the window ledge, and the wide ceiling cornice in matching finish which serves also as a head for the valance-frill over the windows. The corner with its attractive flowered drapery, built-in bench, table and chairs, provides a comfortable fireside nook. In the room corner shown at left is an authentic cupboard equally typical of a later period–18th Century American. The fluted sea shell makes a charming frame for a collection of hobbies or antique china. The characteristic dado on the wall is made with molding-trimmed baseboard and cap. The cornice at the ceiling line is a feature of Colonial woodwork which is widely used in contemporary design. In many of the historical decorating periods, in France and England as well as in America, paint was the finish preferred for paneled walls and other woodwork. By checking with the charts in the Period Chapter (19), favorite colors for each period can be easily selected, also the combinations of colors which were characteristic of special styles. Except for kitchens and other utility rooms, the finish used on wood should be of the flat type, whether in paint or enamel. If you like painted wood, but not too much of it, you can combine one paneled wall with three in some other finish, or use a dado with wallpaper above it. Such backgrounds have been popular in many periods, and they can be adapted to modern rooms by the right choice of panel design. This versatility of wood, and the ease of adapting it to various decorating plans and periods, commends it strongly to the home decorator—especially when remodeling or redecorating is contemplated. Paneling one end of a long room may give it much better proportions because the paneling may be set in from the original wall, with the space between used for closets or other storage. Many other built-in features may be used to increase convenience, and at the same time add the charm of wood, painted or waxed, to the background of your room.

WALLS OF KNOTTY PINE—AN AMERICAN TRADITION

Knotty pine in soft light tones and natural finish is a favorite paneling material in American homes. Though used today in the more livable light tones, it is still Colonial in feeling and is especially appropriate for a traditional room like the one above. The plain plank panels with butt joinings are applied in pioneer fashion—boards of uneven width—a style followed also in the flooring. The massive beams of the ceiling are in keeping with this Early American structural type of room. Built-in bookcases, Dutch-type fireplace with swinging crane for cooking, bright hooked scatter rugs and pine furniture, all follow the tradition. Notice that the coffee table is a cobbler's bench and all the accessories harmonize.

a low paneling running around the walls of a room, from 2 feet 3 inches high to 3 feet—usually up to the line of the window sills—designed to protect perishable wall finishes from injury. It also provides a useful base for mural decorations by lifting the pictures above too much interruption from pieces of furniture placed against the wall. The dado is often finished with a "dado cap" or a chair rail to act as buffer between the wall and the backs of chairs.

Dadoes may be in other protective materials such as stone, tile, composition, linoleum, plastic, etc.; or in simulations of these. They may also be purely decorative bands of paint, wallpaper or other finishes. Sometimes the dado cap or chair rail is merely a flat board some four inches wide, or a molding, or even a narrow trimming border applied at the dado height to break up a too-high wall. A really protective dado of wood or some other substantial material is specially useful in halls, children's rooms, bathrooms—wherever wearability is important.

WOOD PANELING

The beauty of wood paneling—sanded and waxed —speaks for itself. There is dignity in a paneled room, but there is also a warm sense of security and comfort. Paneling is not necessarily elaborate carving and cabinet work, such as we see in pictures of historical period rooms. There are also the simply paneled interiors of comfortable Early American farmhouses and English or French Provincial cottages with their soft wood tones and textures, fine graining and plain moldings.

Paneling is effective in altering the proportions of a room through shape and spacing of the panels. When they are tall and narrow they add height. Dadoes, friezes and horizontal panels reduce height and increase wall length. Paneling on one end wall may help to shorten a room which is too long and narrow, while on two facing walls it gives an oblong appearance to a square room. All-over paneling in warm,

HORIZONTAL PLANKS WITH GROOVED EDGES FOR A MODERN WALL

Interesting possibilities are suggested by this strikingly modern adaptation of plank paneling in which horizontal lines of restfulness provide the motif for the arrangement of wood planks used for walls. Here they are uniform in width, with the slightly more formal grooved type of joining which is often used also in vertical plank paneling. Perfect symmetrical balance in the furniture grouping adds to the effect of dignified restfulness. The deep shaggy texture of the rug contrasts in an interesting way with softly polished wood on the wall and the unusual coffee table in front of the couch. Note that the round lines of this table soften the squareness of prevailing lines in wall and furniture group.

rich tones makes a large room seem smaller and warmer, adds to the coziness of a small, intimate room.

Modern industry has removed most of the drawbacks to paneling as a wall finish by reducing the cost and widening the choice of woods. Developments in veneer production methods have made the beautiful graining and texture of many fine woods available in a variety of panel styles and in stock sizes which can be quickly installed in any average-sized room. With these paper-thin rotary veneers so little wood is required for making panels that even rare and costly woods can now be used without too much strain on the budget. Sheets of veneer may be obtained in such wide sections that a few large panels will cover an entire wall, and still greater variety has resulted from use of new light tones in finishing.

Planks for Sealing Walls: This is the simplest type of paneling and in Early American rooms pine was usually the wood chosen. Pine is still used extensively, as well as various other woods and a great variety of simulated wood finishes. The boards may be used structurally, fastened directly to the framework, or added over any structural finish such as plaster.

Board paneling may be applied vertically or horizontally—this should depend upon ceiling height unless the room is very well proportioned, then it may be a question of personal preference. The very modern designers prefer the horizontal, with flat-band joinings, while the traditional taste is usually in favor of vertical lines, covered by grooves, beads, or moldings. For the plank type of wall one of the most popular among contemporary woods is the knotty pine which now comes in a great variety of stock sizes in planks and panels, adaptable to many types of walls and finishing, and also cut ready for installing built-in partitions, windows, furniture, etc. These planks require the same finish and care as any other paneled wall.

SIMULATED TILE
FOR WALLS AND CEILING

The simple room corner which is depicted in the photograph below illustrates the use of wallboard tiles as a workmanlike background for a desk nook with recessed book shelf and built-in equipment. Acoustic tiles make an attractive, noise-absorbent ceiling. In the photograph at lower left a comfortable studio-type living room is appropriately finished in a pine-and-wallboard combination, sturdy, practical and easy to keep clean. Tailored couch coverings, small rugs and pine furniture harmonize with the simplicity of the background.

IT'S ALL DONE WITH WALLBOARD

The room shown above, which might very well be designed for a young man with a sea-going hobby, illustrates a highly effective and useful wallboard treatment. Here the dado—almost high enough to be called a wainscot instead of a dado—is made of wallboard in pre-decorated, bleached mahogany-simulated wood paneling. It is applied horizontally around the base of the wall and a heavy white rope attached to the wall serves in place of the conventional dado cap. This rope is repeated at the ceiling line instead of a molding (not shown here). The nails holding the white panels are turned into a decorative feature by arranging them in a design and covering each one with an ornamental nail. The bright color scheme is carried out in red and white in bedcover, pillow, curtains, waste basket, picture frames and bracket under the ship model, with blue accents in a book binding or two, and in picture backgrounds. Notice the carrying out of the marine theme by using a lifebelt to frame a round colored seascape and curtaining it to look like a port-hole window.

THREE TYPES
OF DISTINCTIVE
AND ATTRACTIVE
WALLBOARD
TREATMENTS

Bordered Panels: Traditional panels in solid wood walls are set in place in grooves and surrounded with molding, the paneling being raised above the surface slightly or sunk slightly below it. The top and bottom sections of frame holding the panels are called "rails," those at the sides are called "stiles." Shape and size of panels, width of stiles and rails between panels, depend upon the architecture of the room, each period having distinctive characteristics.

Simulated Panels: Moldings may be applied to simulate framed panels against walls grained to imitate stained wood, applied to painted walls of wallboards, plaster, or wood. This type of paneling is easy to apply as the moldings are simply tacked to the wall. The panels are usually rather large with narrow stiles between them, but their shape and size depend largely upon room architecture.

Arrangement of Panels: Panels should be planned so that one large panel or three small ones will come above or behind the spot at which a bulky object such as a couch, refectory table, or sideboard will have to be placed. Variation is more pleasing than a monotonous repetition of the same size all around the wall and makes it easier to arrange furniture in front of a panel center. Guard against having panels too widely separated. If there is some fixed feature in a wall, such as a fireplace or a window group, plan your panels on that wall with reference to the feature, taking out inequalities at the sides of the wall, not in places where they will show most clearly.

When medium-sized panels are spaced at regular intervals, two of them may be used together to make a "frame" for a grouping and should be planned with that in mind.

Painted Paneling and Woodwork: In certain periods and regions most of the wood paneling and trim was painted, as it is today whenever light decorating colors are needed or the wood itself is not impressive in texture or graining.

PLYWOOD AND WOOD VENEERS

Plywood comes in sheets of varying sizes so that it is easily adapted to any type of paneling desired, from Early American plank-sheathed walls or traditional period styles to the wide flat wall surfaces of ultra-modern streamlining. In our present-day plywoods, some 200 foreign and native wood-veneer finishes are to be had in a wide range of prices, making the rich charm of wood paneling available for the average home at a very reasonable price. The process by which plywood is made equalizes shrinkage and resistance to strain, resulting in strong, light wood sheets which are practically non-warping and non-shrinking.

Flexible Veneers: Veneers which may be bent are available in several modern developments providing many unusual and interesting effects. They are in no sense "imitation" or "simulated" wood finishes. They are real wood, cut in paper-thin veneer sheets ($\frac{1}{85}$ inch) and firmly applied to flexible backings—either wallpaper or canvas or one of the new laminated plastic materials. A popular member of this family comes in some fifty different woods and having been made impervious to dampness it can be joined in a perfectly flat effect without danger of separation at seams.

Wallboard has come a long way since it began its career in the form of small spongy-looking sheets of material more like cardboard than wood. The wallboard of today is a stand-in for practically every other wall-surfacing material. It comes in its natural state, or already tinted to eliminate painting, or made up to look almost exactly like various standard wall finishes. There are several advantages peculiar to the use of composition board on walls. Among the different types are those specially treated to make them soundproof, or fireproof, or proof against moisture, vermin and bacteria. In all types they are highly time-saving and sanitary because of their easy-to-clean qualities.

DECORATING WITH WALLBOARD

Prepared tape is a new device which provides a perfectly flat, smooth wallboard surface for any kind of finish by joining sections smoothly, also corners of the boards where they meet at ceiling and wall edges. It comes with a wallboard specially prepared on the edges, with full instructions for using the tape—both on the previously prepared edges and on edges where the board may have to be cut later.

Wallboard Paneling: Today practically all types of paneled walls can be reproduced by combining wallboard with moldings. Specially shaped panels are easily cut from the boards for application over other surfaces, or panels are made on the wallboard background by outlining with applied moldings. The shield type of panel may save a great deal of trouble and expense if you have a really bad break in a plaster wall. Apply a full-length panel—or a smaller one in pleasing outline—right over the plaster, then border and decorate it in any way that harmonizes with the room. You will probably find you have turned a decorative liability into an asset at very little expense.

Other special treatments with wallboard include scalloped border designs for framing windows, doors and openings; panels and borders are also used for simulating a division between rooms, for concealing curtain slots for many remodeling purposes.

COMPOSITION BOARD FOR WALLS IN NATURAL-LOOKING WOOD FINISHES

The two photographs here show how effectively composition board in natural wood finish and soft wood tones may be used on walls and in combination with wood furniture. The room below was done over from a hopelessly unattractive and over-trimmed room to one of simple harmony and comfort. The old fireplace was ripped out, a small window was cut into one large picture window, the old plaster walls were hidden behind wallboard which covers an unneeded door at the left of the fireplace. Built-in book shelves and storage cupboard complete the transformation.

CARING FOR WOODWORK

KEEP IT CLEAN

1. Dust frequently, always with a clean lintless cloth, not too much polish, using a paint brush for crevices or carvings.

2. Try chemically treated dusting cloths, also papers treated with polish, to save time and prevent gumming from wax or liquid polishes.

3. Wash thoroughly when wood is gummy, dirty or streaked—usually not oftener than once a year. For washing solution add 1 tbsp. turpentine and 3 tbsp. boiled linseed oil to each quart of boiling water. Keep this solution hot in a double boiler while using. Change cloths and solution as fast as they are soiled. Cover only small amount of surface at a time, drying quickly.

4. Replace polish lost in washing, being sure to apply oil or wax evenly. Don't leave streaks. Don't use too much polish.

KEEP IT NOURISHED

1. Oils and wax must be rubbed into wood to replace natural substances lost by drying—unless surface has been sealed by varnish; or undercoating of stain, shellac, or filler has been used to protect pores as in "unfinished" oak or walnut. These require only wiping with a soft clean cloth. A helpful amount of moisture can be provided by using humidifiers with your radiators, or a water pan with your hot-air furnace.

2. Choose oil to treat oil finishes. For open-pored hard woods, mix equal parts raw linseed oil and turpentine, rubbing into wood with saturated pad. Repeat regularly or when wood looks dry. For close-grained woods or light colors choose lemon or cedar oil, which will not darken wood, rubbing across grain first. After oil has penetrated, wipe off traces with soft clean cloth, rubbing with grain. This should be needed only once or twice a year.

3. Choose wax to treat wax finishes. Follow directions on container. They are different for different types of wax.

KEEP SHINING SURFACES SHINING

Varnished fine wood, in formal finish, is usually waxed lightly to produce the rich mellow patina desired. To keep it shining, fold a small pad of good paste wax in a pad of flannel for rubbing the surface, then follow with a clean flannel cloth wrapped around a block of wood for polishing. Don't overlook the preparations designed specifically to conceal blemishes, restore surfaces, and keep wood in condition. With little rubbing, these special polishes bring out the deep luster of the finish—and they leave no sticky film on varnish. If film appears, wash with mild soapsuds, a little at a time, rinse and dry. Then rewax.

CARE OF PAINTED WALLS

1. Don't let dust grime their colors. Wipe them down with a long-handled brush or a broom wrapped in cheesecloth.

. . . .

2. Wash them down before they become grayed with dirt. Work from the bottom up to prevent water running down and making streaks through soiled areas. Use plenty of mild, neutral soapsuds in warm water with a soft cloth or large sponge, and work with a circular motion. Rinse with clear water and wipe each finished section dry with a clean soft cloth.

. . . .

3. Use one of the quick-service chemical preparations especially designed to make cleaning painted surfaces less difficult.

. . . .

4. Use the chemical for all smudges, fingerprints, and other small soiled areas. Follow directions on the container.

. . . .

5. On all painted wood surfaces especially exposed to dirt or wear—such as window ledges, cupboard doors, etc.—apply a thin film of liquid wax and polish with a soft, lintless cloth. This will give an attractive finish at the same time prolonging the life of the paint by helping to keep it clean.

. . . .

6. Patch holes in plaster, then cover with paint. Also repaint worn spots. Use sandpaper on the spot, also between coats. Spread paint very thinly at edges.

7. Don't scrub paint or enamel. Keep the surface clean and it will not need scrubbing.

. . . .

8. Don't use abrasives on paint or enamel.

. . . .

9. Do try cleaning enamel with a mixture of one cup of vinegar, one cup of kerosene and one-half cup of water. Shake it up and use it on a soft, clean cloth to wipe the enameled surface. Polish with a dry cloth. Three tablespoonfuls of turpentine or a teaspoonful of baking powder added to any soap-and-water cleaner will brighten the enamel. Or, rub marks lightly with silver polish.

. . . .

10. Do prevent soil by applying a sheet of transparent plastic which you can cut to fit behind a stove or sink, around electric switches or door knobs—wherever grease spatters or finger marks occur.

. . . .

11. Do avoid holes in plaster. Stick a bit of adhesive tape at the point where a nail is to be driven. This usually keeps the plaster from cracking. Another help is to soak the nail for several minutes in boiling water before you drive it into the wall. A small hole in the wall can easily be filled in with a little cornstarch mixed with a few drops of water. Screws driven into plaster may make ugly holes, then refuse to stay in place. You can sometimes remedy this trouble by pushing a wooden match into the hole and breaking it off at the surface to provide a "prop" for the screw. You can also fill the hole with steel wool to brace the screw and hold it firm.

Study of this picture reveals the secret of the room's apparent spaciousness. It is actually a small room, but its feeling of size is doubled by the mirrored wall behind the couch and increased even more by the plain background of walls and ceiling in a soft receding tone of aqua with rug and shutters in a deeper sea-green shade (blue-green). Note the plain draperies in the reflected end of the room, and the plain shuttered windows without drapery which flank the mirrors—all contributing to the effect of space. There is no crowding, because the modern furniture is small in scale,

comfortable but not too heavy for the room. The low sturdy lamp tables with the tall lamps are a very good example of correct scale against the high windows. The opposite wall, shown by reflection, is planned to balance the filled-in wall pictured here. The doorway with its framed panels painted on glass makes an interesting break in the plain side wall. (See reflection in mirrors.) The shaggy rug breaks the monotony of too much smooth texture in walls and fabrics. The two ends of the room show how effectively centers of interest can be created in a room with no fireplace. Note

MIRROR-PANELED WALL

the sea shells on the reflected shelves. They inspired the "marine" theme, and set the color scheme in which upholstery and accessories are tints of off-white and shocking pink. Seats like those in the foreground could be easily manufactured at home with sturdy boxes for bases. Hinged tops beneath the pads would turn them into useful storage spaces. Another object lesson here is the perfect formal balance of the furniture and wall grouping. A line down the middle would divide the grouping into two identical halves. This adds still further to the restful atmosphere of the room.

CHAPTER EIGHT

How to Use Glass for Walls

IN MODERN ARCHITECTURE, glass is used to solve various structural problems, as well as to provide many types of decoration. It is particularly useful in remodeling, either for greater charm or greater efficiency. Ways in which this may be done are outlined below:

Structural Glass Blocks: A section of translucent glass blocks set into an exterior wall in place of a small window would give new life to a dark room and provide privacy without additional expense for curtains and upkeep. These blocks are permanent, never need refinishing, and regular wiping with a damp cloth keeps them clean. Installed between rooms they pass light along from a sunny room to a dark one, with such complete protection that they may be safely used as bathroom partitions. They can be obtained in prefabricated units to fit a great variety of uses, from small inset panels to sections filling the whole side of a room, or in curved shapes for use as bays where windows are not desirable.

Structural Window Walls: Clear glass is now obtainable with insulating properties which make it suitable for structural use in walls when the view outside justifies a large transparent opening. This glass comes in units of various sizes, shapes and styles, ready to be built solidly into the wall, leaving ventilation to conventional windows.

Decorative Glass Panels: Fabric or fine wallpaper panels can be protected with a sheet of plain glass which adds sparkle to your walls at the same time. These glass sheets would allow the use of any type of paper or finish on a bathroom or kitchen wall. There are also glass panels which are only semi-transparent, like antique glass, softly tinted and interestingly textured. These can be used to introduce

A GLASS WALL MERGES THE OUTSIDE WITH THE INSIDE

Primitive charm of Early American plank-sealed walls and furnishings is here greatly enhanced by the modern touch of a glass wall which seems to bring the lovely New England hillside right into the living room. Flagstone-style floors and brick inner partition help merge outside and inside in one continuous picture. When draperies are used on a glass wall like this, hang them in panels so arranged that any part of the opening may be curtained separately.

GLASS BLOCKS PROVIDE PRIVACY

When you need light but wish to eliminate the view the glass-block wall provides a perfect answer. (Stock units are to be had in a variety of sizes and shapes, and many of them are reasonably priced.) Here a graceful curving wall of glass blocks floods a modern living room with light, at the same time diffusing sunlight so that glare and fading of fabrics are minimized. The rounded rug follows the curve of the floor. The draperies, arranged to pull across the window, are made from one of the textured fabrics which require no linings.

GLASS PARTITIONS FOR AIRINESS

Oak-veneered plywood paneled walls and glass partitions give this modern house an individuality all its own. Growing plants soften the austerity of uncurtained glass, and rolled matting blinds provide a screen when it is needed. The bracket device shown here for holding unframed prints makes it possible to change pictures frequently without trouble. Walls like this insure plenty of light for every part of the house, and have their own economy angle since they never need finishing or refinishing.

116

When space is limited dining rooms are often too small for comfort. A mirrored wall above, opposite sheerly curtained windows, would give an airy lightness and a comfortable feeling of space even to a small dark room. In this room the narrow serving table seems doubled, and the way it is placed in front of the glass gives added interest without spoiling the reflection of the room. The curves of the furniture here are in pleasing contrast with the severely straight lines of the background and give a feeling of decoration to the plain room. The effect of space is increased by the oyster-white of walls and ceiling, while warmth is introduced into the picture by peach tones in the tinted mirror and rich dubonnet color in the chair upholstery.

Even a small uninteresting bedroom could be transformed by the treatment given this one, combining smart modern lines with the old-fashioned charm of a white painted floor and traditional furniture pieces dressed up in white paint. Ceiling and three walls are plain off-white, with ivy-covered paper on the fourth wall furnishing the design for a green border around the off-white painted floor. The "puff" in front of the dressing table is made from ordinary shaggy bathroom rugs matching the string rug on the floor. The reflection in the mirror shows how several small windows are made important by ceiling-to-floor chartreuse curtains which drape them as if they were one large window. Instead of a mirrored dressing table you could use two small painted chests of drawers with a sheet of plate glass or mirror across them to achieve the same effect.

The traditional quality of the room at right is given a modern note by the sectional mirrored wall and the light shaggy-textured rug. The mirror shows the book shelves on the back of the bookcase-table as well as on the front. This bookcase takes up no more space than an ordinary lamp table, but is much more useful. Speaking of mirrors, it is worth noting here that fairly large mirror panels have been successfully built up by applying a great many small ten-cent-store mirrors in a solid panel effect to the wall.

MIRROR PANELS, USED ALMOST ANYWHERE, ENHANCE SIZE AND CHARM

a note of color at a strategic spot on a plain wall. A newcomer to the glass field is a flexible cloth wall covering with a surface of small sparkling glass rectangles permanently cemented to the backing. It makes a delightfully gay wall covering for a powder room or bathroom, and panels of it would be attractive for lighting up almost any dark wall area.

MIRRORED WALLS

Applied to walls, mirrors are decorative magic. Strategically placed they can more than double the apparent space, light and air in any room or apartment. To increase the effectiveness of wall mirrors, mirrored surfaces may be used on fireplace facings, window shutters, furniture, cornices and valances, waste baskets and many other accessories. Placed more or less opposite each other, a mirrored wall and a panel or hanging mirror open intriguing vistas and repeat colors where they are most needed. Effectiveness of a lamp, window, or open fire is greatly enhanced when it is doubled by reflection. Small windows draped as one seem much larger when there is a mirror panel between them. Tinted mirrors are to be had in various shades harmonizing with almost any color scheme. In pinkish tints a mirror would reflect warmth as well as light into a cool room. A blue mirror would create an effect of coolness and distance—often very desirable.

Practical Considerations: Mirrors vary widely in quality and price, and the better the quality of the mirror the longer it lasts. So put whatever money you have to spend into the mirror, and not into an

MIRRORED WALL IN A MODERN ROOM

A MIRROR-FRAME ADDS INTEREST

The rooms in this group show the effectiveness of glass treatment for walls as a means of increasing apparent size by opening up vistas. In the modern living room (left) almost the whole room is reflected in mirror panels behind the built-in bookcase and cupboard. Notice the way in which the book shelf at the left is placed so that the mirror forms a background for ornaments on the rounding shelves at the end. The traditional dining room at the right has a sideboard nook completely lined with glass above the dado. This makes a charming background for a fine copy of a Sheraton antique sideboard, and doubles the light and sparkle provided by crystal lamps and white shades. Notice how the glowing color of a flower painting on the opposite wall is repeated by the reflection of the picture just between the two lamps. The walls in this room are papered in scenic wallpaper with a white background and design of Chinese inspiration. The dado and other woodwork are painted Wedgwood blue, while the Oriental-style rug is in soft

elaborate frame. A mirror panel is almost invisibly screwed to the wall and if there is any frame it is a simple wood molding or metal strip. Good commercial quality mirrors are plate glass, roughly between ¼ inch and ½ inch thick, and well silvered. The grinding and polishing given this glass removes surface inequalities and produces its sparkling brilliance and depth of luster. When you take into account the effect of greater space, light and air which a mirrored wall provides without any cost for reconstruction it may well prove a good investment or even a real economy.

INEXPENSIVE MIRRORED EFFECTS

Where there is not too much light, and accurate reflection is not as important as creating a general feeling of more light and air, it is possible to use an inexpensive type of mirror which is merely sheet glass silvered. Still less expensive is what is called "flash" mirror—plain window glass painted black on the underside, and providing a certain degree of reflection. You can often save money by picking up old large mirrors, removing the frames and having them resilvered. But don't throw away the frames. Chapter 38 has suggestions for using old-fashioned picture or mirror frames for trays, shadow boxes, etc.

Mounting and Care: For a large panel, tack a framework of wooden laths to the wall and attach the mirror to it by screws with glass rosette heads or by metal bracket holders screwed to the frame. Be sure the lath base is even and takes up any inequalities of the wall. Don't hang a mirror in direct

MIRROR-LINED ALCOVE SETTING

TO A MODERN MANTEL

tones with blue and pink predominating. Draperies are antique satin in Wedgwood blue with self-toned stripe, trimmed with white-and-blue braid which is used also on the straight fabric-covered valance above. This room relies entirely upon reproductions to create an authentic period atmosphere, and does it with convincing charm. The dining table is an exact reproduction of a Sheraton table, with settings of old crystal beneath a traditional crystal chandelier. The seats of the Chippendale-style ladderback chairs are covered with pinkish leather. The mirror here serves an additional purpose by striking a modern note in an otherwise completely traditional English room. The photograph above is interesting because it demonstrates the opening up of a vista by use of a strategically placed mirror. Notice how it catches almost the whole sweep of the stairway from the hall beyond this living room. In a very light room you could get this desirable vista effect without glare by using gun-metal glass with its soft shadowy quality.

ANTIQUE MIRROR PANELS PROVIDE THE BACKGROUND FOR A ROOM
COMBINING ANTIQUE AND MODERN FEATURES

The possibilities of antiqued glass in modern decorating should not be overlooked. In the living room above it is used effectively to create a feeling of spaciousness in a room which interestingly combines traditional and modern. The clouded effect of antique glass helps prevent the possibility of too much glare in such a wide expanse of mirror. It also helps tie the traditional and modern elements of the room together. The effect of space here is still further increased by an excellent color scheme for a small, light room—cool subtle tones of blue, light olive green and brown, mingled in draperies and slip covers. The modern shaggy rug is in two tones of green, while the tables are finished in a dark brown simulated tortoise-shell effect. Antique brass altar candlesticks have been converted into tall lamps with shades in white—the color used for accent. Notice the pleasing harmony in scale between the height of the lamps, the size of the shades, and the substantial lamp table which is really a circular chest with useful drawers. Figured fabrics are used in this room in correct combination with plain walls and curtains and the geometrical square design in the rug. The mirror wall is combined with glass window walls glimpsed at the left, thus repeating not only the room furnishings but part of the view from outside. An excellent use for antique glass is to install it in a traditional English room. The antique cloudy effect is in the traditional spirit, yet the expanse of mirrored wall provides a touch of modern atmosphere.

LINOLEUM-COVERED WALLS IN A TRADITIONAL HALLWAY DISTINGUISHED BY CLASSIC SIMPLICITY OF LINE

The adaptability of modern linoleum is strikingly illustrated in this charming Federal hallway. The walls are covered with moonstone-tinted linoleum against oyster-white painted woodwork. Note the effectiveness of night-blue linoleum stair treads and flooring, with the border design inlaid in white to frame a French blue rug. The striking color scheme is completed by red upholstery on chairs and sofa.

MARBLEIZED WALL FINISH IN A LIVING ROOM IS UNUSUAL AND STRIKING

The marbleized fireplace wall and door panels provide a dramatic background for the portrait which sets the color scheme for the room below. Blond tones of the wood frame, gold and soft warm gray in the picture background, are found also in the plastic wall-covering with its photographically marbleized surface. Soft honey-colored wool drapery fabric and woven wood blinds match the tones in the picture frame. Self-color scrolls on the wool-and-cotton carpet are in warm light beige-gray. Soft blue-gray upholstery on the chairs repeats the plain wall and ceiling color. The bright red of the lady's scarf is picked up for accent in the covering of the stools. Two French-style side chairs, baroque legs on the glass coffee table, and the almost Oriental design of the broad chairs bring a slightly exotic note into the picture.

METAL PLAYS A VARIED ROLE IN MODERN DECORATION

The room pictured here is a striking example of the modern trend in decoration. It is a symphony in metal, yet there is actual metal only in the graceful curving fireplace facing, and in the mantel, andirons and vase. The glass mirror over the fireplace reflects interesting draperies in cloth spun from aluminum thread. The curved corners at the end of the room, and the end wall above fireplace and shelves have been given a mirror-like depth and brilliance by an aluminum-like finish which creates an illusion of space and depth just as a mirror does. There is color contrast in the book bindings; texture contrast between gleam of walls and drapery and soft dull finish in corded upholstery fabric and deep-pile rug. The wide sweep of the sectional sofa balances the curve of fireplace and wall. Striking finishes and novelty fabrics like those shown here have qualities of super-wearability with elimination of cleaning and replacement costs.

sunlight, nor against a damp wall. Clean with window spray. Use soft cloths only, to avoid scratching.

SPECIAL WALL FINISHES

In addition to the magic of glass on walls there are other interesting wall coverings. Several introduced for modern-style rooms are now widely adopted for many other types of interiors because of special qualities of usefulness or novelty.

Linoleum: Floor linoleum long ago stepped out of the kitchen and established itself on floors all through the house. Now, special versions of it are moving up onto the walls. This hardy and useful finish is no longer confined to the marbleized and simulated wood effects which made it suitable for protective dadoes and paneling. There are many new designs and textures for use in any room where an unusual finish which is also wear-resisting and easy to keep clean is desired. The new linoleum wall coverings are flexible enough to fit around curves and corners. A cove base is often provided to join the linoleum floor smoothly and smartly to walls.

Novelty Walls: In addition to regular composition and plastic wallboards, there are various synthetic textiles; bakelite panels; reproductions of stone, tile and brick; also metallic effects all the way from gold to aluminum. Cork products have found many uses in rooms such as libraries, game rooms and distinctly modern living rooms. When redecorating, by all means look into the cover-up as well as purely decorative possibilities of new finishes for walls.

CARE OF YOUR WALLPAPER

1. KEEP it free from dust. Brush the walls down frequently with a long-handled brush of soft wool or hair, or clean cloth over a broom or a vacuum attachment. Avoid smearing by changing cloths often.

2. WATCH for grease spots—they can usually be removed easily while fresh. Cover them with Fuller's earth or French chalk, leave on several hours, then brush off. Repeat if necessary. Or make a paste by mixing one of the powders with cleaning fluid; spread paste over spot, thinning it around edges; when dry, brush off with soft cloth. For wax, apply a blotter and a warm iron.

3. FINGER MARKS may be removed by dampening them very slightly with cold water and applying Fuller's earth, letting it dry and brushing it off. DON'T RUB.

4. MOLD usually yields to careful sponging with 1 part salicylic acid in 90 parts alcohol. Use a soft cloth or sponge. If this leaves a brighter spot, it will soon disappear.

5. CLEAN old, soiled paper by rubbing it lightly with slices of white bread or art gum, or oatmeal and bran in a bag of open-meshed fabric. RUB UP AND DOWN ONLY. There are also prepared cleaners which must be used according to directions.

6. NEVER ALLOW water splashed on paper to stand. Even on washable paper it may leave marks. Wipe off with soft cloth.

7. ALWAYS CHECK when buying washable paper to be sure it really is washable. If you cannot get what you want in a washable paper, lacquer the paper you buy after it is on the wall.

8. KEEP remnants and scraps of paper for patching damaged places. You can do this easily, especially if there is a design. Cut out around the figures and match the piece carefully with the background. You can also use the scraps for making wallpaper cutouts.

9. WATCH for loose edges where strips of paper join. Pull the paper out gently. Apply wallpaper paste to the wall with a flat brush, then smooth the paper firmly back into place.

WASHABLE PAPERS

TO WASH these use a very mild, non-alkali soap, with warm—not hot—water, and much suds; be sure your cellophane sponge or soft cloth is not too wet—MORE SOAPSUDS THAN WATER; wash from bottom up, a small space at a time, overlapping the edges; rinse with clear water—plenty of clean cloths—and wipe dry. Be very careful not to let water seep into seams, to work its way under the paper and loosen the edges.

CARE OF YOUR LINOLEUM

1. APPLY a coat of special linoleum lacquer to inlaid linoleum as soon as the cement is set. It lasts a long time and preserves the surface. Especially important for floors which must take hard wear. Wax over the lacquer.

: : : : : : : :

2. APPLY a coat of wax to inlaid linoleum without lacquer, if it has already been lacquered at the factory, or to printed linoleum which has been coated at the factory with varnish. A non-rubbing wax may be used, preferably one specially suited to linoleum and similar floorings. Several very thin coats are better than one coat.

: : : : : : : :

3. DRY-DUST daily with a dry, *oil-less* mop.

: : : : : : : :

4. PICK UP spilled food, wipe off footprints and other marks with a damp cloth. Wipe up water promptly.

: : : : : : : :

5. POUR ice water over spilled grease at once to harden it so that it will not penetrate the surface, then scrape it up and wipe the spot with a waxed cloth.

6. USE liquid floor wax to wipe off marks from rubber heels. For rust and other difficult stains rub fine steel wool dipped in jellied soap (mild) over the spot. Wipe with damp cloth, dry and rewax the spot.

: : : : : : : :

7. BEFORE washing with soap and water treat the floor with an application of raw linseed oil and turpentine (2 parts to 1). Let it stay on for several hours then wipe with soft cloth, rubbing surface.

: : : : : : : :

8. WASH only occasionally, with special linoleum floor cleaner or very mild soapsuds; dry and rewax. DON'T WASH TOO OFTEN. With proper care it is not necessary. DON'T use strong soaps or cleaners.

: : : : : : : :

9. PROTECT the surface by using furniture rests on the legs of your chairs, tables and other movable furniture. If you do not have these, wax the ends of the legs.

: : : : : : : :

10. REPAIR loose edges promptly. Lift up and brush out dirt. Apply linoleum cement to floor. Press down and leave overnight under heavy weight. Don't use nails—they may break the linoleum.

CEILING INTEREST AND NOVELTY IN A

The ceiling shown in two views of the room pictured plays a vital role in the drama of the room-setting. The dark walls and floor provide an unusual background for light painted furniture and flowered chintz slip covers. The chintz pattern matches the ceiling paper and ties the ceiling and lower part of the room together. The composition flooring is in spatter finish harmonizing with the Colonial feeling in furniture design and woodwork. A room treated so distinctively must be very well proportioned—as this one is. In spite of the many decorative accessories and the colorful ceiling design, the room has an air of restfulness created by the perfect balance in furnishings and decoration. The fireplace grouping in the picture above balances the secondary center-of-interest grouping on the opposite wall. This in itself is a perfect example of formal balance, with identical units on each side of an imaginary line drawn down the center. (See Chapter 2.) A third center of interest, created by wall shelves and table with windows on each side, is also formally bal-

COMBINATION LIVING-DINING ROOM

anced. The room is an interesting study because it combines peacefulness with drama and creates a very modern effect by means of purely traditional furnishings and materials—the single exception being the round coffee table in blond wood in front of the couch. Everything about this room has been carefully thought out. The mirror above the couch would have been too narrow for the wall space without the group of pictures flanking it. The furniture is all correspondingly small in scale and therefore does not look heavy or crowded in its setting. The whole room is a demonstration of distinction achieved by the use of imagination rather than by heavy outlay for expensive furnishings. Even the small rug uniting the fireplace group looks adequate because of the decorative finish on the floor and the contrast in color which carries out the theme of light against dark. The wood chairs and the hanging wall shelf could be reclaimed from almost any second-hand dealer and easily decorated at home. Draperies are simple to make, easy to hang.

CHAPTER NINE

Ceilings

THE TREATMENT given the ceiling of a room is more important than is generally realized. If you do not like the type of ceiling, or feel it is not in keeping with the decorating scheme you have chosen, or if you have to consider repairs before painting or papering, remember the various insulating boards and composition materials, such as acoustic tile, specially designed for ceiling use. These may all be applied over old or new plaster, used for smooth ceiling effects, or paneled in any contemporary or period designs. Since they are obtainable in all sizes, they may be used with or without decorative joint treatments. They are easy to apply, and offer a solution to many ceiling problems.

Like walls, ceilings may be plain in design, decorated, or paneled. Beams are distinctively a ceiling treatment, and beamed ceilings are found in every period of architectural construction. Each type of ceiling may be finished in various ways to obtain a desired effect. Combinations of finishes often lend interest and contrast when needed in background treatment.

Ceilings and Light: The illumination of any room is more or less controlled through natural or artificial light radiated toward the ceiling and reflected back. Color and texture are the two most important factors in increasing—or modifying—light distribution. We must therefore emphasize their importance in choosing the ceiling finish, whether the material used is calcimine, paint, or paper.

White ceilings are excellent light reflectors and suitable for purely functional rooms such as kitchens. A chalk-white ceiling, however, is not attractive with colored walls. The color contrast calls attention to its joining with the wall, and you have contrast without meaning. White is still a light-reflector, even when it is tinted with a warm tone—so long as you keep it light and clear. In a dark room, use a warm, luminous color in a light tint on the walls and use a ceiling color in a still lighter tone of the wall color. Keep the surface in smooth texture to reflect light. If you want a white effect for a very dark room, tint the ceiling—even if only a little—to bring it into harmony with the walls.

If a room is too light and you wish to modify the light distribution, use a cool, not-too-light color on both walls and ceilings, or a darker ceiling; and keep the texture slightly rough. This helps to absorb light. When figured paper is used, the ceiling should be in the background color of the paper, or a few degrees lighter or darker, provided, of course, that the paper has been selected to tone down the light. If the background color is too dark, the ceiling may pick up a lighter shade from the design. Two-toned patterned ceiling papers are often preferable in a bright room as they absorb light more readily. Having a slightly textured effect, they also hide plaster defects which might pass unnoticed in a darker room.

If your room is of normal, or even more than normal, height, you can exercise greater freedom in the choice of your ceiling color. Contrast between the color on the ceiling and the color on the walls is being used by some decorators with interesting and harmonizing effects. If such a ceiling treatment appeals to you, do not fail to take into consideration the size of your room, proper lighting, and various other factors covered under appropriate headings in this book. Ceilings of rooms not in constant use, such as halls, dining rooms, game rooms, and rooms used solely for entertainment, may safely be painted or papered to suit your fancy—in yellow, blue, or even red—in contrast to the wall color. There is one point, however, to remember if you are using a contrast color on the ceiling of a room—it should be repeated somewhere else in the room furnishings.

It is well to remember, also, that much of the color character of a room depends upon the ceiling. The right tint will reflect a single harmonizing cast over all the objects and colors in the room, which might be described as spotlighting your background with color.

PLAIN CEILINGS

These are usually of smooth plaster, wallboard, or composition; calcimined, painted, or papered. Light-textured plaster may also be used, or simulated textures obtained through applying plastic paint or other textural finishes which may be tinted before application or painted afterward. Wood is seldom used as a plain ceiling, except for a very rustic effect. Extremely rough textures are not used; nor a high glaze, such as enamel, unless for some very special purpose.

Plain Paper for Ceilings: If your walls or floor—or both—are over-decorated, a plain ceiling paper will help to offset this effect. Used in light, receding tones, closely harmonizing with the side wallpaper, it will give an effect of space and roominess, as well as height, to a room. There are many plain ceiling papers on the market, usually less expensive than the matching paper sold for walls. If you wish a plain ceiling effect, but desire a definite wallpaper texture, these papers may be used to advantage, providing a great deal of care is taken in their selection. In choosing them, be sure to hold the ceiling paper above the side wall paper to duplicate as nearly as possible the effect you will get in your room. These ceiling papers come in several different styles, and in a wide range of prices.

1. *Brush Tints.* This type of paper is white on the back and tinted on the face, giving an effect of water-color or flat oil brushed on the ceiling, but with the texture of wallpaper. These tints should be matched with the wall color.

2. *Pulp Tints.* This type of paper is made by mixing coloring with the paper pulp, both sides being alike. In use, it would come under the same general regulations as paint.

3. *Small Patterns.* Many of these are in two-toned effects, which appear plain at ceiling height but give an attractive softened color tone.

4. *Ingrains and Plastic Effects.* These give a textural feeling to the ceiling, and are used when texture would be appropriate.

DECORATED CEILINGS

Decorated ceilings are not often used in modern design, but some formal, period or regional rooms demand them. While not so widely used in contemporary decorating they do fulfill certain definite functions. They give added dignity to a formal room. They introduce an unusual effect, or a note of gaiety, into an informal room. Also, decoration on the ceiling helps furnish a room which seems a little bare, and may be used to correct certain bad room proportions, particularly a too-high ceiling.

Figured Ceiling Papers: Figured papers for ceilings are produced in many charming effects, both to match wallpapers and in separate designs. Patterns range from geometrical motifs to floral effects without stems, festoons and wreaths, clouds and stars, moiré effects, and polka dots. They are usually printed in tints rather than strong tones; but in complex designs the colors may be strong provid-

SUIT YOUR CEILING TO YOUR ROOM

The low-ceilinged room above was reclaimed from an attic and turned into a room any boy would love by the painted sky-ceiling which gives the room height, and the installing of steel corner-casement windows. In order to paint a ceiling in an allover design you can block it out on wallboard panels, then paint in the details before applying the panels to the ceiling. Notice the window cornice and valance which has been continued around the wall as a shelf.

A plain ceiling rounding down onto the wall in the same shade creates a feeling of spaciousness in the room below of normal height and size. Notice the cornice framing the window and uniting bookcases at one side in a continuous grouping with shelves backing the couch. The storage cabinet which ends this unit arrangement serves as a lamp table, at the same time setting off the conversation furniture-grouping in a cozy corner-nook of its own.

MODERN INTERPRETATIONS OF THE PANELED CEILING DEVELOPED IN WALLBOARD

ing there is balance between them. Ordinarily, the higher the ceiling, the bolder and stronger the patterns may be. They may be chosen for use with plain papers on the walls or to harmonize with figured paper, or they may reproduce, in lighter tones, the same motifs used on the walls.

Figured ceiling papers hide small cracks in plaster; smoke and dirt do not show as quickly as on plain ceilings, and it is easier to clean the figured surfaces. The initial cost may be twice as much as that for good plain ceiling papers, but they will probably last twice as long. In a large room they give a furnished effect to the wide expanse of bare surface. Be sure your design is centered exactly.

Borders and Spot Motifs: These are the same types of decorations already described for use on walls. They include painted stencils on washable surfaces; borders and cutouts from wallpaper, chintz, etc.; and a variety of decalcomania designs. These decorations may be used as borders around the edge of the ceiling, perhaps with a corresponding border just below on the wall. They may be scattered over the surface. They may even carry a wall design up onto the ceiling, as when a vine running up the corner of a room flowers into a bunch of blossoms on the ceiling. In rooms used only for entertainment, stars, birds, cartoons, etc., may be painted or pasted on the ceiling. For very elaborate effects, do your decorating on composition wallboard panels before applying them to the ceiling.

PANELED CEILINGS

The paneled ceiling has many varieties and is used in many decorative styles. It is particularly important in period rooms; and if panels are used on the walls, the ceiling panels must be worked out in harmony with them. In contemporary decorating a slightly paneled effect is often given by moldings near the edge of the ceiling, covered with the ceiling paint and looking like molded plaster. This effect is also used between beams. Molding-lines of plaster or real wood moldings applied to the surface often divide the ceiling into sections, either to cover wallboard joining or purely for decoration. Where a large ceiling needs breaking up or the room below seems a little large and bare, wallpaper or cloth panels may be used in the same way as when such panels are applied to walls.

BEAMED CEILINGS

Beamed ceilings may be formal or rustic in effect. They may be plain, painted, stained, or covered with plaster. Ordinarily, the wood of the beams is left showing, painted or stained, while the space between is covered with painted plaster. Beams are attractive in many types of rooms, but remember that they lower the ceiling even when they are in the background ceiling color. Beams in a different color from the spaces between seem to lower the ceiling still

BEAMED CEILINGS AT HOME IN MODERN SETTINGS

Two versions of the beamed wood ceiling are shown in these photographs. In both cases they harmonize with the rustic effect of fieldstone fireplaces and the outdoor atmosphere created by picture windows. Simple contour-type chairs in the living room above are appropriate with the informal comfort of the deep couch, and the built-in book shelves, and the softly waxed composition floor with its shaggy pile rugs. The living room below expresses the same modern idea of comfort in a slightly more formal fashion. The circular couch, in two sections, is upholstered with an interesting deep-pile textured fabric. The material used for the chairs is textured, too, with a sculptured design in self-color. Note the grotto effect of summery plant decorations in the high fireplace; also the note of formality added to the room by long straight draperies and the Oriental-style rug on a polished wood floor.

more and also to make it look smaller just as paneling does. In many rooms this is an advantage, not a drawback, specially when wood paneling is used on walls in high-ceilinged living rooms or libraries. Beams are finished in harmony with other woodwork in your room, unless it is desirable to have the ceiling all one color, in which case they are painted like the spaces between. Beamed ceilings in which the spaces between the beams are left open and the vault of the roof appears above them are confined to very formal rooms in certain early periods or to rustic rooms, depending upon size, design and finish.

HOW TO SOLVE CEILING PROBLEMS

Ceilings have their special contribution to make in solving problems of awkward room proportions. We have already spoken of types of decoration which make them seem lower, of panels and beams which break up over-large spaces. Here are a few other ways in which you may use a ceiling as more than just a covering over the top of a room:

Ceiling Too High: In addition to using a warm, advancing color to make a ceiling seem closer, the following methods can be employed:

1. Use a cornice and treat the ceiling and cornice as one color unit by painting both the same shade. If you are using paper on the ceiling, paint the cornice in watercolor or flat paint to match it as nearly as possible.

2. Bring the ceiling paper down onto the wall and mark the point where it joins the wallpaper with a molding. Contrast between walls and ceiling papers will help also.

3. Use a lightly textured finish in advancing color, in plaster or plastic paint. If you prefer paper there is a special ceiling paper which gives the appearance of a painted ceiling with soft stippled texture.

4. Use the more heavily figured papers in geometrical or other bold designs and in deep colors.

5. Repeat a wall border around ceiling edge.

Ceiling Too Low: Use a receding color. Light tones alone are helpful, but graying any color gives it an even more receding quality than lightening it would do. Soft grays and blues will always look farther away than the warmer ivory, or any pink or yellow tint no matter how light in tone. (See Chapter 4.) It always helps to carry the wall color up onto the ceiling, in the same or lighter tint. Make the joining between wall and ceiling as inconspicuous as possible, perhaps with a plain, rounded cove finish. All-over ceiling paper can be used if you select one with soft receding background colors and an open design which has definite vista quality. This should be used with plain sidewall paper in closely harmonizing tones.

VAULTED CEILING IN A ROOM REMINISCENT OF AN EARLY ENGLISH COTTAGE

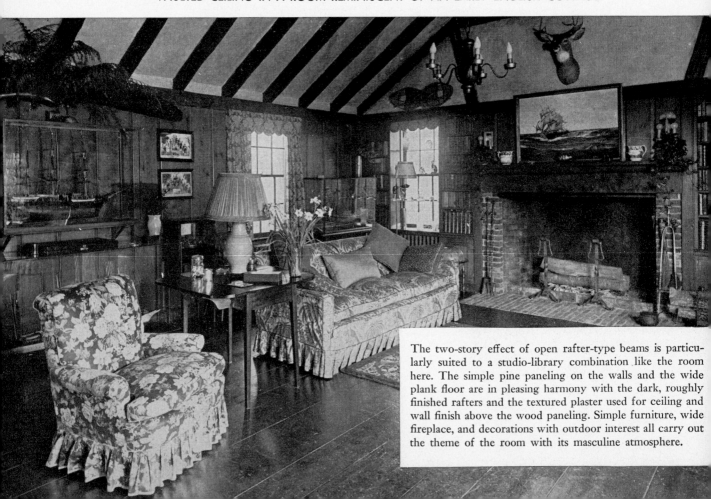

The two-story effect of open rafter-type beams is particularly suited to a studio-library combination like the room here. The simple pine paneling on the walls and the wide plank floor are in pleasing harmony with the dark, roughly finished rafters and the textured plaster used for ceiling and wall finish above the wood paneling. Simple furniture, wide fireplace, and decorations with outdoor interest all carry out the theme of the room with its masculine atmosphere.

CORRECTIVE TREATMENTS FOR
LARGE ROOMS WITH HIGH CEILINGS

Sketches A and B illustrate how decorated sections treated as panels on the ceiling may be used to break up over-large spaces in a long room. If the ceiling is high the solid panels could be used, as in A. Panels made by borders as in B would shorten the space without having the effect of bringing the ceiling down quite so much. One large panel may also be used on the ceiling, with an 18-inch border around the edge. In the picture above, the ceiling is lowered by carrying the design down onto the walls in border effect. A separate border as in sketch C may be used for the same purpose.

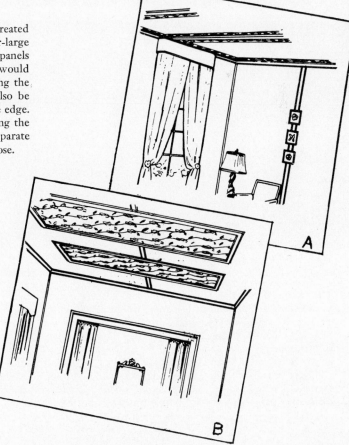

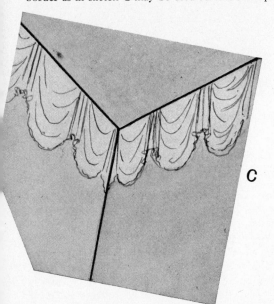

The charm of traditional hardwood flooring softly waxed and lustrous is illustrated in the dining room above where no rug is considered necessary. In familiar herringbone design, the floor is of the type known as parquet. Parquetry and marquetry have come down to us from the days of the Renaissance when designs were built on the floors with small blocks of wood put together like mosaics in stone. Pictorial or floral patterns were called marquetry, geometrical designs parquetry, and for both all sorts of rare woods were used. On our modern floors designs have narrowed down—except in special cases—to simple patterns such as the herringbone weave above or the basket weave made of square blocks with the grain running in opposite directions. Traditional design in this dining-room flooring seems to bridge the gap between the period furniture and the modern built-in storage-serving unit which replaces the customary buffet. The dining table and chairs in 18th Century style seem quite at home against the background of a modern

A FEATURE IN ITS OWN RIGHT

window wall and door. Damask-type curtains, hung on a traverse rod to draw across at night, add glowing color to nature's colors which serve as a back-drop for the scene. Colorful wall paintings contribute additional warmth. The softly textured wall and ceiling are at once traditional and modern in feeling. Another interesting note is the combination of dark mahogany, elaborately inlaid, with the blond natural finish, straight lines and plain surfaces of the built-in buffet with its ample storage and serving space.

CHAPTER TEN

How to Plan Your Floors

FLOORS have regained the importance they had before the over-all carpet of the Victorian Age hid them completely from sight. Not only do we now have all the variety of lovely, mellow woods, we also have a wide range of new types of floorings and reproductions of old floorings in a wide range of patterns, prices and colors.

HARDWOOD FLOORS

The majority of hardwood floors are oak. Hard maple, beech, and birch are frequently used, and occasionally walnut, hazel, hickory, and various others. Maple is harder even than oak and well adapted to the light tones of modern decorating, but its grain is less interesting than that of oak. Edge-grained yellow pine and fir may be used in place of the harder woods on floors where the wear is not too great.

The easiest, least expensive and most widely used floor is one laid with straight narrow boards running the length of a room. The next most popular floor is the parquet, which is made of short boards laid in a geometric design over the whole floor or in a border treatment around the edges with the rest of the boards straight. Floors made of wide planks are usually softwood but occasionally oak is used.

Finishes for Hardwood Floors: Hardwood floors should be stained or bleached to harmonize with furniture or woodwork in the room. Too many contemporary floors are finished in a golden oak shade coated with orange shellac which neither blends nor contrasts with old oak, walnut, mahogany nor with modern light finishes. Unless your floors are completely covered with rugs or carpeting you will find it is worth while to remove this outmoded finish and do the floors over in harmony with the decoration of your room. After stain (or bleach) has been applied to your floors they may be finished in one of several ways:

1. Varnish has gone out of favor as a floor finish. Only the spar varnishes are really durable and their waterproof, alcohol-proof qualities are not usually necessary—*except as a protection for painted and decorated floors.*

2. Shellac is often applied over filler, with or without stain, because it is the quickest and cheapest method of surfacing wood floors. It has its place as an accessory step in proper finishing, but alone it is of little use as a surface because of its short life under even ordinary wear. If you have new floors which have been shellacked, you can rub them down with light sandpaper or steel wool and protect them with a coat of wax. Don't wait for the shellac to wear off in spots.

3. Wax is the most generally satisfactory and attractive finish for hardwood floors. The older the wax coat, the lovelier is its patina and the less often the floor needs to be rewaxed, except at some point of specially heavy traffic—and it is easily touched up at the spots of greatest wear.

How to Wax Wood Floors: Apply a thin coat of good paste wax, allow it to dry, then polish by hand or with a weighted polish brush. Repeat with two or three thin coats. If you prefer liquid wax follow the directions on the container. In general, liquid wax is easier to apply but must be used oftener. The paste wax penetrates better, lasts longer, and does more to nourish the pores. Some decorators recommend a new combination wax-and-stain finish which comes in all the popular shades. There are also self-drying waxes which are said to be slip-resistant, and one which cleans and polishes in a single operation. This may be used on anything from enameled woods to linoleum, hardwood floors, or the refrigerator in your kitchen.

SOFTWOOD FLOORS

New floors in softwoods such as red pine, spruce pine and long-leaf pine are usually laid only on floors where carpets are to take most of the wear. However, if they are properly protected, they can be used almost anywhere, as some of the Early American pine floors have proved. After 200 years of use, they are more beautiful today than ever before. The traditional style of laying these floors in broad planks is suitable for any room fundamentally simple and not too formal in design. The planks may be treated like the hardwood floors already described,

WIDE PLANK FLOORING IS AT
OF FEDERAL

The primitive type of broad plank flooring characteristic of many Early American homes is frequently reproduced today in period rooms and other interiors. For these floors planks in varying widths are laid at random, with ends meeting wherever the length of the boards may bring them and fastened in place with wood pegs. Usually in soft wood, and painted, you will find these floors also in waxed hardwood like the hand-hewn oak plank floors still giving service in many ancient European dwellings. The charming corner group above is an excellent illustration of how well traditional wide plank flooring may harmonize even with rather formal Federal American-period furnishings. The wood-paneled dado, painted a darker color than the wall above, was a favorite wall treatment in Colonial America. Here the graceful lines of the furniture show the influence of French and English styles at the turn of the century (1800), while the clock is one of the banjo models favored by native

**HOME WITH THE DIGNITY
AMERICAN FURNISHINGS**

clockmakers. These wide plank floors in a good quality of softwood, stained, waxed and rubbed to lustrous beauty, can be used in almost any type of room. Their simplicity makes them appropriate for modern as well as traditional decorating schemes, and many modern designers use them either waxed or painted. Wide plank flooring may be made of pine, but because of its tendency to splinter when cut with the grain, many early American floors were made from oak or chestnut planks hewn out by hand, and modern builders use a variety of woods. When they are beautifully finished, these floors are attractive with small rugs of whatever style is harmonious with the furniture and the rest of the background treatment. For example, rugs of the Oriental type would be appropriate with the furniture group shown here, while hooked rugs, or woven rag rugs, would be more at home with furnishings of the simpler Early American types.

with stain and wax finish. They are equally attractive painted and this is the easiest way to handle them if the planks are in need of covering because of imperfections or undistinguished graining.

PAINTED FLOORS

One of the nice things about a painted floor is that it provides such a variety of colors and designs, at so little expense and with charming results. Always use a good quality paint mixed specially for floors. Insist upon a reliable brand of floor paint, or deck enamel. A thin coat of wax applied over the paint and kept renewed whenever necessary will be a great help in prolonging its life. Or you can apply transparent varnish over the paint, using spar varnish if you want the floor to be scrubbable.

A painted floor may make an effective background for a rug or it may double for the rug by supplying all the color and design necessary. If an old painted floor is in good condition you can put a new coat over it provided the new color is darker—but for really good results strip off the old paint and start fresh. For a black floor, make your first coat vermilion, then cover with two coats of black slightly tinted with Chinese blue.

Painted Designs: On wide, even-width boards it is easy to paint a geometrical design in two shades of one color or two harmonizing contrast colors. Give the floor the regular two- or three-coat finish in the lighter tone, then mark the design with chalk, in diamonds or squares, the width of the boards. Give the dark areas in the design one coat of the darker color, then follow with wax or varnish. There are several free-hand methods for painting a variety of patterns for which directions and designs can be bought.

Stencils for Floors: This is another inheritance from New England interiors. They used stencils not only on the walls but also on the floors and contemporary decorators have rediscovered the charm of such floors. Directions for using stencils on floors are the same as those described in Chapter 5. Remember to hold your brush at right angles to the floor and tap the paint on. Here, as in all painted floors, it is important to use a good foundation of two or more coats of paint, the last one being a regular floor paint. In this case, however, it is necessary to choose a finish paint which dries in a very flat effect, otherwise the oil paints used for stenciling will not take hold as they should. A dark stain on wood may serve as a background instead of paint, or a plain composition flooring such as linoleum.

The stencil designs may be in the form of borders or all-over repeated motifs, or a central decoration

135

A PAINTED BORDER IS CHARMING
ON A BEDROOM FLOOR

Designs painted on the floor were great favorites with our Colonial ancestors in the days when carpets were hard to come by and rugs often small and made at home by hand. Today they are being widely used for traditional rooms and special-purpose rooms; also, in highly stylized designs, for modern rooms. Both painting and stenciling are popular methods of floor painting. In the breakfast corner of the bedroom at left a design of trailing ivy leaves was taken from the wallpaper used on one of the four walls of the room. The pattern was enlarged and traced on the off-white painted floor, then filled in with the soft natural green of ivy leaves. Here the quaintly traditional boudoir chair flanks the modern table, set for breakfast coffee. In the room below a stenciled floor is appropriate in a dining-room setting where every detail is traditional. Colonial furniture and accessories are closely keyed to the background of figured wallpaper. white painted woodwork, and deeply recessed window with white ruffled curtains. The floor is painted in a dark shade, the conventional flower motifs stenciled in a lighter color on the surface. (See Chapter 5 for stenciling directions.) For any type of painted floor decoration follow directions carefully; do not neglect the covering coat of hard, waterproof varnish, which makes it easy to keep the floor clean. Renewing it will preserve your pattern indefinitely.

FLOOR STENCILS ARE AUTHENTIC IN AN
EARLY AMERICAN DINING ROOM

and a border may be combined. There is a special advantage in a border if you want to use a rug on the floor part of the time. Choose a design which will harmonize with the rug and space it so that it will frame the rug. Then put a center design on the floor under the rug. In the summer you can take up the rug—and still have a charmingly decorated floor. Be sure to follow the stenciling with a coat of spar varnish over the floor.

Don't forget scale in choosing your design. Conventionalized motifs are generally preferable—and in a border the dominating lines should be horizontal. A Greek key design is very effective. Use stencil patterns in the size which will look best on the expanse of your floor. If they are too small they will look insignificant; if they are too large they will make the room look smaller. This is a decorative novelty with limitless possibilities for introducing charm and color into a room with only a few dollars outlay in money. You may even want to repeat the design in a smaller scale on walls, hangings, or furniture. In using a border, measure the space carefully and lengthen or shorten each section of the pattern accordingly.

EASY-TO-DO DECORATIONS WITH PAINT

Spatter-dash Floors: This method makes a most interesting and charming floor, allowing a mingling of colors which may be very helpful in tying parts of a room together into a unit. The method for spattering is the same as that used for walls and described on page 139, except that a final coat of spar varnish must cover the paint on the floor to protect it from wear. If you prefer white shellac use that as a cover, but it will have to be renewed from time to time and it may leave a film over the paint. Varnish is a little more expensive and takes longer to apply and dry but is a good investment in the long run because of its lasting quality.

For best results use an undercoat of flat paint, then the foundation color, then the spatters, then the varnish. There are two schools of thought about spattering methods but they both turn out successful floors so take your choice. One advocates painting the floor and letting it dry before applying the spatters; the other maintains it is better to apply only about four square feet at a time of the last coat, allowing the paint to set slightly, but not to dry, before spattering.

In either case, apply all the spatter colors without waiting for any of them to dry. The argument for the second method is that the spattered paint will settle into the base and not wear off so quickly. Whichever method you use, tack a temporary dado

of newspapers around the lower part of your wall—unless you want a permanent "dado" of spatter dashes there. If you actually do want a spattered dado, put the papers on the wall along the line you want for the top of the dado. (See Chapter 5.) If your floor has a flat finish use either gloss or flat paints for spatters; but if the background is gloss, use flat paint for them.

This finish is not confined to cottages or cottage-type rooms. Some very lovely and expensively furnished rooms have been done effectively with these floors. They may be left bare or used as a background for rugs. Scatter rugs are attractive in colors harmonizing with those used for the floors. Dark—or black—backgrounds with light or bright spatters are attractive, also lighter grounds with two or three darker colors for the spots. A general favorite is a combination of blue, green, tan, raw umber, and a dull red.

Stippling and Scumbling: Stippling is described under the illustration on page 139. In this process several paint colors are added over a foundation coat as in spattering, and the same irregularity in the effect is desirable. In scumbling, a mottled effect is produced on a floor or a wall by removing a little of the last coat of paint in an irregular design. This is done by rolling loosely crumpled newspaper or wads of cloth over the wet paint, or tapping the surface. Usually the last coat is a little darker than those beneath in order to get mottled effect.

HOW TO PAPER YOUR FLOORS

Very charming and surprisingly durable floors have been made by entirely covering a bad wood floor with an appropriate pattern in wallpaper instead of painting it. Naturally, the paper must be well cemented down and followed by several coats of transparent varnish to insure wearing qualities. For bars, playrooms, etc., this method has great possibilities. Think what you could do with amusing illustrations or cartoons—or with a huge, clearly lettered map on the floor of a map-enthusiast's den!

You may adapt the same idea—in a little more conservative form—to floors in good-enough condition for painting or staining. Turn to the section on cutouts for walls and apply the suggestions in the same way to your floors. Arrange the cutouts in motifs or borders just as you would stencils, following with the protective varnish coats. One advantage of this method over stencils is that you can lay out all the sections of complete design before you paste it down and be sure it is just as you want it. The paper must be well cemented to the floor, or you can glue it with spar varnish, laying down the cutouts as you

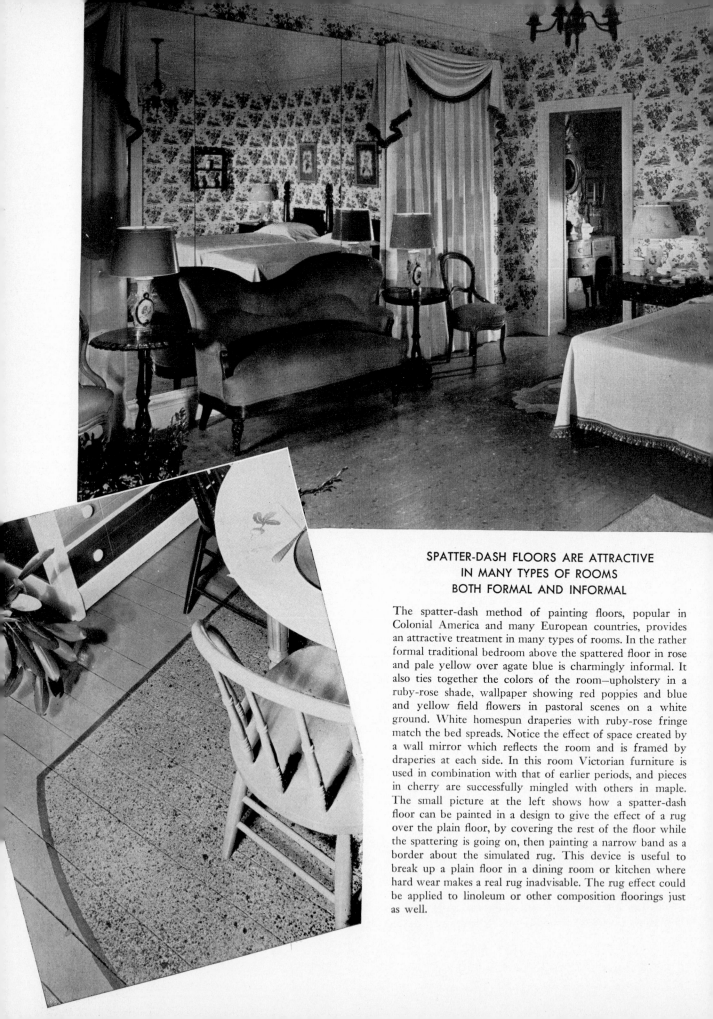

SPATTER-DASH FLOORS ARE ATTRACTIVE
IN MANY TYPES OF ROOMS
BOTH FORMAL AND INFORMAL

The spatter-dash method of painting floors, popular in Colonial America and many European countries, provides an attractive treatment in many types of rooms. In the rather formal traditional bedroom above the spattered floor in rose and pale yellow over agate blue is charmingly informal. It also ties together the colors of the room—upholstery in a ruby-rose shade, wallpaper showing red poppies and blue and yellow field flowers in pastoral scenes on a white ground. White homespun draperies with ruby-rose fringe match the bed spreads. Notice the effect of space created by a wall mirror which reflects the room and is framed by draperies at each side. In this room Victorian furniture is used in combination with that of earlier periods, and pieces in cherry are successfully mingled with others in maple. The small picture at the left shows how a spatter-dash floor can be painted in a design to give the effect of a rug over the plain floor, by covering the rest of the floor while the spattering is going on, then painting a narrow band as a border about the simulated rug. This device is useful to break up a plain floor in a dining room or kitchen where hard wear makes a real rug inadvisable. The rug effect could be applied to linoleum or other composition floorings just as well.

To spatter a floor the brush is held in one hand and struck sharply against a stick or piece of iron pipe in the other hand, as shown above. Black and white are good spatter colors because they contrast well with practically any color you select for your background, but usually the room's color scheme is repeated in the floor. To make spatters small hold the stick about a foot from the floor and use less paint on the brush. To make them larger, hold the stick three feet from the floor with more paint on the brush. The two pictures here illustrate a method for decorating floors which is sometimes preferred because it is easier to use. There is no danger of spattering paint where it should not go and corners can be more successfully handled. This process, called stippling, employs a special stipple brush, or a piece of crumpled paper dipped into a container of paint. Brown wrapping paper is better than newspaper, which is too soft. The piece of crumpled paper is dipped into the paint, then pressed against the floor which has already been painted a solid color. If two or more colors are used, apply them all during the same painting by finishing one section of the floor at a time. This stippling process is not to be confused with the "stippling" described in Chapter 5 for giving a mat finish to wall paint. (See text for more details of these methods.)

139

ATTRACTIVE STYLES IN COMPOSITION FLOORINGS

Flagstone floors are attractive in their proper settings. The flagstone design on composition flooring used for the living room below is in tune with the outdoor atmosphere produced by wide glass walls which seem to make the room a part of the garden outside. Flooring can be bought in this flagstone design, or the outlines can be painted on cement or almost any flooring including various cork and rubber products. Tile floors—or tile effects in composition flooring —are very adaptable to modern or traditional styles. As shown above, with softly waxed finish, the floor makes a charming foundation for furnishings which mingle comfortable modern upholstered pieces with traditional chairs, tables and cabinets. The high-beamed open ceiling, reminiscent of early English architecture, harmonizes perfectly with the modern window wall framing the garden view.

go. When the varnish is thoroughly dry follow with your covering coats, making sure each one is dry before applying another. You might experiment with this method on an attic floor or a back hall before you try it on your living-room floor.

LINOLEUM FOR FLOORS

Among all the processed floor coverings, linoleum is the best known and most widely used. It has long since ceased to be merely useful and has blossomed out into a wide range of colors and hundreds of stunning designs. Patterns are available for "inlaying," others to suit special types and styles in rooms. Or you may make your own design for combining two or more colors in some striking pattern, original or copied from a picture. Modern linoleum reproductions of almost every kind of floor covering are so realistic that no one need hesitate to use them.

It is impossible to visualize the richness of color in linoleum, and the variety of design—running the gamut all the way from traditional to ultra-modern—unless you make a point of looking over the stocks in your favorite store. If no design happens to be just what you want, you can have an inlay pattern worked out which will make a frame the exact size for your rug, or follow the outline of your floor in a border, or pick up some theme in your decorating scheme and carry it out on your floor in proper scale and colors. Remember, this flooring is practically permanent—so take pains to find something you know you can *live with*. If you *should* tire of your color or pattern, however, you can always remedy the situation with paint. This is also useful for covering up the pattern in worn or printed linoleum.

Types of Linoleum: (1) Inlaid linoleum—sometimes called "battleship" linoleum—is a composition of ground cork, linseed oil, and fillers, cemented and pressed onto a burlap foundation. In this stain-proof, long-wearing material the pattern goes completely through the fabric, which makes for durability both because the design cannot be worn off and because it is always possible to match the pattern and insert a new section wherever there has been damage or very heavy wear. (2) Printed linoleum is a cheaper but less durable product—a coating of oxidized linseed oil on a burlap backing. The printed pattern wears off in time and sections cannot be restored or replaced. It may, however, be given two coats of good paint when it begins to show signs of wear.

Where to Use Linoleum: (1) Its cork content makes linoleum a comfortable resilient surface for any working floor such as a kitchen or laundry. (2) Its warmth, its resistance to damage, its durability, all recommend it for such floors as those in children's rooms, nurseries and playrooms. (3) Its appropriate patterns and range of colors, in addition to the utility factors mentioned, make it widely useful in bathrooms and hallways. (4) Smart new designs make it adaptable to any room in the house, as a patterned floor covering without rugs or as an effective rug background. (5) It provides safe and attractive stair-treads and useful covering for work tables, as well as rendering many other special services.

LINOLEUM DESIGNS CAN BE FOUND FOR ANY ROOM IN THE HOUSE

The photographs on this page suggest the versatility of linoleum as a floor covering for living rooms as well as kitchens and other utility rooms. In the bedroom below (left) an old favorite is used—marbleized design with softened color effects and a surface which does not show footprints easily. A small string rug by the bed relieves any feeling of bareness. The living-room corner (right, below) illustrates an attractive way in which inlays can be used to set off sections of floor space and so help create unified furniture groupings for conversation, dining, or other special purposes. Here, the light strip set in the dark floor outlines a corner in such a way that it has the effect of an alcove. Note the comfortable modern sectional chairs put together to make a couch-and-chair group by the table.

STRIPES ON LINOLEUM CAN BE PAINT OR INLAY

The two floors on this page illustrate highly decorative effects achieved with linoleum. In the hallway above inlaid stripes decorate the floor so that no rug is needed. In the dining room shown below the linoleum floor was designed and decorated to match a very unusual color scheme. Modern furniture in limed oak is set against a background of grape and pink and these colors are carried out in the picture above the buffet, lining of the china cabinet, the chair upholstery and the floor covering. Deep grape linoleum is ribbed with peach-pink stripes and spattered with paints in varied colors between the pink bands. You will find many types of linoleum floors illustrated in other chapters.

SPECIA

TYPE OF FLOORING	CHARACTERISTICS
CERAMIC TILE (GLAZED AND TEXTURED)	Cool, serviceable floor, especially in hot climate. Perm Textured variety has great beauty, in warm, rich colors ern version of mosaic faience tile is obtainable in e handle form. Tile comes in bricks or layers. Is simulc many materials.
RUBBER	Somewhat like linoleum, but more soft and resilient. in rolls or in blocks. Wide price range. Many desig colors, also tile effects. Permanent. Damage-proof. proof. Excellent in marbleized designs.
BRICK	Rustic type, permanent floor. Same brick used for floors, on terraces and walks, only more carefully le smoothness.
CORK	Excellent flooring material for warmth, resilience, qu durability. Price range like wood flooring. May be boards as large as 20 x 35 inches, laid in parquet a borders or strips. No slipping. Moisture-proof. Fire ret Easily handled. Laid in mastic cement.
ASPHALT	Promoted to interiors in form of new composition tile fl Brilliant colors. Impervious to moisture. Resilient. Inexp Non-slippery when wet. Accident-proof. Even cigarette wipes off easily.
CEMENT AND CONCRETE	Another case of promotion from sidewalks and are thanks to modern inventions. A new color penetrating coating gives this rough material the appearance of tile, with great ceramic beauty and rich sheen. Firepro manent. Cool.
MARBLE	Marble is the hardest, most permanent flooring. In plain or slightly patterned, it is obtainable in certain varieti fairly moderate price range. It is usually restricted te space which helps from price angle.
SLATE	This may be in regular blocks, blocks larger than tile irregular shapes laid casually. Qualities similar to til
GLASS BRICK	This new development is along same lines as glass b walls. Permanent. Sanitary. Many interesting possibilit
SIMULATED TRAVERTINE STONE	Interesting material made of wood fiber and other ingre Looks like solid stone, but is light in weight. Can be c nailed like wood. Moisture and fire resistant. Comes in blocks or squares. Assorted colors.

USES	CARE	REMARKS
ve for hallways, foyers, sun-rooms, hearths. Suitable ood rooms, especially Early English or Italian styles. in soft textures suitable anywhere. Since tile keeps eat, it may need to be "warmed," in a hall or living oy a few small Oriental rugs.	1. Glazed surfaces: Sweep with soft broom; dust with dry mop; wash occasionally with soap and warm water; dry at once after washing. Polishing increases luster. 2. Soft-finished tile: Wax gives rich sheen, antique patina; treatment and care as for waxed wood floors. For stubborn stains use tri-sodium phosphate. Rinse, dry thoroughly.	If you want to lay tile yourself choose a design without pattern. Look for those which come in series, varying in shape, color and texture.
used anywhere suited to linoleum floors, and in similar Range of brilliant colors makes it especially good for effects. Water-resistance adapts it to kitchens, bath- etc. Durability useful in game rooms, etc.	Treatment and care are the same as suggested for linoleum in this chapter.	Inter-locking tile form, sheets 24 x 36, or large rolls are all easy for the home worker to handle. Cemented in place, like linoleum.
ger confined to outdoor flooring. Waxed and polished, es charming floor for foyer, sun-room or hallway. Also e for rustic effect living rooms, especially Colonial or Provincial.	Treatment and care are the same as suggested for waxed tile floors. Careful waxing is essential to soften the rugged effect of brick.	Don't use a brick floor in a formal room, or with elaborate furnishings. It is charming only in its proper atmosphere.
e for use in almost any room as it takes light polish. only by narrow color range through brown cork tones. nt for play rooms, dance floors, children's rooms, etc. sed in modern-style rooms.	These floors should be cared for according to directions for waxed wood floors already given in this chapter.	In modern interiors, cork sheeting is sometimes used on the walls as well as on floors. With an acoustic tile ceiling, this would make a prac- tically sound-proof room.
e for pergolas, terraces, sun-rooms, play rooms. Pro- afety for kitchen or laundry. Range of colors makes it le wherever tile can be used effectively. Factory-cut nake unusual designs easy to work out in special rooms.	If not waxed, treat as painted floor. If waxed, treat the same as linoleum.	Remember, if you live in a hot climate, that asphalt softens with heat.
rooms, hallways, game rooms, foyers, etc. Lovely akes it adaptable to many rooms as a rug background. ffective in geometric designs marked off with metal perhaps accented by metal medallions.	If not waxed, treat as a painted floor. If waxed, treat like any painted floor waxed.	Don't confuse the new cement finishes with the old concrete paints which wore off too fast to make the floors really serviceable.
ooring for hallways, foyers, etc., in fairly formal homes. e in harmony with wall treatment and other decorative s. Especially good with classic styles, in connection with dadoes, stairs, etc.	Like glazed tile, it requires only washing with mild soap and water.	Marble is really permanent, so be sure you know what you want before you decide to use it.
ve in period halls. May be used in play rooms, sun- etc., where soft finish tile would be appropriate. Often r flagstone design floors.	Should be waxed and polished, like tile. Keep clean and care for in same way as other waxed floors.	Don't use in a very formal room, at least not in irregular, casual designs.
ew floors will undoubtedly be adapted to use in many t rooms in the house, and many styles of decorating.	Easy to clean with soap and water.	Worth checking on for floors, also fireplace hearth and facing.
had in several finishes, adapted to various uses. In ke stone, makes excellent flooring for halls, foyers, etc. very good stair-treads.	Takes fine, hard wax finish. Non-slippery. Care is the same as for waxed wood floor.	May be nailed to wood, or laid over cement, using mastic cement.

OTE: DON'T USE OILS OR ANY SCRUBBING PREPARATION ON ANY COMPOSITION MATERIAL . . . . THEY DECOMPOSE THE SURFACE

Modern decorating takes frequent advantage of the restful, space-enlarging qualities of plain one-color, room-size rugs or over-all carpeting. In this room, keyed to comfort, the restful effect is still further enhanced by long low lines of built-in bookcases and couch. Note the convenience of a built-in radio-phonograph, with special record-album shelves. The specially designed chairs are of laminated birch plywood, and the couch is covered with deep-textured fabric in Chi-

LINE, TEXTURE, VISTA

nese red. Long straight draperies which draw across the windows at night add a touch of dignity as well as friendly warmth. All lighting is of the indirect, concealed type requiring no conventional lamps or fixtures.

CHAPTER ELEVEN

How to Choose Floor Covering

THE FOUNDATION of every decorating scheme is the floor covering. Like walls, they may make a contribution to decorating in their own right or they may serve primarily as a background for your furniture. If you plan to make a feature of your floor by means of design you must neither cover it up with furniture nor have too many other patterns in the room to compete with it. Instead, you will probably select your color scheme from it, key other furnishings to it and build around it. If you choose a plainer floor you have much more leeway in style and quantity of furniture, upholstery, wall treatment and draperies. Because they do simplify decorating problems the plainer types of floor coverings are the most widely used.

Properly selected, floor coverings coordinate all other elements of room decoration. If you already have a fine rug or carpet which must be used you can turn it to advantage by making it the basis of your room structure. Use it as inspiration for your color scheme and adapt your plans to it.

Comfort and ease of care as well as beauty are important factors in floor coverings. They usually represent proportionately a major investment, are apt to be more or less permanent, and should be chosen with an eye to the future. That does not mean you must spend a great deal of money in order to have suitable floor coverings. Many new types of rugs and carpeting have been introduced in recent years which are beautiful and long-wearing but much less expensive than the traditional standard materials.

Each room in the house has its own style, theme and mood—or should have. Each serves a different purpose. For successful decoration floor coverings should fit these special requirements. Bedrooms need

POPULAR RUGS AND CARPETS

Three of the most widely used traditional types of carpeting and rug weaves are illustrated in the rooms on this page. The Axminster weave in 18th Century floral design (below) is shown in a setting which demonstrates correct surroundings for a conspicuous floor pattern such as this. You will notice that walls are plain, draperies have color contrast but no pattern, upholstery is either plain or in a small geometrical design, and the room is large. This makes it possible to use a striking floor carpet without making the room seem over-decorated or too small. The center photograph shows a living room with a plain velvet carpet in the conventional narrow joined strips, used with sturdy modern furniture and large splashy-patterned upholstery fabric. The charm of chenille as a floor covering—in cotton this time—is demonstrated in the living room above. The luxurious room-sized rug was dyed smoke gray to match the background color of gay tulip-print chintz. Handsome cotton velveteen covers interesting tufted chairs that push together in the modern manner to form a love seat in this room where desk and accessories are entirely traditional. The combination of cotton chenille with chintz is a favorite one. In all three rooms the floor covering was chosen as an integral part of the decorating plan, contributing to beauty as well as comfort. With careful planning, it is possible to have these qualities in floor coverings without a large outlay of money. For example· It is better to buy a less expensive type of carpet of the best quality in that type than to select a cheap grade of a more luxurious weave; a really fine cotton rug is more desirable than one in a loosely woven, badly constructed wool fabric. A large rug, like the one in the upper photograph, can be made from several small string rugs sewed together; allover carpeting in a lock weave which does not ravel can be joined together without showing a seam—thus it can be cut into rugs for two rooms and joined later for a larger rug or carpet in one room; large carpet remnants can be made into very good rugs.

something soft underfoot, in colors light enough not to show every speck of lint, every flake of powder. Living-room needs cover a wide range of types and styles but in general the floor is a background for the furniture and should be considered primarily from that angle. Spacious, formal rooms with a large expanse of floor space in proportion to furniture provide an appropriate setting for fine patterned rugs as here their full beauty of design and texture can be displayed to advantage.

CHOOSING YOUR FLOOR COVERING

Carpets Versus Rugs: Choice between carpeting and rugs is a matter partly of taste, partly of utility. In general, carpeting is warmer for a cold climate, rugs are cooler in a hot climate. Over-all carpeting increases the apparent size of a room and makes furniture arrangement easier whereas rugs hold up better because they can be turned from time to time to distribute wear and taken up for a rest during the summer.

As for materials there is little difference between rugs and carpeting. Wool, cotton, linen, silk, rayon, fiber, grass, felt, etc.—all these are used for both. The difference is that carpeting is woven in a continuous strip finished on two sides only; rugs are woven in a great many shapes and sizes and finished at the ends with selvages, binding or fringe. If there is a pattern in carpeting it is all-over and continuous. In a rug it is usually a complete design with a border running around all four sides.

Large Rugs Versus Small: In using a room-sized rug the secret of effectiveness is to have it really room-sized—that is large enough to cover the floor with not more than a foot, or a foot and a half, of floor showing around it.

One alternative to using an undersized large rug is to use several small ones. But they must be carefully selected and correctly placed or they will create an impression of disorder in the room. Small rugs have a great many uses from the standpoint of utility as well as charm. Use them as accents to brighten up a drab floor, bare or carpeted, to provide spots of color and warmth in hallways or rooms where possibility of tracked-in mud makes carpets or larger rugs impractical. If you have a wood, tile or composition floor too fine in itself to be hidden under a large rug or carpet a few well-chosen small rugs may add a desirable note of color, luxury or warmth.

In a sparsely furnished room with a bare or carpeted floor small rugs may be used to break up floor space and help furnish the room. A long narrow room may be shortened by using two equal-sized rugs which break the floor in the middle, or one larger rug with a narrower one at each end in a three-panel effect, or by a judicious combination of large and small rugs.

Patterned Floor Coverings Versus Plain: This is largely a matter of personal taste, providing you select the texture, type of design, and colors which harmonize with your room. If that calls for plain floor treatment and you don't like plain floors, then make your pattern an inconspicuous two-toned design or a very small all-over effect, or look into the interesting textured finishes which create design in a one-color material by cutting it into the nap. These will give you the plain background you need without the flat effect of an unrelieved surface.

1. Plain floor coverings are indicated: (a) In a small room with much furniture. (b) In a room where there is much definite pattern in walls, draperies, upholstery, etc. (c) In a room where restfulness is a primary objective. (d) In a room where a unifying element is needed to blend patterned walls, furniture and accessories into a harmonious whole.

2. Large designs, rugs with borders, etc., are indicated: (a) In a room with wide, open floor space. (b) In a room with not very much furniture and a formal atmosphere. (c) In certain period rooms, discussed in the Period Chart. Note: Remember *design* must always be in scale with your room.

3. Average-sized patterns, all-over designs, etc., are indicated: (a) In an average room where walls and draperies are too plain and livening up is needed—or you are planning such walls and draperies. (b) On floors, where heavy wear is to be expected. Plain rugs and carpets show a path of wear more quickly than those with a covering pattern. (c) In a room where spots, stains and accidents may occur, such as a dining room. A figured floor covering is much less spot-revealing than one with a plain surface. A bold design may be chosen for this purpose, in a dining room where the furniture is rather heavy and needs floor-importance to balance its weight.

Textures on Floors: The texture should be taken into account in selecting any floor covering. If the color of the rug is the same as that of drapery or upholstery in the room, variety in textures is doubly important to prevent monotony.

1. Rich, silky finishes such as Orientals belong in more or less luxuriously furnished, formal, or period rooms.

2. Rough, shaggy, homespun types of finish belong in rooms where usefulness is the primary consideration, where hard wear is to be expected, and where furnishings are simple or approaching the rustic in style.

3. Novelty textures with long, shaggy looped nap, or dull nubby effects with unusual fabrics such as

cellophane should be keyed to unconventional rooms. Used judiciously they can be most effective.

4. Woven cottons or other textures regional in feeling—New England hooked rugs, for example—are best in rooms with corresponding regional treatment or an underlying harmony in style.

5. Deep pile textures create a feeling of warmth and luxury which makes them most appropriate for cool climates and seasons.

6. Flat, smooth textures such as those in many linen, cotton and fiber materials are cool-looking and appropriate for warm climates and seasons, also for semi-outdoor living rooms.

Colors on Floors: In a well-proportioned room, where no odd and unusual effect is being contrived, keep the floor in a lower color tone than the walls. This preserves correct proportions and establishes the feeling of a firm foundation underfoot. If the whole room is very light in its coloring, the floor may be light too, but not quite so light as walls and ceiling.

If the ceiling is too high, a really dark floor will help bring it down. If it is too low, make all divisions as inconspicuous as possible—that is, carry a receding wall color onto the ceiling, and let the floor color tone into the wall in a closely harmonizing shade.

A small room looks appreciably larger with wall-to-wall floor covering in a plain, soft receding color—blue-gray, gray, gray-green, etc. A large room looks smaller with rugs in warm, advancing colors.

HOW TO BUY FLOOR COVERINGS

Having decided the style and type of rug or carpet you want the next important point is getting your money's worth. Floor coverings are usually to last a long time either in the room they are purchased for or one to which they may be transferred later. It pays to spend as much on them as your budget will allow. It also pays to know what you are getting in return for your money. Remember that wool carpet fabrics with a hard twist surface will resist wear better than a soft smooth pile.

Buying Service in Your Rug or Carpet: The chart in this chapter will serve as a guide in choosing the type and style of rug or carpet which is most suitable for your needs. You will notice that those listed as most highly serviceable are made of wool, though many others are satisfactorily durable. This wool, the longest-wearing carpet material yet produced, may be woven into fabrics called "worsteds" or into "woolens."

Wool blends (part wool, part rayon) are lustrous and richly colored. They soil more easily than wool, but also clean easily; they are durable, but not so durable as all-wool. They are less expensive, however, and often furnish a very good compromise between quality and price. If your material is an all-wool pile fabric it is important to be able to judge the construction in weave and the quality of wool used. There are shoddy wools as well as good wools, and listed here are several things you can do to safeguard your purchase.

1. Look at the label. If there is no label, don't buy.

2. Be sure of your manufacturer. A reliable firm does not make false claims for a product.

3. Examine the pile for yourself. You can tell if the wool is springy by pulling out a bit of yarn. You can judge the denseness of the pile by bending the fabric back and pressing your finger down to feel how wide the cracks are between tufts. Good quality means close weave, dense pile, resilience, with pile standing up in bristly, stiff rows. Length of pile is a factor, too, but that varies with different types of carpeting, as you will see in the chart.

4. Examine the back of the fabric. If it is stiffened with jute it means the weave is loose and the carpet will not wear well. You can tell this because the stiffening will show up as a gluelike substance on the back. Also if threads of the weave show up clearly at a distance of two or three feet, it means a loose, poor-wearing construction.

5. Check the color. For satisfactory service the dye should be in the yarn before weaving which means that the color will go evenly from the base of the pile to the tip. If the design is printed on, it will wear off and the colors will become dull and unattractive. Look out also for a "bleached" rug—the colors will be deeper at the base of the pile than at the top.

HOW TO INSTALL NEW FLOOR COVERINGS

There are three different ways to lay a carpet.

1. The traditional method is to have it cut a little larger than the space of the floor, shaped around the hearth or other projection, then laid in place with edges turned under slightly. It is tacked down with carpet tacks to make it stay smoothly in place. Have the edges bound all around before laying, specially at doorways, etc. Do not overlook carpet bindings which come in various colors and may be applied to edges with a hot iron and no sewing.

2. A more satisfactory but more expensive method of laying carpet is to sink sockets along the edges of the floor into which pins are inserted to hold the bound edges of the carpet. This practically makes an over-all rug of the carpet, except that it is cut to

COTTON WEAVES ARE ADAPTABLE AND ATTRACTIVE

Cotton and fiber are no longer confined to two or three standardized weaves and to designs which fit them only for utility rooms or casual settings. In these pictures cotton floor coverings are shown quite at home in a traditional and a modern room. The living room shows modern dependence for variety upon texture and color contrasts rather than upon pattern. The firmly woven cotton rug with its effect of plainness helps give the room a feeling of space which is needed to accommodate rather large modern arm chairs and sectional couch units. Note the Colonial feeling of the scenic print drapery in the dining room, the soft natural-finish maple furniture, and the quaint wallpaper dado.

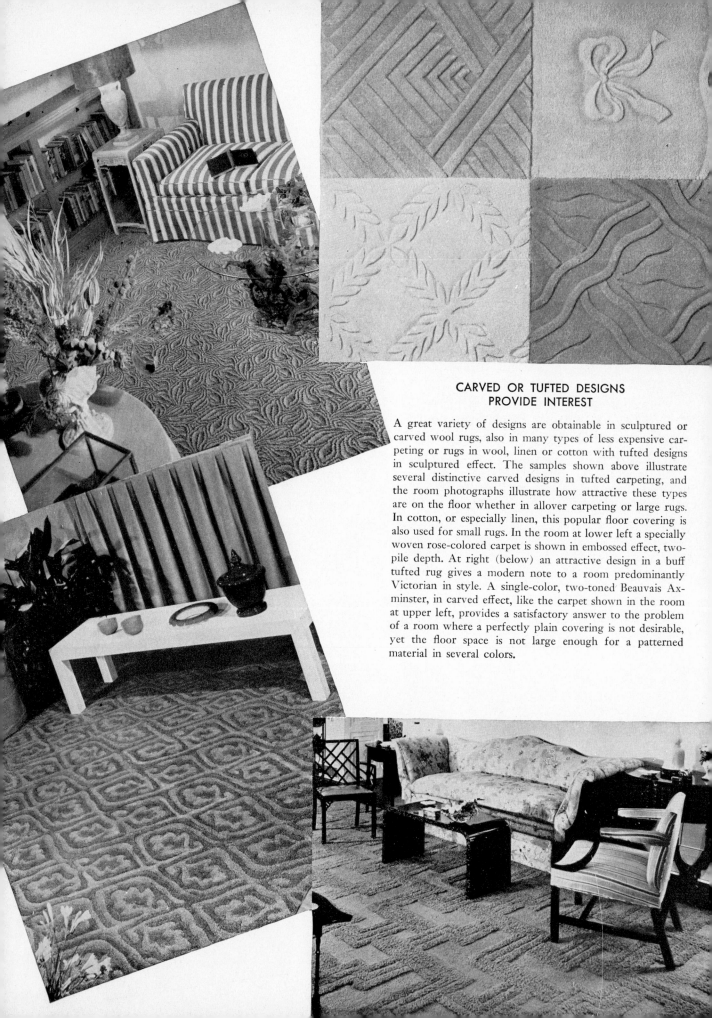

CARVED OR TUFTED DESIGNS PROVIDE INTEREST

A great variety of designs are obtainable in sculptured or carved wool rugs, also in many types of less expensive carpeting or rugs in wool, linen or cotton with tufted designs in sculptured effect. The samples shown above illustrate several distinctive carved designs in tufted carpeting, and the room photographs illustrate how attractive these types are on the floor whether in allover carpeting or large rugs. In cotton, or especially linen, this popular floor covering is also used for small rugs. In the room at lower left a specially woven rose-colored carpet is shown in embossed effect, two-pile depth. At right (below) an attractive design in a buff tufted rug gives a modern note to a room predominantly Victorian in style. A single-color, two-toned Beauvais Axminster, in carved effect, like the carpet shown in the room at upper left, provides a satisfactory answer to the problem of a room where a perfectly plain covering is not desirable, yet the floor space is not large enough for a patterned material in several colors.

PATTERNED CARPETING FOR A LARGE ROOM

In a large room with plain walls, it is often desirable to have pattern in the floor covering. A Beauvais-tapestry style carpet, with a large, softly colored design, provides floor interest in the living room at the left, adding warmth to a room designed for comfort. The size of the room makes it possible to place the large couch and oversized table well out in the room facing the fireplace—an arrangement advisable only where there is a wide expanse of floor space which must be broken up to create a hospitable and homelike effect.

TEXTURE INTEREST IN A CARPET

Many new and unusual textures have been worked out by the makers of today's rugs and carpets to provide variety and floor interest, especially when it is desirable to use only one color in the floor covering. A deep, shaggy pile, like that shown at the right, has a richness and warmth which makes it adaptable to modern or traditional decorating themes. The fact that this effect can be achieved with linen, cotton, or heavy wool yarns makes it possible to provide a wide price range in this type of floor covering. Here a graceful writing desk and chair in French Provincial style are grouped with built-in shelves for accessories and books. The soft green of the carpet is linked with the sunshine yellow of the shelf background by the greenish yellow of the chair upholstery, with notes of color contrast in the desk wood, book bindings, and ornaments. Shaggy, deep-pile weaves are available in every type of floor covering, from broadloom to rugs in many shapes and sizes. Originally made mostly in pastel shades, these lines now include all appropriate floor colors, and are as popular for living rooms as for bedrooms.

"SPATTER-DASH" WOOD FLOOR

For a cool summer dining room (right), simple wooden furniture was made gay and attractive with paint. The floor was brightened by marking the outline of a rug on the painted planks, then using the paints left over from the furniture to fill in that space with a colorful spatter-dash design. (Directions for spatter-dash decoration on page 138.)

PAINT PLUS IMAGINATION

An old bull-fiddle case picked up at a country auction was converted into the set of hanging shelves shown at the left. Shelves were fitted diagonally into the opened case, and the inside was painted a rich glowing Chinese red. The outside was painted white, and antiqued. The result was a hanging wall cabinet which makes an effective background for a collection of small ornaments. In an informal dining room, such as the one shown on this page, the shelves could be used for decorative dishes, making a spot of gay color above a buffet.

type suitable for rugs. It will be attractive in this shape, placed in front of the fireplace or as a center for a friendly conversation-grouping of furniture.

2. Buy strip carpeting which will go with the rug and make a border all the way around, starting at a mitered corner and mitering the other corners also. A figured strip around a plain center might help solve some color problem. You can adapt a carpet from a small room for use in a larger one in this way or by the "oval method" above.

You can always cut up a worn carpet or large rug into strips for hallways or small rugs by using fringe or ironed-on rug binding.

QUALITY OF AGELESS BEAUTY

heaven and the Deity, along with the five-clawed dragon motif traditionally reserved for China's emperor. The rug shown above is another type of Chinese design and coloring which would be equally good as a basis for distinctive color schemes. The background is ashes of roses. Over this some very fine old Chinese patterns are arranged in a wide variety of softly muted tones in mellow blues, yellow, greens and tans. The designs are set off by a narrow gold border with an outer one of interlocking motifs in ivory, blue and rose.

CARE OF RUGS AND CARPETS

Give a new pile rug two weeks for the pile to settle before you use a vacuum on it. Fluff will undoubtedly come off when it is swept but this shedding is merely loose clippings and fibers which will gradually be cleaned off. If you find a loose thread do not pull it out—cut it off.

"Shading" on Pile Rugs or Carpets: This is only the packing down of the pile in some areas more than in others. It shows up on a plain-colored rug but is not noticeable on one with a figured pattern. With tightly twisted yarn rugs, such as the pebble-weaves, this shading is eliminated entirely. The longer the pile, the more conspicuous the difference between the smooth, shiny surface of the crushed areas and the natural dull effect of the erect-pile sections. The difference in color tones is only an apparent difference, not real, and the condition can be temporarily corrected by smoothing out the pile all in one direction with the vacuum cleaner, carpet sweeper, or soft broom. Changing the rug around also helps by shifting the line of habitual pressure in one direction and moving any much-used area to a more protected location. To make your floor coverings last longer:

1. Turn rugs occasionally to a different position to keep wear distributed and prevent marking from heavy furniture. On carpets move the furniture once in a while for the same reason.

2. Move stair carpeting up or down a little when the treads begin to show wear.

3. Where pile is crushed it should be steamed as follows: Wrap your hand in a heavy towel to protect it from steam then hold a hot iron wrapped in a wet cloth over the crushed pile. Don't touch the

SMALL CHINESE RUGS ADD SPARKLE AND DISTINCTION TO A BEFORE-THE-FIRE GROUPING

STRATEGIC SPOT FOR A SMALL RUG

Scatter rugs are often very useful, to give warmth to a bare floor, to tie a furniture group together, or to protect a carpet —as in the Colonial-type living room at the left. In addition to this spark-protection, a small rug may be placed at a point of heavy use to prevent wearing of a path in the carpet. When used on bare floors small rugs become danger spots unless anchored in place by means of non-skid pads, rug cushions, or some other protective device. They should always be placed—like the one shown here—parallel to walls or at right angles, except in front of a corner fireplace, corner cabinet, or some other piece of special furniture. A plain room-size rug in seafoam green matches the color of antique satin used to upholster the three sectional love seats in the living room below. The color theme in this modern living room, taken from nature, is named "Indian Summer." The walls are Indian pink, the draperies Indian pink and bronze striped taffeta, against the soft green of the rug. Huge urns topped by brass trays are used for coffee tables, and a colorful screen in a stylized period design contributes a touch of quaintness to the modern picture. Analysis of the color scheme shows that it is a version of the complementary type—red and blue-green, as represented by Indian pink, bronze and seafoam.

DEEP PILE WEAVE IN A RICH, COLORFUL ROOM

OVAL PATTERNS IN BEDROOM RUGS

Two contemporary versions of traditional styles are illustrated in the bedrooms here. In the one above, the decorative theme is French Provincial. Swag valance and draperies in French blue with rose fringe unite the two windows and make a frame for the dressing-table unit. The bed spread picks up drapery colors, while French imported wallpaper in toile design also repeats the blue and rose tones. Furniture is painted white with gold and blue trim, the boudoir chair is upholstered in cream-colored brocade. A hand-hooked rug ties the whole picture together, with its French floral patterns in pastel tones against a creamy background. In the bedroom at right Early American traditions are expressed in every detail of the furnishings and decoration. Note the white painted dado, the sheer draped and ruffled curtains, the coverings on the high four-poster bed. The most interesting features of the room are the glazed chintz used for both upholstery and wall covering and the characteristic oval braided rug with its striking design in shaded rows accented by strips of black. An oval rug like this may be used with more of the floor showing than is customary with conventional oblong rugs.

material—just let the steam penetrate the pile, then brush in the direction of the nap.

4. Flatten a curled corner by placing a thick newspaper under it and soaking the rug with cold water, then letting it dry with a heavy weight on the edge to hold the corner flat.

5. Don't run an ordinary lamp cord under a rug. The bulge will inevitably mean a line of wear. Instead, have a special cord attached. These are flat and will not cause wearing.

6. Keep the air moist. Too-dry air is as bad for rugs as it is for furniture and woodwork.

Mothproofing a New Wool Rug or Carpet: If your new floor covering is not already treated so that it will be mothproof it is an excellent idea to go over it with a good anti-moth spray which penetrates down into the pile and really protects the fabric. The exposed part of the rug will be fairly safe because of the regular cleaning and the action of light—but dark caves under couches and beds are always danger spots. Remember, if there is any *wool at all* in your rug, it must be treated as if it were all wool so far as moth-care is concerned.

Seasonal Anti-moth Measures: Spraying new rugs to guard against moths does not mean they are permanently safe from invasion. Because moths like dark, hidden places for breeding it is a very good idea to spray the rug cushion as well as the rug and to repeat this each spring before the hot weather arrives. Special doses during the summer will do no harm—specially in the dark areas. Of course, if your fabrics are permanently mothproofed by the manufacturers you need not bother with this.

If you are leaving carpets or rugs on the floor in a house closed for the summer you need to be very sure they are clean and free from eggs or larvae. If they have not been sprayed cover them completely with a blanket of good artificial or pure gum camphor powder—not balls or flakes. Spread the powder thickly, anywhere from ⅛ to ¼ inch, and see that every spot is covered.

CLEANING CARPETS AND RUGS

Routine Rug or Carpet Care: Use a soft brush or a carpet sweeper. Pile rugs should be swept or cleaned in the direction of the nap, specially Orientals. You can make sure of this by brushing the pile back and forth with your hand. It is the sharp edges of fine particles of grit buried at the base of the pile which grind against the pile when it is walked upon and tend to sever the wool fibers.

Periodic Rug or Carpet Care: For a large rug or carpet, thorough renovation should not be necessary oftener than every other year, unless it receives un-

usually heavy wear or is lighter-than-average in color. This complete cleansing should be left to professional skill—the only really safe treatment for a large wool or wool-blend pile rug. It more than pays for itself in longer life and increased wear.

For keeping rugs bright the carpet manufacturers recommend application every so often of special rug-cleaning powders which are brushed into the pile and allowed to stand for a while, then removed with the vacuum.

Cleaning Cotton Floor Coverings: These you may wash—with proper care. Be sure they are all cotton, or cotton and linen, or all linen. Be sure they are vat-dyed for fast color—here is where the importance of a label comes in. Wash them often enough so that the dirt never gets ground in, and use only a mild white soap with lukewarm water. Strong soap and hot water tend to leave a fuzz on the cotton surface. Never hang the rugs over a line to dry. Spread them out on a flat surface and they will not get out of shape. It is better to send the large sizes to a laundry. When wet they are very heavy and hard to handle at home.

Cleaning Special Rug Materials: Brushing is very helpful for flat weaves. Run a vacuum slowly to clean all the way through. A special powder cleaner is good. (1) Cotton and fiber must be treated the same as wool, with powder-refreshers and dry cleaning, but no soap. (2) Grass mats may be scrubbed with mild soap and water and thoroughly dried. If they need refinishing, paint them with a good quality of house paint thinned with one-fourth part of turpentine. The paint must be worked into the fiber, not merely brushed over the surface. (3) Fiber and sisal rugs may be wiped with a damp cloth but not washed or scrubbed. It is best to send them to be dry-cleaned when they are very soiled. They may be attractively refreshed by a coat of special canvas paint. (4) Color of linen rugs may be freshened by wiping with cloth dipped in household ammonia and wrung almost dry. Brush surface when dry. Don't use ammonia on wool.

STURDY, ADAPTABLE TWEED CARPETING

THREE CONTRASTS IN ROUGH TEXTURES FOR FLOOR COVERINGS

Many novelty floor coverings are both attractive and durable. For example, four shaggy string rugs were sewed together to make a foundation for the corner furniture grouping shown center. Plain upholstery and walls provide appropriate contrast for striking plaid draperies ranging from purple-blue to pink, and from dark green to chartreuse. Notice the two chairs which can be put together to form a small love seat. The room (top) is prepared for comfort and repose, with its rose-colored chaise longue, pillow with coral and green stripes, and glass-shelved table close at hand. Geranium-and-rose-striped draperies frame the tall sliding win-

dow. Raffia carpet, and the emerald green of the table, provide pleasingly cool notes for a warm day. Raffia rugs of this type, once considered only for such uses as entry-ways and porches, are now made in many designs and colors attractive in any summer room as well as for permanent usage in many others. The photograph at the left presents an interesting study in modern textures. The satin-smooth natural-finish blond wood of the table, with its useful tray-top and slim straight legs, is set between soft nubby upholstery on the couch and the harsh tweedlike weave of the sturdy, adaptable type of carpeting.

RUG AND CARPET CHART

TYPE	MACHINE-MADE DOMESTIC RUGS AND CARPETS	TYPE	MACHINE-MADE DOMESTIC RUGS AND CARPETS
NOTE: (DEFINITIONS)	BROADLOOM—any carpet woven on a wide loom, 54 inches or more. JACQUARD WEAVE—name used to designate type of loom used for several different weaves, producing wide variety of carpet and rug styles. WARP—cotton threads running the long way of the fabric. WEFT—cross threads in a web of fabric (woof). WORSTED—long straight fibers combed from wool and twisted into hard lustrous yarn.	**CHENILLE**	One of best grades of rug made by machine. Furry, soft weave (from French "chenille" meaning caterpillar), high soft pile with closely woven back giving deep lustrous surface. Very handsome and flexible. Comes in plain or mixed colors and great variety of surface treatments, in standard widths. Available in broadloom sizes up to 30 feet. Easy to identify because of soft appearance when rolled.
AXMINSTER	One of the best-known commercial weaves. Comes in all sizes from 27-inch strip carpeting to 18-foot broadloom. Great variety of color effects in each pattern, resembling hand-woven rugs. Tufts in this weave are mechanically inserted in the fabric and bound down into stiff jute backing, but are not knotted. Easy to identify as Axminsters can be rolled lengthwise but not crosswise. Gives excellent service especially in better grades.	**LUSTER OR SHEEN**	Originally called "American Orientals" the term is applied to any machine-made pile rug which has been chemically washed to soften the colors and give them sheen and luster. Made in Wilton, Axminster and chenille weaves.
WILTON	Solid close weave made of either worsted or woolen yarns on a Jacquard loom. Worsted Wiltons among the best type of commercial floor covering available, and much more durable than the wool Wilton which may seem more luxurious because of depth of pile (varying from ¾ to ⅝ inches deep, depending on quality). Worsted Wiltons are much finer and more lustrous and velvety in texture. Made in narrow widths, either plain, or patterned. Closely woven with low erect pile.	**THREAD AND THRUM**	Flat, pileless carpets woven up to 16 feet in width. Thick cotton warp, thin wool weft and general appearance of tapestry weaves. Available in special colors.
BRUSSELS	Woven of worsted yarns on Jacquard loom, like the Wilton which it resembles in structure except that pile loops of Brussels carpet are not cut. Comes in wide variety of colors and patterns.	**WOVEN LINEN**	Linen fabric woven flat without pile up to 12 feet in width. Comes in variety of textures and patterns. Is reversible, and may be had in standard sizes, plain or bordered or striped.
INGRAIN	A flat, pileless fabric woven on a Wilton loom. Not as popular today as in the past.	**FIBER AND FIBER COMBINATIONS**	Double-faced fabric containing mixture of wool and wood fiber or grass. Takes water without damage and for this reason was originally used for porches or summer rugs but has graduated into other parts of the house. Grass fiber styles (matting) made in Japan are available in 2-foot widths and are sewed together like carpeting. They come in natural straw or light green color and have no pattern except perhaps a colored binder thread. Coco fiber rugs are stronger and brighter in color with floral or geometrical designs. Fibers of many different kinds are combined with linen, cellophane, cotton, etc., as well as wool to create many styles and types.
VELVET AND TAPESTRY	Most of the plain broadloom carpets are woven on velvet or tapestry looms. In the good qualities velvet carpets resemble Wiltons but do not have wool buried in the back which gives the Wilton its resiliency and wearing qualities. In patterned weaves velvets have more color variety as they are printed on the yarn before it is woven. Tapestry carpets are really velvet carpets with uncut pile. They are not popular today because of their uninteresting texture.	**NOVELTY WEAVES**	These include new rough textured modern weaves so popular for use in modern interiors; rugs and carpets with pebbly surfaces that do not show footprints; shaggy string rugs in dark or pastel colors; firm masculine-looking tweed textures; inexpensive fur rugs; new adaptations and combinations constantly coming on the market.
NATIVE CRAFTS		**FINE HAND-WOVEN VARIETIES**	
HAND-HOOKED, RAG, AND BRAIDED RUGS	Typically American. Adaptable to Colonial, Provincial, Victorian, even modern decoration. Make nice scatter pieces especially for bedrooms. Many of them imitated in machine-made types.	**CARVED OR SCULPTURED RUGS**	Carved rugs are made by shearing the surface of high-pile handmade rugs. Design is usually carved on single colored surface. Great variety in designs, colors and textures, depth of pile, quality of wool, closeness of tufting. Comes in many modern designs which make them particularly suitable to modern rooms. Many tufted types are now made by machine in the style of these carved rugs or carpets.
NAVAJO ALGERIAN SWEDISH PEASANT	Native types of floor coverings used extensively in modern decoration. Navajos made in flat hand weave with large pattern, usually in color combinations of white, gray, black and red. Extremely serviceable. Algerian rugs are handmade with high pile. Designs usually geometrically worked out in beige, gray, white and black. Swedish handmade rugs are very colorful. Some in high pile weave, also in flat ones. Available in great variety of patterns.	**SAVONNERIES AND AUBUSSONS**	Handmade weaves from France. Formal in design and delicate in color. Savonnerie weave is high-pile, Aubusson flat tapestry. These handsome rugs are appropriate in formal rooms and many period type rooms.
NUMDAHS	Colored felt rugs with gay floral or bird designs in embroidery. Made in Northern India. Suitable for country homes or summer floor coverings.	**ORIENTALS**	Orientals are hand-woven, distinguished by the care with which they are made, by closeness of weave and fast colors. They are bought not only for their great beauty and wearing qualities, but for enduring value as well. Persian Orientals are among the finest types with soft harmonizing colors and graceful patterns with stylized designs using plants, birds and animals in their motifs. Indian rugs are more brilliant in color, more pictorial and naturalistic. Turkoman or Bokhara rugs are always red in color, usually in geometric designs. Caucasian rugs resemble them except that other colors than red are used in the designs. Chinese rugs, woven from silk, come in lovely patterns with pastel colors predominating.

This is not intended to be a complete spot-removal guide—only a ready reference for the stains most often occurring on rugs, carpets, or upholstery. Quick action saves much time and trouble later, because a fresh stain comes out easily. The longer it stays in the more firmly it becomes "set" and the more difficult it is to remove. Another advantage of immediate treatment is that you know what caused the spot and so can apply the right remedy.

REMOVING STAINS FROM RUGS AND CARPETS

TYPE OF STAIN	TREATMENT	TYPE OF STAIN	TREATMENT
ACID . . . Battery	Must have immediate treatment as it eats into the rug. Saturate spot with borax solution to neutralize (1 oz. to 1 pt. water), then absorb gently with sponge or blotter. NO RUBBING. Repeat until you are sure all acid is absorbed.	DIRT	Brush thoroughly with soft brush. Then sponge with mild warm soapsuds, and rinse carefully with clear warm water.
ACID . . . Lemon Vinegar Etc.	Acids like these affect colors, and must be sponged off at once with a solution of 1 part ammonia to 4 parts of water. Colors are sometimes restored by this.	EGG	Scrape off excess with blunt knife before treating. Sponge or swab with cold water. If traces remain after spot is dry, sponge with carbon tetrachloride.
ALCOHOL	Alcohol spots should be dried out at once with absorbent cotton or blotting paper. Continue alternately moistening with a wet sponge and drying, until part is clean. If there is discoloration, apply diamond dyes (dissolved in denatured alcohol) with a brush to the spot. Experiment first with color, of course.	GREASE	Remove grease spots caused by butter, lipstick, oils and fats, vaseline, butter and butter substitutes, gravy, sauces, etc., immediately with a knife, then sponge or swab with carbon tetrachloride, which is sold under various trade names. Apply with soft cloth, taking up soil as it dissolves with clean cloth or blotter. Another simple method is to sprinkle the spot with Fuller's earth. Lay a clean blotter over this and iron with a warm iron. Use fresh powder and clean blotter and repeat treatment until grease is dissolved. Remove powder with vacuum cleaner or brush. Rub toward center to avoid rings.
ANIMAL STAINS	These stains vary in composition, and usually cause discoloration which cannot be removed entirely. CLEAN AT ONCE. Sponge thoroughly with salt solution (½ cup salt to 1 quart lukewarm water). Then sponge with weak ammonia solution (1 part in 20 parts water).	GRASS	Sponge with denatured alcohol.
BLOOD	Blot up as much as you can with white blotting paper, or cheesecloth. Sponge spot with salt solution of ½ cupful salt to 1 quart cold water. Then rinse with lukewarm water and dry with clean cloth.	INK	Take up freshly spilled ink with blotting paper or soft cloths. Then sponge spot with lukewarm water. Old and stubborn stains call for professional cleaning.
CANDLE WAX	Scrape off excess wax with blunt knife. Place blotter on stain and press with warm iron. When traces remain, sponge with carbon tetrachloride, and treat as for any other grease spot.	IODINE	Apply first pure alcohol and then lukewarm soapsuds made with very mild soap. Rinse with clear water.
CANDY	Sponge with cloth wrung out in hot water, if not chocolate; use warm, not hot water, for chocolate. If traces remain, use carbon tetrachloride.	LIQUORS WINES SOFT DRINKS, ETC.	Dump salt on spot at once to prevent stain from spreading and to absorb liquid, brush off with soft broom, then sponge with cool water.
CHEWING GUM	Soften with carbon tetrachloride. Let stand a few minutes, then remove carefully with dull knife. Use more than one application carbon tetrachloride if necessary.	NAIL POLISH (Enamel)	Treat with carbon tetrachloride and a drop of banana oil. Sponge carefully.
CHOCOLATE	Sprinkle with powdered borax; then soak for fifteen minutes with cold water. Remove gently with cloth and cold water. When dry, remove borax with vacuum cleaner or whiskbroom.	PAINT	Fresh paint, if moist, can be removed by cleaning gently with a cloth wet in turpentine. Old or difficult stains should be removed by professional cleaner.
COFFEE	Apply clear lukewarm water and dry with cloth or blotter.	ROAD OIL TAR ASPHALT	Sponge with a cloth well moistened with carbon tetrachloride. Change the cloth as it becomes soiled and continue until no more color comes off.
CREAM (OR MILK) ICE CREAM CREAM SAUCES CREAM SOUPS	Sponge or swab with warm water. When traces remain, use carbon tetrachloride. When ice cream contains chocolate, treat according to directions for chocolate.	SHOE POLISH	Apply carbon tetrachloride and blot with clean blotter. Repeat treatment, using clean spot on blotter each time.
COCKTAILS	Use clean cold water, then "squeeze" spot dry with clean cheesecloth. If cocktail contains fruit juices, you may have to resort to professional assistance. Try coarse powder-like corn meal, or chemical powder especially prepared for rugs. Remove the powder after it has soaked up the stain and dried with vacuum cleaner, or brush it off.	WATER RINGS	Sponge whole area lightly with cold water, and spot itself with carbon tetrachloride or chloroform.

There are several outstanding and unusual features in the plan worked out here for matching rooms, each one designed to be used as a combination sitting room, study and bedroom by one of two daughters in a family. Distinctly modern are the upholstered sofa-type day beds, the big arm chairs, the wall treatment with simulated bricks and climbing vines, the wall-to-wall shag carpet which goes through the doorway without a break. Yet, in this present-day at-mosphere, the graceful Empire lines of the side chairs and the glass-and-plastic coffee table are perfectly at home, also the sturdy Georgian-type knee-hole desk. The furniture plan is repeated in the two rooms, creating an effect of one room, but giving each girl her own bed and study corner; different arrangement in each room prevents any effect of monotony. There is a pleasant contrast between the textured upholstery fabric used on the modern couches, and

CHAPTER TWELVE

Doors and Doorways

YOUR DOORS need not be accepted as they are just because they happen to be a part of the walls. A door can be taken out completely and replaced with a different type at comparatively small expense. New openings can be cut or old ones closed up and filled in. This has been made practical by the development of many stock models in doors and a variety of built-in devices all ready to install. If it is not practical to make structural changes, there are still many ways in which your door situation can be improved.

Types of Doors: Each of the traditional furniture periods has its own distinctive door treatment and the definitely European period styles are now the only types which must be made to order.

Doors include not only the conventional type of hinged single door but also many other varieties, such as sliding doors, folding doors, Dutch half-doors; French window-doors and French inside-doors; double-swung doors, glass-paneled doors, ventilated doors. They all serve special purposes and in the right place are very useful aids to decoration.

Finishing Door Trims: If your doors are reasonably satisfactory, you have only to be sure they are correctly treated. For the wood facing (trim) around the opening there is a simple rule which should very seldom be broken. If the door and wall are alike in color, make the trim that color too. If for some reason they are not the same color or the same shade, match the trim with one or the other of them. The reason for this is that a narrow line of color separating a door from its background looks thin and ineffective against a large expanse of wall. If you want the door featured, its mass is great enough to make it an effective spot of color with or without the

SPACIOUSNESS, LIGHT, AND AIR

the lustrous material with which the chair seats are covered. Accessories and occasional pieces in the two rooms vary, representing individual tastes of the occupants. Note the ingenious window cut into the wall and fitted with shelves— a decorative as well as useful feature. Above the day bed a glimpse can be caught of a long book shelf also set conveniently into the wall. The green of leaves against walls of off-white is a pleasant color note.

KINDRED DESIGNS IN DOORS

The sketch (left) shows a traditional door with well-proportioned panels in a simple attractive design. The same design is modernized in the door of the modern living room decorated in Mexican style. Notice the height of the door and the evenly spaced small panels which decorate it without loss of the one-panel effect. There are several interesting points in this room. One is the glass wall with the door set into it and sweeping draperies which can be released to cover the glass. Another is the bracket console on the wall, highly decorative but taking up no floor space. The tile floor is cool and appropriate in this hot-weather house. The sleek upholstery of the arm chair and the soft wax finish of the tile provide texture contrast with the shaggy rug.

162

band of trim; but if you don't include the trim in the color-picture of the door, *do* include it in the wall background color. Exception to this is when a door is decorated by lines of color around panels, etc., and the trim is made part of that design.

Finishing Doors: Ordinarily it is better to match both door and trim to the color of the wall background. This makes the room seem larger and gives you more leeway in your choice of pictures and drapery. However, there are occasional exceptions to this decorating convention, as when the walls are painted or papered but the woodwork is some fine unpainted wood. In this case the wall color should be keyed to the wood tones, with both the trim and doors in this wood. Another exception is when a door is emphasized as a special device to help break up a large expanse of wall, or to balance some prominent feature such as an important window, a fireplace or a tall piece of furniture. Then the door alone, or the door with its trim, would be set off by treatment in contrast to the walls.

SINGLE DOOR PROBLEMS

If your home is average in size, or smaller than average, the chances are that you have too many doors rather than too few. Or you may have one which fills the wall or swings open just where you need space for furniture. It often happens that one door is never closed because no privacy is needed at that point, while some other door is never opened because the traffic goes through a different opening. In both these cases the doors are equally useless and should be operated upon at once. On the other hand, they may be very useful where they are, but add nothing to the beauty of your wall composition.

Restyling: You may want to change the face of your door because you do not like its style, because it is out of harmony with your room, or for some more practical reason. Whatever the root of the problem, there are many simple ways to remedy it. A few of them are suggested here.

1. Making only one door in the room a contrast while the others are left to match the wall may be a useful device when several doors in a foyer or hall lead to various obscure places such as closets and passageways. If these doors are painted like the wall, while the front door and the door to the living room are finished in a more conspicuous color, it may help relieve the confusion which makes guests so frequently open the wrong door. Try this idea in a living room, also with several dead-end openings into closets or side hallways.

2. In halls with little wall space, as in kitchens lined with white cabinets, painting doors in a con-

TURNING A DOOR INTO A WALL DECORATION

When a door is needed to balance some architectural feature such as a window or to break up a large wall space and make a room look smaller it can be treated as a decorative panel in a frame. The sketch above illustrates a way in which a plain door can be made more interesting by stenciling, painting or applying cutouts to the panels. If you are doing this you should be sure that the panels are well proportioned before you emphasize them with decorations. When decorative treatment is used on a door, as shown in the above photograph, the design should usually be repeated at other points in the room either on walls or furniture.

RESTYLING DOORS

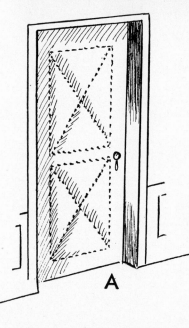

The modern foyer shown here has several distinctive features. Notice the narrow, bracket-type shelf-table attached to the wall with no legs to interfere with floor cleaning. A mirror doubles the space of the small hall and provides a striking background for flowers. The rubber floor in granitized pattern harmonizes with the marbleized finish of the door. Paneled in the modern style with composition material it illustrates how restyling could be used to give a door new smartness. Flat composition panels like these can be applied over any type of finish and are not expensive to use. Sketch A shows an ordinary door converted into modern style by the simple device of fastening leather panels (or imitation leather) over the original small panels and decorating them with a design in ornamental nailheads. (If necessary use wallboard backing.) Sketch B makes a ventilating device out of a paneled door by having a design cut out to allow the passage of air and a certain amount of light. A door like this would be useful between a hall and living room.

A

B

trast color often provides a welcome note of decorative interest. In this case, the wood in movable window parts is often painted the contrast color also. This color idea may be used anywhere you feel the need of a bright note just at the spot where a door happens to be. You cannot put furniture there, so you can only get your color by applying it to the door.

3. When doors are attractive and well arranged they may provide an inexpensive way to bring color and design into an informal room with too-plain walls. You can use the edges of panels as frames for stencils, cutouts, or colorful prints.

4. Using one plain panel for the face of a door provides an excellent answer to several door problems. You can use it to change the style, to provide a decorative highlight, or break up a large wall space. In all these cases the process is the same. The difference is only in the surface finish of the panel.

A thin sheet of plywood or composition board, attached to the face of the door by nails or cement, makes a flat sheath panel over the entire door, flush with the edges. In a bedroom this may be covered with some of the quilted fabric used on a headboard for the bed. In a living room it may be faced with a variety of highly decorative finishes.

If there are so many doors that they give a cluttered feeling to your wall, use this same one-panel device in reverse. Finished in exactly the tone of the wall, the plain surface will make the doors surprisingly inconspicuous. This treatment is even more effective when the wall is papered. Paint the trim to match the background of the paper used on the wall and use the same paper on the doors to retire them almost completely into the background. Give this treatment to all subsidiary doors and leave one or two main doors in their original form, unless they are not attractive or decorating balance calls for a different division. Or conceal an unwanted door by placing a screen in front of it, only making sure the screen is large enough to cover it entirely, frame and all.

Mirror treatment for doors is in a class by itself because there are so many ways in which it can be made to contribute. The modern style of applying the sheet over the whole door takes away any bedroom feeling from a mirrored door and makes it a charming answer to a door problem anywhere in the house. It serves the same purpose as a mirrored wall, providing a sense of space, light reflection, and general airiness.

Superfluous Doors: These are a real opportunity. In many rooms there is a door practically never used. Take it out of its frame, remove the hinges, and fill

DUTCH DOORS
ARE BOTH USEFUL
AND
ATTRACTIVE

Doors can often be made more useful with very little trouble. In the picture a double Dutch door provides light and ventilation for a little Colonial dining room, with a valance above the door which makes it look more like a window than a door. This Dutch-door treatment may be used to solve a problem of too little light or air. It is a very simple matter to substitute a Dutch door for the conventional type or to have an ordinary door made over into a Dutch door, as shown in the sketch. You will find a Dutch door particularly useful for a child's room or nursery.

REMODELING IS AN EASY WAY TO MAKE DOORWAYS INTERESTING AND USEFUL

When a wide archway is not needed you can always convert it to usefulness by means of built-in units which add charm to both connecting rooms and at the same time provide needed storage space or shelves. In the Colonial-style dining room above such a unit has been installed to fill up a square opening between two rooms. For ventilation the door has been fitted with louvres, while the lower panels have been retained in harmony with the traditional paneling of the door at the left which also supplies the design for the woodwork of the built-in partition. Notice here that the recessed shelves are the depth of the built-in section, while no doors are provided for the storage around them. This storage space opens into the room on the other side which has shelves at the sides and cupboard space with doors below. Sketch A suggests another way an opening can be filled in or French doors can be removed and the space filled in as illustrated. Here the living-room side is shown with the space at each side of a new single door used for book shelves, ornaments, etc. On the other side the space could be paneled with decorative fabric, wallpaper or other material. B, C and D illustrate three methods for concealing an archway between rooms, at the same time dramatizing the wall by draping it continuously from doorway to walls and framing the wall with a valance or cornice.

FILLING IN AN
UNUSED DOORWAY

Above, book-filled shelves are built in around a closed-up door opening to provide interest and color as well as convenient storage space below the shelves. In a dining room the same arrangement could be used for dishes or silver. In this room the dark wall makes a dramatic background for colorful bindings, coral upholstery and creamy white draperies made long and full to be drawn across the windows. Softly neutral carpeting, lighter than the walls, a light ceiling and wide window spaces keep the room from seeming too dark. Traditional furniture is in harmony with the dignity of the window treatment, the background woodwork and the tall early 19th Century urn-stands which flank the windows.

A TALL SCREEN
HELPS MAKE
TWO ROOMS OUT OF ONE

In the room above, a screen covered with wallpaper, like that used in the dining end of the room, provides a feeling of privacy without loss of light or air from the window-wall of the living room end. The low combination lamp table and cupboard also increase this feeling of separateness, without obstructing the view. Sturdy comfort is suggested by the simple yet graceful lines of tables and chairs, a bit traditional in feeling but modern in the use of natural wood tones and softly rubbed finish. The color scheme is interesting in its use of nature's greens topped by a soft sky-blue ceiling, with white for contrast and flower-red for accent. The muted blue-gray of the carpet links the indoor color harmony with the clouds and water outside the picture windows which make up one wall of the living room.

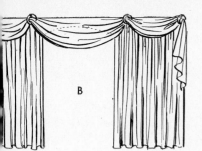
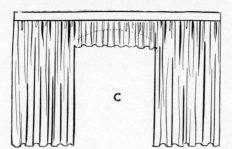
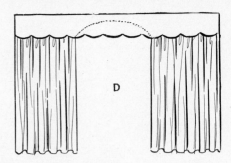

THREE SUGGESTIONS FOR CAMOUFLAGING AN ARCHWAY BETWEEN ROOMS
THROUGH WALL-TO-DOOR DRAPERIES HEADED BY CORNICE OR VALANCE
TO DRAMATIZE A COMMONPLACE WALL

in the opening with shelves, as in the sketch on page 166. The trim may be removed, or retained as a frame. Save the discarded door. You may find an unused end of a hallway where you can have a badly needed closet installed by using the door or you may cut it down to make doors for lower parts of two corner cupboards built into a room where needed space is wasted by empty corners. Covered with a sheet of wallboard and set across two painted wooden saw horses the door would make a wonderful table for a picnic porch, a game room, or a sewing room.

Restyling Double Doors and Doorways: If you live in a hot climate you may find good use for these large openings, but anywhere else their disadvantages outweigh any possible advantages. Often two small rooms connected by the opening would be much more livable and attractive if they could be made into one larger room, specially where a living room and small dining room are involved. If that is impractical, keep the doorway but take out any old-fashioned doors or grill-work and give the opening one of the interesting new treatments illustrated. Look into the possibilities of pleated partitions which open and shut like an accordion and take up no space at all when they are pushed back. They come in many attractive fabric finishes to harmonize with any decorative style as illustrated. (See Chapter 17.)

Restyling an Archway: If the opening is an unattractive, outmoded type of arch more drastic treatment will be needed. Have the arch filled in with wallboard, if possible, to make a square top, then treat the opening in one of the ways illustrated. If this cannot be done there is a device you can use to cover up an arch and add a strikingly beautiful note to the decoration of your rooms. It sounds expensive, but it need not be carried out in expensive materials.

For informal rooms soft cotton dress fabrics would be charming. This treatment uses a wallboard panel in each room cut to fit across the top of the wall from the ceiling down to the bottom of the arch. The lower edges of these panels are straight or cut in a graceful design and covered with fabric

MODERN DOOR PANELS IN A TRADITIONAL ROOM

The door in the picture above is made dramatic by the use of dark mirrored glass for paneling. The same glass is repeated on the cornice over the draperies and the black tone is picked up by lampshades. Ordinary mirrors could be used in the same manner to cover up uninteresting door panels and provide a reflection needed for some decorative purpose. The plum-colored carpet and turquoise upholstery in this room are accented by off-white draperies and couch upholstery. Notice the alcove arrangement of game table and chairs, making a center-of-interest group in front of the interestingly draped window. Textured fabric on the couch harmonizes with raised-figure effect of draped material.

167

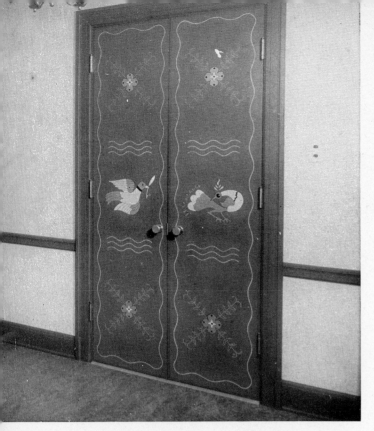

EASY DECORATIONS FOR DOORS

An entrance hallway needs color for warmth of welcome. It needs finishes easy to take care of and durable in their nature. The Pennsylvania Dutch hallway above fulfills all these requirements. The walls are covered with maize linoleum, while the floor is in blue linoleum with a marbleized pattern which does not show footprints. The woodwork is painted a soft dark blue. The doors here provide the special feature for the hall. Covered with inlaid linoleum, they are carved and nail-studded with Pennsylvania Dutch motifs including the two central figures typical of this style. Any ordinary door can be treated with panels in a design to match a special period or region, and linoleum is easily applied.

In the sketch group above a suggestion is offered for making plain French-door panels more interesting by application of framed flower prints within alternate panels. If you desire the view between rooms completely blocked you can use prints in all the panels on one or both sides of the glass. If only on one side you need sheer glass curtains on the other.

like a window valance. From beneath the valance the walls are curtained with the fabric, from the edges of the doorway to the corners of the room. They should be full enough to draw across the opening if desired.

In a more formal room a deep swag drapery hung across the top of the wall in three deep loops with the one in the middle dipping low enough to conceal the archway might be used in place of the valance. Or you can hang your drapery from a narrow cornice strip at the ceiling from wall to wall, with floor-length curtains at the sides of the wall and a flounce above the opening just deep enough to conceal the arch.

DOUBLE-DOOR PROBLEMS

Filling in Double-Door Openings: If connecting rooms are large, and an opening is not needed for purposes of traffic, light or ventilation, you can gain wall space by removing the trim and filling in the spaces with wallboard. If the joining shows you can cover the line with a decorative wallpaper border to make a panel; or hang a fabric panel over the inset; or fill the space with book shelves on the living-room side and shelves for some other purpose on the dining-room side. Another happy solution is to use a mirror panel on one side or on both. If you need a passageway between two rooms, narrow it to a single door and fill in the space at the side with shelves, cupboards, or mirrors. If no remodeling is possible, use drapery on the entire end wall, or place large decorative screens over the opening.

French Doors: When French doors open out as windows they are charming and useful, but as interior doors they are usually out of place. They do not give the privacy doors are designed for, and too often they are placed most inconveniently from the standpoint of furniture arrangement. However, they are often in a doorway leading from a living room to a hall where some kind of door is needed, so they must be retained or substitute doors installed.

1. If possible take them out and replace them with one of the new types of single door closings already mentioned.

2. If you must keep the glass doors, fit bright bird or flower prints over the glass panels on both sides; or on one side, using the conventional glass curtains on the other.

3. You can fit mirror panels into the panels over the glass, on both sides; or on one, covering the backs of the mirrors with curtains or prints applied to the glass.

4. You can face the doors with plain sheathing as described above for single doors.

INGENIOUS USE OF LIVING SPACE

The photograph above shows how a wide doorway, built between two sets of useful and decorative shelves, may be used to convert an overlong room into an attractive combination living and bedroom. The slight raising of the bedroom floor level adds interest, and emphasizes the division without lessening the feeling of spaciousness created by the wide opening. Note the effective way in which the end wall has been treated as a picture, with wall designs framing the dressing table window. The bedroom side of the shelves can be filled entirely or partly with shallow drawers or cupboards.

An extra partition is often very useful, with or without a doorway. The reading and conversation corner above illustrates a modern and very useful method of creating a room-within-a-room, without having to build either a partition or a doorway. Prefabricated storage units like those shown are available in so many different dimensions, designed for so many different uses, that they can be fitted into any room. They are finished on the back to fit smoothly together, thus providing a real "wall" between two parts of a room. They may also be used back to back, so that storage facilities are available on both sides. This is particularly useful where an alcove effect is desired in a living room, for use as a library, dining room, den, or home office. The units above eliminate need for a doorway, combining with furniture to set off the space. When a real doorway is needed, it can be incorporated in the wall units, as in the two small photographs at each side. Units may be built up to reach to the ceiling, forming a complete wall, or they may be kept lower to serve as a partial partition, high enough to serve the desired purpose, without cutting off air and light from the enclosed section.

WINDOW WALLS
WHICH
PROVIDE
THEIR OWN
DECORATION

CHAPTER THIRTEEN

What to Do about Windows

THE WORD WINDOW is said to be derived from "wind-eye." Certainly that describes two window functions we must never lose sight of. Windows were designed to let in air and light while allowing those inside to look out. In most dwellings they are still keyed to climate, region and architectural periods.

Types of Windows: 1. The double-hung, two-sashed type common in Colonial houses has one large pane in each half of the window or a number of smaller panes. This is the tightest movable window and the easiest to weather-strip.

2. The casement window in the small-paned English style is usually shorter than the double-hung but admits more air because its full length swings open, either in or out, from the sides of the window frame.

3. The French window is hung like a double casement from the side frames of the window but extends to the floor and serves as both window and door.

4. The bay window is made by a group of windows set at an angle to each other or in a curve to form a recess or small alcove in the wall of a room.

5. The dormer window is one set into a gable which rises from a sloping roof. The window itself may be double-hung or casement.

6. The picture window is a modern contribution to the greater usefulness of windows. The window-wall would not actually be classed as a window but takes over some of its functions.

Remodeling Windows: If your windows are out of harmony with your style of decoration, inadequate, badly placed, or hopelessly out of scale, look into the new developments which make it possible to replace them with windows of a different style,

The lovely woodland scene revealed outside the windows of the room above emphasizes the desirability of a type of window so wide that it combines a plain glass wall section with casement windows at each side. The simple unlined draperies pictured here are full enough to be drawn across the side parts of the windows with the central section uncovered. The dramatic picture of a curved window (left), with the flower box set in to carry the straight line of the wall inside, is a striking example of how effectively the old and the new can mingle in decoration. The room is traditional in furnishing, but window treatment, plain walls, mirrored chimney breast and light shaggy rug are all refreshingly modern. Growing plants provide relief from any effect of bareness in the large uncurtained window space. If you have a drab uninteresting room with not enough windows it will be worth your while to install a new wide window, or to increase the size of the room by adding a bay window. You will find many styles, both traditional and modern, which come ready for use. The cost in many cases is surprisingly modest for an alteration which will mean so much in terms of both beauty and comfort.

TWO TYPES OF MODERN WINDOW STYLING

A dark room close to a street can have privacy, with plenty of light and air, by installing a glass-block wall section. Transparent side windows providing ventilation and a glimpse of the street can be lightly curtained if you prefer. A glass-topped table adds to brightness of room above by reflecting soft filtered light from the glass blocks of the wall. In the well-arranged modern room below, wide aluminum-framed panes seem to bring the trees into the room itself. The drapery is carried back on the wall so that it will come just to the edge of the window and frame the view without interference from glass curtains. Tall built-in book shelves at each end of the room balance the window, and the two small couches with reading lamps form a center-of-interest furniture grouping where the view can be enjoyed. Large plain areas in floor, wall, and trimly tailored slip-cover fabric give additional importance to the figured drapery framing the window, and to the textured effect of books on shelves.

or to unite several windows into one. This remodeling is not so expensive an operation as one might think. Practically all types of windows are available in stock units, and are ready to install. Double-hung windows may be removed in favor of one of the casement types. French doors may be substituted for windows opening on a porch or terrace. Even bay windows, picture windows and window-walls can be bought all ready for incorporating in your present wall. Some styles are more expensive than others, but in each type inexpensive models are included in the price range.

WINDOW TREATMENTS

In their early days curtains and draperies were intended to increase the usefulness of windows, not lessen it. Thin curtains next to the panes, called glass curtains, were introduced because the primitive cloudy glass had been improved so that it was transparent and something was needed to soften glare and help to prevent people on the outside from seeing in. At night long heavy draperies were pulled across windows for warmth and greater privacy. An additional set of curtains was often used and called under-curtains or draw-curtains. These were lighter in weight but heavy enough for protective purposes. Installed between glass curtains and over-draperies they controlled light and air when over-draperies were not drawn or when they were confined to decorative side curtains.

Today, curtains are used in exactly the same way except that rolled window shades or Venetian blinds are usually called upon instead of draw-curtains to control light. A simple rule sums up the essence of contemporary window decoration: The walls around the windows are "draped" rather than the windows themselves, and these draperies play a leading part both in room composition and in helping to correct structural defects. This innovation in window dressing, simple as it is, has changed certain basic decorating practices. Style no longer requires that window treatments be limited by the size and proportions of window openings. You can have all the light you need and all the decorative drapery you desire—neither one interferes with the other.

TYPES OF WINDOW CURTAINS AND DRAPERIES

There are three main types of window decoration—glass curtains, light-controlling draw-curtains, and over-draperies. In more elaborate types of decorating work all three may be used on one window. More often two sets are used and in many cases only one.

LIGHT-CON-
TROLLING
CURTAINS IN
DUTCH STYLE

DUTCH
CURTAINS
ARE COMBINED
WITH
OVERDRAPERIES

In the small homelike living room (top) functions of glass and draw-curtains are combined in semi-opaque curtains divided in the center, Dutch style, so that the top can be closed and the bottom left open, or the reverse. All four curtains can be pulled back to give a clear view of the trees outside the window. They are in correct length—the lower one just to the sill, the upper one overlapping so that from the outside the effect is that of one long curtain on each side. To relieve the plainness of these curtains the window is framed in a border cut from the same knotty pine (or simulated pine wallboard) used for sealing the walls. The rustic theme of the room is carried out in simple pine furniture with rubbed finish, accented by conversion of once-primitive household articles into new usefulness. Note the lanterns made into lamps, the cradle turned into a handy combination storage and coffee table, the quaint flower container in the corner, and the amusing table by the arm chair. A plaid fiber rug relieves plainness, and the small furniture in scale with the room keeps it from seeming as small as it is. The arm chair is as comfortable as a much larger piece would be, and the love seat fits nicely under the window where any sofa would have crowded the room. In the other room an attractive curtain arrangement combines full floor-length draperies in heavy coral fish-net with Dutch-type draw-curtains of cotton taffeta plaid in coral, turquoise, and deep beige. The beige screen is topped by a scalloped valance of plaid matching the window valance which joins the two windows and the space between in one long unbroken drapery treatment. Wall and ceiling are light beige, fiber rug deep turquoise. Dark wood in dining room furniture harmonizes with dark floor, stained and waxed. Green accents in ivy, laurel leaves and chair-seat stripes complete the picture which successfully combines graceful curves of traditional furniture reproductions with modern feeling in background treatment.

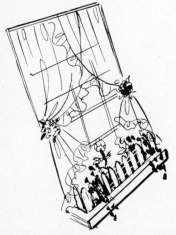

CRISP
SUMMER
FRILLS

VALANCE INTEREST FOR A DOUBLE WINDOW

Several types of glass curtains are illustrated in the rooms on this page. With rayon over-draperies, appropriate glass curtain materials would be marquisettes, nets, and gauzes in silk or rayon. Other materials often used for tailored glass curtains are theatrical gauze, mesh filet, celanese, ninon, and various new sheer synthetic novelty fabrics such as spun glass. In the room at the left effective use is made of sheer glass curtains hanging straight and properly full exactly to the window sill. Two small windows are given importance by being curtained as one and the graceful curves of rayon taffeta over-drapery are in pleasing contrast with straight lines of glass curtains and valance board above. The curtains are simply hemmed, and the width of the hem is right for their length. Plain fabric was chosen in this room for window treatment because of patterned material on wall and floor. The "Rule of Three" is applied by keeping ceiling, wood-work, drapery and chair plain, combined with floral wall pattern, and the geometrical design on both the floor and couch. Color of plain surfaces is taken from the back-ground wallpaper color with dark wood and dark sofa fabric to provide accent. With exactly the same size and style of windows and the same kind of rayon fabric used for drapery as in the room at the left the window treat-ment in the room above it illustrates the much softer and less formal effect when ruffled tie-backs are used next the glass instead of plain tailored curtains. Ruffled curtains may be long, as in this picture, or sill length, and may be hung with or without over-drapery. They are usually in some crisp white material such as organdy, point d'esprit, lawn, dimity or cushion-dot scrim. Ruffles of self fabric may be from 3 to 6 inches wide, sometimes even wider. The ruffled curtain is most at home in bedrooms, children's rooms, kitchens, and any type of informal room, but is not confined to these. In fine net or organdy, deeply flounced, it may be used in quite elaborate interiors, usually with Co-

TWO WINDOWS CURTAINED AS ONE

174

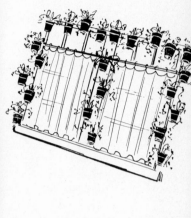

GROWING PLANTS
FOR
COOLNESS

CONTRASTING RUFFLES ARE DRAMATIC

lonial or Victorian feeling. Embroidered organdy and batiste
are appropriate for dressy effects. Curtains of very fine permanent finish ruffled organdy are so striking that they are
really at their best with only an organdy valance and no
over-drapery at all. In this case they may be ruffled straight
around instead of just on front and bottom edges as is customary. The double ruffle shown here gives additional airiness to the crisp white of the curtains and helps soften rather
severe lines in wallpaper and over-drapery. Graceful curves
in curtain draping, in round lamp base and shade, curved
lines and upholstering on chairs all contribute softening
notes. When light needs softening, ruffled glass curtains of
the tie-back variety may be hung straight to the floor as they
are in the picture above (left). This treatment is a third
example of dressing a conventional two-window arrangement as one unit, and shows once more how effectively the
styling of draperies can alter the atmosphere of a room. This
combining of ruffled glass curtains, hung straight, with
draped frilled hangings of patterned chintz, turns the two
ordinary windows into a charming picture. Figured drapery
is effective against a background of simple polka dot paper.
Large, splashy pattern combines with plain ceiling, monotone
fiber rug, and small unobtrusive geometric design of upholstery and wallpaper. A valance ruffle like this one at the
top is often used as a finish when ruffled glass curtains are
hung at a window without over-drapery. Note correct position of tie-backs, one-third of the curtain length from the
top. The crossed draping in the room at lower right illustrates another popular style of hanging ruffled glass curtains.
Draped high over aluminum-frame windows, then cascading
to the floor beneath long straight side draperies, they join
the stripes of the wallpaper in giving added height to the
room. Ruffles and scallops on draperies, bed dressing and
slip cover offset plainness in floor and ceiling.

HIGH DRAPING FOR LIGHT AND AIR

It all depends upon the style of room decoration, the window itself and its relation to the room. Except for certain period treatments the secret of smart, good-looking windows is simplicity in draping, combined with correct length and sufficient fullness. To be effective all curtains must be carefully made and well hung, with the right rods, fixtures and accessories. Never forget that matter of fullness. If you must choose between skimpiness in expensive fabric and graceful fullness in something at half the price, by all means take the latter. Make up for any fine-fabric deficiencies by attractive colors and trim tailoring in every detail of making and finishing.

GLASS CURTAINS

As the name glass curtain implies, these sheer or semi-sheer curtains are hung next to the panes. They are made in a great variety of styles. They should be full—two times the width of the window, or even two and a half if they are very sheer. They are usually in a light color tint. These curtains may be hung on a traverse rod as draw-curtains with pulleys, or shirred tightly top and bottom casement fashion; or they may hang free from frills or pleats or a plain casing at the top. (See Chapter 14.) They may reach just to the sill, or—if the rod is outside the frame—to the bottom of the window apron or to the floor. Never end them part way between the apron and the floor. It is always correct to make them the same length as over-draperies they are used with, except that they should never be long enough to lie on the floor even when the draperies do. In sill length, on a rod placed inside the window frame or on the sash itself, they are often called "sash curtains."

In style, glass curtains may be straight or tied back, ruffled or plain, elaborate or simply tailored, softly lustrous or crisply starched. They may be hung in many combinations, with or without draw-curtains or Venetian blinds. In small rooms or those with simplicity as a keynote, glass curtains are often used alone in some appropriate style or material. The effect of windows covered only with transparent curtains is to make a room look more large and airy. When glass curtains are hung with no other drapery various types of headings will add smartness to their appearance. Such a heading might be a flounce, French or cartridge pleating, shirrings with or without a heading, or rows of fine cording.

The type of sheer fabric you select for your glass curtains should be keyed to the style of the draperies and the other furnishings of the room. When dressy materials are used for upholstery and floor coverings they call for finer, more elaborate fabrics in glass curtains.

DRAW-CURTAINS FOR LIGHT CONTROL

When three sets of draperies are used the middle set is installed on a traverse rod between glass curtains and over-draperies. Taking the place of shades or blinds, they must be long enough to cover the glass curtains, heavy enough to shut out light in the daytime and provide complete privacy when closed at night. Glazed chintz, raw silk or pongee, casement cloth, taffeta, monk's cloth—any soft opaque fabric—may be utilized for these curtains. They may be in a color which matches or blends with the over-draperies, or they may carry the tone of the wall background. If your room needs an additional note of liveliness they may even be worked out in some gay accent color used in the drapery or some other part of the room. Remember these are utility curtains. They should be plain and well tailored, finished with a plain hem or an appropriate fringe.

DRAPERIES

Even the simplest draperies represent a real investment in any room where several windows or large bare wall spaces demand decorative treatment. Give serious thought to this problem before you buy the yards of material which will be required. Be sure the type of fabric and the style you choose suit both your room and your window needs. Over-draperies are usually a pair of curtains at either side of one window or group of windows, plain or draped, with or without a valance across the top. They are hung on various types of rods or poles, and may be used alone or in combination with glass curtains or draw-curtains, or both.

Drapery Design: This varies in accordance with the shape of the window and the needs of the room. Each wall is a decorative unit in itself as well as part of the room composition. A check list of the elements of composition as they apply to draperies may help you make the best selection.

1. Line is expressed in the outline and folds of the curtains, and must be related to the lines of the room. In the average room some type of valance gives unity and completion to the window picture, but if the ceiling is too low it is best omitted. Long lines in draperies which hang to the floor are more graceful than when they are shorter. If radiators or other obstacles interfere you will have to use short curtains at least on one window or use one of the many methods suggested in this chapter to avoid the obstacle. Adequate fullness is essential to grace of line. Decide whether you should keep drapery lines straight or drape curtains back by studying the balance between straight lines and curves in the room. If

LONG, FULL
DRAW-CURTAINS
ARE EXCELLENT FOR
WIDE WINDOWS
OR GROUPS
OF WINDOWS

In the photograph above both straight full over-draperies in a heavy dark fabric, and long sheer glass curtains are made as separate draw-curtains to be pulled across in front of the window if desired. Curved and extension rods are extended some distance over the wall on each side to insure light and air. The window is a modern-type steel casement which can be quickly and easily installed anywhere to replace a small old-style window or to fit a new opening. This one is set out from the wall slightly, with glass ends forming a shallow bay to help make a picture of the window. With no view outside worth "framing," narrow glass shelves are set in and small pots of growing flowers are spaced along each shelf and the window sill. On the floor below tall plants in decorative flowerpots complete the picture. Game table and reading chair make this a charming center-of-interest window treatment, and framed flower panels at the left carry the window theme into the room. A hobby collection of colored glass or other decorative objects could be used instead of plants on the shelves. Both sets of draperies are finished at the top with French pleats to control fullness and glass curtains are placed just inside the drapery instead of next to the glass in the recess. When the sheer curtains are drawn the window plants show through them; at night the over-draperies closely pulled together provide a warm cozy background for an evening's game. No lamp is needed because of indirect lighting installed above the molding to reflect down into the room. The charming effect of full over-draperies pulled across windows is shown in the living room at right. When two or three windows at the end of a room would seem crowded by individual curtaining, you can always make the end wall dramatic by continuous over-draperies.

A CORNICE, A SHAPED VALANCE, AND TWO DRAPED SWAGS

The window at left above illustrates several interesting points. Full, straight, lined over-draperies are made more formal by being installed under a wood cornice which conceals the rods and covers the tops of the drapery. The lace glass curtains are sill length so that they will not interfere with the table which is part of the picture, while the drapery just clears the carpet. The drapery fabric, with a crinkle effect previously produced only by French hand-looming, looks like a priceless museum textile. Actually it is a machine-loomed fabric made from nylon yarn with its well-known practical qualities of endurance and cleanability. Glass-curtain fabrics woven of nylon retain permanent shape, meaning perennially fresh curtains with no stretching and no ironing after washing. Note the cornice box here. You can get almost any style of ready-made cornice in wood, metal, plastic, composition board or other materials and have it cut to fit your space; there are also metal and plastic types with extension features. Wood cornices with traverse tracks built into them eliminate need for rods or poles and make the whole drapery-hanging installation very simple and quick. Cornices are usually in plain color to match walls or woodwork, but they may also be in contrast color or decorated with borders or other designs. (See Chapter 14.) In the window treatment at center above traditional style in furniture blends charmingly with traditionally patterned fabric and a graceful formal valance. Compare this deep fabric-covered valance, boxed over a valance board, with the narrow wood cornice in the picture at left. They illustrate the difference between cornices, which are comparatively limited in design and usually not more than

six or seven inches deep, and valances which may be any depth (in scale with the window) and are practically unlimited in design. All types of valances—like cornices—hide rods, ropes, curtain poles or pulleys. In addition to that they are part of the drapery design. They must be in harmony with the type, style, period, and decoration of the room. They are often made of the same material as the draperies, but when the ceiling is high enough contrasting fabrics like those in the middle illustration are very effective. The graceful draping of the swag valance in the picture at right above is traditional in style, while projecting festoon ring fixtures are practical and modern. These large decorative rings are sturdy and easy to install. The drapery slides in and out, so that it can be changed at will to alter the window effect. When draperies are used to enlarge a window the rings can be placed at any desired distance beyond or above the window frame. The straight full curtains hide the wall at the sides and the curve of the swag conceals any part of the wall showing above the top of the window. The window illustrated here shows glass-curtain treatment above radiator grille. The combination of curved swag, graceful cascades, and long straight folds in drapery and curtains makes this a window treatment which could be adapted to almost any living room, bedroom, or dining room. The small bay window on facing page shows a charming treatment in French Empire style. Notice the classical lyre design of the cornice, the formal draping of the swag valance, the striking combination of plain and figured fabric. The French book cabinet and the quaint candelabra harmonize with the drapery framing them against a background of sheer glass curtains.

178

there are too many straight lines already, use curves in your draperies. If you have too many curves, balance them by long straight folds at the windows.

2. Scale and proportion affect both the way draperies are hung and the type of pattern in the fabric. With normal windows it is usually better to hang draperies so that they just cover the top and side trim around the window. Crowded inside the frame they make the oblong of the window appear too long and narrow. Exceptions to this rule might be when the woodwork is unusually beautiful and the window unusually large, or when a large window is deeply recessed in the wall. In this latter case the drapery may be inside, or a frame around the outside opening with only glass curtains in the recess close to the windows.

Size of patterns in figured draperies is also a matter of scale. In small rooms small designs give small windows better proportion. In large rooms large patterns for large windows are much more harmonious. If windows are small you should make them *look* larger by grouping them in a unit treatment, or spreading draperies out around them if they are not close together. If you need clear window space for light, or windows are too small to be attractive, keep all the drapery on the wall, letting it just hide the inner edges of the frame.

3. Color and texture are closely tied in with scale. Strong contrast color in draperies makes windows seem larger and the room smaller. So do fabrics in heavy coarse texture, or lustrous finishes like velvet and satin. Light, transparent curtains have the opposite effect and make a room seem larger when they are used alone at windows, as do any draperies closely toned in with the wall background. (For details about choosing colors to suit various conditions see Chapter 4.) Do not have too many different types of texture in one room. They will create a restless feeling just as too many colors or patterns will.

4. Balance is important. When several single, separated windows are distributed on three or four walls they seldom balance each other. The easiest remedy is to make them less conspicuous by giving them simple curtaining, with less drama in color or pattern or preferably both. If the windows are grouped on one wall, or can be made into a group, they may be much more dramatically treated—but don't forget to work out some center of interest on the opposite wall to balance your group.

5. Suitability enters deeply into every phase of decorating. Applied to draperies it means several very definite things. (a) Rich fabrics, elaborately draped valances and swags, curtains sweeping the floor for six to twelve inches—all these belong in very formal or elaborate rooms no matter what period their dec-

Draperies like those in A below, with flounces frilled or otherwise trimmed, would fit nicely into a feminine bedroom scheme. In the plain treatment sketched here the tiered style can be adapted to almost any room. In sill length, omitting the lower flounce, it would be appropriate for a child's room or a kitchen. Incidentally, it is an excellent way to re-use old draperies or other fabrics. Without a cornice the top flounce can be used all the way across as a valance. The draperies illustrated in sketch B are smartly marked with large monograms repeated on the bed cover. In sketch C the curtains are only sill length because two enormous wine-colored Turkish towels were used to make them. Instead of a valance the top is finished with a swag treatment of soft heavy rope.

UNUSUAL DRAPERY EFFECTS

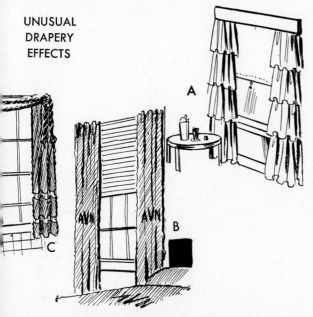

SMALL WINDOWS MADE IMPORTANT

In the picture at left above, a small window in a large wall space is transformed by draping. A decorative pole placed above the top of the window and extending beyond the trim is used to hang full straight draw-curtains with a draped swag valance. The drapery over the rod—in contrast color and lined with the curtain material—hides the wall above the window when the curtains are drawn apart.

Windows may be framed instead of draped. In the picture at the right above, the frame is made from glazed chintz gathered through the middle to make double ruffles. Here there are two windows so they are joined at the top by one long ruffle and the space between them made more important by a row of framed prints. The chest below the window can be built in, or several small chests of drawers could be placed side by side to give the effect of a built-in feature. If there had been a radiator here it could have been enclosed in a grille and the chests installed at the sides just the same.

Three windows in a bay are shown on the facing page (upper left). For an informal room the curtain treatment here is both charming and practical. Hung on continuous curving rods, which come conveniently assembled in sets for various combinations of draping, the valance and draperies are designed for good light control as well as window interest. The flowered cotton valance holds the three windows of the bay together when double-tiered draw-curtains of flowered fabric are pulled aside in either tier showing soft sheer white glass curtains next the panes.

WIDE VENETIAN BLINDS NEED SPECIAL DRAPING

The floor-length Venetian blinds for a boy's room above are in beige with red tapes to match the red and beige plaid of the drapery. The dramatic valance, which can be made by anyone handy with a needle, is covered with textured beige fabric bound in red and laced together on the drum section by red silk cord. To balance the tall narrow window the drapery is hung mostly over the wall with the inner edges just covering the edges of the slats. In the feminine bedroom (right) the Venetian blinds have three tapes as they often do when used with an unusually wide window. Here blinds and tape match the neutral off-white tone of walls and woodwork. Ruffled tie-back draperies in soft flowered fabric cascading to the floor take the place of glass curtains in this summer window treatment. The crisp white frill of the bed cover and the blue fiber rug on the floor add to the feeling of airy summer coolness. Note correct high draping for crossed curtains—one third of the curtain length from the top.

CURTAINS FOR A BAY WINDOW AND A CORNER

Two ordinary windows which are placed at unequal distances from the corner offer a difficult curtaining problem as in the sketch above (right). The solution shown here turns the corner into probably the most charming spot in the room. Ruffled sheer glass curtains, floor-length, relieve the plainness of over-draperies. A trimly tailored pleated valance at the top covers rods and pulley mechanism of the drapery while uniting drapery and curtains in a single picture.

That even a small bay window may bring a sense of spaciousness to a small room is shown by the photograph below. The classic simplicity of line in woodwork and draperies gives the little dining alcove an air of serene and gracious charm. Simulated columns at the entrance to the bay and the deep wall cornice of the room continued above the windows make any kind of valance unnecessary. Note the Venetian blinds carried to the floor for unbroken line, and the graceful looping of draperies which lie on the floor at the bottom. This looping illustrates again the correct proportions between the draped section of the curtains and the skirts, usually one third of the distance either from the top or the bottom—never in the middle of the curtain length nor in the center of a window. Draping here is done by means of a cord run through the folds at an angle, pulling the curtain up to the desired curve.

CONTINUOUS CURTAINING AROUND A CORNER

LEFT, GRACEFUL DRAPERIES FOR A DINING NOOK

When corner windows are very wide, as in the above picture, and you want over-draperies which pull across to cover the whole space at night, it is better to divide the fullness which would be needed and drape the corner as well as the outside frame of the windows. The use of Venetian blinds without glass curtains is another reason for this style of draping as it covers the ends of the slats evenly. With no glass curtains the frilled valance which conceals traverse rods and pulley cords also softens the severity of so many straight lines. The round lamp and curving design on the shade also help in this. A corner window with a view is always an excellent place to use blinds without glass curtains, with a padded seat built in around the corner to provide storage. A hinged lid can be made under the pads, or the front panels can be made into doors. Contrast tapes are effective on the blinds here because they pick up the dark stripe in the pad cover fabric. Windows like this, as well as window seats, are carried in stock.

oration may happen to follow. (b) The heavy but not necessarily extravagant materials used in fairly formal rooms include many silk, cotton and rayon versions of reps, damasks, brocades, satins, heavy taffetas, velours, velvets, and also the heavier types of printed linens and cretonnes. Wherever possible these should be long enough just to clear the floor. (c) The medium-weight fabrics used for over-draperies in the average room, such as poplins, broché silks, chintzes and thinner taffetas, linens and cretonnes, are more attractive in floor length, but may end either at the window sill or the apron just below it. (d) In informal or rustic rooms, simple, short draperies are preferred such as monk's cloth, homespun, hopsacking, or various other fabrics such as almost any washable vat-dyed figured cotton, unbleached muslin, crash, denim, and even bed-ticking.

6. Room coordination is essential for harmony. Drapery design follows a simple rule already referred to as the "Rule of Three" which applies to any fairly large fabric area in the room, including wallpaper and floor coverings. This rule calls for one plain fabric and one patterned, while the third may be textured, geometrical in design, or with soft over-all shadow pattern of some kind. Followed with discretion, you will find this rule is almost a magic formula for avoiding what decorators call a "busy" room, meaning one that is not restful because it is too broken up, or seems cluttered.

WINDOW SHADES AND VENETIAN BLINDS

Types of Shades: Modern two-toned shades are both cheaper and simpler to use than the old-style, double-set type with a dark shade behind a light one at each window. The two-toned finish makes it possible to present a unified window effect from the outside by having a uniform color on the back of all shades in the house or apartment while on the inside each room may have its own harmonizing shade color.

Serving the same purpose as the traditional outside or inside window shutters, Venetian blinds are the most effective way of controlling light without sacrificing ventilation. They are usually of wood, but may be had in aluminum, plastics, steel, and other materials. Unless installed inside a deep window jamb or under a valance they require a cornice to cover their mechanism. Venetian blinds can be used with drapery or glass curtains alone. However, the blinds are usually more attractive when the edges are concealed by drapery and the lines of the slats softened by sheer glass curtains over them.

Types of Blinds: Blinds usually match the wall color or the woodwork, with self-toned or contrast-ing tapes. If you want to change the color of the tapes buy pin-up tapes in any color you wish and apply them over the old tape. Bamboo makes light attractive window blinds. In its natural color it blends well with the blond or bleached woods often used in present-day rooms. Slat porch shades arranged to roll from bottom to top are easily adapted to the new wide windows.

BAY WINDOWS AND CORNERS

With the development of many types of bay windows in stock models, ready to give spaciousness to crowded rooms or to bring a flood of sunlight into dark ones, proper treatment has become increasingly important.

Types of Treatment: The popularity of bay windows has resulted in the designing of so many new types of window and drapery fixtures that you will find the mechanical solution of your bay window problem surprisingly easy. Any good store will tell you about the newcomers in this field and advise you how to use them. Whatever else you do with a bay, treat the windows as a drapery unit even when there is some space between windows. Make the drapery scheme conform to the draping of any other windows in the room both as to design and material.

Unit treatment may be carried out in one of several different ways: (1) A continuous cornice or valance may follow the tops of the windows around the curve (or angles), with glass curtains or draperies—or both, in many different styles and combinations—hung continuously around the bay. (2) Glass curtains alone may be hung around the curve inside the bay, with headings, while the cornice or valance is carried across the ceiling in front of it. In this case the drapery curtains hang at each side of the recess, as they would at any large window.

If the glass is practically continuous around the corner, curtain the whole space as one window with over-draperies only at the outside edges. If you want to get a corner window effect when two ordinary windows are close to a corner you can drape the wall in the corner and use the same material at the outside of the two windows, with glass curtains between. The importance of corner windows calls for a decorative heading of some kind for the curtains. Ornamental poles, cornices, valances, swag draperies —all find a place in corner window treatments. Often both the glass curtains and the draperies are hung on traverse rods with traveler pulleys for better light control and for privacy after dark. Every possible drapery need has been met by rods, poles and fixtures designed to make draping straight around corners no more difficult than any double-window treatment.

COMFORT
IN A COUNTRY
LIVING ROOM

Friendly and hospitable, this simply furnished room is as fresh and
original in spirit as the unusual landscape window above the fireplace.
Soft blues and grays, with touches of green and sunshine yellow, seem
to bring into the room the restfulness of field and sky outside the uncluttered picture windows. Rag carpeting over wide-plank floors, raftered
ceiling, bird posters, all are in harmony with the plank and stone walls
in natural tones of soft gray. Notice the comfortable couch, easily converted into a bed, with storage space under a bookshelf at the back,
also the combination bookcase and lamp table. Furniture like this, with
simple modern lines keyed to comfort, would be at home in any informal
living room, study or recreation room.

A BRIGHT FRAME
FOR LOW CASEMENT WINDOWS

This living-sleeping room, with twin couches, quaint beamed ceiling, and
built-in chest, takes its gay color scheme from the flowered linoleum rug.
In order not to exclude light and air, the small windows are curtained
only with a suggestion of side drapery and a narrow frilled valance—
just enough to frame them with color. Note how the blue of fireplace
wall and ceiling picks up the blue of the sky outside.

THREE DRAMATIC WINDOW TREATMENTS

These two square walled recessed bays are practically identical in size but at opposite poles decoratively speaking. The bay window (right) with its curved French Provincial panels and drapery frame is the essence of everything traditional. Delicate lines of dressing table, soft feminine sweep of frilled over-drapery, contrasting simplicity of full straight transparent glass curtains—all these belong to a bedroom window treatment which could be effectively reproduced with wallboard paneling and colorful inexpensive chintz draperies combined with a draped dressing table to match the curtains. It is the draping, the fullness, and the ruffled finish which give the window picture its distinction. In direct contrast is the dressing table and window treatment of the square recessed bay in the picture above. Translucent glass panels at each side of the window behind the dressing table, textured white draperies almost severely straight in line, glass accessories and table top—all give expression to the very latest interpretation of the modern spirit in decoration.

When corner windows are even on the two walls and extend to the corner a stylized drapery design like that at lower right is charming and smart. The full sheerness of glass curtains and the splashy floral pattern on over-draperies are both set off by plain painted walls and square boxed lines of the fabric-covered valance. Stripes in the couch cover suggest correct combination in the room between fabrics plain, striped, and floral. The round coffee table is large enough to be in scale with the window picture where a small table would look lost, while its curves and those of the tall vase and flowers counteract possible severity of many straight lines.

SOME
PROBLEM
WINDOWS
AND HOW
TO MAKE THEM
INTERESTING
AND
ATTRACTIVE

A long group of square small windows like those in the photograph above can hardly be successfully curtained except by covering the whole wall with drapery. When light and air are necessary a scheme like the one worked out for the four-window group above is the best solution—window decoration is achieved with none of the view cut off. Especially adapted to an informal interior, the plate-rail shelf here with its gay curtain, bright plates and bits of ivy balances the group below made by the sofa and two lamp tables. The row of prints between window and couch fills in the wall space and completes the picture. In the sketch on facing page another suggestion is offered for setting off a window of this type by a border of small framed prints.

If balance requires a window with drapery at a spot on your wall where there is no window you might try the plan used in the room at right. A large colored landscape print is installed at the appropriate place and covered with a framework enclosing glass panes like the real window panes in the room. With draperies matching those at the windows an amusing effect is obtained, along with the desired balance. Note the old wooden commode which has had its top lifted and the space filled in with growing plants. Note also the interesting result secured by hanging the two prints on colored tapes (or ribbons) from the ceiling, and the unusual cornice at the ceiling line.

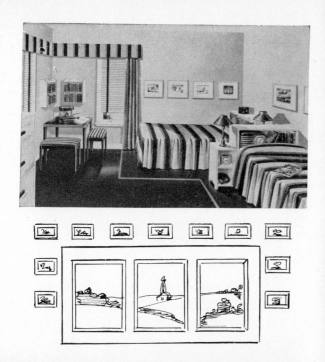

This framework set around an ordinary insignificant window in a hallway turns it into a striking and important decorative feature. Small lights installed behind a glass frame into which photographs are fitted provide subdued illumination in a dark corner and greatly increase the dramatic effect. Note the additional drama of dark wall with heavy white cornice and double curtains in soft white opaque fabric. In the small picture above left are shown simple draperies suited to younger taste. Tailored simplicity in the drapery, and in the valance carried around the corner, harmonizes with the furnishings of a room designed for two boys. The window treatment and the floor design combine to give the study corner an alcove effect.

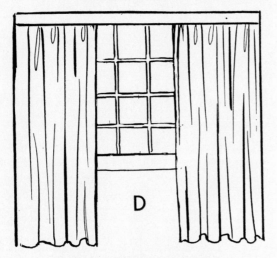

TRICKS FOR IMPROVING
BADLY PLANNED WINDOWS

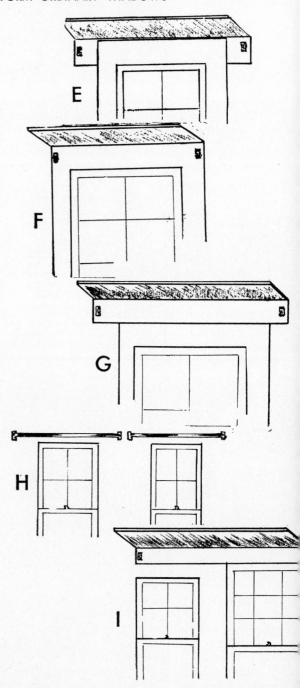

In sketches A, B, C, D we see the same kind of small window changed completely by different treatments. In sketch B it is apparently lifted to the ceiling by use of a valance over the wall above the window and its lines are brought to the floor by side draperies to give an effect of height to the room. The same window, cut in two by short glass curtains (C), looks noticeably shorter and wider than the original window. When a long cornice covers the top and side curtains drape the wall at each side (D), the same little window would pass quite well for a large double window. In the panel of plain window sketches illustrating the same principle we have (E) a valance board set outside the frame to increase the apparent width slightly. In sketch F the same window would appear quite a little narrower. In sketch G the valance board is placed well above the window frame to make the window appear taller, and to balance the height it also extends beyond the line of the frame at the sides to make the window seem wider. In sketch H two windows are connected by wide rods extending beyond their frames. A still better solution in this case would probably be to use one long rod of a type available in the shops which can be extended to any length with no danger of sagging. By using a valance over these windows you can easily drape them as one unit. In Sketch I the valance board is shown making this unit of two windows and also evening up unequal heights.

The two separated windows shown in sketch J, draped separately, are merely windows in a wall. With very little additional expense you can make them a focus of interest in your room. One way is shown above. A long draped swag valance ties them together in a unit, full sheer glass curtains soften their lines, and the panel between them is filled with a sheet of mirror glass which opens vistas and adds depth.

DRAW-CURTAINS AND VALANCES FOR A CHEERFUL BREAKFAST ALCOVE

DECORATIVE FRAMES MAY SUBSTITUTE FOR DRAPERIES

Where windows are badly proportioned or too small, but are greatly needed to admit light and air, make them decorative by framing instead of draping them. In the picture above one frame is made by knife-pleating a crisp cotton fabric and attaching it to the edge of the trim. Little cutouts in matching color on the panes add to the gay effect. Another bright idea is to make a valance out of striped chintz to look like the edge of an awning, then cut the side pieces on the bias so that when they are applied to a frame they will look like small barber poles. The edges of this valance are bound with cloth to match the darker stripe. A summery variation of this would be to make the valance green and white, put a lattice frame of white slats or bamboo in the window space and train vines on it. A row of white pots across the sill for the vines would be more effective if you lined the sill with green tiles or green linoleum. The bay window at left, large enough for a table and six chairs, makes a comfortable dining spot in a large regional-style kitchen. The full valance flounces and draw-curtains are made from gaily colored cotton dress fabric to match the color scheme set by the plaid pattern in the linoleum rug.

The dramatic window treatment in this photograph is a striking illustration of the effectiveness of continuous curtaining around a bay. French pleats are used to control fullness both in sheer glass curtains and over-draperies. By use of curved rods these over-draperies are drawn together when desired in both directions, meeting at the center of each window. The lustrous texture of the drapery is effectively contrasted with the raised design on the upholstery and the geometrical pattern of the textured acoustic tile ceiling. The modern light fixture, the smart dark strips on the

IN THE MODERN MANNER

arms of the chairs, a mirrored coffee table top, and soft pile carpeting make this a center-of-interest window typical of the best in the modern style of decoration. Chairs like these, designed for comfort and long wear, are often saved from heaviness by use of strong but lightweight frame material.

CHAPTER FOURTEEN

Effective Curtains and Draperies

YOUR WINDOW TREATMENT can do any number of things for your room—from merely furnishing the best possible supply of light, to providing a dramatic climax and center of interest. It can pull a decorating scheme together, or correct architectural defects.

Contemporary window treatments—especially many kinds of corrective curtaining—call for increased width in draperies with simple lines but deep voluminous folds, placing greater stress than ever before upon color, design, and texture in fabrics. This does not mean that you must pay an exorbitant price in order to have attractive windows. It does mean you must know the effect you want to create before you begin to shop for your materials, and then get the best possible value for whatever amount of money you can spend.

WISE BUYING

Draperies may, and often do, run into high figures because of the quantities required. But color and grace are the two most vital factors in choosing draperies, and in modern fabrics charm of color is not confined to expensive materials. Color runs riot over the counters devoted to budget-priced chintzes, cretonnes, rayons, cottons, and a host of novelty fabrics. As for grace, that is largely a matter of enough fullness to give you the lines you want. Soft, voluminous folds of a budget-priced material are many times more effective than skimpy lengths of some lovely and costly fabric. This bears repeating: Buy plenty of yardage in the best grade of a less expensive fabric-type rather than sacrifice fullness or basic quality for the sake of some higher-priced type of material.

In other words, a good firm mercerized cotton sateen hung gracefully full is both more wearable and better looking than silk or rayon satin in a flimsy weave or sparingly used.

Inexpensive dress materials often substitute with marked success for conventional drapery fabrics. These may be particularly useful if you are looking for patterned hangings. The narrower width in which dress fabrics are woven usually means seaming for drapery use and the seam will be much less conspicuous in fabric with a pattern. The fabric chart on page 417 lists not only traditional curtain and drapery materials, but also many dress fabrics which may be adapted to drapery and curtain purposes.

HOW TO BUY SERVICE IN DRAPERIES

Whether you are buying your curtains and draperies ready-made, having them made, or making them yourself, serviceability in fabric is vitally important. All window-draping materials are exposed to constant siege by two of the worst fabric enemies—strong sunlight and dirt. They may be sheer glass curtains or heavy lined draperies, but they must be able to stand up under repeated washing or cleaning of some kind—unless they belong to the group of plastic synthetic materials which are free from all the old trouble-making fabric qualities. Looking exactly like the various traditional textiles, or with special textures, sheens, and beauties of their own, they will in time make care and replacement of draperies a negligible factor in choosing them.

In the meantime whether you are looking for draperies in an old or a new type of fabric it is important to know what you are buying. There is no electric eye which will reveal the hidden factors of wearability in a fabric, but there is one course of safety—manufacturers' labels. These should accompany the fabric, whether it is sold by the yard or in draperies already made up.

Fabric Labels: Labels should give you all the information you need for wise buying. Labeled fabrics have been put through various tests to determine the degree of service they will give, and the information is printed on the label for your guidance. Strength tests indicate the length of wear you may expect. Cleaning tests report on cleanability and the method approved by the manufacturers—machine-washing, hand-washing, or dry-cleaning. Directions for cleaning and care should also be on the label. Other information should include (1) the degree of shrinking or stretching when properly cleaned; (2) degree of color fastness in cleaning and in sunlight; (3) type and durability of finish. Keep your labels as long as the fabric lasts. Use them as guides for cleaning and care. If there is some special finish it may last a long time with right care yet disintegrate rapidly under the wrong kind of treatment.

Buying Curtains or Draperies Ready-Made: The fabric label on ready-made products should give the same information as that described above. But in addition to fabric quality there is also workmanship to consider. It is this alone which insures proper hanging and lasting satisfaction whether in sheer glass curtains or in heavy over-draperies. Check the following points before you invest in ready-made draperies or curtains.

1. Fullness. Be sure the curtains follow the rules in this chapter for fullness, according to the type of fabric and the width of the window where they will be used.

2. Length. If the fabric is not pre-shrunk and there is no label allow 1 inch to the yard for shrinkage of rayon, 2 for cotton.

3. Finish. Hems should be straight and neatly finished, all stitching securely fastened at the ends by return stitching. Ruffle-seams should be deep enough to hold through many washings, with no raw edges showing.

4. Hems and Headings. Check these to be sure they are as deep as they should be. Glass curtains should have top hems from 2 to 3 inches deep for headings, bottom hems from 1½ to 3 inches except when hems at bottom and on both sides are all 1 inch doubled. Drapery headings should be from 3 to 5 inches, bottom hems from 2 to 3½ inches. One hem is often fastened with bastings only for easy length adjustment.

5. Valances. If there is a valance of any style which comes with the curtains or draperies be sure it is deep enough to allow adjustment to the height of your window. The average proportion is ⅛ to ⅙ of the distance from the floor to the top of the window dressing, but if you are using a valance for some special corrective purpose this proportion may need to be altered. It will also be affected by the width of the window and the proportions of the room. Try a pattern on the window before you start shopping. You can take it with you and be sure you are buying one which can be adjusted to your need.

HOW TO MEASURE YOUR WINDOWS

Hasty measurements or careless computation of yardage may have serious consequences, specially if you are buying fabrics with designs which must be closely matched. Check your measurement and yardage figures before you start out to buy. Don't measure one window in the room and assume that it speaks for the others. Even when windows are sup-

190

posed to be the same size they may show surprising variations when carefully measured. Use a steel tape or a yardstick of wood or metal for large areas. Cloth tape measures are handy for close work, but may stretch and prevent real accuracy when used for long spaces. The diagram on this page will serve as a guide for your measuring.

1. For length of rod, when sill-length glass (or sash) curtains are to be set inside the window frame, measure from jamb to jamb following the line in the diagram from H to I.

2. For length of rod, cornice, valance, or pole between brackets, when curtains are to be hung over the trim, measure from A to B in the diagram—that is, to the outside edges of the trim. (If curtains are not set inside the frame, they must cover the trim entirely, never stopping half-way.) When draperies extend beyond the window, to widen it, measure beyond A and B to the points you have selected on each side.

3. For length of glass curtains to be hung inside the window frame, measure from the top of the window sash to the sill (C to D). Hung this way inside the jamb, curtains never go *below* the sill.

4. For other sill-length curtains or draperies measure from the top of the window trim to the sill— from G to F.

5. Add width of the apron just below the sill if you want apron-length curtains (E to J).

6. If curtains have to be longer than the apron, carry them all the way to the floor, from A to K. Never let them end at any point between the floor and the apron unless it is to clear some object such as a radiator or window seat. If curtains or draperies cannot be made to reach the floor when they are moved from one home or apartment to another, don't leave them dangling. Cut them off to the apron or the sill and use the pieces for valances or some other purpose.

7. If your over-draperies are to be very formal, add 10 to 12 inches to floor-length measurements for a sweep or for looping up with tie-backs.

HOW TO ESTIMATE MATERIAL

Buy a little more than your measurements call for and use leftover pieces for accent touches in the room or save them for possible repairs and remodeling. This is much better than taking a chance on running short of material. Make a little chart for each window and include in your list everything which goes into the dressing of that window—curtains and draperies (right and left), ruffles, valances, tie-backs, trimming, lining. Leave a space opposite each item for the amount of material you estimate as needed. In making up figured fabrics the extra yardage required for matching patterns may take care of small items such as tie-backs, or even of plain stretched

DIAGRAM FOR TAKING CURTAIN AND DRAPERY MEASUREMENTS

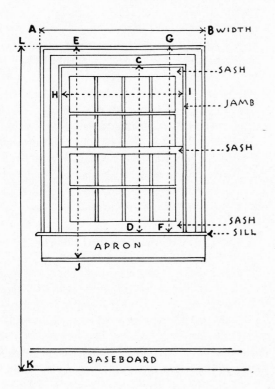

The diagram left will help to clarify the measuring of your windows for curtains and draperies. When the directions speak of "sill length" or "floor length" the measurement is taken to that point, but in making and hanging the hem should clear from ¼″ to ½″. Because so many sills and floors are not even it is always wise to hang all curtains before the hems are turned (or seamed) so you can pin them up at the point which looks best in case there is unevenness. It is safer to let draperies hang two or three days with hems only pinned or basted. Fabrics often stretch a little after hanging and it is much easier to make the necessary adjustment before the final hem is put in than to alter it afterward. If hangings are to be draped try them out before final hemming to be sure enough allowance has been made. All draperies hang better with some form of weighting along the lower edge. For use at the mitred corners of hems the best weight is a small round disk covered with the curtain fabric and tacked in place or anchored by a piece of twill tape drawn through the disk and stitched to the inside edge of the hem. There are also small triangular pin-on weights very convenient for draperies which have to be laundered or dry-cleaned often. For lightweight fabrics such as taffeta, chintz, and many other drapery materials, it is more satisfactory to insert hardage weights in the hem by tacking the tape lightly along the line of the hem where it is to be turned up. For glass curtains use round string weights basted into the hem.

valances. With plain fabrics, every one of these will have to be added to your estimate.

Allowances in Computing Length: Put down first the length of one finished curtain—whatever length you have chosen. Add to this as follows:

1. Shrinkage Allowance. If your fabric has been pre-shrunk your label should tell you so and in that case you need make no allowance. If it has been tested for shrinkage, the label should report the maximum percentage you will need to allow. One per cent on the label will mean not more than ½ inch per yard; 2 per cent works out approximately ¾ inch per yard; 3 per cent calls for an allowance of about 1 inch per yard. If fabric has not been tested, allow 2 inches a yard for safety if it is cotton, 1 inch a yard if it is rayon. Remember that non-washable fabrics may shrink in the dry-cleaning process. When curtain fabrics are not pre-shrunk, have them shrunk before making them up if that is possible.

2. Bottom Hem Allowance. For straight transparent glass curtains all hems are best doubled, as the light shining through makes an attractive pattern of the crossed threads. The lower hem width is usually proportioned to the length of the curtain, from 1½ to 3 inches. (Some people prefer a uniform 1 inch hem down both sides and across the bottom of transparent curtains.) For heavier materials, the lower hem should be from 2 or 3 inches deep on straight hanging curtains to as much as 12 inches on those which are draped back or spread out over the floor. All lower hems (except very heavy or lined draperies) should have triple thickness of material. Add twice the width of the bottom hem to the length allowance.

3. Top Hem and Casing Allowance. Headings for curtains gathered on a rod vary from 1 to 2½ inches and are formed by the top hem. The casing should be large enough to allow the rod to slip through easily, usually 1 to 1½ inches. For sheer curtains with stiffened pleated tops allow for two thicknesses of fabric under which the buckram stiffening is folded to prevent its showing through, while in heavier material the heading is formed by making a hem the width of the buckram (usually from 3 to 5 inches) plus 1 inch for hem turn-in under the edge of the stiffening. A safe allowance for the top hem is to add 8 inches to length measurement.

4. Design Allowance. In figured fabrics the bottoms of pattern motifs should start at the same level on all the curtains in the room, and near the bottom of the curtains. The simplest way to figure extra yardage for this is to add the entire length of one "repeat" to each individual curtain length measure.

5. Draping Allowance. For any type of draping the curtain must be longer than if it were to hang straight. Make a few inches allowance, and test before finishing the hem.

Estimating Width: Do not include selvages in your measurements as they will be cut off. In place of them add whatever you are turning under on the edges for hems which are sometimes the same width front and back and sometimes deeper at the front edge. For over-drapery with a curved rod or valance board allow several inches at the back edge for fabric which is carried around the curve to the wall—this is called a "return." The fullness itself is a matter of fabric, window width and style of drapery. A good rule for average-weight glass curtains is to allow for fullness twice the width of the window space they are to cover—with a little less if they are heavy net and three times the window space if fabric is very soft and sheer.

If curtains and over-draperies are made to be drawn together, the width before pleating must be at least double the width of the space which will be covered when they are drawn, and with many fabrics should be even more. If over-draperies are fixed in place at the sides they should look as if they *could* be drawn across the window, and that means they should hang very full, just as draw-curtains do when they are pulled back. Since fabrics come in widths of 36, 40 and 50 inches and average windows are from 36 to 48 inches wide, materials can often be used on average 3- and 4-foot windows without cutting or seaming. But don't sacrifice your effect to save adding a part of a width to each curtain. The general rule is double width for average weight fabrics, a little more if they are very soft, a little less only when they are unusually heavy and stiff.

Measuring for Ruffles: The secret of successful ruffles and flounces is plenty of evenly distributed fullness. Measure all edges of each curtain to which ruffles will be applied, and double this for fullness. For bias ruffling in a very sheer crisp fabric you need a little less fullness, probably one and one-half times the length of the curtain edges instead of twice. Depth of curtain ruffles depends upon what you like. The traditional width is from 3 to 6 inches but present-day styles often employ flounces as deep as from 6 to 9 inches. This may take a little more fullness—specially at corners.

Estimating Extras: Figure gathered or pleated valances just as you do the straight flounces described above, allowing for hems and headings as you would for the curtains themselves. Measure for shaped valances, allowing for finishing of edges, margin for fastening over rods or valance boxes, and returns at the ends, usually 3 inches extra in width and 3 inches at each end. If material is figured, be sure to allow for centering the pattern exactly.

LINING GIVES BODY TO DRAW-CURTAINS AND VALANCES

Continuous valances over lined draperies fitted with pulleys for drawing them over the windows provide distinctive window treatment in the room above. The drapery is used, without glass curtains, in front of recessed casement windows which allow for a long window seat. Both valance and draperies are bound with grosgrain ribbon giving a trim tailored effect. The "Rule of Three" for fabric combinations is exemplified here in figured draperies, plain colors for rug, wall and ceiling, with geometrical stripes in the couch upholstery and diamond-shaped windowpanes. Note the graceful line of the shaggy oval rug which adapts itself so well to the curving outline of the room.

EASILY MADE SWAG VALANCES AND USEFUL ACCESSORIES

Swag valances draped in formal style to give a period effect to brocaded draperies are shown in photograph at right above. The swag is made of contrast material, edged with beaded fringe, and draped from rosettes or rings. Instead of tie-backs, rosettes are placed at a correct point for low draping, two-thirds down from the top. Here this low draping line increases the tall formal effect of the window treatment. The sketches at right illustrate uses for a device which is very helpful in dressing windows. Rings in metal, wood, glass, or plastic are mounted on arms attached to the wall or window frame and used both for swag valance and draperies and for looping back curtains. They are adjustable on their rods for turning at the most convenient angle. The sketches show three very simple swags used over plain sheer curtains to give a window an appearance of being dressed up. Allow one and one-half times the window width for draped part of swag, cutting the cascade ends on the bias. When you don't want to go in for expensive draperies, remnants of fabrics left from slip covers or cushions may be fashioned into swag valances which bring the windows into the decorative room scheme with almost no expense. This is also a practical way to use up good sections cut from discarded draperies. On the other hand swags may be very full and carried one-third of the way down the window, or all the way to the floor to make complete side draperies. The draping arm and a rosette pin (shown at extreme right) are available in many styles and materials.

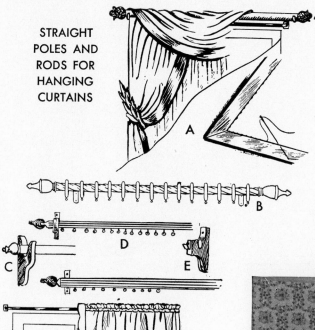

STRAIGHT POLES AND RODS FOR HANGING CURTAINS

SMALL BAY WINDOW DRAPED LIKE A SINGLE WIDE ONE

A charming use of ruffles in a contrasting fabric is illustrated in the small country living room pictured below. The miniature bay window with its full sheer floor-length glass curtains has been utilized to provide needed floor space for a chair-and-table reading group. The shirred valance across the top and the draped chintz at either side make the whole window treatment a very important item in the decoration of the room. The effect is greatly enhanced by the plain wall at the window end of the room. The drama of the figured drapery would have been largely lost if the flowered wallpaper had been continued over the wall behind it. Quaint charm in the figured paper, the flowered draperies and the Colonial furniture is given emphasis by the simplicity of the plain self-striped rug in the living room and the square hooked rug on the bare floor in front of the entrance door with its interesting and appropriate panel design.

Traditional for hanging the heavier type of draperies is the ornamental wood pole with carved ends projecting just beyond supporting brackets. These poles are always finished to match other wood in the room, painted, stained, or in natural light tones. A variant of this pole is the black iron or bronze rod with ornamental wrought ends. A conventional bracket pole is shown in sketch A with drapery looped over it to form a valance. An ornamental metal draping "arm" harmonizes with the formality of pole and drapery. With this type of pole rings are ordinarily used, as in sketch B, either sewed to the back of the curtain or provided with small loops for hooks attached to the top hem. This pole is mounted on concealed brackets instead of on the customary wooden type shown in C. This special bracket which allows the drapery to go past it makes it possible to use the pole to extend width of draperies and make a window appear wider while the bracket remains attached to the window frame. The concealed bracket may also serve as a support for the center of a very long pole or rod. In D and E the rings are inserted in a slot instead of being slipped over the pole by unscrewing the decorative end. Wood poles may be used for fixed side draperies, draw-curtains, or softly draped

curtains and valances. In normal size they are fairly thick and only drapery headings which are attached to rings are suitable to use with them. (No casings.) In the group marked F are illustrated some of the uses for rods or poles of types which fit between two sides of door or window jambs, also the flat-fitting rods used mostly for sash and shelf curtains. In top sketch the sash curtains are of the double-tiered Dutch type sometimes hung in this way on a casing over a small rod, and sometimes with rings as draw-curtains. Glass curtains shirred over flat rods and stretched between top and bottom of French door panes in casement-curtain style illustrate one important use for small flat bracket rods. With the set-in types the pole is supported by small sockets attached to the jamb at each end. These rods can also be had in metal with a small suction cup at each end which holds them firmly against the door or window jamb without nails or screws. They come cut to measure with a spring which makes them adjustable. The adjustable types are useful anywhere, and are especially suited to light-weight drapery or sheer curtains. To fill in a fan-shaped transom over a doorway or window (as in G) a curved rod is fitted with a glass curtain shirred over it and gathered

GAY DRAPERY FOR A CENTER-OF-INTEREST WINDOW

In the living room below voluminous folds of flowered chintz frame the window and make a picture of the whole window group. The valance is a simple ruffle across the top of the window, but it is dressed up by the same lacy ball fringe used to edge the draperies. The flowered fabric is used in correct combination with the plain slip cover and the plaid design of the fiber rug. Note the love seat and the small arm chair which make a conversation group and still allow space for convenient radio, phonograph and record-storage cabinets doubling as lamp tables. The vista from this living room into the sunroom is made interesting by folding shuttered doors which take up no space when not in use and provide ventilation when drawn. The built-in book shelves used as a semi-partition with the folding shutter doors suggest a useful way to set off one end of a long narrow room.

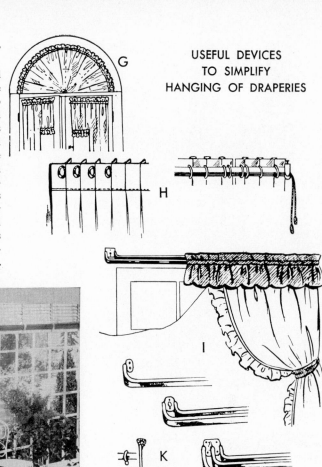

USEFUL DEVICES TO SIMPLIFY HANGING OF DRAPERIES

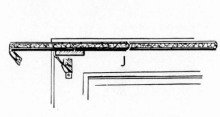

into a rosette at the middle of the lower edge. For draperies to hang from any arched opening over a door or window a curved rod is supplied with rings or hooks for shaped drapery tops. Arched rods are sometimes applied to the wall above a window and filled in with shirred curtains or used for long draperies to give increased height to a short window. Sketches marked H show a conventional pulley arrangement for draw-curtains, which may be glass curtains, under-curtains or over-draperies. These are usually called traverse (or traveler) rods. Here the rings are attached to the curtain and then slipped over the rod. A more convenient device is to use rings with small loops through which hooks fastened to the curtains are inserted. There are many styles in these rods, from those which are hidden under a cornice or pulley to those which are very ornate and part of the decoration. They are used in front of windows, in doors and archways, and as movable partitions to curtain off space for special uses. In the group of sketches marked I are shown the widely used rods with curved ends fitting into side brackets. They may be round or flat. They come with one rod, two, or three, all fitted into the same bracket, so that they can be used for three sets of curtains; or for crossed

tie-back curtains and valance. Usually bought in extension form, these useful rods make practically any combination of draperies, curtains and valances possible. They are sketched here in their usual flat style. In buying extension rods be sure they are long enough to be solid and not sag when extended. Sketch J shows a curved-end extension rod designed to carry draperies beyond the window on each side without the necessity of nailing a block on the wall to hold the curtain rod. Except where a casing is used, curtains are attached to rods by means of various types of rings and hooks. For lighter-weight curtains and draperies the hooks are often pinned into the folds of the fabric. For heavy over-draperies sewing is safer. In sketch K can be seen the ring with a loop into which hooks are inserted, and three types of these hooks. One is the pin hook which is fastened in the curtain at each group of pleats, or at regular intervals, and then hooked into the loop in the ring. The long shaft of the middle hook is sewed to the curtain and is particularly useful for supporting deep pleats. The small hook at the left is sewed to drapery or curtain, and the ring next to it shows the little loop through which the hooks are thrust. These loops may be sewed directly to the curtain.

195

SHIRRED TOPS FOR
SHEER GLASS CURTAINS

The simplicity of the modern dressing room above is relieved by the soft grace of the window treatment. Straight sheer glass curtains are finished at the top with a deep shirring band corresponding to the width of the hem which just clears the floor although over-draperies rest upon it. French pleats are used to control fullness in these lined draperies and the illustration shows the space which is left plain at the inner edge of each curtain before pleating begins. Deep folds indicate graceful fullness when draperies are pulled together over the window. Note the interesting fireplace and book-shelf arrangement, also the softly polished tile floor with its shaggy modern rug. Glass-topped dressing table and round stool furnish curves offsetting straight lines, while texture provides contrast and variety between sheer gleaming glass curtains and lustrous drapery fabric used with rough textures of rug and the pile fabric upholstery.

FLAT PLEATS GIVE GRACE TO

That flat pleats make effective headings is illustrated by long over-draperies used without valance in the living room above. Draperies like these are often used to add height to a low-ceilinged room. If the window is short, Venetian blinds or window shades can be used to conceal the wall space above the windows. There is an interesting combination here of traditional and modern feeling, with accessories, occasional pieces and Victorian-tufted chairs contributing period touches to plain modern wall treatment, comfortable slip-

TYPES OF HEADINGS AND

When there is no over-drapery, cornice or valance to conceal the top of hangings the heading becomes a very important consideration in the window design. A plain ruffled heading with casing is shown in sketch A. B shows flat pleats used for drapery fullness and attached to rings slipped over a rod. The reverse side of the drapery shows how these pleats may be stitched underneath to hold them in place (B-1). This stitching is a useful device when drapery needs to be widened by piecing, as in remaking, or is made up of several narrow lengths of material. Sketch C shows the formation of box pleats at the top of a curtain. Flat pleats are especially adapted to heavy, stiff fabrics which are difficult to control. Cartridge pleats illustrated in sketch D are made by stitching a pleat down from the top as if for French pleats or box pleats. However, in this case, the stiffened pleats are left to form rolls which may or may not be filled with cotton to keep them in shape. They may be used with even space between or grouped.

**EXTRA LENGTH
FOR GRACEFUL DRAPING**

VOLUMINOUS FOLDS IN DRAPERY

covered sofa and soft shaggy rug. Note the convenient 18th Century "dumb-waiter" round table, also the working out of formal and informal balance. The mantel arrangement with its flanking lamp tables and windows shows formal or identical balance. The grouping of two large chairs with the table between opposite a large sofa is an equally good example of informal or occult balance. Here the objects are different, but they are arranged so that they seem to balance each other in size, scale, weight and importance.

ATTACHMENTS FOR HANGING

The group of sketches at right illustrates three methods for attaching pleated curtains to the rod or pole. In the middle (1) a casing has been applied to slip over a rod. This is practical only where draperies or curtains are to remain in a fixed position on the rod. The two outer sketches show hooks to insert in rings (2), and rings applied to the curtain (3). At lower right is shown the method of making French or pinch pleats. They may be left to fall in loose round shape something like a triple cartridge pleat; or the projecting pleats may be pressed into three sharp, flat pleats called "pinch pleats"; or the folds may be flattened and pressed almost like box pleats. French pleating is better for softer and more pliable types of fabrics than for those of a heavy or wiry weave. To simplify making of French pleats two products are available. The patent washable pleater shown at top left is stitched on the back of your curtain or drapery and takes the place of other stiffening. Another device works with a drawstring through slots in buckram.

A decorative window treatment above—in which lustrous spun rayon on a cotton back gives a two-toned effect to stripes of dusty rose, blue and white—shows a heading of pinch pleats with gracefully looped over-drapery. Sheer glass curtains in this case are apron length, while the drapery lies on the floor a few inches to allow for better draping. For this drapery treatment a valance board may be used but is not necessary. A casing attached to the back of the pleats can be slipped over a curved extension rod since the draperies are not intended to be changed from the position given them when they are put up. To cover the window the shaped tie-backs with rings at the ends are simply unhooked. The high draping (approximately one-third of the way down from the top) is not only correct but is often very convenient. If a radiator were below the window instead of the table, this draping would make the curtains swing clear at each side.

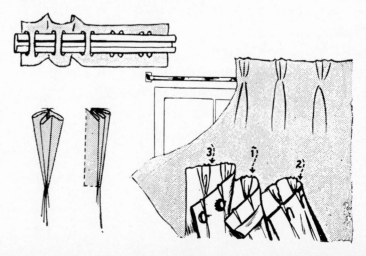

EFFECTIVE DRAPERIES FOR A WIDE PICTURE WINDOW

Treatment like the one given this window is very simple to work out. Straight glass curtains are arranged here to draw across the picture window, and long formal over-draperies can be pulled across the window in front of them. The soft lustrous fabric adapts itself beautifully to the simple draping of the shallow valance which frames the window without cutting off the view. In this case a straight length of drapery material is pleated in at the ends of a shallow cornice box and the upper edge of the material is fastened over the top of the frame while the lower edge is draped.

In the sketches shown here A illustrates how easy it is to put up a valance board by resting it on top of the window trim and supporting it by angle irons or small brackets. The average width of the board is 3″ or 4″, though it may be wider if it is necessary to bring the draperies forward to hang in front of shelves or a radiator below a window. If there are two or more windows in a group, run the board straight across above all of them and dress the group as one window. If the tops of the trims are uneven attach a block of wood to the wall to support the angle iron or bracket at one end—or both. Use strips of wood on the wall (or two blocks) when the board is to be lifted above the window top for height or extended beyond it for greater width. To attach glass curtains and drapery behind the valance use any kind of arrangement you like best in the form of molding curtain tracks, or rods attached to the underside of the board itself, or fixtures on the window trim. Only make sure that glass curtains, over-drapery and valance have space enough between them so that the draperies hang freely and grace-fully, especially if you are using pulley or traverse tracks. Detail drawing A-1 shows the method of applying a stiffened valance around the board. Thumb tacks or hooks and rings

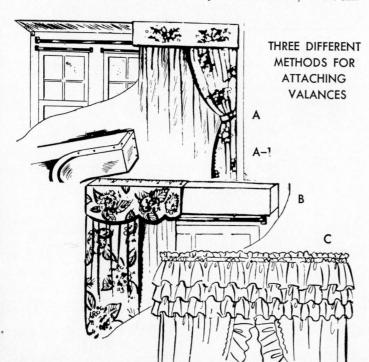

THREE DIFFERENT
METHODS FOR
ATTACHING
VALANCES

A

A-1

B

C

FORMAL DRAPERIES
FOR DRAMATIC FLOOR-LENGTH WINDOWS

The bay window above shows an unusual and interesting combination of straight drapery panels with deeply draped-back curtains at each side of the bay. Architectural traditional woodwork, combined with tall windows, gives an air of dignity to the room, while the casual arrangement of modern furniture strikes a note of quiet comfort and homelike charm. Note the use of dark walls and draperies in the sun-flooded room, with a pale yellow ceiling and deep tawny yellow carpet to reflect the sun and furnish cheerful contrast to the olive green walls.

DRAW-CURTAINS TO DRAMATIZE ORDINARY WINDOWS

In the living room below, windows are given importance by being treated as one large window. The shaped valance extends across the group, with overdraperies and glass curtains covering both the windows and the spaces between them. Note that the color scheme of this living room is also the over-all theme for the other rooms shown. In the dining room above, opening into the living room, the colors are repeated exactly, and the draperies are the same. In the bedroom, green is still the dominant color, but in stronger tones with lavish use of white, and red is still the accent color.

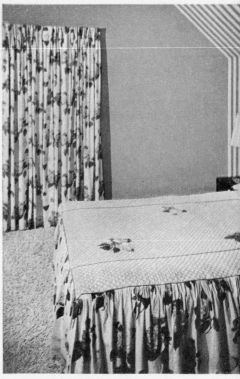

WELL-PLANNED DRAPERIES FOR A BAY WINDOW

The cloth-covered valance in the picture above is made with a stiffened foundation following the curve of a fixture placed near the ceiling above the bay windows. Both sheer glass curtains and draperies are made to draw over the windows on a long curving rod supported by concealed brackets. The effectiveness of contrast banding is shown here, the color of the plain dark band being picked up from one of the shades in the drapery pattern.

ANGLED RODS ALLOW CHINTZ OVER-DRAPERIES TO BE DRAWN BACK

attach it at the back and hold it in place. Sketch B illustrates a method for using a cornice box as a foundation for a valance. The valance is usually of the same fabric as the over-draperies but it may be a contrast to them in color or design. It is important to have a stiffened fabric valance deep enough for the window and to have the curves come at appropriate points for the drapery hanging beneath them. (Sketch B.) The finished valance may be fastened to the board by tape on board and valance edges, with buttons or snaps to make removal for cleaning easier. The ends of the valance (like the edges of over-drapery) must always make the turn around the corner and reach the wall where they are tacked or hooked to the edges of the window trim. A simple shirred or ruffled valance (sketch C) is the easiest of all types to make and install. It may be in several tiers as shown here or in one deep flounce all the way across the window, or may fill in between side draperies. The flounce may be attached like any other valance to a board but this type adapts itself easily to a casing and a rod. It is the least formal style of valance and is frequently used with sheer draperies and informal chintzes when a casual effect is desired. The edges may be finished to match your curtains.

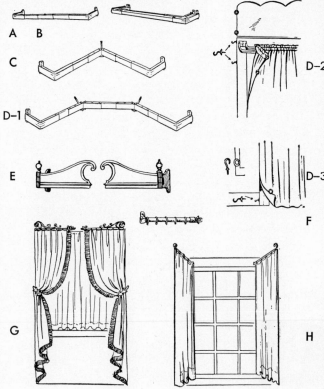

Modern adjustments and improvements in extension rods guard against sagging. Corners and curves and angles are provided with special braces so that the rods can be used around bay window curves and corner window angles without interference with your drapery. Sketches A and B illustrate a very convenient type of extension bracket rod with square elbow corners which add to the effect of using a valance board. These come in single and double sets which are made by using two rods with arms in slightly different lengths. In sketch A, a specially helpful device is shown in which splicing is used to build the rods up to any desired length. Sagging is prevented by a special rod support. Sketches C and D show how simple it is to curtain bay windows and corner windows by using extension rods adjustable to various-sized spaces and angles. Outside edges of curtain drapery or valance should hang straight and smooth against the wall. Sketches marked D-1, 2, 3 show how this effect can be achieved by using ordinary cup hooks screwed into the wall or the baseboard. The small rings sewed to the edges of the curtain, top and bottom, and also to the valance, are fastened firmly over the hooks, holding the edge of the curtain taut and insuring a trim tailored line at the outer edges. Sketches E, F, G and H show several types of swinging bracket cranes with rings and loops for attaching drapery. The window H suggests a way to curtain a man's room for plenty of air and no frills by using one of the plain swinging cranes. The window in G illustrates a more formal use of the crane in a treatment appropriate for a living room or dining room where more light may be needed at some times than at others. Fringed draperies are looped up with metal (tie-back) arms harmonizing with the decorative crane used as a heading for draperies. Sketch E is an interesting example of modern improvements applied to traditional styles. The swinging wood bracket in a period design is set out from the wall in cornice effect, with concealed rods at the back of the swinging sections to hold draperies. Slots in the "returns" (the wooden arms which hold the front away from the wall) carry a full-length rod for glass curtains. There are many variations of these useful and attractive fixtures, in both wood and metal. They may be concealed by the shirred casing of the curtain, or they may be a decorative feature used as a heading for the drapery they carry. They are favorites for casement windows, French doors opening inward, and for regulation windows where it is desired to let in the maximum light and air.

MODERN DEVICES FOR INSTALLING DRAW-CURTAINS

they may be pleated before the tape is applied. The sliders are fabricated, for easier laundering, and the wood track moldings are available in a great variety of sizes and shapes. They come with 1, 2, or 3 slots for triple curtaining or curtaining with valance. Curved sections are to be had for turning corners. Sketch I shows a curtain hung from a ceiling molding (left) as well as a regulation window treatment.

A useful method for hanging curtains or draperies without the necessity of installing rods and brackets is illustrated above. A slot in a narrow molding or wood track is attached to ceilings, to walls, to tops of windows, to under sides of valance boards, to cornices, to shelf edges—wherever curtains of any type are to be hung. A slider tape stitched to the top hem of the curtain contains small sliders at intervals which are inserted near the end of the track and provide the necessary fullness. Curtain tops may be plain or

Sketches above illustrate a modern form of traverse track used in place of the ordinary rod or pole arrangement. One sketch shows the front of the track and the other illustrates from the back both the return which gives it a cornice effect and the special overlapping feature which allows draperies to close securely, shutting out every particle of light and any chance of a draft. If you use one of these, allow a little more unpleated margin for this overlap on the inside edge of your draperies.

HANGING CURTAINS AND DRAPERIES

If your curtains and draperies are not properly hung they lose most of their effectiveness no matter how handsome your fabrics or how good your tailoring. Fortunately, there is no necessity and no excuse today for badly hung curtains. Every possible curtain-hanging need has been met with fixtures which do not warp or sag, are easy to install, and keep their trimness indefinitely even with the most casual sort of care. Hidden parts are sturdy and furnished with recent mechanical devices to make operation easier. Decorative parts are carefully designed to harmonize with major furniture periods and styles. Best of all, even the finest stock fixtures are so moderately priced that it is wise to invest in strong, well-made, handsome fixtures.

They should not be elaborate and conspicuous. Far from it. Theirs is a supporting role in your window-drama. They should not be allowed to draw attention away from the drapery, but neither should their importance be overlooked.

Before you settle upon the style you want for your new draperies pay a visit to the house-furnishing section and the drapery department of your favorite store. You will almost certainly find new ideas which will help you plan your window treatments and enable you to turn out a really professional-looking job. Do not attempt to put up your new draperies on old fixtures unless they are firm, sturdy, and adequate for smart styling of your windows.

CORNICES AND VALANCES

Cornices are extensively used to cover the tops of curtains and draperies, to conceal rods and pulley cords, and to tie two or more windows into a group by extending across all of them. Usually made of wood, metal or plastic, cornices vary from 4 to 8 inches in depth.

Cornice Finishes: A cornice may be perfectly plain and painted like the wall or woodwork, or it may be made highly decorative. Beaded moldings, ornamental carving at the top, or applied designs from wallpaper or fabric may be used. Glass, tin, plaster, straw, cork, leather, etc., are all novelty materials which make effective cornice facings. Mirrored cornices are particularly striking and are frequently used in modern decorating plans. Traverse cornice pole sets are new, and specially easy both to install and use when you want draw-curtains of any type. These cornices come in stock sizes, and in styles adapted to modern and traditional architecture.

Valances may be casual or formal, simple or elaborate, depending entirely upon the style of your window treatment. Aside from their purely decorative qualities valances provide the easiest and most effective method for correcting bad window arrangement or inappropriate window style. Technically, a valance is always installed by means of a valance board (or an enclosed box like a cornice) except for certain flounce or swag styles. In practice, however, it is possible to attach even a stiffened valance by a casing near the top to a flat curved rod in such a way that it gives the effect of being attached to a conventional board. This is not recommended, since valance boards are easy to install, but it may be useful in emergencies or in temporary quarters.

Types of Valances: Like cornices, valances may be made of wood, metal, or plastics, or be faced with mirrors or any of the other decorative novelties mentioned. The difference is that the valance is considerably deeper than the cornice, being usually from $\frac{1}{5}$ to $\frac{1}{8}$ the length of the hangings, and offers a greater variety of types. Shaped valances may be cut from plywood or composition board attached to the valance board. These can be painted or covered with wallpaper to match the wall behind them. They may also be stenciled or treated with cutout designs and borders. The variety possible in designing valances is endless but they fall in general into several groups, all illustrated by pictures and sketches in this chapter.

Fabric valances may be the same as your drapery; or they may be a contrast material, or some novelty such as leather, quilting, or braided panels. With plain draperies a figured valance is often effective, and the reverse. Heavier fabrics may serve for a valance over sheer draperies, but sheer fabrics are never used for valances unless the curtains below are of the same sheer material. The flat stiffened valance covered with fabric must be carefully made and attached with precision to the valance board. The lower edge may be scalloped, carried straight across, or cut in any shape which suits the style of your drapery.

GLASS CURTAINS

When sheer curtains are used with over-draperies they should be carefully harmonized with each other as to color and texture. To accompany silk taffeta or rep the best choice is fine net or gauze. With chintz, use a coarser net, voile, organdy, or a similar fabric. With linen or cotton rep a heavy net or a sheer casement cloth is most appropriate. With brocades and other fine silk or rayon fabrics, use silk or rayon gauze, marquisette, and other sheer silky textures. In general, heavier over-draperies call for heavier glass curtains, while finer fabrics need the

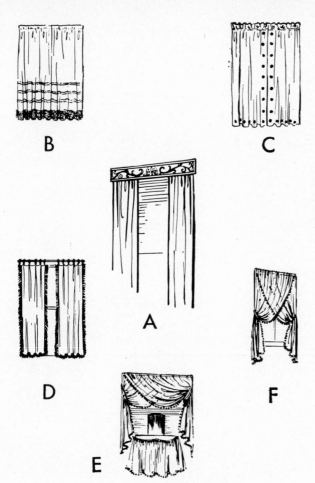

B

C

A

D

F

E

ATTRACTIVE BUT INEXPENSIVE WINDOW TREATMENTS

Sketch A (above) shows a cornice used with plain semi-sheer glass curtains and Venetian blinds with no other curtains or drapery. Sketches B, C and D illustrate ways in which inexpensive fabrics can be made into attractive glass curtains for use alone or with over-draperies. Sketch C shows a row of coin-dot embroidered motifs done in color around the edges of a pair of sheer curtains. Sketch B illustrates the use of an open fabric with lengths of colored yarn drawn through the meshes of the weave. This is easily done with a blunt needle or even a small bodkin. If the weave is too close for this, tie the yarn to a thread in a needle and pull it through after the thread. Sketch D shows a different type of fabric of a heavier homespun weave raveled out around the edges to make a self-fringe. Whip over the edges to prevent more raveling. Many other novelty ideas will occur to you, such as appliquéd cutouts and borders, stenciled motifs or applied bandings. Striped linen dish toweling makes gay dinette curtains. Note the three different styles in headings. For attaching sheer curtains by rings, as in D, reinforce the tops with tape or muslin. Lowly cheesecloth at almost nothing a yard is used to make the sheer tie-backs and the dressing-table skirt in sketches E and F. They illustrate two styles of draping for crossed curtains, both on two rods, one in front of the other. The ball fringe added to extreme fullness gives these curtains an air of real charm. A trick in keeping cheesecloth curtains fresh and lovely is to dip them in thin starch after laundering, stretch them out on the line to dry, and hang without pressing. They will look like new.

INSTALLING CORNICES

Sketch A (below) shows a simple cornice finished like the wall background. A plain cornice such as this may easily be used (instead of a valance board) as a foundation for various types of valance treatments. The detail drawing (B) demonstrates one method of installing poles or rods in a cornice. If you do not want to have the slots in the cornice itself you can merely use the box to cover any type of regulation rod or pole you prefer to use. The detail drawing (C) shows one design in a very popular type of adjustable extension cornice. These may be obtained in many styles and in sizes from 36″ to 120″. Ready-made cornices, cut to measure, are obtainable in any size whatsoever. A cornice may be the same height and width as the window, or extended to make it seem wider, or lifted to make it seem higher. With a low ceiling or a short window a cornice is often better than a valance. Its narrower width detracts less from the height of the room. When the top of the cornice is lower than the ceiling make a cover for the top to protect curtains from dust.

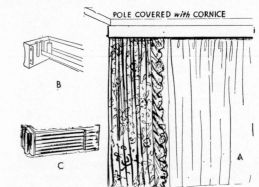

POLE COVERED *with* CORNICE

B

C

A

DECORATED CORNICE AND SIDE BORDERS GIVE UNITY TO A GROUP OF SMALL WINDOWS

In the gay morning room below a cornice over the window continues down the sides to make a frame for the window. The wallpaper dado of grayed yellow-green, yellow and white, with geranium-red accents, sets the color scheme for the room with its neutral off-white walls and ceiling. The provincial design on the cornice repeats the dado colors and semi-sheer draw-curtains (bound in geranium red) are a soft yellow. The serviceable rug is in the grayed yellow-green tone and wall shelves are painted red. The cheery outdoor effect of the room is emphasized by red geraniums and green plants and vines in bowls and window boxes. Bird prints correctly grouped above the sideboard are framed in the same soft maple used for the furniture.

THREE OF THE MANY STYLES IN SHEER RUFFLED TIE-BACKS

Fine sheer net or organdy used without other drapery can be made quite formal by the style of draping. In the photograph above, net—floor length and very full—is rounded at the bottom and all edges are finished with a narrow scalloped trimming. Tops of curtains are crossed under a shallow valance board which supports a double-draped swag-and-cascade valance. Tie-backs are correctly placed well below the center line of draperies. Dressing-table skirt is decorated by lines of the curtain trimming and a turned-up edge of this at the bottom. Note the interesting wall treatment. The plain broad stripes of the paper have been decorated on the dressing-table side of the room by application of wallpaper border in a lacy flounce design harmonizing with the sheer draperies. Around the mirror this border is arranged like a draped flounce. The attractive window at right (above) illustrates a popular style of dressing informal windows where plenty of light is needed. Short ruffled tie-backs are hung on a curved-end bracket rod over the window trim while straight ruffled sash curtains below are attached to the sash. Embroidered scalloped edges for the ruffles add a touch of color to the traditional whiteness of this type of curtain. The quaint wallpaper design goes well with simple Colonial-style furniture and gay old-fashioned oval rug. A style like this may be utilized for cutting down and remaking glass curtains. The summery effect of crisp sheer white used with figured chintz is shown in the room at right. A contrasting flounce on chintz draperies gives accent and tone to the window treatment, further emphasized by cutouts of the chintz applied to a white window shade behind the glass curtain frills. Note the low tie-back line.

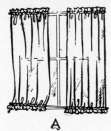

A

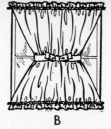

B

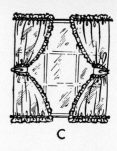

C

VARIOUS METHODS FOR ATTACHING
GLASS CURTAINS TO CURTAIN RODS

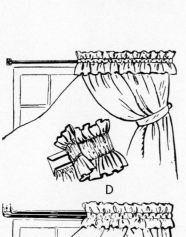

D

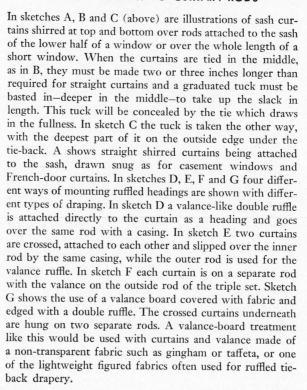

E

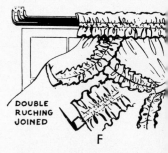

DOUBLE
RUCHING
JOINED

F

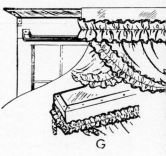

G

In sketches A, B and C (above) are illustrations of sash curtains shirred at top and bottom over rods attached to the sash of the lower half of a window or over the whole length of a short window. When the curtains are tied in the middle, as in B, they must be made two or three inches longer than required for straight curtains and a graduated tuck must be basted in—deeper in the middle—to take up the slack in length. This tuck will be concealed by the tie which draws in the fullness. In sketch C the tuck is taken the other way, with the deepest part of it on the outside edge under the tie-back. A shows straight shirred curtains being attached to the sash, drawn snug as for casement windows and French-door curtains. In sketches D, E, F and G four different ways of mounting ruffled headings are shown with different types of draping. In sketch D a valance-like double ruffle is attached directly to the curtain as a heading and goes over the same rod with a casing. In sketch E two curtains are crossed, attached to each other and slipped over the inner rod by the same casing, while the outer rod is used for the valance ruffle. In sketch F each curtain is on a separate rod with the valance on the outside rod of the triple set. Sketch G shows the use of a valance board covered with fabric and edged with a double ruffle. The crossed curtains underneath are hung on two separate rods. A valance-board treatment like this would be used with curtains and valance made of a non-transparent fabric such as gingham or taffeta, or one of the lightweight figured fabrics often used for ruffled tie-back drapery.

SPECIAL POLES AND ACCESSORIES FOR CURTAINING CASEMENT WINDOWS

As shown in sketch C (below), the use of concealed swinging cranes over stationary side-window panes, together with semi-transparent draperies, allows a maximum of light and air from the window. The effect would be softer if shirred glass curtains were used on the panes with the side draperies shown here. Draperies can be hung on short rods attached to the wall at each side of an inswinging casement, or by rings over ends of a long pole extending beyond the window. In this particular style of window (C) a valance could be used over the stationary upper panes. In sketch A, a more formal treatment, the heavy, lined over-drapery is attached by rings to an ornamental swinging crane. This is a favorite treatment for windows and French doors which open in. Glass curtains are usually shirred over panes when draperies like this are used. Sketch B illustrates the fact that any type of valance or swag over-drapery may be used with outswinging casements. Here a formal drapery is made by drawing heavy soft fabric in 50-inch width through large glass valance rings. If you want a valance over an inswinging window you must place it above the window so that it just covers the trim, and extend the board beyond the window for the side draperies.

C

A

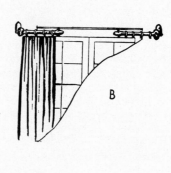

B

complement of finer weaves in sheer materials. For crisp tie-backs and other frothy ruffled curtains use cotton materials such as dotted Swiss, *point d'esprit*, sheer nets and organdies, either in permanently starched finish or with starch added in washing.

Treated nylon and such novelty fabrics as spun glass may represent more of an initial investment than other sheer materials, but in contrast to their usually short life these lovely fabrics are practically indestructible. The spun glass fiber fabrics are entirely unaffected by air, moisture, sun or dust, and will never become faded or yellow.

Types of Glass Curtains: Straight glass curtains should be very full (two or three times window width). They may have plain hems or be finished with deep fringe across the bottom to weight them and make them hang gracefully. Various novelty finishes are also used. When you need the utmost amount of light from your windows but still want them to appear decorative use one of the many types of ruffled tie-backs. They may be elaborate or simple, formal or informal, but they are always attractive if they are properly made, hung and cared for. The ruffled tie-back is probably the most popular American curtain, partly because of its adaptability for use with or without other drapery, and partly because of our Colonial tradition.

Ruffles are sometimes applied the length of the curtain at a distance back from the edge, as well as along the edge, and these curtains are either tied back, or allowed to hang straight.

Fine organdy used for ruffled tie-backs is so inherently decorative that it should rely upon its own charm and not be combined with over-draperies nor even with swags or valances of other fabrics. Make a frilled organdy heading, drape the curtains singly or cross them in a more elaborate style—but treat them as draperies covering the entire window trim.

Tie-backs for Ruffled Curtains: For ruffled curtains tie-backs are usually made of the curtain material and also ruffled, but they may be worked out in various other interesting ways. The length of the tie-back depends upon the amount of fullness which is to be held in, and varies from 14 to 20 inches. It is usually finished at the ends with rings or loops which are caught to a hook on the window frame. With sheer ruffles, wreaths and bouquets of artificial flowers bring a charming touch of summery colors to crisp white curtains. The most important point to consider in draping any curtain is the correct placing of the tie-back, either well above or well below the center of the curtain which should never be pulled awkwardly tight. Allow soft graceful curves on all draped edges. Try out your effects before you settle upon the final point for tie-backs.

Unlined Draperies: Glazed chintzes are often better unlined, as this allows the luminous effect of light shining through them to intensify their colors. Many fabrics are woven purposely so that the interest of the weave will be increased by light behind the drapery. These are colorfast and should not be lined. Semi-transparent draperies, of course, are never lined.

Drapery Trimmings: Even a simple cording or piping helps give a finished effect to draperies. Narrow grosgrain ribbon is a favorite binding or edging for light-weight materials and many varieties of woven strips or tapes in narrow bands known as gimps and galloons are traditional for trimming all heavier materials. They may be simple, or very decorative with glistening metal or cellophane threads interwoven through them. Fringes come in every type of finish, from the washable ball fringe to the most elaborate edgings made of bouclé, chenille, and the handmade tassel and ball fringes.

Drapery Tie-backs: Transparent glass curtains are never looped back, but almost all other types of draperies and curtains may be used with tie-backs of some kind if you prefer. Fabric tie-backs in the heavier drapery materials are always stiffened, and made either from the drapery fabric or some contrast material used for trimming. Many types of smart cord and tassel tie-backs can be bought and assembled. Heavily fringed tassels are very decorative. Informal tie-backs may be made of rope, knotted at the ends, and looped about the draperies. Before you take the trouble to make any kind of fabric tie-back, look through the shops for some of the distinctive novelty fixtures available.

Lined Draperies: The reasons for lining draperies are several. A lining greatly increases durability by protecting the curtain fabric from exposure to sun, dirt and dampness. It also insures better hanging and more grace in the drapery. Even glazed chintzes are often lined for wearability with a very thin silk, rayon or mercerized mull in a tone which does not change the color effect. Sateen is the universal lining material when the lining does not show. For most draperies the best lining color is a warm rose tan, but if they are made of printed fabric with a light ground, white or off-white is better.

Interlining makes certain fabrics hang much better, and may be used to give a rich graceful appearance to a material which might otherwise look a little light in weight for important draperies. For portières in doorways, or for draperies on swinging cranes, the additional weight of an interlining is helpful.

COMBINATION OF FABRICS IS OFTEN THE ANSWER

For successful alteration of draperies and curtains, study the photograph and sketches shown in this chapter. The wide flounce all around chintz draperies in the photograph would add several inches to their measurement and the valance above would lengthen them still more. Notice the combination of quilted fabric and chintz, with cutout appliqués. This attractive dressing-table chair can be made by cutting down the legs and back of an ordinary wooden chair and making a slip cover of the chintz. Chintz draperies which had been used in a room with several windows could be remade into a set like this. Also, ruffles in a different fabric may be used to increase the width and length of straight glass curtains which are converted into tie-backs. By using a wider ruffle even more fullness and length could be added to the curtains. If they are still too short you can piece them at the top under a ruffled valance which matches the ruffles

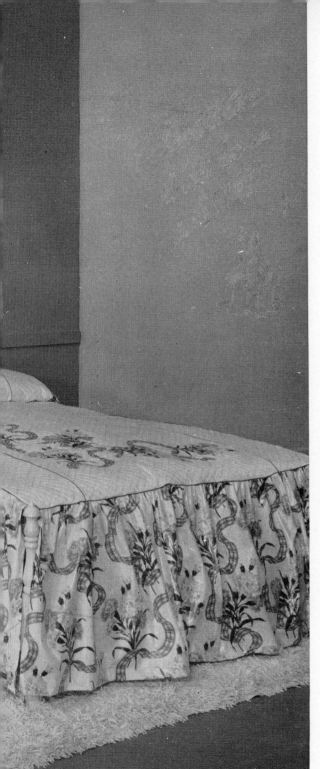

TO REMODELING PROBLEMS

on the curtains. This same kind of ruffled valance can be used over straight sheer curtains to cover piecing, or a pleated valance may serve the same purpose over heavy draperies. Light curtains may be edged with darker fabric, or darker curtains may be edged with light. If the curtains are pieced at the top, use flounce material opaque enough to cover the piecing. Ruffles all around (like those in the photograph) may be used also on glass curtain tie-backs.

CHAPTER FIFTEEN

Remaking Curtains and Draperies

THE PROBLEM of what to do with partly worn or faded curtains and draperies is often encountered. There is shrinking which was not sufficiently allowed for in buying or making; there is the day following moving day when draperies too good to be replaced must somehow be adapted to different sets of windows and a different background, and so on. In this chapter you will find suggestions which may be adapted to fit your particular needs. If not, you may be able to combine two or more of them in some way which will be helpful and they will serve as guide posts in working out your special problems.

In addition to re-using curtains and draperies at your windows, remember many drapery fabrics can be turned into upholstery for small chairs, slip covers, bed spreads, etc., by means of clever "piecing," by dyeing faded fabrics, and by combining materials.

REMAKING STRAIGHT GLASS CURTAINS

Sheer fabrics used for glass curtains usually give way first over the lower sections of the windows where sun and dust have most direct access to them. Here is a list of problems with suggestions for solution:

1. When straight floor-length curtains show signs of wear you can cut out the worn parts and make the curtains over into short straight Dutch half-curtains attached to the upper and lower sashes of the window sill; or you can use some kind of edging for frills around the two sections of the curtains, leaving the upper parts long enough for tie-backs while those over the lower sash hang straight.

2. With straight sill-length curtains worn at the bottom you can use the good top parts on the lower

section of the window, leaving the top uncurtained, or combine good sections from curtains for two windows to make double sash curtains for some other window.

3. When sheer straight curtains are worn or damaged for a few inches, or even as much as a foot, at top or bottom the bad sections can be cut off and the curtains treated according to the suggestions listed later for remodeling too-short curtains or draperies (page 210). Sometimes they can be given enough extra length just by taking out top and bottom hems and substituting facings, then adding wide fringe across the bottom.

4. If straight glass curtains are too small all around for your window you can always increase their size by putting flounces around them and turning them into ruffled tie-backs.

5. If sheer curtains are not full enough for the window you want to use them with you can widen them by following suggestions for widening draperies (page 211).

6. Don't forget that several fine quality sheer curtains with too little good material left for use as curtains may provide enough yardage for such things as dressing-table skirts, bed-canopy ruffles, lamp shades, etc. (See illustrations in this chapter.)

REMAKING RUFFLED GLASS CURTAINS

If you can match your fabric cut off the worn ruffle, making a new wider ruffle around the curtain. If you cannot match it, use other material with the same basic weave but some different finish. For instance, on dotted Swiss curtains use plain Swiss ruffles, or on plain curtains ruffles of the dotted fabric. Ruffles may be a different color, matching over-draperies or a dominating color in the room. If curtains are much too narrow join pieces of matching fabric to the front edges underneath the ruffles and put ruffling around the edges of the new pieces, making two ruffles down the length of each curtain. (See illustration page 211.) If you also need to lengthen them, carry the new pieces and the ruffles around the bottoms. Other adjustments in length can be made by use of alterations at the top which are the same as those used for lengthening draperies and straight curtains.

REMAKING DRAPERIES

When draperies are too far gone to be re-used at windows always save the good sections for use in other places. Scraps of cretonne are useful for bags, shelf curtains, or house aprons. Before you discard draperies as draperies be sure there is no way to re-use them at windows. You can sometimes combine several pieces for smaller windows in a different room. Good parts of two pairs of draperies can often be utilized to make one pair by joining the best parts of the four draperies into two. Seam them and hide the seams in the fullness, or make a feature of the seams by use of trimming bands, up and down, or across—whichever way your piecing has to go. Worn edges and bottoms can be cut off and the draperies adjusted by the same means as those listed for lengthening and widening. Here are a few suggestions which may help you:

1. One attractive use for salvaged sections of drapery material (or of sheer curtain fabric) is to make them up in the tiered style illustrated on facing page. The graduated flounces can be attached to plain lining material, or to lengths of plain sheer fabric, or to muslin salvaged from old sheets. They can be edged with trimming, narrow ruffles, or binding. This is an excellent way to utilize old drapery or curtain materials, or any other appropriate pieces of fabric you have on hand. For small short windows, flounces may even be made of worn linen napkins, dyed to match your room colors. Another possibility is to use old straight curtains or draperies as the foundation and add new flounces. A valance is attractive with tiered draperies, and may be either a top frill continued across the window on a rod, or a stiffened shaped valance, or a cornice box.

2. If your fabric is really good but there is not very much of it use it for edging, or for bands across the bottoms of other draperies; or try combining it with appropriate materials in the form of valances. Soft rich fabrics are particularly good for the easily made and easily put up festoon or swag valances which may be used alone, or over sheer curtains or as a heading for draperies. (See Chapter 14.)

DYEING FOR ECONOMY AND CHARM

3. Lined draperies may be made economical by the re-use of old drapery fabric for the lining. If the color is not right, you can strip the fabric of color, then dye it in any shade you like. It may give new life to an old pair of unlined draperies to line them with a colorful contrasting material salvaged as above. By draping them back so that the lining shows in a cascade effect, you will make your old draperies look like something entirely new. Plain fabric lined with cretonne often proves very attractive, just as does figured fabric lined with plain material in a gay color. (See illustration on facing page.) If the cretonne colors are not exactly right to go with the plain material you can dip the figured fabric in a weak dye bath which will change the color tone and still leave

SUGGESTIONS FOR
RENOVATING DRAPERIES

the design showing. Be sure to experiment on samples first.

Modern dyes and tints come with full directions for use and if the directions are followed carefully good results are invariable. One advantage of dyeing is that miscellaneous leftover pieces of fabric can be brought together into color harmony which allows their use in the same room. Extraordinary results have been obtained with inexpensive pieces of new cretonne in which colors were a little garish by dipping them in a weak solution of a neutral color like tan or gray.

Old linen or cotton sheets come out surprisingly well after a trip to the dye pot and may be used for many informal types of draperies and curtains. For remaking cretonne draperies inexpensively try combining them with unbleached muslin dyed to match

This photograph demonstrates interesting remake possibilities. The soft lines of the swag drapery are in a design suitable to almost any type of window except one in a strictly tailored or modern-style room. Here, for a bedroom, it is adapted to a double window and dressing-table arrangement developed in soft blue taffeta, with old rose taffeta lining and roses to hold draping and dressing-table swags. Note the correct draping of the taffeta curtains, with the roses placed well below the center of length at the side. You may drape curtains above center, or below, depending upon the effect you want. But grace of line disappears if the draping cuts their length in the middle. A dressing table like this could easily be turned out from a shelf or plain wooden box placed on its side to give an open front, the stool might be any discarded piano stool or round keg. The curtain lining could be made from old curtains cleaned and dyed to contrast with the outside, which would be very attractive in an inexpensive flowered chintz or dress fabric. Or faded chintz curtains could be revamped to line plain fabric, new or redyed. In the photograph at left tiered curtains are shown made from bordered fabric in a design which could also be worked out with plain material and an appliquéd border made from remnants, sewing leftovers or re-used draperies. Draperies too narrow or short can be cut into tiered sections and combined with other materials to fit any window. Notice the border applied on the floor above, and used also to make a "skirt" shade for the lamp. Chairs like this could be made in almost any home workshop with boxes for foundation and framework backs of heavy padded molding. Cushions and slip covers would complete the job.

DEEP FLOUNCES FOR WIDENING
CURTAINS OR DRAPERIES

The charming window treatment at right could be easily
adapted to enlarging old draperies without quite enough
fullness, or to the use of dress fabrics which are too narrow to be effectively full without piecing. Here blue and
white checked gingham was given sufficient width by the
addition of wide white frills, repeated around the edges of
the bed cover. With fullness controlled by French pleats,
and draped correctly high over full frilly white glass curtains, these draperies turned an ordinary window into a picture. Note the summery effect of artificial African daisies
tucked into the tie-backs and picking up the orange and
yellow in the plaid fiber rug. The walls of the room are
fresh blue and the ceiling lime yellow, with these colors
carried into chair upholstery and flower prints on plain
walls. The color scheme is interesting as an example of how
the three primary colors can be used by muting them a little.
Here the blue and yellow are both soft shades, and the red
of the third primary color appears only as an element in the
orange of the rug and in red accent notes in the chintz on
the chair and in the flower prints.

As shown in sketch A, too-short draperies ruin appearance
of any window. Several methods are illustrated for correct-

HOW TO ADD LENGTH
WHEN DRAPERIES
ARE TOO SHORT
FOR A WINDOW

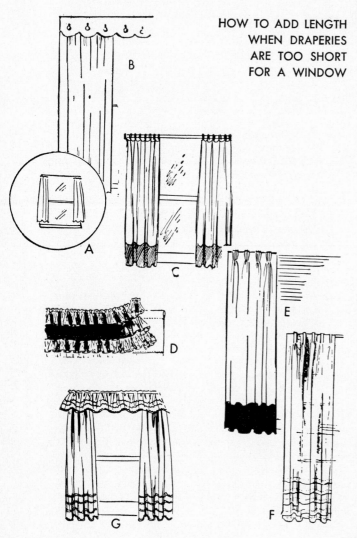

ing this situation. In sketch C a double hem (or a faced
band) of fabric is added at the bottom of each curtain. This
fabric should usually be a little heavier than the fabric above
it, but as nearly as possible the same color. The effect is
richer if there is contrast in weight and texture rather than
in color, although when the drapery or curtain is very long
a contrast in color as well as in texture may be desirable.
With sheer curtains (as shown here) these bands may be
added with hemstitching, rick-rack braid, narrow insertion,
or other suitable trimming. With heavy fabrics (sketch E)
a welted cording or piping makes a very handsome heading
for the band without being too conspicuous. If your draperies are of brocade or a heavy-ribbed fabric, velvet or
velveteen will make effective bands. For soft silk or rayon
curtains in ninon or marquisette, rayon jersey or some soft
novelty fabric would be attractive. With draperies of napped
materials such as velvet or velour use a heavy upholstery
satin for the hems. If you still have not enough length, lower
the curtains as in B by attaching them below the pole, or
piece the tops of the draperies and cover the piecing with a
valance of the fabric used for the hem (see B). Sketch G
illustrates draperies or curtains lengthened by adding rows
of trimming to camouflage a lengthened section. The piecing
at the top is covered by a valance, also trimmed. The shirred
valance shown here is especially good for thinner materials
and may be in one flounce or a triple flounce as shown in
D. Flounced valances are equally good for lengthening ruffled tie-backs or any kind of ruffled curtains. Pieces can be
added above French pleats, or any other heading, to go
under a smart shaped valance like the one in sketch B. In
sketch F sheer curtains are shown with tucked pieces stitched
on under tucks to look as if they were part of the original
plan. This device is a very good one to use with any unlined fabric which is not too heavy. In this sketch note the
cartridge pleats used at the top to control fullness.

210

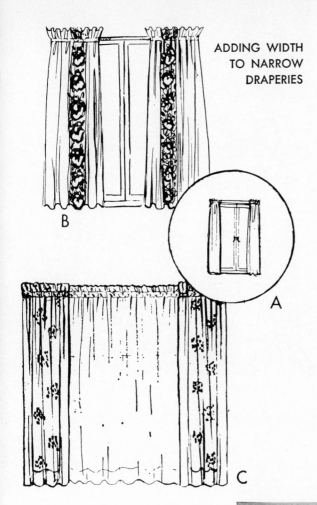

ADDING WIDTH TO NARROW DRAPERIES

B

A

C

The very modern living room below combines black cotton with wide applied strips of soft Delft blue felt for draperies and slip covers. Bands like this can be set in instead of applied if plain draperies need widening. Sketch D shows a method for stitching together narrow lengths of fabric in several harmonizing colors to make very effective draperies. After the seaming they can be pressed into pleats which will bring the folds over the seams so that each drapery will look like a solid piece of fabric in various color tones. This device is often very useful when you have a chance to pick up remnants, or have one pair of draperies which must be expanded for use on more than one window. Sketches B and C illustrate two attractive methods for widening too-narrow draperies or curtains (as in A). Sketch B shows a band of figured fabric set into the drapery from top to bottom. If necessary, additional bands could be added at the outside edges. In sketch C a pair of figured draperies and a pair of plain are combined where the originals were too short as well as too narrow. The plain fabric is used to make a border completely around the figured panel. This same device can be used by combining plain centers with figured borders; old draperies can be enlarged with new material. Sketch E shows a different method for lengthening and widening draperies. The band at the top is stitched to the curtain instead of being used as a valance to cover a piecing seam. The same kind of band is applied as a double false hem added to the drapery at the bottom and up front edges. This trimming fabric is also used for tie-backs. The sketch shows a casing applied to the top of the band to give the effect of a valance without use of a valance board.

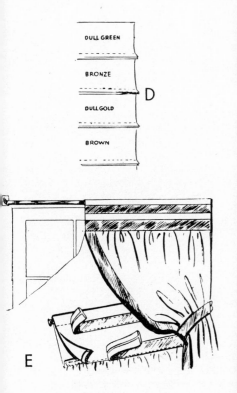

DULL GREEN

BRONZE

D

DULL GOLD

BROWN

E

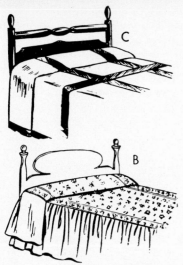

TURNING DRAPERIES INTO SLIP COVERS

The group of smart bed and slip covers above could be made of plain drapery fabric, new or dyed for re-use, combined with chintz flounces made of leftovers or remnants. The wall background of striped paper sets off the plain and figured fabrics to advantage. Patterns are available for these covers, shown here in solid-color glazed dimity with gay violet-patterned borders. Notice the smart heavy cording and large buttons on the chair slip cover, and the graceful lines of the table. A table cover like this is easy to make and allows the use of a table not good-enough looking to be refinished but sturdy enough for service. A fabric circle is cut with its diameter twice the height of the table plus distance across the top (allow for flounce in measuring).

MAKING USE OF LEFT-OVERS

A made-over skirt applied to a kidney-shaped dressing table (as shown above) with center front opening for the arms to swing out adds charm to a bedroom. The ruffle could be in plain color matching the ribbon used for bows. Note that the fabric in the photograph above is used also for lamp shades and mirror frame. The first step in transforming curtains which have outlived original usefulness is to rip open seams. Then remove stitches from all ruffles, etc., launder and iron pieces, dyeing if necessary. Apply patterns as to new material. In sketch C (above) pieces of fabric are seamed together to make an attractive tailored spread with seams covered by stitched bands in a contrasting color or texture. B illustrates a type of spread very well adapted to combination of salvaged materials. In sketch A is shown the decorating effectiveness of a chintz shade used with plain valance and side draperies. These shades are also attractive in windows where sheer tie-back curtains are used with or without over-drapery. They may easily be made from remnants or leftovers, especially when the fabric is glazed chintz. With figured over-draperies try applying cutouts from the pattern to the lower part of the shade.

HOME CLEANING FOR DRAPERIES

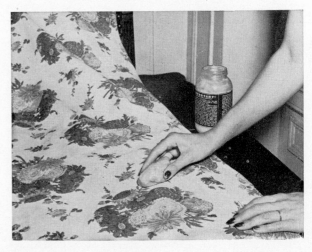

Non-washable chintz draperies are being cleaned above with wallpaper cleaner, molded into a soft, flat ball. Smooth draperies on a large table and work as directed. This cleaner can be used on chintz lampshades also, or upholstery.

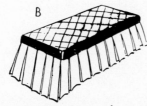

COMBINING QUILTED FABRIC WITH PLAIN OR PATTERNED MATERIALS

These sketches show a decorating scheme for use of new material or re-use of old. Here the leftover drapery material is dyed in a light tint and combined with two quilted mattress pads dyed in a contrast (or darker) tone. The bolster roll on the bed can be made from heavy buckram and used for pillow-storage. The stool (A) can be made from any old keg, or from an unused piano stool. The box (B) makes an excellent storage-chest placed under a window or at the foot of a bed. You can use an ordinary packing box in the size you want, lining it with oilcloth or glazed quilted fabric. Hinge the top for a lid and pad it to make a cushion-seat. Use a band of trimming or a fold of fabric or a narrow pleated frill around the edge of the lid. If you have a dressing table (or want one) you can dress it in the same fashion.

The photograph below suggests a way to reverse the combination of quilted and plain or patterned materials. A set of curtains from two windows would supply the chintz shown here for over-drapery, bed-spread top and bindings. In this set the quilting is in dark green sateen, the chintz in a flowered pattern on a pale blue ground. Notice the flared circular cut of the quilted skirt and its use as a covering for the headboard of the bed.

This photograph illustrates use of wallpaper cleaner for Venetian blinds—a method which saves both time and hands, while it leaves slats smoothly clean. Be sure to follow directions in using cleaner.

one of the colors in the pattern. It comes out of the dye bath with a finish almost like French linen. For sheer glass curtains a very thin cheesecloth can be dyed yellow, orange, pale green, lavender, coral, or some other pastel tint. Dried without pressing, it comes out in a crinkled effect which is charming when the curtains are made very full and softly draped. You can edge the cheesecloth with inexpensive cotton ball fringe dyed the same color. Leftovers from silk or rayon dress material, or fragments of old draperies may be dyed for swag valances. A full skirt from an evening dress can be dyed and used for tiered curtains or a dressing table skirt. One word of caution: Test your shade on a sample after it is dry. Dyed or tinted fabrics always look darker when they are wet.

If draperies are lined the lining must be taken out and dyed separately, otherwise it may shrink differently and spoil the hang of the draperies.

REMAKING WINDOW SHADES

It is extraordinary how much decorative window shades can do to bring new brightness into an informal room. Glazed chintz and light-weight cretonnes are excellent fabrics if you want figured patterns on the shades. If you are using material with figures be sure the motifs are centered on each shade, and in the same place on all shades in the room. When you are cutting fabric allow for a 1½-inch hem on both edges, to be put in by hand or machine. For a decorative effect finish the bottom of the shade with cotton edging or fringe in the background color of the fabric.

Decorative Window Sills: Try decorating your sills and protecting them at the same time by fitting them with glass, mirror, or colorful tiles which match your draperies or your room colors. Carefully fitted sections of linoleum or other composition wall and floor materials may be used in the same way to make decorative window sills. If the sills are deep, lined covers for them are attractive made of the fabric used for over-draperies.

COMFORT AND CHARM, WITHOUT CROWDING, IN A

Clever planning and buying made this double-duty room into a complete, attractive one-room home, with a comparatively small outlay of money. The room is long and narrow so a dining alcove has been created by building in a closet at one side of the double windows (draped as one), and using a pair of tall six-fold shutter screens to set off the alcove and conceal the kitchenette at the other side of the window. A sealed-in fireplace and chimney breast is made

into a center-of-interest feature by facing it with mirror panels which broaden the room by reflecting the opposite side. Addition of twin chests helps provide a second small alcove, out of traffic lanes, for game table and chairs. The bed-couch is flanked by a writing-table desk (with book shelves below) and a chest of drawers instead of small occasional tables. Furniture is in blond wood in ready-made stock models. The love seat at the left of the couch is made up of

CHAPTER SIXTEEN

How to Buy Furniture

NO ARTICLE of furniture in a room, not even a tiny accessory, can live to itself alone. It must be an integral, and integrated, part of the whole. Before you start out to look at furnishings make a plan-model of your room (see page 36), then work out just what you *think* you are going to need. This plan should take into account the same factors as your original room-composition plan including suitability, comfort, family activities, comparative permanence of your present quarters, and so on. List everything you want in the room. This will include, first, all items indispensable for the proper functioning of the room—enough chairs, tables, lamps, etc. Second, additional things which fill in the outlines of your picture—special comfort, luxury or beauty items. Third, accessories.

PLAN YOUR BUYING

After a few exploratory shopping excursions you may change this plan, but never change it on the spur of the moment. Before you buy any major piece of furniture try out the alteration as it will affect your floor plan and the composition of your whole picture. That handsome, inviting lounge chair you couldn't resist on the spacious floor in the furniture department may be so large when you get it home that it will look like an elephant in a herd of deer when you put it with your other chairs. So take home its measurements and see what happens when you place the proportioned model on the floor plan just where it is to stand in relation to the rest of the furniture.

Budget your money as nearly as you can, concentrating on the indispensables. Then start out on a

REMODELED ALL-PURPOSE ROOM

twin chairs slip-covered like the drapery. These can be used separately if desired. The modern shaggy room-sized rug is gray in a little darker tone than the gray of the wall. The couch is in soft dark green and the plain chair in rosy red. The white textured cotton background of the drapery fabric is splashed with rosy flowers and green foliage, making up a gay complementary color scheme against a neutral background in walls and floor.

tour of inspection before you make any permanent decisions. Check the prices you have only guessed at with those you find in reliable shops and revise your estimates accordingly. *Do all your shopping on paper* before you begin to buy, then you won't be rushed off your feet either by your own enthusiasm or by super-salesmanship. From the lowest, up to the medium grades, the price of furniture is related to the actual *value* of the piece with reference to design, basic wood, construction and finish. From that point on you are paying not for more durability, nor satisfaction, nor even beauty, but for various special qualities and refinements—novelty, superfine fabrics, exotic or rare woods, handwork, unusual grain in veneers, or the intangible of limited production. These are all desirable in their place, but they are not essential in the average home and are often obviously inappropriate in simple surroundings. So, if your budget has limits, shop for *values.*

BASIC FURNITURE

Wise buying means spending the larger part of your budget on the articles which are expected to stay in service longest and must therefore stand up under wear. When you buy basic furniture you judge it as you would judge a basic dress for your wardrobe. That means you will put your money into good fundamental construction, quality of materials, and enduring beauty of design. If it is upholstered furniture you are buying choose quality in a muslin cover and change slip covers from time to time to harmonize with a new color scheme or decorating program.

Whatever the type of furniture buy the best quality you can afford; but be sure you are paying for *quality,* not for useless decorations or some transitory novelty. Don't buy cheaply made, run-of-the-mill furniture and label that "economy." Instead, dig up some old furniture which is sufficiently substantial and well put together to be worth cutting down, refinishing, or otherwise doing over.

If this is not possible, buy something in the frankly inexpensive class, but good of its kind. If you can't even do that, fill in with tables and side chairs from the unpainted furniture department of the store, or even from the kitchen section. Paint these attractively, decorate them in harmonious designs; or rub them with stain and wax them, or dress them up with pads and fabric slips. When you are ready to replace them they can always be made useful somewhere in a bedroom, kitchen, hobby room, hallway, or porch.

One major piece of real distinction combined with comfortable and attractive but frankly temporary articles will do more for your room than a compromise which spreads your money out over a roomful of mediocre furniture. Also, *too little* furniture is always better than *too much.*

Take Time to Shop Around: Furniture buying should always be done in stores you can trust and in such stores the salesmen are usually both intelligent and accommodating. State your problems frankly and ask them to let you study the stock before you decide on your purchases. In many larger stores you will find there is a decorating department where you can get expert professional advice without cost. Naturally, if you place no monetary strings on your buying program these specialists may serve their stores by steering you into higher spending brackets; but their real function is to create good will for the store and if they know that involves money-saving in your case they will cheerfully work on your problem from that angle.

Unless you live in a very small place don't confine your shopping to one store. Nothing is more annoying than to accept something you don't really want, then after it is too late run across exactly what you were looking for in another shop. Another advantage of shopping around is that you will discover many charming or useful things you had not known about. Manufacturers are continually bringing out new time- or space-saving furniture. Unless you are a confirmed shopper the array of plastics in all forms, ingenious double-duty designs, improved lighting devices, will amaze you. There are chairs with storage space beneath hinged seats, built so they can be shoved together for love seats. All types of new folding and expanding furniture are available.

Buying in Pairs or Sets: Buying in pairs is an excellent idea for chairs, small tables, chests of drawers, lamps, even love seats. Pairs will help you work out restful balanced arrangements; but do not be tempted to buy suites—not even bedroom suites. They are usually stiff and stereotyped. Your room will have more charm and more personality if you do your own harmonizing of separate pieces and work them into a plan which expresses your own taste.

For a dining room it may be necessary to buy a certain number of matching pieces—two arm chairs alike, for example, and a set of chairs for the other seats at the table. But don't think you have to invest in the conventional table, sideboard, serving table, and set of chairs. You will find many suggestions in pictures in this book for assembling your dining room pieces in a way which will express real charm and individuality.

For anyone on a budget this emancipation from the suite idea is a real blessing. It means that you can start with one really good piece and gradually surround it with things which do not match, but

TWIN CHESTS IN BEDROOMS ARE CONVENIENT AND SMART

The attractiveness as well as the convenience of buying in pairs is illustrated in the two bedrooms on this page. In the upper picture twin chests create a dressing-table nook in an alcove by combination with a mirror and a mirrored table which fit exactly into the space. The wood is in soft blond finish, against aqua walls and rug. The butterfly decorations are bright-colored cutouts pasted on the wall. Notice the use of the ottoman for a comfortable dressing-table seat. When not needed it makes a chaise longue out of the arm chair. In the room below the twin-chest idea is carried out in traditional mahogany and traditional type designs, proving that this convenience need not be confined to furniture in the modern style. Notice the effective way in which double windows at the end of the room have been draped with draw-curtains under a continuous valance to make a frame for the bed. Where floor space is limited you can often find twin chests made without legs which can be placed on top of another chest rather than side by side as in these pictures. The upper one should have fewer drawers than the lower, and if it is slightly smaller that will not matter. In buying chests remember that even in the traditional models you will find many styles made up so that a section of the chest opens to form a desk when needed. Don't overlook the possibility of small twin chests for bedside tables and end tables. They take up no more space than conventional tables and serve many more uses.

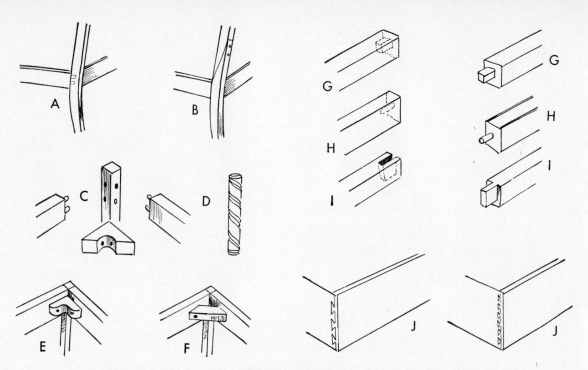

ESSENTIAL POINTS IN SOUND WOOD FURNITURE CONSTRUCTION

These sketches will give you an idea of what to look for in the way of solid construction when you are buying wood furniture. The hind legs of any article of furniture should be part of the design—not just sticks to prop up the back of a chair or desk or chest of drawers. Sketches A (right) and B (wrong) illustrate why one method is so much stronger than the other. In A you will see outlines of the mortise-and-tenon joining which is one of the approved methods for holding furniture parts together. In sketches C and D you will see how this type of joining works and why it is so solid and substantial. The cylindrical pegs shown are called dowels. The grooves serve to permit the escape of air and prevent air pockets in the glue which is used to strengthen all types of joinings. Sketches C and E show how a chair post should be joined to the chair rails. The central figure is the chair leg. In the correct method (E) dowels are used with a corner block screwed in for additional reinforcement. F shows the wrong kind of corner block, not fitted into the corner, and nailed in place instead of being screwed. Nails are not used anywhere in well-constructed furniture, and screws only in bracing this corner block. Check any piece

of wood furniture which must carry a load by these sketches, also wood frames for upholstered pieces. Sketches G, H, and I show the three tested methods for solid joinings—G, mortise and tenon; H, dowel; I, tongue and groove. Sketch J illustrates a dovetailed hand-made joining of the front and side of a drawer, also a machine-made dovetail joining. The larger size dovetailing is characteristic of hand-made construction. Drawers should always be put together with good glue in dovetail joints—never with nails or screws. They should not only be properly joined, they should also be finished on the inside (underside, too) and separated by dust-proof partitions. A three-ply panel makes the best bottom for a drawer because it does not warp. The use of good wood, such as mahogany or oak, in the sides of drawers and their general finish are helpful clues to the quality of construction throughout the piece. In sketch K correct usage is shown in turning out a curved furniture leg. The piece is cut from solid wood, not made up by glueing on a knee curve. In L correct use of plywood around a curved corner is contrasted with the wrong method where a separate piece is inserted at the curve making for weakness at a critical point.

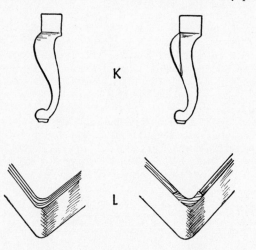

SMALL CABINET BAR BECOMES A USEFUL MODERN CONSOLE-CABINET WHEN THE DOORS AND TOP ARE CLOSED

SECTIONAL UNITS OFFER MANY COMBINATION POSSIBILITIES

In addition to the unit grouping of twin pieces of furniture, modern design has introduced a wide variety of assembly units. Here are shown a few interesting examples of what can be done in this way. The cabinet at upper right consists of several sections put together on a separate base. The record cabinet has a door which doubles as an occasional table or even a small writing desk. The cabinet at the left is prepared for a radio or television set. Notice in this room the modern lines of the cabinet and mirror combined with the quaint old flower print in an oval frame and the French Provincial-style chair with its tailored upholstery cover of blue and white bed-ticking. The soft over-all rug is in tufted cotton; the chintz of the slip cover is repeated in the shade of the pottery lamp; the pattern of the paper used for wall and ceiling is reproduced from a design in which printed pages of a book are scattered at random over-

lapping so that only the paper of the printed pages forms a background. The black and white print creates an exceptionally soft and lovely grayed effect. The dressing table at the left is made up of two small chests (which would serve equally well as bed tables) flanking a small occasional table exactly the same height and width. Notice the dramatic pattern of the woven cotton rug used on a painted wood floor. The useful furniture alcove above is created by grouping of desk, shelf, and table units all made with flush surfaces to fit smoothly together. The desk has a pull-out shelf for a portable typewriter, a letter file drawer on a double-extension slide and two book shelves set into the back. The contour chair is made with a light bentwood frame. The table-and-chair dining unit which helps enclose the alcove is part of the assembly group—which can be had in light or dark finish and arranged in many groupings.

do blend in a subtle harmony which is much more pleasing.

A great deal of the furniture which is planned for selling as units, or combinations, or double-duty furniture is developed in modern style and modern materials, but even if you do not like modern furniture it may give you ideas you can translate into traditional pieces. Two chests of drawers side by side, with a big mirror covering the wall behind both of them, in any design which allows them to be placed flush with each other so that there is no gap between them, will give you the same space-saving convenience as some specially built unit pieces.

straight and curved lines, between horizontal and vertical lines. Don't let monotony creep in. Use harmonizing but different textures and colors, and planned contrasts. Develop your taste by studying pictures and model rooms—then trust it. When you outgrow the room—through further education—do it over. You can always manage this once you learn to do it on a step-by-step basis, one thing at a time.

This step-by-step method can also be applied to a room which you are slowly redecorating over a period of time. Your problem is to fit a few new pieces harmoniously into old surroundings, yet make them an adequate nucleus for the lovely new room you

SPACE-SAVING CONSOLE-CABINET

The furniture groupings on these pages illustrate several important points in buying. The pieces are all well built and beautifully finished, whether modern or reproductions of traditional forms. The modern cabinet is a type very well adapted for use in a living room, dining room, or combination of living room with dining room or bedroom. It will also serve in a foyer or hall instead of a console table. This

18TH CENTURY CREDENZA AND CHAIRS

adaptability is one of the advantages of modern design. A chest like this takes up no more space than a console table but is much more useful. The same advantages may be had from the credenza and the small commode in the two center pictures. These are shown here in hallways but they could be used equally well in any other room. The credenza type of furniture is particularly good in dining rooms and double-

Many other adaptions will suggest themselves if you go through the shops with your eyes and your mind open. And if you do this *before* you buy, the new ideas can be harmoniously incorporated into your original plan without upsetting your budget calculations.

Don't Go to Extremes: Whatever your decorating scheme, keep it livable. Don't make your room a museum of period furniture or any other type. Combine your antiques, or your period reproductions, or your modern pieces, with others in appropriate design and harmonious feeling. In every period and every region, from the earliest days down to the very latest mode, there have been examples of good furniture—and bad. So in any style or period look for grace in design. Don't forget balance between

hope will some day emerge from the chrysalis of the old. In this situation don't let the old things limit your choice too seriously. It is much better to get a few things you really want for your new nucleus, then spend a little money (plus time and thought) to bring the rest of the room temporarily into focus with these. This may often be done inexpensively by the use of color in paint, by all-concealing slip covers, by gradual elimination of the worst offenders against harmony.

WOOD FURNITURE

In buying new furniture, there are three values to be checked—design, construction and finish. The first is largely a matter of taste. As your taste becomes trained by looking at pieces accepted as right for whatever period or style they belong to, you will be able instinctively to recognize whether the lines of a piece of furniture are good, mediocre, or bad. There are no hard and fast rules in this field—only the general principles of grace, suitability and comfort.

With the high development of precision machine work, hand construction is no longer the exclusive hallmark of quality it was once considered, and much fine wood furniture is turned out at least partly by machine. The finest finishes are still done by means of patient hand work, but new finishing

employed instead of hand work. In this group it is safest to avoid carving and elaborate design. By sticking to simpler forms you can put all the money allowed for your purchase into basic quality; at the same time you will save future work taking care of the furniture.

3. "Low Grade"—which goes by the trade name of "borax furniture"—is sloppily designed, made of inferior woods, and put together in whatever way is quickest and cheapest, decorated with pressed wood glued on in imitation of carvings, and usually finished with thick stain under a coat of shiny varnish. If you *must* buy anything in this group select

SMALL COMMODE WITH HEPPLEWHITE CHAIRS

duty living rooms. The grouping of chairs and cabinet is something to keep in mind when you are buying, also the accessories to go with the cabinet. In both of these groups balance is achieved by proper size in ornaments and wall decoration plus matching chairs in harmonious period and scale. By planning your group in advance you can be sure of having it harmonious as it should be. If you want a con-

EIGHTEENTH CENTURY CONSOLE-CARD-TABLE

sole table instead of a chest you can still get double service by selecting one like that shown in the picture above. The back makes a lovely frame for flowers or other ornament and can be let down to convert the table into one the right size for cards or lunching. Notice the chairs in these pictures. If you have even one chair-tipper in your home, don't buy any small chair without stretchers for reinforcement.

materials, veneers, for instance, are changing even that.

Grading Furniture: In general, furniture falls into three groups, with certain definite characteristics for each group. This applies, of course, to new furniture—not to antiques.

1. "Standard" designates the best in construction, design, and finish. It is usually the most expensive, with only the finest materials in all the concealed parts as well as in those which show on the surface. Edges and turnings are clean. Carvings (in the wood itself) are clear and sharp.

2. "Medium" includes many intermediate grades in which the pieces are usually very well constructed, though materials are less fine, less hand work is used, and the new commercial finishing methods are often

a design stripped free of all camouflage, carvings and other decoration.

The danger points in buying wood furniture are not in those pieces which come clearly under the three group headings, but in those which fall into a sort of transition zone between. It is here that a rudimentary knowledge of construction will be really worth while for you.

Furniture Woods and Veneers: Cabinet woods are such familiar friends as mahogany and walnut, maple and oak, with several other woods occurring less frequently. Among these are birch, beech, sycamore, gum, poplar, pine, hickory, teakwood, rosewood, ebony. Novelty woods such as laurel, ash, harewood, zebrawood, and many other rare varieties are used for special types of furniture. Some of them are not strong enough for solid construction but have a very beautiful grain which makes them useful in the form of veneers. Many types of modern strong laminated plywoods are also valuable in making furniture, and veneers have always played an important part in fine woodworking. Solid wood must be used for areas to be carved and for structural parts of beds, chairs and legs of tables, etc. But for flat and curved surfaces beautifully grained veneers of more expensive woods are often desirable. The only caution here is that while good modern veneering is done with glues stronger than the wood itself, and is very satisfactory, the cheaper veneers are applied carelessly, with inferior glues, and will soon crack or peal away from the foundation wood.

How to Judge Construction: Good construction follows very definite rules. Examine the joints first, no matter what type of furniture you are buying. In all grades except the lower brackets, joints are carefully fitted together by one of the methods illustrated here (page 218). If there is hardware, check that. It should be in scale with the piece and in harmony with its design. If you are buying a chair you should sit in it to be sure it is level with the floor.

Rock a table to check on the same thing. Carefully examine a large chest with drawers after you get it in the place where it is to stand in your home. If it seemed all right in the shop and yet is not even on your floor, this is probably a defect in the floor. Use a small wedge to level the chest of drawers so it will stand true. Leaving it on the uneven surface often causes it to settle and throw the drawers out of line enough to interfere with their smooth working.

All these qualities of good construction are obtainable not only in the best, or standard, grades of furniture, but also in the better medium grades. It is only in low-grade furniture (no matter what price is asked for it) that you find splintery wood in drawers, butted joints nailed or glued together, cheap stained veneers posing as solid woods. This fraud can be easily exposed by examining the edges of the wood. Whether or not the table top or chair seat is solid will show up on these edges. Plywood or veneer may in many cases be better for surface sections than solid wood—but not in low-grade furniture.

How to Judge Finish: Nothing else has yet equalled the exquisite soft velvety gloss—the patina—imparted to fine antique furniture by years of careful waxing and polishing over an original finish applied long ago by painstaking hand craftsmen. The object in modern reproductions is to produce as nearly as possible this antique effect.

All the best (standard) grades of furniture have a finish entirely done by hand. The process is exacting and necessarily expensive—but it is more effective

TRADITIONAL PIECES CLEVERLY DESIGNED FOR MORE THAN ONE USE

In your shopping expeditions be on the lookout for occasional pieces which not only have charm but also serve several purposes. The nest of tables shown in this group is especially interesting because of the arrangement of the two large tables side by side under a top table long enough for use as a coffee table.

The traditional library steps above make charming end tables and provide extra storage for odds and ends which always need to be kept out of sight.

Portable or folding tables are very useful. This small butterfly table would take up very little space at the end of a couch or beside a chair, but opens to a tea-table size. The table next to it has sides which make it easy to pick up like a tray and move it about.

Attractive and convenient, this modern-style drop-leaf but-terfly table has casters large enough so that it rolls easily about and acts as a portable serving table as well as dining space for two. Top and shelf are surfaced with blond lino-leum.

This all-plastic group illustrates the ethereal delicacy of transparent plastic, which is nevertheless as strong as any well-constructed furniture. This unusual table is set for en-tertaining, for which it is well adapted with its heatproof and damage-proof glass shelves. Notice the flower bowl on the lower shelf which becomes part of the graceful table design. In buying tables try to keep them in proper heights and in scale with the furniture they will be used with. Tables placed at the ends of sofas should reach to the top of the arms and should set the standard for all other end tables in the room. If you cannot buy these in the same height cut off the legs to bring them down. Don't buy small unsubstan-tial coffee tables. In front of a couch oblong tables should be sturdy, long and low—as much as five and a half by two and a half feet. A round coffee table should be at least 30 inches in diameter, and all coffee tables should come just below the edge of the couch, usually not more than 11½ inches from the floor.

than any of the easier methods in general use. A fine finish should be of eggshell softness, with no glare, showing the grain of the wood clearly even when it has been stained.

Medium-grade furniture is sometimes hand-fin-ished, sometimes machine-finished, and sometimes has a combination of the two. The machine finish is often applied by spraying quick-drying shellac, varnish, or lacquer over the stained surface. One ad-vantage of the new synthetic lacquers (entirely dif-ferent from Oriental lacquer finishes) is that they can be made comparatively resistant to heat, moisture and alcohol. With some of these lacquers a very satis-factory effect is achieved, but it is usually still better when it has been rubbed down afterward by hand. You can improve medium-grade furniture by home treatment and give it a much softer sheen—but don't pay first-grade prices for any medium-grade finish.

Low-grade furniture has what you would expect of this class—the cheapest possible finish. This usually consists of staining (which fills up the pores of the wood to conceal the lack of fine grain) in colors chosen to imitate some better wood than that used in the construction. A coat of shiny gloss varnish fol-lows, undimmed by rubbing down. Even this can be improved by working on it at home, but don't waste strength and time on *new* furniture. If you are going to expend that much effort on a new piece, it is much better to put your money all into better construction and buy the unfinished furniture available in great variety in the stores. Doing over a really cheap finish means removing what is there and starting over—not just refining or touching up. That much work is usually wasted on a poorly constructed piece with a short service-life ahead of it.

UPHOLSTERED FURNITURE

Upholstered furniture is more difficult to judge than wood furniture because of two factors, fabric finishes and cushioning. The cushioning is entirely hidden by the coverings and a large part of the wood framework is covered too. You cannot very well take the chair to pieces before you buy it, so you will have to rely on a few construction clues and on the reputation of the retailer or manufacturer.

Prices range through a very wide field—from less than ten dollars for a little occasional chair up to hundreds for the finest workmanship and materials in a large chair or sofa. Your only safety is to refuse to make a heavy investment in this type of furniture unless you are satisfied that you are buying value. Don't think your upholstered furniture must be large and heavy in order to be comfortable. The lighter, more graceful designs may be just as comfortable, or even more so. It is a matter of construction and line, not bulk. But don't forget to consider also the size and tastes of the people who will use the furniture—specially chairs.

Importance of Labels: If possible, insist upon a label before you buy any piece of upholstered furniture. Many states now require labels attached to all upholstery stating the exact contents of the inside materials used for both built-in spring sections and loose cushions. All the following items below may not be covered on the label, but some of them will be.

The best framework wood is birch, white ash, rock maple, hickory. Gum, poplar, soft maple, basswood, and pine are also satisfactory materials. Make sure that construction follows the same principles of joining as good wood furniture—dowelled, and strongly glued, with legs part of the frame. A firm framework is doubly important in a sofa, which must be prepared to carry the weight of several people. A test for rigidity of the framework is to lift one end from the floor. If the sofa responds to the lifting with no swaying or warping along its length, it is probably well enough made to be a good buy. If the wood is one of the strong varieties mentioned above it should hold that strength over a long period of time, given a reasonable amount of wear. Check to be sure the frame has the correct corner blocks, bracing all four of the legs. When these blocks are placed only at the front corners, and not at the back, support is lacking just where it is needed most. This is a defect often found in cheaply built frames. (See page 218.)

The springs in well-constructed upholstery are made of coiled, finely tempered metal with closed ends, set close together, and tied with heavy French cord. This tying and sewing hold the springs to the webbing with from four to eight strings and the coils are also tied to each other. Cheap construction uses open-end springs too far apart and too loosely anchored with flimsy twine. The springs soon break loose from their moorings and poke through the webbing or the upholstery. Between these two extremes are many grades.

The best material for filling in over the springs is long-stapled, curled horse-hair, usually covered by a layer of cotton felt which keeps the hair from working through the covering. Less desirable grades of hair range down to the short bristles of hog hair which is straight and lacks resilience. In a really well-made chair the filling is about 80% horse-hair with 20% cotton. Kapok, which is sometimes used, starts out by being light in weight and resilient, but disintegrates after a period of use. Moss, African fiber, tow, excelsior, and other such materials are found only in the cheapest grades of upholstery. They soon pad into lumps and masses.

COMFORT IN FURNITURE DOES NOT DEPEND UPON SIZE

The small arm chair above is shown as a reminder that comfortable chairs do not always have to be large, overstuffed models. Chairs of the boudoir type, properly upholstered, may be used for pull-up chairs in living rooms to provide comfort at table or fireside. The small sofa grouping below—a charming example of formal balance with chairs in

light, graceful English Regency style—proves that furniture may be compact enough for a small room with no loss in comfort. Love seats (shown below), used alone or in pairs, give the same feeling of luxury as a large sofa without crowding the room. They are even more useful when you buy them in sections which can be put together as love seats or couches and used later in a larger room in one unit as a full-sized sofa.

A CHAISE LONGUE AND A USEFUL SUBSTITUTE

It is often possible to work into your plan restful furniture which takes up less space than full-sized couches or sofas. Also, the smaller pieces are less expensive while probably serving your purpose equally well. A chaise longue may be had with the type of cover shown here, or in one of many other styles including tailored upholstery. These useful pieces fit into a corner or fireplace grouping where other furniture might be too bulky and use up too much wall space. The oversized chair and hassock combination pictured has several advantages. It doubles for a chaise longue, and its rounding back makes it fit nicely into a corner.

The webbing is one of the important clues to good upholstery. You can see it if the salesman can be induced to loosen the muslin tacked over it on the bottom of the chair or sofa. In a good piece this webbing is strong and tough, tightly anchored to the framework, with the springs firmly anchored to it in turn. A red line down each side of webbing strips is an indication of quality. In a piece with arms the sides should be covered with burlap to keep the stuffing in place, *not* with the cardboard which is sometimes found in shoddy construction.

Cushions are important and are used on most of the older types of couches and easy chairs. Cushions with springs, found in cheaper grades only, are less comfortable than those without springs and less attractive in appearance. They look stiff, even when new, and they soon develop lumps under hard wear. The most satisfactory filling for loose cushions is a combination of white or gray goose down with about 20 per cent feathers. These help keep the down fluffy and at the same time add body to the cushions. Duck down and chicken down have a slight odor in wet weather and are used only in lower grades of furniture.

Upholstery Fabrics: The fabric covering adds a large item of cost to a couch or a big chair because of the yardage required, and no fabric will stand up under heavy wear without showing it. For this reason many decorators advise spending most of the money on the construction features of upholstered furniture and buying only a moderately expensive covering which can be renewed when it shows too much wear or soil. Many people prefer to buy a piece in its structural muslin covering and make inexpensive slip covers to tide over until they are ready to have the covering done. This makes it easy to have springs, stuffing, webbing and loose cushions checked at that time with whatever restoration seems needed. This will considerably lengthen the life of the piece. If you don't like regulation slip covers, you can make them in the style of upholstery and sew them into place. (See Chapter 21.)

If you decide to buy pieces already upholstered, check seams, design-matching in fabric, general tailoring. Above all, make sure that loose cushions are really loose, not attached at the sides; and that they are really reversible, not covered with lining fabric on the underside. Care in checking these two fabrics may double the life of your upholstery.

Exposed Wood Parts on Upholstered Furniture: The style pendulum has swung away from elaborate carvings on legs, backs, arms and other exposed wood sections. Contemporary decorating recognizes the fact that in the average home today there is little time for dust-collectors of any type. Also in all cases where price is an object the extra decorations add to cost without making a real contribution in return. Carving is still lovely in formal drawing rooms (with no servant problem), but the smart new plain designs are more satisfactory in the average home. They also take much more kindly to the useful slip cover vogue than do the more elaborate pieces. The simpler and smoother the lines, the easier it is to make your slip covers fit smoothly and trimly.

Rubber for Resilience: Apparently the perfect replacement for the usual complicated spring-and-padding method is the use of foam-rubber cushions. This foamed latex is molded to fit, cemented to its base, and covered with fabric. Plywood or metal can be used with it and the result is a chair light, strong and amazingly comfortable.

Advantages of Rubber: Besides lightness, rubber makes housekeeping much easier. The cushions are always fluffed up just as they should be, never needing to be shaken and struggled with after someone has spent an hour in a chair. No moths or other vermin can make any impression on this material. It gives off no lint or feathers. It is the last word in comfort. Soft and buoyant, it can be molded in shapes to fit over the springs, arms and backs of chairs and sofas built in any of the traditional styles. In short, this latex, whipped up into a foam and molded into shape, takes the place of springs, or supplements them, equally well. Used on modern

CIRCULAR SECTIONAL COUCH UNITS BOTH ATTRACTIVE AND ADAPTABLE

style contour-shaped chairs as straight padding it provides as much real comfort as the deep luxurious upholstery we have been used to thinking essential. It is adaptable to all types and styles, and is combined with durability which eliminates need for repairs.

BUYING VALUE IN SLEEP EQUIPMENT

In shopping for mattresses and springs you are under the same handicap as when buying upholstered furniture—the things you are really paying for are hidden from sight. The best rule is to buy from a store you can trust and take the advice of a conscientious salesman. Also—as with upholstery—labels are very important. New improvements in sleeping equipment are constantly being made both for comfort and long wear. A good innerspring mattress will be resilient and buoyant. Lasting comfort depends upon structural design, quality of construction, grade and tempering of wire, strength of all materials used. Manufacturers of good mattresses make certain service guarantees. Find out what these are. Your label will tell you that, also about materials and care.

Solid mattresses are filled with various paddings from inexpensive blown cotton which soon forms in lumps to felted cotton mattresses which give reasonably good wear. Curled animal hair is the best and most lasting mattress filling. In order of values the types of hair are horse tail, cattle tail, horse mane and hog hair. A curled hair mattress can be (and should be) reprocessed and rebuilt every five to seven years. Kapok is soft but not highly durable. As in upholstery, latex is being used both alone and in combination with innerspring units. (See Chapter 21.) An inner-roll border usually indicates a better type of mattress while a mattress cover is always a good investment. There are many grades and types of springs, with box springs as modern favorites. Often these are sold in a unit with a corresponding mattress in matching cover-fabric.

If you expect to use it for any length of time, never spend money for a spring or mattress of poor quality. With a limited budget put your whole investment into the mattress and springs and let the bed-frame wait. For a very small sum you can have the box spring mounted on feet, then treat the bed as a studio couch. Or you can make a headboard by decorating the wall at the head of the bed. If your space is limited don't overlook couches or sofas which can be converted into double beds at night. The sofa-bed has been developed so that it equals in beauty and quality of workmanship any couch you would want to buy for your living room. Also, in Chapter 17, you will find suggestions for built-in beds for regular use or for emergency guests.

SOFAS SHOULD BE SCALED TO THE ROOMS IN WHICH THEY ARE USED

Never go out to shop for a large piece of furniture such as a couch without knowing exact dimensions of any piece you plan to buy. You should also outline on your floor plan where it will go and measure the space it must fit into. Remember that the front of the conventional davenport takes up more space than the back. The large sofa in the modern manner is beautifully proportioned and would be charming in any room large enough to be in scale with it. The interesting textured effect of shot silk upholstery fabric in light blue is set off by contrast of flat pillows and walls in tangerine color. The lamp with chartreuse base provides color accent and the dramatic flower arrangement balances the picture. Notice the adjustable arms which can be raised or lowered at will. Advantages of sectional pieces like those on opposite page are obvious. The chair at left can be joined with others like it to make a love seat or couch. The curved seats could serve alone as love seats, and pushed together would make up one of the new curved sofas so useful for practical furniture grouping in modern and traditional rooms.

The charming small room (right) shows a successful attempt at redecorating by means of salvage from second-hand sources. The chairs are Victorian vintage, also small tables and accessories. A slip cover with a figured frill brought the old sofa into harmony with the other furnishings. Chintz in a Victorian pattern, like the frill, is made into draperies which tie the two windows together by a continuous valance and can be drawn across at night as far as the mirror in the center. Inexpensive all-over carpeting and plain painted walls are used to give the room a feeling of space.

BUYING ANTIQUES

If you think the quaintness of some old-appearing chair or table or chest of drawers will add a note of charm to your room by all means buy it—at a sensible price. But don't be lured into making *investments* in antiques, unless you have delved pretty deeply into the matter. And don't spend money for old pieces which cannot be restored to usable condition. Examine them carefully and thoroughly before you buy. Your home is not a museum and the chances are you have no space which should be given over solely to display purposes. It is much better to buy a good modern reproduction than to put more money than you can afford into a piece which offers no proof of its value as an antique and is not in condition to serve a useful purpose in your scheme of living. It was once possible to pick up rare bargains in antiques in this country, but those days are practically over. Most authentic pieces have been absorbed by the trade.

ON THE TRAIL OF A BARGAIN

Auctions, second-hand stores, junk shops—these are fascinating places to anyone who has a liking for doing things over, and they are often life-savers when your furniture needs exceed your budget. Here antiques are not a stock-in-trade. You may be lucky enough to pick one up, but it will probably be a by-product of your expedition rather than its objective. The thing you may reasonably expect to find is a needed article of furniture which is still fundamentally sound but needs minor repairs, alterations, or refinishing—or all three. Brush up on your knowledge of construction before you go into one of these places. (Finish is less important because that usually has to be done over anyway.) Be on your guard against paying more than the used article is worth just because it is appreciably less than you would pay for something new. Remember to count in the cost of repairs and refinishing when you compare prices with new pieces in the same class.

The small room above illustrates the effective way in which a feeling of space can be achieved by clever use of built-in furniture. Books and ornaments fill the fireplace wall on shelves built at each side with one row above the mantel. Below the interesting picture window, with its casement side windows for ventilation, shelves take care of the radio in ad-

dition to books or magazines. The corner desk has excellent light from the window, and would be solid enough to use for a typewriter as well as for writing. The shelf-bench beneath the other casement window is grouped with an easy chair and a sturdy coffee table to make a conversation corner-with-a-view. Color is given the whole room by the

COMFORT

colors of nature outside the window, bindings of books, rich tones in the rug, window draperies, and chair upholstery. The draw-curtains illustrate an interesting method of hanging draperies without sacrificing a full view from the window. The track on which they are hung continues at each side around the corner at the ceiling line.

CHAPTER SEVENTEEN

Building In Furniture

FURNITURE actually built into your rooms is good investment. You have the benefit of plentiful storage without sacrifice of an appreciable amount of floor space. You achieve a feeling of space and restfulness because you have more room in which to spread out and arrange the movable items of furniture. As you have seen from pictures in this book, built-in units may also add greatly to decorative effect.

If you want the built-in effect but would like to be able to take pieces of your furniture with you when you move you will find your answer in the many new flexible units which can be reassembled in different groupings to adjust to different wall and floor spaces in new quarters. (See Chapter 28.) Another advantage is that they come in stock models and you can add to your grouping from time to time as your furnishing plans develop. To make these units look really built-in—and also to make them really easy to care for—look for those with a base resting solidly on the floor, and see that the backs fit tight against the wall at the top. This can be insured by sawing out just enough of the baseboard to slip the pieces in. Be sure to keep the sections of baseboard so that they can be replaced when you want to move the furniture out.

If you have a dado or paneling which will not allow the section to be taken out you can either have the back of the furniture hollowed out to fit over the projections, or have a temporary molding strip applied to the back, across the top and down the sides as far as the open space extends. This is usually the most practical solution. Finish the molding as nearly as possible like the furniture before you apply it. If you match it well it will not be noticeable at all.

READY-MADE BUILT-IN EFFECTS

The interesting arrangement shown in the two pictures on this page is so simple that it can be easily duplicated in any home—and so useful that most homes would welcome it for at least one room. In the living room below it solves the problem of making a studio couch look extraordinarily like a handsome daytime sofa by use of substantial book-filled table-shelves at each end to support tailored cushions placed where sofa arms would be. The shelves at the back, designed to appear built in, are in three sections—two long and one short. Easy access to the storage space below the shelves is provided by doors at the ends; and the space is large enough for card or game tables, tennis rackets and other awkwardly shaped articles as well as many smaller things. Notice the twin tables placed in library-step effect against the book shelves. If still more shelf space were needed these could be bookcases too. Huge flowers splashed over the chintz are very effective against the plain background of the room, and the graceful curves of a coffee table in the French Provincial manner, together with round lamps and shades, counteract a predominance of straight lines. In the bedroom picture we see exactly the same shelf assembly providing a headboard for two studio couches dressed as regulation beds. The bedside table between them is formed by a shelf-door in the middle unit which was concealed by couch cushions in the other picture.

THE SAME SHELF UNITS IN A LIVING ROOM

PLYWOOD TOP AND WASHABLE FABRIC FOR A GAY TEA-TABLE

SHELVES WITH FOLDING DOORS PUT A WALL TO WORK

In the small living room (right) one entire wall has been fitted with narrow shelves which take up little floor space but make housekeeping very much easier. They are concealed when not in use and made decorative by paneled folding door-screens painted to match the woodwork in the room. Here the section fitted with a shelf-leaf that drops down to make a serving counter is being used for a refreshment bar. It would do equally well as a desk or a serving shelf in a living-dining room. One section could be fitted with drawers—or with filing cases for a home-worker. The shelves can be built in or made at home and set in place, or several tall bookcases can be fitted into the space. Notice texture contrast between the soft cotton floor-covering and the burnished effect of upholstery fabric—also the mirror panels which make the small room seem twice as large. The smart plaid wall panel (below) makes an effective background for hanging shelves. Note the book with a fabric cover put on diagonally. The fabric-trimmed desk and chair are trimly smart and serviceable. This is a quick, easy way to cover up marred finish and the coated material is so easily kept clean that pieces of furniture treated in this way could be used even in kitchens, nurseries or playrooms. Any soft pliable oilcloth, or stain and waterproof fabric, could be used following these models.

SIMPLE SHELVING MAKES A USEFUL CORNER

Built-in book shelves and desk provide a work corner in the "den" shown below, with a glimpse of the attractive flagstoned patio outside. Note the panels above the desk with concealed lights installed behind them.

BRIGHT FABRIC PROVIDES AN EASY WAY TO REFURBISH FURNITURE

OFFICE BUILT INTO A BEDROOM

The sketches below show two ways in which a writing shelf may be built into a wall or a corner in any room of the house from attic to kitchen. It is an easy, inexpensive, space-saving way to provide convenience at strategic points in a busy household. The ship-shape bedroom working unit in the photograph above shows how efficiently a small room may be adapted to meet more than one purpose and still not seem crowded. Instead of being built in, as shown here, a unit like this could easily be made up from three unpainted chests of drawers finished at home by painting or waxing. Plywood boards, mitered and braced in the corner, would make a strong inflexible bridge between chests, and a surface of linoleum cemented on would be both attractive and serviceable. A corner-desk arrangement is very convenient for anyone with typewriting to do.

In figuring out innovations, don't overlook the versatility and enduring usefulness of book shelves and shelves for collections or hobbies. For most books and most rooms 10 inches is a satisfactory width for shelves, and vertical spaces between them should be 10, 11 and 12 inches—the largest space at the bottom, graduating upward. A solid base at the bottom, or a storage unit with doors, will keep the books cleaner. A 14-inch shelf may be needed for very tall books. Open shelves of any kind are attractive when they are lined in a contrast color—unless the room is too small for that treatment.

Unit furniture is available in very fine woods, with fine cabinet work and finish. It is also to be had in substantial but inexpensive pieces left unpainted for home finishing. These are worth while if you are on a budget because they can be given harmonizing finishes and used to fill in until you can have the kind of things you really want. They can always be refinished then and used for kitchen, nursery, game room, sewing room, or made-over attic room. With plastic waterproof finishes they may even be moved onto the porch, and they can always be made gay and colorful for sunroom or dinette. With this inexpensive furniture you may not always be able to find pieces without legs or feet of some kind, but these can usually be sawed off with resulting improvement in the appearance of the chest, cabinet, or whatever it may be. Look specially in Chapters 16 and 28 for further details about built-in and unit furniture.

ICEBOX INTO CUPBOARD

The junk-shop icebox (below) furnished doors and base for the useful and attractive cupboard built into a corner—equally appropriate for china in a dining room or as a display cupboard for ornaments, collections or hobbies.

EASILY BUILT-IN DESKS FOR CONVENIENCE IN KITCHEN OR DEN

BUILT-IN BEDS ARE PRACTICAL, COMFORTABLE, AND INEXPENSIVE

The bedroom in the photograph above was reclaimed from unused attic space by the use of wallboard, and made into a completely furnished room by the addition of ingeniously planned built-in furniture. The bed is a box spring and mattress set into a frame made by storage units and shelves. French-pleated draw-curtains are used to control daylight, and reading lights are attached under the shelf at the head of the bed. Units like these can be bought and assembled if you are not carpenter-minded. The couch-bed shown above is built into a nook at the side of the fireplace to provide a useful couch by day and a comfortable emergency sleeping place at night.

FINISHING AND DECORATING

Reclaiming old furniture is usually not difficult and it is often exceedingly interesting. Sawing off unnecessary trimmings, cutting down ungainly height, turning dark muddy stained surfaces into satin-smooth natural finishes, applying gay trimming bands and colorful motifs—all you have to do is use your imagination and follow manufacturers' directions for applying a wide variety of improved finishes of every type.

Varnish and paint removers are much easier to use and more effective than they once were. There are kinds which stay moist until the old finish is ready for removal which means you do not have to work against fast drying-out, nor keep adding more remover. Bleaches and stains are available for every type of wood and every possible shade, including the new blond and nude tones. Rubbed finishes are soft and lovely. Glazes and antique effects are distinctive and smart. Paints and enamels can be obtained in an ever-increasing range of tints and shades so that it is rarely necessary to attempt any color mixing beyond a little lightening with white, darkening with black, or graying (softening) with a mixture of the two.

Plastic wood and stronger-than-ever glues make repairs easy—but never depend upon ordinary glue. It must be the special kind made for wood repairing. With the help of light strong plywood, composition wallboards and ready-to-use moldings you will find many rebuilding and building-in jobs quite within the range of home efforts. Also there are many stock models in woodwork, built-in features, windows, mantels, mirror panels, etc., all with directions for installing which are keyed to the technical limitations of the home carpenter.

If you want to resurface a chest or cabinet with plain flat sides, drawers and doors, or to put a new top on any piece of furniture, don't overlook the possibilities of linoleum which can be cemented on without previous refinishing. Wall linoleums specially are light and easy to handle and make a durable, practical, easily cleaned surface. They are inexpensive because remnants will do nicely. By cutting off legs and substituting a wide molding base, covering surfaces with linoleum and adding new-style drawer pulls an old-fashioned tall dresser can be transformed into a smart low modern console-chest for any room in the house. The linoleum requires waxing, as wood does, but self-polishing linoleum wax is much easier to apply than wax for wood.

Linoleum tops are very effective in contrast colors with blond or painted furniture. With darker painted or enameled surfaces they can be matched so exactly to the rest of the finish that it is almost impossible to distinguish a difference except by the greater resilience of the composition material. These tops are not only damage and soil resistant, they also minimize breakage when used on coffee or dressing tables. They cut down a typewriter's clatter when they are applied to desk tops. The only tools you need are a sharp knife and a cement spreader which you can make yourself from a piece of cardboard 6″ x 4″ with the longer edge cut into saw-like teeth. The cement you can get from the dealer when you buy the linoleum.

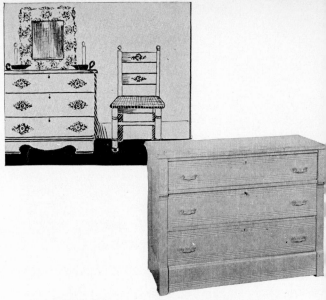

TRANSFORMING OLD CHESTS OF DRAWERS

The cutouts above show a very ordinary old-style chest of drawers used with its duplicate as a base for the two charming furniture pieces in the pictures at left, and (right) on facing page. In the easily added superstructure needed to get a dining-room cupboard effect, sides and shelves are made of plywood which you can have cut into the right lengths and shapes in the shop where you buy it. If you prefer you can simplify the design by eliminating the curved sides and keeping the edges straight. Repainting, then decorating with gay peasant designs in bright colors, will give you the delightful cupboard you see at the left. The designs may be painted semi-freehand, stenciled, or made with cutouts of some kind. Decorated chairs and flower prints carry out the peasant motif of the cupboard patterns. An equally useful version of the same style chest of drawers appears in the bedroom work-corner at the right. By placing the sturdy chest a comfortable distance from the corner and using shelf brackets on chest and wall to support the plywood shelf a streamlined work-table and storage unit is improvised. Note the useful bulletin board set inside a redecorated picture frame.

EASILY BUILT-IN STORAGE SPACES

The sketches (left) show wallboard and plywood used to take advantage of space ordinarily lost where dormers and sloping roofs are left in their natural state. In sketch A, spacious closets are built in under the eaves, while in B a dormer window is made a center of comfort and usefulness by a window seat with drawers below. In the photograph a modern type of wall cupboard is installed in a small linoleum-floored hall to provide convenient storage space. With the mirror above one end, the top of the cupboard serves in place of console table. Units like this can be bought, or they can be made at home of wallboard or plywood, and installed in a hallway anywhere in the house. They are shallow enough so that they would not be in the way even in a narrow passage. Outside the kitchen they could be used for cleaning cloths and small supplies. Upstairs they could substitute for a linen closet, or carry the overflow from bathroom medicine chests, and one unit might even serve as clothes hamper. For a child's room they could be made with blackboard panels. In a small den or study they would hide a generous amount of papers, tools or other hobby and working equipment.

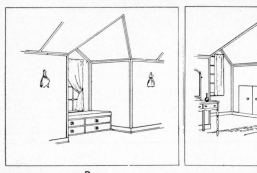
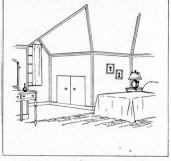

B   A

MAKING A SMART MODERN COFFEE TABLE

The "before and after" table (right, center) shows how easily
an obsolete piece of furniture may be converted into something very useful and attractive. The present vogue for large
round substantial coffee tables inspired the transformation.
The central pedestal was eliminated and the legs sawed off
to make the table correct coffee-table height. Filling in the
caster holes with plastic wood made it possible to reverse
the legs and show the graceful curve at the ends. For the
rest, the old finish was removed and the table painted in a
light pastel color with a slightly darker band around the
outer edge. Leaf designs were then painted at random over
the top. For increased wear a sheet of heatproof glass cut
to fit the top would protect against dirt and spilled liquids.
A circle of colored linoleum could be cemented to the top
in place of the finish shown, or fabric could be used under
the glass. For success with fabric it is best to cut a circle
from stiff, thin cardboard, then stretch the fabric over it and
glue it firmly in place around the edge of the underside.
This can be cemented to the wood and your fabric will
always be trimly in place under the glass.

ATTRACTIVE BUILT-IN DINING-ROOM FEATURES

Small dining rooms profit especially from built-in furniture
with its ample storage and serving space. In the room shown
at right the shelves and cupboard are built all across one
end of the room, making other wall furniture unnecessary
and providing floor space for an attractive breakfast group
in front of the window. Notice the breakfast table with a
central storage section and leaves which drop when not in
use. This room is coolly dressed for summer with a linoleum
rug in floral pattern and soft tones of green, peach and
ivory. Simple draw-curtains, split bamboo shade and pots
of growing plants all add to the impression of coolness. The
wallpaper decorations are unusual and interesting. The border is continued across the window like a cornice and a pattern is made up from the stripes in the paper to serve as a
background for a flower print with painted wood frame and
wide contrasting mat. This is an effective means for giving
a small picture importance on a large wall space. Alone it
would be completely lost.

FABRICS PLAY AN INTERESTING AND IMPORTANT ROLE

In the living room above fabrics are used for contrast in color, texture, and pattern. The simulated brick wall is a light turquoise color, the draperies are of textured raw silk in a deeper shade of turquoise. The combination of boldly patterned upholstery fabric with plain seat cushions on the curved sofa is unusual and interesting. Loose cushions with deep tailored hem borders match the draperies. The deep-piled cotton shag rug is made with stripes of mustard yellow and terra cotta. Green and gold are other colors used in the decorating plan, with black for accent. The chair by the desk is upholstered in a mustard yellow textured fabric, with black and turquoise fringe—the same as that applied at top and bottom of the gold-colored lamp shade. The stylized scenic pattern of the printed fabric adds life and movement

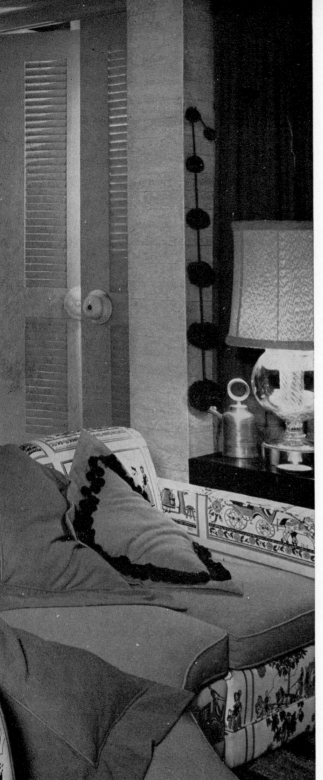

IN MODERN ROOMS

to a room where plain surfaces predominate. The desk is an interesting example of modern assembled furniture. Three chests of drawers, each with a sliding shelf, are placed side by side, with the small cabinet-and-shelf unit on top of the large central chest. Notice the doors, with large knobs and louvred panels to increase ventilation.

CHAPTER EIGHTEEN

How to Use Home-Decorating Textiles

FABRICS are important to the home decorator. They may inspire the whole color scheme. They may provide a large part of essential interest and variety, and they are important to comfort. The warmth and softness which make any room home-like and welcoming can be supplied only by means of decorative textiles in appropriate colors, interesting textures and attractive designs.

In addition to a seemingly endless variety of fabrics specially woven and designed for decorative purposes, most of the traditional dress materials also are utilized in contemporary decorating and must be included in any comprehensive list. Decorating fabrics may be a major expense in your plan, or they may come well within a limited budget. You can judge by sight the colors, designs and textures which appeal to you, but you must know something about fabrics in order to select those which will serve as well as please you.

HOW TO BUY FABRICS

Today's reliable manufacturers have given you one answer to the problem of wise buying—fabric labels. These should tell you the basic fiber and weave, also any variations from standard. They should inform you as to durability, washability and cleanability. If the textile requires any kind of special care or treatment the label should tell you that too.

Interpreting Your Label: In order to understand fabric labels it is necessary to understand the nature of the different fabric types and to know what you should reasonably expect from them. These types are determined by fiber and weave. Durability depends upon the combination of these two factors.

237

The most durable of all natural fibers is pure silk, with ramie, mohair, wool, linen, cotton and rayon following in that order. Any combination of two fibers will produce a fabric a little less strong than one woven entirely from one kind of fiber.

BASIC FIBERS

There are five basic fibers, each one with its special suitabilities—with the exception of rayon which is sometimes classed as a synthetic rather than natural fiber and may be used to reproduce almost any characteristic fabric woven from the other four. Synthetics are in a class by themselves and will be discussed later.

1. *Cotton* is the most widely used vegetable fiber, having more than two hundred kinds of cloth made from it. Several processes are used to increase wearability or improve appearance in cotton weaves and your label should inform you if they have been used. *Mercerizing* adds to life and luster by strengthening the fiber, and increasing its absorptive power so that it takes dye with great brilliance and clarity. *Controlled Shrinkage* means that the fabric has been processed to keep shrinkage to a minimum. *Sanforizing* compresses the fabric and moves the yarns closer together making the weave stronger and cutting down shrinkage to within three-quarters of one per cent. (This process may also be used on rayon.) If fabrics are to be washed you must know the degree of shrinkage in order to make allowance in buying. *Starchless Finish* is often used to keep sheer fabrics crisp without starching—the original stiffness returns with ironing. *Glazing* gives the fabric gloss, stiffness, greater resistance to soil. When it is labeled "Permanent" your fabric is washable without loss of glaze. But follow washing directions on the label.

2. *Linen* is the second most important vegetable fiber and is made from flax. Its smooth yarn is woven into a crisp, cool fabric with lustrous finish and absorbent qualities, used for many varieties of cloth. *Ramie* is a vegetable fiber which may be used as a substitute for flax. Its threads have the luster and strength of silk but not its elasticity.

3. *Silk*, an animal fiber taken from cocoons made by silkworms, is spun into threads which are finer than human hair but strong and elastic. This lustrous fiber is the most beautiful of all natural fibers. When silk yarn is "weighted" with metal it is cheaper but less durable.

4. *Wool*, taken from the fleece of the sheep, has fibers covered with microscopic interlocking scales which make it one of nature's most effective insulators. Pure wool, taken directly from the sheep or lamb, is strong and resilient but soft. It is made into

two types of yarn—*woolen* and *worsted*. The fibers used for woolen yarn are short and curly, loosely interlocked and twisted together for weaving soft warm fabrics. The longer fibers used for worsted yarn are combed, laid parallel to each other and tightly twisted for weaving into harder-surfaced fabrics. *Reprocessed wool* is new wool woven from fibers reclaimed from scraps and remnants accumulated by manufacturers of textiles and clothing. *Reused wool* is made by changing back into fiber wool which has been made into fabrics and *used by the consumer*. Every wool fabric label should tell you which of these wool products you are buying. The price you pay should be in scale with these classifications. *Mohair* is made from the hair of the Angora goat. It is closely allied to wool, lustrous, resilient and enduring. There are wide differences in mohair fabrics based upon the quality of fiber, closeness of weave and height of pile.

5. *Rayon* is a vegetable fiber as the basic material comes from specially processed cotton or wood pulp. Celanese and bemberg are developed from the same source. The fibers are heavier than silk, without its elasticity, and may be either lustrous or dull. In white fabrics rayon never turns yellow with age as silk does. Two types of rayon yarns produce two different types of fabrics. *Filament Rayon* is a long continuous thread woven into silk-like fabrics such as taffeta. *Spun Rayon* is made by cutting filament rayon into short pieces the length of cotton, linen or wool fibers, and spinning these into yarn for weaving fabrics which resemble cotton, linen, or wool. It is these "rayon staple" fibers which are used in various blended yarns.

DYEING TEXTILES

One thing your label should tell you is whether the dyes in the fabric are fast to washing, also to sunlight, and this must guide you in buying. If you cannot afford dry cleaning make sure your fabrics are washable. If they must be used where they are constantly exposed to sunlight make sure they have at least a high resistance to fading and protect them with linings if you are not sure. When fabrics are *stock-dyed* it means that the raw fibers were dipped in the dye bath before the thread was spun, a method not often used. When cloth is yarn-dyed it means the threads were dipped before they were woven and this is generally accepted as the most satisfactory method. The third method, called piece-dyeing, is the least reliable as the fabric is not dipped in the dye until after it is woven.

Printed Patterns: Early textile designs were painted by hand on each piece. This art is still practised in

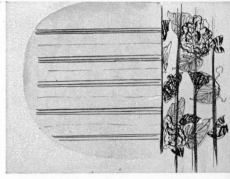

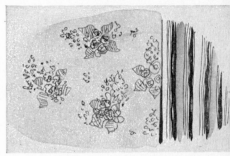

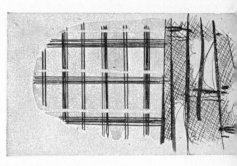

COMBINING PATTERNS EFFECTIVELY

The rule governing combinations of patterned materials with other designs and plain surfaces is exemplified in the photograph and sketches here. In the photograph the definite scenic pattern of the wallpaper would create a feeling of confusion and show to much less advantage if the draperies were also figured. When the figured material is on walls the area is so large that it is usually better to keep most of the upholstery as well as all the draperies in plain fabrics, simple geometrical design, or a shadow pattern. You will notice that the floor and ceiling here are plain. The sketches at right demonstrate effectiveness of various combinations of figured motifs with stripes or plaids. In all these cases floor and upholstery coverings would be plain or nearly so.

Comfort is the keynote of the modern bedroom (right) with its trim tailored lines and its restful monochromatic color scheme. Contrast in texture and tone provides the necessary variety to prevent monotony. These textures, modern in weave and finish, are all called "tweed" because of the basic weave but several distinct surface finishes are shown. The nubby-textured couch upholstery fabric in a dark rich shade is contrasted with the light cotton rug which again is in contrast with a dark floor. The dark note is carried on by striped tweed draperies behind a dressing table of dark lacquered wood. Here texture contrast is afforded by the gleaming finish of the wood. The bedside table and lamp base are also dark. The light-colored draperies, stool and bed-coverings are in a tweed fabric with a slightly lustrous finish. The wall shows a smooth plaster contrasted with doors and bed-wall in panels of a photographic plastic finish modeled after the roughly woven texture of the bed-cover fabric. The blond wood frames of bed, mirror, chaise longue and floor-lamp bases are in soft natural finish contrasting with the gleaming lacquer of the dressing table. Another contrast note is in cushions on the chaise longue made from the dark glossy satin. Notice here the use of curves in the head of the bed, lamp shades, stool and dressing table to offset the predominance of straight lines and rectangles.

Sheer crisp fabrics in fresh white are perennial favorites for bedroom use. On the bed at upper left dotted Swiss is combined with sheer embroidered flounces and a top of coin-dotted Swiss in yellow, green and red on a white ground to make a frilly traditional treatment for a little girl's quaint sleigh-type four-post bed. The third photograph shows the softness of gleaming light-weight taffeta with its adaptability to feminine draperies and bed coverings. Notice the softness, also, of the full flounces made from rayon sheer glass curtain fabric, and the interest provided by texture without pattern—except for stripes in the wallpaper setting off the bay window bed-alcove.

made-to-order designs but most commercial fabrics are printed by one of several methods.

1. Block printing is a hand method which produces beautiful patterns in very soft, lovely colors. It is complicated and costly and is usually used only on very fine linens which justify such an expense.

2. Roller printing is the accepted method used for printing the majority of good quality fabrics. The designs are etched on the rollers, a separate roller for each color. The last one carries the background color and the design is repeated at regular intervals over the fabric. When the design appears only on the warp threads a mottled or faded appearance results and these are called warp or shadow prints.

3. An inexpensive process of stamping the design and color on the face of the fabric is unsatisfactory and the pattern is short-lived. If you want service from your textiles avoid this type of printed pattern.

TEXTURE IN FABRICS

Texture is an important factor in suitability. For hard service choose close strong weaves in soil-resisting textures—mohairs rather than velvets, glazed chintz rather than soft printed linen. Use smooth textures to reflect light in dark rooms or corners, nubby or pile surfaces if there is too much light. Elaborate silk and rayon fabrics are always formal; linen, wool, cotton and simpler rayons are formal or informal depending upon color, weave and pattern. Many coarse rough textures are adapted only to homespun interiors, but others in special designs and finer materials are suitable in almost any type of room. Each case must be decided on its merits. (See Fabric chart for various fabric uses and suitability.)

However, there are certain general guiding principles in the combining of textures in a room. As with color, mingle different weaves and textures for the sake of variety and interest—but not too many, and not too different. Keep to an underlying similarity of type. Don't mingle textures which are completely unfriendly. For example, a delicate silk brocade and a rough primitive fabric such as denim or coarse homespun do not ordinarily belong in the same room. With rep and denim combine monk's cloth, cretonnes and kindred fabrics. Handsome cotton and wool damasks combine well with fine chintz, various conservative novelty weaves and the better grades of sateen. Expensive hand-blocked linens may be used with almost any of the finer fabrics, including silk brocade and velvet. Heavy satin is often combined with sophisticated rough novelty textures for the strong contrast characteristic of the modern school, but it is an effect at home only in more or less modern rooms.

CONTEMPORARY TEXTILE TRENDS

Modern weave and design have introduced many innovations into the field of decorative fabrics. Texture has taken on new importance. Unusual combinations of basic materials have been used to obtain distinctive effects. Along with this has gone a new approach to color and design with a dominance of clear bright color and stylized patterns. Geometrics play a leading role. Many patterns are built around definite architectural motivation—designs planned to make a room seem larger, smaller, higher or lower.

Hand printing has been revived, and reversal to quaint historic scenic design in softened colors goes hand in hand with startling modernistic abstractions in vivid shades. Inspiration for ideas has been sought in all parts of the world, many of them founded upon importations of primitive fabrics from South America and Mexico with their sturdy Indian weaves and gay colors woven into the fabric, in stripes, checks or plaids. Favorite hues in these are clear bright turquoise, electric pink, and pure golden yellow—often against a background of neutral wheat color which makes the fabrics effective with the bleached woods of much modern furniture.

Manufacturers have come into the picture with new and more attractive versions of many old favorites—like the pinwale cotton corduroy which is so soft and drapable, so rich yet subtle in its pastel colorings, that it fits into almost any type of room and any fabric need from upholstery to lamp shades. Cottons have been perfected to an almost unbelievable degree of beauty in richness of color, variety of weave, and adaptability to all styles of decorating. Most of them have been made fadeproof and shrinkproof for greater durability and ease of care. Many of them have been given the plastic treatments mentioned below.

Synthetic Fabrics: 1. Plastic or synthetic materials are used to coat or impregnate invisibly all sorts of fabrics making them permanently resistant to water, stains, soil, fading, wrinkling. This means delicate pastel tints in draperies or upholstery can be had without the constant cleanings which wear them out. Luster will not come off, soft nubby fabrics won't be harmed by the dust they catch.

2. Plastics used for basic fiber materials carry this improvement even farther. Nylon was our first wide-scale introduction to the versatility and beauty of plastic textiles. These sheer drapery fabrics which are soft but strong, non-sag, resistant to tearing, fast-drying and permanently set in size and shape, eliminate most of the trouble and time once spent keeping glass curtains clean and in order. Nylon draperies and upholstery in many types have the same desirable

Coated fabrics of many types provide new durability as well as new beauty of surface in today's fabrics. The glazed chintz used for draperies and slip cover (left) was chosen with such a large amount of light background showing that it would make ordinary chintz difficult to keep fresh—these permanent glaze finishes require only daily dusting and occasional wiping with a damp cloth to keep them fresh and literally spotless. Notice in the chintz slip covers the careful placing of a large motif in the center of each back panel and each cushion seat. Also, the same point in the motif is placed at each side of the front flounce, and the panels above it repeat the same section of pattern for a unified picture.

How very charmingly waterproof, coated fabrics can be draped and manipulated is shown in the table-curtain-and-chair group below. With a wide diversity of patterns these fabrics are ideal for kitchens, dinettes, nurseries, playrooms, bathrooms, etc.

MODERN FABRICS FOR EASY CARE

qualities, and curtains may be laid in pleats which are not destroyed by washing or cleaning.

3. Casein from skimmed milk provides a synthetic base for warm fluffy yarns woven alone or in combination with wool or rayon into fabrics for blankets or warm soft draperies.

4. Coke, limestone and salt are synthesized to produce beautiful fabrics of every type from simulated leather to sheer draperies—all waterproof, windproof, mothproof, mildewproof, impervious to most acids, oils and solvents, and easily cleaned with soap and water.

5. Glass, aluminum and other metallic substances, have been spun into fine threads for use in soft gleaming fireproof and dustproof draperies and upholstery materials.

VARIETY AND CHARM IN SIMPLE COTTONS

Emergence of cotton as an all-purpose basic fiber for a great variety of weaves and fabric types is one of the interesting textile developments of contemporary industry. New cotton fabrics carry prints of a kind previously seen only on fine silks. A heavy glaze finish makes balloon cloths look like taffeta without making them less washable. Mercerized broadcloths and plain poplin are finished with a luster like that of real silk, while satin stripes and checks on ginghams and chambrays give these fabrics a brand-new sophistication. Cotton gabardines and many novelty weaves have designs in the beautifully soft tones associated with hand-blocked drapery fabrics. Black as a background color is combined with vivid prints in all the bright but subtly blended colors characteristic of the modern palette. The charming recreation room (left) with its open-beamed ceiling and walls of grooved wood is made interesting by the bamboo used for furniture bases and the completely cotton fabric treatment. The rugs are braided cotton, the chairs and cushions are covered with twill printed in a windowpane plaid, the couch upholstery is a textured cotton which resembles monk's cloth woven on a gigantic scale. Notice the correct balance between patterned design in draperies, geometrical design in upholstery and rug, against a plain wood background and combined with plain fabric on the couch.

DISTINCTIVE AND ORIGINAL DESIGN IN A MODERN FABRIC

In the photograph of a living-dining room above, a very modern interpretation of chintz pattern is shown in a room where the wall at the fireplace end is covered with chintz instead of wallpaper. The fabric ground is white with the design made up from South American travel posters in cerulean blue, pink and chartreuse. The plain wall is cerulean blue and two very modern *banquettes* are upholstered in pink leather. The large table at the right folds up into the wall when not needed for dining, games, or some other special purpose.

CHAPTER NINETEEN

Period Styles — Home Decorating

FAMILIARITY with historical periods is not necessary in order to create a charming and livable room—but it may be very helpful. A working acquaintance with the more important periods is usually a fruitful source of inspiration—and you may turn out to be one of those for whom the subject is filled with romantic interest. You will certainly find that there is nothing mysterious or difficult about it. "Period Style" is merely a term used to cover the designs in furniture and decoration popular during any given era in some particular country.

Every good design—in a house, fabric, or wallpaper—has a distinctive character or "feeling." Getting so you can recognize that feeling is important. It is also fun. It will give you more confidence in making your decorative plans. It will help you harmonize your old furnishings with new, or work out a brand-new scheme which will be appropriate and in good taste but keyed to your own special likes and needs.

It is neither desirable nor necessary to *copy* period rooms in homes. Modern comfort and convenience are considered more important than an exact reproduction of some special period, even if it happens to be a favorite style. Make good use of such a period style as a guide in planning your home, but distinguish between guidance and slavish imitation. Living in a world brought closely together by air travel, radio, motion pictures, a home need not express only one national influence in decorating—Spanish, Italian, French, English, or any other country—or one definitely limited period. Even one room that is 100% a certain period—Louis XVI, or Elizabethan, or Victorian, for example—would have a slightly musty, unlived-in flavor. Decorations too starkly modern, on the other hand, may be too cold in feeling.

A home which truly expresses charm and individuality should represent an accumulation of personal experience as well as intelligent application of such things as scale, balance and color harmony. This element is the secret of appeal in many of the most charming Colonial American homes. Analysis reveals a strong Clipper Ship influence in decorations brought from all parts of the world—grass cloths from Java and Sumatra, wallpaper from China, rugs from the Orient, drapery fabrics from India. Combined with domestic products of the day, they provided a mellow and colorful background for Early American furniture mingling harmoniously with quite formal and elegant 18th Century English pieces.

With the aid of the charts, sketches and photographs in this chapter you will be able to recognize characteristic features of whatever period happens to appeal to you most. At the end of the chapter you will find suggestions for successfully mingling two or more periods in the contemporary manner, and for successfully combining historical periods with modern styles.

ROOMS FROM FAVORITE ENGLISH PERIODS

The photographs on this page illustrate six of the great English decorating periods which have most strongly influenced American styles. The "Hall" at upper left has the small square paneling, decorated ceiling, tall diamond-paned oriel windows, and stone floor of the English Renaissance. Characteristic features: oak for furniture; boxlike chairs, and high-backed bench (settle); Elizabethan refectory table with melon-bulb legs, and bench; "wainscot" arm chair; distinctive fireplace, in shape called "Tudor arch." (See Chart No. 2.) The 18th century cottage interior at upper right is timeless. Medieval in structure and background finish, its counterpart may still be found in England. Characteristic features: oak for beams and furniture; rough plaster; 17th century settle and stool; Queen Anne influence in open dresser with pewter dishes; Windsor arm chairs, hoop-and-spindle type, origin of American version so popular in Colonies; Jacobean gateleg table; diamond-paned casement windows; gaily colored print draperies; flagstone floor, small hooked rug. (See Chart No. 3.) The Georgian bedroom at the left illustrates "Chinese Chippendale," with its straight square legs and pierced fret. Characteristic features: Chinese wallpaper; gay, amusing overmantel decoration with raised plaster designs, white or polychrome Chinese figurines; painted dado and cornice; waxed wood floor, Chinese rug. The drawing room at the left is furnishe l in style predominantly Hepplewhite of 1770–80, with classic treatment of walls and fireplace from a slightly earlier period. Characteristic features: shield-back arm chairs, graceful sofa; French influence in decorated commodes, Aubusson-type rug; drumtop table, "sofa" table, secretary, slightly later Hepplewhite-Sheraton style. In both background and furnishings, the dining room at lower left typifies the work of Robert Adam between 1770–90. Characteristic features: painted plaster walls, ceiling, with low relief designs in Graeco-Roman manner; side table, pedestals, urns, in mahogany, parcel-gilded ornamentation; pedestal extension table (compare American Duncan Phyfe); classic columns, garlands, borders, widely imitated by American Federal; wall niche, painted wall panels; classic draperies; Oriental rug. In the small drawing room at lower right Sheraton furniture is shown against a painted, simply paneled background of 1780. Characteristic features: simplified version of classic Adam themes in mantel, door, window treatments; delicate lines of arm chairs, tables, spinet piano, secretary; wall sconces; parquet floor, Aubusson-type rug. Two side chairs are Hepplewhite. (See Chart No. 4.)

(Left to Right, and Top to Bottom) *UPPER PANEL* (GOTHIC): French Canopied Chair of State; Two Italian Chests (1400–1500); French Chest with Tracery; French or Flemish *Credence;* Gothic Arch Panel Carving; Furniture Carving Detail; Italian Sacristy Cupboard (1450–1500); Flemish Cupboard (1450–1500); French *Armoire,* Linen-Fold Panels; French *Credence* (1400–1500). *LOWER PANEL* (RENAISSANCE): Armchair, Square, Box-like Lines; Low Bench or Stool; Italian Heavily Carved Frame, Stool, Chest (1550–1600); Mortise-and-Tenon Joint, for Furniture Construction; Baluster-Type Pedestal Support, Classic Pilaster, Spiral-Type Leg with Bun Foot; Characteristic Decorating Motifs—Leaf Ornaments, with *Cartouche* between them; Oblong Linen-Fold Panel, Nulling, Gadrooning; Refectory-Type Table, Lyre-shaped Support; Flemish Draw-Table (1600); French X-Type Chair (1600); French Carved Table (1600)

EARLY EUROPEAN PERIOD STYLES
DATES—1200 TO 1650

CHARACTER-ISTICS OF PERIOD	GOTHIC—SIMILAR DEVELOPMENTS IN ALL EUROPEAN COUNTRIES Approximate Dates—1200 to 1500	RENAISSANCE—ESPECIALLY IN ITALY AND SPAIN Approximate Dates—1500 to 1650
TYPES OF FURNITURE AND WOODS	Little furniture used. Large decorated chests, ancestors of modern "double duty" furniture, used for storage and traveling; also, with pads, for seating and sleeping. Seats: mostly stools, trestles, benches; chairs—tall, box-like, often with draught-blocking canopies and drapery—reserved for nobles. Beds: huge, paneled, often built into room. Oak most common wood, others used locally. Construction by mortise and tenon joints.	Renaissance style in furniture followed revival of classic (Greek or Roman) forms in architecture. Credenza, typically Italian. Period of refectory table, draw-top table, chest on stand. Beds: set on low platform, often without any footboard; triangular headboards, carved or covered with leather or velvet. Chests highly decorated. Woods: walnut and other fine woods used in addition to oak (Continental Europe).
DISTINCTIVE POINTS IN FORM, DESIGN, DETAIL	Architectural Gothic lines influenced decoration. Furniture large in scale, massive, elaborately carved with figures, gargoyles, pointed arches, other typical designs. "Linen-fold" panels modeled after folds in chalice napkin at religious ceremonies. Motifs naturalistic, painted early in period, later carved.	Furniture still straight-lined and simple in form, massive in scale, but with elaborate carvings, polychrome, inlay, and metal ornaments. Introduction of X chairs. Characteristic features: heavy carved pedestals, lyre-shaped supports, classic columns; conventionalized motifs; classic and other themes (see sketches); cupids; grotesque animal and human forms used in carvings.
FLOORS AND CEILINGS	Floors of stone, often strewn with rushes for warmth, making stretchers necessary on tables, chairs, etc., to keep feet from litter on floors. Ceilings open beamed, arched, with carving.	Floors of marble, mosaics, tile. Oriental and peasant-made rugs, braided rush mats. Ceilings decorated, colorful, often painted or heavily beamed, very elaborate in Italy and Spain.
WINDOWS AND DRAPERIES	Windows: tall arched frames divided into small lights by tracery; rich, heavy draperies to keep out draughts. Glass, becoming clearer and more widely used in windows, made rooms lighter so that glaring colors could be softened slightly without loss of cheerfulness.	Windows: architectural treatment, often with columns and decorated panels above; arched openings for windows and doors. In Southern countries, windows smaller and recessed in thick walls, with rich hangings on ornate metal poles, or wall decorations centering around the windows—especially in Spain.
FABRICS AND COLORS	Early fabrics: woolen and linen, embroidered or painted in simple colors, naturalistic or conventionalized designs, for hangings and cushions. Later rich silks and velvets. Colors, in paint and textiles, crude and brilliant.	Textiles: fine velvets, silks, brocades, etc., with classic motifs, local themes, elaborate patterns, gold threads; decorated leather; gold trimmings and fringes, nails, decorative fabric bands. Colors: strong; blue, yellow, green, russet, crimson, Venetian red; black; gold and silver lavishly applied.
ACCESSORIES, ORNAMENTS, LIGHTING	Principal metal: wrought iron much used for ornamental finish on chests and cupboards; also metal work. Metal rush-light holders suspended from ceiling or fastened to wall as brackets. Accessories mostly utilitarian—vessels used for eating and drinking.	Wrought iron, silver, bronze, polychrome, used for candelabra. Accessories: silver, Venetian glass, enamels, potteries, mirrors, paintings, statues, tapestries, elaborately decorated screens, andirons, lanterns. Tiles used for many decorating purposes. Accessories used for pure decoration as well as utility.
REMARKS	What is usually called the Gothic period, beginning some 350 years before the Renaissance, covers a wide range of development in the decorative arts from early crude simplicity to later luxurious elaboration. Same forms appeared in secular and religious architecture and in decoration. The pointed arch, foliated ornament and tracery are Gothic sign manuals.	The Italian Renaissance was the source of inspiration for the rest of Europe. It marked a tremendous advance in the art of comfort, with the beginning of upholstery, and great increase in quantity and variety of furniture, as well as elaboration in all forms of decorating. Later development, based on curves, called "Baroque." (See French periods.)

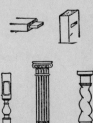

Oak Cupboard (1500);
"Wainscot" Chair (1600)

Court Cupboard (Chest-on-Stand, 1600); (Right)
Elizabethan Refectory Table,
Pedestal Legs, Bulbous Turnings

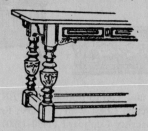

Early English Carving Details (Right);
Above, Typical Motif; Below, Table
Edge and Characteristic Melon-Bulb
Leg of Elizabethan Refectory Table

ENGLAND AND THE RENAISSANCE—THE "AGE OF OAK"
DATES—APPROXIMATELY—1500 TO 1700

CHARACTER-ISTICS OF PERIOD	TUDOR AND ELIZABETHAN (HOUSE OF TUDOR) Dates—1485 to 1603 (Henry VII—Henry VIII—Elizabeth)	JACOBEAN AND RESTORATION (HOUSE OF STUART) Dates—1603 to 1689 (James I—Charles I) (Charles II—James II)
TYPES OF FURNITURE AND WOODS	Styles essentially solid; masculine in feeling; dignified, even sombre. Many of the low Gothic chests became cabinet chests on legs. Paneled beds in box-like stalls gave way to huge canopied four-posters. Characteristic pieces: refectory draw tables with bulbous carved legs; stools; benches; straight chairs with box-like bases; wainscot chairs, with panel backs. Court cupboards typically English, also Welsh dressers. Woods: usually oak; Scotch pine (deal) next in favor; some use of chestnut and walnut.	Masculine feeling still dominant in styles which evolved directly from Eliz bethan into new types of furniture, with increased use of upholstery. Seatin chairs emerged from box-type to present forms; simple sofas developed—rec elongated chairs. Distinctive pieces: gate-leg tables; day beds, caned, w sloping headboards and no footboard or back; tall clocks; small stands; rou tables first introduced. Woods: oak remained favorite until after 1660 wh walnut came into its own in England.
DISTINCTIVE POINTS IN FORM, DESIGN, DETAIL	Forms still straight-lined and simple, large in scale, massive, especially wall furniture. Chairs growing lighter; cushions for added comfort on hard wood seats. Motifs for painting and carving: classic Renaissance themes with traces of Gothic; oak and ivy leaves, acanthus leaf, fleur-de-lis; Tudor rose and grape very popular. The lower Tudor arch replacing Gothic for all purposes. (See illustrations for typical shape.)	Forms still straight lined, with abundant carving, but size and heaviness duced. Bulbous leg of Elizabethan tables replaced by lighter and more gra ful designs; spiral turning, and Flemish scroll characteristic of Charles II f niture. Characteristics: chair backs high and narrow, ladder type or cane carved or upholstered, now at comfortable angle instead of straight; twiste leg style for tables definitely late Jacobean, also half-spindle forms appli to cabinet fronts, etc.
FLOORS AND CEILINGS	Floors: stone, followed by oak planking; "Turkey carpets" imported, in strong colors and clear designs; "Turkey work" rugs made at home by pulling wool through coarse fabric, leaving loops, tied on back, cut for pile on top. Ceilings: ornamental, with beams and rough plaster; geometric plaster designs in relief; open-timber construction; usually rather low for size of rooms.	Floors: wood, developed from wide planking to include parquet and inlaid signs, with patterns in colored woods; often covered with Oriental ru Ceilings: open-beam construction; beamed with plaster panels; decorated designs in paint and plaster. Closed ceilings still proportionately low, so times plain with decorative cornice.
WINDOWS AND DRAPERIES	Windows: large casement, small panes; architectural beauty of design called for simple hangings; wrought iron poles carried full heavy draperies which pulled across windows. Fringes and trimmings in gold, silver or strong colors.	Windows: Leaded casements popular, sometimes in form of bays; groups windows might be built on top of each other, with stone or wood mullions tween. Hangings rich, specially in later part of period under French influen
FABRICS AND COLORS	Fabrics: rich damasks and velvets, brocades, brocatelles; leather; needle-points; East India hand-painted cottons; embroideries in silk or wool on linen. Famous "Tree of Life" pattern, introduced from Orient, equally famous in England. Textures: from firm and rich to coarse, rough effects. Colors: strong, clear, bold; preferably reds, greens, yellows, blues, in deep rich shades.	An age of fine fabrics in England: velvets, silks, damasks, brocades for uph stery. Window hangings, cushions; portieres introduced for wide archways; lo velvet hangings drawn at night around four-post beds. Elaborate texti leather, used for upholstery, with heavy handmade silk fringe. Exquisite e broidery, crewel, needlepoint, popular. Colors: brilliant, concentrated larg in textiles.
ACCESSORIES, ORNAMENTS, LIGHTING	Metals: wrought iron for candlesticks, andirons, hinges, etc.; brass and bronze for handles, knobs, ornaments. Accessories: tapestries, paintings, mirrors widely used, especially on stone walls; Chinese pottery, silver, pewter, heavy earthenware brought in by foreign trade.	Metals used less than formerly, but inlays of metal, ivory, marble, rare woo introduced from Italy. Accessories: Oriental pottery, tapestries, painted la scapes, hunting scenes, mirrors framed and hung in panels of walls. Crys chandeliers designed for candles introduced from France.
REMARKS	The Renaissance came later to England than to some other countries. Italian models inspired designs, but they were adapted to English Gothic, resulting in furniture noted for solidity, with designs cruder and simpler but naively charming. England was still in the "Age of Oak" when the continent had turned to walnut.	The end of the Restoration (1689) marked the beginning of the Age of Wal in England—also the end of Gothic themes in decoration, and the growth the Continental influence already shown under Charles II in the use of S-an curves in chair and table legs, known as the Flemish scroll. Oak was still us but largely in cottages and country homes.

English Decorated Chest (1650);
Jacobean Chair, Tall Cane,
Back with Characteristic Detail,
Carved Stretcher, Scroll Feet

Jacobean Highboy (1675–1700),
Typical Apron, Stretcher, Bun Feet

Late Jacobean Chair, Cane Seat
and Back Insets, Spiral Stretche
Carved Front Stretcher; Jacobe
Gateleg Table, Spiral Turnings

(Left to Right, and Top to Bottom) Walnut Marquetry Clock (1700). WILLIAM AND MARY: Typical Double-hooded Cabinet Top; Chest-on-Stand; Furniture Leg with Inverted-Cup Turnings and Bun Foot; Table with Apron and Curved X-Stretchers. QUEEN ANNE: Typical Highboy with Cabriole Legs; Fiddle-Back Chair; Detail of Broken-Pediment Cabinet Top with Acorn Finial; Cabriole Legs with Club Feet; Wing Chair with Cabriole Legs, Shell Carving on Knees. EARLY GEORGIAN: Cockleshell Ornament, Popularized under Queen Anne; Parcel-Gilt and Walnut Mirror (1730); "Swan's Neck" Broken Pediment, Flame Finial; Detail of Foot Types—Scroll, Pad, Ball-and-Claw; Ornamental Motifs—Chinese Fret, Beading; Chair of "Lion" Period Showing Development from Queen Anne; Walnut Drop-Leaf Table (1720); Triangular Broken Pediment; Acanthus Leaf Carving Motif; French-Style Bracket Foot Used on Cabinets; Detail of Mirror Frame Showing Rococo Carving: Chinese Lacquer Cupboard which Foreshadows Chinese Chippendale Vogue

ENGLAND'S "AGE OF WALNUT"

CHARACTER-ISTICS OF PERIOD	WILLIAM AND MARY Dates—1689 to 1702	QUEEN ANNE Dates—1702 to 1714 (Dutch Influence)
TYPES OF FURNITURE AND WOODS	Furniture developments included: the tallboy (highboy), chest-on-chest, secretary desk—all descendants of the old chest-on-legs; cabinets with drawers; slant-top and knee-hole desks, with provision for writing materials; corner cupboards (with or without glass doors) to house china collections; gate-leg tables, tea and gaming tables; refectory tables disappeared. Walnut replaced oak, with veneers and highly polished wax finish, sometimes over varnish. Lacquering, japanning in red, blue, green, black, gold, were popular; also inlay and marquetry—colorful woods such as yew, cherry, holly, etc., combined with ebony and ivory in elaborate floral or herringbone designs.	Many distinctive furniture pieces mark this period, including: secretaries, cabinets, tallboys, lowboys (often used for dressing tables); the high-backed wing chair called "Queen Anne," many kinds of small tables, tilt-top, etc.; gate-leg dining tables; grandfather clocks. Period originals include: Windsor chairs, of wood; upholstered love-seats, developed into settees with backs like twin chairs; camel-back sofas, with outward curved arms and five cabriole legs; upholstered stools called "squab cushions" used with big chairs in chaise longue effects. Beds little changed—elaborate fourposters with testers. Carved mahogany first began to replace walnut, inlays, etc.; woods beautifully polished; paint and lacquer popular. Construction more scientific, pinned joints, glue, etc.
DISTINCTIVE POINTS IN FORM, DESIGN, DETAIL	Feminine influence began to appear in rich but confused styles marking transition between English Renaissance and Dutch styles. Furniture generally smaller in scale, forms still basically rectangular but curves gaining importance. Chair backs high, in carved wood with cane or upholstery; bedposts very tall, fabric often covering all wood; all-over upholstery popular. Characteristic details: straight legs with trumpet and inverted-cup turnings and bun (flattened ball) feet, replacing scroll legs; flat, carved stretchers, often in X shape; double-hooded cabinet tops; triple-arched aprons on lower section of high chests of drawers; appearance of Dutch style cabriole leg with pad feet and single shell carved on knee; Dutch tulips and butterflies in decorative motifs; distinctive ivory jessamine flower inlays; flowing seaweed pattern in marquetry.	Period marked by strong feminine influence, greatly increased comfort. Chairs first made to fit human form, with backs "spooned" at shoulder line. Scale smaller, but chair and sofa backs higher. Curved, flowing lines supplanted straight, first time in England; symbolized by general use of cabriole leg, conventionalized version of animal's leg with knee, ankle and foot (or bird's claw). Characteristic details: side chair backs in unbroken "line of beauty" curves, with fiddle-shaped splats plain, pierced, or carved; cabriole legs, plain or with scallop shell on knees, no stretchers; duck, pad, web and scroll foot; club foot later replaced by ball-and-claw; bracket foot developed on chests; broken, swan-neck, and scroll pediments replacing hooded tops on cabinets, etc.; acanthus leaf and cockleshell principal motifs for carving; Chinese themes in lacquer.
CEILINGS FLOORS AND	Floors marble or parquet; planks used in simpler homes. Rugs hand-made at home; Orientals, Aubusson and other types imported from France. Ceilings higher; decorated, or plain with deep ornamental cornices.	Floors usually wood, often in exquisite inlay or marquetry; marble still used. Oriental, Savonnerie, Aubusson, rugs popular, also needlework carpets in "Queen Anne stitch." Wilton carpets, 1701. Ceilings: plain, or with painted decoration.
WINDOWS AND DRAPERIES	Windows tall and narrow, harmonizing with high ceilings; panes now clear glass, and larger; double-hung type increasing. Draperies hung with cornices, valances, over-draping, to cut down great height of windows.	Windows still tall, narrow, increasing use of double-hung type. Hangings rich: figured velvets, satin damasks, chintzes, pulled across windows under deep, shaped lambrequins and valances. Trimmings used on draperies.
FABRICS AND COLORS	Fabrics for all decorating purposes increasingly rich and beautiful. Designs of English flowered cotton materials inspired by Indian prints. Famous Tree of Life design (Oriental) popular. Beautiful tapestries, needlepoint, crewel embroideries, widely used. Colors still strong and virile, but with touch of feminine subtlety; reds softened to rich rose; yellow in greenish shades; green in yellowish tones; blues with reddish tinge. Favorite accent colors, black and gold. (See Wallpaper, above.)	Fabrics: French influences shown in rich, smooth textures, beautiful damasks, brocatelles, brocades, tapestries, crewel embroideries; gilded, embossed leather for upholstery. Upholstered pieces trimmed with fringe, gimp, nails; chintz-like printed cotton popular, with free use of foliage and flowers in smaller-scale patterns than Jacobean. Colors: warm but subdued; Chinese rugs, Chinese porcelains influenced color schemes; soft crimson reds, blues, golds, deep yellow, turquoise, off-white, various shades of green.
ACCESSORIES, ORNAMENTS, LIGHTING	Metals: bronze, brass, silver, replacing wrought iron for fixtures and candlesticks; iron painted, when used; designs less massive, more graceful; teardrop hardware characteristic. Popular accessories: Chinese porcelains, other Oriental ornaments; portraits; mirrors with elaborately carved frames (often lacquered); Dutch and English porcelains; heavy crystal chandeliers; firescreens; clocks of every type, including the new tall "grandfather" styles.	Metals: brass for hinges, handles; iron on country pieces only; bronze, painted iron, for fixtures, etc.; silverwork greatly improved; gilt used to touch up carvings or molded plaster. Accessories: Oriental, Dutch, English porcelains; portraits; tapestries; fire-screens; tall clocks; crystal chandeliers. Many mirrors, in two sections to avoid tax on large mirror sheet; edges beveled; frames carved; tops in same curve as top of chair backs.
REMARKS	Most notable development of William and Mary period was increasing emphasis upon comfort in furniture. The vogue of the upholstered wing chair which began then has lasted until the present. Dutch influence William brought in from his native Orange combined with English traditions to produce the comfortable, versatile furniture characteristic of Queen Anne's reign. These short but important periods were so closely linked that many characteristics of each appear also in the other, which makes them appropriate to use together.	Later Queen Anne styles heavier, more elaborate, leading into Early Georgian when mahogany replaced walnut furniture. "Gesso" ornament much used—plaster carved in low relief, gilded. Around 1725 came "lion mask" motif—lion's head carved on knee of exaggerated cabriole leg, lion's paw (instead of claw) grasping ball at foot; "Satyr mask" carvings. Chinese forms came in, with fretwork, beginning tremendous Chinese vogue. Some very beautiful pre-Chippendale pieces produced, in carved mahogany with natural graining.

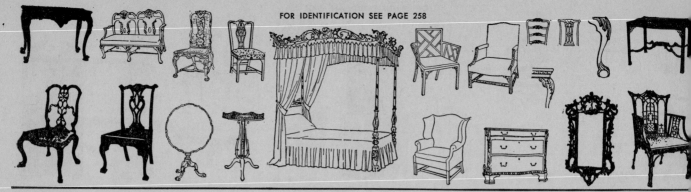

CHARACTER-ISTICS OF PERIOD	THOMAS CHIPPENDALE Active Period—1735–1779 (Dutch, Gothic, Chinese, French Influence)	GEORGE HEPPLEWHITE Active Period—1760–1786
TYPES OF FURNITURE AND WOODS	Chippendale made all kinds of furniture except conventional sideboard, using instead long serving console, often between separate pedestal ends. Sofas and settees developed on Queen Anne lines: arched backs, stuffed, upholstered; cabriole or straight legs; sometimes rolled-over arms. Furniture types include: break-front cabinets, slant-top desks, secretaries, with straight, serpentine, block, or bombe fronts; bow-front chests of drawers; many small tables, often tip-top, specially with tripod base and carved pie-crust or scalloped edge, or gallery-top with pierced metal edge. Early Georgian beds, already changed from fabric-covered types, now exposed foot posts with carved finish of pine-apples, vases, burning torches; in changes carried farther by Chippendale, canopies retained, but only headboard and posts curtained, canopy cornices elaborately carved, posts gradually lowered. Woods: mahogany with exqui-site chiseled carving, rich color, and French polish for soft brilliant luster. Strong construction, perfect joinery. Various woods for gilding and Chinese lacquer.	Hepplewhite was famous for his chairs, also many other kinds of furniture. These include: a great variety of large and small tables; bowed-front cabinets and desks; typical serpentine sideboards, usually with convex center and con-cave ends; square tapered legs with spade feet, oval inlays in front; chests of drawers with bowed fronts, aprons at bottom, and beautifully proportioned splayed bracket feet; comfortable sofas, with soft cushions, graceful outward-rolling arms, six (or more) legs without stretchers; originations—tambour-front desks, drop-leaf tables having one end oval, one square, for double size when together; special window seats for Georgian windows. Mahogany still favorite finish, in smooth surface with brilliant grain; low-relief carving; popu-larized satinwood and hand-painted medallion decoration; used grooving and reeding plane. Woods: various fine woods for marquetry, veneers and inlays. Structure: slender lines made furniture less solid than Chippendale, with stretchers sometimes needed; frequent use of veneer over soft wood base.
DISTINCTIVE POINTS IN FORM, DESIGN, DETAIL	Chippendale designs passed through several phases under influence of Dutch-English, French, Gothic, Chinese styles. Scale smaller than early Georgian heaviness, but still massive, gradually growing lighter, always graceful. Char-acteristic details: cabriole leg with ball and claw foot, heavily carved knee; later, straight leg with grooving or carved fretwork; Greek key, Chinese de-signs, etc., sometimes stretchers; distinctive squared chair backs, with top rails in "yoke" or "Cupid's bow" forms. Types of chair backs include: vase-shaped splat, pierced and carved; splat and allover backs in ribbon, Gothic, Chinese patterns; Chinese cross-hatched splats, or carved pagoda-shaped tops; ladder-backs (pierced horizontal rails). Cabinets had straight or swan-like pediments, bracket feet; secretary doors had thirteen panes of glass set in lead frames. Favorite motifs: acanthus leaf; eagle head; Greek and Chinese foliage, flowers and fretwork; bamboo forms; ribbon patterns; cabochon ornaments. "Chippen-dale Gothic" and "Chippendale Chinese" indicate two distinct periods within this period.	Hepplewhite's sytle carried out his written purpose—to "unite elegance and utility." Less magnificent than Chippendale, in smaller scale, furniture dis-tinguished by lightness, refinement, grace, exquisite finishes. Influenced by the French of Louis XV and XVI, he emphasized curves and beauty of proportion. Characteristics: legs straight (except on French-style pieces), square or round, plain, fluted or reeded; usually spade or thimble feet; front chair legs perpen-dicular to floor, back legs curving out. Chair back separated from seat (joined only by continuation of back legs), in distinctive types: shield, oval, camel, heart, wheel; detail of decoration and central splats varied, including interlaced urn, urn shapes, ribbon patterns, "Prince of Wales" plumes, in painted motif decoration, low relief carving, or inlay. Favorite motifs: plumes (three ostrich feathers), wheat blossoms, garlands, honeysuckle, leaf scrolls, swags; fluting, reeding; oval classic patera, painted classic figures. Serpentine curve in top rail of shield chair back often repeated by Hepplewhite in table and console top, sideboard shelf, four-poster bed cornice, cabinet pediment.
FLOORS AND CEILINGS	Floors: waxed wood, plain or parquet; sometimes marble; planks or tile in cottages; Wilton rugs and carpets popular, often with plain ground and floral borders in damask-like designs; imported rugs from Oriental countries; Savon-nerie and Aubusson from France. Ceilings with deep ornamental cornices.	Floors: same in general as earlier Georgian, except for softer colors in rugs and carpeting, and increasing French influence on English designs. Ceilings sometimes plain, but with increasing use of molded plaster decorations in Adam style.
WINDOWS AND DRAPERIES	Windows: fewer in number and smaller, but still narrow and high, capped by broken pediment; typical "Georgian" arrangement—two windows with rather wide space between, hung with trimmed overdraperies, straight or caught back, under deep, shaped valances. Chippendale loved lavish draperies.	Windows: Hepplewhite interest shown by window-seat designs, also hangings specially selected to go with his furniture; deep trimmed and shaped valances; headed overdraperies usually held back gracefully in a deep inverted V.
FABRICS AND COLORS	Fabrics: rich, beautiful textiles, used for hangings, in silk and velvet weaves; English printed linens and cottons; French toiles de Jouy; rich, heavy fabrics for upholstery; also colorful tapestry, worsted damask, Spanish tooled leather, close-stitch embroidery. All colors soft but still vigorous and virile: green, green-blue (like turquoise); rich yellow, green-gray, brown, yellow-brown; lacquer red; gold (especially on black lacquer).	Fabrics: Hepplewhite preferred silks and satins, especially in narrow stripe de-signs; he liked the serpentine patterns of French styles; also designs of ribbons, festoons and tassels, shields, circles. Colors, softer than any used before: white, gray, gray-green, buff, pale yellow, bluish-green, greenish blue spe-cially characteristic, with soft pinks and pale blues also.
ACCESSORIES, ORNAMENTS, LIGHTING	Metals: silver pieces, skilfully worked, French rococo influence in elaborate designs; brass, bronze, pewter for accessories, lighter than previous styles; elaborately fretted brass drawer handles and key plates. Mirrors, framed in open-work carving, gilded. Portraits. Pottery and porcelain for tableware, ornaments, vases and figurines; Delft, Dresden (Meissen), French, Chinese wares imported; English wares, Lowestoft, Bow, Derby, Chelsea, Worcester, Bristol, and many others. Lighting: candlesticks, candelabra, sconces, chan-deliers—made of brass, silver, crystal; sometimes painted iron in simpler homes.	Metals: silver made more popular by discovery of Sheffield plate process (1742); fine workmanship; rococo French styles gradually replaced by simple classic designs; Hepplewhite and following designers eliminated elaborate Chippendale drawer pulls, substituting simple oval brass plates with beaded molding and center decoration; other metals little changed. Wedgwood, Spode, other fine potteries and porcelain used for various decorative accessories, in addition to those listed under Chippendale. Portraits popular, also landscapes, sporting prints, engravings. Mirrors with large elaborate open-carved frames. Lighting: see other sections of this chart.
REMARKS	Sound yet spirited, Chippendale designs at first developed early Georgian styles, thus serving as a transition between Queen Anne and the late Geor-gians. His book, "The Gentleman and Cabinet Maker's Directior" (1754) be-came a model book for English country cabinet makers, also many fine American craftsmen. Genius enabled him to combine forms and motifs from French, classic, Chinese, Gothic sources with great harmony and beauty, and he was considered by many the greatest English furniture designer.	Designed with great charm, Hepplewhite furniture had a wide vogue and many followers, partly because of his posthumous book "The Cabinet Makers' and Upholsterer's Guide" (1788). Horsehair stuffing came in and was used by him, and he saw the end of the "Age of Mahogany" in England (about 1770). He made wardrobes and chests of drawers in place of the highboys and lowboys which gradually came to be made almost exclusively in America. Working out Adam designs as well as his own, he marks the transition from Chippendale Georgian to the new classical Georgian styles (neo-classic).

GEORGIAN DESIGNERS
DEN AGE"

VERGING TOWARD AGE OF SATINWOOD

ROBERT ADAM, ARCHITECT (In firm with brothers)
Active Period—1762–1792
(Classic and French Influence)

THOMAS SHERATON
Active—1790–1806

Adam first introduced ensemble idea in interiors, making no furniture himself but designing every piece in the room, also all decorative details, to fit his architectural background. Sideboards, consoles, settees, cabinets, tables, bookcases, chairs, all show classic qualities of fine proportions and symmetrical balance combined with delicacy. First modern-type sideboard, all in one piece (1775), attributed to Adam design; pedestal extension table also introduced. Typical pieces include painted commodes, small desks, dressing tables, as well as all larger pieces. Woods: some mahogany, much satinwood; sycamore, natural, or dyed gray and called "harewood"; tulipwood, holly, ebony, used for exquisite inlays; light colored woods for veneers, pine for painted pieces. Finishing: low relief carvings, narrow moldings, decorated painted panels, gilding and parcel gilding, marquetry, all characteristic. Marble used for table and console tops. Wedgwood plaques applied to furniture panels as well as to walls. Pedestals and painted half-moon consoles popular.

Sheraton made many of his earlier pieces himself, later putting his efforts into designs and drawings for other cabinet makers to follow. He specialized in small pieces of furniture for ladies' boudoirs, liquor and knife cases, etc., but designed furniture of all types in use at the time, including kidney-shaped desks and tables, wardrobes, sectional bookcases. His long sofas famous; solid backs with wood top rail, graceful legs, arms upholstered or curved lime. Sideboards masterpieces of design; long, graceful, fronts straight or bowed, often with deep convex ends; brass gallery across back typical, also fitting of cabinet section for liquor storage; knife boxes still used. Invented "pouch" work-or-sewing-table; known for Pembroke tables—folding leaves supported by brackets, instead of legs as in earlier periods; designed many types of beds, including first known twin beds. Woods: usually mahogany for dining rooms, library, bedroom pieces; painted wood, for drawing rooms; various fine woods in veneers and inlays. Structure very durable despite delicate appearance.

Characteristic Adam details, also formality of design, appeared in furniture and background. Lines and motifs classic, after Pompeian models (Roman city decorated by Greek artists). Furniture light, graceful; forms basically rectangular, with straight lines or curves; fine balance in combination of straight lines with circular. Details: legs straight and tapering; square, with spade or block feet; or round, and plain, fluted, or reeded, with turned or molded feet; panel decorations; classical fluting and garland designs for low-relief carving; decorated underframing for tables; fluted frieze or apron. Chair backs: square, round, elliptical, shield-shaped, upholstered, or filled with carved wheel, lyre, urn, etc.; solid or openwork. Motifs, all classic, mostly Pompeian: Grecian honeysuckle and fret; oval patera and rosette; urns and vases; swags of flowers or drapery; pendant husks; endive, pineapple, acanthus leaf, fuchsia, all in classic feeling; Greek key, wreath, and fan; human figures, often mythological; classic animal themes such as ram's or lion's head, goat's foot, griffon, various birds. Lovely Italian-style paintings on furniture panels.

Sheraton's earlier designs strongly influenced by Adam and by Louis XVI styles; later by Greek curves of Directoire and Empire. Designs similar to Hepplewhite, but scale smaller, more delicate, with straight lines predominant. Sheraton used more underbracing; sideboards usually had convex instead of concave corners; he left part of seat frame showing—Hepplewhite drew seat covers well over apron. Characteristics: legs straight, tapered, very slender, usually round, but sometimes square; fluted, reeded, grooved; feet natural, collared, spade, or thimble; later legs sometimes spiral-turned. Chairs: S-shaped arms; backs square, with top rail straight or central panel rising slightly above it; space between lower rail and seat; ornamental lattice-type splats, often with urn or lyre design in center panel; some caning used; Directoire curve in back of later models. Details: reedings, inlays, borders of light woods, narrow inlay contrast bands; turnings, but little carving; first to use porcelain plaques to decorate furniture. Favorite motifs include: swags; the star, cockleshell, fan, disk, sunburst, rosette; also other Adam ornaments.

Floors: hardwood or marble, but often with overall carpeting; floor covering woven in special design for room ensemble; rugs to fit shape of circular, oval, elliptical, octagonal rooms. Ceilings: plaster, with delicate cast plaster relief ornament; straight moldings; arabesque forms; spiderweb designs.

Floors: hardwood or marble, with floor coverings corresponding to influence of period—Adam, or (later) French Directoire and Empire. Ceilings: in simpler homes, usually flat plaster, painted; in more elaborate interiors, molded plaster of Adam styles most frequent.

Windows: new type, called "Palladian" group, with arched center window flanked by two side windows shorter and narrower. Architectural orders (columns, pilasters, etc.) in slender, Pompeian style; classic architectural door and window entablatures. Draperies classic, with formal draped swag valances.

Windows: either Georgian or Adam types, with classic influence in draperies increasing toward end of period. Architectural door and window treatment continued, with slender classical pilasters, cornice and frieze.

Fabrics: textures smooth, rich, but delicate; designs smaller, graceful, feminine; classical and mythological themes; silk and velvet weaves for hangings and upholstery; leather still used for upholstery; embroideries less popular; horsehair introduced. Colors softer and lighter: white, grays, blues, mauves, yellows, corals; old white (like marble), gilt, subtle greens; also special soft shade for background and furniture called "Adam green"—popular in America.

Fabrics: Sheraton favorites, plain stripe and flowered silks, also gold and silver brocades; chintz, toiles, printed linens popular in period, especially for bed draperies—always elaborate in Sheraton designs; knotted fringe widely used for bed valances. Colors in pastel tints, soft and lovely: Sheraton's favorite, blue; frequent color schemes, blue and white, blue and black, very pale blue with yellow.

Metals: brass, silver, and other Georgian metals, worked in classic designs; ormolu mounts introduced (see French periods). Ornaments: jars, urns, vases in Greek forms; marble and bronze busts; mirrors in typical Adam frames, or made part of wall—set in doors, over mantels, in panels; plaster casts, or reproductions of antique statues or urns, set in semi-circular wall niches; Wedgwood Jasper ware, in white classical relief designs, against blue, green or black, used for plaques and accessories—specially vases like Greek and Etruscan models. Lighting: fixtures part of room ensemble; sconces and candle holders; wall mirrors with candle brackets; silver and crystal chandeliers.

Metals: in general, same metals and same uses as in other later Georgian periods; brass in delicate designs for sideboard galleries especially typical; hardware in earlier styles like Hepplewhite (drawer pulls, etc.); about 1795, new brass drawer pull comprising round, square, rectangular, or hexagonal base with lion's head in center holding in its mouth a round brass ring. No fretted outlines after Chippendale. Ornaments: typical late Georgian, with classic lines and fine detail in pottery, porcelain, silver, vases, other accessories. Mirrors with characteristic Sheraton frames, usually square across top with narrow decorated panel in classic frieze effect. Lighting: like other late Georgian periods.

Robert Adam and his brothers used the firm name "Adelphi" as their trademark and worked from the background to the furnishing and decorating, carrying the same motifs through walls, ceiling, floor and furniture in a room. Their furniture designs were executed by skilled cabinet makers, among them Chippendale, Hepplewhite, possibly Sheraton, and this makes it difficult sometimes to identify pieces. Often typical Sheraton lines are modified so that the piece is called "Adam-Chippendale" or "Adam-Hepplewhite." Also, popularity of Adam architecture influenced designers of pottery, rugs and fabrics.

Sheraton, last of the great Georgian designers, is specially important because he gave so much time to drawing and designing and had so many subscribers to three editions of his book, the "Cabinet Maker's and Upholsterer's Drawing Book" (1791-93–1802). His designs were used by cabinet makers in England and America, and his influence was very great. Because he got his effects through purity of line and perfect proportions, his style has a timeless quality which makes it very adaptable to modern use. Earlier pieces particularly fine. Chinese influence persisted through all the "classic" periods.

(Left to Right, and Top to Bottom) ENGLISH REGENCY: Typical Sofa with Rolled Ends, Flared Legs, Striped Upholstery, Wooden Frame; Graceful Chair, Showing Similarity to English Sheraton and French *Directoire*, with Curved Back Line, Flaring Tapered Legs, Classic Decorative Motifs; Detail of Cornucopia-Type Leg. VICTORIAN: Typical Armchair, Showing Regency and *Directoire* Influence in Scroll Back, Curved Back-and-Arm Supports; Corner Shelf, Popular for Display of Ornaments; Mother-of-Pearl Inlay on Chair Back; Settee Showing Combination of Louis XV and Empire Forms with Victorian Detail; Characteristic Side Chair; Table Leg Showing French Influence in Cabriole Curve and Knee-Carving; Mid-Victorian Chair with Tufted Seat, Short Legs, Louis XV Back Influence; Armchair Showing Typical Late Victorian Exaggeration—Too-short Legs, Awkward Curves, Too-high Back, Top-heavy Carving

AGE OF SATINWOOD

BEGINNING OF THE MACHINE AGE

CHARACTERISTICS OF PERIOD	French *Directoire* Influence	ENGLISH REGENCY PERIOD 1810–1820	French Empire Influence	Louis XV Influence	ENGLISH VICTORIAN PERIOD 1837–1900 (Approximately)	Goth Reviv
TYPES OF FURNITURE AND WOODS	Furniture styles were influenced by *Directoire* and Empire interpretations of classic. Typical English designs less stiff and formal, seating furniture more comfortable than French models. Characteristic pieces: sofas with rolled ends, flared cornucopia legs, often with Sphinx arms (used also on chairs); many tables and pedestals with tripod base; dining tables with pedestal bases, flared legs; bookcases and shelves with copper wire screening covering front. Chairs: typical Greek circular (*klismos*) back, or Empire back with top rail slightly rolled over; front and back legs both flaring slightly outward. Woods and materials: rosewood; mahogany with reddish finish; various ornamental woods; considerable ebony or black lacquer, used with gilded or brass mounts or inlays; small furniture pieces often of wood painted black with gold banding; marble popular for table tops, mantels, etc. Construction: cheaper and less finished, with joinery less perfect than preceding periods.			Victorian decoration was a confusion of types and styles, usually drawn fro Regency or other past periods but modified beyond recognition by a search f novelty, and by adapting styles to machine manufacture. Many varieties of f niture pieces produced, especially: large horsehair sofas; many small "extr sofas and love seats; what-nots, hanging corner shelves; chairs in every typ size, style, including "Morris" chair originating in Arts and Crafts rev movement led by Wm. Morris and others toward end of period. Woods an materials: black walnut, heavily carved; mahogany; ebony; carved rosewoo sometimes with ebony or mother-of-pearl inlay; marble widely used for fur ture tops, mantels. Construction: early types of machinery replacing ha work, with loss in solidity of structure as well as in beauty of finish. Cheap production accompanied by over-elaboration in everything, usually with t worst features of previous styles chosen for models and furniture design.	
DISTINCTIVE POINTS IN FORM, DESIGN, DETAIL	Heavier (antique) Greek or Roman forms replacing Pompeian slenderness, with scale larger than Georgian designs and feeling more masculine. Greek curve dominant in all decorating, combined with straight lines. Characteristic details: cornucopias, animal heads, chariots, tripods, worked into structure of furniture, in classic manner. Chairs: backs and legs with Directoire curves, often lyre-shaped splats (see Chart No. 7). Decorative ornament: brass mounts, ormolu, fret. Popular motifs: various leaves, honeysuckle, laurel, ivy; also rosettes and crossed arrows.			Furniture forms: large in scale, clumsy and heavy, badly proportioned. Inspir tion drawn from Regency, Greek, Turkish, Gothic, Venetian, Egyptian styl in addition to Louis XV—the strongest influence. Louis XV curves distorted, e aggerated, in low, writhing lines of tables, chairs, other furniture. Charac teristic details: low legs, high backs; heavy carving, much meaningless ging bread ornament; inexpensive pressed gilt metal often applied to wood, imit ing French ormolu; much tufted upholstery. Great variety of motifs include as favorite designs: fruits, flowers, leaves, bouquets, scrolls.	
FLOORS AND CEILINGS	Floors: Entrance halls often black and white marble squares; other floors usually wood, with room size carpeting in allover leaf and flower pattern; rugs also used, with floral border and center ornament, or in designs recalling arrangement of Roman floor mosaics. Ceiling: high, plain or with plaster center decoration and decorated cornice.			Floors: new, machine-made Axminster allover carpeting very popular, becau of many colors possible in the design as compared to Wilton; strongly color natural flower patterns most widely used; hardwood floors also used, wi flowered rugs. Ceilings: high, usually with molded plaster design and orna decorated cornices.	
WINDOWS AND DRAPERIES	Windows: Double hung, or French casements to floor, both with large panes of glass. Elaborate draperies, rich satin or silk; often in striped fabrics; also in two or three contrast colors through use of deep swag valances or folds of fabric draped over ornamental poles; much fringe trimming; classic draping lines; voluminous folds, often in plain lustrous silk weaves. Cornice headings, pleated valances also favored.			Windows: tall; often hung with lace curtains, attached by rings to heavy orn mental poles or headed by deep gilded cornices called "bonnets"; heavy si and satin overdraperies, with complicated draping and elaborate trimmin tassels and glass-bead fringe popular; formal, lambrequin-type valances wide used, with fancy cornices and tie-backs.	
FABRICS AND COLORS	Fabrics: Silks, satins, damasks lavishly used; stripes popular; also small scale patterns, classic themes, geometrical designs. Colors: much stronger and brighter than preceding periods, with dark shades popular, such as browns, deep reds; sharp contrasts, and strong accents; liberal use of gold and gilding; favorite shades included Chinese pink, bright yellow, light or sea green, buff, apricot, salmon, lavender; contrast colors in wide, bold stripes popular.			Fabrics: several new materials introduced; horsehair and plush used for u holstery with walnut, brocade and satin with rosewood; development of chin one Victorian bright spot, with really good patterns based on natural flowe and grasses in bright, attractive shades. Colors: new synthetic dyes, harsh tone, faded easily, furnishing reason for gloomy parlors, closed to sunligh Favorite color scheme: tomato red carpet, dark green walls, dark wood, mu gilding.	
ACCESSORIES, ORNAMENTS, LIGHTING	Metals: brass mounts; ormolu ornaments; classic lines and styles in silver continued; all metalwork and lighting fixtures simpler in design under classic influence, with Greek, Roman and Egyptian motifs. Ornaments: accessories after classic models, urns, vases, jars, etc.: marble busts popular, usually of famous Greeks and Romans; pedestals often lower section of column shaft; mirrors widely used. Lighting: fixtures of same general type as those used in French *Directoire* and Empire rooms; light and graceful, with classic lines and themes; silver and crystal chandeliers and other fixtures.			Metals: pressed gilt metal ornaments; black iron around fireplaces; much hea silver plate. Accessories: profusion of ornaments, all kinds, called "bric-brac," mostly useless and unattractive; statuary, from blackamoors to molde plaster hands; all sorts of complicated forms and figures in glass, metal, chin glass domes protecting stiff waxed flowers; large, gilt-framed mirrors; dague reotypes, beaded pictures, many prints and paintings on walls; "antimacassar (tidies) over upholstery (to protect it from macassar oil used on hair). Lightin elaborate designs in traditional chandeliers, sconces, etc., with gas jets par replacing candles, usually in central fixture hung above a "center table."	
REMARKS	Regency rooms and furniture were still well proportioned, all details showing classic and French *Directoire* influence; severity and simplicity marked a reaction against elaboration, but dignity and charm were preserved. As the period became so-called "English Empire," then merged into Victorian (1820–1837), furniture became heavier, often clumsy and awkward, with gradual loss of distinction and beauty. The same tendencies were reflected in backgrounds, and in all decorating detail, not only in England but also in mid-19th century France and America.			In this first "machine age" pride of craftsmanship was lost, with machine ef ciency not yet achieved. Lacking any real style leadership, it was a general drab period, imitative and artificial, though a few really fine pieces emerge and some of the chairs and smaller pieces are quite usable in proper surroune ings. On the whole, it was an era of confused design, without balance in a rangement, motivated largely by a tasteless display of possessions. Styles we intricate, curious, with occasional touches of picturesqueness or quaint charm Efforts of the Pre-Raphaelites (Morris, Rossetti, Ruskin, and others) to restor medieval styles resulted only in addition of some Gothic themes and motif	

FIRST GREAT BOURBON STYLE

GOLDEN AGE OF FRENCH STYLES

CHARACTER-ISTICS OF PERIOD	LOUIS XIV—THE "SUN KING" Reign, 1643–1715—Regency 1715–1723		LOUIS XV Reign, 1723–1774	
	Baroque Influence	Renaissance-Classic Influence	Rococo Decorations	Oriental Influence
TYPES OF FURNITURE AND WOODS	Under Louis XIV, first really national French style evolved from magnificence of Italian, Flemish, French Renaissance. Typical pieces: *armoire* and chest-on-stand, later partly supplanted by commodes and bureaus; tables usually rectangular, often very large, X-or-H-shaped stretchers, carved sides, marquetry; architectural consoles (attached to wall); sofas, benches, stools with squab cushions; ''rest-beds,'' ancestors of *chaise longue*; huge beds, elaborately draped, in fourposter style or with canopy over part, but no front posts (as in ''angel beds''). New furniture types: ''confessional'' chair introduced; toilet and night tables; writing-table-bureau, fore-runner of desk-cupboard (secretary). Woods and materials: oak for woodwork and large pieces; walnut, chestnut, sycamore, beech, ebony, for chair frames, etc.; many rare, colored woods for marquetry and inlay. Marble for table tops, also porphyry, alabaster, colorful stone mosaic. Finishes: some waxed wood; much paint; imitation of Chinese lacquer; heavy gilding and parcel-gilding; veneers of wood, horn, ''Boulle'' work. Structure: panel construction left visible; furniture solid and heavy, with underbracing; carving, and turned woodwork, on frames.		Age of comfort; intimacy instead of dignity; feminine influence. Typical pieces: chairs, upholstery or gilded cane; *fauteuil bergere* most characteristic (see glossary, p. 430); *marquise* (wide bergere); *causeuse* (''gossip''), easy arm chair; *confessional*, large bergere-type wing chair, often with matching *tabouret* (stool) to put together like *chaise longue;* many sofas, including day beds with fabric-covered headboards; beds (smaller than formerly), canopied four-posters, alcove beds, also low head and foot board with draperies hung from crown or valance above; console tables, movable or attached to wall; ladies' work and powder tables; ingenious dressing tables; graceful cabinets, commodes; huge wardrobes. Innovations of period: *tambour* desk; firescreen; corner cabinet; hanging wall shelves; *chiffonier*, small piece with drawers (about 1750). Woods, materials: walnut, mahogany, oak, rosewood, cherry, apple, pear, ebony; for inlay, veneer, etc., rare woods in light tones or colors. Marble for table tops, gay red, yellow, orange. Finishes: some natural wood; usually paint; much Chinese lacquer, called ''Vernis Martin.'' Structure: construction disguised under veneers and continuous curves; fine workmanship.	
DISTINCTIVE POINTS IN FORM, DESIGN, DETAIL	This splendid, florid, formal style, based upon Renaissance classic and Baroque elements, was combined with increased interest in comfort. Forms: basically rectilinear and classic, broken by carving and Baroque embellishment. Scale: large but well proportioned; massive. Lines: early period straight, classic, combined with compass curves, only when necessary; later period began tendency toward Baroque S-and-C scrolls, bold and sweeping. Characteristic details: legs (early), short pedestal type, some inverted cup turnings (like English William and Mary); later legs, modified cabriole (see English Queen Anne), with block or carved hoof foot (called ''doe's foot'' leg); chair arms long as seat, straight or scrolled, sometimes upholstered; seats square; chair backs high, broad, rectangular, tops square or slightly bowed; chair frames carved, with solid upholstery, or caning (introduced about 1690); cabinet fronts straight or slightly serpentine. Decorative detail very elaborate: scrolls, carvings, heavy moldings, inlays, veneers, metal mounts. Favorite motifs: classic themes (early period); conventionalized acanthus, lotus bud, other floral forms, broken by gadroon; concave cockleshell and Louis XIV sunburst specially distinctive.		During childhood of Louis XV, court life turned away from great salons to smaller rooms, boudoirs, etc., emphasizing daintiness, charm. Scale: smaller, lighter, to fit rooms. Lines: in revolt against classic forms, all straight lines avoided; free, flowing curves; many S-and-C scrolls, large at top, small at bottom; classic symmetry replaced by optical balance (page 28). Characteristic details: cabriole leg exclusively; doe's foot replaced by scrolled leaf foot or dolphin head; no stretchers; serpentine, bombe, or circular fronts on desks, cabinets, etc.; chair arms short, flaring, often with small pads; serpentine shaping of seat, rails, back; back lower, wide, slightly arched. Embellishment: lavish rococo designs, but light and gay, with less carving; much marquetry; parqueted panels, with distinctive diagonal or cross grained veneers; porcelain plaques, mirrors applied to furniture panels; painting in ivory, soft tones of yellow, gray, green, with fine lines in white, gold or color; metal mounts. Motifs: lozenge, cartouche; shells; pairs of doves, other birds; Cupids, hearts; pastoral figures, rustic tools; grotesques; satyrs; allegorical figures; arabesques; musical instruments; foliage, scattered flowers, nosegays, crumpled ribbons.	
FLOORS AND CEILINGS	Floors: occasionally black and white marble squares; usually parquet; Oriental rugs; increased use of French rugs, *Aubusson* in flat tapestry weave, or *Savonnerie* pile weave, usually in elaborate Baroque scrolled, deep bordered patterns with central motif. Ceilings: central portion with design in heavily molded plaster, or scene painted by such artists as Charles Lebrun.		Floors: oak parquet, herringbone or block pattern; or marquetry with contrasting woods; Oriental rugs, in soft colors, light ground; *Aubusson, Savonnerie* rugs, with rococo patterns, delicate in coloring. Ceilings: deep, ornamented plaster coves, rounding down to molding or cornice; plain center often decorated with large paintings of birds, figures, etc., against blue-sky background.	
WINDOWS AND DRAPERIES	Windows: floor to cornice, French type; architectural treatment given doors and windows, with decorated moldings and cornices; panel embellishments above doors. Draperies: elaborate window hangings of rich silk fabrics under valances of fabric, shaped and draped; ornamental tie-backs, placed low.		Windows: tall, floor to cornice; French type; tops arched or square; mirrors often placed between. Draperies: curtains full, very rich; deeply scalloped fabric valances; bordered edges; graceful curves in draping; feminine feeling of period expressed in beauty of fabrics and trimmings for window draperies.	
FABRICS AND COLORS	Fabrics, very rich and gorgeous: large formal patterns, often worked with gold and silver threads; brocades, velvets, damasks, brocatelles, taffetas, some prints; for upholstery, heavy silks (above), also leathers, serges, tapestries, needlepoint, with trimmings of gold or silver nail-heads, or rich hand-woven fringes. Colors vibrant, strong, fairly dark: crimson, grass green, intense blue, gold; later, lighter tones such as ''aurora'' (yellowish dawn-pink), flame, flesh, amaranth (purple).		Fabrics: brocades, damasks, satins, moires, velvets, taffetas; printed cottons, toiles-de-Jouy (introduced by Oberkampf, 1759), white ground with scenic repeats in colors; patterns, reduced in scale, scrolls, ribbons, flowers, shells; Oriental themes; for upholstery, appropriate silks (often flowered), also leather, needlepoint, pastel-colored tapestries (Beauvais), special designs to fit chairs and sofas; taffeta for summer slip-covers. Colors: all softer, lighter, in muted tones; gold accents; white, gray, cream; pale tints of rose, other pastel tones.	
ACCESSORIES, ORNAMENTS, LIGHTING	Metals, very important for embellishment and accessories: silver, gold; bronze, copper (often gilded); brass, tin, silver, applied and used in inlay, ironwork hinges, elaborate lock-plates; bronze corner mounts typical; *ormolu* developed by Andre Charles Boulle, cabinet maker to the King, used for mounts, motifs, moldings made of cast bronze, chased and gilded. Boulle also invented a new veneer (named ''Boulle work'' after him) made of tortoise shell, inlayed in interlocking patterns with ebony, brass, bronze, copper, German silver. Tapestries: industry developed, with Gobelins, Beauvais, Aubusson, products widely used as wall decorations. Mirrors: Louis XIV hobby, all types used everywhere (''Hall of Mirrors'' at Versailles). Pottery, etc.: Chinese porcelain; Delft ware; native wares, often with Chinese patterns. Lighting: chanceliers of silver, copper, gilded wood, even crystal, already in vogue (from Italy), developed greatly during period; wall sconces of metal, gilded and carved wood with ormolu; elaborate *girandoles*, with branching candle brackets, often mirrored.		Metals: finely worked ormolu mounts; metalwork for clocks, lighting fixtures, shelf ornaments, exquisite in chiseling and finish; wider use of furniture rails and galleries; ironwork favored for stair rails, console tables, shelf ornaments; gilded bronze andirons and other accessories. Potteries, etc.: increased use of glass, Venetian style; Pompadour encouraged Oriental vogue, with imports, Chinese patterns for all decorating materials (called *chinoiseries*), monkey motifs (*singeries*), also Turkish themes; Chinese porcelains; exquisite French Sevres ware, specially in rose, king's blue, gold, later in du Barry rose and apple green (only Sevres factory allowed to use gold); porcelain collecting a hobby, as in Queen Anne England. Tapestries still used, in softer colors, also Chinese lacquered screens. Portraits, other paintings, with picture and mirror frames in carved wood. Mirrors widely used; ''trumeau'' mirror specially distinctive (mirror combined with picture inside frame). Lighting fixtures largely wall sconces and *girandoles*, in bronze and silver; also crystal chandeliers.	
REMARKS	From the time of Louis XIV, France became a leader in decorative styles. The Regency period (1715–23) marked the transition between classic splendor of Louis XIV and the romantic decorative era of Louis XV. Basic forms and architectural outlines of Louis XIV were largely retained in Regency styles, with free S-and-C scrolls introduced in symmetrical arrangement. Veneers of polished walnut, mahogany, rosewood, replaced ebony. Full-bodied Louis XIV colors were softened slightly, more feminine. All lines lighter, scale smaller.		This Louis XV period has frequently been called a climax of art in its relation to interior decorating, with its qualities of originality, richness of detail, beauty of line. Yet some time before the end of the reign a reaction against the rococo, and in favor of classic forms had already begun. Motivated by discovery of Herculaneum and Pompeii (1738–48), encouraged by Mme. Pompadour's interest in them, the new movement was well under way when Louis XVI came to the throne (1774).	

LAST OF THE BOURBON STYLES —

CHARACTER-ISTICS OF PERIOD	Classic Influence	LOUIS XVI—1774-1789	FRENCH PROVINCIAL Developed 1700-1800 (Approximately)
TYPES OF FURNITURE AND WOODS	By accession of Louis XVI, Europe had already returned to classic forms and themes, charmed by delicate beauty and grace of Pompeian-Greek decorations and furniture. Typical pieces: *boudoir* furnishings increased in variety—small desks, work tables, tiny cabinets, three- or two-drawer commodes, chiffoniers, secretary desks; tea-tables, breakfast tables; card-tables very important; consoles with fluted legs (often semi-circular); extension dining tables (4, 6, or 8 legs) widely used; marble-topped commodes in all rooms (drawers, or paneled fronts); roll-top desk introduced, often with secret drawers, ingenious devices (like other writing furniture); chair designed in sets; short-legged *bergère* sets (ancestors of modern unit furniture), two chairs with long seats to put together like day-bed, or regulation seats to fit into large stool placed between them (first, in Louis XV period); typical sofa, and settee, straight back and ends. Beds: distinctive small four poster, with light, open frame supporting small canopy; also small bed, upholstered head and foot-board, equal height; sofa-type bed, upholstered back. Woods, materials (similar to preceding period): walnut, sycamore, satinwood, etc.; oak carcase work, beech chair-frames; mahogany, more toward end of period; marble furniture tops, gray, neutral. Finishes: some natural wood, high polish; mostly soft gray or ivory paint; veneers; Japanese black-and-gold lacquer supplanting colorful Chinese type. Structure: simple and lighter than previous period, but strongly built.	During era of Louis XVI, scanty furniture of smaller provincial homes was still crude, Gothic or Renaissance in form and types. High-back, comfortless chairs with turned woodwork, had bareness disguised by covers and hangings of coarse woolen materials. By the time of Louis XV, greatly simplified versions of court styles were being copied in provinces by local craftsmen, who began—toward end of century—to fuse elements of Louis XV and Louis XVI design into a naive but charming style called French Provincial. Characteristic pieces: huge *armoires* (in place of closets); cupboards, sideboards; large oak tables, benches; metal-fitted dressers; cherry armchairs, colored linen upholstery; *credence* sideboard invented at Arles, in Provence (huge base under small cupboard); cupboards like open-shelf Welsh type; sideboards, uncovered top for serving. Bed (important and distinctive feature): built into alcove, with curtains or paneled doors; or massive four-poster, heavily curtained with blue and white or red and white checked woolen, usually set in alcove. After 1750 greater variety—commodes, secretary desks, new types of tables, wall shelves, tall clocks. Woods: walnut, beech, local fruitwoods, oak (long after discontinued elsewhere). Finishes: light woods stained darker, waxed; oak sometimes stained black, like ebony; natural woods beautifully waxed; occasional piece in colorful paint, but little paint or gilt. Structure: sound, honest construction, but wood not always well enough seasoned to prevent warping.
DISTINCTIVE POINTS IN FORM, DESIGN, DETAIL	Revolt against rococo, with return to natural, simple, rectangular forms. Scale: still smaller than Louis XV; beautiful proportions, symmetry. Line: graceful union of straight lines with curves, usually in circles or ovals. Characteristic details: straight tapered leg (square block form at top with square rosette ornament), decorated by fluting, reeding, beading, some spiral turning; no more cabriole; stretchers reappear; chair backs square, sometimes arched or hooped, varied by circular, oval, or lyre shapes; upholstery or caning, backs and seats; chair arms short, slight curve; chair farms, leg, back, straight, curved sides and front. Embellishment always delicate in scale: right angle and symmetry in ornament again; simpler carving, low relief, surface patterns; marquetry, inlays, in conventional classic or checkered designs; cameo-like inlaid plaques, low relief or painted porcelain; ormolu mounts; brass moldings on drawer edges, etc.; *chinoiseries* still popular. Motifs, pastoral or classic, Pompeian type: rosettes, medallions, garlands, swags, scrolls, festoons, paterae (see English Adam period); acanthus leaf, pomegranate, myrtle, wheat sheaves; pleated ribbons, ribbon bows; baskets of flowers, gardening tools; lyre, urn, flaming torch, trophies, animal heads, mythological figures; classic architectural forms—columns, volutes, etc.; favorites of Marie Antoinette were roses and foliage, swan, shepherd's crook.	The curving character of Louis XV lines and forms gradually became basic to French Provincial, with Louis XVI modifications, some trace of *Directoire* later but no Empire influence. Strength of Louis XV type shown by prevalence of typical modified cabriole (doe's foot) leg, with long S-curves, sometimes used in crude form even on peasant kitchen tables. Lines: in better pieces, graceful, dignified, with irregular free curves softening outlines, but no extreme in design or decoration. Scale: ranging from large and heavy in cruder peasant pieces, to feminine delicacy in some finer furniture; average desk, chair, small to-medium in size, but sturdy and substantial, with good proportions. Characteristic details: many chairs with turned wood frames, large homespun-covered cushions tied to backs and seats; rush seats frequent; ladder-back chairs; lyre-shaped backs, various other typically Bourbon details, local modifications; benches and settles, cushions, and straight, turned legs; later, cabriole-leg upholstered chairs appeared in better homes. Embellishment: Louis XV panel irregularly curved shape, became distinctive for door, cabinet or wall panels, decoration centered on armoire doors and bed frames or alcoves; carving simplified; a little marquetry used. Motifs: less elaborate of the typical Bourbon themes, mingled with peasant motifs and art; successful merging of Louis XV with Louis XVI distinctive of these styles.
FLOORS AND CEILINGS	Floors: usually oak parquet; Oriental rugs in soft tones; Savonnerie and Aubusson (latter most popular) in period motif patterns. Ceilings: plain, except in very elaborate rooms, then painted cloud-and-sky effects.	Floors: tile, or wide oak planks, waxed; hand-made gros-point rugs, in floral patterns; in more formal homes, Aubusson, Savonnerie, Orientals. Ceilings low; heavy exposed beams, except in better houses.
WINDOWS AND DRAPERIES	Windows: cornice-to-floor French type; door, window trim, delicate classic entablature; decorative panel above—relief carving, or painted motif in circular or ellipse-shaped frame. Draperies: daintier than former periods, less voluminous; headed by cornice treatment or lambrequin-type valance (usually straight). Typical drapery fabric motifs: small flowers sprinkled on light ground; small flower sprays on stripes.	Windows: short casements, set in thick walls, with deep ledges. Draperies simple cornice or valance treatment, with full draw-curtains in checked or *toile*-style fabrics. Like English and American cottage styles. Later types, in better homes, simplified versions of Louis XV and Louis XVI drapery fabrics and styles.
FABRICS AND COLORS	Fabrics lovely, but lighter weight than before, less expensive: weaves listed for Louis XV; exquisite patterns of famous Lyons silks and toile-de-Jouy cottons; motifs distinctive, symmetrically placed—small pastoral landscapes, classic figures, scenes (often in medallion-frames); stripes; small, delicate floral or other characteristic patterns. For upholstery: fabrics, tapestries, needlework, with pattern designed to fit seat or back; also tooled leather; brass nail trimming, with no gimp or braid. Colors, even more muted at first, stronger later: white and gold for walls gradually replaced by off-white, or soft, delicate shades of gray, green, blue, pink, gray-blue, fawn, greenish-gray.	Fabrics, ranging from fine silks and real toiles-de-Jouy, in current patterns, to hand-made woolens and checked ginghams: blue-and-white or red-and-white checked wool used for bed-hangings; printed cottons (sometimes quilted), percales, calicoes, chintz-types; gay, charming, home-made textiles and embroideries of all kinds, in original designs, distinctive for upholstery, hangings, wall coverings; plaid pattern popular; simpler types of silk fabrics used, specially striped satin. Colors: early use of bright wall colors tended later toward neutral grays and white; in general, favorite shades were bright reds and blues, with browns and warm greens next; also yellows, tans and cream.
ACCESSORIES, ORNAMENTS, LIGHTING	Metals: ormolu mounts; brass for small railings, moldings; silver, brass, beautifully worked. Porcelains: Chinese, European, imports; exquisite French pieces (Sevres, etc.), with period motifs, Chinese patterns. Beautiful clocks, screens. Terra cotta nymphs and satyrs by artist Clodion, famous. Exquisite knick-knacks—small paintings on ivory (miniatures), etc. Mirrors: square or rectangular, shaped tops elaborately carved, many trumeau style, oval shape. Lighting: fixtures smaller, lighter; exquisite classic designs. Ormolu, silvered bronze, marble, alabaster, tole, glided wood, crystal, biscuit ware, porcelain, for sconces; silver and crystal chandeliers; oil lamps introduced.	Metals: pewter largely used instead of silver; wrought iron for cleverly made fittings, andirons, etc.; copper for decorative cooking utensils; tole for candlesticks, lighting fixtures. Potteries: brown casseroles; brightly colored pieces from Rouen and other French makers placed on walls or shelves; Quimper ware popular, made in a fishing village, and decorated with local scenes in gay colors, finish purposely crude. Simple colored glass pieces widely used. Other accessories: those typical of period, depending on degree of prosperity in home. Chinese porcelains often found in later years. Lighting: tole, simple iron, brass, candle fixtures.
REMARKS	Symmetrical balance, emphasized under Louis XIV, now even more important, but without over-formality and heaviness. Louis XVI styles, with their refinement and perfection in detail, carried on the traditionally feminine feeling in French decorating which had marked its early divergence from the masculine interests and tastes dominating all earlier English developments. As the Louis XVI period had begun before the death of Louis XV, so revolutionary themes began to appear here and there before the Revolution—tripod-base tables, caryatid supports, Sphinx heads and other *Directoire* motifs.	It is a mistake to think of "French Provincial" styles as merely crude and peasant-like. They include also many local interpretations of court styles, worked out by excellent craftsmen for provincial homes of lesser nobility or the wealthy merchant class, in styles following a few years after Paris originals. One characteristic all these styles had in common—the houses were meant for pleasant, comfortable living rather than display. This fact combined with merging of elements from the great Bourbon styles to create a graceful, but sturdy style, with special aptitude for mixing with other styles of similar origin.

THE REVOLUTION

NAPOLEON'S EMPIRE

FRENCH *DIRECTOIRE* (Directory) 1789–1804 (Including Years of Revolution, Consulate) Pompeian Influence	EMPIRE—1804–1814 Greek and Roman Influence / Influence of Conquered Countries

While the Revolution ending the reign of Louis XVI made no definite contribution to French styles (except to eliminate monarchistic symbols wherever possible), the four short years of the Directorate (1795–99) developed a very characteristic style which persisted through the Consulate, to the period which began with Napoleon's coronation as Emperor (1804). This style combined Louis XVI elements of classic lightness and grace with a still stronger classic influence which tended toward severity in backgrounds. Typical pieces: daybed-sofas, head and foot-board equal height, modeled after classic couch, type made famous by Mme. Recamier; upholstered sofas often high at one end with back sloping toward lower arm at foot, forerunner of Empire mode; light, graceful sofas and settees with backs and ends straight, or scrolled slightly outward; many small tables (round, oval, rectangular), made after Grecian models with animal form details; rectangular commodes, simple pilasters or columns at ends; tall Pompeian-type tripod pedestal-tables; light, decorative chairs in Greek styles, gracefully curved to fit body; bed placed with long side against wall, equal height head and foot-board, canopy hung above and supported from wall. Woods, materials: ebony and light fruitwoods popular, also mahogany and chestnut; marble commode and table tops. Finishes: fine polishes, light paint, some gilding. Structure: unstable economic conditions made cheaper construction necessary, with lower quality, less perfection in detail.

Empire furniture often sacrificed comfort to classic authenticity. Typical pieces: couches for dining (Roman style), with low tables; rest-beds in one piece, raised and in Grecian roll; couches and sofas, Greek rolled arms, often no backs; sofas, one end of back higher, arms and legs in simple Greek curves, upholstered but with ormolu-mounted wooden frame; beds (usually against wall or in alcove), head and foot-board alike, several types—low four poster without tester (pineapple-topped posts), "gondola" ("boat") bed, "sleigh" bed; beds, backless sofas, often with bolster at each end; tables, usually round, all sizes, central support, or legs joined by shelf at bottom, with mythological monsters, caryatids, classic columns as supports; one table often in center of room; rectangular cabinets, commodes, consoles, etc., caryatid or column supports at ends. New types: "jardiniere" table, often with plaques of Sevres porcelain; portable dressing table mirror, swinging in frame attached to small drawer; "drum" stool; upholstered Roman-type stool, curved arch supports (also in *Directoire*). Woods and materials: rich, dark colored woods, specially mahogany stained deep red, solid or veneer; ebony; some amboyna, elm, apple, pear; also (for chairs) rosewood, yew, walnut, beech; oak carcase work. Finishes: paint, gilding on metal mounts; fewer moldings; large plain surfaces veneered in rare woods, grain emphasized; high polish. Structure: solid; cross pieces, truss supports, often used; chair legs in one piece, floor to arm.

Styles combined almost austere simplicity with direct charm, showing definite feminine influence expressed through Greek forms. Scale: both furniture and decoration small, delicate, but with excellent proportions. Lines: straight lines and rectangles combined with Greek curve and scroll to produce effect of great grace, restraint, slenderness. Characteristic details: front chair legs delicately turned, round, straight and tapered, back legs swung outward; few stretchers; seats square or round; backs designed with long, slow, sweeping curves, ending in typical outward scroll at top; upholstered, or filled in with palm leaf, crossed arrows, beneath top horizontal panel with urn or diamond decoration; arms straight or rolled outward, sometimes with swan support. Embellishment: painted ornamentation, largely replacing carving and other modeled forms because of greater adaptability to changing modes of period; no marquetry. Motifs included Pompeian Greek, and revolutionary themes: mythological bird and animal motifs suggested by ancient vases and frescoes, replacing floral and pastoral designs of Louis XVI; arabesques, festoons, rosettes, swans, urns, lyres, popular; also revolutionary pikes, clasped hands, Liberty caps, victory torches, military trophies, fasces (bundle of sticks with axe in center); geometrical patterns widely used in diamonds, circles, stars, stripes, lozenges, ovals, octagons.

Style of obvious richness, formality. Ancient Roman forms dominant. Scale: massive, heavy. Lines: geometrical, rectangular, straight, severe, without grace; except for classic curves in chairs, sofas, etc. Characteristic details: four chair legs flared, to front and back; or, back legs flared, front legs vertical, straight, term-type (round or square); typical feet included ball, scroll (often with leaf shoe), dog's paw, winged claw, bear's and lion's claw; chair backs, either Greek *klismos* type, or curved to fit body, slight back roll in top rail (see *Directoire*); lyre-shaped splat, or cross-rail between seat and top; Sphinx, swan, favorite arm supports. Embellishment: some turnings, little carving, no marquetry, inlays only in metal (silver); much elaborate ormolu, sharply outlined, but not fine workmanship; plaques of Sevres ware, or classic Wedgwood, in white biscuit on blue, applied to furniture. Motifs of period included symbols of conquest, also typical themes from conquered peoples (Rome, Egypt, etc.): crossed swords, drums, spear-heads, winged victories; obelisks, pyramids, Sphinx-heads; winged griffins, lion's paws, swans; mythological divinities, heroes, monsters; Greek, Roman, Pompeian swags, garlands, arabesques; horn of plenty; pineapple, lotus, palm, conventionalized leaves and flowers; specially imperial eagle, conqueror's star, laurel leaves and wreath, Napoleonic insignia—the bee, or capital N (often in center of victory wreath).

Floors: oak parquet; occasionally marble; rugs in small patterns, with characteristic motifs of period, in *Aubusson and Savonnerie* weaves. Ceilings: plain, with rounded cove above light frieze or cornice.

Floors: tile, marble, oak parquet; bare floors popular because of "antique" feeling; large carpets more popular than rugs. Ceilings: high; usually flat; plain, except for occasional molded plaster ornament around center fixture.

Windows: French type, room height, panes fewer and larger; door and window casings usually flat, circular or square top, door panels with characteristic motifs. Draperies: elaborate hangings, draped over spear-head poles or hung by large brass rings on decorative brass rods; swag valances typical, cascade or jabot at each side of window; wood fringes and classic borders. Cornice seldom used for drapery. Formal line and contrast colors characteristic.

Windows: simple classic treatment, door and window openings, wood or marble; door panels often diamond-shaped, or decorated; tall French windows, sometimes wide with arched tops. Draperies: voluminous, elaborate, rich, of heavy silks patterned in strong contrasting colors; formal draping and tiebacks; deep swags (often crossed) as valance; side jabots; heavy fringes, tassels, gold trimming; sometimes three sets of draperies in contrast colors.

Fabrics: satins, moires, other richly colored silks; formal classic patterns or very narrow stripes; toiles-de-Jouy in landscapes or typical motif designs. Colors: popularity of strong, deep tones increasing, with Pompeian frescoes and mosaics now serving as inspiration for positive, brilliant shades such as earth reds, deep yellows, Pompeian red and greens, black. Restraint of this style makes balance in use of strong color essential.

Fabrics, rich, distinctive; luxurious weaves, strong, vivid colors, conventional repetition of spaced motifs in characteristic spot-pattern designs: satins, damasks, brocades, moires, small-patterned velvets; lampas; woolens with silk or satin appliques in designs or stripes; fine (often scenic) toiles-de-Jouy; additional, for upholstery, tapestry, worsted damask, leather; upholstery trimmings, fringes and gimps. Colors: bold, contrasting; walls in grays, greens, chalky pinks; also dark tones of brown, deep green, maroon; favorite shades, wine reds, royal purple, bright blues and yellows, emerald green, black, violet, with much actual gold or gold color for trimming (also other metals).

Metals: brass used for lion-head drawer pulls, claws, other decorative purposes. Accessories in general carried on from Louis XVI, still with more emphasis on classic in line and motifs; urn, lyre shapes used in wall sconces, vases, etc. Statuary popular, bronze or marble. Paintings by the artist Jacques Louis David much admired; many designs of his inspiration worked out by decorators of period. In accessories and lighting fixtures, as well as in larger decorating forms, classic motivation combined symbols of republican Rome with pure Greek themes, and a strong reaction against pomp and display of the entire Bourbon era.

Metals: much gold and silver ornament; ormolu used everywhere, gold-encrusted, but cheaply cast, not finely chiseled; ormolu key-hole coverings, accessories, bronze ornaments. Potteries, etc.: fine porcelain vases and urns. Other decorative objects: pedestals, with large urns or marble statues, often in wall niches; harps; mirrors in Empire frames; bronze and marble busts. Lighting: previous types of fixtures and holders continued, with typical Napoleonic motifs of period, greater severity, wider use of Egyptian themes; candelabra with caryatid supports distinctive. Classic architectural forms applied to frames, fixtures, many accessories.

Because of the short period of time involved, and overlapping influences, it is often difficult to know where *Directoire* ends and Empire begins. Many of the classic forms and lines are similar, the chief difference being in scale and feeling, with *Directoire* lightness and charm swallowed up in the massive, heavy style fostered by Napoleon. Essence of *Directoire* decoration was sincere effort to achieve a true interpretation of classic Greek and Roman forms and feeling. The close kinship which links *Directoire* styles with English Regency and American Federal designers is due to the classic charms of Pompeii.

All distinguishing marks of the period are closely related to Roman Empire characteristics, with broad, austere surfaces, sharp edges and straight lines, unvarying symmetry in design and arrangement, combined with symbols of power. This grand style retained none of the grace and gaiety of previous periods. It had many elements of Louis XIV style, such as masculine feeling, large scale, symmetry, vibrant color, classic motifs, yet does not mix well with early pieces and not at all with later Bourbon periods. After the Empire, French styles degenerated, but were first to emerge into definitely Modern forms.

CHARACTERISTICS OF PERIOD	EARLY AMERICAN PERIOD 1608–1720 (Approximately)	AMERICAN GEORGIAN PERIOD 1720–1780 (Approximately)
TYPES OF FURNITURE AND WOODS	Early American furnishings were brought from Europe, copied from such pieces, or made from memory, often with local or individual modifications and touches. Based at first upon Gothic-Renaissance cottage forms, reminiscent of the Tudor oak period, they had distinctive local motifs and characteristics (as "Connecticut chest," "Hadley chest," etc.). These low chests with hinged tops, paneled and decorated sides, one or two drawers at bottom, evolved later into chests of drawers; chests-on-legs developed into cupboards, paneled and carved like European court cupboards; early, crude, desk-boxes became the "Governor Winthrop" slant-lid desk; corner cupboards came later; early tables, crude Gothic trestle or "hutch" (chest) type; later, Elizabethan refectory types, then Jacobean gateleg; a distinctive New England table had turned legs, pine top, molded stretchers, wide overhang, curved edge apron (often with drawer); space-saving drop-leaf tables popular, among them "butterfly" table in unstained maple (originating in Conn. about 1700); chairs were stools, benches, settles, wainscot chairs, Brewster and Carver, then Jacobean, William and Mary types; beds, tester-canopy four-posters or spool-turned, also trundle beds, cradles. Woods: oak, pine, maple, walnut, beech, ash, cherry, elm, cedar, cypress. Finishes: natural, waxed, or paint. Structure: sturdy, braced with stretchers, made with wooden pegs, hand-wrought nails used later. Resemblance to French Provincial.	Increased comfort, combined with beauty, set keynote for Georgian period in America, with certain deviations from English prototypes; also, earlier influences persisted longer, as in English provinces. Typical pieces: simple fiddle-back chairs, with rush seats; American Windsor chair (gradually replacing ladder-back), made with straight, turned legs, set in seat at slant (instead of English cabriole legs), hickory instead of oak, several types of back—hoop, fan, comb, most popular, all without English splat—usually nine spindles and shaped saddle-seat; rocking chairs, as early as 1745; William and Mary, Queen Anne types in chest-on-chest with simple molding top finish, lowboy and highboy (called "tall-boy") in maple as well as walnut and mahogany, all Georgian drop-leaf tables popular (gate-leg, Pembroke, etc.), also tripod base tilt-top tables, hinged card tables; Georgian dining room pieces; sofas, couches, day-beds, wing chairs; chests of drawers, slant-lid desks and secretaries, knee-hole desks; beds, canopied four-posters (often tent-type), later posts lower, no tester top. Woods: maple, pine, cherry, pearwood, walnut, then mahogany and bird's eye maple or curly maple for inlay and veneer instead of English satinwood. Finish and construction: like English models, with books by Georgian cabinet-makers as text-books; country furniture cruder but sturdy, often charming, usually painted; typical Windsor chairs in black or bright paints.
DISTINCTIVE POINTS IN FORM, DESIGN, DETAIL	In forms, scale, general design, and many details, Early American styles followed English models, through Tudor and Jacobean periods, into William and Mary. Characteristic details: simplification, often crudeness of decoration and finish; rush seats generally used for side chairs; typical straight-line chairs, such as ladder-back, banister-back, had turned arms, legs, and stiles, with back legs, which continued up as back supports ending above top rail in mushroom-type finial; loose cushions more frequent than upholstery on chairs, stools, benches; later, Jacobean-type chairs had caning, cane or rush seats, with cushions, S-and-C scrolls, spiral-turned legs, scroll feet; late in period, William and Mary style tables and other furniture, introduced characteristic trumpet-shaped legs, inverted cup turnings, etc. Embellishment: by 1680, Gothic style of elaborate carvings replaced by simpler types of decoration; low relief carving, painted designs, specially on chests and cupboards; also turnings, strap-work patterns, applied split spindles (very characteristic); wooden handles, round or oval. Motifs: Tudor rose, acanthus, arcaded panel, sunflower. Regional decoration and motifs, Pennsylvania Dutch: unfinished wood for utility pieces, with gay peasant-type decoration on "bride chests" and many smaller pieces; paintings, in bright colors, included animals, people, flowers and foliage, checker-board and zig-zag designs, scallops, rosettes, other naive, simple motifs in conventionalized patterns. Early period styles lasted in country houses into 19th Century.	American-made furniture of this period was Georgian in line, scale, form, feeling, following a few years behind English models, much less ornate, and often characteristically modified in some details. Distinctive points: short cabriole legs ("bandy" legs), ending in club foot, later in claw-and-ball, or lion's paw foot, used on early wing chair with arms rolling horizontally or vertically; later Chippendale type wing had cabriole, or straight grooved leg, often carved skirt; followed by Hepplewhite type, with taller wings, back and wings sometimes in serpentine outline; Hepplewhite-type, straight, slender legs came in just before Revolution. American buffets narrower than English style; cabinet doors the same, usually with thirteen leaded glass panes. Distinctive American originals: "Goddard" block front desks, chests of drawers, cabinets; fronts cut from solid wood block, with three vertical panels, two outer ones convex, center one concave, shell motif at top of each; bracket foot; curved line in legs and scroll pediments; French-type carving ornament; Louis XV irregular panels on cabinet doors; made by firm of John Goddard, R. I. cabinet-maker, in mahogany, sometimes maple, cherry, walnut. Embellishment: veneering, cross-banding, in walnut and butternut, soon after 1700; some carving, but simpler than European types; decalcomania decorations popular, also paintings and stencils. Motifs (varying with localities): pineapple cones for newel and bed posts; rose, acanthus leaf, cockleshell; tassels, scrolls; shells, leaves, husks, gadrooning; French wreath, delicate *Chinoiserie*, favorite Philadelphia designs
FLOORS AND CEILINGS	Floors: wide planks laid with wooden pegs, oiled and polished; rugs small; hand-woven, or braided rags in hit-or-miss pattern, or hooked rugs in geometrical or floral designs. Ceilings: low; exposed timbers from hand-hewn logs, oiled, perhaps stencilled; later, some wood paneling, or plain plaster.	Floors: wide boards still, in country homes, with hand-loomed rag carpets, hooked and braided rugs; beautiful parquet in finer houses, sometimes marble in halls; Oriental rugs; imported "Turkey work" and needlework; English Wilton carpets and rugs. Ceilings: higher, plain or with delicate molded plaster
WINDOWS AND DRAPERIES	Windows: small; casement type; small rectangular or diamond-shaped panes, set in lead, English cottage style; early, iron shutters (for protection); double-hung sashes only after 1700; dormers occasionally; larger windows in warm South, often in French style, specially in later houses. Draperies: simple, sill-length cotton or linen draw curtains; sometimes with simple valance; silks found more often later; more formal in South, and toward end of period (see American Georgian).	Windows: larger; often with folding shutters, or Venetian blinds (later in period); windows recessed in deep walls, sometimes window seat below; French windows in Southern houses. Draperies: short chintz, calico, or sheer ruffled curtains in simpler bedrooms and country houses; floor-length draperies in formal rooms, straight or draped, made of imported textiles; shaped valances, or draped swags, often with jabots; elaborate fringes, tassels, tie-backs.
FABRICS AND COLORS	Fabrics: homespun, hand-woven wools and worsteds; also cottons and linens; imported calicoes; with India prints, and printed cottons in chintz style later; occasionally English damask, brocade or needlework, used for cushions or wall decoration; leather or "Turkey work" for early upholstery. Beautiful hand-woven coverlets are distinctive, also exquisitely pieced quilts. Colors: after more somber tones of early Puritan days, reds, blues, greens, and yellows used in cheerful shades, largely in fabrics against soft wood tones.	Fabrics: early, English printed cottons, Indian prints, hand-blocked prints made in America; imported damasks (silk or silk-and-worsted), crewel embroidery on drill cloth, drill cloth; later in period, imported velvets, brocades, brocatelles, reps, serges, also chintzes and toiles-de-Jouy; for upholstery, leather and haircloth also used. Colors: shades of English periods; painted wall colors, white (favorite), cream, pearl tones, gray-blue, mustard, Georgian green, red, brown.
ACCESSORIES, ORNAMENTS, LIGHTING	Metals: early, pewter for cups, basins, tankards, candlesticks, etc., instead of silver, brass, or porcelain; wrought iron for andirons, other fireplace fittings, hanging lanterns, candlesticks, stands, and typical decorative hinges—H and L, strap, cobra, rat-tail, butterfly shapes—in scale with doors; copper cooking utensils, warming pans, etc., used for decoration also; brass for hinges later, also silver-plating; brass and silver accessories used increasingly toward end of period. Other accessories: porcelain ware, brought from England, also local ware after 1700; pieces of armor; guns and samplers on walls; pictures and maps (English types); few mirrors until after 1700; clocks also rare, usually wall type with open weights. Lighting: fixtures simple but charming; primitive oil lamp (Betty-lamp) of iron or copper, often hung from base for table use; floor candle-stands, with adjustable arms, of wrought iron and wood; simple wall shelves and brackets for candlesticks; sconces and center fixtures later, of brass, copper, pewter, even silver; these metals also for single and group candlesticks.	Metals: in finer homes, brass replacing wrought iron for fireplace fittings, fixtures, etc.; silver replacing pewter, with fine silversmiths (Paul Revere, many others). Potteries, glassware: Oriental porcelains; English wares, Staffordshire, Wedgwood, Worcester, Chelsea, Derby, etc.; slip-pottery, also Stiegel glass (tones of purple, blue, red-violet), from Pennsylvania; "Jersey glass" by Wistar (dark blue, turquoise, amber, green, brown). Pictures: imported engravings (also made in America after 1729), mezzotints; botany prints, silhouettes, oil portraits. Mirrors: increasingly popular after 1700, Queen Anne two-piece type at first, after 1750 in various Georgian styles; mirrors attached to small box of drawers for bureau top typical. Clocks: very important, with fine clock-makers such as Willard family; first tall case clock made 1722, many after that; also shelf, wall clocks, enclosed weights. Lighting: many imported fixtures; elaborate wall sconces of silver, cut glass, brass, bronze, pottery, often with tin or mirrored reflectors; candlesticks and chandeliers of brass, silver, glass, crystal; glass "hurricane" shades typical American style.
REMARKS	The terms "Colonial" and "Early American" are loosely used, many writers applying Colonial to furniture brought from abroad before the Georgian era, and Early American to pieces made here during that same period, others using it to cover American styles up to 1820. Varying national backgrounds of New World settlers influenced development of definite regional styles, with certain characteristics in common resulting from pioneer conditions shared by all. New England homes were echoes of Yorkshire cottages; Pennsylvania Dutch settlements reflected medieval German forms, while Philadelphia developed from Quaker simplicity into a center of Georgian elegance; Charleston, New Orleans, and other Mississippi and Gulf cities, were strongly under French influence; Florida and the West Coast were Spanish in tone. These regional influences have persisted to some degree through all periods.	Much fine early Georgian furniture was imported by the Colonies, and by 1750 American craftsmen had produced really distinguished pieces modeled after them—the highboy being a notable example. By 1760, the Chippendale vogue had crossed the water to become an American favorite, followed by Hepplewhite styles. The classic Adam influence was felt just before the Revolution, and carried over into the Federal Period, influencing backgrounds particularly. In Philadelphia, fine cabinet-makers such as William Savery became apostles of Chippendale, turning out much fine furniture classified as the "Philadelphia Chippendale" school.

AMERICAN FEDERAL PERIOD
1780–1830 (Approximately)

During this period American designers and cabinet makers of real distinction were developed, among them Samueal McIntire and Duncan Phyfe. Hepplewhite models were followed, then Sheraton, with Adam influence; later styles adopted English Regency, French Directoire, Empire, characteristics. Typical pieces: Hepplewhite serpentine-front sideboard popular; dressing tables; Hepplewhite and Sheraton several-part tables, extension dining tables, hinged card tables; Pembroke tables, many small tables (tilt-top, three tiered, etc.), drum tables; tambourine desks; scroll-pediment secretaries, china cabinets, bookcases; dressing tables; bow, serpentine or straight front chests of drawers, sideboards, etc.; chairs, sofas, like English models; "Martha Washington chair" distinctive; beds like earlier period, but lighter, more delicate lines; heavy Empire "sleigh" bed later. Original development: "Hitchcock" type chair (early 19th Century); partly handmade, partly by machine; turned legs, rush seat; slender, based on Sheraton-Empire types; back in gentle curve, horizontal slats in various designs; painted; decorated with gilding, decalcomania, painting, or stencils. Woods: same as earlier periods; specially favored, white walnut, mahogany, maple, pine, cherry, beech, yellow poplar, apple, pear, red gum instead of mahogany (called "bilsted"); also, satinwood, rosewood. Finishes: fine polish; paint; Oriental lacquer; japanning. Structure: like European, often very fine, as in Phyfe, etc.

During the best years of the Federal Period (1795–1818), much exceptionally beautiful furniture was produced in America, before it began to reflect Empire heaviness. Scale: light and delicate, but substantial, with very fine proportions. Lines: cabinet makers and designers followed English models (late Chippendale, Hepplewhite, Adam, Sheraton), with French influence introduced later through refugees (after French Revolution); American country-made pieces sometimes a little clumsier in line and proportion than European prototypes, but fine work of men like Phyfe unsurpassed in beauty of line. Special Phyfe characteristics: delicacy in form and detail; use of mahogany; graceful proportions; Grecian curved line in chair backs and legs; lyre motif for chair backs, sofa arms, small table pedestal supports; concave flared table and sofa legs; tripod-base table; metal feet and casters often used (specially brass animal-paws on table-leg tips); typical decorations, reeding on legs of chairs or narrow panels, exquisitely fine carvings, profuse use of acanthus leaf motif, some ormolu mounts and ornamental brass hardware, with Directoire and Empire motifs appearing later. Embellishment (Federal Period): in general, same as European models, but characteristically simpler in detail and ornament; fine veneering and inlays used. Motifs: classic themes of English and French models; special development of eagle motif, symbolizing new American Republic, used wherever possible; Phyfe's classic lyre outstanding, with strings often in ebony or brass for contrast with rich red mahogany.

Floors: wide planks, beautifully polished; fine parquet flooring; marble occasionally in halls; Oriental rugs brought by merchant ships; also English Wiltons, Brussels carpets; later, Aubusson and Savonnerie rugs from France. Ceilings: like European, Adam styles in molded plaster popular; later, plain.

Windows: French type in South, also appearing in other sections; usually recessed in deep wall; Palladian type popular; simple molding trim, often with "ear" effect at top; occasional arched tops over doors and windows; inside shutters; Venetian blinds. Draperies: ruffled tie-backs, chintz curtains, in simpler rooms and homes; finer homes, elaborate trimmed draperies in imported silks, formal English or French styles; boxed cornices; fabric valances, straight or shaped; also swag, jabot.

Fabrics: beautiful imported silks, chintzes, printed linens, toiles-de-Jouy; also exquisite laces from France, silks and embroideries from China, brocades, satins, velvets, taffetas, moires, lampas—all other typical English and French materials; also (for upholstery), plush, tapestries, crewel embroidery, needlepoint, "linsey-woolsey," haircloth, leather; stripes, solid colors, patterns of period in France or England. Colors: similar to European; soft blues, grays, olive green popular; Duncan Phyfe favorites, grays, blues, greens; stronger colors later, also U.S. flag shades.

Metals: brass andirons, fenders, candlesticks, hardware, pitchers, some ormolu mounts, etc.; beautifully worked silver tableware, accessories, fixtures, etc. Potteries, glass: all types fine imports, especially French, English and Chinese porcelains; Stiegel glass; Sandwich later (after 1825). Mirrors popular; typical English and French designs; Chinese or rococo carved frames, with leaves or scrolls, painted white or gilded; sometimes candle brackets attached; "Constitution Mirror," architectural frame, simple pedestal, fluted pilasters, scroll pediment (often eagle in middle), gilded carving; "Bull's Eye Mirror," convex glass, heavy circular frame, rich carving, eagle at top (sometimes candle brackets); Sheraton-type, gilded wood frame, painted panel at top. Clocks: fine local products in tall-case, shelf, wall, cuckoo types, specially Williard banjo. Pictures: oil portraits; prints—classic, historical, fruit or flower, etc.; patriotic scenes (painting or decalcomania) on clocks, mirrors. Lighting: earlier types; also beautiful crystal and silver fixtures with drooping prisms (candleholders, sconces, chandeliers); mirror-girandoles popular. Miscellaneous: European style urns, vases, etc.; world-globes typical.

French influence strong in parts of South, "American Empire" styles lasting into Victorian period. Elsewhere, French influence more modified by local designers, with late Bourbon and Directoire feeling more pronounced. American Victorian styles reflected all English characteristics (see Chart No. 5), with John Henry Belter's heavily carved rosewood furniture leading. Representative features: wallpaper in strong colors, large patterns; imitation tapestry and embossed leather; ceilings with plaster ornament, painted beams, deep coves; heavy, clumsy woodwork in golden oak, mahogany, birch, cherry; elaborate, swathed draperies; intricate parquet floors of colored wood; black walnut furniture; horsehair and plush upholstery; cords, fringes, tassels; jig-saw ornament; Currier and Ives prints; steel engravings, statues, mottoes, what-nots, bead curtains, tidies; over-elaborate colored glass, etc.

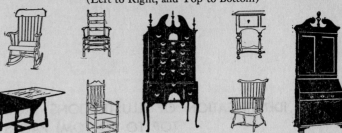

EARLY AMERICAN: Boston Rockers; Butterfly Table, Original Connecticut Design; Ladder-Back Chair; Banister-Back Chair; Walnut Highboy, Queen Anne-Type Broken Pediment, Flame Finials, Shell Ornament, Cabriole Legs, Acorn Drops on Apron; William and Mary-Type Lowboy; Fan-Back Windsor Chair, Saddle-shaped Seat; Early Georgian Bookcase Desk, Panel Doors, Bracket Feet

AMERICAN GEORGIAN: Chippendale-Type Piecrust Tilt-Top Table, Tripod Base; High-Backed Wing Chair, Cabriole Front Legs, Stretchers; Mahogany Highboy (1775), Cabriole Legs, Broken-Scroll Pediment; Chippendale-Type Armchair; Chippendale-Style Wing Chair, Lowered Back, Cabriole Legs; Armchair, Chippendale-French Influence, Ribbon-Back; Chippendale-Type Armchair

AMERICAN FEDERAL: "Martha Washington" Chairs— Armchair, and Wing Chair with Rounding Back; "Bull's Eye" Mirror, Carved Frame Topped by Eagle; Hepplewhite-Type Chest of Drawers (1790), Serpentine Front, Oval Brass Drawer Pulls; Chippendale-Type Ladder-Back Armchair; Sheraton-Type Sideboard (1790–1800), Inlays, Concave Corners, Straight Slender Legs; Georgian-Style Armchair; Federal *Girandole*, with Eagle and Candle Brackets; Sheraton-Style Bookcase-Desk (1800)

POST-FEDERAL: Duncan Phyfe Chair, Empire Influence; Sheraton-Type Chair (1800); Duncan Phyfe Lyre-Back Chair; Armchair, Sheraton and *Directoire* Influence; Sheraton-Type Dressing Table (1800); Gilt Mirror (1810); Victorian Chair; Low Victorian Chair

IDENTIFICATION OF ILLUSTRATIONS FROM PERIOD CHARTS, (LEFT TO RIGHT, AND TOP TO BOTTOM) PAGES 250, 251, 253, 254, 255

ENGLISH GEORGIAN DESIGNERS....Pages 250-251

CHIPPENDALE: Side Table, Showing French Influence (about 1750); Mahogany Chair, Showing Development from Early Georgian Types (1740); Settee with Double-Chair Back, Reminiscent of Queen Anne Style; Ribbon-Back Chair, Typical Chippendale Top Rail, Cabriole Front Legs, Claw-and-Ball Feet; Late Queen Anne Chair, with Elaborate Carving, Showing Transition to Georgian Forms; Pie-Crust Tilt-Top Table, Tripod Base, Ball-and-Claw Feet (1760); Chair with Typical Vase-shaped Splat, Ribbon Design; Tripod-Base Table, Lyre-shaped Support, Metal Fretwork Gallery Top (1760); Characteristic Chippendale Bed, Showing French Influence in Rococo Carving of Canopy Top (1750); Chinese-Chippendale Chair, Cross-hatched Back and Arms; Sturdy Wing Chair, Lowered Back; Armchair, Chinese Carving on Arms, Legs, Stretcher; Chest of Drawers, Characteristic Bow-Front, Bracket Legs, Carving (1760); Chippendale Detail Group—Ladder-Back Design, Table-Corner with Cabriole Leg and Acanthus Leaf Carving on Knee, Characteristic Ribbon-Back Splat with Top Rail in "Yoke" Form, Typical Acanthus Leaf Carving on Knee of Cabriole Leg with Ball-and-Claw Foot; Mirror with Elaborate Gilded Carved Frame (1750); Fretwork Table, Chinese Influence (1760); Chinese Fret Chair, Pagoda-Top Back (about 1760)

HEPPLEWHITE: Typical Shield-shaped Chair Back; Elaborate *Girandole* (Candle Holder, about 1785); Hepplewhite-style Sideboard, Rounded Corner, Slender Graceful Legs; Legs, with Typical Thimble Foot, Spade Foot; Favorite Late Georgian Chair Seat, Tapered toward Back; Greek Key Border Design (Fret); Hepplewhite Mirror (about 1780); Chairs with Distinctive Shield Backs, Straight Tapering Front Legs, Plain Back Legs Slightly Flared

SHERATON: Typical Secretary, Showing Fan-shaped Base of Broken Pediment, Graceful Design of Glass Door Panels (1790); Characteristic Chair with Lattice Back, Slender Lines; Armchair Showing Typical Upholstered Arms, Horizontal Back Sections, Fan Decoration (1790); Detail, Characteristic Chair Back, Central Part Raised above Straight Top Rail, Vase-shaped Splat; Graceful Pole-Screen (1790)

ADAM: Typical Chair, Wheel-Type Back, Graceful Lines; Mantel Showing Characteristic Classical Design—Column Supports, Garland and Rosette Decorations on Frieze and Fireplace Facing; Settee Showing Greek Influence and Similarity to French *Directoire* Styles; Adam Side-Table Showing Marble Top and Decorative Underframing; Carving Detail of Characteristic Adam Fan-shaped Motif

FRENCH BOURBON STYLES....Pages 253

LOUIS XIV: Term-Type Furniture Legs—Table Leg and Armchair Leg; Gilded Wood Side-Table, Pedestal Leg, Cross Stretchers (1680); Typical *Armoire* (1700); Gilded Wood Upholstered Armchair, Pedestal Legs, Cross-Stretchers; Carved Hoof Foot; Boulle Pedestal, Ebony with Brass Decoration; Console Table, Gilded Wood, Marble Top (about 1710)

LOUIS XV: Gilded Wood Frame, C-Scroll Design, Carved Foliage; Louis XV Desk, Rootwood Marquetry, Beautiful Inlay; Oak Armoire, Irregular Panel Outline; Detail of Panel Carving from *Armoire*; Typical Beechwood Side Chair, Cane Back, Cabriole Legs; Carving Details of Chair Back, Table Edge, Cabriole Leg; Upholstered Beechwood Daybed, Graceful Curved Ends, Cabriole Legs (1760); Walnut Wing Chair, Cabriole Front Legs, Stretchers; Painted Oak Upholstered Armchair (*Bergere*); Typical Carving Detail; Painted Wood Console Table, Shellform, Free Foliage (1760); Chaise Longue, Curved Frame, Cabriole Legs

LAST OF BOURBON STYLES....Page 254

LOUIS XVI: Typical Carving Detail; Favorite Bed, Toile-upholstered Headboard and Footboard; Popular Flower Garland Design; Small Commode, Delicate Legs, Brass Gallery; Console, Decorated with Mask and Leaf Forms (1785); Armchair (1780); *Secretaire*, Companion Piece to Commode at Right; Commode, Ormolu Flower Festoons on Black and Gold Lacquer (about 1790); Late Louis XVI Armchair, Velvet Upholstery (1790); Side Chair, Classic Feeling, Fore-runner of *Directoire*; Leg and Arm Post of Typical Armchair; Oval Frame, Gilded, Laurel Leaf and Ribbon Motif (about 1780)

FRENCH PROVINCIAL: Typical Chair Back, Cabriole Leg, and Foot; Characteristic Armchair, Modified Louis XV Forms, Simple Checked Upholstery; Typical Mirror Top; Commode, Louis XV Type Cabriole Legs, Curved Apron, Irregular Door Panels

POST-BOURBON STYLES....Page 255

DIRECTOIRE: Doric Capital (Classic Column Head); *Directoire* Armchair, Back Slightly Scrolled Out, Front Legs Straight, Back Legs Flared; Ionic Capital

EMPIRE: Armchair, Back in Greek Curve, Winged Arm Supports; Empire Armchair with All Four Legs Slightly Flared; Corinthian Capital; Empire Ormolu Mount, Military Motif; Typical Empire Ormolu Decorating Pattern; Characteristic Bed, Ormolu Mounts, Conventionalized Leaves and Roman Heads (about 1810); Mahogany "Psyche" Mirror, Classic Treatment of Posts (about 1810); Massive Commode, Enriched with Ormolu Mounts, Caryatid Supports at Ends (about 1816); Desk-Chair Showing Typical Circular Back, Greek *Klismos* Type (about 1810); Favorite Empire Diamond-shaped Design for Ormolu Mounts and Other Decorations; Post-Empire Chair, Showing Greek Curves Still Dominant; 19th Century French Chair, with Empire Flared Legs, Curved Back; Arabesque Motif; 19th Century French Chair, Showing Empire Influence, but with Poor Proportions Similar to Those of English and American Victorian Styles

ROOMS FROM FAVORITE FRENCH AND AMERICAN PERIODS

Feminine grace of the Louis XV period, combined with comfort is shown in the 1740–60 *boudoir* at upper left with its low arm chairs and chaise-longue daybed. Characteristic features: delicately carved wood panels; plain ceiling, decorated cove-cornice; free curves in furniture; carved marble mantel, curved opening. In the Louis XVI *salon* of about 1780 at upper right note straight lines, greater simplicity, square fireplace opening. Characteristic features: painted chair frames; classical feeling in garlands, mantel design; commode and secretary in decorated wood veneer. (Chart No. 6.)

Following the primitive simplicity of homes built during the first hundred years of the Colonies, many homes were designed and furnished in the more luxurious styles of later English periods. Often pieces from several periods were charmingly combined, as in the Massachusetts dining room (1700–25) shown at the right. Characteristic features: painted plaster walls, painted wood paneling and pilasters on fireplace wall; fireplace with simple mantel shelf, tile facing; built-in cupboards; Jacobean gateleg table; walnut side table (inlaid), walnut chairs, clock, highboy, all after William and Mary style; wide-plank floor; Chinese rug. (Compare with English Charts No. 2 and No. 3.)

The typical Colonial bedroom at right has charmingly stenciled walls, combined with a fireplace wall with white-painted, simple plank paneling. Characteristic features: four-post bed, tester flounce; maple and painted beech for furniture; highboy, dressing table, and mirror, all in American Queen Anne style; wide-plank floor, small hooked rugs. The dressing table stool dates back to a period before 1750, the Boston rocker and the sewing table came in much later—about 1840. Despite many touches reminiscent of England, the general effect is definitely American. The four-post bed was found in every type of bedroom; the highboy continued for many years to be an American institution.

The drawing-room below, with walnut paneling, shows Gibbons influence in overmantel carvings (English Chart No. 3). Characteristic features: Queen Anne style in burl-walnut furniture: tall clock and secretary-desk; high-backed wing chairs, settee; side chairs, fiddle-back splats; cabriole legs. The dining room at lower right illustrates English influence in late 18th century America. (English Georgian Charts.) Characteristic features: mahogany for furniture; Sheraton style, with grace and lightness; elaborate woodwork; polished floor, Oriental rug. Note similarity of extension pedestal table with Duncan Phyfe designs (American Chart No. 8).

SECTIONAL FURNITURE GROUPED AROUND A MODERNIZED VERSION OF A

The living room above with its modern furnishings shows an interesting use of draw-curtains alone to control light and air. The draperies at side windows are floor length, and sill length at the middle window in order to clear a book shelf placed there and doubling as a lamp table for the couch. A radiator would have called for this treatment, also. The

special feature here is that the deep valance-curtain is on its own traverse rod with pulley and can be drawn independently of the drapery curtains to obtain many different combinations of light. When the longer curtains are closed at night on a rod placed just above the lower edge of the valance, the short ones above can be drawn back to provide

COLONIAL DUTCH OVEN STYLE FIREPLACE

air. The fireplace with its convenient pocket for storing wood, the plain mantel and the slightly raised hearth are interesting. So also are sectional couch pieces, use of plain surfaces relieved by texture in the rug design, and the complementary color scheme—soft green walls, chartreuse curtains, soft red upholstery, neutral gray rug, and blond wood.

CHAPTER TWENTY

Modern Styles in Home Decorating

MODERN DECORATING is a term used to include aspects of present-day practice which depart widely from traditional or conventional models. By definition modern is a fluid style based upon a continuing effort to adapt furniture and backgrounds in form and function, to the changing moods of contemporary life. It avoids mere prettiness, seeks simplicity through elimination or ornament on structural forms, and unites the direct and incisive quality of straight lines with the softening effect of sparingly used curves. Adapting design to function, it is streamlined for comfort and beauty in the modern manner.

Backgrounds and furniture share in the simplicity features of functionalism. Flat smooth surfaces are without applied ornament. Long continuous curves combine with long, low straight lines to produce an effect of restfulness and comfort. Notice in the pictures that this restrained use of curves is constantly employed to offset any effect of too much straight line or too many angles. Simplicity of paint makes it popular for backgrounds, which also employ plastics, new composition materials, new photographic finishes, modern designs in wallpaper, and a great variety of synthetic, plastic, and natural fabrics draped or plain.

Color is relied upon in modern interiors to make up any decorative deficiencies in the way of ornament. It is used according to the same rules of harmony outlined in Chapter 4 except that brighter tones are employed and textures are emphasized, while more striking contrasts and unusual effects are sought in the way of shading and modifying colors.

261

SPACE-SAVING ARRANGEMENTS WORKED OUT WITH SECTIONAL FURNITURE

The rooms shown here illustrate several outstanding features of modern decoration. In both we have plain floor covering, long low lines of comfort and repose, with effective use of often-wasted corners through furniture designed especially for them. We have glass for tables and mirrors, fabrics in interesting textures. In the room below the corner-saving is worked out in a sort of alcove formed by a built-in shelf and storage unit at the right. The desk placed against this increases still more the alcove feeling in the corner. Corner tables like the one used here are built especially to take the place of end tables when sectional couch and chair units are put together in this way. Attractive wallpaper is

in a typical modern geometrical design with horizontal feeling. The patterned fabric used for part of the upholstery shows impressionistic styling of natural objects in textile design. Observe the restfulness and feeling of ease created by absence of small cluttering decorative objects. The room above makes its space-saving corner arrangement by running combination book-shelf and storage units around the corner, where the curved shelf section ties them into a unit. The two upholstered chairs can be shoved together if necessary to make a love seat. As in so many modern rooms the walls and ceiling are plain with only a slight cove-curve to join them and no molding.

MODERN BEDROOMS EMPHASIZE SOLID COMFORT

The charming bedroom below is an example of modern design carried out in lovely soft color harmonies combined with low lines and formal balance for restfulness. Modern use of beautiful wood graining is shown in the bleached mahogany used for the plain-paneled surface of beds and chests of drawers. The rich honey tones of the wood are emphasized by a plain rose-beige wall behind them. The other walls are covered with wallpaper in a stylized floral design in which the principal colors are rose-beige and chartreuse. The chartreuse textured carpet provides a harmonizing floor background. The bed and chest assembly is made up of separate units, but put together like this they give the effect of a solidly built-in furniture unit. Even in a small bedroom such an arrangement of twin beds and chests (with the taller chest shown at the left) would provide all the storage space two people would need. The child's room above illustrates how modern ideas may be adapted to the youngest members of the family—and to a reclamation problem for an attic or other rooms. Here the walls were done over with wallboard, painted. Windows were enlarged and plain dark blue waxed linoleum cemented over rough plank flooring. The cheerful soft red of the curtains is repeated in painted toy shelves which combine with a hanging wall cupboard to create a modern alcove effect for the bed in the corner.

The use of glass in modern decoration is strikingly illustrated in the dining room at left. Wall-size sliding windows are of insulated glass. Oak table and console in light natural finish are decorated with bands of mirror set into grooves around table legs and between console drawers. Chairs have mirror insets in the backs and the console top is a heavy sheet of mirror. The whole picture is reflected by a mirror-paneled wall behind the console. The top of the table is thick solid heat-proof plate glass. The chairs, unusual but comfortable looking, are upholstered in rough chartreuse textured fabric. Treatment in the manner of this room, even though more simply carried out, would make any small dark room into a sparkling, brightly cheerful dining spot. Installation of windows like these is a simple and not expensive process. For time and labor saving as well as extra beauty you can have sheets of glass mirror cut to fit the top of your present table and console. The mirror will hide scarred tops. If you prefer transparent glass you can hide the scars by cementing a colorful sheet of linoleum over the wood to show through the glass. Even extremes of contrast in modern usage may be very attractive as in the refreshment corner at left. A tiny bar like this can be installed in the corner of any dining room, living room, hall or game room. This one is made dramatic by use of the new "nude" wood tone, white

Colorful linoleums give variety to table and desk tops, every type of stain and heatproof plastic is utilized for finishes, accessories, or important pieces of furniture. Gleaming lacquers reminiscent of the Orient are used often, specially in conjunction with Chinese motifs and designs in wallpaper and accessories. It is interesting that Oriental Chinese designs are worked into modern decorating schemes with the same success they achieved in the days of Chippendale.

Without the aid of traditional ornamentation it is impossible to hide flaws in workmanship and construction is therefore emphasized rather than concealed. Materials are never made to look like something they are not. Metal is called metal; maple is plainly maple; neither one is grained and stained to make it look like mahogany or walnut. The finishing processes used have for their purpose the best development of individual grain, color and texture in each species of wood. If a light tone is desired a naturally light wood is used, perhaps with a little additional bleaching or rubbed-in paint to bring out some special beauty of the grain. In modern decorating it is necessary to think in terms of the wood tones in your furniture. Accent colors and background colors should provide complementary contrast (Chapter 4). Since most of the unpainted woods are in blond finish, such neutral tones as ivory

and tan do nothing for them. For grayed wood tones you will find grays, greens, blues, and yellows make good backgrounds; for warm, light wood tones choose pinks, pinkish beige, greens, and blues.

In order to achieve variety without applied ornaments the modern craftsman works with many different materials. From all over the world, choice cabinet woods are brought to the designers' studios to be used in producing effects previously undreamed of. Such foreign woods as amboina, bubinga, macasser, narra, makore, padouk and thuya have become familiar names in modern workrooms. Glass in some form is used for many types of structure and finish. Aluminum, stainless steel and chromium plate furnish moldings, joining strips, decorative accents. Cork veneer, velvety in texture and warm in coloring, provides surface finish for walls, floors and wood furniture. Plywood and paper-thin veneers are used for large panel effects and to form the rounding corners and curved cornices popular in modern rooms. Translucent lampshades of wood veneer mounted on parchment carry the wood theme even beyond the frequently used wood bases.

In the absence of conventional decoration textiles play a leading part in supplying necessary interest in design, color and texture. Just as new woods have been used, so a great many new styles in weave and texture have been worked out to counteract mo-

paint on wood with the grain showing through. Here the white bar and stools are set on a floor of stark black linoleum. Terra cotta and nude shades are combined in a crisscross rough cotton covering for the comfortable chair beside an extra large cocktail table of glass combined with nude and terra cotta wood. This rubbed paint finish on wood, with the grain showing, is as effective in colors as in white. A modern contribution to seating comfort is the natural contour or form-fitting design so often used for chairs. That functional shaping of back and seat produces a chair in which heavy upholstery is not needed for comfort. The chairs shown here make good use of a primitive method of interlacing fabric or leather strips—once the only kind of "spring" used to support mattresses for sleeping. For these chairs broad-textured tapes are interwoven to adjust themselves to body contour. Modern upholstered furniture varies from the more or less traditional, with new fabric coverings, to all sorts of new basic frames and shapes. The chairs around the table in the picture at the right follow the contour idea, but this time upholstery is added in a tweed-like fabric. The furniture wood is natural birch, also used for the picture frames. Modern armless chairs may be used singly or pushed together for love seats, couches and various groupings.

notony of plain surfaces; new types of synthetic fabrics have added still more variety and richness. You will notice in some of the pictures in this chapter that various types of primitive art—Mexican, South American, Swedish Peasant—are harmonious with the modern decorative idea. Wherever simplicity of line and strong bright colors are used modern designers seek inspiration.

In furniture, ease of handling has brought about wide use of light metal tubing, bentwood, and laminated wood strips in making frames for chairs, settees and tables. Grace and lightness are natural attributes of these flowing lines, and economy is also served by ingenious designs which avoid costly joinings without sacrifice of solidity. Chairs are scientifically planned to fit the anatomy and the purpose for which they will be used. They may have backs which automatically adjust. They are made in sections for all sorts of helpful combinations. They have comfort built deeply into their sturdy construction.

The newer types of movable furniture are light in weight and may be easily shifted about—an important feature for assembly units with separate sections. The heavier pieces which stand against the wall and are not meant to be moved are usually built with a base reaching to the floor so that they have the convenience of built-in furniture which requires

no bothersome cleaning underneath. Tables that fold into the wall, cabinets attached to the wall to leave floor space free, dining tables which expand or contract, groups of large pieces which slide together when not in use like the familiar nests of occasional tables, all these and dozens of other ingenious devices are characteristically modern. They are made highly practical by the smoothly finished sides which make unit groupings easy to work out. Many of these furniture groups are standardized in dimensions, yet there need be no monotony in their use. The wide range of grains in woods, of colors in paint and lacquer, added to the versatility of the groupings provide an endless variety of effects, all with a pleasing sense of spaciousness.

Mass production, which means that unit furniture—to be installed as if it were built-in, or assembled as you like in your rooms—makes available at comparatively reasonable prices this furniture for practically every part of the house. You will find that many of the space- and labor-saving pieces will mingle charmingly with traditional furniture you already have or wish to buy. Professional decorators mix pieces in really good but simple traditional design with definitely modern furniture because of the warm personal note they add to the simplified lines and forms of the newer decorating style. The only thing to remember is the old principle of harmony.

MODERN FURNITURE GROUPS

The furniture on this page illustrates various types of modern design. The circular desk (left) fits equally well against a wall, as here, or into a corner. The one combined with book shelves receives light from a glass-brick wall—a favorite modern device for introducing light without sacrificing privacy. The interesting space-saving unit furniture in the picture above is planned to fulfill the highest number of functional purposes with a minimum of care and space. The handsome sectional book shelf and cabinet in dark wood veneer has several uses and comes in light finishes also. The section at the left is a general utility cabinet with shelves on one side and cork-lined trays on the other making it useful as a beverage cabinet. The unit at the right is a drop-front desk with a drawer between the book shelf and the desk. The broad stripes used for wall treatment are as distinctively modern as the design of the chairs which flank the furniture assemblage. The sections (left) in light wood may be arranged as here or at various angles, in alcove effect, or fitted into corners, or as individual pieces. They are adaptable to several different types of rooms. At the left is a desk-chest; the unit next to it is a chest of drawers; next to that a dressing table, another chest of drawers, then a table with one drawer which may be used as a dressing table, a writing table or a console table for the hall. Each of these units is the same height, 30 inches, and the same depth. Their smooth modern surfaces make it possible to join them so they look like one continuous streamlined furniture unit with built-in effect. Sleek simple lines give distinction to the dining-alcove group at the left. Notice the convenient drawers in the table. Dramatic contrast provides a theme for the group below.

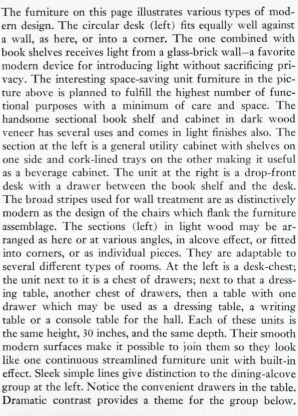

CURVING DESIGN FOR SOFAS INCREASES THEIR USEFULNESS

Upholstered furniture has been affected by the modern ideas of functionalism and comfort just as all other aspects of decorating have been. The difference is partly in basic design but more often in arrangement and line. As shown in the two rooms on this page, chairs and couches are lower than average, deep, and luxuriously upholstered with textured fabrics plain or almost plain. With the practical idea of adapting furniture to available space modern designers have put out most of their upholstered furniture in sections which can be put together to make small love seats or chaise longues for a small apartment or expanded almost indefinitely into long couches to provide seating for large groups of people. The curved design for couch units makes an arrangement which fits gracefully into a corner or into a conversation group facing window or fireplace. An interesting observation about this curved design is that the chairs and

couches can be easily arranged in a semi-circle for watching a television performance. The handsome room below shows more or less conventional upholstery used on sectional pieces which make up the over-large curved couch by the fireplace. In this room Chinese accessories are harmoniously used with modern furnishings and background. The room above is distinctive in its complete departure from tradition. The circular couches here are in interesting new design. In pale gold textured fabric with peach pillows they are highlighted against walls of pale peach, with soft gleaming draperies in the same color framing an unusual lighted wall panel which provides a center of interest for the furniture grouping. This is painted to look like a tall birdcage built into the wall with tree branches, birds and open sky making up the picture. Floors are painted a deeper shade of gold than the couch, the cabinet is a Mayan Indian design.

UNUSUAL
TREATMENT
FOR A CORNER
IN A
LIVING ROOM
OR DOUBLE-
DUTY BEDROOM

Some of the earliest of the modern ideas came to America from Sweden. Simple lines, blond wood, textured surfaces, and clear bright colors distinguished their decorative designs, with a touch of native peasant craft-art added. Furniture and decorations in this classification are called "Swedish Modern." The couch-bed above, with bright colored stripes in textured upholstery fabric and square bolster rolls fitted around a built-in shelf and storage space, is typical of the solid comfort usually found with Swedish designs. Notice below the box spring the band of plain fabric which carries on the dark line of the wood table base. A low glass mirror-panel fills the wall space between glass table-shelves. A charming design in metal makes a frame for the glass coffee table by the couch. The wall is covered with paper simulating cork, and banded on the joinings with narrow strips of chrome metal. These carry on around the wall at dado height as shown on the curved surface at right. The square bolster and storage-shelf arrangement is one that could be used to give distinction to any studio couch in a crowded room. The upholstery-like design of tailored mattress and box-spring covers is very smart and serviceable. There is nothing to take off if you want to make up the couch as a bed except the bolster rolls with the pillows inside. The simple livable combination of bedroom and study shown below unites Swedish peasant-type wallpaper in blue and white, and handcraft-style braided rugs, with a modern blond wood assemblage of sectional furniture. Notice the interesting design of the arm chair by the desk, upholstered in soft light blue textured fabric. The companion chair at the right is in the same type of fabric in dark blue.

THIS SWEDISH MODERN
COMBINES
PEASANT MOTIFS
WITH SECTIONAL
FURNITURE

The three rooms on this page illustrate several major—and international—features of the period known as "Modern." They all have uncluttered, restful backgrounds, a certain sparseness in furnishing, simple lines, high ceilings, doors and windows, architectural lighting. In the American room shown at right the walls are painted a neutral tone to show off the strong colors of modern paintings, the furniture is severe in line, but comfortable, showing the use of a glass-like plastic in side chairs and decorative veneers in wood furniture frames and table. The English room (above) adapts traditional forms to a modern setting in a greater degree than the other two. The furniture mingles Chippendale-style pieces and accessories with couch and easy chair in bulky modern over-stuffed style. The modern theme is further carried out by use of functional glass and chromium, concealed lighting (combined with an 18th Century chandelier), and a blue and silver color scheme in sharply divided masses. In the French room (below) the accent is on the modern use of textures and forms, combined with an Oriental motif in decorative accessories. Note the wide veneering of the walls, the curved line of wall and furniture, the needlework mural in Chinese design above built-in bookcases in the fireplace alcove—also the delicate side chairs which strike a traditional note.

The fireplace grouping in the room above shows modern upholstery material used at the left in a heavy tweed-like weave on a modern sofa; at the right a firmly woven diagonal twilled fabric with a slight sheen covers a modern version of the traditional wing chair. Table and fireplace accessories of transparent plastic are as modern as smoothly paneled walls and the large painting framed with molding in the same design as that used for the fireplace below. No-

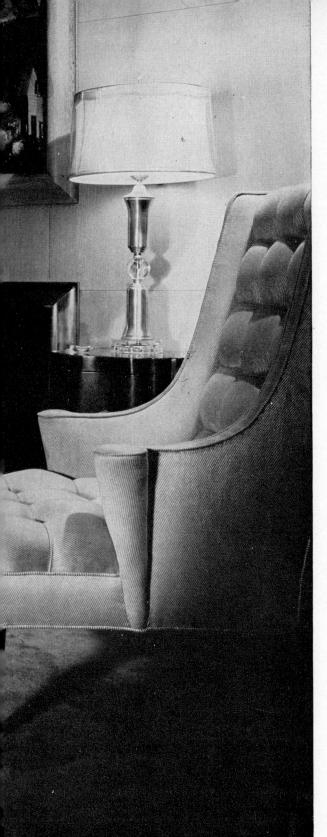

LOOSE-CUSHION TYPE OF SOFA

tice here the tall lamps suitable for reading. The string rug which ties the fireplace group together is placed where protection is most needed in order to conserve the pile carpeting of the room.

CHAPTER TWENTY-ONE

Upholstered Furniture and Slip Covers

UPHOLSTERED FURNITURE must be carefully selected. It usually represents a comparatively large portion of your furnishing money, and it is expected to make a major contribution to the comfort as well as the beauty of your home.

Fabric Suitability: Fabrics used for upholstery must be harmonious with all other textiles in the room. In general they should not be too conspicuous but should serve rather as a bridge between draperies, walls and floor coverings. A large bold pattern makes a chair or couch seem smaller and should be used only on a large piece of furniture with which it will be in scale. (For general principles governing the combination of room fabrics see the text and illustrations in Chapter 13.)

Avoid too many different patterns in upholstery and be careful about harmonizing texture and color as well as design. If you have an over-large and ungainly chair or sofa you can make it less conspicuous by using upholstery in the same color as the carpet or the wall or a neutral tone which merges with them both. If you have a particularly lovely piece use contrast color in the upholstery to make it stand out. If you want to make a chair look larger use a bright warm color to cover it.

The design of any fabric to be used on side chairs is important because these are often stood against the wall where both outline and color of the back are conspicuous. For small upholstery chairs leather or leatherette is good, also stripes in velveteen, satin, taffeta, oilcloth or felt—depending upon where they are used. Small occasional arm chairs with good proportions and design may be effectively employed to furnish accent color by being covered in bright tones, striking designs or glossy fabrics.

POINTS ON CHOOSING FABRICS

Fabric Types: Each room in the house has a special affinity for different types of textiles, although some may be used anywhere depending only upon color, use and pattern. Taffetas and other silks or rayons—plain or with stripes and figures—are charming in bedrooms, boudoirs, and small formal but gay living rooms. Damasks in some form are very adaptable. They do not wear as well as brocatelles and brocades, but are all right where there is less hard usage. For heavy-duty furniture, rely upon mohair, twill, velveteen, velour and other such weaves.

Textures: With the introduction of new fabrics textures have achieved a new importance and much more leeway is allowed in combining them than the old traditions approved. It would still be out of place to use fabrics such as denim or monks' cloth in a room with a silk velvet sofa and a fine Oriental rug, but many of the rough-textured rayons and silk or rayon blends would be perfectly at home there. For use with the more delicate types of period furniture fine fabrics should be selected in traditional designs. For the more massive types of the earlier periods select heavier materials in bolder patterns and weaves. Smooth-surfaced fabrics resist dust better than rough-pile weaves but may not wear as well.

If you cannot afford a really good covering for upholstered pieces it is usually better to buy them in muslin and use slip covers permanently or even temporarily. One solution for this problem lies in a type of upholstered furniture which can be obtained covered in a sturdy inexpensive rep fabric but made with provision for separate upholstery covers to be fastened on so that they fit as smoothly and tightly as the rep upholstery itself. This rep undercover is sufficiently good-looking to serve alone until you can afford the finish you really want. Or you can use conventional slip covers with the rep doing duty while they are being cleaned. An advantage of this system in addition to the economy angle is that the fitted covers fastened over the rep may be removed like slip covers and just as easily kept clean.

Periods and Fabrics: If you have furniture with a particular period feeling you can emphasize it by appropriate upholstery. In the early days of Colonial American and English styles, use of upholstery was largely confined to cushions for hard wooden seats. These were usually covered with homespun in strong reds and blues with occasional mixture of green and gold. Velvets and brocades gradually came into use over real upholstery padding, also embroidered materials, India prints, and damasks in silk and worsted. As furniture became more formal on both sides of the ocean tapestries and large designs were used,

hand-blocked linens with conventionalized motifs and large patterns reflecting Oriental influences. At the same time chintz and cotton prints in small neat patterns were employed for less formal interiors.

Needlepoint, crewel embroidery and striking conventionalized designs continued into the late 18th Century period when colors became softer and more subdued and rich brocades and damasks were widely used. All through this period chintz was popular in flower designs as well as a great variety of scenic and classic patterns. Under the Chippendale influence furniture fabrics were made with many Chinese motifs. Adam, Hepplewhite, Sheraton and Duncan Phyfe were partial to stripes and small all-over patterns. Early 19th Century models carried the classic revival into upholstery fabrics through repetitions of many Greek and Roman motifs. The familiar black horse-hair of Victorian pieces is not necessary to carry out the feeling of the period. A great variety of chintzes were used, and any chintz-like fabric will be harmonious as upholstery on furniture of the middle 19th Century. Ginghams are at home in French Provincial as well as Early American and similar style rooms.

SLIP COVERS

Rules for selection of patterns and colors in slip cover fabrics are more or less the same as those which govern upholstery except that usually larger patterns are appropriate with the all-over fabric cover. The chief difference is in the type of material used. While many slip cover fabrics are suitable for upholstery, and many upholstery fabrics are used for slip covers, there are ordinarily certain definite types of textiles most appropriate for slip cover use. Materials are usually intended to be washed. They must also protect the upholstery, and they must be easily tailored. Medium-weight fabrics are best with glazed or unglazed chintzes, cretonnes, plain and printed linens heading the list. Striped taffetas, satins, sateens and silks, cotton reps or mattress ticking are used for sturdy covers, and almost any type of closely woven cotton material may be suitable for certain decorating schemes. Avoid loose weaves which allow dust to sift through and are easily pulled out of shape.

Service in Fabrics: Unless you are planning to have your slip covers dry-cleaned it is very important to buy fabrics which are preshrunk and color-fast. If you have no label which covers this it is better to test the fabric before you buy it, or at least before you make it up. A good way to do this is to take a sample square ten inches each way, run a row of machine-stitching around the square one inch from the edges, then wash and iron the sample. By measur-

EFFECTIVE USE OF TEXTURED FABRICS

STRIPES AND TAILORED LINES FOR STYLE

Among upholstery fabrics few are more serviceable for heavy-duty furniture than some of the modern rough-textured varieties. In the library-living room (top) the comfortable sofa is upholstered in heavy material with a woven textured diagonal pattern. Textured fabric is used also on the chairs, in a striped design this time. The sofa covered with striped damask-type fabric (center) illustrates the slip-cover type of upholstery. The very modern twin lounging-sleeping couches (right) are put together in a space-saving corner arrangement. The upholstery is in coral wool combined with cotton print fabric in chartreuse, coral and blue which is also used for draperies in the room. The cushions are boxed so that they stand firmly against the wall to provide a back for the couch.

ing it again you can tell approximately how much you will have to allow for shrinkage. You will know also whether the colors run. If it is color-fast but shrinks a quarter of an inch in that nine-inch piece, you will know that the shrinkage is an inch to each yard. You can allow that much in making, but it is still better to steam the fabric thoroughly, or soak it in cool water, then dry it and iron it before using it.

There are dozens of attractive designs for slip covers, many of which you will see illustrated in this chapter. Basically they are made in the same way and doing them at home is not so difficult as you may think. If you can afford to have them done by your favorite department store, or in a neighborhood shop, you will be sure of results and will be relieved of the labor involved in making them. But if you are budgeting it is much better to put the money available into the best possible fabric quality and do the work yourself.

Patterns for Slip Covers: Recently pattern companies have designed and put on sale a variety of patterns covering the basic upholstered pieces designed for the average types of sofas and chairs. Even if your furniture varies from this average in size or shape you can find a pattern which will approximate your need and can be adjusted to fit. If you are hesitant about using the direct patternless pin-on method for cutting your fabric, try one of these patterns. If necessary get some very inexpensive muslin or cambric or use pieces of old sheeting to make a cloth model before you cut into your fabric. One advantage of a pattern is that it will tell you exactly how much material you will need.

Fabric Requirements: The average upholstered arm chair with a pleated skirt and no loose cushion takes about 5 yards of 50″ material, 6½ yards of 36″ material. If there are cushions, each loose cushion

EFFECTIVE FABRIC CONTRAST

will take about 1½ yards of 50″ material. For a large club-type of chair increase the figures above by a yard of 50″ material and about 2 yards of 36″ material. Wing chair figures are approximately the same as those for a club chair. The average sofa needs 10 to 12 yards of plain 50″ material and 4 yards more if the back cushions are also loose. These measurements are for fabrics plain or with small figures in the design. For large patterns additional allowance must be made for centering motifs and matching the pattern. It is always better to be on the safe side and buy extra material. You can use it for cushions, small chair upholstery or lamp shades.

Working Without a Pattern: If you are making your covers yourself, without patterns, the secret of success is literally to make your slip cover *on the chair or sofa.* Start with the back and seat, pinning the material to the chair, then pinning the seams before you cut them. Use colored tailors' chalk to mark seam lines. Do plenty of basting—on the chair if necessary. Follow curves carefully with chalk lines. Allow an inch and a half or two inches for seam adjustments and if there is a definite motif in the fabric pattern be sure to center it on the back and on the cushions. Space your fabric so that the same motif appears on the two arms and any other opposite spots. If there are stripes place one in the exact center of the back, etc. Run them from front to back on the seat, not across.

Pin and cut in this order: chair back, seat under pillow, front panel; then take the inside arm, the outside arm, and the wing if there is one. Baste care-

LEATHER UPHOLSTERY FOR A MAN'S CORNER

Leather is a traditionally masculine fabric, as shown by its popularity in club rooms, offices, and bachelor apartments. In the photograph below it is shown on a sturdy chair designed to appeal to masculine taste and comfort. Notice how much at home the leather upholstery is against the wood-paneled walls with built-in shelves for ornaments and books.

SATIN-STRIPED FABRICS ARE ADAPTABLE

The fireplace group in the bedroom above shows two charming comfortable chairs upholstered in chartreuse and beige satin stripe fabric, which is also used for the side chairs in the room. Notice the mirrored facing about the fireplace which reflects the bed with its quaint headboard shaped like the back of a Victorian sofa. The floor is covered

fully and try on before stitching. When you do the back of the chair leave a two-inch flap for a placket at the left side for a slide fastener. Leave the flounce until the end, allowing from two to three times the plain measurement for gathered or pleated flounce fullness. For inverted pleats, at corners only, allow about ten inches for each pleat. Don't forget to leave from six to eight inches of fabric on the back and inside arm pieces for tucking in around the seat. At any strained points cut the fabric for smooth adjustment, and wherever there is extra fullness ease it in if possible or, if necessary, take it up in darts.

The more tailored the cover is, the more professional it will look and the better it will stand up and

back in seamed sections to correspond with the seat cushions. At the back of the sofa arrange two zipper closings, one at each end. Follow original upholstery construction lines in seaming and trimming both in the body of the slip cover and in the cushion coverings. Always make loose cushions alike top and bottom so that they can be reversed for longer wear.

BED AND COUCH COVERS

Suggestions for various types of tailored and frilled covers are to be found in illustrations in this chapter. For large beds or couches it is often necessary to join more than one length of fabric and the best method is to use a design which will bring the joinings where you can apply a decorative finish. The trim, tailored effect is all-important in making a studio couch a decorative asset instead of something to be put up with in a room. A two-piece arrangement in which the mattress is covered separately is usually easier to keep looking trim than the one-piece style. It is also easier to handle if you are using the couch as a bed. Bolster rolls are attractive on beds and particularly useful on day beds and studio couches. They may be round or square and used for storing pillows or bedding.

Regulation bed spreads may be tailored and trim or frilled and flounced and very feminine. They are made to be accompanied by bolsters or matching pillow cases or with an extension at the top which folds over flattened pillows to give a finish to the picture.

TO TRADITIONAL OR MODERN DESIGN

with a twisted yarn broadloom carpet in a soft peach tone. Walls and woodwork are painted willow green and the design of the chintz combines deep pink, chartreuse and tones of green. The room is an illustration of how attractively traditional and modern themes can be mingled in contemporary decorating.

keep its shape. To get this tailored effect use welting or upholstery trimming to finish the seams. In either case be sure these are preshrunk and color-fast. Trimmings are usually in self color on plain fabric but they may be in contrast to match an accent color of the room. With figured materials trimmings are usually in one of the colors in the pattern. In using very light chintz you can protect the flounce from soiling quickly by edging it with a plain band of fabric matching the trimming color. Before you begin to plan your slip covers investigate the special attachments on your sewing machine if you are not already familiar with them. You will find these devices a great help in your work.

For a sofa, proceed in the same way, making the

COTTON UPHOLSTERY FOR A CHILD'S ROOM

This mother-and-daughter set of chairs is specially designed for nursery or bedroom. Exactly alike except for size, the two comfortable wing chairs are upholstered in pink cotton fabric with white eyelet petticoats which could be made removable for laundering. A folding mahogany tea table and a small hand-woven rug complete the picture.

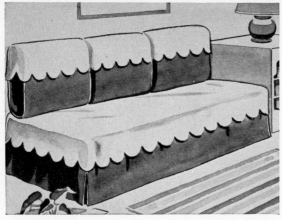

THREE TYPES OF SLIP COVERS

For any slip cover choose a fabric and style in harmony with your room. This is illustrated by the pictures above and at the left showing the same sofa with two different slip-cover treatments. In a room with Victorian accessories authentic Victorian charm is achieved by using a sweetheart rose fabric and moss fringe edging with a full gathered skirt and fringe-edged cushions. An original touch is the multi-stitched heading along the top edge of the skirt which helps to provide a framework for the fringed cushions. Against the modern background suggested in the picture at right above a sleek modern effect is given the sofa by a tailored cover in wild mulberry fabric with an all-over huge leaf design for the inside arms and back. Heavy rope-corded edges add sharpness to the lines of the sofa and provide an unusual decorative touch. Notice the distinctive finish given to the skirt by a combination of box and inverted pleats at corners. The studio couch at the left illustrates how this article of furniture can be given an inexpensive but distinctive slip-cover treatment. A plain tailored sheath cover is topped by contrasting semi-covers which can be in a light color because they are so easily removed for laundering. Tops like this would also freshen up an old cover.

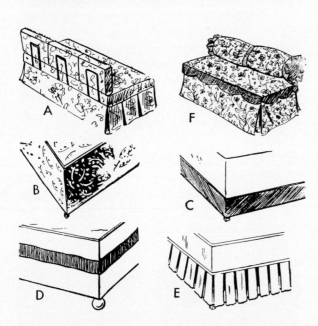

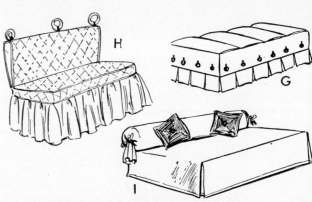

USEFUL IDEAS FOR COUCH COVERS AND STORAGE-SEATS

The sketches here may help you solve some slip-cover problem for a studio couch or suggest a useful camouflage for storage boxes. Sketch A illustrates frames obtainable in the shops for holding cushions firmly upright and giving your couch a much neater appearance. B, C, D and E show four different ways of making attractive couch covers. When a flounce is used—pleated like this one or gathered—an effective and convenient way to handle the slip cover is to make a separate sheath for the mattress and attach the flounce to a plain sheet of material fitted over the top of the springs. The flounce keeps its shape better if it does not have to be removed and making the couch up as a bed is greatly simplified. Always carry a flounce all the way around a couch cover so that you can reverse it for longer wear. In sketch I is shown an effective use of a long bolster roll to provide a "back" for the couch. In a corner a second shorter roll can be used at right angles to the long one. In G a flat steamer-type trunk is converted into a convenient seat by a slip cover with a padded top. F and H illustrate two devices for turning packing boxes into comfortable seats.

TRIM FITTING IS IMPORTANT IN MAKING
ALL KINDS OF SLIP COVERS

The beautifully fitting slip cover on the chair at right illustrates how closely a well-made slip cover resembles upholstery. The secret is to follow the structural lines carefully and to use fabrics which will not shrink with washing. Striped glazed chintz combines smartly with plain glazed chintz in this cover. Combining two materials is an economical way to make use of remnants or to make over drapery fabrics into slip covers. The two chairs above are identical beneath the slip covers, showing the different style effect achieved through the use of different fabrics and patterns. One chair is strictly tailored while the other is just as definitely feminine in effect. In the sketches at A we see three types of seat slip covers which can be used on straight chairs such as the one at B. In sketch C the top of the back is also covered. The entire back of any chair can be covered to match the seat if you fit a pad over it and anchor it firmly in place. It may be necessary to use a shaped sheet of composition board or heavy cardboard to cover openings in the wood frame. You can make the padding yourself from cotton batting or buy padding by the yard. The tables and stools in the sketches are all made from old unattractive bits of furniture or from boxes and kegs made into substitutes for furniture. In these cases small pieces of left-over fabrics are used for the slip covers.

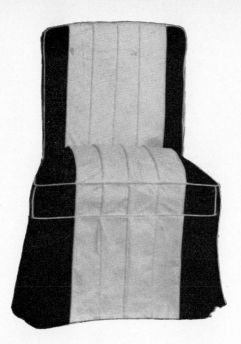

STYLE VARIATIONS ACHIEVED THROUGH USING DIFFERENT SLIP COVERS ON A SIMPLE SLIPPER CHAIR

The interesting thing about this page of slip-cover designs is the variety. In each of the ten photographs the chair is the same small slipper chair and the fabric is the same heavy cotton twill in a deep glade-green shade with white for trimming—yet each cover has a personality of its own. Not one of them would be difficult to make. Among them you may find just the suggestion you have been seeking for a slip cover which will add a note of real distinction to your room. They can all be worked out in many different fabric and color combinations.

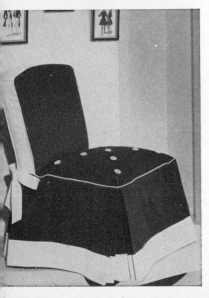

RUFFLED GINGHAM PICTURE FRAMES

Fabric slip covers may be used for salvaging or giving new charm to various small furnishings and decorations. Picture frames and mirror frames are not hard to make and they help tie the accessory into the room color scheme. They may also cover up shabby or ugly frames. They are especially useful for children's rooms, as shown above.

SUGGESTIONS FOR DOUBLING SERVICE LIFE OF UPHOLSTERY OR SLIP COVERS

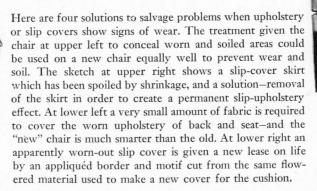

Here are four solutions to salvage problems when upholstery or slip covers show signs of wear. The treatment given the chair at upper left to conceal worn and soiled areas could be used on a new chair equally well to prevent wear and soil. The sketch at upper right shows a slip-cover skirt which has been spoiled by shrinkage, and a solution—removal of the skirt in order to create a permanent slip-upholstery effect. At lower left a very small amount of fabric is required to cover the worn upholstery of back and seat—and the "new" chair is much smarter than the old. At lower right an apparently worn-out slip cover is given a new lease on life by an appliquéd border and motif cut from the same flowered material used to make a new cover for the cushion.

DRESSING TABLE SKIRTS

Skirts for dressing tables have so many different shapes and styles that it is impossible to do more than suggest a few which are both attractive and practical. Skirts may be of any material suitable for draperies but they are usually matched either to window draperies or bed covering or both. No matter what fabric is used any gathered or pleated skirt should be made very full. By covering the top as well as the sides of the dressing table you can use almost anything for its foundation. A shelf attached to the wall by a bracket, two orange crates with a board across the top, a box the right size and shape—anything at all in the right size can be covered and used. The same thing goes for a stool to be placed in front of it. Use the same drapery that you do on the dressing table for covering an old chair with the back and

DRESSING TABLE TREATMENTS

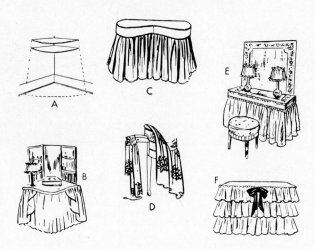

A and B suggest ways in which corners may be utilized for dressing tables. In C and D are shown two more versions of the kidney-shaped table. D illustrates a convenient method for attaching a skirt to any type of dressing table—fasten a tape with snaps to the top of the table with matching tape sewed to the top of the skirt. This makes it easy to unsnap the skirt for washing or cleaning. In sketch E a small table or shelf could be used for the dressing table. A cutout design is applied around the mirror and under the glass of the table top. When a table with a drawer is used you can make the front of the skirt in a separate piece and attach it to a flat board screwed to the front of the drawer so that the whole front will come forward when the drawer is opened. For a narrow drawer make the separation at the edges of the drawer. If you make a skirt like that shown in F you can use material from an old sheet for the foundation, dyeing it to match the flounces, applying it slightly full, then sewing the flounces to it. Here, if there is a drawer, only the top flounce needs to have a separate section for the drawer. When a dressing table needs a stiff heading under a band of shirring or pleating—as in some of the illustrations shown—cut a strip of buckram to fit the top of the table and cover with fabric. Stitch to inside edge of skirt under the shirring.

legs cut down, a box with a padded top, part of a barrel, a nail or butter keg, an old piano stool—the list is almost endless.

CARE OF UPHOLSTERED FURNITURE

Regular care pays dividends by prolonging the life of your upholstered furniture. It is much easier to prevent unsightly smudges on backs and arms of chairs than to remedy the situation after it has become serious. In general, the smoother the fabric the easier it is to keep clean and the deeper the pile the more careful you must be to see that cleaning gets down to the roots of the fibers. Slip covers should usually be washable; they should be kept clean. After washing they are sometimes difficult to iron especially if they have corded or trimmed seams. The best procedure is to press them as well as you can, then put them on the chair, dampen slightly the parts which need further ironing and run the iron over them on the chair. Don't wash glazed chintz unless the label says it is *washable*. Always clean upholstered furniture thoroughly before putting on the slip covers.

Routine Upholstery Care: Brush or vacuum all upholstered furniture regularly. If you must clean upholstery quickly by beating dust out of it use a small stiff brush and lay a dampened cloth over the part you are beating to keep dust from flying over the room. Use the upholstery attachment on the vacuum weekly or oftener. Don't overlook crevices, sides and backs, undersides of cushions. Crevices and dark places generally are breeding places for moths, and the best preventive measure is frequent cleaning with brush or vacuum.

To keep cushions in shape plump them up often with your hands and air them occasionally in front of an open window. Never beat a cushion filled with down, and never use the vacuum on it. Suction is too strong for down. Set upholstery cushions up on their sides at night and replace them in the morning. This will help them keep their shape and last longer. Be sure to reverse loose cushions once a week to distribute wear.

Cleaning Upholstery: Smooth fabrics can be kept looking new and fresh by wiping them over frequently from the day you buy them with a cloth saturated in cleaning fluid. This will remove surface soil and keep the colors bright. Using an all-purpose cleaner like carbon tetrachloride, apply the cleaning fluid with a piece of cheesecloth. Light straight strokes and over-lapping of cleaned sections will avoid rings. Glazed chintz upholstery must be merely wiped with a soft cloth and *no liquid* unless it has a permanently glazed finish.

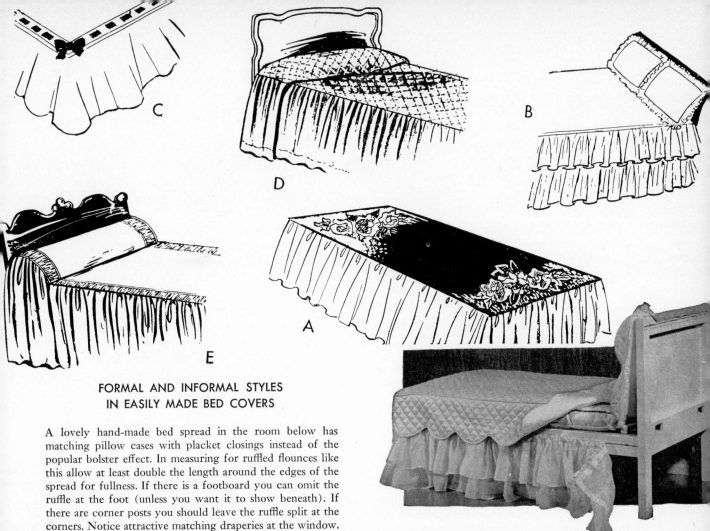

FORMAL AND INFORMAL STYLES
IN EASILY MADE BED COVERS

A lovely hand-made bed spread in the room below has matching pillow cases with placket closings instead of the popular bolster effect. In measuring for ruffled flounces like this allow at least double the length around the edges of the spread for fullness. If there is a footboard you can omit the ruffle at the foot (unless you want it to show beneath). If there are corner posts you should leave the ruffle split at the corners. Notice attractive matching draperies at the window.

The bed shown in cutout above illustrates an easy device for attaching flounces to the wooden frame of the bed by a slot molding like that often used for hanging draperies. Here the headboard is covered by means of the same device. To get the same effect—an underskirt with a spread over it—without this molding you can attach the flounces to a fitted piece of muslin placed over the springs and under the mattress. The headboard can be covered by making a fitted slip cover, using a shaped piece of plywood or composition board in front of the headboard if the outline is not attractive. The sketches in the group demonstrate various styles in bed coverings. Sketch A shows the possibility of combining two fabric pieces, dark and light, and thus utilizing perhaps dyed muslin from sheets or material from worn draperies. To brighten up the plain effect cutouts from chintz are appliquéd on the top. If it has to have piecing the seams can be covered by bands of appliquéd cutouts. Remember always to center any middle strip and make both sides identical. In B a double flounce is used in light-weight fabric for both spread and pillow covers. In C a flounce is given fullness by circular cutting. D shows the popular bolster style with additional length to fold under and over the pillows. This piece may be made separate if you prefer. In the very formal spread used at E bands of shirring outline the edges of the bed and the flounce is graduated at the top end to allow for a bolster effect over the pillows without destroying the even floor line of the flounce. Measure carefully if you are making a spread like this.

EFFECTIVE FABRIC COMBINATIONS

The bedroom pictured above illustrates the use of a fabric canopy and flounce matching the spread on a Colonial four-post bed. Patterns and directions are obtainable for making various styles of "testers," canopies and bed draperies. The two windows are made into a dramatic center-of-interest by the dressing-table mirror panel between them and by continuous draping with the flowered chintz across tops of windows and mirror. A satin stripe in the chaise-longue cover provides the desired geometrical design combined with plain background and flowered chintz. Notice how the modern line of the mirror-paneled dressing table and the trim tailoring of the chaise-longue slip-cover-type upholstery harmonize with the 18th Century bed, chair and accessories. In the traditional bedroom shown below a dark soft silky fabric makes draperies and bed cover with appliquéd borders cut from the striped chintz used for dressing table and chair. Notice the same border applied above the wall dado and over the head of the bed to frame a picture. It is also used as a ceiling line border carried across the top of the drapery like a cornice (not shown in picture). The attractive little chair could be copied by cutting down an ordinary chair and padding the back and seat for comfort.

QUILTING OR RUFFLES

The comfortable bedroom above could be done in quilted rayon fabric combined with striped taffeta, or it could be worked out with cotton quilting and bed-ticking or dress material for the stripes. A long-wearing woven cotton rug like the one shown would harmonize in either case because of the smartly tailored style of draperies and coverings. The dressing-table stool could be made from a piano stool or a small keg. In this case the top could be kept removable and the inside used for storage. Note how well the tailored fittings combine with traditional furniture and flowered chair. The room below shows how fresh and charming ruffles can be when they are made in the light background color of flowered chintz and applied to bedroom decoration. Here all the ruffling is set on under narrow heading strips of decorative banding with touches of color which tie them into the decorative scheme. This same color is used for the headboard on the bed. The dressing table is fitted with arms to swing open and the skirt section is divided in the center for this. Note the plain wall and floor, which are restful as background for so much gaiety. The chintz is carried into the adjoining bathroom and even used as an outer covering for shower curtains.

POINTS ON CLEANING

For more drastic cleaning of upholstery use one of the soapless lathers which clean by chemical action and do not wet the fabric when correctly used. In general these are applied with circular motion over a small area and wiped off before you proceed to another section. Each one has specific directions as to just how it should be used. If you follow these you can do a really good renovating job at home. These cleaners, however, should be used on the whole chair or couch to keep one spot from looking brighter than the rest. Homespun upholstery should never be brushed after cleaning, but pile fabrics should be brushed up with a soft brush in the direction of the nap. If the nap becomes flattened you can revive it by steaming just as for carpets; repeating several times ten minutes apart. Brush while damp with a soft brush; when fabric is thoroughly dry, brush against the grain for new, sleek luster. (See page 280.) For twist upholstery fabrics there is a dry-cleaning preparation which can be brushed into the fabric, allowed to dry, then removed with the vacuum.

Cleaning Leather and Simulated Leathers: Real leather can be cleaned with saddle soap or other mild soap suds or by rubbing the surface with a soft cloth dipped in milk or beaten egg white. After cleaning wipe with slightly damp cloth then rub dry with a soft dry cloth and polish until surface is shining. Follow with one of the commercial leather-conditioning dressings to feed the leather and prevent splitting—unless you have done your cleaning with a special product which cleans and conditions at the same time. Never use any cleaners other than those mentioned or some product designed for use on leather. Never use furniture polish, oil, varnish or shellac on leather. For simulated leathers clean with a damp cloth or if necessary use mild soap suds and remove with a damp cloth. To prevent cracking follow the washing with a thin coat of petroleum jelly. If you find a hole in a leather-covered table-top you can camouflage it by getting a candle in matching color, melting the wax, pouring it into the hole and smoothing it out before the wax has had a chance to harden.

Spot-Cleaning Upholstery: It is important to remove spots as quickly as possible after they occur. For heavy-pile fabrics procedure is practically the same as for carpets. For lighter-weight materials follow the same rules as those for the care of all fabrics. When using cleaning solvents be careful not to remove fabric finish or to leave cleaning rings. Apply the solvent just outside the spot and rub with circular motion toward the center, bringing the spots to a head rather than spreading them. Use fresh clean cloths for rubbing as the stain comes out. Never use too much cleaning fluid at a time. This floods the spot and spreads it. For various types of stains not covered in the chart on page 159 treat the fabrics as you would any similar dress materials. For fresh stains or spots always try an application of Fuller's earth or French chalk. When this is allowed to stand for awhile and then wiped off it often takes the stain with it. For fabrics not injured by water a damp cloth or a light sponging with soap suds will sometimes help. To remove dog and cat hairs stroke the surface lightly with a damp piece of sandpaper, a damp rubber sponge or a new special brush which cleans away hairs as well as lint with magic speed.

Cleaning Slip Covers: If you wipe glazed chintz covers every day with a clean cloth they will stay clean over a long period of time. This applies also to smooth satin or other glossy surfaces. Textured cottons and various other rough weaves which collect dust may be kept clean by brushing with a whisk broom. Fabrics which wrinkle easily require frequent washing. Before washing slip covers brush bindings to remove dust, baste any pleats smoothly in place, make any necessary repairs. Wash only one large print piece at a time and never wash covers with two different print patterns together in the tub. After the last rinsing blot the water out with a towel, press when almost dry and replace on the chair or couch. Finish pressing on chair if necessary. (See page 280.) A tightly rolled newspaper pushed down at each side and at the back of the seat will hold the cloth firmly and prevent wrinkles.

CONSERVATION MEASURES

Upholstery Repairs: Plastic surgery with ordinary adhesive tape or one of the ironed-on tapes will often prevent major injuries. Cut the piece of tape an inch longer than the tear and slip it underneath, bringing the edges closely together over it. For the press-on tape heat it first by holding it against a hot iron to melt the glue. After the tape is in place beneath the edges with all ravelled threads tucked underneath place a heavy object over the spot and leave it until the tape is thoroughly dry.

Moth Protection: Use a liquid moth spray to protect upholstery fabrics. If a slip cover is over wool upholstery remove the cover every now and then and see if there are any traces of moths. Brush all the seams of the slip cover before replacing it. If upholstered furniture is being stored treat all wool fabric with moth spray and cover the whole piece with a clean muslin sheet. Cheap muslin will do for this purpose or an old sheet.

The living room above illustrates today's trend toward mingling of traditional with modern decoration. Use of a subdued modern background emphasizes glowing charm of color, beauty of period furnishings and accessories. This well-planned room is notable for its feeling of comfort and ease. A modern mirror-facing around the fireplace, and modern mantel design, frame a traditional grate. The slip-cover type of upholstery on right-and-left-armed chaise longues and on

armless easy chairs is in a beige and gold satin stripe—the chair in the middle is covered in slate-blue satin like the occasional chairs in the bay window. Pale lemon yellow for walls and woodwork makes an effective background for bay window draperies in deep rose and tones of blue with touches of yellow on beige linen. The "Rule of Three" is carried out here by plain background, flowered hangings and striped upholstery. An Oriental rug in soft gold, rose,

CHAPTER TWENTY-TWO

Living Rooms

IN CONTEMPORARY HOMES the living room is the center of family life and the most important room in the house. Successfully decorated and furnished it provides for all shared interests, and also for as many individualized activities and hobbies as convenience allows. This marks a modern reversion to an ancient way of living, in contrast to Victorian standards and ideas. During the hundred-odd years of Victorian influence houses had everything except a living room. They had dining rooms, parlors, libraries, studies, dens, nurseries and sitting rooms. Large establishments added drawing rooms, boudoirs, and servants' quarters—but no living room.

It is only since the turn of the century that we have once more centered our homes around a communal "living room," going back in spirit to the English Great Hall which made up practically the entire dwelling of that period. Here family joined guests and retainers to carry on all domestic activities from dancing and eating to working and sleeping. Many a modern multiple-duty room serving as a one-room apartment recreates almost literally activities of that early all-purpose living room except that modern ingenuity camouflages uses and compresses various activities into neatly compact space limits. More and more today's living rooms are planned to combine dining- or guest-room equipment with furniture needed for purely living-room purposes; this trend has influenced furnishings to a certain degree by introducing many new types of combination fittings such as those illustrated in Chapters 17 and 20.

Formal Living Rooms: The degree of formality varies widely, but the existence of a formal room usually means that the house is large enough to take care of relaxation as well as specialized interests and activities of the family in other rooms while primarily social pursuits are carried on in the living room. With this in mind, furniture grouping should be planned for flexibility, for diversified lighting, for convenient accessories at all strategic points where people may gather for music, games or conversation. In a room like this there should be several centers of interest with fixed seating arrangements for three or

SUBTLE HARMONY

wine, gray and blue has the muted over-all motifs which can be used with an outstanding floral pattern in draperies. A round, mirror-topped coffee table with curved legs combines with 18th Century porcelains and crystals to provide relief from straight lines. The color scheme—pale yellow and soft yellow-beige combined with a second primary color in grayed blue—uses the third primary, red, for accent in softened tones of wine and rose.

PENNSYLVANIA DUTCH PIECES ADD INFORMAL CHARM

The traditional living room above shows a center-of-interest fireplace grouping, in formal balance, with seating provided by twin right and left banquettes. These sofas are simply covered in chartreuse tweed with pillows in green and white stripe and tomato red. The color scheme is carried on by olive green walls and by draperies with a white ground and bright colors in a distinctive pattern called a "vegetable seed-package" print. The very modern concealed lighting back of the cane and oak ceiling-line molding is in contrast with quaint wall lights, authentic Pennsylvania Dutch furniture in pickled pine, and accessories of the period. The simple homelike atmosphere is increased by a grass matting rug in natural tan with a border painted in Swedish design. Woodwork in pickled oak, small potted trees and an old portrait over the Colonial-type mantel add to the unusual and special charm of this room.

more people in each group, enough local light and chairs easily moved to increase seating capacity wherever it is required. General lighting should be soft and flattering, and supplemented by special light over tables or other centers of activity.

Furnishings should be adapted to the size of the room. Carpets or room-sized rugs are usually most practical as they are not in the way of furniture and do not interfere with easy movement of chairs. However, a formal room—almost always fairly large, with clear floor space in the center—will display to advantage a large Oriental-style rug which harmonizes with the traditional furniture appropriate to the room's dignity.

In such a room fabrics can be used which are notable more for beauty than for long-wearing qualities.

This type of room is not apt to be in continuous use and such fabrics as fine silk and rayon damasks, brocades, satins, velvets and tapestries are therefore practical and appropriate. Keep the purely decorative aspects of furnishings in harmony with the formality of large pieces and general decoration. Murals, large pictures, mirrors and fine objects of art all belong here. If small prints or etchings are used, group them to give the effect of one large picture.

Informal Living Rooms: The real family living room may have a touch of formality if it is large enough. It may be crisply fresh and gay, or it may be definitely on the casual, lounging, restful order. Its decoration is keyed to comfort and convenience of the family first, guests second. Restfulness and ease will be primary considerations, ornaments more

FEDERAL AMERICAN LIVING ROOM WITH RESTFUL PLAIN WALL AND CARPET

Two views of this living room illustrate many points in furniture and accessory arrangement. Entirely traditional in feeling, it still has a modern air of solid comfort. In the view above we see a fireplace wall with set-in book shelves flanking the mantel. An uncluttered effect is produced by the nice balance of small accessories—mirror, mantel ornaments and grouping of small pictures at each side. The fireplace wall is balanced by center-of-interest arrangements on right and left walls. At the left the space between window draperies is filled by a hanging shelf in dark wood to provide an effective background for a hobby collection of dog figurines. The comfortable writing table-desk below has accessories which carry out this same hobby theme. On the right wall a comfortable slip-covered sofa is the center of a group of chairs

and tables with tall lamps for comfortable reading. The picture grouping is particularly interesting as a demonstration of how to give importance to a collection of small pictures. The group of four, all the same size, above each lamp table balances the larger group arranged above the sofa to carry the whole composition up for balance with the other walls. Observe that the pictures used in a group are selected and framed to give unity and balance in that group. The dark mats of those in the central group are very effective against the birch-bark walls, as is the dark background color of the chintz at the windows. The gray carpet and light gray upholstery of the open arm chairs is given life by using red on the other chairs and the blue of dog-patterned slip-cover chintz which carries out the hobby theme of the room.

BOOK SHELVES ARE APPROPRIATE IN LIVING ROOMS

Book shelves distributed around the combination living room-library above have been given an interesting recessed treatment at the sides of the fireplace. The wall at each side and above is built out beyond the chimney breast to frame shallow shelves, narrow mantel, over-mantel treatment in an unusual but highly effective manner. Simple moldings outlining fireplace and shelves make a separate inner frame for a panel in which a recessed shadow box displays a ship model in full sail. The panel-light above shows up in dramatic fashion this ship and 18th Century mantel accessories. The contemporary trend toward incorporating into living rooms various elements of convenience and special equipment is illustrated by the room at left. One end has been set off as a working center by a wide archway and a rolled screen for privacy when necessary.

or less limited to convenience. Unless the room is very small arrange the furniture as suggested above in groups, but groups here should be centered about definite family interests.

Color schemes should have a warm homelike, friendly feeling. Unassertive backgrounds are usually more satisfactory in the long run, with dramatic or striking features confined to smaller areas or purely decorative objects which can be changed if they be-

CENTERS OF INTEREST—CONVERSATION AND REFRESHMENT

Damask and velour are appropriate upholstery companions in the early 20th Century room above with wallpaper keyed to the classic romanticism of the picture over the sofa. The fine quality of damask suits the graceful lines of the small sofa while the large solid chairs, Victorian in feeling, are upholstered in a sturdy pile material which is equally suitable to their heaviness and bulk. Notice the tall lamps, at an excellent height for reading, modeled after 20th Century kerosene glass lamps. The lower photograph at right shows how a corner of a room has been utilized for a wood-paneled bar with its attractive shelf arrangement across the window. The green and white stripe of the awning outside is part of the picture—picking up the green of the rug in the room. A bar like this is at home in a living room or dining room as well as in a special entertainment room.

come tiresome. For year-round living it is important to adapt living-room furnishings to climatic changes by slip covers and other devices. (See illustrations, Chapter 21.) Remember that smooth fabrics both look and feel cooler, pile or rough surfaces look and feel warmer.

Carpeting on the floor gives a feeling of spaciousness to a room that may have to be fairly well-filled with furniture, and adds to quietness by absorbing

TRADITIONAL BABY GRAND PIANO IN HARMONY WITH AMERICAN GEORGIAN STYLE

Arrangement of pianos is difficult only when there is not sufficient space. In any large-enough room a piano can and should be made a major center of interest. In the completely modern room at right this is accomplished by placing the piano where the player faces the room and providing a dramatic background in the large round mirror which reflects an interesting flower arrangement. Notice the reliance upon texture for fabric interest, the curved corner into which a curved arm chair fits nicely, also the cove lighting around the entire ceiling line. In the room above the traditional baby grand piano is placed in an alcove—an effective background for a grand piano. The location of the alcove gives the piano a commanding position in the room, with the bay-window center of interest balancing the fireplace wall. Colonial mantel, Washington family scene and Mt. Vernon style andirons are in harmony with 18th Century furniture

and accessories. Walls and woodwork are painted spice color, repeated in a slightly deeper spice-tone broadloom carpet. Chintz draperies with shaped valances are in pale blue cretonne with a pattern of roses and baby chrysanthemums in autumn colors; fireplace easy chairs are upholstered in turquoise damask. A wing chair on the other side of the room has a slip cover of the chintz, illustrating a rule often useful when using chintz for window draperies. Making a slip cover from the drapery chintz for at least one important chair in another part of the room gives a desirable feeling of unity and balance to the room picture. Notice that both of these pianos are placed with the straight side along the wall and the curved side toward the room. This arrangement saves floor space and brings the more attractive side of the piano into view. The curve often provides a niche—as in the modern room at right—for a chair (or love seat).

NOTES ON PIANOS

1. If your piano is an unattractive upright, do not be discouraged. Retire it into an alcove or corner and make it as unobtrusive as possible by painting it to match the wall behind it.

2. Play the piano at least a few hours each week to exercise the strings and keep them in good condition.

3. Have piano tuned three times a year. Have it "voiced" every three years.

4. Leave keys exposed during the day. Too much darkness yellows the keys.

5. To clean piano: wipe keys with cloth slightly dampened with denatured alcohol. Dry with soft cloth. Never use soap on keys as it stains ivory.

6. Clean sounding board by inserting a piece of dry cloth under the strings. In grand pianos insert beginning at the base side and pull toward the treble. Avoid pressure on the keys.

7. Place small bags of para-crystals or nuggets in piano to keep moths from felt pads.

8. Never use polish or oil on the case. Dust with soft untreated cloth.

sound. It is better to have floor coverings in the conventional relation to walls, which means the darker tones at the base of the room. However, do not choose carpets or rugs so dark in tone that they will show every fleck of dust. Also avoid textures which are easily crushed into paths of wear.

Occasional furniture and service accessories must be carefully thought out. They are too often casually scattered around and so uncoordinated with each other and with the room background that they make the whole place seem cluttered and unrestful—"busy" is the decorating term for such a room as opposed to restful. (See Chapter 2.) While each major chair, couch or sofa needs a resting place conveniently near for lamps, ashtrays, books, etc., it is not necessary to have all of these in the form of small tables. One larger table may serve several chairs in a group. The tables themselves may be varied by substituting small chests of drawers, book shelves, etc. (See Chapter 16.) The important thing is to have surfaces available where each person may place a glass, cup, plate or ashtray. No matter how many types of tables you use, remember to keep end tables approximately the same height throughout the room.

Special Living Room Features: If the living room is to be used for games or hobbies, be sure to make provision for their use and storage. Wherever possible, use game tables in some decorative form and let them stay set up in a convenient corner, alcove or bay window instead of having them put away after each using. If you have musical instruments they must be very carefully considered from the standpoint of greatest effectiveness functionally as well as decoratively. In modern rooms, radios, phonographs and phonograph records are usually provided for by built-in cabinets, conveniently placed but inconspicuous. Where no such provision is made avoid elaborate ornate cases. Select those in harmony with your furnishings if possible and place them where they will be most useful—usually in a center-of-interest grouping for those of the family who are interested.

PIANO CASE IN BLOND WOOD
IS AT HOME
IN A MODERN ROOM

TELEVISION ALCOVE
WITH DRAPERIES
TO DRAW ACROSS

The combination library and man's living room above illustrates an excellent way to put an alcove to work—also several other points it is well to remember if you are planning a library nook in your home. Here the curved wall of the step-up alcove is lined with shelves, the lower one planned to hold unusually tall volumes if necessary. More shelf space has been allowed than is required for books and gaps are filled in with accessories, trophies, or hobby collections. The fireplace wall in this picture is interesting because the treatment could be used as a model for revamping the end of almost any room. This type of simple wood paneling and mantel design, even the convenient built-in cupboard above the fireplace, are available in various woods at reasonable prices. A smoking rack like the one at the right can be made

TRADITION OF EARLY AMERICA

at home, or a hanging book rack can be bought and converted into a smoking rack or a frame for hobbies. Brass fireplace accessories, and large slip-covered wing chair drawn up to the hearth, suggest cheerfulness and comfort. The saddled horse on the table-stand, trophies on mantel and shelves, fitted golf bag ready for service—all these provide clues to the room-owner's special interests.

CHAPTER TWENTY-THREE

Points on Libraries and Dens

CONTEMPORARY living conditions often crowd out traditional types of rooms once considered essential even in medium-sized homes or apartments. This necessitates working out new ways for taking care of the functions those rooms fulfilled. When a living room is used as a combination of living room with library or studio it may be treated so that the best features of both types of room are included.

LIBRARIES

If you are planning a library, or a library nook, remember that the primary essentials for library comfort are adequate storage for books, proper lighting, comfortable furniture arrangement for study and relaxation, and a general atmosphere of quiet and peace.

Books and Book Shelves: Books should be easily accessible and for this reason they are no longer stored behind glass. Even in elaborate libraries open shelves are installed to house them, and the shelves are always made to seem part of the architectural structure of the room. If you are building removable shelves, or buying them, cut out the baseboard behind them so that they will fit against the wall and look built-in. If you cannot do this, cut out the shelves at the back so that they will fit snugly over baseboard or dado. If possible, close part of the lower shelf space with doors for storage of papers, equipment, etc.

Adjustable shelves are very convenient but often too complicated for home carpenters. If your shelves are not adjustable be sure they are spaced so that the lower ones will take care of taller books while small books will fit nicely into the upper ones. Provide space on a low shelf for those extra-tall books which so often have to be laid flat on the shelf. Test partitions to be sure they are close enough together to keep shelves from sagging when they are filled with heavy books.

If the ceiling is not too high, shelves are often built straight up to the ceiling line, or almost to that point. Often they are finished at the top with curved headings and the upper shelves reserved for decorative objects. Whenever shelves are above comfortable reaching distance provide a library step and use upper shelves for books least frequently referred to. Reference books should always be within easy reach and close to a well-lighted desk or table. To keep clutter from your shelves, plan to build in a closet either in the room or just outside in a hallway to serve as a convenient "stock room."

Furniture: A flat-topped desk or table large enough for spreading out papers, blueprints or maps should be in every library. A reference or work table with a top which can be lifted slightly at the back like a drafting table is very helpful if you have much reading or studying of large books to do. Chairs should be the right height for desk or table and made comfortable with pads or cushions. If a typewriter is included in equipment be sure it is placed where it can be used with ease. A comfortable easy chair (or several, depending upon the size of the room) is a must even for a small library. If possible include a couch or chaise longue or ottoman-chair for real relaxation. Accessory tables and equipment follow the same rules of convenience as for any living room.

Lighting: Dark, light-absorbing walls and heavily curtained windows are no longer considered correct treatment for libraries. Even if dark wood is used for paneling and shelves because of its feeling of cozy warmth, or because the style of the room demands it, wall spaces and ceiling in white or pastel tones help reflect light and offset dark wood areas. Windows should be curtained and draped to control light but not obscure it. Very sheer glass curtains in white, cream or sunny yellow, should be combined with draperies which just cover edges of window panes rather than hang over them. This holds true even when full draw-curtains are designed to pull across the windows at night—a favorite treatment for library windows because of the feeling of warmth and privacy.

Artificial lighting must be carefully worked out. Modern fluorescent lighting is particularly desirable where reading or work is to be done at night. The shelves should be well lighted, or a "trouble" light provided. This is a shaded and protected bulb on a long cord which may be carried anywhere it is needed for reading titles of books on shelves. Don't forget that proper placing of mirrors may be utilized to reflect and increase light where it is needed. Many modern libraries make extensive use of new types of concealed lighting. (See Chapter 37.)

Decoration: Traditional dark color schemes once considered essential for libraries with their walls of dark-paneled wood, furniture upholstered in leather, have been replaced by a wide variety in colors and treatment. The soft restfulness and warmth of wood for paneling and shelves is still popular but may be obtained in new natural or honey-colored finishes just as well as in dark conventional wood tones. Plain draperies in background color are usually more desirable than patterned fabrics because the books themselves provide design and color. However, if you wish to strike a gayer note, use figured fabrics in which designs and colors are not too conspicuous. Hangings may be in any style provided they follow the rules for good lighting mentioned above.

Wood paneling is attractive for walls because it blends so well with the architectural lines of shelving—and with the help of present-day stock paneling or imitation wood materials you can indulge a taste for wood on your library walls at comparatively small expense. Many novelty fabrics, wallpapers and composition materials are also admirably adapted to library use, but walls should be kept plain because of book jackets which provide texture as well as design and color. Floors and ceilings should contribute to quietness. With ceilings this is easily accomplished by use of sound-absorbing acoustic composition boards. Floors may be made noiseless by wall-to-wall carpeting, large rugs, or some noiseless flooring such as cork. Floor coverings may be plain or figured. Self-tone figured carpeting is restful, while the rich colors of Oriental rugs blend harmoniously with the colors of books on shelves.

DENS AND HOME OFFICES

A library or a quiet corner of a living room may serve as a small den or office, or a special room may be fitted up somewhere on the premises. Aside from requirements of technical equipment necessary for avocation, vocation, or hobby, the principles of lighting, comfort and furnishings are the same as those mentioned for libraries. Shelf space is usually required for books and magazines, or for special books, materials, and possibly records. When a hobby involves activity it should always be segregated in some way from other household activities. But when it consists of collecting decorative objects they may be made part of a decorating scheme for whatever room in the house they seem to be most suitable and adapted.

STUDIOS—MODERN AND TRADITIONAL

The two studios pictured here demonstrate the basic principle of studio decoration—individuality. The studio-living room is usually designed as a workroom for one person which means that comfort of guests or other members of the family is a secondary consideration. The studio in the lower picture shows the traditional high ceiling and open-raftered finish associated with remodeled barns, old mills or other buildings so often taken over by artists for their quarters. The brick chimney and fireplace intensify this effect. Built-in cabinet and couch-bed provide comfort and convenience by day and adequate sleeping quarters if necessary by night. A studio like this can easily double as a guest room or guest house. The furniture is simple but comfortable. Growing plants and flowers combine with bright drapery and couch cover to soften the austerity of exposed rafters and brick. The upper picture illustrates many features of modern studio-living room design. Very new tiered studio windows with modernistic light control devices, use of straight lines in geometric feeling for desk, fireplace-treatment and furniture—these are as distinctive as they are modern. The striking combination of black for floor and lacquered furniture with white or light colors in upholstery and cabinet trim is another modern note which gives this studio a highly dramatic quality. Here, as in the traditional room (right), flowers and plants are used to soften austerity.

LIBRARIES IN THREE ATTRACTIVE STYLES

The three rooms on this page illustrate three typical interpretations of the library idea in contemporary homes. The room in the picture at left demonstrates how inexpensively a small room might be transformed into a charming library retreat or combination library and workroom. Book shelves like this could be installed easily, and the furniture is comfortable but simple. Early American chairs harmonize with the primitive wide plank floor which may either be painted or stained and waxed to match the pine used for furniture and book shelves. Draperies frame the window but do not obscure the light which filters through very sheer glass curtains. The radiator is enclosed in a continuous line with the book shelves, with a removable louvred section at the front.

At left we have a library developed according to the most modern theories of decorating. Combining library and study features, this room illustrates the use of structural lines in design. The desk is built around a column flanked on each side by recessed built-in book shelves. Both walls and column are covered with parchment-toned linoleum, while desk top and all other darker trimming strips are in linoleum with pigskin finish. The floor linoleum is a marbleized pattern in tan with flecks of brown and cream. A parchment shade on the lamp, and furniture upholstery in brown and cream, carry out the analogous color scheme ranging from cream through brown. The center picture in the group is a charming example of the traditional library. Wood-paneled walls in soft waxed pine serve as background for rich shades in book bindings and an oil painting which depicts a colorful old sporting scene. Traditional 18th Century wood furniture shows how well mahogany or walnut can be combined with lighter wood tones such as pine. A capacious well-lighted desk and a modern easy chair create the feeling of quiet comfort essential in successful library decoration.

DISTINCTION TO THE ROOM

carpet ties the room together, adding its own note of restfulness and charm. Notice the fireplace grouping which solves a problem in arrangement due to the opening of doors on each side of the fireplace. The placing of the couch and the two large chairs allows a fireplace grouping, with space at each side for traffic lanes leading through the doorways. Notice the paneled doors which seem to be part of the wall.

CHAPTER TWENTY-FOUR

How to Treat Fireplaces and Mantels

IN A RECENT POLL of young people planning homes more than eighty out of every hundred reported that they considered a fireplace essential for completing a room. The answers came from young people who had not grown up in the tradition of fireplaces as necessary heating agents. The poll therefore throws an interesting light on the close link which still exists between "hearth" and "home"—a link so fundamental that many languages employ the same word for both.

Certainly from the decorative standpoint nothing else yet worked out can compete with the fireplace as a center of interest about which to build any type of living room, formal or informal. Where there is no fireplace, and one cannot be installed, it is necessary to devise other focal points for grouping furniture and many successful plans have been worked out. (See Chapter 2.) But don't dismiss your fireplace dream easily. If the chimney is properly arranged it is neither as difficult nor as expensive as you may think to build in a fireplace.

FIREPLACES THAT WORK

When Building a Fireplace: If you are having a fireplace built be sure the specifications call for correct relation between the various elements of the fireplace. Size of chimney and flue, width and height of opening, depth and angle of side walls and back, position of throat and smoke shelf—all these should be checked. Size of the fireplace opening should depend upon size and style of the room and the kind of fuel to be burned. The rustic, primitive types of fireplace are usually larger than those in more formal styles. The "great big fireplace" which people often

GROUP OF COLONIAL AMERICAN FIREPLACES

The traditional fireplace group on this page suggests transition stages of one type of fireplace through several generations in American homes. In the photograph at the left is an authentic old Dutch-oven fireplace with typical flagstone hearth, rough stone construction and plain board mantel. Grooved pine paneling, rag rug, wooden rocker and checked table cloth all belong to the original background and furnishings of the room as much as the primitive gun hung ready for action on hooks above the mantel. The picture at upper right illustrates an attractive contemporary version of this type of fireplace. Detail has been carefully thought out. Painted wood paneling for the chimney breast, combined with scenic wallpaper everywhere else on the walls, is as Colonial in feeling as the furniture, hooked rugs, slate hearth, black wrought-iron fireplace fittings, pewter on the mantel, and the lighted candles. In the picture at lower left appears a more modernized adaptation of the same Dutch-oven type. Roughly finished cut stone has been used here to build the fireplace, and the Dutch-oven spaces are converted into convenient cubbyholes for storing fuel. The mantel has become heavier and more important to balance the heavy beams of the ceiling in a rather large room. The *petit point* fireplace screen, powder horn, and huge iron kettle for kindling combine with the hooked rug and Windsor chair to create a friendly Colonial atmosphere in the room. The picture at the upper left shows a fireplace all ready for cooking, equipped with swinging crane and kettle. The Dutch-oven section has a door paneled in natural finish white pine like the rest of the woodwork, while heavy molding supports the mantel. Brick fireplace interior, plastered facing with iron decorations, and cement hearth, give a finished appearance to this fireplace and harmonize with the carved cornice and the beautifully paneled walls. Huge pewter plates, rows of cups, hurricane lamps and candle brackets are all appropriate accessories. This picture was taken in a dining room, so the small Colonial rush-bottom chairs flank the fireplace and no furniture is grouped around it. Note the dark painted floor in wood planks of unequal widths, also the unusual "antique" texture of the rag rug.

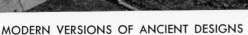

MODERN VERSIONS OF ANCIENT DESIGNS

The group of pictures on this page shows the very interesting connection between ancient fireplace forms and the latest types of modern design. Above is a faithful reproduction of the quaint hooded fireplaces which marked the first medieval step away from primitive cooking and heating fires placed in the center of the hall with only cracks in walls and roofing to carry off the smoke. Rough stone, primitive carving of the frame around the recessed fireplace, hammered metal of the hood are in delightful and historically authentic contrast with finely finished panels on the doors of the book shelf-cupboard at the right. Note the raised floor of the fireplace, wrought-iron fixtures, and mantel-like plate-rail just below the ceiling line. In the contemporary room at upper right the overhanging hood principle has been translated into brick, used also for the floor. Textured plaster walls, single-panel door in natural blond wood finish, simple book shelves suspended by metal chains, and shaggy fur rug, all mark this studio room as distinctly modern. The two pictures at right illustrate the same interesting contrast between ancient and modern. In the one above a different type of hooded fireplace appears. This corner installation follows the design of early fireplaces in Scandinavian countries. For some reason corners were always preferred and the sides of the fireplace were cut away to show as much of the fire as possible. Hearths were always raised, sometimes up to a foot or more. Here the Scandinavian fireplace is framed by pine-grooved paneled walls in a studio room with recessed built-in book shelves and accessories which are harmonious in feeling with the fireplace. The chimney breast is of molded cement with brick and tiles for base and trimming. Over-all carpeting in soft brown is in tone with brown stained wood. Draperies are tan and blue, ceiling painted in robin's egg blue. The modern room at lower right has many earmarks of contemporary design, but the hooded fireplace is closely akin to those of Northern Europe just described.

demand is suited only to a great big room. A large fireplace should burn large logs and such a fire would be unbearable in a small room. A small fire looks lost in a cavernous fireplace, and much of the heat actually is lost. A 30-inch fireplace well filled with blazing logs looks better and gives out more heat than a 48-inch opening with the same fire.

If you need real heat from your fireplace investigate those types which include circulating air devices for greatly increased heat, also distributing it more evenly and widely. In a small fireplace a depth of 12 inches provides draft, but one of 16 to 18 inches allows larger wood to be burned and provides greater safety against logs falling out. For an average room (15 x 20 feet) a fireplace opening from 30 to 36

inches wide is customary. For a larger room, width is increased proportionately, and depth must be added in the same ratio.

FIREPLACE FITTINGS

Fireplace tools and fittings are usually also decorative accessories and should harmonize with the style and size of the fireplace. Ornamental wood baskets and coal scuttles are attractive if they are in keeping both with the fireplace treatment and the room. Unusual baskets and other containers often make distinctive fuel containers. A long-handled brush is both ornamental and handy for keeping the hearth neat—also an old-fashioned bellows to stir up a sleepy fire. The thing to remember is that large, crude fittings of rough iron belong with large crude fireplaces of fieldstone or brick. Small finely wrought fittings are dwarfed by a large opening and their delicate grace is lost. Brass is the one material which may be used with any fireplace, but it must be in tools that are scaled to the dimensions of the fireplace and harmonize with it in design.

Andirons: A metal fire basket may be used instead of andirons, but most people prefer the traditional fittings. They are usually made in brass, black iron or gray Swedish iron, but have occasionally been decorated with gold or silver overlays and ornaments. Modern designers have introduced many new designs making use of the new plastics, even those which are transparent. A new device is a log rest of heavy iron which is placed over the shanks of the andirons, inside the fireplace, to take the strain from them. These are particularly useful under heavy logs, and in a large fireplace burning extra long logs several of the rests may be used between the andirons.

Tools: Pokers, shovels, brushes, and tongs often come in sets with a rack-and-stand arrangement, though with more primitive types of fireplaces they are usually hung about the fireplace or under the mantel. In design and material they should harmonize with other fireplace equipment. Tongs should be sturdy enough to lift large lumps of coal or logs of whatever size you expect to burn.

Fenders: These railings are most often made in polished brass, though silver and silver plating have been used when that metal was more harmonious with fireplace treatment and room decoration. They should be the same size as the hearth, forming a border for it. They often add an authentic touch to period rooms, and in proper design a fender gives distinction to many types of contemporary rooms.

Firescreens: There are many types of metal screens, most of them folding so that they can be set aside when not wanted. They are in black to go with black

TWO FIREPLACES WITH THE CLASSIC LINES OF AMERICAN GEORGIAN AND FEDERAL PERIODS

iron fittings, in brass or trimmed with brass to harmonize with brass fittings, or in other special finishes.

MANTELS

When fireplaces were first cut into chimneys there was no mantel shelf—only a plain opening in the chimney with the fire built on a hearth in front of it and an overhanging hood to collect smoke. When the fires began to be built in a recess set into the chimney the mantel shelf appeared and remained through many generations an important part of fireplace design in most countries. In recent years modern designers have often reverted to the original plain facing or molding about a fireplace opening with no suggestion of a mantel, but in the average room some type of mantel is still preferred.

Types of Mantels: Rough stone with simple wood plank walls is appropriate for game rooms, country cabins, and in rustic-type rooms. The mantel then is a plain shelf of stone or heavy wood. Period and regional rooms require mantels in harmony with their other decorations and furnishings and these traditional styles furnish models for most of the mantels used in our contemporary decorating. Many of them are appropriate and charming and with the proper finish are at home in almost any room. Others left over from the days of later 19th Century monstrosities are towering creations with tier after tier of dust-catching fretwork and grilles. These require drastic treatment. So also do those over-heavy massive types in brick or masonry inherited from a somewhat later generation.

Size of Mantels: Many rooms have been spoiled by mantels out of scale—too high and narrow, too low and broad, too large, too small, too light, too heavy for the wall space. There is no hard and fast rule about size because every room is a separate problem, but for the room with average proportions these figures are helpful: In English- and Colonial-type rooms the mantel shelf is usually from 44 to 54 inches above the floor while in the French styles it is slightly lower —from 36 to 48 inches in height. The width of course should be in pleasing proportion to the height. If proportions are wrong it is usually not too difficult to correct them.

Materials, Finish and Facings: Many materials have been used for mantels and mantel supports but wood, marble and carved stone have always been favorites. Stone and marble usually belong to period types, and if you have one you must either adapt other surroundings to it or replace it. Wood, on the other hand, can be easily altered in style and appearance by paint and removal of superfluous ornaments. A wood mantel and frame should harmonize with other woodwork in the room unless you want to emphasize the fireplace by contrast treatment. If the fireplace is so unattractive that you want to make it as inconspicuous as possible use the old remedy—paint everything paintable in the background color of the wall behind it.

Facings are important—and useful. An outmoded fireplace with brick facing can be modernized simply by hiding the bricks under a smart mirrored facing, sheathing them with one of the many fireproof plastics, or cementing a layer of tiles over them in a colorful design which may be traditional or modern.

A MODERN FIREPLACE, AND A MODERN INTERPRETATION OF EARLY AMERICAN PINE

303

A delightful use of accessories in the small living room above illustrates several interesting points. The narrow shelves which flank the mantel used for 18th Century pieces are given a very modern air by light-panels inset at the top. Simple mantel decorations harmonize with the Colonial background of painted paneled wall and azalea-patterned

paper on the other three walls. Over the small console sideboard a round Colonial mirror is flanked by a symmetrically balanced arrangement of small pictures and crystal candelabra. A vase filled with Mexican huckleberry leaves gives a touch of green to the fireplace group with quaint coffee table and small hooked rug. The color scheme in this room

ACCESSORIES THAT HARMONIZE

combines coral with bayou green and copper. Flowers on the wallpaper are in deep peach and white against a soft coral ground; the painted wall is done in a pinkish terra cotta while the tiered draperies are made of cotton taffeta striped in pale green, coral and beige. Maple, cherry and pine woods are mingled in various pieces of furniture.

CHAPTER TWENTY-FIVE

How to Use Accessories and Accents

ACCESSORIES should always be considered as accents, but accents do not always have to be accessories. Accents are often confined to such small touches as piping or trimming on upholstery, hangings or cushions. They may be worked out through a flash of color in a fabric design or a scatter rug. They are usually bits of contrast color placed at points needing emphasis—that is, *accent*.

Under the term "accessories" is lumped a vast array of decorative objects ranging all the way from utilitarian pieces such as clocks and ashtrays to the purely ornamental field of pictures, statues, hobby collections, bits of pottery, etc. In choosing accessories the personal element must be taken into account more than anywhere else in decorating, but even here a certain amount of planning and coordination is essential. Many a lovely gracious room has been ruined by too many accessories all crowded together like a dealer's badly arranged display.

If you are one of those who cannot resist bits of charm in the way of bowls, vases, ashtrays, candlesticks, and all the other colorful odds and ends you find in the shops, you probably have a large and growing collection on your hands. You bought them because you liked them, and for the same reason you want to use them. The solution is simple. Sort them out in groups which harmonize with the furnishings of various rooms in design, feeling or color—then re-assort each group so that it divides into two or more, each made up of the number of pieces you can effectively fit into your decorating plans for the different rooms. Install the various pieces where they will show to best advantage, leave them there for awhile, then put them away and arrange a second group in their places. It often happens in such a division that one group is in the lighter tones appropriate to summer color schemes while another group is in richer colors adapted to the warm shades of a winter decorating plan. In that case use one with your winter hangings and save the other to go with summer draperies and slip covers.

USEFUL ACCESSORIES

Working Accessories—Full Time: Clocks, ashtrays, screens, bookends, lamps—these are constantly used and must satisfy a utilitarian as well as a decorative purpose. Most people have clocks which keep fairly good time, screens are usually high enough and substantial enough to hide what they are supposed to hide; but ashtrays, bookends and lamps too often fall short of fulfilling their mission. Ashtrays should be large enough to hold an accumulation of ashes if necessary, heavy enough not to tip over, and designed to prevent half-burned cigarettes or cigars falling on the outside and burning the table. They should be of some material easily kept clean by washing, without constant scouring and polishing. Also, there should be enough of them so that at least one is in easy reach from every seating place in the room. Bookends should either be the type with a flap under the books to insure steadiness, or have a base heavy enough and large enough to support them. Lamps should be weighted in the base to make them safe and shades or inverted bowls should not be so large and heavy that they overbalance the base.

Part-Time Workers: Vases, bowls, trays, candlesticks—these are all articles designed for utility but in most cases used only on special occasions. They should be well designed for their functional purpose, pleasing in outline and not weighted down with too much fancy ornamentation. If they are not really attractive in appearance keep them put away except when you are actually using them, or try redecorating them with enamel, lacquer or brightly colored pictorial motifs.

PURELY ORNAMENTAL

The variety of non-utility articles which come under the heading of ornamental decoration is limited only by the imagination of the human race and the backward reach of historical research. Every kind of material has been used in the creation of countless designs and patterns. Today we draw upon the crude simplicity of primitive (also some extremely modernistic) pottery, the dust-catching fretwork and carvings of early rococo and later Victorian decorating styles, the graceful perfection of line in the Greek vase or statuette, the subtle color

On these pages is presented almost a complete object lesson in correct use of different types of accessories. It is worth while to analyze various treatments straight around the room which is shown in two views. Starting with the mirror-paneled fireplace above, the wall is made important by ceiling-high draperies at each side in a pomegranate and green print on white. In the center hangs a barometer clock over the mirror with small French-style tables and tall lamps at either side. In this traditional room a sectional sofa is divided in the modern style to make a short chaise longue on one side of the fireplace and an arm chair on the other. The elephants bearing ashtrays introduce a picturesque and colorful note. A graceful 18th Century French-style cabinet at the right with a display of interesting china is tall enough and large enough to provide a balance for the fireplace group and for the two seating groups shown at the left and on the opposite side of the room (see facing picture). The H hinges on the cabinet doors are characteristic of Early American and European furniture. It is a detail worth noting if you are striving for a period effect. A third center-of-interest grouping includes twin modern-style easy chairs upholstered in the drapery chintz and flanking a large low reading table. The bowl of flowers is correctly arranged here—kept low so that it will not interfere with visibility between occupants of these two chairs. Proceeding to the facing picture and moving to the left past the chair-and-table group we come to an attractive small sofa or love

DECORATIVE
FRENCH WALL CLOCK

seat interesting in design and upholstered in textured modern fabric trimmed with moss fringe edging and deep fringe around the bottom. The large 18th Century mirror is flanked by two groups of small pictures framed alike to build up the composition on this wall and balance the other walls. Mirrors may be hung (as this one is) like pictures, with frames or metal clamps; or they may be applied directly to the wall with decorative screws. Unframed mirrors—known as Venetian mirrors—often have decorations in the glass itself around the edges in place of any frame. Remember to place mirrors where you want a sense of space, not at the end of a room which is already too long. In hanging them follow the same rules as for framed pictures. In this room 18th Century urns make appropriate lamps for traditional tables. Notice on the table at the right the correct groupings of accessories in graceful balance and rhythm. The tall lamp dominates the group made up of several objects in varying heights arranged in pleasing relationship to each other. In grouping accessories remember that except where pairs are used for formal balance odd numbers work out best. The crystal candle-chandelier (with electric candles) harmonizes with the formality of the room, its period feeling and the height of the ceiling. Apple green walls and sofa provide a color foil for the complementary accent color of pomegranate in the drapery flowers and the pink tones which mingle with beige in the Oriental rug. The light rug shows to advantage against a dark wood floor.

harmonies and superb finishes of Chinese porcelains, the sleek gleam of metals, glass and plastics in modern contributions to the purely artistic side of home decorating. A few really fine accessories are worth waiting for. In the meantime you may find exactly the color you need in a bit of inexpensive pottery with a nice glaze and good lines. Don't be afraid to use it. It will be quite at home with the finer pieces.

Through the maze of colors and designs there are certain changeless principles you can depend upon to guide you:

1. From your point-of-view nothing is beautiful unless it will enhance the beauty of the room which is to be its setting.

2. No matter how perfect any object may be artistically you can dim its beauty by placing it against an inharmonious background and increase its charm by the right setting.

3. Apply the rules of composition and color combination in Chapter 2 and Chapter 4 to the choice and arrangement of all accessories and you will find them very useful aids to effective decoration.

Suitability: The personal element is so strong in selection of accessories that we might almost say anything is suitable if you like it enough. In practice, however, objects whose chief value is sentimental can usually be worked into your bedroom rather than your living room. Try to find a place for some over-large article of real merit in a hall where there is little furniture. But don't just set it down there— make an appropriate setting by building in a niche, making an illuminated shadow box or otherwise "framing" your treasure. The more real art value a piece has the more environments it will harmonize with—if it is suitable in color and scale—but don't carry this too far. Pieces of crude peasant art which are charming in a simple homespun and knotty pine living room would lose their appeal in a setting of formal silk fabrics and polished mahogany, while a crystal chandelier would look most out of place in an Early American gingham-draped cottage.

This brings us to the matter of period suitability. It is not necessary to limit yourself to accessories in the same period as the dominant style of your room, but you can use characteristic decorative objects effectively to help create any desired period feeling. Typical accessories of every period have been reproduced by contemporary manufacturers and you will have no difficulty finding what you need to help establish an authentic atmosphere. With the right wallpaper, slip covers and accessories you can give a pleasing period flavor to a room filled with nondescript furniture—and spend comparatively little money on the project. (See Chapter 19.) In modern backgrounds distinctively modern accessories are usually found, but many of the earlier styles may be called upon to break the severity of plain surfaces characteristic of modern design.

Arrangement: Each grouping of accessories on table, dresser or mantel should be a minor composition harmonizing with the background and with the over-all room picture. Balance and scale are very important. Small accessories for small rooms, large accessories for large rooms are obviously desirable. The illustrations in this chapter demonstrate the grouping of small objects with correct and pleasing observance of the rules of balance and scale. Study these pictures for all the finer points.

Color: It is in the working out of a color scheme that accessories can render you real service. If they are dull and characterless, or in too many colors jumbled together, they can rob your room of all distinction. On the other hand, if you work out your accent colors so that they fall at strategic points and place your accessories at those points you can bring out and point up the beauty of your furniture and hangings. It will also help make your room a complete composition which at the same time expresses you. The bright color you select for accent contrast should be carried through all the various groupings in the room, but often all that is necessary is a touch of the color in an object as small as a lacquered cigarette box or an ashtray. Remember that woods and metals have color and this must be taken into account in arranging accessories made from natural wood, silver, brass, pewter or copper. Glass and transparent plastics have so much brilliance, whether clear or colored, that they may be used to brighten up a dark corner but should not be placed where light is not needed.

TYPES OF ACCESSORIES

In addition to the classifications already mentioned there are many small articles of household furniture which must be included under the heading of accessories. Waste baskets are too often ignored entirely or are flaws in an otherwise charming picture. They are very necessary in all types of rooms and may easily be made attractive enough to justify their existence. They may be covered with expensive tooled leather or fabric, they may be mirrored, they may be handpainted. They may be equally good looking covered with laced-up fabric to match your draperies, or with wallpaper to match the walls. Stencils or cutouts may be applied to inexpensive baskets and the tops finished with upholstery trimming.

Brass, copper and pewter kept softly shining are additions to almost any room in the form of candlesticks, fireplace accessories, clocks, wall sconces, etc.

BUILDING WALL INTEREST THROUGH CORRECT HANGING OF PICTURES
AND MIRRORS IS AN IMPORTANT ELEMENT IN DECORATING

When a picture is hung alone it must be large enough for the space it is to fill, important and beautiful enough to be emphasized, harmonious with the room in subject, design and coloring. It should be placed in the center of a wall panel when there is one. Always hang pictures and mirrors "blind"—no wires showing—and flat against the wall. The rule for height is to place the center of an individual picture or the central picture in a group at the eye level of a person average in height—unless some special adjustment must be made with relation to a piece of furniture below the picture. Hang your largest picture over your largest piece of furniture if possible. Oil paintings, and good reproductions on dull paper, are usually framed without glass. Gilt frames are still used with period pictures but contemporary taste calls for simpler framing than in the past even in period rooms. Often an old picture may be used in a modern setting merely by transferring it to a new simple frame. Wood frames may be used in stain, natural colors or enamel, and a wash finish on plain wood is a modern favorite. Portraits, florals, Chinese

tures grouped above—an excellent illustration of one way to use small pictures with frames and mats. Generally speaking, mats are used for prints, etchings, lithographs, water colors, photographs, and wash drawings. The mat should not be too conspicuous, but it is very important. The first objective of mat and frame is to display the picture to the best possible advantage. A second objective is to provide a decorative bond between picture, wall and room furnishings. With the right mat you can often use very simple inexpensive frames, old ones refinished, or even bound sheets of cellophane. If you like a change of pictures now and then look for some of the modern "holders" which are fastened to the wall, allowing one print to be slipped out and another inserted. A very large mat may give new importance and interest to a good small print, and using plain mats will make it possible to hang a few well-chosen pictures against gaily patterned walls. The mats should be in a neutral transition tone linking wall and picture colors; the plain areas serve as a break between patterns in backgrounds and pictures. Mats

pictures, unstylized nature themes are essentially ageless and may be adapted by proper framing to almost any room. Others are definitely dated, require appropriate framing and are at home in some rooms, out of place in others. Novelty framing must be carefully keyed to the picture and the room. An example of this is shown in the picture above right where two oil paintings are framed alike in fruitwood with mats of scalloped copper set off by brass nailheads in a solid line. Designed like 18th Century mirrors this novel framing style harmonizes perfectly with traditional wood paneling, Early American table, hurricane candlesticks, statuette lamp, and antique china plates on the wall. Grouping here is noteworthy. The pair of pictures and the paired plate arrangement on the wall balance the length of the table. On the table itself symmetrical balance of accessories (lamp and candlesticks) is kept from stiffness by optical balance between the two books and a shallow tray filled with growing plants. Complete formal balance is carried out in the picture above left where identical tables and lamps flank the sofa with pic-

are usually heavy soft-finished cardboard in white, off-white or soft pastel tints, but other materials have been successfully used. Wallpaper, linoleum, plastics, mirrors, textured fabrics, linen, metal foils—even blotting paper and straw matting—may help to harmonize your pictures with their background. Whenever possible make them a part of the grouping nearest them—and never forget the importance of scale, line and balance in their relation to each other, their surroundings, and to the wall or panel space. Small pictures which are merely interesting spots on a wall may be beautiful and effective in a group. A series of similar prints may be arranged inside one large frame, or in panels outlining a doorway, or they may turn a corner behind a furniture grouping into a dramatic center of interest. Plan each picture grouping in some organized, symmetrical design—you will find many illustrations in this book which will help you do this. Never place a picture or group "off center" in a panel or wall space, and never use a stair-step arrangement unless you are hanging them on a stair wall.

DON'T THROW AWAY
DISCARDED PICTURE FRAMES

New uses for old frames are shown on this page. You will recognize one of the frames in the handsome shadow-box wall shelf which serves as a background for display of small accessories. This is easily made by building a shallow wooden box with evenly spaced shelves fitted to the opening in the frame. You can paint the frame any color you like, with an antique finish for additional interest. The interior may be painted the same color or a contrast shade; it may be lined with mirror panels in which case the shelves might be made of glass or mirror; an attractive lining could be made from fitted pieces of linoleum. To use a frame like this as a setting for flowers or a growing plant you would merely omit the shelves (see page 314), but you would probably want to use a smaller frame. The oval frame is shown in the upper right corner serving on a buffet as a cheese tray. This was accomplished by fitting a piece of plywood over the entire back and fastening it securely to the frame. The tray shown is painted coral, decorated with a wavy striped design in black and scalloped white bandings with black dots. Again an-

tiquing adds interest. The third frame is transferred into a useful tea or cocktail table by fitting a piece of plywood into the opening and attaching the frame to a homemade base. The base of a discarded table could be used, or cut down legs from an old table or chair, or a folding luggage rack. This table is painted blue and white, antiqued, with the carvings decorated in color. A sheet of glass, linoleum or mirror could be used over the plywood. An inexpensive way to have a glass top on a table or other piece of furniture is to buy salvaged or traded-in plate glass from a glazier and have it cut to your measurements. Smooth the edges of the glass with emery paper or coarse oilstone and place it over your painted, waxed or fabric-covered surface. If you want to paint the glass itself it is easily done by giving it a coat of enamel and placing it paint side down when thoroughly dry over several layers of paper on the surface to be covered. This must be flat and smooth under the papers. Many other articles around the house can be salvaged by this same type of decorating.

Avoid too elaborate designs both because they are harder to keep in condition and because they interfere with the patina which is the chief charm of burnished metal. Wrought iron is particularly appropriate in simple interiors such as Colonial or Early English.

One use of metal often overlooked in contemporary homes is its decorative function in the form of hardware. Today doors are usually hung with hinges more or less concealed and little more attention is paid to knobs and keyhole plates. If you are working out any kind of period furnishing be sure to check on the type of hardware characteristic of the time. Whether it was iron or brass it was placed on the surface and many beautiful designs were worked out which greatly enhanced the beauty of doors to which the hinges and plates were applied.

Knobs and pulls for drawers were also beautifully designed and keyed to the style of the day. Brass

door-knockers are characteristic of our own Colonial period. French hardware expresses all the essential elements of contemporaneous furniture design. Many of the old styles in hardware have been reproduced in modern metal-working shops and your dealer can probably help you select fixtures or hardware which will bear the stamp of the period you are working out in your room. For contemporary decoration chrome metals and plastics provide beauty, in labor-saving materials requiring little care.

Pictures: It is not necessary to spend a great deal of money in order to have attractive pictures on your walls. Many lovely reproductions are available including practically all the fine historical paintings. Pictures may be expressions of your own personal taste or they may be chosen purely as accents to the color or design of your room plan. Frames should form a transition bond between the wall, the picture and the furnishings in the room. They must also make other small occasional pieces to accommodate metal bowls for flower containers.

Hobby Collections: Don't use hobby collections for decorations unless they are decorative. Fortunately, many of them can be used to add beauty as well as interest to a living room or any room to which they are adapted by their nature. For example, a collection of period china table dishes would be specially appropriate in dining-room cabinets while china bowls and figurines would be most at home in a living room although either one can be fitted into any room where space is available. In choosing a background always try to work out something which will display as well as house your collection. An assortment of colored glass bottles and jars shows to best advantage placed where light shines through the glass. A bay window with glass shelves, or a glass partition between rooms, makes an ideal cabinet for any colored glass.

HINTS ON CARE OF ACCESSORIES

Don't throw away broken crockery or porcelain unless it is badly shattered. There are professional menders of valuable accessories and the others you can take care of yourself if you follow directions on the containers in which special mending cements are put up. The secret is to hold the broken edges together for ten or twelve hours by means of strong rubber bands or cord. Once the cement is set the piece will be practically as good as new. To protect your furniture paste pieces of thin felt or moleskin on the bottom of flowerpots, candlesticks, all heavy ornaments.

Cleaning Marble and Ivory: To clean marble objects make a strong solution of sal-soda combined with Fuller's earth, coat the marble with the paste and leave it on twenty-four hours before washing it off. If ivory objects are all in one piece they can be safely cleaned with soap and water. If several pieces are glued together, rub the surface with a piece of raw lemon dipped in salt. After the juice has dried on the ivory rub it off with a damp cloth.

Care of Metals: In addition to the commercial metal cleaners here are some suggestions. To brighten pewter, drop a lump of potash in a quart of water and soak the pewter article in this for twenty-four hours, take it out, rub all over with a cloth dipped in olive or mineral oil and follow by a brisk rubbing with a dry chamois. Modern pewter is often made free from lead and is non-tarnishing. Its brilliant finish is indefinitely preserved by careful washing and thorough drying. It can be cleaned with metal polish if high brilliance is desired. Never put pewter over a flame or in an oven or leave it near gas fumes. Connoisseurs

DRAMATIC SCREEN WITH SHADOW-BOX PANELS

Folding screens can be more decorative and more useful than most people realize—and they are not difficult to improvise or actually make at home. You can buy frames to cover at home, or get one with an inexpensive finish and do it over yourself with new paint and new panel decorations. Screens may have only three sections, or as many as six without being too heavy to handle. Many types of novelty screens are almost ceiling high and may serve as complete partitioning in emergencies. Modern designers make extensive use of such devices.

A CENTER-OF-INTEREST HOBBY DISPLAY

The general rule for housing hobbies is to seek out a harmonious background which will display your special collection to the best advantage and to make sure of protection also for objects which are perishable. Ordinary-sized glass or china may be displayed on open shelves, but such things as fragile miniature pieces, and dolls with cloth garments, should be guarded by glass against breakage and soil. Glass-enclosed shelves are always good. For tiny objects an excellent device is to store them in tables with hinged glass tops and shallow box trays beneath where the miniatures may be arranged on colored fabric which brings out lines and colors. You can convert an ordinary table into a "display case" by having a flat box made and attached to its top. Don't forget the value of mirror backing for shelves to repeat color and show the back as well as the front of a bowl or vase. In the china collector's room shown below the use of glass shelving and inset panel lighting insures good illumination for the entire display. Never crowd a display.

GROWING PLANTS FOR RESTFULNESS AND BEAUTY

Shown above are three attractive and unusual ways to bring into your home the fresh green of growing plants. An old-fashioned pine commode (at right) has its top turned into a flower box filled with ferns and ivy. The foliage prints on the wall are framed with mats made of pressed leaves and flowers under glass. At the left a shadow box with shelves, made from an old picture frame, is dramatized by the rich dark green of ivy leaves. The lattice-brackets (center) support decorative bowls holding small flowerpots to be filled with plants or vines.

of old pewter prefer it unpolished, in its natural soft dull tones.

Brass and copper may be cleaned with turpentine or one of several commercial polishes or with a homemade mixture of paste consisting of equal parts vinegar, flour and table salt. Rub the paste on the metal and remove with hot soapy water after it has dried. For badly tarnished pieces apply the paste thickly and leave it on for several hours. Oxalic acid (label it poison) is effective but must be carefully used. Wear gloves and apply it with a dish mop. When it has turned white wash it off with a wet cloth and polish the metal with a dry cloth. To make the gloss last longer after this process squeeze fresh lemon juice over the surface of the metal.

The soft turquoise patina of oxidized bronze is obtained by a chemical process. It should be protected by a thin coat of pure wax, replenished occasionally. If the bowl or vase is to be used for flowers give it a weekly waxing and change the water every twelve hours.

Clean silver accessories according to the directions in Chapter 26 for table silver. The cotton spoken of there, or treated paper which comes in sheets, should be kept conveniently near silver articles and used often. In this way you will avoid frequent thorough polishing.

When metal fixtures or ornaments are too badly worn to be restored by polishing, try covering them with colored Chinese lacquer. Use a primer first which you can get at a silver dealer's. You can salvage any articles which are worth keeping because of good lines and useful qualities.

Care of Pictures: To take care of paintings and frames you must know what not to do. Don't wash or clean the painting itself. If it has been properly varnished all it will need is dusting with a soft cloth. If it is soiled and grimy turn it over to an expert restorer for treatment. Dust gilt frames with lamb's wool duster or a feather duster, using a light touch. Never use water or alcohol on gilt. To brighten a dingy frame apply a light coat of paste wax and polish gently after it has dried for a few minutes. Wooden frames should be cared for just like fine wood furniture or woodwork.

Care of Mirrors: Mirror frames are treated in the same way as picture frames. The glass is cleaned by the same process used for windows. Don't hang a mirror where it will be hit by direct rays of the sun for a long period at a time—it will gradually become cloudy and eventually have to be refinished. If bare spots appear on the back of a mirror try repairing them by covering with tin foil secured to the glass by means of shellac, dark paint or glue. Whatever cleaning method you use be careful about using too much liquid. If the mirror has a frame, the liquid may run down inside and eventually spoil the reflecting finish.

FRESH FLOWERS AND GREENS
MAKE EFFECTIVE
AND CHARMING ACCESSORIES

Arranging cut flowers is a highly personal matter. Below are shown four arrangements for shallow bowls which are interesting and dramatic. Flower stem-supports are essential, and stiffness must be avoided. A movable double tray table like the one at lower left is something every housewife could make use of. It will save many steps and make for pleasanter serving at home meals or parties. Note the low-kept flowers. The three charming flower arrangements above illustrate effective handling of tall flowers in small-mouthed vases. The first essential is to avoid crowding which automatically eliminates grace. Strive for naturalness, considering the way the flower stalks grow on the plant. When you are arranging apple blossoms, dogwood and other flowers with little natural foliage let the beauty of the branches show. Notice the slightly irregular outline which would be made by a line drawn around the outside edge of these groupings. This is the line of grace and naturalness. It usually has a triangular effect, but not with equal sides. In order to keep flowers fresh, clip the stems and change the water daily. See that all leaves below the water are removed because the water is poisoned by decaying vegetable matter. It is easier to arrange flowers in jars or vases with spreading tops especially if they are a full-leaved variety. For economical brightening up of a room try the effect of bowls filled with Mexican huckleberry or laurel leaves. Alone or with a few flowers these long-lasting greens are very effective. In the fall autumn leaves serve the same purpose, alone or as a background for fall flowers which may be changed often.

Perfection in line, detail, and finish makes this furniture a faithful reproduction of that found in many a Federal American home. Notice the English Regency influence in the comfortable chairs around a table in Duncan Phyfe style. The Oriental rug and the crystal chandelier are both in harmony with the period furnishings. An interesting point here is the

successful use of modern background notes in a traditional room. The wallpaper is in broad stripes, above the painted wood dado, and the draperies are modern both in style and fabric. Framing windows at each side of a mirrored sideboard alcove, they are topped by a shaped valance which runs straight across the entire wall, uniting windows and alcove in

316

WITH TRADITIONAL DIGNITY

a very effective picture. The dark valance, picking up the color of the dark figure in the drapery pattern, affords dramatic contrast to the heavy wood cornice finished with light-colored paint to match the dado. The side draping can be released at night to cover the window completely, just as conventional draw-curtains would do.

CHAPTER TWENTY-SIX

Points on Dining Rooms

DINING ROOMS have been highly conventionalized in the past, both as to furniture and its arrangement, but the trend toward freedom of expression in home decoration applies here as well as elsewhere in the house.

DINING ROOM COMFORT

There are certain requirements for comfort and convenience which must be taken care of in any dining room. Table size should be adjustable. Figure that for each additional person you must allow an additional twenty-one inches of table space, and for comfortable serving there must never be less than three feet of space between the table and the wall or any piece of wall furniture. The average table is between twenty-nine and thirty inches high and a comfortable chair to go with it has a seat seventeen to eighteen inches from the floor. If you are improvising or remodeling a dining table from some other piece of furniture remember that these are comfortable heights for dining.

The shape of the table should conform if possible to the proportions of the room. Chairs should not be too large, but large enough for comfort. Two special chairs, possibly upholstered, may be used at the head and foot of the table even if they are somewhat different in style from the side chairs. In a large enough dining room where much entertaining is done a small arm chair for each place at the table is a worthwhile luxury. Traditionally, refectory tables appropriate with Italian, Spanish, or early English styles should be accompanied by low benches for seating, but modern ideas of comfort usually cause a substitution of chairs in harmonizing design. For easy serving a

317

The two dining rooms on this page are very different in theme, style and atmosphere but they both express the interest and charm essential in a dining room. The one at the bottom is a faithful contemporary interpretation of Georgian design in fine reproductions. A Sheraton-design table harmonizes with Chippendale-design ladder-back chairs and other furniture in 18th Century style. A crystal chandelier and other crystal accessories carry out this period feeling. Formal draperies of heavy cotton fabric are in a deep champagne color; chair seats are upholstered in turquoise matelasse. The color scheme is centered in mural paintings on three walls picturing early days in New York from City Hall to Central Park and in a Persian rug with jewel and floral motifs in tones of green, blue, gold and rose on a soft ivory ground. The room is not very large considering the size of furniture used in it, but is given a sense of spaciousness by open vistas of the murals on the walls and by mirror panels covering the fourth wall. Scenic wallpaper or photographic murals can also be used for effective wall panels. The one at the left is Early American with extension refectory table, simple chairs and small corner cupboard all in soft rubbed pine. The same period feeling is carried out by a painted floor and an oval braided cotton rug. Notice that the table is placed near the wall beneath the window out of the center of the room where space is obviously needed for a traffic lane between the hall and other parts of the house.

DINING ROOMS RECALLING DIFFERENT PERIODS IN AMERICAN FURNITURE

Dining rooms, whether traditional or modern, can often be made to render additional service to the household without lessening their usefulness or attractiveness as dining rooms. The photograph at the right illustrates this in a traditional room where one end has been set apart for a tea-and-conversation group in front of a wide center-of-interest window. The small table would serve equally well for breakfast, or a late-evening snack, or as an overflow game table in a house where the living room is sometimes crowded. It could also accommodate an overflow of guests from the regular dining table. The oval Duncan Phyfe-style table, the Chippendale arm chairs, wing chair and small "bachelor's chest"—all are shown to advantage against the 18th Century background of the room. Between the white-painted dado and cornice, the red-cabbage-rose wallpaper, with off-white ground, is very effective. The quilted fabric used for drapery borders and chair seats is designed to match the paper, while the rest of the drapery material and the wing-chair upholstery are in the off-white background color. Plain carpeting keeps the bold figures in the pattern from creating an effect of restlessness. The room below is conservatively modern. The plainness of walls, sectional storage cabinets, draperies, and fluorescent lighting fixture, is pleasantly warmed by the Oriental rugs and the scene framed in the wide window. The table placed at one side rather than in the center allows the room to be used for other purposes than dining, since it leaves space in front of the window for a game table or easy chairs.

SUGGESTIONS FOR SPECIAL COMFORT IN DINING ROOMS

TRADITIONAL THEMES FOR DINING ROOMS

The rooms above are interesting to compare. They have many points of similarity and yet the one at the top creates a feeling of simple homelike charm while the one below it is dignified and formal in addition to being comfortable and beautiful. Since the table, chairs and sideboards are all in fine mahogany and all faithful reproductions of 18th Century pieces, and in both cases the floors are covered with plain carpeting, we must turn to walls, draperies and accessories for explanation of the difference. In the room at the top the walls are paneled simply and painted; draperies are informal ruffled chintz draped back without glass curtains; accessories are confined to a bowl of fruit and candlesticks on the table, three porcelain pieces on the sideboard and a plainly framed picture above it. In the room below walls are covered with handsome scenic paper; draperies are long and formal, made straight to draw across the windows; accessories are period silver pieces such as the tea set on the console at right, the low flower bowl on the dining table and the tall branched candlesticks on the sideboard.

USES FOR EXTRA DINING ROOM SPACE

Dining rooms are doubled in usefulness through an informal breakfast, snack or entertainment bar installed at one end or in an alcove or corner. In the room at the top of the page an interesting arrangement is worked out at the end of a dining room in which simple Colonial feeling is expressed in knotty pine furniture, converted lanterns for chandelier lights, and etched glass hurricane candlesticks on the table. The bar with its rail and slip-covered stools has a French Provincial air with curves edging the shelf above it and painted vines decorating it. Sometimes a built-in unit like this may be all that is needed to give real distinction to an ordinary dining room. In the room below it a commonplace alcove is transformed into an attractive background for a period piece of furniture by a mirror panel and glass shelves. An alcove like this could just as well be turned into a small bar, either through building in equipment or installing one of the many models which can be had in styles to harmonize with any type of furnishings. The mirror panel is attractive and would give a feeling of additional space in a small room.

To prove that charm is not confined to formal furnishings a sideboard is shown above which was reclaimed from the dreary-looking marble-topped bureau beside it. In this case the process was very simple. The top was removed, the mirror taken out and turned lengthwise for hanging over the chest of drawers. The rest was merely a question of refinishing, painting, and decorating the mirror both on the frame and around the edges of the glass. It is shown here with a lacquered kitchen tray for fruit, and home-decorated bottles flanking a bowl of ivy. In a dining room with painted furniture and peasant designs in gay colors this piece would make a charming buffet or console serving chest.

heatproof table near the swinging door to the kitchen is advisable and may be concealed behind a decorative screen, possibly repeating motifs and colors of draperies on the opposite side of the room.

DINING ROOM BACKGROUNDS

Dining room settings should be interesting, cheerful and gay without being busy, restless or disturbing. Table decorations come in the same classification. They should be as charming as you can make them but low enough not to interfere with visibility across the table. Except for some very special function they should not be so dramatic that they interfere with the quiet sociability which makes for pleasant dining.

Don't forget balance of large wall pieces when arranging dining room furniture. Try to place a tall cabinet where it will balance a fireplace, a window, or some other piece of furniture. As for the table, convention places that in the center of the free floor space but you do not have to follow this rule. If there is a lovely view you may want the table in front of a window at an angle which will allow everyone to share the view. Many modern dining rooms have had an end or a corner converted into an informal dinette-bar for regular food "snacks" or for liquid refreshments. Throughout this book you will see suggestions along these lines which you may be able to adapt to your own uses.

DINING EQUIPMENT

Equipment in the way of silver, dishes and linen is so highly personal, so much a matter of individual taste and budgeting that little can be said about it of a general nature. One thing, however, it is well to keep in mind. Contemporary manufacturers have developed highly decorative table settings at comparatively low prices so that it is possible to set a colorful, charming table without a large outlay for dishes and silver. These include china, unbreakable plastic dishes and attractive substitutes for table silver.

Traditional linen is beautiful but expensive. Here again modern design has come to the rescue of the budget by utilizing many peasant styles and color effects in cotton or rayon for gay informal tables, also by substituting various kinds of place mats and runners for the traditional large tablecloth. If you can afford it, fine linen is still the same good investment it was in great-grandmother's day, but while you are accumulating a supply of it your table need not suffer from loss of attractiveness. Study the illustrations for suggestions on setting a lovely table. Selection and use of other dining room accessories follow the same principles outlined for accessories in Chapter 25.

CARE OF DINING ROOM EQUIPMENT

Cleaning Silver: Wash silver in soapy water and always rub it lengthwise in polishing or drying. Keep it away as much as possible from tarnishing agents such as eggs, matches, salt, fruit juice, rubber and gas. Have a roll of paper, or a jar of cotton (both specially treated by impregnation with tarnish remover) handy by the sink to rub over any piece as soon as it has become tarnished. Do not put silver away until you have removed the stain. Use this same treated cotton wadding or paper on silver accessories, candlesticks, any other decorative pieces. It is useful also for emergency jobs on copper, brass, aluminum or pewter.

For general silver cleaning there are the old reliable silver pastes which always turn out beautiful silver. When pieces are deeply carved or ornamented there may be dark areas at the base of the raised designs. If this occurs wash the articles in hot soapsuds containing a few drops of ammonia, then use a soft brush to remove all traces of polish and impart a brilliant luster.

Tarnish Prevention: To prevent tarnish put silver away in a drawer or cabinet with a small open jar of a special preparation containing odorless chemical crystals which absorb tarnishing gases in the air. If the storage space is kept tightly closed one jar will keep silver bright from four to six months without polishing. Another device is to line a drawer or small wooden chest with treated cloth which you can buy by the yard. Use thumb tacks or anti-tarnish glue you get from a jeweler to fasten the cloth. Don't use ordinary glues. They have tarnishing animal fats in their composition. Another don't—never store silver in a cardboard box nor leave such a box in the drawer with it. Unless the cardboard has had special treatment it probably contains sulphur, a tarnishing agent.

Table Linens: Linen table covers are very easy to take care of. If white linens are badly stained soak them before washing a few minutes in a tub of soapy water with a cup of chlorine bleach added. Wash in the same water, rinse three times, and hang on a line with a fold over the line to keep the shape of the piece. Iron while quite damp with a hot iron, on the wrong side first, then the right. Iron thoroughly dry and don't always fold in the same creases. For colored rayons and cottons test for color fastness, then wash as for any similar fabrics—unless you have a label to guide you. Remember that rayon needs a cool iron. If you live in a hard-water area use a water softener in washing napkins and tablecloths, to keep white clear and colors bright. Don't forget that linens take dye beautifully. When a tablecloth has worn thin in spots you can salvage the best parts of it for dressing table skirts, small window draperies, or napkins and table runners by means of the new easy-to-use dyes.

Care of Fine Table Settings: Here are a few don'ts which will help prolong the life of your fine crystal or china:

1. Don't wash several dishes at a time. Put them in and out of the dishpan one by one, and don't use a dishpan without a folded towel in the bottom.

2. Don't hold fragile dishes under running water, and don't let any dishes stand until food particles have dried on them.

3. Don't use strong soaps or any scouring powders.

4. Don't subject glass or china to sudden changes in temperature.

5. Don't stack or hang up fragile cups.

For the rest, dry with a clean lintless towel and stack with paper napkins between plates. Keep them covered and you won't have to wash them just before using. Cellophane, oiled silk or waxed paper are dustproof and inexpensive. For glasses, use a dish mop and handle stemmed goblets with special care. Use a soaped camel's hair brush for getting dirt out of cut crystal glasses or ornaments. A little ammonia for sparkle may be used, but not too often.

VARIETY IN TABLE SETTINGS

Three lovely table settings here combine the charm of candles, silver, crystal and china with the satiny gleam of Irish linen damask. The "flower" centerpiece at upper left, arranged on two levels, is ingeniously devised of fresh vegetables. The lush tropical lilies are really carrots. They are sliced very thin with an ordinary double-blade potato peeler, soaked in cold water until they curl, then speared onto match sticks with pins. A raisin makes the center of each flower and the foliage is dark green spinach leaves mingled with lighter-hued salad chicory. Four candles are effective in the center of the table. In the small picture they are shown accompanied by three bowls of blue grapes sprayed with gold powder to form a handsome autumn table decoration. Notice the attractive sparkle given the table by graceful water, champagne and wine glasses correctly placed for serving. The table setting at the center is dramatized by an unusual centerpiece and white china against a colored linen table-cloth. The simplicity of design in silver, glass and china intensifies the note of drama. At lower left is a unique table arrangement in which a beautiful white Irish linen dam-

ask cloth, richly glazed pottery and interesting silver are set off by a brimming basketful of freshly gathered, perfect, home-grown vegetables used as a centerpiece. The picture at upper right demonstrates how beautiful a table can be with a mat at each place on a polished table top instead of the formal linen cloth. Notice here the distinctive design of pedestaled glasses and unusual handles of the silver. At lower right a small table is set in a dinette for a schoolday breakfast. White dishes are used on a cloth made from four Irish linen dish towels with bright red stripes and checks. The napkins are made of plain white toweling edged with red rickrack braid.

The glass service shown in the above picture has a large shallow matching bowl used for a centerpiece. This is arranged with flowers kept low in order not to interfere with conversation across the table. A "yellow" table below expresses the cheeriness of spring. Organdy place mats are yellow matching daffodils dramatically arranged in a low crystal bowl which harmonizes with the glasses. A graceful flower arrangement like this is accomplished by means of a rack placed in the bowl to hold the stems. Glasses are in an American design with terraced foot and bubble-like bowl.

DRAMA AND BEAUTY IN

White damask cloth, bright-hued plates, pottery serving dishes, star-Christmas tree, gold and silver angel chorus, decorate the buffet table in the center of the group which is set for a Christmas-tree-trimming party. The table (above left) is ready for New Year's Day callers. Notice the balanced harmony between the silver candelabra and the bowl of flowers and fruits in harmonizing tones ranging from pale pink to deep purple. Textured white cloth, muted gleam of Danish silver and soft candle-light make this table a picture to be remembered. When using candles, chill them for several hours in the refrigerator before lighting to keep them from dripping. The Easter table at lower left has a snowy damask cloth, leaf-green plates and a most unusual centerpiece. A bouquet of pink and white tulips with white pear blossoms

The dinner table above, with its fruit centerpiece and formal silver service, illustrates the classic loveliness of satin-smooth damask for table-cloth and napkins. The wedding table below also draws upon the beauty of damask, in this case a plain weave with monogrammed decorations. The shining crystal dishes are specially suitable for wedding refreshments, and the flowers are arranged with unusual grace between glass candelabra fitted with deep cups for protection against dripping candles.

FESTIVE TABLE SETTINGS

is set in a container made from a Savoy cabbage with all its crinkled green outer leaves intact and the heart carved out to hold a bowl of water for the flowers. At the upper right a coffee-and-cake service is shown with lovely Irish linen runners, their lacy cutwork borders dramatized by the dark table showing through. Notice the effective arrangement of flowers in a low silver bowl between tall candlesticks. For a Saturday night studio party after a football game nothing could be more attractive than a hearty beans-and-cider supper served in the warm glow from an open fire. This lengthened-out table with a striking Irish linen table-cloth in bright red and white checks is set with highly glazed pottery plates and cider mugs in a soft green, with a centerpiece of glowing red Indian corn and dark green leaves in a wood salad bowl.

The above room is in the French Provincial manner, with recessed bed and simple graceful curves in furniture. Floral motifs in wallpaper and other decorations are characteristic notes. A special advantage of the recessed-bed arrangement is that it not only provides an attractive setting for the bed group, it also allows additional closets to be built in at each side. Twin *poufs* at the foot of the bed, together with the sculptured carpet and the straight window draperies under

COMFORTABLE BEDROOM

a mirrored cornice, strike a modern note in the traditional harmony. Combined qualities of grace and sturdiness give French Provincial styles a feminine appeal, yet they are not too elaborate to satisfy masculine taste.

CHAPTER TWENTY-SEVEN

Points in Decorating Bedrooms

IN BEDROOMS beauty is important—but comfort is the first word and the last even in the planning of your furniture arrangement.

BEDROOM ARRANGEMENT

There is less leeway in the placing of bedroom furniture than any other kind because of certain fixed requirements in a room with such a definite function to perform. Beds or couches must be placed, if possible, where morning light does not shine in the sleeper's eyes. They must be kept out of draughts. They must not be in the way between the closet and the entrance door or dressing equipment. They must have fairly large wall spaces whether they are placed lengthwise or at right angles to the wall. In most bedrooms these various considerations reduce the number of possible bed locations to one or at most two. Twin beds pose a special problem, often solved by placing two couches in front of a common headboard. If the room is small, look through this book for pictures of other suggested twin bed or couch arrangements.

Placement of the rest of the furniture must be planned with reference to the location of the bed or beds, also according to special considerations of func-

327

tion and convenience. Dressing tables should have adequate lighting both by day and by night. Chests of drawers should be accessible. Never plan a bedroom without convenient small tables, and comfortable chairs which should be included if there is room for them. Adequate artificial lighting is important, especially for those who read in bed.

BEDROOM BACKGROUNDS AND FURNITURE

Bedrooms should not be decorated with colors, patterns or textures which are unrestful. Strongly outlined wallpaper patterns, for example, which carry the eye from one point to the other in constant movement are not conducive to repose. Flat paint is better than light-reflecting gloss enamel. Window arrangement should allow plenty of light for daytime cheer, but should also be planned for light control if the room is used for resting during daylight hours. Make sure that small rugs are placed where they are most needed. (See Chapter 11.)

The style of your bed may be anything you like from a stately draped four-poster in a traditional bedroom to a studio couch in a bed-sitting room. Modern designers have worked out flexible combinations of harmonizing individual pieces which allow free play for personal needs and tastes. All you have to do is make sure that the various pieces are related in feeling, design, color and finishes.

Contemporary ideas of convenience have resulted in fundamental changes in interior arrangements of bedroom chests of drawers and storage cabinets even when the exterior is traditional in style. Chests of drawers designed for masculine use are made with several of the deep drawers a man likes for stacking his shirts and underclothes in uniform piles. Those intended for feminine use are equipped with one or two fairly deep drawers with the rest of the space given over either to shallow drawers or still shallower sliding trays concealed behind cabinet doors to avoid the broken-up surface effect of so many drawers.

Provision for many things formerly kept in bureau drawers is made by fitting up closets to make the best use of the storage space there. (See Chapter 36.) Many a modern bedroom dispenses entirely with bureaus and dressers. Instead one whole wall, or a large part of a wall, is given over to built-in drawers, shallow cupboards and closets, and cabinet doors concealing many sliding shelves of various depths.

DRESSING ROOMS, CLOSETS AND MIRRORS

Adequate full-length mirror provision is a bedroom must, even if it is only a narrow door panel.

In contemporary rooms this need is often taken care of by converting a closet into a small mirror-paneled dressing room, or building in such a unit within the room. If the bedroom has its own bathroom this may be converted into a combination bath and dressing room, leaving space in the bedroom for such additional features as a desk, bookcases, etc. Proper storage space is an absolute essential for bedrooms. It is not expensive to build in additional closets provided the room is large enough. (You will find suggestions for closets and storage units in Chapter 36.) Don't overlook the possibilities of corners. Built-in corner cupboards, with decorative wood doors, may take care of shoes, hats and many other awkward articles of apparel. Dressing tables may be improvised anywhere in space otherwise unused—in corners, in front of windows, over radiators, etc.

COMFORT IN THE GUEST ROOM

Don't use a guest room as an overflow spot for furniture not needed in the rest of the house. If you must do that, recondition it and redecorate it so that it will look as though it all belongs together and with the room it is in. This can usually be done easily by means of paint and slip covers plus a little home carpentry.

Have closet space free from family clothing. Be sure to make some arrangement for a guest who wants to write letters home, even if it is only a tiny table with a drawer and a supply of writing materials and postage. A small easy chair—a chaise longue, if possible—with a reading light and a book shelf would appeal to the guest who likes an occasional moment of privacy. A thermos bottle or pitcher, a drinking glass and a flashlight are thoughtful notes, also a small ironing board built-in or parked in the closet. If possible add to this a small iron, also a radio near the bed.

Other comfort notes include an extra blanket on the shelf, a chest of drawers with additional towels and soap, and a folding rack for luggage. Equipped with canvas strips these racks cost very little and may be easily fitted up for extra service. Cover the top with a bright-colored piece of canvas or striped bed ticking or heavy cretonne and run a border of matching upholstery braid around the edges. It may be used this way for an extra seat or placed beside the bed with a tray on top to double for a bedside table.

If the room is very small, study the chapter on closets and install all the storage devices you can in the guest room closet to save space in the room. Even if the bedroom is not crowded it is a nice idea to make the closet into a miniature dressing room.

EARLY AMERICAN
AND FRENCH
PROVINCIAL THEMES
IN TWO
CONTEMPORARY
BEDROOMS

The bedroom shown in two views on this page is an outstanding example of what color and pattern can do toward creating distinction in an average-size room with no outstanding architectural features. A sense of spaciousness is achieved by a neutral background of off-white in paper and ceiling and plain carpeting in soft receding moss green. Additional height is given a low ceiling by satin stripes in the paper and straight floor-length hangings under ceiling-high valances. Quaint old beds are painted white to match woodwork, spreads and many of the accent accessories. The striking pattern of the chintz is dramatic against the shadow-striped walls and plain floor, its pattern accentuated by the plain overspreads on the twin beds. Pennsylvania Dutch bureaus in black with gold and flower decorations are dramatically effective against the white walls, and the black finish is repeated on Victorian tufted sofa and footstools. The color scheme is an unusually effective version of the complementary rose and green. The rose-and-foliage pattern of the print is on a white ground, the sofa is upholstered in chartreuse, and the still life pictures over the beds pick up the deep green of the carpet. The room is given a modern touch of drama by combining period accessories with the very modern framing and style of the two pictures. Notice also the door with its bolection molding trim and modern flat panel treatment. The bed tables are interesting because the use of chintz as slip covers makes it possible to utilize irreclaimable tables or even boxes for this purpose. The room shown in the photograph at right is a contemporary interpretation of Louis XV themes. Three walls are papered in a floral pattern of morning glories in green and deep fuchsia on a white background which matches white paint on woodwork and the fourth wall at the head of the beds. Rough-textured green satin is draped over the windows and over the entire remainder of the wall to make a frame behind each of the beds, or a solid background of drapery when the tie-backs are released. The stretched valance from wall to wall is of the same fabric and the long straight glass curtains beneath are very full and sheer. Headboards of the

twin beds, tufted stool and easy chair are upholstered in white and fuchsia flowered rayon satin harmonizing with fuchsia satin bedcovers. The Louis XV beds and other furniture pieces are painted old cream white with touches of gilt. Small fluffy white rugs are used at strategic points on a bare wood floor. A room like this could be developed quite inexpensively by using chintz and modern textured cotton fabrics for draperies and covers, and refinishing old furniture.

329

GUEST ROOM PROBLEMS

Double Service from Guest Rooms: Few of today's homes can spare a whole room set aside exclusively for an occasional short-time or week-end guest, but if you have an extra room you can put it to very good use and take care of your guests too. The plan is simple. Furnish it as a bed-sitting room with a studio couch and concealed dressing arrangements, then add whatever is needed to make it serve other purposes between guests. Decide what that purpose shall be and equip it accordingly. If you make it into a study or a den for some man in the family, see that masculine comfort is provided for. If you need it most for your own private sitting-room it will require little more than the guest equipment already there.

In many families a guest room has been successfully combined with a sewing room by addition of a few special built-in double-duty features which completely concealed all traces of sewing activities. A very successful guest-sewing room can be worked out in any fairly large room, specially in a converted attic where plenty of storage space can be built in under the sloping roof. In any case, build in shallow drawers and cupboards along one wall for all sorts of materials and sewing gadgets. Install a well-lighted full-length mirror, and make a glass-topped skirted table to set over the sewing machine and turn it into a dressing table. If you have a portable machine, use a section of your built-in wall for a drop-leaf shelf which makes a cabinet for the machine when closed and a working table when open. While your guest occupies the room put the machine away and use the arrangement for a writing or typewriter-desk.

On another wall install a large decorated panel of light but strong plywood or wallboard, folded up against the wall. This should have legs at the upper corners which look like part of the design but drop down to support a cutting and work table. If this panel is lengthwise of the wall it will take up less space in the room. If desired you can have useful built-in shelves in the wall behind it. If there seems to be no wall space for this table, place it behind a studio couch and make it large enough to cover the couch when it is down in working position. The working side should be faced with cork or other similar composition material into which pins and thumb tacks may be stuck. Have a measuring strip painted along the entire outer edge with inches, half inches and quarters marked.

If you have a dressmaker's dummy and no room in the closet for it, build in a corner cupboard with a decorated wood door, a built-in ironing board, and an extra shelf or two above the figure.

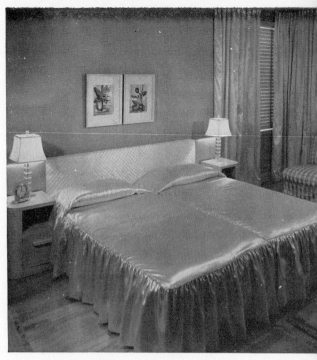

MODERN SIMPLICITY IS THE
KEYNOTE ABOVE,
COLONIAL CHARM BELOW

FOUR VERSIONS OF BEDROOM COMFORT AND CONVENIENCE

The rooms in this group are charming expressions of the new and the old in bedrooms. The room at left has a modern space-saving arrangement which allows the comfort of twin beds without sacrificing much more floor area than one double bed would require. In this case a headboard is arranged with table-chest units to look as if they were all one piece. This same arrangement could be carried out in a home workshop by slip-covering a headboard extending beyond the beds and placing twin tables or chests in front of it. The beds could be twin studio couches made from box springs mounted on short legs. Simplicity of modern decoration is given richness and beauty here by bed spreads and draperies of lustrous rayon satin. Fringed cotton rugs on a wood floor, slip-covered chair and small plastic smoking table are all attractive features of contemporary room design keyed to comfort and easy care. The Colonial room below is equally expressive of Early American comfort with its canopied four-post bed, spatter-dash floor, its cheerful wood-burning fireplace, slip-covered wing chair and convenient secretary-bookcases. Pale green wallpaper is combined with white painted woodwork in dado, mantel and cornice. Notice that the large flowered chintz in pink and green used for chaise longue, bed and draperies is combined with plain painted surfaces plus geometrical design in small diagonal lines of the wallpaper and checks on the red chintz of the wing chair. All accessories, from clock to fireplace fittings, harmonize with the period character of the room.

The simple homelike little bedroom above, Colonial in feeling with plaid wallpaper, candlewick spread and wing chair, would make a comfortable room for a maid, a guest, or a younger member of the family. Below is shown an interesting use for a small space which is little more than a passageway between other rooms. It is converted into a bedroom for family or emergency use by installing small twin beds which may be used side by side or one above the other as shown here. Addition of a small-scale arm chair and a combination drawer-and-shelf furniture unit, with extra reading lamp serving both bed and chair, makes the tiny space a self-contained bedroom. An oval braided cotton rug matching the one in the living room-dining room beyond harmonizes with rubbed wood furniture and simple Colonial design.

The two dressing tables shown below are modern in design but combined with accessories in traditional feeling. They both employ a slightly incurving line at the front for greater convenience. The one at the left is in lacquer with plastic legs and supports harmonizing with the plastic legs of the tufted stool. The table at the right in traditional wood is used with mirror and leather-upholstered seat both late 18th Century in design. The modern note here is the glass top with an open shelf below for cosmetics. Notice in both cases the use of small cotton rugs to protect the carpets on the floors. The dressing room above is for a lady who likes efficiency as well as charm in the business of dressing.

Designed like streamlined kitchen cabinets, against a background of mirror with glass shelves at each side for perfumes and ornaments, everything needed is instantly accessible. A small closet on each side was built in to make this alcove effect with mirrored walls. The dressing-table stool harmonizes with the Regency draperies reflected in the mirror and the period love seat below them. Crystal wall sconces add another note to this union of modern and traditional features. A dressing table unit along these lines could be assembled inexpensively or built in across the end of any ordinary bedroom. (For draped dressing tables see Chapter 21.)

The problem of a special room which might double as a living room for a guest and provide additional living space for the family when not needed for this purpose is cleverly solved in the room below. The chief feature of this room is a traditional breakfront cabinet with plenty of storage space and a desk front which can also be used as a dressing table because a lighted mirror has been placed in the middle section usually reserved for books. Glass curtains hide cosmetics and dressing equipment when the doors are closed. The rug is an interesting innovation—woven from long-wearing viscose fibers very attractive in texture and colorings. In the room above, the corner arrangement of twin couches is varied by an interesting feature which provides headboards, table, concealed light, and a panel for the clock. The coffee table is large enough so that it can also serve as breakfast tray.

HOW TO CONVERT ONE ROOM INTO A

The complete one-room home pictured above (two views) demonstrates that it is not necessary to sacrifice either comfort or charm because space is limited. Attractive modern folding partitions shut off sleeping and cooking alcoves when they are not in use. Built-in shelves for books and dishes (with storage beneath) provide a shallow window alcove for the table. A waxed linoleum floor, with two shaggy rugs, makes a smart, easy-to-care-for floor. The soft, restful, antique green used for background walls and ceiling creates a

CHAPTER TWENTY-EIGHT

Points on Double=Duty Rooms

MODERN DECORATION is more or less responsible for the contemporary popularity of double-purpose rooms—sometimes triple-purpose or more. In the types of rooms illustrated in this chapter charm and convenience are made possible by clever planning and ingenuity in creation of double-duty or built-in features. Most of these could be duplicated in your own home.

TYPES OF DOUBLE-DUTY ROOMS

Rooms used for several distinct purposes come under two general headings. There are double-duty rooms which are intended primarily for one purpose and have additional functions added; there are those planned as one-room apartment homes in which living, sleeping, cooking and eating are all equally important. With both types devices such as built-in furniture and sectional, flexible units are valuable to help solve problems of accommodating varied activities in small space.

Whichever type your room is you will probably need to make it seem as spacious as possible, and you can use to good advantage all the suggestions made in various chapters for increasing the apparent size of a room. You will need plenty of storage space for concealing equipment when it is not in use. Keep decorations and furniture simple in order not to give any impression of crowding.

Two-Purpose Rooms: In the case of living rooms which give up space for dining nooks or turn sofas into overnight guest beds, special furniture and equipment may not be essential but are almost always helpful. Bedrooms can be converted easily to double for studies, dens or workrooms. Dining rooms

COMPLETE AND ATTRACTIVE HOME

feeling of space in the room. It harmonizes with soft yellow upholstery on the side chairs, and off-white used for the wing chair, bedcovers, folding partitions and rugs. The floor is in a deep gold tone, the chaise longue in a deeper green than the walls, the draperies are green and white. With red touches for accent, the whole effect is colorful and gay, yet at the same time cool and restful. Notice the deep storage drawer built in beneath the lower bunk bed, and the deep wood cornice carved across both window and shelves.

MAKING USE OF AN ALCOVE FOR A GUEST ROOM
WITH FOLDING DOORS FOR PRIVACY

Double-duty rooms—which may do triple duty or even more—are often modern in design rather than traditional because the modern school has put special emphasis upon this phase of decorating. However, many successful rooms have been worked out by applying the same kind of engineering to traditional furniture and arrangement. It is often possible to revamp the interior of an "antique" to make it serve many new purposes without changing its appearance at all. Also, if you can find twin pieces, you can often combine them in a manner which is modern. Designers of the room shown on this page (three views) have cleverly mingled modern styles with traditional touches which accent the room and give it a richer flavor. In the photograph at right we see the fireplace corner with an overhanging cupboard effect and decorative panels instead of a mantel. The sectional couch, or love seat installed in an alcove made by a built-in closet at the left, comprises two pieces with bolster-roll pillows movable in either direction to the length of the cords. Notice the back rest and the recessed shelf with a reading light set in above it. The coffee table has leaves which extend almost to the length of six feet and convenient drawers for storage of small articles used in serving. The long drawer at the bottom is specially made to accommodate trays and slides in both directions. Sand color walls harmonize with draperies in natural color cotton casement cloth trimmed with rows of moss upholstery fringe in deep tobacco brown—which is also the color of the cotton string rug. Couch and arm chairs are upholstered in heavy textured plaid combining tones of beige, brown and dark blue with threads of lighter blue. Henna and light blue accent colors are used in the panel decorations and in accessories. In the view above, the guest-room end of the living room is shown with a glimpse of the dining section at the left. Privacy is made possible when desired by deep doors which at other times fold back flat against the wall taking up almost no space at all. Behind the doors at the right we get a glimpse of a closet which fills up the rest of the wall space and is completely equipped to provide everything a guest might need. There is even a small desk for writing behind the doors. Day bed-alcove walls are finished in terra cotta paint matching the leather used for furniture tops and various other decorations in the room. The day bed is covered with the same casement cloth used for draperies, the inset pieces dyed terra cotta. A row of small drawers between shelves over the couch is a novel and useful device. Inset panel lights above the shelves make other lighting unnecessary at this end of the alcove. Textured light blue fabric is used for webbing on contour chairs in natural light wood. Here another dark brown string rug is on the floor. The table at the right is particularly interesting. Designed after an old-fashioned "Lazy Susan" it can be used at this low level for a library or reading table, and screwed up exactly like a piano stool to the correct height for games or dining. It is finished like the other specially designed pieces in a soft beige color with tiny spatter-dashes in various tones of tan, cream, brown and henna. The window at the left is fitted as a serving counter from outside the room. At upper right is a view of the semi-partition which breaks the room in the center by jutting out from one wall only to provide extra wall space on the living-room side and cupboard space on this side. The central section of the cupboard lets down as shown here to provide an informal breakfast or refreshment serving table. Part of the cupboard equipment is a television set.

There are many features of special interest in the room on this page with its alcove-end providing additional sleeping space as well as dining facilities. The living part of the room, with traditional furniture and wallpaper in a traditional design, is modern in its utilization of space. By covering both couches with the same slip-cover material—narrow green and white stripe made up on the bias, and mitered to give a diagonal effect—a unified grouping is made between a large sofa at the left and the studio couch at the right. The book shelf used as a table in the corner between them is accessible from the front. The most striking feature of this room is the use of the wallpaper as a floor finish. In a rich deep green with motifs in gold and white this paper is laid over several thicknesses of heavy paper, each one held in place with varnish. A special varnish is applied over the wallpaper to prevent wear and make it quite feasible as a floor covering. Notice the lamp

shades made of the upholstery fabric and the nice grouping of accessories. In the lower picture we see the stepped-up dining alcove with a semi-partition topped by growing plants. An old center table refinished is used as a small dining or refreshment table. A built-in couch or day bed beneath the windows has cupboards below it and large storage cupboards at each end which make supports for the bolster rolls and act as lamp tables. The fluffy light-colored string rug on the floor matches the smaller one at the other end of the room. The short windows are curtained with semi-transparent gold over-draperies in casement cloth and very open net glass curtains. The day-bed cover below is of the gold cotton fabric. The upholstery on the French Provincial chairs is the same green and white stripe as that used on the sofas, the arm chair at the left is in gold. A room like this furnishes sleeping accommodations for three people if necessary.

A MODERN CABINET MAKES ONE-ROOM
HOUSEKEEPING EASY

Sometimes a room may be used for several purposes merely by virtue of one piece of furniture which combines the uses of several. The four-purpose cabinet shown on this page is one of these. Closed, as it is in the picture above, no one would suspect that the dining table at the left is stowed away when not in use behind the two doors on the lower section of the cabinet. Bookcase units flank these doors, two small drawers above them are used for silver storage, and the long drawer pulls out to become a desk as shown in the picture below. This picture also reveals the dish cupboard space and the desk fittings behind the upper doors. The third picture illustrates use of one half the table, left conveniently close to its base. A unit like this could be equally useful for home workshop purposes instead of dining. The table would provide plenty of working space for papers and typewriter.

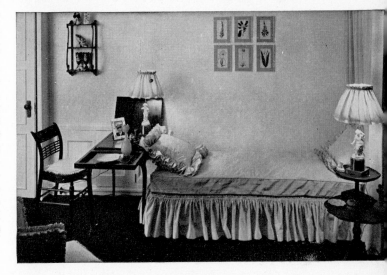

MAKING THREE ROOMS OUT OF ONE

An awkwardly long room is usually both unattractive and inconvenient. In the group of pictures shown here such a room is divided into three activity areas which may be thrown together as one room or separated into three private zones by drawing curtains across the ceiling. This particular arrangement planned for two young girls gives them an entertainment unit, as shown at upper right which can be used for dining. Built-in book shelves, fern-filled grate, modern sofa and slip-covered chair turn the small area into a charming living room. Walls throughout are soft pale pink with black rugs and bowknot chintz in pink and black against a white ground. The sofa is covered in a textured fabric a little darker tint than the walls. The next unit provides sleeping quarters for one roommate, as illustrated in two views (top left and center right). The one above provides a view through into the living room and shows the chest of drawers which turns a sleeping cot into a studio couch by making a corner into which it fits—as you will see at the right. The draperies between this unit and the living section are repeated to partition off the third area, which is the second girl's bedroom illustrated at lower right. Here a new note is introduced by plain fabric used for bed covering and for drapery which conceals the back of a mirror panel making a headboard for the bed and facing toward the rest of the apartment. There is a mirror covered by the bowknot drapery on the other side when it is drawn back from the opening. The two front sections are designed to be thrown together for mutual entertaining, but if one wishes to entertain alone—or the roommate who occupies the "front bedroom" wishes to retire—the double draperies pulled across the opening insure privacy. The most interesting point in this plan is that it is all achieved by means of furniture arrangement and draperies without the expense of building in any partitions.

can usually be turned into double-purpose rooms with great advantage to the entire family, since this room is otherwise used only for short periods of time each day. It is quite possible to continue using your dining room for eating purposes and still make it a full-time partner with other rooms as a center of home activities. The possibilities of such a room are described below.

Converting Old-Style Dining Space into a Busy, Useful Room: A conventional average-size square dining room in a household where space is at a premium and time-saving means much can be transformed so that most of the working activities of the family-at-home are focused there. A large opening on the living-room side of a dining room can be partially closed in and the space filled in with three storage units. The one at the left, with open shelves above and closed cupboard below, can be painted like the rest of the woodwork, perhaps in a soft green with the inside of the open-shelf section painted a dark rich green against which dishes can be effectively displayed. The lower cupboard space can be used for dining room storage, while the section at the right would do for books on open shelves painted like the others and with storage space below. The central section can be treated as a cupboard with double doors over the upper part opening above an oblong extension table placed at right angles to the storage units. This table would serve for dining and also as an evening game table, the games being stored in the cupboard above it. Extended, it would provide a cutting table for sewing.

On the opposite wall low book shelves, cupboards, blackboards and two built-in desks around one corner would take care of the children's evening homework. The other corner could be fitted with corresponding book shelves, radio, a desk at right angles to the wall for use of the grown-ups in the family. The built-in units in the two corners should be connected by a linoleum-covered counter running the entire length of the wall under the window, providing typewriter and sewing machine storage space beneath it as well as plenty of shelf room for papers, sewing materials and other equipment. With smart streamlined blond wood furniture, one or two comfortable easy chairs and windows enlarged to picture-window size, a room like this might well become the most treasured room in the whole house—as well as a really delightful dining room.

One-Room Apartments: In working out a successful one-room apartment real double-duty, space-saving devices are almost necessary. They may be built-in, bought and installed, or improvised at home. The pictures in this chapter will illustrate many of the most up-to-the-minute ideas in this field.

SWISS PEASANT DECORATING THEME

As masculine in atmosphere as the preceding room was feminine the combination living and dining room on this page—with sleeping quarters for two—could be worked out in very small space. Against a background of ship-shape trimness and gay peasant colorings, Swiss chairs and table are appropriately grouped with the winter sports equipment displayed against the wall. The color scheme is masculine in

BOOK SHELVES SERVE AS A SEMI-PARTITION

The double-duty room on this page has a semi-partition made by book-and-ornament shelves extending halfway from the wall at the left in the picture above. The other side of this partition is used for a small electric kitchenette cooking unit. In both sections of the room modern lines and background are pleasantly mingled with authentic antiques and reproductions. The picture above has a bell motif, carried out through a collection of bells of all sizes and types arranged on part of the shelves at the left. The bell theme is applied to the draperies by means of rows of fringe made up of tiny red and brown wooden bells applied in rows around the front and bottom edges of gold-colored casement-cloth draperies. Walls are deep beige. Floors are dark gray with a spatter-dash design in bright colors and string scatter rugs in yellow. The modern desk especially designed with a sloping top is painted henna, a color which is picked up in the chintz used for upholstery and repeated in the interior finish of the book shelves. A modern sofa is upholstered in heavy brown textured fabric. The coffee table is an authentic old cobbler's bench and the knitting box at the left was once a blacksmith's nail box. Notice the modern indirect lighting panels above the book shelves—and the quaint old student's lamp on the desk. A final touch of traditionalism is in the painting over the sofa, modernized by being hung without a frame. In the section of the room shown below only the cooking unit is modern. The Dutch door with Colonial iron hinges, the Lazy Susan table, the corner cupboard and the candle-chandelier all belong to the early days of America.

IN A COMPACT HOME FOR TWO

its use of cigar browns with autumn yellows on walls and in couch-bench upholstery. Bright chintz curtains are in browns, rusts and yellows. The gay little rugs are brown and yellow on a dark brown floor. The drapery chintz is used like paper on one wall at the dining-nook end of the room. The little dish cupboard has a door which lets down to form a table.

This attractive sunroom is connected with the living room only by curtained French doors at each side. This makes it possible to indulge in bright colors without fear of clashing with the more conservative living-room color scheme. Several cardinal principles of sunroom furnishing and decorating are very well illustrated in this picture. White bamboo chairs with red cushions are as comfortable as those in any living room. Lamps—smart black and white with patent leather shades—are well placed for reading. The built-in table between the French doors adds to convenience by recesses for radio and books. Sunrooms are always made doubly attractive by growing plants, provided they are kept healthy

and fresh looking. In this room the green of the ivy and other plants, all in red containers, provides the color note for a striking complementary color scheme of red and green combined with neutral black and white. Note the moldings applied like latticework behind the ivy pots; also the wood cornice which runs completely around the room and provides cover for the tops of window shades and draperies. This gives unity to the room and window picture. Split wood rolled shades like these are particularly suitable for the wide window spaces of sunrooms. Off-white side draperies here are developed in plain material, also the upholstery—which is correct where much design is supplied by plant leaves or

CHAPTER TWENTY-NINE

Sunrooms, Porches and Terraces

FRESH AIR LIVING is so pleasant as well as healthful that it needs no recommendation to most of us. What we do need is to learn how to keep the places designed for that kind of living from looking like just another living room—or an annex to the junk yard. Most ordinary furniture which is not too elaborate or formal can be adapted by proper decorating or camouflage to sunparlor or terrace use, but the color scheme and general decorating plan should be just as carefully worked out as for any room in the house. For successful sunroom or terrace furnishing you must always keep their special functions in mind. A sunroom should be airy and gay in warm weather, cozy when it is cold; always comfortable, informal and easy to care for. A porch or terrace must always harmonize with the exterior of the house in type and color.

Sunroom Windows: With a large expanse of windows some kind of light control is needed even if you have outside awnings. This may be provided by Venetian blinds or draw-curtains, but for variety's sake you may prefer to use something specially appropriate rather than just to repeat window treatments used in other parts of the house. For this reason split bamboo shades and other split wood shades, rolled down from the top or up from the bottom, are sunroom and terrace favorites. If draperies are used where there are few flowers they may be gaily patterned, but if many flowers or plants are in the room these will be more effective in combination with plain or striped fabrics. A cornice or valance over the whole window space, with drapery only at corners or outside edges, is preferable to having the space cut up by a narrow patch of drapery at each window division.

SUMMER LIVING

flowers. Geometrical designs may also be used with plant decorations. Red and white awnings carry out the inside color scheme, as awnings should when they seem almost a part of the room. Some kind of wheeled table is indispensable for hospitality when a sunroom is far removed from the kitchen. The table shown here is complete for service, even to a drawer at the end for storage of linen and silver. The floor of this room demonstrates the dramatic possibilities of waxed linoleum, shown in a checkerboard-type design of large black and white rectangles. A floor like this is easiest to keep in condition in a sunroom, at the same time offering an endless variety of striking and appropriate patterns.

Cretonnes, printed linens, sailcloth, twills, duck, all informal cottons may be used for curtains and draperies. Long-wearing dirt and weatherproof novelty fabrics are specially appropriate both for draperies and upholstery in sunrooms or open-air living rooms. If glass curtains are used with over-draperies be sure they are substantial enough to stand up under constant exposure to sun and dampness; avoid delicate silks and rayons. Long-wearing sheer spun glass, nylon, and other synthetic fibers are perfect for situations like this, while light filtering through their soft luster adds great beauty to the room.

Floors: Floors in sunrooms should be easy to keep clean. Waxed linoleum and composition floor coverings in distinctive patterns, or softly waxed tiles, are most suitable. Rugs should be cotton, Kashmir, hooked straw, fiber, or some combination of these. They should be gaily colored and small enough for easy cleaning. Porch floors are often of wood and should be painted to match house shutters if these are blue or green. If the shutters are yellow or white you will find that light gray or black is effective on the porch floor. Do not use ordinary floor paint for porches. For wood choose a special porch or deck paint, and for cement use one of the new long-wearing cement paints. Rugs in waterproof fibers may be used even on open porches but they should be taken inside when the weather is too bad. Waterproof canvas paint can be used to restore color or protect fibers.

Furniture: In period furniture only those styles which are primitive or regional in feeling are suitable for sunroom use without drastic alteration. For example: A Windsor chair in natural pine finish might fit in nicely, but if you have a Victorian piece you want to use you should cut off the furbelows and paint the wood, or hide the whole piece under a slip cover. The most popular special furniture for sunrooms, terraces, and all open-air living, is made of reed, rattan, wicker, bentwood, plastic, spun aluminum, painted wrought iron, bamboo, and certain special woods. In general, next to metal, fibers which grow in marshy places stand up best under exposure to weather.

California redwood and cypress are satisfactory woods when used for modern types of outdoor furniture. They are both durable if they have been properly prepared and if you give them correct care. Redwood, which comes in its own natural color, must have an oil finish to keep it from cracking under exposure to weather. Cypress, generally in a soft silvery gray tone, is practical only when it has been kiln-dried. Before buying either of these woods find out whether they have been given these treatments.

WINDOW WALLS GIVE YEAR-ROUND COMFORT

The two photographs above illustrate different uses for modern wide built-in windows in sunrooms. These large windows are heralds of the construction innovation often called the "solar house" in which sunlight is utilized to furnish auxiliary heat as well as light. To make large windows practical, all sizes are obtainable in stock models with double panes of glass which provide insulation equal to an 8-inch brick wall. These panes are permanently sealed together. Many large windows are equipped with devices which make it possible to lift them entirely out of their frames in the summertime, or slide them back against the walls of the house, turning any room into a temporary open-air living room. One advantage of the flood of light afforded by transparent walls is the relief of eye strain. What we call glare is attributed not to too much light but to the sharp contrast between areas of light and shade caused by small bright window spaces. In the room above extensive use is made of bamboo. It frames the window and makes trellises at each side. It is also used to panel the dark chocolate brown wall which frames enlarged vacation photographs, books, and a center-of-interest furniture group. The other three walls are cream. The bamboo furniture is simple but comfortable, with upholstery in tan and brown. Growing plants are grouped (as they should be in sunrooms), not scattered spottily around the room. Split bamboo which makes the rolled shade is particularly good with the bamboo decorations in the room, but would make an attractive shade for any informal sunroom. The waxed linoleum on the floor carries out the analogous color scheme in tones of orange, brown and tan to which the green of the plants adds a contrasting note for accent. Note the interesting round bamboo table with brown linoleum top and plants grouped around a cylindrical fish bowl. The room in facing upper corner has sliding glass doors which turn the screened porch into an extension of the living room. Straight, full draperies can be drawn across at night for warmth and coziness.

BAMBOO, METAL, GLASS, IN A SUNROOM

The sunroom above demonstrates how effectively bamboo may be combined with wrought iron in sunroom or terrace furnishings. Windows here are dressed with glass curtains and over-draperies, both on traverse rods so that they can be drawn across the windows. Bamboo-trimmed cornices and dado are especially effective with split bamboo rolled shades, bamboo flower boxes and hanging vine supports. Wrought-iron tables with glass tops are charming and labor saving for sunroom use. These small iron glass-topped tables may be purchased in nests and are very useful—no tops marred by cigarette burns or wet glasses. All-over carpeting is not appropriate for sunrooms but a large rug like this one of cotton and fiber is both suitable and decorative. Small rugs may also be used in sturdy weaves over a background floor of painted or waxed wood, tile or composition flooring.

SUNSHINE FOR CHEERFUL BREAKFASTING

A very popular use for sun porches is shown in this picture where the breakfast table is set to take advantage of early morning brightness. Window boxes with green plants and vines filter and cool the light. Draw-curtains in soft green with a matching stiffened valance are a little deeper in tone than the cool soft green used for walls. Split-wood shades are off-white, like the woodwork, while the linoleum rug in bright coral, gray and white, provides warmth in a complementary color scheme. The coral is repeated in slip covers not shown in this picture.

345

Hardy hickory is an old-time favorite which is even more attractive in modern adaptations.

Don't be afraid to combine painted wood furniture with pieces in hickory, rattan, reed, bamboo or metal. The new light weatherproof metals and plastics will amply repay investments made in them as they seem destined to last practically forever. Combined with the new synthetic fabrics which are literally unaffected by sun, weather, soil, or mildew, this new furniture is worth whatever it may cost. It mixes well with traditional outdoor or sunroom pieces which means you can acquire a chair or a table at a time to replace other furnishings as they reach the point where they are no longer worth repairing or renovating. Remember one thing when you are buying or making over furniture for a sunroom or porch. Don't buy it, and don't spend time or money on it, unless it is going to turn out really comfortable and durable.

Care of Outdoor Furniture: Do not neglect proper care of your outdoor furniture. A little care taken to bring cushions and small pieces inside at night or in wet weather and to condition all furniture before storing for the winter will greatly prolong life and attractive appearance. Painted wood must be kept painted and protected with spar varnish. Natural wood finishes must be kept oiled to shed water and prevent moisture soaking into the pores. If your furniture and cushions have been exposed to rain dry them off afterward with a soft cloth. Watch your wrought iron for flaking off of paint, or rust spots at joints. If you encounter rust do not wait for it to spread. Use sandpaper on the spots to smooth the surface, then rub with a solution half water and half kerosene to eliminate any remaining rust. After drying with a clean cloth, paint over the spots with red lead and let that stand forty-eight hours to dry thoroughly. Now you can touch up the spots with enamel which matches your finish. For finishing and painting wrought iron see page 349.

Many types of summer furniture are moved into game rooms for the winter, but if they are to be stored see that they get proper care before they are put away. Dust, then wash rattan and wood with clear water, let dry, apply a thin coat of spar varnish. When this is quite dry wrap each piece in paper before it is stored. If paint is cracked or peeled use sandpaper, then touch up the spot, or remove paint entirely and refinish.

Canvas cushions, awnings, or any parts of furniture made from canvas or similar heavy fabrics can be given new life as well as beauty by being painted with a special canvas paint which is not expensive and is very easy to use. It makes the surface actually water-repellent, and also discourages moths and mildew, without making the fabric stiff or subject to cracking. This paint comes in a dozen attractive colors including black and white and a soft silvery gray called "aluminum." It may be used for painting stripes or designs over a solid color or to cover up bold stripes and designs with a solid color. Applied to brand new canvas it is an excellent conservation measure as even new canvas exposed to sun and rain needs protection to prevent deterioration of fibers. If cushions or canvas on summer furniture are dull, soiled or faded, give them a coat of this paint before putting them away.

Comfort: Plenty of waterproof cushions, pads and ottomans for extra seating are useful on terrace or lawn. They are easily made at home, and you can keep them in a box converted into a window seat by the use of padding and slip cover, or a shallow storage closet built in against the house wall to take care of games, cushions, and all odds and ends which would clutter up the porch or terrace. Several beach rolls should be included in equipment for sunning, relaxing, or exercising. You can easily make these yourself of waterproof canvas and cotton padding. One or two gay beach umbrellas, with tables and chairs, will turn any spot on lawn or terrace into a pleasant hot weather entertainment center. Don't forget the comfortable folding arm chairs with canvas seats and backs which can be stored away in small space. They are useful even for emergency seats in living room and dining room. Small folding tray-tables are a great convenience and can be made by painting ordinary camp stools to use as bases for gaily decorated lunch trays of papier-maché, wood, fiber or tin.

CHOOSE OUTDOOR FURNITURE FOR BEAUTY AS WELL AS WEATHERPROOF SERVICE

For real outdoor use painted wrought-iron furniture stands up under bad weather with less care than any other type of traditional outdoor furniture. In modern light-weight designs it is airy looking and attractive for hot weather. There is just one precaution—it is not always comfortable so be sure your furniture can pass that test. In the lower left picture of this group the table and chairs set out for dining in a corner of the garden are light and graceful in design but sturdily constructed. Red and white waterproof chair cushions, the red beach-roll on the grass, and the modern wooden porch chair with seat and back of red interwoven tape are so gay that a festive spirit is assured. The glass-topped table makes linen or place mats unnecessary. Furniture like this can be salvaged from discarded wrought-iron restaurant or garden furniture by adding upholstered seats and refinishing the frames. In the top picture are shown the solid comfort and attractive design typical of modern styles in sturdy pickled pine furniture. These chairs, upholstered with a gay waterproof fabric, have been placed with the matching table in a shady setting on a flagstone terrace in front of a small studio summer house. Furniture like this may be used in any outdoor living room—or game room—and would fit into many sunrooms. The third picture in the group introduces modern design in traditional long-lasting hickory, with woven cane and weatherproof upholstery. The flower stand and vine trellis, also of hickory, would provide an attractive screen at the end of a terrace or porch. The furniture here is placed outdoors on the grass, but it would do just as well for a porch or an informal sunroom. The terrace pictured below makes use of wood for dining table and benches, in combination with iron for chairs and small tables. Notice the built-in storage box which provides convenient table space on its top.

347

MAKING THE MOST OF A TINY TERRACE

In the living room with terrace shown at upper left, an interesting complementary color scheme of Caracas green and coral, combined with neutral Nubian brown, is carried out against a background of neutral off-white for walls and woodwork. The small terrace admits a flood of light allowing use of brown in over-all floor covering and rayon satin draperies which draw across the window-door. Upholstery is in green and coral. Note the mirrored cornice which extends around the room, also the straight stiffened valance edged with fringe. The tiny terrace requires light delicate furniture, but its colors and those of the awning are keyed to the room inside—white painted furniture, brown linoleum floor, green plants, coral seat pads and awning stripes.

AN OPEN-AIR FIREPLACE HAS MANY USES

Nothing is more delightful than a crackling fire in a glass-walled room, or on an open porch or terrace. If you have a chimney which goes through the wall of any kind of outdoor room or terrace by all means canvass the possibility of opening it to install a simple fireplace. The illustrations here show two very simple types of fireplaces which could be installed for very little money. The one pictured at the left is appropriate for a house in Colonial or regional feeling while the other one would be adaptable to almost any style of architecture. When an open-air fireplace is equipped for

picnic cookery—supplemented if necessary by a few electric gadgets—a good time is guaranteed. If you can't achieve a fireplace for cooking, do save up for a movable broiling grill and other accessories for turning an open-air terrace into a picnic spot. In the summer a fireplace can be made a center of decorative interest by banking it with greens as shown in the picture above. The comfortable furniture here is made of sturdy water-resistant wood with upholstery which is moisture- and fadeproof. The wide boards of the porch are painted to match the wall of the house.

GAY OUTDOOR TABLE AND CHAIR MADE FROM THE DISCARDS BELOW

TUB AND TABLE
SALVAGED
FROM THE JUNK HEAP

This group of pictures demonstrates the power of saw and paint brush. In the cutout illustrations can be seen the raw material from which a delightful table and chair were fashioned for use on terrace or porch, for a picnic in the yard, or even for meal-serving in a basement playroom. To make the chair out of an old barrel, saw away half the staves sixteen inches from the bottom. Fasten several cleats inside to support the seat, which is allowed to project two inches beyond the front edge. By hingeing this seat and lining the barrel with oilcloth a convenient storage spot can be had. The barrel must be sandpapered to remove splinters and rust. This one was then painted white and decorated with gay colors. The top scallops are pink with red swag edge. The huge strawberry painted on the seat is red and green. (For greater comfort a round unattached seat cushion would be useful.) The swag below the seat is red, and the hoops are yellow, blue, and red. If your furniture is to stay outdoors, varnish over the paint and antique the surface. The table which was bought for almost nothing was treated with paint remover and sandpapered, painted white and then decorated in bright colors like those used on the barrel. The amusing heart-shaped rug on the floor could be cut from an old rug or a piece of heavy felt, bordered with rug fringe and decorated with appliqués cut from colored felt. The paint manufacturers have instructions and designs for making the decorations shown and many others.

A successful hallway must fulfill its primary purpose as a passageway which means that its furnishings must usually be arranged against the wall or in a niche or corner. This leaves the floor space largely visible for more decorative effects than are desirable in rooms where furniture breaks up the design. In the picture above, flooring of deep red linoleum in shaded monochromatic effect is set off by an interesting

inlaid border in white, designed to follow the outlines of the floor. Soft white linoleum on the walls is flecked with red in a Parian marble design. White woodwork and red linoleum stair treads complete a dramatic background. The window draperies are also dramatic, yet very simple and easy to make. The straight draperies arranged to draw across the window and the swag valance are in French blue, both

ENTRANCE HALL

edged with self-toned moss fringe. The handsome ceiling-line cornice carried across the front of the bay window serves as a cornice heading for the draperies. Plants on the window ledge provide a green accent note of contrast for the red of the color scheme. The mirror, small cabinet, light graceful chair and stool all harmonize with the traditional style of the woodwork and the period design of the floor.

CHAPTER THIRTY

How to Have Harmony Between Rooms

IF YOUR HOME is anything larger than a one-room apartment you will have to give some thought to the place as a whole even if you are only decorating or doing over one of the rooms. Most rooms in a house or apartment open into one or more adjoining rooms. In many homes and apartments a central hallway (or a foyer) serves architecturally as a unifying element, but people too often forget that it should also be decorated with that function in mind.

HALLWAYS, VISTAS AND ALCOVES

Entrance Hallways: Entrance halls vary widely, from a tiny apartment foyer to a wide central hallway the full depth of the house or a spacious reception hall which is a room in itself and is furnished as such. They have one thing in common—the entrance hall is the first thing and the last thing your guests will see when they come to your home. Make sure they carry away with them the impression you want them to have. Entrance halls are often less well heated than other parts of the house and for this reason warmth as well as welcome should be expressed through furnishings and decoration. In general, use furniture of more slender proportions against light smooth walls, thicker or more massive pieces against darker or rougher walls.

DISTINCTIVE HALL TREATMENTS

Colors may be stronger in halls than in other rooms, wall and floor decorations bolder and more striking, furniture chosen with more thought for novelty and less thought for comfort. Halls are built to serve first of all as passageways and they must

351

never be cluttered up with unnecessary objects. At the same time almost any hallway can be made interesting and attractive by clever planning—and possibilities for unsuspected usefulness are legion. Decoration of halls must always be influenced by the style, theme, and colors used in the rooms opening into it. If doorways are large and usually open there must be a direct relation. If doors are smaller and often closed the link between rooms and hall may be less obvious but it should never be ignored.

Lighting Halls: Never leave dark gloomy corners in your halls. If no outside light can be brought in by use of glass in windows or partitions, provide pleasantly shaded lamps of low candlepower for tables, or lights in wall sconces. Inexpensive "pin-up" lamps are useful for this purpose. (See Chapter 37.) A mirror panel at the end of a dark hall, or a wall mirror hung where it will reflect light from a lamp or window, may produce all the additional lighting you need.

Walls and Ceilings: Hall ceilings are often high in proportion to small floor areas and dark warm colors will tend to lower them. If the color is brought down for a foot or two on the wall it will increase the effect even more. Wall panels are good, also deep cornices, and spreading designs or horizontal stripes in paper. A dado is doubly useful. It helps break up high walls and at the same time protects them. In wood, plastic, linoleum, or other composition materials which can be easily cleaned it guards the vulnerable lower part of the wall against accident and soil. Following a stairway, the dado also helps link lower and upper halls with a band of color. The dado may continue in the upper hall or stop at the first doorway.

If the hall is large any appropriate wall finish can be used, but if it is small select a cool receding color or a design with perspective. Walls in a small hallway are ideal places to use bold scenic paper because there is little furniture to break up pattern, no one stays in the hall long enough for it to become tiresome, and large scenic patterns with lines receding into distance will "open up" a tiny hall amazingly. Add a strategic mirror panel and double the illusion.

Furniture and Its Arrangement: In your entrance hall try to include a mirror, a wall table and at least one chair no matter how small the space. By careful attention to scale you can usually achieve this. An attractive console shelf will do for table, a padded stool or bench for seating. Give them importance by framing them with a decorative design on the wall, or by beauty of finish and coloring. Because there are comparatively few pieces of furniture in a hallway each one should have some special quality of individuality or distinction. In the average hall

there is space against one wall for a grouping of a console and two chairs. In crowded quarters, don't forget the utility value of a commode or small chest of drawers instead of the table. With slightly more room you may be able to include a love seat, a small sofa, or an interesting old chest placed on the opposite side of the hall, with some wall decoration above to balance the group of table, chair and mirror.

Furniture used in an entrance should be keyed in style to important living room pieces, but matching is not necessary or even desirable. Better let your hall have an individuality of its own, governed by its proportions and special needs but related in feeling with adjoining rooms. Appropriate novelties, antiques, or cabinets for hobbies—all may find a home in the hall if they do not crowd it or interfere with traffic.

SUGGESTIONS FOR SUCCESSFUL HALLWAYS

In many hallways (away from the entrance) a nook, or bay window, or by-passed corner is large enough to be treated as an alcove room and fitted up for reading, games, a small bar, a writing desk or some other activity. A large bare upper hall may be greatly improved by turning one end into a sewing center, or a spot for working on some hobby. These halls are often well lighted, and a homemade storage window seat, with a small rug, a table and a few comfortable slip-covered chairs, will give you all the benefits of an extra room.

Floors and Flooring: Floors are important because they must be prepared to take punishment, yet they are allowed more latitude in design and color than those in any other room in the house except a play room. Quiet is important in a passageway, but carpeting is often ruled out because of the cleaning problem, specially if there are children. Cork, linoleum, or some other felt-base composition flooring is next-best for deadening sound. At the same time these products are sturdy and easy to care for. In slightly mottled or marbleized designs they show dusty footprints less than with a plain surface. A coat of special linoleum wax now and then gives them a soft luster and helps keep them clean. Inlaid borders and large striking designs are very effective in these cork or linoleum floors. If rooms open together, floor colors must be related by harmony or planned contrast. Rugs may tone in with each other or small rugs in the hallway may contrast with a large rug in the living room. With small rooms you can increase the effect of size by carrying the same wall and floor colors, or analogous shades, through the hall and adjacent rooms.

DUTCH COLONIAL SIMPLICITY
CONTRASTED WITH
FEDERAL FORMALITY AND ELEGANCE

MODERN TREATMENT—TRADITIONAL THEME

The hallway picture below shows a striking group in which modern materials and sharp color contrasts are used, while furniture and floor design are reminiscent of the French Directoire period. Brilliant colors and bold design make this arrangement suitable for a small apartment foyer, especially when it can be seen from an adjoining room. Black linoleum flooring is inlaid with yellow, black mirror-based seat is upholstered in bright yellow leather, and the sunburst mirrored clock is also yellow. The pale yellow foyer wall makes a background for the panel "frame" about the group. The border is an appliquéd design of green, black, orange and white ending just below the ceiling line.

The two entrance halls on this page (above) show wide variation in type, style and treatment but they both share one characteristic essential for hall decoration—they present a charming and memorable picture to anyone entering the house. A dark, cluttered, or nondescript entrance hall may ruin the effect of a really beautiful house or apartment to which it leads. In the picture above left a cheerful bright entrance hall shows how a small amount of space may be utilized to advantage. Everything about the little hallway would breathe welcome to a guest. Pleasantly Dutch Colonial in feeling, the beauty of simple paneled painted woodwork is enhanced by decorative wallpaper in appropriate period design. The wide plank floor, hooked rug, pine table and flat corner cupboard all fit into the picture. Ruffled sheer white Colonial curtains at door and window admit a cheerful flood of sunlight. Notice storage space in the lower part of the wall cupboard, and figurines in the cabinet above—an excellent spot for a hobby collection. The Dutch half-door with the top which can be opened for additional air has a special charm in these surroundings. It is interesting to observe how easily a cabinet-door-and-window unit like this (including a closet built in at the left of the door) could be installed in a gloomy entrance hall and transform it completely. These can be had in stock models. The hallway at upper right shows a fascinating arrangement of spiral steps in a modern adaptation of the circular staircase widely used in the Federal period of American decoration. Arched bay window, draperies, clock, crystal chandelier and chairs are all typical of the period. But the round fringed rug strikes a definitely modern note.

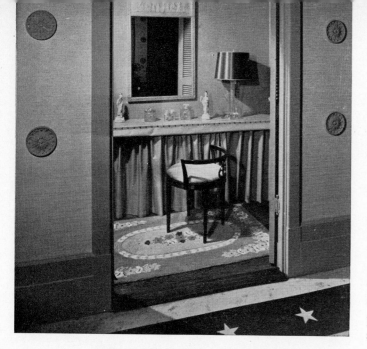

SMALL FOYER WITH POWDER ROOM

A powder room is a very desirable addition to any entrance hall even if it has to be installed in a small converted closet. If you have no available closet but do have a little extra space, it would be worth while to utilize the space by enclosing it with wallboard to make a tiny room like the one shown here. The foyer below is a very good example of small space attractively treated. The flooring is beige marbleized linoleum inlaid with black and beige border. Imitation grass-cloth wallpaper on the walls is in soft natural beige. Medallions are painted in turquoise like ceiling and woodwork. A Hepplewhite-style commode in mahogany with satinwood inlay harmonizes with two period benches upholstered in beige and coral-striped moiré—and provides extra storage space ever-useful in a small apartment. Another excellent feature of this foyer is the ceiling-high mirror panel with the lamp in front of it which doubles both apparent space and light from the lamp. Opening from the foyer the powder room above carries out the same color scheme—turquoise woodwork and dressing-table skirt, accented with coral in the leatherette dressing-table top and lamp shades. The background of the needlepoint rug with its floral rose pattern is also coral.

Draperies and Accessories: Windows and door panels should be curtained for the softening effect. If light is poor you can use sheer materials such as silk, rayon, or nylon gauze, in white or soft sunny yellow. If you have the usual single window, or window group, make your draperies as gay or as striking as you like or your general plan allows, unless you want them to match those in a neighboring room. For privacy and light control use any of the standard methods—draw-curtains, shades, or Venetian blinds. There should be enough wall decoration—mirrors, pictures, tapestry, panels—to keep the walls from looking bare and cold. But plan these decorations specially for your hall. Don't hang things there just because you can't find any other place for them. If the staircase wall seems bare you can carry a line of suitable pictures in "steps" up the wall—an arrangement which should never be used anywhere else.

Stairways: Use some kind of carpeting on your stairs if you possibly can. Many inexpensive woven materials come in attractive colors and weaves. Use them until you can afford finer fabrics, then cut the old stair carpeting down to make back stairs more quiet, or for kitchen halls and porches. Stair carpeting is important for several reasons. Bare treads are noisy and often very disturbing. Carpeting makes them quieter, more comfortable, easier to keep in condition, and safer, specially for children and old people.

In addition to these practical advantages a carpeted stairway makes the hall appear more inviting and hospitable and adds needed color. Like a dado, the carpeting unites the lower and upper floors by a line of color sweeping upward. If you do not use carpeting, and have composition flooring in the hall, save wear and tear on the treads by covering them with the same flooring. This also carries the hall color upward. If the hall flooring has a pattern, use the same flooring material for treads in a plain color matching the background of that on the floor.

PUTTING HALLS TO WORK

In the section on built-in features you will find many suggestions for turning waste space in halls into useful storage or utility areas. In Chapter 36 ideas are sketched for installing new hall closets or making the most of those you have. Always survey your hall space and check your budget with the possibility of building in a small utility lavatory in a back hallway to save trips upstairs, and a powder room off the entrance hall for the convenience of guests.

Powder Rooms: These may be full-size rooms with full equipment for dressing, lounging, and coat stor-

ROOMS WITH NO DOOR BETWEEN MUST BE KEYED TO EACH OTHER

In the country library and dining room shown above, dramatic color contrast is used to link the rooms in harmony, rather than the more customary device of gradual transition in color. However, this is made attractive and pleasing by carrying the same floor and ceiling colors through the opening, by confining the basic scheme to the same colors in each room, and by repeating the main color used in each room as an accent in the other. Wood in light natural tones is used for furniture throughout. Note the dark green of living room walls repeated in the foliage of the flower arrangement glimpsed through the opening, the deep rose of the second room picked up in the living room.

PAINTED BRICKS
FOR INFORMAL FIREPLACE SETTINGS

In a game room, an enclosed terrace, or an informal living room, a brick wall or chimney breast may be made attractive by means of paint and decoration. In the game room above, with its large old-fashioned Dutch-oven type of fireplace, water-thinned paint in creamy white makes an appropriate background for an Indian rug and growing plants. Rubber tiling on the floor is good looking as well as practical. Storage space built under the stairway provides cupboards and shelves to take care of game room supplies, special dishes, and wood for the fireplace. During warm weather, the Mexican furniture and gay folding yacht chairs can be moved to a porch or terrace. The brick chimney breast at the right is kept from giving an impression of heaviness by the book-filled shelves filling the wall above and around it. Note how the rich red of the hearth is repeated in the armchair upholstery, and picked up by many of the book bindings. The shelves are painted in the same creamy white used for the fireplace facing; the yellow ceiling and lamp shade seem to reflect the yellow firelight flickering behind polished brass andirons. Note the curtain-type screen, safe and easy to handle. (For many other fireplaces, see Chapter 24.)

age, but they are usually just large enough for essentials. They may even be tiny converted closets or alcoves. Planned only for occasional and probably festive use, they may be as light and gay as you like in decoration—even amusing and frivolous. However, they are most effective when they are keyed, in color at least, with the hall from which they open.

Really good mirrors are essential, and a triple-mirror of some kind will increase your popularity as hostess. A three-fold mirrored screen often solves this problem, or even a triple dressing-table mirror. At least one full-length mirror panel is very desirable and need not be expensive. An old mirror can often be taken out of its frame, reconditioned, framed in simple molding and attached to the wall or the inside of the door. If you can afford mirrored glass for walls it will make a cubby-hole powder room look like one of generous proportions. In any case be sure that you have at least a good clear mirror over your dressing table.

This dressing table is the next essential. It may be only a shelf with attractive cover and drapery skirt, but there must be provision for all essentials. If there are no drawers in the dressing table a series of small decorative shelves on the wall flanking the mirror may hold toilet necessities and sewing supplies in decorative containers, or if there is room have a diminutive chest of drawers in the corner. A stool or chair should match dressing table decorations, and a second chair should be included even if it is only a folding camp stool concealed by the dressing table skirt. Your own ingenuity will suggest other clever devices. Put yourself in the guest's place and do your furnishing with that in mind.

Lighting is important. If there is daylight the window should be sheerly curtained for daytime use and provided with blinds or draw-curtains for privacy at night. Place the dressing table where it will receive the best light from the window, and arrange artificial lighting with make-up in mind. (See page 389.) An excellent idea is to have a good "candid" mirror over the dressing table, with an all-revealing light, then hang another mirror in a corner where it will receive only a subdued light so that the effect of make-up may be judged as it will appear in the softer lighting of living room or dining room.

HARMONY BETWEEN ROOMS

The problem of decorating adjoining rooms is easily solved in the case of conventional bedrooms which usually open only into a hall, dressing room, or bathroom. On the bedroom floor of a house sufficient unity can usually be achieved by use of related or neutral colors in the hall and avoidance of

STEPS ADD INTEREST TO HALLWAYS

The vista shown in the above picture, leading from an apartment foyer into a living room, illustrates an important principle of harmony between rooms which should be expressed in both color and feeling through underlying kinship rather than exact matching. The living-room decorations here are in early 19th Century style, only a little removed in history from the later Victorian period to which chairs and love seat in the foyer belong. Light beige tones of simulated-wood paper in the hall provide an easy transition to soft brown walls in the living room. Flowered cretonne draperies there blend with the floral design of upholstery in the foyer, which in turn picks up its colors from the blue, green, brown and yellow used for stenciled motifs beside the doorway. These are in a stylized pattern derived from early 19th Century French designs, and furnish a coordinating element between the two rooms in style as well as color. The room below is an interesting example of harmonizing when two vistas open from the same room. In the vista at the right, which shows a hallway and a corner of the dining room, unity is carried through by means of woodwork and matching archways at each side of the hall. As you look up the steps to the right the Colonial theme is carried along the landing into the room on the upper level through the use of hooked rugs, toile slip covers and Colonial-type furniture. Wide plank floors used in all the rooms and hall help create a feeling of unity.

jarring contrasts between walls or decorations on opposite sides of a connecting door. But in apartments or one-story bungalows bedrooms must usually be brought in some way into the over-all picture. The same principles then apply as those for any adjoining rooms.

For keying rooms in a house together the course of least resistance is too often followed—use of the same background color throughout. This may be desirable in very small quarters because it increases a feeling of space, but it means you must try doubly hard for variety and interest through diversity of textures and decorating color schemes. The best method is to work out a logical sequence of colors through walls, floors and draperies, linking rooms with hallways and with each other. When a group of rooms and a hallway can all be seen from one central point select a key color for the group then use it in varying combinations and shades. Soften it for the foundation color in one room, use it as a secondary color in another, as a bright accent color in a third. By following the principles of color harmony (see Chapter 4) you can work out a different color scheme for each room, yet they will all be harmonious.

HOW TO TREAT ROOMS OPENING TOGETHER

When two or more rooms open directly into each other the arrangement offers possibilities for working out vistas and perspectives which are both charming in themselves and help to create an impression of spaciousness. In many houses the living room opens with arches or double doors into one or more other rooms in addition to the hallway—usually a dining room, library or sun porch. The rooms in any such combination should be linked together by some harmonizing element. This does not mean they must all be decorated alike. They serve different functions and call for different treatment. There may be sunlight in one room and not in its neighbor, which will affect the color schemes. A formal, traditional living room may open into a den designed for solid comfort, informality, and relaxation. In this case mood, theme, and composition will be different in the two rooms, and the materials used not at all alike. A way must be found to harmonize the two without violating their essential characteristics.

Gentle Transitions: An archway or an open door should not mark an abrupt and disconcerting contrast between walls and backgrounds brought together at the opening. The transition from one to the other should be gentle. For this you must establish a thread of underlying unity running through mood, theme and style, and color.

NO "WASTE SPACE" IN THIS HALLWAY

The hallway illustrated above does almost everything you could ask a hallway to do. It provides charming vistas to anyone entering the front door, both into the living room and up the graceful stairway. A glass-paneled Dutch door at the back means there is always plenty of light and air. Sturdy marbleized black linoleum flooring with dramatic Chinese Chippendale design in yellow provides a smart floor easy to keep clean. Black linoleum stair treads carpeted in red matching the Chinese red of the Chinese Chippendale table in the hall carry the color up the stairway. Hall chair seats and draw-curtains in the living-room doorway are in the same red. Outdoor colors of sky and garden visible through the living-room window and the Dutch door in the hall are brought into the house through soft blues and greens in living-room draperies and upper hall wallpaper. This is an interesting point demonstrating the attractiveness of harmony between different rooms or sections of the house when both are visible from an observation point such as the entrance hall provides here. The use of the stairway wall for book shelves is another point in this transition harmony. Colors of the books tie living room and hall together. The unusual arrangement of built-in book shelves has several advantages. It turns a usually blank wall space into an interesting and colorful background and the books are easily accessible. Also there is no delicate paper to show soil and fingermarks along the stairway. Shallow shelves like this could be built in along almost any stairway. If you have books without adequate living-room wall space for them this plan may be your solution. Ceiling and woodwork are soft ivory, repeated on the living-room walls and ceiling. The unique feature in this hall is one which does not show until demonstrated. (See sketch at right.) The space under the stair landing is used—as in many halls—for a large roomy coat closet with every convenience for family and guests. But in this hall the space between the landing and the foot of the stairs has not been wasted. It is filled by three sliding compartments, each operated by a gentle push against the outside panel. A hidden latch clicks, the panel opens and the compartment inside slides out. These hidden drawers take care of an endless number of the things that usually fill closet space all over the house—as you can see in the sketch.

Transition Devices: If you have your entire house decorated in some particular period or regional style, then color is all you need watch—but it takes real ingenuity to harmonize rooms in which a variety of tastes must be expressed and the rooms are not held together even by any distinctive architectural motif. If you must use fundamentally different types of furniture in connecting rooms, apply camouflage to the most antagonistic pieces and introduce a few neutralizing pieces in a style somewhere between the two extremes. Search for fabrics and colors which can be harmonized with both rooms and use them freely. Synchronize floor treatment as much as possible. Use double-faced hangings or screens at the opening. Wallpaper and borders often help solve the problem. You may not achieve a perfect transition, but you will have rooms you can live with until something more drastic can be done.

If your two rooms serve much the same purpose—for instance, a living room and sun parlor, or the old-fashioned parlor and living-room arrangement—the safest solution is to work out plans definitely related in mood, theme, composition and color. Related does not mean *alike*. Contrast of some sort is preferable to avoid monotony, but it must be contrast closely harmonized and so related that the two rooms can be regarded as one large canvas or as twin pictures designed to hang together on one wall. In this case contrasts are better worked out in details than in background treatment. Let the background supply the unity which will bind the two rooms together and provide the harmonizing element. For instance:

Many houses have a living room which opens with very little architectural separation into a living porch which may be much lighter than the room itself. In this case, select a harmonizing color scheme in which one of the light-producing colors appears in its cool aspect in the living-room background (pale yellow), deepening in the lighter room to a warmer version of the color (orange). The mood and theme need not be identical, but they should be closely akin, with the porch expressed in a slightly gayer and more informal type of decoration, furniture, and rugs. But be sure the feeling in the two rooms is essentially the same. Carry color accents and decorative moods through both of them, and merge the types of furniture as you approach the opening. In other words, make your transition gentle.

Connecting Two Rooms with Dissimilar Purposes: When the wide opening connects two rooms with

THREE UNITS IN ONE HARMONY

In the room below advantage was taken of the long, narrow proportions to subdivide the space into three separate room areas without actually using any partitions. The living-room end was arranged on a large shaggy rug as if that were one room, with the sofa facing the fireplace. Its extra long back, at the edge of the rug, divides the room from a "hallway" with a writing table and two chairs placed against the back of the sofa. A door to the dining-room end is formed by two large folding screens, which separate without concealing. Looking from either end, the effect is dramatic and the sense of space is preserved with no loss of room character. Mirrored doors increase this feeling of spaciousness.

different functions, such as a living room and a dining room, a different approach is required, but the transition must nevertheless be gradual. The living room is probably keyed to a restful mood and theme, carried out in soft colors relaxing to eyes and mind. Strong colors are used for accent, but sparingly, in order not to disturb the restful atmosphere of a room in which many hours at a time will often be spent.

The dining room, on the other hand, should be gay and cheerful, or interesting and dramatic. The atmosphere should be without strain but need not emphasize restfulness. This allows a more lavish use of color, dramatic walls, and large-patterned fabrics— if the room is big enough to carry them. The chances are that you will want less conventional furniture here than in the living room. To link the two rooms, pick up the bright accent colors you have used in the living room and make them the basis of your dining-room gaiety. Introduce the living-room background colors somewhere, in upholstery, drapery, or even accessories. Then the magic wand of color will draw the rooms together into a harmony of contrast, without detracting from their distinctiveness.

Harmonizing with Wallpaper: Wallpapers may often be found in harmonizing sets and this is one of the most convenient methods for linking rooms. In these sets the design may be the same with colors reversed, the background color in one being used for the major design-color in the other. Again, the same design may come in several color combinations each harmonious with the others. Sometimes colors and design are both repeated varying only in scale and tone. A group of colors may be worked into several different designs, some large and bold, others smaller and quiet.

It is obvious how these sets could be used to introduce unity in a series of rooms. By adding a plain paper or using paint in one of the dominant shades the possibilities can be expanded still farther. You can easily make up your own "sets" by assembling, for example, (1) a paper in large open design for the hall, (2) a plain paper in the same background color but a lighter shade for the living room, (3) scenic vista panels against a darker shade for the dining room. You can also combine stripes, or geometric design, in one room with florals in flanking rooms, possibly with a floral border to head the stripes.

Borders can always be utilized in this way to increase unity by bringing design colors from one room into others or forming a continuous line from one room to the next. Pattern, color and texture in draperies may be used to help out this linking of rooms. In a good many shops it is now possible to find fabrics included in the matching sets described above, various textures, colors and designs being assembled in groups for use together.

Vistas: Whenever you achieve a lovely, satisfying transition, emphasize it by reflection in strategically placed mirrors. No other device is so generally helpful in making rooms seem larger, lighter, airier. Mirrors emphasize charm by repetition. At transition points they tie rooms together by bringing a picture of each into the frame of the other. Their possibilities are endless. If it seems impossible to repeat a particular color note at a certain spot where it is needed for balance, scale, or harmony, try introducing it by reflection in a mirror. This is specially good when the color note is in the next room and you want to bring it through the opening for transition purposes. Vistas, mirrors and hallways all play major roles in linking rooms together.

ALCOVES

Recessed areas, large or small, must be included in the general mood and theme of a room, but they should form a picture within a picture. They are often most effective when set off from the general background by walls in a different color or design. The secret here is contrast—but keep within the spirit of your composition by combining in a strikingly different way the same elements you use in your over-all picture.

If the walls of your room are light and for contrast you want a dark wall in a dining niche or balcony, pick up one of the minor colors in your drapery, wallpaper, or slip covers and use it for your alcove wall. For unity, be sure to introduce some decorative motif from the room into the alcove by means of drapery, upholstery or accessories.

When alcoves are large enough they may be used for various extension living purposes. Many built-in features sketched in Chapter 17 may be adapted to alcove transformation. Proper equipment will give a large alcove a double-duty character, keeping it in harmony with the room it adjoins without limiting its special usefulness. A built-in couch bed and storage space added to the regular furnishings, for example, would provide emergency guest quarters. Book shelves, desk and reading light would convert it into a cozy library or study. It makes an ideal spot for game or hobby equipment and enjoyment. If you have an alcove like this, and an upright piano which you don't want in your living room, turn the alcove into a small music room. If the piano is old, paint it to harmonize with the alcove decorations. With a phonograph and radio plus comfortable seating arrangements you will have a center your family will love for music and relaxation.

ALCOVES FOR USEFULNESS AND INTEREST

Alcoves are often regarded as nuisances, while as a matter of fact they are almost always opportunities for creation of unusual and interesting effects. In this group of pictures three different types of small alcoves are cleverly utilized. The one in the center picture with its corner windows has been converted into a quiet retreat for conversation, lounging or reading, and gaily dressed up with plaid slip covers and valance. The upper picture shows a comfortable Early American living room with a small alcove which makes a charming picture with its built-in storage window-seat, deep ledge for flowers or plants and sunny latticed windows. Either of these two alcoves could be easily converted into dining or game table nooks by the addition of a table and small chairs. The alcove bed in the sketch at right illustrates a space-saving arrangement which at the same time provides a distinctive bed treatment. Several variations of this device are useful and attractive. An alcove is often built in, with the space at the sides utilized for closets while storage drawers or cupboards are built in above and below the opening. Another variation is to turn a living room into an emergency bedroom by fitting up an alcove like this with a studio couch, using cushions at the back as well as the ends.

The Early American theme used in decorating the young girl's room above often has a strong appeal to youth—even the most modern—and is a frequent selection. The canopy bed in this room designed for the daughter of the family is set into a mirror-paneled recess which is the only modern note in the room. Plaid cotton taffeta in pink, green and white makes a canopy for the bed, a frill around it, drapery for the back behind the headboard and a deep flounce beneath the bed spread. The same fabric is used to cover the chairs. Furniture of maple in authentic Colonial designs, hooked rug

COLONIAL BEDROOM

floor coverings and Early American accessories furnish a room which any girl should love. Walls are painted chalk pink and draperies are striped cotton taffeta in pink, green and white used with shaped valances and frilled glass curtains. From silhouette to prints, the atmosphere is authentic.

CHAPTER THIRTY-ONE

Rooms for Youngsters

IT IS IMPORTANT wherever possible to give the younger members of the family rooms of their own where they can follow their own pursuits and hobbies and satisfy (within reason) their own tastes in decoration. The room should be furnished so that they can entertain their friends there. If a youngster has a room alone an extra couch or bunk will be a welcome feature for hospitality to overnight guests.

When a room must be shared, twin bunks or beds are recommended with twin chests of drawers, desks and tables, all arranged to give each occupant of the room a little private center of activity and relaxation. As soon as youngsters are old enough it is better to make some kind of division between the two parts of the room. If the room is large enough, and the placing of doors and windows allows it, an actual partition can be built in with composition board, or made by tall book shelves placed back to back. Modern tall folding screens can be used, or one of the movable partitions which operates from a molding applied to the ceiling. (See picture on page 334.) Other devices for setting off two parts of a room are described on pages 336 and 339.

Closets and Storage Space: By utilizing contemporary ideas for furniture, closets and cupboards which are built in or appear built in you will be able to provide adequate storage space without large expense. For younger children closets should be specially fitted with low poles for hangers, low shelves and hooks. (See Chapter 36.) Always have an automatic light in the closet so that they can see what they are doing, and a safe step-stool if they need to reach higher. If they have attractive, cleverly worked out closets, with easily reached shelf space and plenty of cupboards and drawers, most children will soon

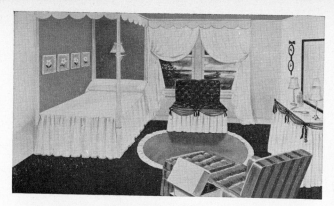

FOR AN OLDER GIRL, AND A YOUNGER ONE

Feminine in feeling, but simple and easy to arrange, the room above would be suitable for the girl who likes traditionally dainty effects expressed through modern adaptation. Simplicity of plain painted walls is very modern. So too is the deep blue painted floor with a small round cloth rug of lighter blue; but the four-poster bed and the swag drapery on window seat and dressing table are reminiscent of great-grandmother's day. The painted valance around the bed is a novel substitute for the old-fashioned tester flounce. It continues over the windows to form a cornice for the draperies. White used for bedcovers, draperies and dressing-table skirt is bordered with pale blue topped with rose swags in blue, and the upholstery of the chaise longue easy chair is in blue and rose. The dusty rose of the ceiling is carried down onto the walls behind the bed, with remaining walls white. The white flower prints are on blue mats with white frames. Shaped cornices of the type used in this room can be bought in various styles in composition board. The rug could be made of felt with edging of heavy shirred fabric. Unbleached muslin, or white cotton, would be charming for the draperies, and the swags could utilize remnants or dyed leftovers. Any ingenious girl could make the storage-love seat

in the window by having a hinged lid and a board back attached to a packing box. The box could be lined with oil-cloth and the padded back and cover could be tufted like those used here which are in dark blue with rose stitching and buttons. The room above would appeal to the girl of conservative tastes who has not yet quite outgrown childhood affection for her dolls and toys. Simple pine furniture and fiber rug are serviceable and attractive. Ruffled curtains in criss-cross style are draped back with bows made of the fabric used for bed spread, slip cover and lamp shades. The study-desk with its reading light and globe is placed in the window alcove where it will be framed by the curtains and adequately lighted.

take pride in their ability to keep them in order.

Furniture: Chairs in scale for size and correct for posture are important, specially while youngsters are still growing. All the furniture should be in scale with this growth, which means that it must be changed from time to time. For this reason unit furniture is specially desirable. Twin low chests of drawers can be placed on top of each other to make space for larger articles of furniture needed later. New units can be added to book shelves to make them taller. The smaller tables from a nest of tables can often be used in a child's room, with the larger ones retained for some grown-up room. Desks, tables and chairs should be replaced as soon as they are outgrown, but this need not be a too-expensive process. The smaller articles for the earlier stages can easily be made by cutting down old pieces and dressing them up with the gay paint, decorations and slip covers children love.

In buying new furniture make sure that it is well constructed, sturdy and comfortable but also attractive. You can often find pieces which may be utilized later in other parts of the house or adapted to changes inevitable in taste as well as in size of grow-

ing children. (For suggestions on remodeling furniture, slip covers, etc., see Index.)

Decoration: For young people from high school age onward decoration of their rooms ceases to be partly a matter of adjustment to size and becomes an individual problem, except that allowance must still be made for the rapid changes in tastes and interests usually associated with youth. For this reason as much use as possible should still be made of inexpensive furnishings or converted pieces beautified by decorations and fabrics. Fortunately most young people like to plan and help create these things themselves, especially if they are allowed to exercise their own ingenuity and skills.

For younger children everything should be sturdy, washable, easily kept clean—as nearly as possible damageproof. Washable paint, paper, linoleum or novelty composition materials are advisable for walls. If you cannot refinish the entire wall you can use one of the materials mentioned for a washable dado carried as high as little hands can reach. Floor coverings should be durable and easily taken care of. For warmth, quiet and cleanability linoleum is excellent, also various other types of composition flooring.

COMPACT COMFORT IN A BEDROOM-STUDY

The room above with clipper ship motif and maritime-patterned draperies, was designed as a comfortable study-bedroom for a young man with a ship hobby. It is interesting because it could be so easily transposed into suitable quarters for the young daughter of the family who wants a room she can use on occasion as an informal living room. The only changes necessary would be to work out a color scheme more delicate than the red, white and blue used here, and substitute her more feminine hobby. Furniture is in natural finish pine, walls and ceiling are soft blue, woodwork and lamps are white. Red and white toile for curtains and slip covers, cherry red for day-bed cover and shelf linings, with a homespun rug in soft

ORGANDY FOR AIRINESS

dark blue complete an ensemble colorful enough to appeal to any boy. Notice the effective mingling of books and accessories on the shelves—which the average boy could build—and the correct arrangement of two large pictures lined up to balance the size of the couch below. The very feminine bedroom above could never be adapted to masculine occupancy, but its crisp white organdy and white printed chintz would appeal to many girls. The walls are soft blue-green, the rugs pink, and the chair pale gray—colors repeated in the pattern of the chintz. Notice the draperies extending over the wall at each side of the window to serve as a frame for the dressing table without covering the window.

Rugs or carpets should be sturdy and simple, large enough and heavy enough not to get in the way of youthful activities. Heavy woven cotton, linen and fiber rugs which can be washed or easily cleaned are best. Wood floors may be waxed or painted but should not be slippery.

Fabrics for draperies and all other purposes should always be washable, and made up in attractive but simple styles. Color and pattern are both very important to children, and they should always be consulted before a choice is made. Even very young children have some decided color preference, and if they are allowed to help select the color scheme, then given a final choice of several appropriate materials for walls and draperies they will feel that the room really belongs to them. This will go far toward providing the pleasant environment which is so necessary to a child's best interest and happiness. Letting youngsters help plan their rooms is also a good way to educate them in fundamental principles of good taste and decorating standards.

Don't forget the difference between the tastes of boys and girls. They both like bright gay colors such as red, blue and yellow, but feminine preference

usually tends toward the daintier pastel tones such as pink and baby blue, while the boys like their colors in the stronger primary hues. With both you will have to guard against their love for pictures and decorations and patterns. A judicious use of these is essential—always keyed to childish interests—but too much pattern is as fatiguing to young eyes as to older ones. Unless the room is used just for play and recreation, it should be restful as well as gay. Girls usually choose softer fabrics for draperies, with crisp ruffled sheers for curtains, while boys prefer sturdy fabrics in tweedy or nubby weaves, often in bold stripe or plaid designs. Most boys like plain built-in furniture with a "ship-shape" atmosphere, while girls love dressing tables with frilly skirts and a "grown-up" air.

For younger children a large cork pin-up board on which they can display their own efforts or keep pictures which intrigue them can be placed low and framed to harmonize with the room. It can be moved up later on the wall and utilized by teen-agers for the ever-changing pin-up pictures, snap-shots, dance programs, memoranda and clippings which reflect their developing interests or hobbies.

THREE ROOMS FOR BOYS

The three rooms in this group are carefully planned both to fill the needs and satisfy the tastes of the average active-minded boy. In the bedroom above right light natural finish pine has been used to build in complete equipment for storage, working, dressing and study. Reading light over the bed, books and radio beside it, provide comfort for relaxation. Window draperies and bedcovers, gaily colored but simple, and sturdy blue woven rug are definitely masculine in tone. Any ordinary room could be converted in this manner by installing ready-built units fitted flat against the wall to look as if they were part of the original construction. The photograph directly right shows what can be done with an attic to create the kind of retreat a boy would love because of the feeling of privacy and independence it would give him. Much of the work of remodeling a room like this can be done by the boy himself. Storage space is provided under the built-in bunk. Closets and shelves under the eaves take care of clothes and sports equipment. Built-in book shelves behind the bed also provide radio space. The desk at the window could easily be made by remodeling two old chiffoniers, cutting off the legs and connecting them as shown here. An easy way to modernize them is to use linoleum for resurfacing drawers, sides and tops. Folding porch chairs are inexpensive but comfortable, and the phonograph case with its record-storage rack is easily built in. The color scheme here shows that free rein was given to an imaginative young man's fancy—soft light brown painted floor, beige painted furniture and woodwork, pale azure walls and dormer, canary yellow dado and ceiling. Drawer pulls and phonograph-cabinet lining are coral, while the rug is blue, brown and coral plaid on a yellow ground. Venetian blinds are yellow too, in this room which is big enough to serve as a neighborhood entertainment center as well as a boy's bedroom. The above photograph illustrates what can be done, with very little expense, to convert an unused basement-corner into a combination den, workshop and hobby room for the boy of the family. Easy-to-apply knotty pine (or wallboard) can be used for walls, combined with painted plywood for sturdy shelves and cabinet doors. This compact many-purpose unit, built entirely by home construction, shows how waste space can be put to work.

TWIN COUCHES IN A STREAM-LINED STUDY

Two boys in a family may give rise to a furnishing problem when there is only one room which both of them must use. A studio-couch atmosphere is usually preferable in a case like this. There are several attractive arrangements which may be worked out to save space and make the quarters ship-shape. The room below is modern in its lines, an interesting arrangement of day beds with a table between giving a streamlined effect. Plain background, simple draperies, book shelves, and plaid design of a sturdy fiber rug are in harmony with the masculine feeling of the room. Note the trim lines of bedcovers and the suspension desk with a convenient bulletin board above it.

BEFORE-AND-AFTER BEDROOMS

GAY ATTIC ROOM FOR A CHILD

This delightful room for an older child (below) shows what can be done by converting an attic into a roomy combination playroom and bedroom for a boy or a girl. The taste of some little girls might call for more frills and that of some little boys for more simplicity, but the gay awning ceiling, the table for games or eating, and the ledge above the window for pet toys would appeal to almost any youngster. Two comfortable chairs are provided for grown-up visitors, but otherwise the decorations and furnishings are kept in scale with its young occupant.

The dreary bedroom shown at upper left is a replica of too many rooms in which some younger (or older) member of a family is expected to feel happy. The "after" pictures show what can be done to make over such a bedroom with an expenditure of very little money and not too much labor. Studying the alterations in these pictures we see how two entirely different rooms can be evolved out of the same original. In both cases major operations were the same so those are described first. The bureau with its simple design needed only to be reconditioned by tightening up the drawers and removing the ugly old finish. The rickety table by the bed was merely cut off above the point where the four legs went into a center post. This lowered the top about six inches and the table no longer looked unbalanced and spindly. The bookcase table shown in the young man's room was very easily made from plain boards sawed the right size and nailed together in proportions to fit a grooved frame removed from a discarded picture. Fastened on with finishing nails, the frame concealed the plain boxlike construction of the shelves. The mirror was replaced in each of these rooms by a mirror reclaimed from a second-hand store and finished to match the room. The old one, which was too small to balance the bureau, was used elsewhere in the house. The bed required the most drastic treatment. The headboard was cut down to the same height as the footboard and the scalloped ornamental top of the old headboard (without the posts) was used to finish the new lowered headboard. The job of transforming the rest of the room was done entirely by means of paint and other decoration. The picture at the left shows the room finished for a young girl, gay with frilled draperies and bedcover. Walls are painted soft sunny yellow, the floors painted soft dark green. French gray enamel for the furniture matches the tone of the stitched rug with its colorful border of yellow, black and rose. In the same room adapted to masculine taste (above), background walls are painted Empire green, floor a darker green. The furniture is distinctive in combinations of French gray and dark green enamel, with touches of red on the top rail of the bed footboard, knobs of the two lower bureau drawers, and tops of bureau and little table—which is here used as an occasional table beside a Windsor arm chair in natural pine. The dark felt rug is brightened by stitched-on appliqués in red, gray and green. Inexpensive draperies are made from lengths of calico with a quaint formal pattern in deep red, hung under a valance of dark green felt with a red top-border. The same double Dutch glass curtains so uninteresting in the first picture are attractive here because the over-draperies allow their fullness to be pushed together, doing away with the skimpy effect.

The nursery above is quaintly Early American in theme. Blue and white checked gingham is used to cover the walls, to make window draperies, for a skirt around the cradle,

and to make cushions for a comfortable old-fashioned rocker. Washable woven rag rugs on the floor, and a useful double shelf easily made at home complete a simple, charming

THE NURSERY

nursery plan, at the same time functional and easy to keep clean. Nursery furniture can be easily made by cutting down and refinishing full-size pieces.

CHAPTER THIRTY-TWO

Points on Nurseries

A SEPARATE ROOM for a baby is not always possible, but it is always desirable. If you can convert a room close to yours into a nursery by all means do it. The schedule necessary for a baby or a young child requires quiet at many times when equally necessary activities of older children and adults make the average home anything but quiet. When a separate room is out of the question it is important to set aside a part of whatever room is used with some kind of temporary partition which can be closed for daylight darkness and comparative quiet. It may be an alcove, or a corner of your bedroom, made into a temporary nursery. In any case the principles are the same as those for a separate nursery room as far as it is possible to apply them within the framework of another room.

Before you design a baby's room or buy equipment it is advisable to look ahead a bit. For example, if you plan a family of several children who will use the same nursery furniture it is not an extravagance to fit up the room with only infant necessities in mind. But if it is to serve one child through progressive stages of growth it is much more sensible to spend money in the beginning only on absolute necessities, or on furniture which can be adjusted to later needs. In planning for a small infant there are only two absolute necessities—baby's comfort and mother's convenience. Elaborate frills and furbelows once considered essential in a baby's environment have been replaced by decorations equally dainty but much simpler and more sanitary.

A NURSERY FOR THE NEW BABY

A nursery should be planned first of all with comfort, convenience and efficiency in mind. Walls and floor should be finished with the needs of the growing child always in mind so that redecorating of the background will not be necessary when you replace infant furniture with sleeping and play equipment for the toddler.

Light and Air: Light and air should be well regulated in any nursery and provision must be made for

367

that. Place the crib or bed where light will not shine in the child's eyes to disturb early morning slumber or an afternoon nap. Venetian blinds are particularly useful in a nursery because light can be dimmed while fresh air is admitted. They should be painted in the background wall color. Later on they can be brightened by painting or covering the tapes. Draw-curtains may be used for light control, but they should be washable and always kept fresh and clean. If sheer glass curtains are needed to soften light use them with shades or blinds but not with over-draperies. Select simple fabrics such as gingham and organdy, or some of the various treated and synthetic materials so easy to keep clean. Ceiling lights should be covered with reflector bowls and lamps placed where they will be out of the range of vision. Night lights should be deeply shaded.

Comfort and Convenience: During the early months of its life an infant needs only a comfortable place in which to sleep—bassinet, cradle or crib. All other equipment is for the convenience of whatever grown-up is acting as nurse. Some kind of chest of drawers is essential for storing the baby's clothing and supplies. A table will be needed large enough to hold bathing necessities and scales, but any table can be used for this purpose if it is protected by an oil-cloth cover. Even a large kitchen table will do. A comfortable chair must be provided, also a straight chair without arms. A screen is useful to prevent drafts and help control light. This can also be used to hide undecorative equipment. An electric hotplate and a small nursery refrigerator are very convenient. They are both nice to have in a safe spot in the older child's room for use when lunches are served there or young guests are being entertained.

DECORATING THE NURSERY-PLAYROOM

When the same room is used for sleeping and play it should be a little quieter and more restrained than a room devoted entirely to daytime activities, but fundamental requirements are the same. It is much better to start with a very simple background for the baby. In the early formative months a baby's mind is highly impressionable and the things he sees should be simple and pleasant, easy to understand. Complicated objects in his environment will only confuse and puzzle him. So leave the decorations until later, and let the growing child pass judgment on changes or additions as they are made.

Walls, Ceilings and Floors: Start with colors and finishes which will provide appropriate backgrounds for later developments. Paint or paper should be washable, in pastel tints chosen with the light-exposure of the room in mind. (See Chapter 6.) Wall

BASIC FURNITURE FOR THE NURSERY

Above, an adjustable crib and chest of drawers is supplemented by a matching costumer with shelves for shoes. There is a comfortable low adult arm chair and a soft washable chenille rug on the linoleum floor. The furniture is solidly constructed, with washable finish, made gay and attractive by colorful Danish designs. Notice the amusing paper, with one wall left plain so that pictures can be changed with changing tastes.

FURNITURE AND DECORATIONS FOR CHILDREN

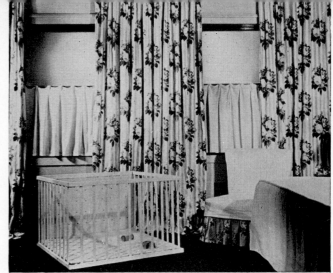

A SOLUTION FOR THE NURSERY-IN-BEDROOM PROBLEM

When the nursery must be part of your bedroom one solution is to curtain off a corner by installing slotted moldings on the ceiling with special traverse tape-fixtures as shown here. These allow curtains to be drawn when desired and they come with moldings which curve around corners making a complete little room of the section set aside for baby's equipment. An alcove is better still, but the attractive possibilities of a corner arrangement are shown in the pictures above—two views of the same room. A slotted molding is used on the ceiling, and also around the crib allowing the chintz flounce to be detached easily for washing. An over-blouse slip cover for the chair protects the chintz and is charming in the same fabric used for ceiling partition-curtains and door drapery. Cutouts from the chintz are appliquéd on bed spread and door curtain, also pasted in a design on the walls and on a chest of drawers with conveniently divided top. One small chest flanked by twin cupboards or shelves could be substituted for this special piece of nursery furniture. The picture at the right shows the other side of the room where a closely related chintz pattern in a larger design is used for draw-curtains over windows with short sash-style glass curtains. Notice the play pen which has one side covered for protection against drafts.

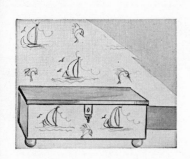

At lower left is a charming modern group of three pieces assembled as a unit for a child's room. With their simple lines and peasant design pieces like this could be made at home and decorated with free-hand painting, stencils or cutouts. At upper left the same pieces are shown in plain enameled finish, with contrasting color for the drawers. The shabby old kitchen table (center right) was made into the useful attractive nursery table just below it with very little work and almost no expense. The sawed-off legs are painted Chinese red. The rest is white enamel with a Bermuda blue border around the edges of the top and a wavy red line with two rows of blue dots along the sides. Alphabet, numbers, and amusing figures complete the decoration. If you are crowded for space you can cut down and decorate an old bridge table which can be folded and put away. There is hardly any limit to the cutting-down possibilities of full-size furniture to nursery scale, and for growing youngsters it is often wiser to save on these earlier pieces and buy new things when they can be on a more permanent size basis. The sketches illustrate possibilities of decals or cutouts for nursery walls and furniture.

linoleum is excellent, also many washable composition wallboard or plastic finishes. Floors are best in linoleum or composition flooring which will not be harmed by water and can be easily washed. Wood floors in a nursery are more serviceable when they are painted and protected by waterproof varnish. Washable rugs should be kept in place by rug cushions to prevent accident.

When the child is old enough to have more variety in his surroundings, you can begin really dressing up the room. This will probably include stencils or cutouts or figured paper on the walls, but remember to keep them washable. Many children love decorated ceilings which they can see when they are lying down, and there are many papers specially designed for walls and ceilings of rooms for children of various ages. These come in washable finish and in a wide variety of designs—story book characters, favorite friends in the animal kingdom, flowers, birds, airplanes, cartoons, peasant motifs—the list is endless. Let them choose what they like, and always buy a little extra for repairs and also for cutouts which they can make themselves and paste on their furniture or on the screen they have taken over from their infant nursery.

If floors are plain, stencils and cutouts can be used there, too, or you can buy composition floorings in patterns specially designed for children's rooms. (See Chapter 10.)

Furniture: All nursery furniture should be sturdy, compact, easily cleaned and free from dangerous protruding corners or sharp edges. Paint or enamel in a hard finish is usually best, but make sure it is not lead paint. Young children often try to cut their teeth on a piece of furniture and there is danger of lead poisoning.

The crib which succeeds the early bassinet may be bought in a style which allows converting later into a small bed which will carry over until the child is large enough for a regular bed in small scale. Some quite large children need a bed with crib-rails to keep them from crawling out, and these can be bought with detachable rails for later use. There are charming designs in this type of bed in French Provincial styles, also Early American as well as contemporary styles.

Furniture should be arranged so that there is plenty of free floor space for games and toys. Adequate storage space must be provided for all clothing, toys, games and equipment—and it must all be where the child can reach it. Low shelves, with easily opened chests, cupboards and drawers can be built in, or bought in units, or made at home.

Provisions for Activities: Every child's room should have a large low play table with addition later of

The photographs in this group comprise three views of the same room, all shown because of the exceptional charm of this nursery-playroom and suggestions which could be taken from it for working out at home. In the picture above are several interesting features. Wall paintings are done on panels with a background in the same soft pastel blue used for the painted sections of the walls. The double bed with its quilted cotton spreads and chintz pillow covers has a removable partition and heavy pulley ropes by which it can be lifted bodily up against the ceiling when more floor space is needed for play. (The mechanism for this is safely out of reach of children's hands.) The floor is painted a dark blue, spattered in white and decorated with large white-painted circles spattered with pale blue. The charming little tea table and chairs shown here are made from salvaged soda-

something to be used for a desk. A dado made of slate or washable composition not only protects the wall but provides an outlet for the drawing and writing urge. The wall above the dado provides an attractive background for a stenciled or painted or cutout border, in frieze effect, carrying the child's favorite story characters cartoon-style around the room, or for purely decorative designs.

Wallpaper friezes for children's rooms also come in a great variety of colors and designs and are excellent to use above the dado. A molding ledge topping the dado makes a good place to keep pencils and crayons. A cork section could have large sheets of water-color paper thumb-tacked to it for more ambitious art projects. This panel could be moved up on the wall later and framed for a pin-up board, while the dado could be painted.

You do not need to buy a complete outfit of nursery furniture, either for the new baby or for a child's room. Kitchen tables, chests and chairs may be painted and decorated for use of anyone taking care of the child. Adequate cupboard space and good work-table top are both provided by some of the utility bases sold with kitchen equipment. Old furniture may be remodeled, or inexpensive pieces may be found in the unpainted furniture departments of the stores.

COMPACT NURSERY-BEDROOM FOR TWO YOUNGSTERS

This light, cheerful room is keyed to children's comfort, and carefully planned for their convenience. Good light is insured by the wide window, and by fluorescent wall lamps for reading in bed. A dark dado minimizes inevitable finger marks on the wall; the white string rug, effective against a dark red linoleum floor, can be easily washed. The table desk is large enough for two. Neatness is encouraged by the amusing clothes hangers, and by storage units beneath the window.

DOUBLE ROOM SUGGESTIONS FOR YOUTHFUL NEEDS

The one-room apartment shown above makes use of a sleeping device which would be most useful in a bedroom-study for two young people or older children. The modern accordion-type doors would hide the sleeping bunks, as they do here when pulled in front of them, and provide additional closet space instead of the kitchenette arrangement shown. In the cheerful room below, designed for two boys, the simple appropriate furniture is both sturdy and attractive. Smartly dark wall treatment is made practicable by the flood of light from window-walls at one side of the room. Use of orange-red combined with the light rug color and boldly pat-terned wallpaper provides dramatic interest.

THREE VIEWS OF A CHARMING
NURSERY PLAYROOM

fountain equipment cut down and enameled in soft white. Gay slip covers with frilled trimmings of plain blue are in crisp glazed chintz—pink and white on blue—with a dogwood design. Notice the circus theme carried out in bed lamps as well as in pictures. The view (upper right) shows the blue and white striped wallpaper used on two walls and across the ceiling to suggest a circus tent. This treatment would be very good for a too square room, giving it more pleasing proportions. The cupboard is made up of two separate pieces and its simple lines could be easily followed in home construction. Glazed chintz makes a slip cover for the lamp and for an old boudoir chair reclaimed for adult comfort. Green ivy, colorful toys and pictures provide accent notes for the room. In the right photograph the striped ceiling is shown. There is a light in the horn held by the

monkey on the trapeze. A third cabinet combines with four shelf units (placed on two bases) to frame a large smartly plain blackboard with crayon shelf below. Twin tables put together with a double-drawer case in the middle to provide desk space for two children could just as well be made from a long kitchen table with legs cut down. Blue and white paint, chintz cushions and heavy white cotton cords dress up round cheese boxes used both for seats at the desk and for storage. A touch which would delight a child is the clown riding the globe on the bookcase. This room demonstrates that imagination is the principal ingredient needed to turn out a delightful room for children. If you haven't a carpenter in your family you can assemble cabinets, shelves and tables from inexpensive unpainted wood items in the shops and finish them with washable enamel.

SIMPLE COMFORT FOR THE GROWING CHILD

The room seen below in two views was furnished for a new baby, then adapted to the needs of the young child at very slight expense. Pink and white color scheme became yellow, green and beige, with Chinese red accents. Substitution of a bed for the crib was the only major alteration. Addition of a corner-shelf-desk, table, and a few accessories completed the transformation.

TRANSITION IN THE NURSERY

The room below is designed to adapt itself to the changing needs of the daughter of the household over a period of several years. Notice the studio bed with its built-in framework of shelves, and other pieces of simply designed sturdy furniture. A padded box under the window provides extra seating as well as useful storage. The colorful linoleum floor is warm and easily kept clean, and a soft shaggy rug by the bed adds a note of comfort. Parchment-linoleum walls are attractive and cleanable. This room would do just as well for a boy, with few changes except window treatment and bed covering.

The converted attic room above would delight any masculine member of your family. Its colorful decorations combine with trim lines, convenience and comfort to create a restful haven in even the busiest household. The floor of waxed navy-blue linoleum with small soft gray shaggy rug is easy to care for as well as beautiful. The walls and ceiling are made of self-color insulating wallboard which needs no other finish. Its soft sky-blue color makes the room seem more cool, airy and spacious, while its surface is made doubly

attractive by white stars painted all over it at random and the impressionistic map painted in red and white on the window wall. For warmth and color against the cool background red has been used for mattress cover and cushions of the couch, for window draperies, and for the seat pad on the Windsor chair. The built-in desk with roomy drawers beneath is balanced by a built-in closet at the other end of the wall (not shown in picture). Note the shelves built in around the radiator and over the couch, also the convenient

WASTED ATTIC SPACE

storage drawers in the wooden box which forms a base for the couch. The globe on the book shelves is in soft green, which is used as an accent color. The decoration around the ceiling light carries a touch of red to relieve the severity of the plain white shade. A room like this can be built into almost any attic with very little expense or trouble. The wall sheathing comes cut to measure and is usually grooved in such a way that it can be put together with ease and accuracy even by a home carpenter.

CHAPTER THIRTY-THREE

How to Make Use of Attics, Basements

IF YOU LIVE in a house the chances are that your attic is used mostly for storage of things you will never need, your basement area occupied by heating equipment, shelves for canned goods, and possibly a laundry. Your family are probably more or less crowded in the living parts of your home, or at least you would like a little more space for healthful and profitable encouragement of many home activities. There are few houses in which a charming and comfortable extra room of some type would not be welcome.

The average attic or basement can be converted to fill these needs. The conversion may be done in a very inexpensive manner by your family itself over a period of time, or you may consider the results worth a real investment in materials and labor. Many suggestions given in this chapter are adaptable to either approach. New furniture and fittings have been specially designed by manufacturers for game and play rooms, but in most families the challenge of doing over and converting previously unusable furniture will add to the fun.

REMODELING ATTICS

The first step in converting an attic to greater usefulness is to go through the things you have stored there, sifting out everything that may be usable and putting them to work. Next sort the remainder and discard every item which cannot justify its being kept. You will undoubtedly discover that what you have left to be stored can be taken care of in the smaller storage space available under the eaves after you have put in partitions to convert the major floor area into one or more rooms. It will help to build in

BOOKS, MUSIC, GAMES, FLOWERS, ADD TO A CHEERFUL ATTIC ROOM

low shelving for labeled boxes and all small objects.

Heat Problems: The chief objection to using an attic for living purposes is usually too little heat in the winter and too much in the summer. The problem is partly solved by using insulating wallboards or panels to conceal rafters and build partitions. The insulating quality of the boards prevents overheating from the sun in hot weather and helps to retain heat in the winter. Used for both walls and ceiling, these are easily installed by attaching them to a framework of crating-lumber nailed to rafters and studs. Composition boards come in a wide variety of finishes adaptable to any type of decorative effect. (See Chapter 7.)

If possible extend your heating pipes to the attic room. If this cannot be done there are small electric heaters in the form of small stoves or artificial fireplace grates. Sometimes it is possible to build the room around a chimney wall so that an opening can be made either for a small grate or a Franklin stove. In one house a chimney which went through the middle of the new room was made into an attractive feature as well as a source of heat. It was painted to match the walls, and an opening was made in one side to furnish draught for a Franklin stove. Tall book shelves were placed against the other three sides.

Floors: Attic floors are often good enough to be finished by painting, either plain or in decorative fashion. (See Chapter 10.) If you prefer you can use one of the many charming linoleums, or other composition floorings, cork or inexpensive novelty carpeting.

Lighting: If windows are inadequate and the room is to be used in the daytime, either make the most of the small openings by curtaining around instead of over them and using only light-reflecting colors and surfaces on walls and ceiling, or enlarge them by replacing with one of the many types of windows now available in inexpensive stock models. Many of these are specially built to provide insulation as well as light.

Varied Uses: These attic rooms may be used for bedrooms, sitting rooms, bed-sitting rooms, hobby, study or work rooms, dens or emergency guest rooms. One family made a complete little kitchenette apartment for convenience of visiting sons or daughters. If you use a converted attic room for a maid's room give it the same careful decorating attention you would give a guest room. Another possibility for attic space is to partition off the whole length and make it into a playroom or game room along the same lines as those suggested for basements.

REMODELING BASEMENTS

Rooms for entertainment, games, hobbies and special avocations may be built into basements and also into unused garage space, attics, spare rooms and enclosed porches, but of them all the average basement will prove most satisfactory. Many new

The dreary attic in the small picture was transformed into the pleasant room at right with very little expense and trouble. Composition board applied over roof rafters and studs is painted in soft beige and green. Pre-decorated composition board made the end walls and the built-in storage spaces. Beveled joints were used on the walls, stock molding strips painted in a soft henna to cover other joinings. Henna paint lines the shelves and is used for the padding on the built-in window seat. The old floor is painted a soft dark brown. Rug, bed spreads and cushions in tones of blue-green complete the colorful ensemble with touches of white. The combination living room and bedroom shown at left illustrates use of knotty pine grooved paneling (or wallboards in knotty pine finish) for building a room into a dormered attic. A two-toned wall-and-ceiling finish, with scalloped border matching scalloped window cornices, gives individuality to the room. The wood of the simple furniture is in soft natural finish harmonizing with the darker wood tone in the background. Fabric designs show how various remnants, or leftover drapery fabrics, can be combined so long as their colors harmonize and designs are not too obtrusive. In this case soft tones in the sturdy wall-to-wall carpeting on the floor help to tie the various fabrics together while tones in the braided rug repeat their colorings. Flowers are part of the room decoration, and pin-up lamps provide additional light over the couch. These useful fixtures are hung on the wall with picture hooks, their wires connected with the nearest base outlet.

BEFORE-AND-AFTER ATTIC

houses have the basement planned for easy converting into a game room and in recent years this term has come to include practically all informal entertaining done by any members of the family.

Walls: If you are remodeling your basement you will probably have to wall off the sections used for heating and laundry purposes and face the walls and ceiling of your game room with composition boards, wood or simulated wood. If the walls are plastered brick you may need only whitewash or special masonry paint, but the average basement requires more than this for year-round use. Walls and ceiling are often damp and too crude in appearance to make an attractive room. Also plumbing and heating pipes usually need to be concealed.

False walls and partitions are easily built on 2 x 4 wood studding to give you the dimensions you want, cover up any unsightly objects and allow easy building in of shelves and storage spaces. In case of dampness you must be sure to waterproof walls and ceiling by special masonry paint before erecting studding or applying wall-finishing materials. Choose wallboards or wood facings with insulating and moisture-resistant qualities. These are no more expensive than other types and will give much better service in a basement. For details about wall and ceiling finishes see Index.

Floors: You may have a cement floor which is good enough to be marked off in flagstone effect or other designs and painted with one of the new special paints for cement floors. When these finishes are waxed they give the effect of tile and may be very effective. If the floor is damp, asphalt floor coverings are advisable as these are impervious to moisture. Otherwise any flooring material may be used such as wood, cork, linoleum, etc. For active games and dancing waxed wood, linoleum and cork are best.

Lighting: Windows in basements are almost always small, and darkened by being set below the surface of the earth with only a small excavation for light. You can help remedy the daylight situation by making larger excavations outside and using curtains inside which do not shut out any light. Translucent glass block partitions between game room and laundry or heating unit may also help solve the lighting problem. One necessity will almost certainly be the installing of additional electric wiring with outlets to take care of adequate night lighting for all centers of interest or activity in the room. These are easily added if you are putting up new partitions or wall facings. If you are not building anything in, be sure that the extra wiring is carried around walls in safe non-conducting plastic casings and connected with floor plugs to eliminate necessity for using dangerously long extension cords.

Storage: In refacing your walls and ceiling be sure to allow for storage space of all equipment which is not decorative or is only used occasionally. Closets for extra folding chairs and tables, game boards, children's toys and work materials should be made with plenty of shelves and hooks. Build in extra closets here for outdoor game and sports equipment of all kinds used by the family, with special racks and compartments to keep them in order. These would include such things as fishing tackle, hunting gear, golf bags, skates, also equipment for baseball, football, tennis, croquet, etc.

Hobbies: If there is space enough, and you have a camera enthusiast in your family, build in a small dark room. A carpentry bench in one corner with cupboards and shelves built into the corner and special lighting fixtures is a very useful addition. Decorated screens around this corner would make the room entirely festive on special occasions. Don't forget a "reading corner" with comfortable chairs, good light, and shelf space for book-minded members of your family.

Bar Equipment: For adult entertaining a bar is important whether you serve real drinks or only soft drinks and refreshments. If there are children, let them have one end of the room with low shelves and special closets for their toys and a miniature "milk bar" for themselves and their guests. Building your larger bar into a recess made by false walls on each side of it will give you space for dish cupboards, food storage and a small sink, all behind closed doors, with a locked compartment if desired.

Basement Cooking: Here, as in the attic, it may be possible to open a chimney and install a fireplace. Do this if possible. It may be very simply and inexpensively finished as to mantel and facing and nothing adds more to good cheer than an open fire. If you can do this, keep the fireplace in harmony with the style of your decorations and equip it for broiling, corn-popping, etc. If the fireplace is impossible, a small stove, electric grill or charcoal grill should be provided for barbecue picnic meals or midnight snacks.

Decoration: As for decoration this is one room in the house where you can try anything in the way of color and design. Be as gay as you like with paint, paper and fabric. But don't be drab. This room is not for resting, but for amusement and activity. Many special papers are designed for use around the bar as well as for gaiety in the rest of the room. It's a wonderful place for indulging your fancy for cutouts, stenciling and free-hand painting. If you have any budding artists or cartoonists in the family this is a good place to let them have free rein. Colorful maps in large scale, easy to follow, are attractive wall decorations. Whenever you get tired of the decorations you can always change them. A framed cork "pin-up" board is both useful and amusing.

Furniture: With the exception of special game equipment, furnishings are often made up of pieces

BASEMENT RETREAT—KEYED TO COMFORT

A room especially adapted to relaxation and entertainment, like the one above, may be in a reclaimed basement or anywhere in a house or apartment where a room is not needed for its original purpose—a spare bedroom, for example, or a "white elephant" dining room. This picture illustrates a combination den, library, living, game and hobby room, with emphasis on masculine appeal. The cannon, the crossed swords on the ivory-painted brick chimney breast, and other accessories all indicate an interest in things military. Below the book shelves are storage spaces for papers or entertainment essentials. The walls are of mellow pine, the low comfortable arm chairs are upholstered in bright green sailcloth. Rectangles of green and white linoleum provide a floor which is attractive and at the same time useful for table-tennis, dancing, or other social activities. The low table is set for a friendly game. Lamp shades of red and white stripes provide the necessary bright note in a complementary color scheme of green and white with red for accent.

The amusing "Gilbert and Sullivan" bar room (right), with its Victorian air, provides both refreshment and music for guests in the basement game room glimpsed through the doorway. The color scheme of black and turquoise is enlivened by the gay turquoise and white of the canopy. Ball fringe and accessories are in keeping with the period, and the floor design of notes from a Gilbert and Sullivan opera provides an unusual touch of drama. Pictures from the operas on the walls help carry out the theme.

salvaged from the rest of the house. This is entirely satisfactory provided you remember two things—everything must be comfortable, durable, keyed to relaxation, and decorated so that the miscellaneous pieces are brought together into harmony. This can be done by means of paint, upholstery, remodeling and slip covers. (See Index for details.) Eliminate any object which impedes traffic or catches dust, unless it is absolutely necessary. With most families a radio and phonograph are "must" equipment for music and dancing. If you have an old upright piano your new room is an excellent place for it. Paint or decorate shabby pieces of musical equipment and add a new life of usefulness to their past. If rugs are used, have them small enough to be rolled up easily and put out of the way.

BEFORE-AND-AFTER BASEMENT

This all-purpose room was reclaimed from the dreary basement shown in the little picture above. The walls were plastered and oaken beams installed for a rustic effect, but less expensive composition wallboard could have been employed just as effectively. Asphalt tile in marbleized finish makes a colorful floor in which brown, gold, blue and red predominate. The stairway was remodeled with easy-to-install stock fixtures, and a real storage closet was built in behind shelves and service bar. A dining table with comfortable chairs and bench is conveniently placed between the service bar and a cooking grill built into the corner. This is gay with red brick used for lining, trimming, and serving shelf. Shelf linings and stair rises are painted red, while the upholstery combines blue, red and off-white with a soft mellow brown like the wood tones. The pipes on ceiling and walls were hidden by beams, and beams were placed around the ugly post in the middle with additional seating provided around it. Wrought-iron fixtures, lamps and all other accessories are harmonious with the room. Flooring like this, which is moistureproof, is comparatively inexpensive even with decorative insets which are cut and ready to install.

GILBERT AND SULLIVAN PROVIDE THE THEME

ALCOVE REFRESHMENT BAR IN THE BILLIARD ROOM
ABOVE COULD BE DUPLICATED IN A DINING ROOM

The carefully planned kitchen above has every kind of up-to-the-minute labor-saving device hidden behind its sleek exterior. The automatic electric stove, conveniently placed between the dinette and the sink, is supplemented by an electric toaster and an electric broiler; it has its own special light, and plenty of table space for use in preparing and serving foods. The serving counter which separates the dinette from the kitchen is made doubly convenient by the

CHAPTER THIRTY-FOUR

Efficiency and Beauty for Kitchens

MODERN KITCHEN

cupboard below, with doors opening on both sides for ease in putting dishes away. Gaily striped draw-curtains at the window above the sink pick up the colors of the pattern in the linoleum on the floor.

SCIENCE AND ART have joined hands to make the American kitchen of today a combination of beauty and utility undreamed of only a few years ago. Along with this has gone a contemporary trend toward making kitchens attractive and livable as well as efficient. The illustrations in this chapter demonstrate how really easy it is to achieve your ideal in the way of a kitchen without burdensome expense.

Whether it is large or small the most important thing about a kitchen is that it should provide working and storage space so arranged that the least possible effort is required in cooking, serving and cleaning. Kitchens are built in every size and shape but no matter what type yours may be you can find a way to arrange the necessary equipment for maximum working efficiency. If you are in doubt when you are buying new equipment you will find there are a number of manufacturers of kitchen furnishings who provide a planning service free. They will look over your floor dimensions and their engineers will report to you the best arrangement for your special problems and floor space. Lighting and wiring are important. They will advise you about that, too. (See Chapter 37.)

It is not difficult to work out your own plans if you follow a few key principles. Every kitchen should contain three centers of operation: (1) A food storage center which includes the refrigerator, cupboards for condiments and non-perishable foods, with special containers for vegetables, bread, etc. Here, also, should be located utensils used in storing and preparing food. If possible locate this unit near an outside door which makes stowing away of foods from market or delivery easy and quick. (2) The sink and cleaning center should be surrounded with

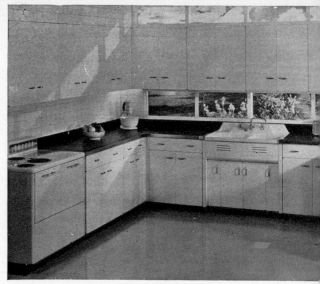

LIGHT, AIR, AND A VIEW MAKE A CHEERFUL KITCHEN

The kitchen at right above was remodeled from a conventional room (not shown) in which two separated windows took up valuable wall space and equipment was scattered at intervals around the room. Here it is shown made over into a compact U-shaped working unit by the use of composition board for enclosing the sink, building in cupboards and resurfacing walls and ceiling. Enamel-tile effect in soft peach is used for walls, harmonizing with linoleum in deep peach color on the floor. Black linoleum for counter tops and baseboards provides effective contrast for cupboards enameled in an off-white glossy finish. Glass is charmingly employed in panels above and below a bank of cupboards, allowing plenty of light. The upper one provides a sky panorama, while the lower windows frame gardens outside. The cost of installations like this is surprisingly low. At left is shown an L-shaped arrangement of kitchen working centers and the use of louvred glass both in cupboard doors and entrance door. Translucent glass-block panels which are not transparent are very useful for partitioning off kitchen space from other rooms without shutting out light. A waist-high or shoulder-high partition of glass block or louvred glass can also be used to create a small dinette.

enough storage space for everything used at this point. (3) The cooking center should have space for all the utensils and dishes necessary for actual cooking within easy reach from the stove.

Arrangement: The ideal arrangement for a kitchen is to have the equipment lined up along three walls in a U-shape so that refrigerator, sink and stove are connected by an imaginary triangle (called the "triangle of efficiency") with as nearly as possible equal sides and the points at the three centers of activity. If you have a kitchen in the shape of an L your triangle will be different in proportion, but you can keep the same relationship between working units. One very good solution is to place your sink across a corner between stove and refrigerator.

Many small kitchens have equipment ranged along two walls in a long narrow room, or there may be only space for equipment on one wall. Still try to keep the efficiency relation between units. If you have a very large kitchen the wall space would undoubtedly provide much more storage and working space than you need, while the triangle arrangement would involve long walks back and forth across the floor. Here the best solution is to divide the floor space by locating equipment at right angles to one wall at the point where it will make a U-type arrangement just large enough for your needs. The

rest of the room can be used for a dinette or breakfast room, a hobby room for someone in the family, a sewing room, or a playroom where an eye can be kept on the children while you work.

The amount of working counter space you have will depend upon the size of your room. A good rule is to plan for as much as you can fit in by streamlining all your lower kitchen units in a continuous, closely fitted together arrangement with all tops level at a convenient working height. If they are stock model units you may have a space at the end or between two cabinets where they do not fit exactly into your wall space. Utilize this by filling in the top with a board and building a rack below for trays.

Apply some of the principles of mass-production efficiency to your own kitchen. The first thing you will want to work out is an arrangement which will place all necessary material within reach of your hands while you are standing at any one of the working centers in your kitchen.

One way to achieve this is to apply the system you can see in any carpenter's shop—the large work surface. For you this will probably be thirty-two to thirty-six inches from the floor. Add to this a pull-out shelf sturdy enough to use for beating and chopping at the best height for those processes, five or six inches below the work shelf; also a narrow shelf on

NEW KITCHENS FROM OLD WITH THE AID OF UP-TO-DATE STORAGE UNITS

The three rooms on this page show how kitchens can be transformed from dreary depressing spots to efficient work rooms, charming in their own right. The dark, gloomy room above required comparatively little basic alteration to make it over into the attractive kitchen shown. A prison-like window above the sink was cut down to the sink, providing a view for anyone working there. An inset panel light installed above it takes care of after-dark activities at the sink. A panel of decorative wallboard in tile effect at the back of sink and counter, linoleum flooring and counter surface (with efficient built-in storage units) complete the transformation. The kitchen in the center had a modern stove and plenty of light but everything else was drab and inconvenient. Here metal was used to top the new storage units and for the sink. Marbleized linoleum made a smart new floor and streamlined cupboards replaced the old-fashioned inaccessible storage units. The refrigerator was moved to the proper spot to make an L-shaped working arrangement. Again a special lighting panel is set in above the sink. The makeshift kitchen at bottom required a little more doing over to make it into a streamlined room with metal sink and counters, attractive walls papered above a wall dado and linoleum floor. In renovating your kitchen don't overlook the advantages of modern metal finishes which require no scouring to keep them clean and shining. Some housewives like one counter near the stove in metal, one in linoleum and one in wood. Among woods, laminated maple is a favorite choice.

the wall between the working surface and the cupboards above which will take care of all the small things you need for your activities at that particular counter. Between the shelf and the counter provide racks and hooks for knives, spoons, measuring gadgets, etc.

If you have enough counter space divide it up so that all baking supplies and equipment are at the spot where you have the best surface for rolling out dough. Set aside another space near the refrigerator for salad mixing. Unless your kitchen is very small you will find it is a great labor-saver to duplicate constantly used supplies and articles in various locations. A can opener attached to the wall at each opposite side of the room will save many trips back and forth.

Special Conveniences: All-metal sinks are worth investing in if you can manage that in your budget. There is no more chipping or scouring. A damp cloth wipes them clean. The new double sinks arranged for dishwashing without a pan are time-savers. Faucets placed high and at one end of the sink prevent many accidents to fragile dishes. A shelf on the wall half-way between your storage cupboards and the part of the counter set aside for serving is a great help. Make it wide enough for your dessert dishes, coffee-serving paraphernalia, etc.

Don't overlook the convenience of attractive hanging shelves in glass or wood for handy storage of small supplies. Also, a couple of old cheese boxes painted and decorated make attractive trays or wall shelves for spices and condiments. A bathroom cabinet with a mirror provides first-aid remedies and a place for make-up materials. A child's slate hung on the wall with a slate pencil attached is an easy way to keep daily track of supplies, menus, etc. Oilcloth covers for your cook books and a special shelf for them will save both the books and your time.

KITCHEN STORAGE

Your chief concern in the question of kitchen storage should be to have as much of it as possible. The next consideration is to have it as conveniently arranged as the space will allow. In many a crowded kitchen, where everything is behind something else, there are many square feet of unused space on walls or in corners which could easily be converted into usefulness. Most shelves are too deep and too far apart. The answer to this is to have adjustable shelves if possible, and have shallower cupboards for everything except the large articles.

If you must use the regulation cupboards you can have half-width shelves built in between the wide ones for all the smaller dishes. You can partition off

A GROUP OF KITCHENS

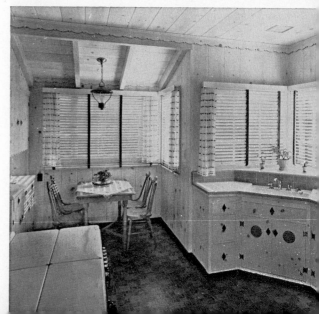

CHEERFUL, HOMELIKE, AND WORKABLE

For those who like hominess in their kitchens—something a little more reminiscent of the old-fashioned country kitchen—the rooms in this group are designed. Working units are as compact and efficient as those in the modern kitchen above, but these are differentiated by softer finishes and living-room touches. In the room at upper left walls and door are covered with light pine wall linoleum, with mahogany linoleum for counter tops and back-splash. Twin benches by the fireplace—made from an old railroad-station bench—turn the fireplace area into a dinette when the drop-leaf table under the window at left is rolled between them. The table is fitted with large wooden castors for moving. Light beamed wood ceiling harmonizes with the walls, also with the floor of golden brown linoleum. The homelike kitchen at lower left is finished throughout in knotty pine. The wood is blond white, with accents in the kitchen in red. The flood of sunlight controlled by Venetian blinds, the interesting corner-sink arrangement, the wood ceiling with scalloped cornice—all help to make this an unusually attractive room. Wood finishes have personality and versatility. They may be stained in light natural tones, partially hidden by a thin paint coating or "wash," or completely covered by enamel. When lacquered or dull-varnished, knotty pine is cleaned easily with a damp soapy cloth. The third room (left) solves a problem many a mother encounters—where to put an active child for play when she is absorbed in kitchen duties. In this original design the bay window is made into a nursery "annex." Over-draperies of dress fabric are hung high, with short sheer sash curtains to admit abundant sunlight. Shelves are installed for toys, and wooden

gates carrying nursery-rhyme characters separate the play area from the rest of the room. Light in the bay window is provided by an ordinary round white glass bowl fixture painted to resemble the "man in the moon." Cabinets and shelves are attractively decorated above a convenient dining shelf at the left. Linoleum floor and enameled walls provide the background for this pleasant, livable workroom. Gaily decorated kitchens may be very modern, or they may draw their inspiration from provincial Europe as in the room above. Here, decoration is centered about a dinette built in across the corner, but quaintness is given to cabinets also by stripes of bright-colored cellophane adhesive tapes bordering doors and drawers. A door of tongue-and-groove wooden planks is appropriately fitted with old iron hinges. Double Dutch draw-curtains at the windows control the light and their gay borders carry out the peasant theme. Floor linoleum is laid in a simulated rug design with bright colored motifs on a neutral ground. The dinette table is a curving shelf nailed to the wall with a smaller shelf above it for radio and potted plants. An old jeweler's clock dressed up in a coat of paint and decals is flanked by a pair of old porch lanterns and framed by a wallpaper border. Rush-bottomed chairs are painted red and decorated with decals. Flowering plants on the window sill, and decals on a home-made shoe box below, add more color to this cheerful corner. The room at lower right brings color in from outside by means of the wide windows. Bright curtains and blooming plants on the sill complete the window picture. Notice the popular rounding counter-bar providing dinette facilities. This is often used in modern kitchens to mark the dividing line between dinette and kitchen. The room at lower left has a dado of composition board tiling in Chinese red, a color repeated in counter and table tops, chair seats, Venetian blind tapes and open shelves. Walls and cabinets are white enamel. A row of red apple decals may be used to cover nailheads in applying the composition board to the walls.

some of the space with sheets of wallboard to make "filing cabinets" similar to record cabinet divisions for platters, shallow dishes, baking pans, lids, etc. These partitions can also be installed in deep drawers to increase their usefulness. For storing kitchen linens, knives and forks and many small gadgets, a cabinet fitted with shallow sliding trays is a great convenience. Next best thing would be shallow drawers. For knives, forks, spoons, etc., have partitions built into these drawers or trays. For standing flat dishes safely at the back of a cupboard, nail a flat-type curtain rod along the shelf.

If you have a large enough kitchen you can build in a very useful closet for food supply storage. Even if it is not large it can be arranged to hold a great deal by being lined with ten- or twelve-inch shelves around three sides from floor to ceiling. This leaves space in the center for a permanent step-stool for easy reaching to upper shelves. These doors, as well as all other kitchen closet or cupboard doors, can be utilized for racks and small railed shelves which will take care of many small articles, jars, cans, etc.

If your kitchen is crowded you may be able to convert the broom closet into a convenient food storage cupboard and build in a long, shallow broom closet against a wall outside the kitchen door, or even on a porch. Another interesting use of hall space is to build a low, shallow cupboard with shelves for parking empty bottles which are to be returned. The shelf above makes a convenient place for resting shopping bags while you are unloading them. For more storage suggestions see Chapter 36.

DECORATING KITCHENS

Make your kitchen decorations as bright and as cheerful as you can but work it out in colors that are not too brilliant or aggressive—except for accent notes. For backgrounds cool, soft tones such as green and blue will make the room seem larger and create a restful atmosphere. Yellow tints from pale cream to maize will make it look bright and sunny. Peach, apricot or pale salmon will impart a warm cheerful tone.

If the kitchen is very small the woodwork is usually painted to match the walls either exactly or in a slightly lighter or darker shade. In larger rooms, or those where more decorative snap is desired, the woodwork may be done in a contrasting color—apple green, for example, with cream walls, or a soft green-blue with apricot.

Finishes for Kitchen Walls and Floors: Plain plaster walls with enamel finish are the least expensive and are always attractive. A well-equipped kitchen has a kitchen exhaust pan over the oven which pre-

KITCHEN EFFICIENCY DEPENDS ON PLANNING, NOT ON SIZE

Wider use of glass in kitchens is a modern contribution to efficiency and charm in one of the most important parts of the home. Above, a typical rectangular kitchen was transformed into a room planned for pleasant living as well as convenient working by replacing a solid wall at the end of the room with a diagonal line of tall glass doors. These can be thrown open in summer to include the porch made from the rest of the floor space. Adjustable-top wheeled tables arranged for a view of the garden can be rolled out onto the porch for outdoor dining. They can also be adjusted to the height of the sink for use when needed as extra counter space. A waxed linoleum floor has a plain inlaid border attractively designed to follow the diagonal wall. The flood of light makes it possible to use a dramatic color scheme here in black, Chinese red and beige. Walls are black, also chair legs, Venetian blinds, linoleum cove-baseboards and linoleum counter tops. Red is used for ceiling, window frames, chair seats and pulls on the drawers which take the place of cupboards for pot and pan storage. Cupboards and drawers are finished in beige. Floor linoleum is beige with black and red design and red line setting off the border. Red flower shelves and pots filled with green vines are strikingly effective against the black walls. The modern contention that kitchens do not need to be large in order to be charming and efficient is demonstrated by the pictures on the facing page. The one at the top center is hardly more than a closet yet it is distinctly workable. A wooden "lunch counter" built out from the wall provides dining space, with stools which take up very little room. The paper on the wall with its pattern of squares is effective—and the squares are used for writing in specially interesting menus. The tiny kitchen at upper right has charm and style. It is not crowded or cluttered, because every inch of space is put to work. Slides pull out to make a dinette or a working surface. Comfortable chairs fold up to be put away when not in use. Walls, ceiling, cabinets and chairs are all in a

soft shade of cool, receding green to help push walls back. With this, dark blue linoleum is used for counter tops, splash boards and slides. Marbleized linoleum on the floor in a lighter blue is decorated with strong diagonal bands in darker blue and white—a device which helps make the room look larger. Red accents are in the glass-covered flower prints on upper cabinet doors and in artificial flowers arranged under mitered glass panels to frame the windows. Cupboard doors, without knobs, are opened by slipping the fingers into a recess under the frame. Inside the cupboard shelf space is increased by simple little wood platforms which divide the shelves into compartments on different levels for convenient storage of dishes in various sizes. Tilt-front bins under the cabinets provide extra storage for everything from bread to salvaged string. Even in this miniature kitchen a convenient double-size sink is provided, with full-sized stove and refrigerator and plenty of counter space. Below, three views of a "Pullman kitchen" picture another small room treated in a highly imaginative style. Stove and storage cupboards (center left) are flanked at the right by a novel vegetable-bin door (below), and by an alcove with camouflaged storage and sink units and dinette stools.

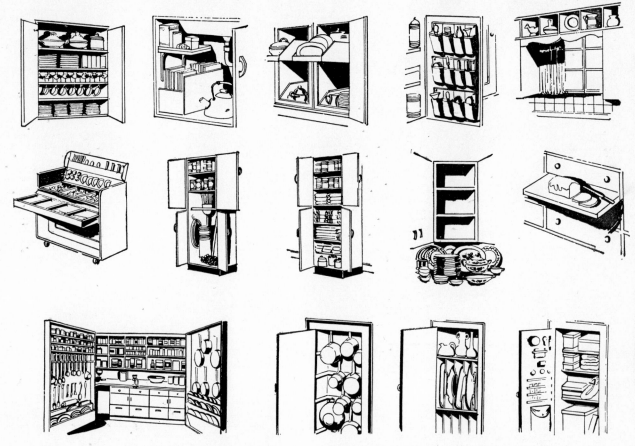

SUGGESTIONS FOR SIMPLE, EASILY INSTALLED LABOR-SAVING DEVICES

vents wall discoloration from grease and soot. This means that enamel will stand up very well even under long wear. Wallboard paneling with various types of hard surfaces, many of them in simulated tile effect, are suitable. Asbestos tile, genuine ceramic tile, vitreous glass tile—all of these are more expensive than paint or enamel but permanent and very easy to take care of. Structural glass brick which admits light is an increasingly popular newcomer in this last group of permanent finishes. Don't overlook it if you are remodeling. Used for inner partitions or semi-partitions it walls off space without cutting down light.

Linoleum and several varieties of washable paper provide colorful, durable and charming walls. To protect painted or papered walls behind stove or sink apply a panel of heat-resistant glass or transparent plastic; or use a decorative panel of moistureproof and fireproof wallboard.

Linoleum is the number one favorite for kitchen floors but there are many other materials which may be used. Any of the composition floorings are suitable; varnished cork is excellent because of its resilience underfoot; colorful ceramic tile (six inches square) makes an easy-to-install flooring which is not often used but is worth investigating. It is perma-

nent, shows no wear, needs no care except wiping up with a damp cloth, and comes in really wonderful colors. When this tiling is put down by being floated on a type of mastic (cement) which never hardens the mastic gives it a resilience which makes the floor comfortable to walk on or to stand on for hours at a time.

Window Treatments: Kitchen windows are usually needed for light and air. Venetian blinds are always desirable with or without curtains. If the room is sunny, roller shades should be double—one in a dark color for hot summer days. Draw-curtains may be used to control light, and in that case are usually the type known as Dutch curtains which can be manipulated separately top and bottom. Swinging bracket rods are often desirable. Glazed chintz is occasionally used for side draperies but curtaining is more often confined to crisp sheer fabrics, plain or ruffled. On the market today are innumerable curtains in made-up models showing much originality and ingenuity in color and design. The favorite background is white or cream with the color in embroidered dots and patterns, or in various kinds of trimming. Gingham is often most attractive. If windows are near a sink it is sometimes wiser to choose water-

LABOR-SAVING DINETTES MAKE HAPPIER HOUSEKEEPING

The breakfast nook at left is separated from the kitchen by open shelves at the end of the stove. Corner windows provide a flood of light for working efficiency, also cross ventilation with a kitchen window. Gay yellow—with soft blue for contrast, green and white for accent—makes the room a cheerful place for breakfast even on the gloomiest day. On bright summer days, a green awning can be lowered to shut out glare.

The dinette below is planned to serve many household needs, in addition to providing a pleasant setting for fam-

ily meals. Open shelves have storage space below where various equipment can be stored when not in use. Sturdy comfortable chairs and a long table solve the problem of evening homework space for youngsters, away from distractions of grownup conversation. They are equally useful to the housewife for sewing, mending, or writing, during daytime between-meal periods. The bright coral, off-white and green color scheme is cheerful by daylight or lamplight. Note the warm tones of the brick floor, waxed and easy to care for. A translucent glass window admits plenty of light, while screening the view from the street.

A REAL HOME-CENTER KITCHEN

A kitchen like this is literally the "heart of the home." Ample window space provides plenty of light, making possible the use of an overall blue background—floor, walls, woodwork, ceiling. Red for contrast, with white and green for accents, adds a note of gaiety to the restful blues. Black wrought-iron Colonial hardware, effective against the light paint of doors and cupboards, harmonizes with quaint lamps, colorful old dishes, a hooked rug, and mother-and-daughter rockers.

ADDITIONAL SUGGESTIONS FOR SIMPLE, EASILY INSTALLED LABOR-SAVING DEVICES

proof fabrics. If they are too close to the stove shirr them top and bottom to keep them from blowing.

Many people prefer no curtains in the kitchen and use other means of decorating. One attractive finish is to frame the tops and sides with ruffles on curtain rods. Another treatment is to use shaped pieces of composition board—a cornice or valance carried down both sides of the window and decorated to make a frame as for a picture. You will see various other ideas illustrated in this chapter.

Decorating with Paint and Paper: The kitchen is one of the rooms where you can give your imagination free play in devising decorations. You can have a Dutch kitchen, Mexican, French Provincial, Swedish, English, Colonial—all according to the way you dress it up. To get whatever atmosphere you desire use stenciling, wallpaper cutouts, or free hand painting. Choose characteristic motifs and apply them as borders on the wall, as panels on your cupboard doors, as spot decorations or borders on chairs or other furniture. You can even make borders around the ceiling and put a garland around your central light fixture.

If you are modern-minded you can use geometrical or impressionistic designs. Some people like lace doilies pasted on the inside of glass cupboard doors. One amusing kitchen was decorated by having colorful food pictures, with recipes underneath, photostated and blown up to fit the various panels of all the cupboard doors. Painted lines set them off with the effect of framing. So call upon your imagination and throw away your inhibitions when you begin to plan your kitchen decorations.

DINETTES AND DINING NOOKS

If you are fortunate enough to have space for a dinette, or even for a let-down table shelf, you can create a gay breakfast setting guaranteed to start the day right. Perhaps you have a butler's pantry which does not pay its way in service for the space taken up. Remove part of the wall and make it into a dinette opening into the dining room or into the kitchen— or both. A semi-enclosed dinette is much cheerier and more airy than when such a small space is entirely shut off from adjoining rooms. If it is large enough, you can reserve part of the space for storage cupboards. You will find a wealth of inspiration for planning dinettes or dining nooks from the rooms pictured in this chapter.

DRAMATIC CONTRAST IN DECORATION, AND UP-TO-THE-MINUTE

The bathroom above is equipped with many fittings designed for comfort as well as for streamlined beauty. On both shower and tub walls vertical rods are placed to lessen the very real danger of injury from slipping. A utility rack is fitted across the tub for essentials of bathing and make-up. These racks may be had in great variety and a wide range of prices. Here a mirror serves vanity purposes, at the same time providing a support for book or paper for the comfort of those who like to read and relax in the tub. Decorative curtains can be drawn across the tub and toilet alcove if desired. When space is available the modern practice of sepa-

rating the toilet from the rest of the room by enclosing it in some way, or installing it in a closet just outside, avoids delays and makes it possible to use the tub section as a dressing room. The stall-like partition enclosing this tub is a very useful device, its flat top providing a safe resting place for bath salts or bubble-bath preparations in decorative containers. Notice the deep flat window sills, which serve the same purpose. The wash basin has enough flat surface so that objects can be placed there for a few moments without danger of catastrophe, also convenient towel rods at each side. The table with shelves provides attractive storage for a supply of

CHAPTER THIRTY-FIVE

Points on Bathrooms

AMERICAN BATHROOMS have long been the envy of the rest of the world—yet in most homes they still leave room for improvement. Ideally every house should have a lavatory-toilet-powder room on the first floor in addition to the one or more bathrooms on the bedroom floor, but this is not always possible in practice. Where bedrooms have private baths it is not difficult to add dressing-room features which greatly enlarge bathroom usefulness. It is when several members of a family have to share the facilities of one bathroom that problems really become acute.

Architects and builders, cooperating with manufacturers, have come to the rescue of families in this situation with plans for a new type of bathroom. In the first place, these will be planned to utilize every foot of space. There will be adequate storage for towels and all other supplies, arrangements for sitting down at a dressing table or for bathing and dressing the baby.

Many of these plans call for extra walls and curtains which divide the room into four separate compartments—bathing, washing, dressing and toilet—each one accessible without disturbing the occupant of another compartment. Clever working-out of space and new types of translucent partition material make these bathrooms practical even in surprisingly small floor space. If you are planning a new home look into the possibilities of this four-way bathroom arrangement. If you cannot manage the innovation because of space or money limitations—or if you are remodeling an old bathroom—concentrate on methods for putting every foot of free space to work both on walls and floor.

UTILITY FEATURES

Developments in use of glass, plastics and composition materials have transformed the bathroom picture. The variety of materials, old and new, used for walls, dadoes and floors furnishes a wide range from which to choose, and suitable materials are available in almost any price bracket.

GADGETS FOR CONVENIENCE

fresh towels. Fluorescent light tubes flanking the mirrored door of the medicine cabinet are placed correctly for most effective lighting. In this case the daylight is also in the best location—facing those who use the mirror. For make-up or shaving the light should always shine in the face of the person looking into the mirror, not into the mirror itself. Venetian blinds are decorative, even without draperies, and admit light while protecting privacy. Notice the comfortable low stool for aid in dressing, the well-equipped manicure table, the unobtrusively flat scale for keeping track of weight. Plaid paper on the upper wall carries on geometrical theme.

Walls: The first requirement for bathroom walls is that they should be washable and moistureproof, at least up to the height of a dado or wainscot. Vapor-resistant enamel for woods or plaster, tile, linoleum, hard-surfaced washable wallboard and other composition materials, plastic finishes, special wall oilcloths and washable papers are all durable and easy to care for. Marble is used in luxury bathrooms, and glass in various forms is being introduced more and more into every type of room. Tile is the old standby, but is now more often simulated than real. Asbestos wainscot tiling with a baked-on enamel surface is easily nailed into place on the wall; also a compressed fiberboard, scored like tile and specially treated to resist moisture. In addition to plain linoleum there is a special linoleum tiling made up of small tiles easy to apply by spreading a special adhesive on the back and pressing them into place. Opaque white or colored glass, etched glass and mirror panels all make very attractive walls.

For the walls above the dado many washable papers are available which are inexpensive because of the small amount needed for the space. If you like plaster, you can paint walls and ceiling with vapor-resistant enamel. If you are doing a room over with wallboard there is a special plastic coating-plaster for use in bathrooms. Woodwork should always be finished with enamel, but not in too high gloss.

Floors: Tiling and linoleum are the two most popular bathroom floor materials. Both are durable, decorative and easy to clean. (For types of tiling see Chapter 10.) When either tiling or linoleum is used in matching designs on both walls and floor a very striking decorative effect may be created. New cement finishes and other floor plastics make attractive bathroom floors. Bathroom rugs, of course, should be washable. There are endless varieties to choose from, with some form of cotton as the leading contender for favor. Most popular rugs are chenille and string, with hooked, braided or rag rugs most appropriate in Early American settings.

Equipment: The trend in bathtubs is toward a flatter bottom with a broader rim which may be used as a seat while taking footbaths or bathing children. If you have no shower you can easily install one over the tub or in a separate enclosure if there is room. (See illustrations.) Modern tubs come in various shapes, some of them fitted across corners to save floor space.

Bathtubs, washbowls, toilets and porcelain fixtures come in various colors as well as white. All new metal fixtures are in metals which stay bright without polishing. Washbowls are larger and many of them have small drain-shelves at the sides for extra convenience. If you have one which leaves a gap between

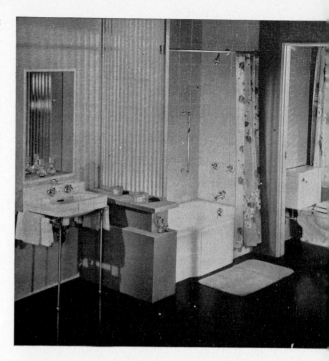

GLASS MAKES IMPORTANT CONTRIBUTIONS TO MODERN BATHROOMS

Glass plays a role which is highly functional as well as decorative in modern bathrooms and four different types of its usage are shown in the quartet of smart rooms on this page. You will notice that all but one have the very convenient side racks for towels attached to the washstand. In the bathroom at the bottom clear glass is used for a separate shower, easily installed in any room with sufficient floor space. In the room at top (above) a glass-block partition screens the tub from the rest of the room. In the

room above glass blocks are set into an outer wall to admit a flood of softly tempered light with no sacrifice of privacy. Note the fluorescent lights on either side of the mirror. At the bottom a fluted form of translucent glass makes a partition at the foot of the tub. A two-tiered storage cabinet between the glass partition and the washstand provides convenient shelf space. Notice the modern design in the wash bowl made with a double shelf behind the bowl. In this bathroom a small closet is utilized for the toilet.

itself and the wall, fill up the space with a glass shelf to provide counter space and to keep articles from falling on the floor at the back. There should be more than one washbowl if possible, or a special small round bowl for cleaning teeth.

Lighting: New types of fluorescent lighting are particularly useful in bathrooms when they are used for dressing and make-up purposes. There should be a central light snapped on by a switch at the door and not fumbled for over the washstand. In addition to that special make-up and shaving lights should be provided wherever needed. For further details and suggestions see Chapter 37. Many bathrooms are deficient in electric outlets. Any electric equipment such as shaving razors, curling tongs, heaters for the room or the baby's milk bottle, radios, clocks and sunlamps should be taken care of by conveniently placed outlets.

SPECIAL BATHROOM FITTINGS AND EQUIPMENT

Many a bathroom considered "too small" seems that way only because the space is not fully utilized. Examine your bathroom. You will find that enough shallow cupboards, shelves, closets (and possibly even drawers) could be built into or against the walls, fitted into corners, or filled in around stationary equipment to make the room as convenient, compact and workable as a ship's galley.

Bathroom Cupboards: Clever planning has been used to make many a bathroom an efficient aid to housekeeping. The one small medicine cabinet and conventional clothes hamper which make up most bathroom storage are inadequate even for the needs of one person to say nothing of a family. Is there space between the foot of your tub and the wall? If so, use it to build in a small closet with narrow shelves on one side and short clothes pole for hangers to take care of night-clothes and dressing gowns during the day. If this space is not available there may be a corner or a free wall section where a closet could be placed.

If you have an old-fashioned tub you can build a framework around it with doors which open to reveal storage space beside the sloping bottom of the tub large enough to take care of all your bedroom-section cleaning equipment. If there is space at either end build in ceiling-high closets. The lower section of one wall cupboard can be built with a door that opens out to serve as a clothes hamper. Study the equipment in the various bathrooms illustrated and see if there are not many features which could be duplicated in yours by means of wallboard or plywood. Also, look through the shops for new types

MAKING THE BEST USE OF SPACE
IN SMALL BATHROOMS
AND SUGGESTIONS FOR REMODELING

of double-duty bathroom furniture and equipment—for example, a clothes hamper with a front opening, drawer above, and shelf on top for toilet extras. You can buy many pieces in unpainted materials, decorate or paint them to match your color scheme or cover them with washable paper, linoleum, etc.

Bathroom Furniture: A stool or a small slipper chair is very useful, preferably covered with water-proof material to match your shower curtain. If you can possibly manage it you should build in or install a dressing table with a stool or chair which can be shoved under it if necessary and a good make-up mirror above it. A corner shelf or even a ten-inch board shelf supported by brackets on the wall, with an attractive skirt decoration, would serve this purpose very well. Bathroom scales and a waste basket are necessities rather than luxuries. Dress your waste basket up to match your other decoration unless you buy one in some of the lovely plastics which are used also for bath stools and other furnishings.

Two things are seldom adequately supplied in bathrooms—mirrors and towel racks. There should be enough racks to take care of all large and small towels and wash cloths without crowding—a separate rack for each person if possible. There are movable racks to be found in the stores, also rods which can be fastened to the wall by suction cups. Bathrooms are comparatively small rooms and mirror space

To glance at the attractive bathroom at left nobody would guess that it doubles for a laundry on occasion. With soft gray walls and ceiling, the rich red linoleum floor is very striking. Border stripes are in silver gray. Red is used for chair upholstery, bath mat, shower curtain, towel monograms and a band around the ceiling-light panel. A convenient suspended dressing table with a mirrored lid is fitted with sliding trays to hold creams, lotions, and all make-up necessities. As for the laundry angles—the towel rack becomes a clothes-dryer and washing equipment is revealed at the washstand. The built-in cupboard arrangement at the left conceals a small laundry tub next to the washstand, with a drawer below it for towels. Under the wash bowl is a tilt-front clothes hamper. A lid over the tub (when it is not in use) makes extra counter space. The medicine cabinet is double size with two mirrored doors so that one side can be used for ordinary bathroom necessities while the other holds washing powder, soap and other cleaning materials. The whole room is flooded with light from the recessed panel overhead. Less decorative than this plastic rack, but equally useful, is the type of clothes dryer which can be lowered from the ceiling by a rope and pulled up again after the clothes are hung. There are also folding floor racks which stand up or can be hooked over the shower-curtain rod by the base and hang upside down from there. Some of the colorful plastic racks or those made from glass and stainless metal are decorative enough to be left in the bathroom as towel stands when not needed for drying clothes. Notice the wide flat tub edge for comfort in bathing children and sitting on the edge of the tub in the process of dressing. Decoration is often all that is needed to make an unattractive bathroom gay and cheerful. Such a transformation is accomplished in the room above through wallpaper, pictures and drapery. Twin cabinets are fitted in at either side of the washstand, and a dressing table with a mirror at the left.

The "before" and "after" pictures at right tell an interesting story. Without any change in fixtures an out-of-date bathroom was transformed into an individual and very attractive room. A black marbleized linoleum floor with white pin stripes provided a foundation from which the room was built up. Painting the outside of the tub black against a black wall made its ugly lines practically disappear. White pin stripes on the walls, white brackets and vases harmonize with the draperies as well as the floor. A dressing-table shelf with plain black linoleum top, black Venetian blinds and lamp shades, black toilet and chair seats carry out the dramatic theme. Inexpensive white muslin with black braid stitched on for stripes makes draperies and skirts. Color is provided by bright bunches of variegated artificial flowers, with the same colors repeated in a bath mat. A black painted bird cage decorated with flowers is suspended over the old light globe. The clothes hamper is hidden beneath the dressing-table skirt. The use of artificial flowers here in bunches, and framing the dressing table mirror suggests the charm of having real live growing plants in a bathroom. A bird cage hung from the wall can be used for growing vines, blooming plants in small pots are charming on window sills or glass wall brackets. The imaginative treatment given the little bathroom here will doubtless suggest many ideas which you can apply to your own. The bathroom directly above demonstrates the informal charm of pine in soft light natural finish, or washed pastel color, used in a modern bathroom. Remodeling could be easily done with this workable wood, building in storage units and shelves wherever space allowed. Notice the small, compact wash basin with the convenient flat ledge at the back, and space-saving towel racks. The tub has a convenient rod which helps prevent slipping on the smooth porcelain of the tub.

makes them seem larger as well as increasing their convenience. If there is room for a deep triple mirror or a mirrored screen try to manage one; otherwise attach a full-length mirror panel to a wall or a door. A dressing-table mirror should be good in quality even if it is small. A separate compartment near the washbowl with a shaving mirror will be greatly appreciated by the man of the house. A small special cabinet for his use will please him too.

BATHROOM DECORATIONS

Make your bathroom as gay and colorful as you like, only remember not to clutter it up with too many strong colors. Unless it is unusually large such treatment will make it seem crowded and closed in. A two-color scheme is usually best. If a three-color scheme is preferred, use one of them for accent only. If the bathroom adjoins the bedroom select colors and decorations which will harmonize with those of the bedroom. Remember that all colored articles displayed, all colored fixtures, all mirror or picture frames must be considered part of the color scheme and harmonize with the background and furnishings. This includes monograms and decorations on towels, which should be in the accent color chosen. You will find suggestions for appropriate color schemes in descriptions of bathrooms in this chapter.

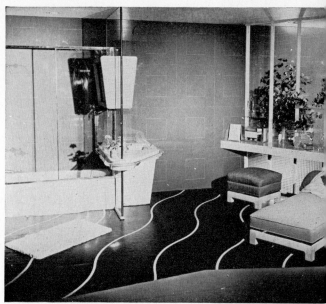

TWO UNUSUALLY INTERESTING BATHROOMS AND SOME DECORATING SUGGESTIONS

The bathroom in the upper left corner has twin lavatories flanking a dressing-table unit with linoleum counter top. Wide mirror panels over both lavatories seem to carry the window draperies straight around the walls. The smart suspended cabinets allow full spread to an attractive linoleum floor with center in dusty pink separated by a white strip from a mahogany-colored border. Coral linoleum covers the walls, and shower curtains match the draperies in a plaid pattern of turquoise, pink and white. Notice the fluorescent lighting above the mirrors. In the large bathroom directly above a very modernistic design incorporates a comfortable chaise longue and dressing-table stool with innovations in convenience. Walls are of bright blue vitrolite, the chaise is turquoise piled high with tawny orange and pink pillows, the stool is done in the same tawny orange. The tub has a ceiling-high glass partition at the end dividing a shelf for bath accessories on one side from a wash-basin unit on the other. A towel rack completely encircles both shelf and basin. Above, a two-way medicine cabinet is set into the glass with doors opening on one side toward the washstand and on the other side above the tub. At the left, mirrored doors conceal a toilet and a closet. Bleached oak, glass and mirror are used for dressing table and washstand, bleached oak for the furniture in definitely modern design. Against a charming marine wallpaper (in the picture at lower left) various plastic fittings are shown for bathroom use. Some of them are in transparent plastic used alone, others are smartly combined with underneath finishes in black or chromium. Just above a set of attractive shower fittings and towels dresses up a simple bathroom. These are made at home by appliquéing cutout flower designs in graduated sizes on towels and shower curtain. The motifs can be cut from washable glazed floral chintz or fast-color sateen-type cotton prints where flower, leaf and stem patterns can be separated from the over-all design. The appliquéing can be done by using the zigzagger attachment of your sewing machine. Plastic-coated fabrics are available for shower curtains which could be charmingly decorated in this way, and the colors can be matched in plastic shower-curtain rings.

Backgrounds are no longer confined to white or a few pale colors. All the various composition, tile, or linoleum fabrics for both walls and floor are designed in striking patterns and color combinations. Special patterns have been designed for bathroom wallpapers and also various types of cutouts and borders which may be used to brighten up a plain surface. Dadoes come in marbleized designs as well as tile. Special made-to-order inlaid designs can be worked out in linoleum for your walls as well as for your floor.

Fabrics: Fabrics designed for bathrooms are obtainable in many charming designs and textures. These are treated to resist steam and water and have many new long-wearing qualities. Follow the same rule as for other rooms when you are using patterned draperies. Flowered curtains for shower, window and dressing table are much more effective against a plain background. There are many fascinating waterproof and steamproof materials on the market in addition to the old favorite rubberized silk. Ordinarily it is better to use the same material for other draperies as that used for shower curtains. If this is not possible be sure that they harmonize closely. In draping bathroom windows remember that you can drape outside the window trim and conceal the too-narrow or too-small proportions often found in these windows. (See Chapters 13, 14 and 15.) Always include the rug and bath mat in your color scheme.

CHILDREN'S BATHROOMS

If you have a special bathroom for the children you are as fortunate as they are. Manufacturers have put out really wonderful equipment for children's comfort, and an adult bathroom is much easier to take care of without the additional items needed for children's convenience. For small children there are square tubs with two seats in opposite corners to make bathing a game. There are low toilets and special low washstands and cabinets. There are very attractive decorating schemes worked out with wallpapers and draperies, specially for young tastes.

If the children must share a grown-up bathroom there are many things you can do to make life easier for them as well as to encourage good habits. If you cannot install a special low washbowl with an undersize medicine cabinet and mirror you can at least build a sturdy step-stool for use with the washbowl. And you can have a small cupboard or chest of drawers or medicine cabinet placed low enough against the wall so that they can manipulate doors and keep their own supplies there. Low towel racks—and names on their towels—will encourage cleanliness.

BUILT-IN WARDROBE AND CHEST OF DRAWERS

The photograph above shows a very convenient built-in cupboard, storage and dressing-table arrangement which can be made of wood or composition board combined with plywood. Here the whole wall was enclosed with wallboard to create closets on each side of the partition. Instead of the drawers shown cupboard doors could be used in front of a bank of shelves or sliding trays. Shallow shelves provide the least expensive of all storage for clothes or linens folded

IN THE MODERN MANNER

flat and a cupboard door gives them sufficient protection. Shallow closets and drawers are often more convenient than the deeper ones, and many modern designers fill a whole wall with them, cutting down the floor space only a foot or less.

CHAPTER THIRTY-SIX

Points on Closets

CLOSET ENGINEERING is a modern contribution to comfortable attractive homes and easy efficient housekeeping. Old houses are usually very poorly equipped as to closet space. Those more recently built may have enough space allocated to storage but it is very seldom arranged for maximum convenience and effective use. If you cannot solve your own storage problems you can obtain expert advice from professional closet engineers who will tell you how to get the utmost out of the closets you already have and figure out where additional storage can be made available in all sorts of unexpected places. They will build in equipment for you, or supply it in unit form so that it fits as if it were built in but can be taken out and transferred if you move.

CLOSET DECORATION

Closets should have a character of their own but like alcoves they should also harmonize with the room adjoining. If you line your closets with paper or fabric be sure it is of a type which can be kept clean by wiping with a damp cloth—washable paper, glazed chintz, plastic-coated material of some kind, linoleum or oilcloth. There are so many of these that you can easily match your closet up with any color scheme or style of decoration. If you use ordinary wallpaper don't forget to protect it with clear lacquer for easy cleaning.

For linen or dress closets quilted fabrics are favorites both for linings and shelf covers. These are available in some of the easily cleaned fabrics mentioned above, with shelf edgings to match linings all the way from trim tailored effects to those which are wholly fluffy and feminine. Carry out the decorative scheme in hangers, garment bags, boxes, hat stands— all accessories used in the closet.

For protection of garments or linen many new plastic covers and cases have been devised. These have the double advantage of being completely dust-proof and allowing their contents to be seen so that no time is lost looking for some particular article.

Glass shelves above the hangers also show at a glance what is up there. All such materials add sparkle and charm to a closet.

Decorative schemes for closets are as varied as those for rooms. Having worked out the engineering angle of convenience you can indulge your fancy in the matter of decoration providing you keep equipment and trimmings easily cleanable as well as harmonious with room furnishings. Line drawers and trays with the same material used for shelves or walls. It is an attractive note in any room where drawers are in use.

CLOTHES CLOSETS

Clothes closets are found in all sizes and shapes. No matter what type you start out with careful planning will make it serve its purpose better. Closets should be arranged so that they help keep clothing in good condition, make it easy to get garments out or to put them away, and provide the greatest possible amount of diversified storage. Rods, hooks, and shelves should be supplemented wherever possible by drawers, shallow sliding trays and racks of various kinds.

There are many special fittings which increase accessibility in clothes closets, also the number of garments which can be taken care of without crowding. Remember that crowding of garments defeats the purpose of the closet which is *to keep clothing in condition*. At least twenty-four inches should be allowed for the width of the hangers on a rod. If there is not that much space in a shallow closet use short rods and put them crosswise instead of lengthwise. There are bracket rods which fold up against the wall when not in use, and extension rods which pull out to make garments easily visible. These are indispensable in small closets or those which are badly shaped, and often useful to make the most of space even in a large closet. A long hook or wooden peg attached to a wall may substitute for the bracket fixture and take care of several hangers. Special hangers mounted on handles make it possible to use a high clothes pole for a double tier of hangers. Men's suits can be easily hung in this way in a part of the closet where there are no shelves. You can make a pole for putting up regulation hangers by fastening a hook to the end of a broomstick.

Take advantage of all the specially built storage units put out by manufacturers of closet equipment, and look for corners where you can build in attractive cupboards with shelf or hanging space. Wide, shallow cupboards should have two doors, sliding doors, or the accordion-pleated type of closing which slides back without taking up any additional space.

THESE CLOSETS ARE PLANNED AND DECORATED

Three essentials of successful closet designing are protection, accessibility and attractiveness. In order to have any or all of these qualities in your closets you must have order. Order means a place for everything with articles which are often used in the locations easiest to get at. For help in working out convenient plans study the pictures, sketches and text in this chapter. Above you will see two views of a charming closet planned by a closet engineer to take care of a woman's needs and at the right, one specially designed for a man. These are both compressed into small space, but also serve as models for installations in larger space where that is available. The woman's closet is lined with blue quilted satin and fitted with plastic rods for handbags and other accessories. Below the partition these serve as shoe racks. At the right an enclosed glass cupboard and a series of drawers in graduated depths take care of hats and lingerie. Hand-made blue satin hangers match the lining. A closet like this can be converted into a closet dressing room by the addition of a mirror and shelf either on a wall or on the inside of the door. The man's closet is definitely masculine just as the other is definitely feminine. Drawers, shelves and cupboard are all in softly finished natural wood. Sloping shelves with moldings take care of shoes. Clothes hangers are specially made to fit coat shoulders and have blue plastic monograms set into the center. In larger space dressing facilities added to this equipment would make a dressing room out of the closet. Shelves and drawers like those shown in both closets can be either built in or bought in units and installed. Sketch A illustrates effective use of two closets built in, with space between for a dressing table. Full-length

FOR MAXIMUM USEFULNESS
FOR BEAUTY

mirror panels on each of the doors would make a convenient double mirror for dressing. Notice the cellophane hat box. Garment bags also may be made of cellophane which makes it easy to see what is inside. If you have cloth garment bags try stitching cellophane windows in the panels which hang at the front to eliminate groping. This is safe even in moth-proof bags. A dressing table like this can be made from a table, shelf or box which fits into the space with a round keg for the dressing-table stool. Leaving one side of the closet for extra long garments is an excellent idea. An adaptation of this is to plan your closet so that rods are placed on two levels to accommodate longer and shorter garments. In a larger closet three levels can be arranged, one for evening clothes, one for day-length dresses, one for jackets and skirts. The low rod is very useful where children must share a closet. A reverse arrangement which has the same benefits can be worked out by having the rod high enough for the longest garment, then placing chests of drawers beneath at two levels to fill up part of the floor space. Leave enough space free for the long articles and gauge the width of the chests by the space needed above them for two shorter lengths of garments. This stair-step arrangement can be carried out with shelves, trays or boxes with cupboard fronts as well as with drawers. B and C show twin closets arranged for a woman and for a small child. The mirror and tray on the door convert the closet into a small dressing room. Low rods are convenient in hall closets or in children's closets, while various kinds of racks are useful for odds and ends or for special purposes. A great variety of these can be found in the shops.

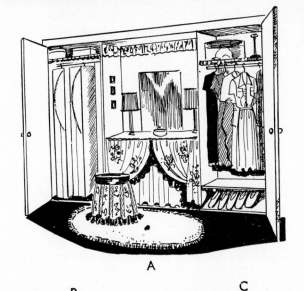

A

B

C

Entrance Hall Closets: Coat closets should be kept for the family's outdoor clothing and for guest use. If you have a small hall closet apply your ingenuity to making the most of your space. It should have a rack for dry umbrellas which can be made at home by installing a narrow shelf near the floor with two curved-end enameled curtain rods at intervals above it. This could be either on a closet wall or on the inside of the door. A twelve-inch shelf along one wall a few inches from the floor will take care of rubbers and overshoes. If you need the storage have a drawer built under this. Racks with solid sides on closet walls or doors are invaluable for caps, gloves, mittens, muffs, handbags, etc. If you prefer you can use a small chest of drawers or narrow shelves for this purpose. If you have no powder room fasten a mirror to your closet door with a shelf below it for the convenience of guests.

If you have no other storage place for luggage you can have the top shelf widened so that it will take large suitcases without difficulty. An ornamental roller shade or decorated bamboo screen suspended from the walls at the ceiling would conceal the contents of the shelf and protect them from dust. If this closet must double for a game closet you can build a low "fence" along one end to hold such things as card tables, golf bags and tennis rackets upright.

SPECIALIZED CLOTHES CLOSETS

When you install rods for clothes hangers remember that outdoor garments are bulky. If there is room it is helpful to install one of the folding bracket rods at the front of the closet for guest use. Long hooks or stands for hats are important. If you have stands be sure the bottoms are weighted and they are not so high that they are top heavy. These may be very decorative in colored plastics or in wood painted to match the woodwork. For coats, hangers should always be of the broad, shoulder-shape variety, wide enough to carry the whole shoulder width of a man's overcoat. Never forget to have a good clothes brush in plain sight.

Bedroom Closets for Women: Treatment for a woman's closet depends upon whether it is to be purely a storage closet or to include some dressing-room features. It is often very economical to work in extra drawer space in a closet in order to cut down the amount of furniture necessary in the bedroom. For long evening gowns place a special clothes-hanger rod high enough so that the dresses will hang above the floor, allowing sufficient space for your entire supply. Now estimate how much rod space you need for dresses in daytime length, and fill in the floor space below with a deep drawer or a box

with a hinged front. Use the rest of the rod for hanging short articles such as skirts, jackets, etc., and fill in the floor space below that with a chest of drawers or a bank of sliding shelves.

This stepped-up floor effect, from the evening gown section to the jacket section, will take advantage of every inch of floor space. Use magazine racks on walls or inside doors for the handbags which are always inconvenient to store in a dresser drawer. Use a man's tie rack if you have a supply of belts. The perfect arrangement for hats is to build a corner cupboard in your bedroom or dressing room or in the hall outside your bedroom door. You can fill it with shelves the proper height for the particular type of hats you wear, or copy the kind of small revolving hat tree used in millinery showrooms. Don't overlook cellophane covers for hats. If you want to keep hats in your closet arrange shelves just high enough to take transparent hat boxes or hats on low stands. You can make shoe bags yourself for your closet doors, or you can have a set of shelves made with seven inches between shelves.

Don't overlook the uses for doors suggested from time to time in this book. If you have two doors for your closet you can put a full-length mirror on the inside of each one for an excellent dressing aid. For adults the mirror should be almost six feet from the floor at the top. If it is to be used by children too it should be no more than fourteen inches from the floor at the bottom.

Bedroom Closets for Men: Many items of special equipment have been turned out for men's closets. Men often like the closet arranged for easy dressing, and a little careful planning will make that possible. There are multiple hangers to keep clothes free of wrinkles. A cabinet or chest of drawers for a supply of socks, shirts and underwear cuts down trips between dresser and closet. Shoe racks with shoe-cleaning equipment and a convenient stool for putting on socks and shoes save more time. A tie rack and a mirror on the door simplify the tie problem. Ties and scarfs keep their lines much better if they are hung on racks instead of being folded in drawers. A garment carrier which slides out at a touch brings an assortment of suits into view for quick choice. Many convenient arrangements have been worked out by closet engineers for men's closets of all types and sizes, all designed to save dressing time as well as space.

Men's clothes will keep their shape much better, with less pressing, if you use the large, heavy wishbone hangers. If coats are hung without crowding they will reshape themselves and wrinkles will disappear. Shelves for hats should be provided, also hangers for trousers.

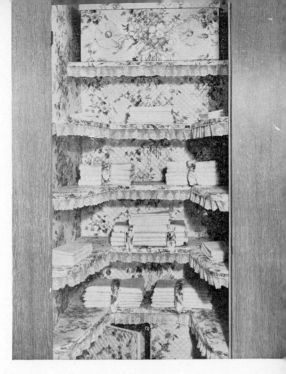

In the dressing room above storage was provided by building in composition-board cupboards and shelves, then redecorating the whole room with wallpaper and enamel. The background of the paper is in dusky charcoal, while the design is rose pink matching the rose pink of enamel, draperies and rug. The linen closet at right illustrates a clever use of space. The U-shape of the lower shelves makes it possible to store small articles on the sides where they will be easily accessible and not lost among larger piles. A straight shelf at the top for a large box and enclosed space at the bottom provide storage for blankets or comforters. A charming washable glazed chintz, quilted and edged, provides an attractive background for stacks of linen. The U-shape makes room for stepping into the closet and if a small stool is always kept there you will be able to make the best possible use of the entire space. Don't forget a closet light. The two illustrations below show convenient storage units which can be built in or assembled in closets or dressing rooms. The closet at the left is built into a passageway between bedroom and bathroom, making this into a small dressing room (dressing table at right not shown). Notice boxes covered with the same quilted fabric used for lining closet and shelves. The sliding trays shown here are less expensive and often more convenient than drawers. It is a good idea to have some of them very shallow for easy access to flat articles. Special storage boxes are obtainable to match closet fittings or you can cover ordinary boxes yourself. If you do this it is a good idea to incorporate a cellophane window in the front so that you can see what is inside. As a substitute for this keep a small pad and attached pencil on the shelf or tied to the box for listing of contents. The unit (right below) is developed in painted wood with shelf trimmings and attractive fittings on the upper shelves. Be sure to line drawers or trays with the same paper or fabric used for trimming or walls. The Swedish peasant motif of the wallpaper border is repeated in the stack of round wooden boxes at the left. An assortment like this is picturesque and useful for storage of sewing equipment, fabric and trimming scraps.

IDEAS FOR INCREASING SPACE

Installing shallow, prefabricated storage units may make a small bedroom doubly useful. In this room they cover all of one wall. In an overlarge room, deeper units can be used, on more than one wall. They come in so many different dimensions that it is easy to fit them to the wall space. In the bedroom illustrated here, closet-units flank a center section with drawers and storage cupboard. Above these are other units for storage of articles not in regular use. These may reach to the ceiling, or a smooth panel may fill in the space to carry out the effect of a wall. This room makes good use of streamlined matching units for dressing table, drawers, and cupboards fitted with shelves and convenient sliding trays. Storage facilities like these can also be built in, to fit any particular space. For use in other parts of the house, units come specially equipped for storing linens, food, dishes, collections, overshoes and raincoats, umbrellas, topcoats, games, sports equipment, photographs, stationery and other such supplies, books and magazines, radios, phonographs and record albums. There are also units designed to serve as writing or typewriter desks, dressing tables, chests of drawers, and various types of office equipment.

IT PAYS TO PLAN YOUR CLOSETS

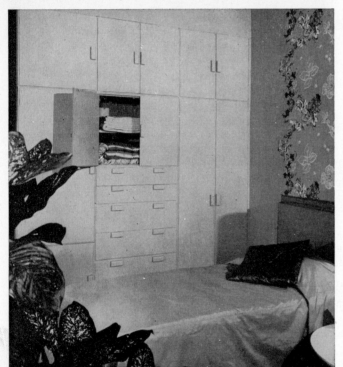

The "step-up" closet below at left is an illustration of well-used space. Storage-steps make it easy to reach top shelves, at the same time providing a seat for putting on socks or shoes. This photograph illustrates effective use of a very small space. For a larger closet, both the hanging space and the sliding-tray cabinets could be enlarged. The center closet is fitted up for special storage purposes, probably in a hallway. Racks for card tables are especially worthy of notice. Called a "carousel" closet, the one at the right is gaily decorated to suit its name. The distinctive feature here is the turntable device (like a "Lazy Susan"), which could be installed in any closet deep enough for it. The platform revolves on ball-bearing parts, making any special garment or accessory instantly available at the front of the closet. Three upright poles, stemming from a center pole, form a triangle with connecting rods which hold clothes-hangers and garment bags. Each upright pole has projecting hangers for hats, purses, and belts. Conventional shelves above the "carousel" take care of hat boxes, etc., for articles less often used.

INSPIRATION FOR COLOR SCHEMES FROM PICTURE OR FABRIC

In the living room above, a brightly colored Chinese portrait sets the color scheme and also provides a theme—as shown in pagoda-shaped cornices and Chinese-patterned fabric used for draperies. The wall color repeats the soft green of the portrait background, while the bright red of the costume is matched by the Chinese red of sofa upholstery and lamp base. Dark green touches in the painting are picked up in the color of the coffee table, in the picture above the desk, in drapery bandings, and in green-leaved plants. Accessories are keyed to bits of white in the lower part of the picture, and to its red-gold frame. Modern lines of furniture, and smart modern composition flooring, merge harmoniously with the Chinese theme and coloring. Illustrated at right is the corner of a room in which the color scheme stems from chintz used for draperies. Here again the complementary red-green combination is shown, this time in combination with neutral brown. The white of flowers is repeated as accent color. In each of these rooms, a flooring of natural cork tiles is used in place of other floor covering. The resilience of cork cushions footsteps, and absorbs sounds, while its insulating qualities provide warmth in winter, coolness in summer.

MODERN USE OF COLOR
IN A TRADITIONAL ROOM

Areas of strong color are modern in feeling, yet reminiscent of many
early 19th Century color schemes. In the living room above, this use of
color harmonizes with the clean lines of modern furniture, in combination with a fireplace and accessories typical of the ante-bellum South.
The rounded end of the room, the curved mantel with its fine porcelains,
the graceful chandelier, the Victorian love-seat — all are in the American tradition of the first half of the 19th Century. The shaggy deep-
piled rug, and the bookshelves above the chest of drawers, are as modern
as the chairs and end tables, yet they blend into a harmony characteristic of many contemporary rooms in which traditional and modern
themes are successfully mingled.

AT-A-GLANCE CHARTS

FACTS YOU WILL WANT TO KNOW ABOUT
COLOR, WALLPAPER DESIGNS AND FABRICS

HOW TO USE THE COLOR FAMILY CHART

Each of the following color schemes is merely a guide to help you work out a plan which appeals to you and is suitable for your room. They are made up of colors which have stood the test of being used together in attractive rooms, in the relationship given in the chart. You can shift them about in your room, so long as you keep the proportions approximately the same. You can often adapt a living room scheme to a bedroom by using lighter and softer tones of the same colors, or the reverse. The more dramatic combinations listed in the chart can often be used for entrance halls or dining rooms, as well as living rooms; or you can translate a restful living room combination into brighter, stronger tones for those rooms, using a larger proportion of the bright accent color. If you are doing over a room only partly, and some of the colors you have cannot be changed, look through the chart until you find a plan which includes those colors. You will then be able to give your room harmony by using the suggested combinations in selecting your new fill-in colors. If you want to make changes in one of the color schemes given, you can check the colors you would like to substitute by using the color wheels on page 405 to make sure that your new combination will be pleasing.

DIRECTIONS FOR USING COLOR COMBINATION CHARTS

COLOR WHEEL NUMBER 1 illustrates color combinations in which the three primaries are used together, or the three secondary colors, or three tertiary colors. The three points of each triangle link the colors used in this TRIAD COLOR SCHEME. The rule for success is to use only one of them in a strong, bright tone, in small areas, with the other two in softened (or grayed) tones.

COLOR WHEEL NUMBER 2 illustrates the color pairs which are effective together through contrast. This is called the COMPLEMENTARY COLOR SCHEME. As the arrows indicate, the pairs are exactly opposite each other on the wheel. One should be used in a bright tone for smaller areas, the other in grayed tones and larger areas.

COLOR WHEEL NUMBER 3 illustrates the use of a color with the two which are next to its opposite on the wheel, one on each side. This SPLIT COMPLEMENTARY COLOR SCHEME follows the rule for complementaries, and may include the direct contrast color also, if desired. For example, yellow may be used with blue-violet, and red-violet, with or without the true violet shade which comes between them.

To avoid confusion, not all of the triangles are indicated. Cut a piece of paper the size of the triangle and lay it with the top point at any color you choose. The other points will rest on the correct colors.

COLOR WHEEL NUMBER 4 illustrates how an ANALOGOUS COLOR SCHEME is developed by using colors which are related because they are side by side on the wheel. Any group can be used, all around the wheel, as indicated by the dotted lines. For an accent color you can use a contrast color opposite any one of your group. For instance, in the yellow-orange to red group, complementary blue could be used for accent (shown on color wheel 2).

Black, white, gray and other definitely neutral tones can be used with any combination of colors.

The VALUE SCALE shown here is in black shading up to white, but this shading is the same for any color. For example—strong, intense, vivid shades of red tones will deepen to reddish black as more black is added, and go in the other direction from light red to pale pink to pinkish white as white is added.

WHAT DECORATORS MEAN WHEN THEY USE THESE COLOR TERMS

HUE: Each section in the color wheel is called a hue. To change a hue, another color (not black, white or pure gray) must be added to it. Every hue has a different wave length from every other hue. Mixed with its complement equally it produces gray.

PRIMARY COLORS: Also called "normal," also "fundamental." Primaries are the three pigment colors which cannot be produced by any mixture of other pigments. These are red like that of a geranium flower, yellow like that of ripe lemons, blue like the deep clear hue of a sunny southern sky.

SECONDARY COLORS: Secondaries are the three colors which are produced by mixing two of the three primaries in equal amounts. Red + yellow = orange; red + blue = purple (or violet); yellow + blue = green.

TERTIARY COLORS: Tertiaries are the colors produced by mixing a primary with a secondary, the exact shade depending upon the proportion. Red + orange produces shades such as russet, burnt orange, coral, etc. Red + purple—mulberry, amethyst, orchid, etc. Blue + purple—heliotrope, periwinkle, lavender, etc. Blue + green—turquoise, aquamarine, bottle green, etc. Yellow + orange—maize, primrose, flame, etc. Yellow + green—jade, Nile, olive, chartreuse, etc. Mixtures of complementaries not included because these produce shades of gray—a neutral. Some authorities consider, also, the shades produced by mixing two secondaries as tertiaries, such as slate, citron, buff, sage, etc.

COMPLEX COLORS: All colors which are made up of more complicated mixtures than those producing secondary and tertiary colors are called complex.

NEUTRAL COLORS: Black and white are considered neutral. Also all those tints and shades in which tones of gray or brown predominate.

TINTS: The light tones resulting when white is mixed with a color. Much white makes a color cold.

SHADES: The dark tones resulting when black is mixed with a color. Much black deadens the color.

TONE: Each hue has many tones. By tone—or tonal value—we mean the relative strength of the hue as it approaches black or white at the opposite ends of the value scale. Mixed with white, a color is "pale" in tone; mixed with black, it is "dark" in tone. The upper and lower extremes of any color would be white (or very pale gray), and black.

CHROMA: This term is used interchangeably with value, tonal value, and intensity. The chroma of a color such as yellow is "light"; the chroma of a color such as Navy blue is "dark." When a color fades, it loses chroma.

LUMINOSITY: This term is used to describe a quality of warm clear colors in light-reflecting tones and finishes, such as light golden-yellow. Clear white is also luminous. Literally "luminous" are only metals in gold, silver, platinum, or clear plastics.

A FEW TESTED COLOR COMBINATIONS

YOUR FAVORITE COLOR	SUGGESTED COLOR GROUPS TO USE WITH IT
RED	Green, gray, blue (for accent)
SCARLET	Light blue, ecru (or Navy and taupe)
CRIMSON	Pearl gray, mauve
GARNET	Sapphire blue, mauve, pearl gray
CARDINAL	Marine blue, turquoise, gray
WINE	Black, old blue, beige
ROSE	Flesh, light blue, green
OLD ROSE	Blue in various shades
CEDAR ROSE	Blue, cream
PINK	Green, orchid, blue for accent
ORANGE	Violet, light blue, indigo for accent
BURNT ORANGE	Electric blue, light brown
SALMON	Turquoise, lavender
HENNA	Peacock green, royal blue, gray
PEACH	Rust, blue, tan
MAIZE	Powder blue, pink
YELLOW	Violet, blue, green
PRIMROSE	Lavender, dusty rose, soft green
SOFT YELLOW	Brown, French blue
GOLD	Soft gray-green, deep red
DARK GREEN	Brown, beige (or sage green and gold)
MYRTLE	Heliotrope, yellow
SOFT GREEN	Rosewood, deep violet
TARRAGON	Heliotrope, pearl gray
CHINESE JADE	Rose, ivory
NILE	Cornflower, orange
LIGHT GREEN	Rose, dark green, mauve
BLUE	Yellow, sand, orange for accent
COPENHAGEN BLUE	Burgundy, gray
FLEMISH BLUE	Olive-green, cardinal
LIGHT BLUE	Orchid, champagne
DEEP PURPLE	Orange, gray
VIOLET	Green, light and dark shades
LAVENDER	Green, mauve, gray
HELIOTROPE	Light blue, cream
HYDRANGEA	Old rose, primrose yellow
MAUVE	Emerald green, dark red, brown
BROWN	Orange, tan, cardinal for accent
GRAY	Violet, crimson, lavender.

BASIC PRINCIPLES FOR WORKING OUT A COLOR SCHEME

1. DOMINANT OR CONTROLLING COLOR

   Decide on your dominant or controlling color, which may dominate by covering a large area or by strength of color in a smaller area. Decide whether your foundation or background color is to be the dominant or a secondary color. Plan to use a large amount of quiet background color, a small amount of bold, strong color. All large foundation areas should be in light or grayed tones.

2. GRAYING

   Clear colors are gayer, more cheerful, but grayed tones are more restful, their harmonies more subtle. Mixing gray with bright colors brings them into relation with other colors in the room. As . . . red and yellow in bright tones seem to clash. Mixed with gray, they become rose and tan and go very well together. Use this principle also in buying materials. Avoid too much graying. It gives muddy tones, dirty grays, flat greens. A little gray goes far.

3. RELIEF AND CONTRAST COLORS

   Decide on relief and contrast colors and bring them into all parts of the room composition. Remember the order in the amount of space allowed each one—foundation, then relief, then contrast. All colors—including background colors—should be keyed to the dominant color. Soften strong contrast colors

with white. Contrast is less in lighter tints. Soften darker contrasts with gray.

4. ACCENT COLORS

   Use pure bright intense colors only in accessories, etc. Distribute them so they will not be spotty. The smaller the area the brighter the color may be. The larger the area the softer the tone should be. Don't use large amounts of pure bright color.

5. KEYING

   This is another means of creating harmony. A key color is the one about which the color scheme is built—the dominant, or controlling color. All other colors in the room must be "keyed" with it—harmonized. Two colors in which any part of a third color is present will be linked together. Example: To key red and yellow to each other, mix them both with a little of the third primary hue—blue. Violet and green will result, and these are harmonious to use with your strong tones. Remember this principle in buying as well as mixing colors. A lovely print or art object will have these tones keyed for you, and you can use them for your own composition. The safe rule is to avoid too many colors and too strong tones except in accents, etc. Most colors will "go together" if you soften them.

COLOR AREAS AND SAMPLES

PROPORTIONATE SAMPLE SIZES

1. WALLS .... 24" x 24"
2. FLOOR .... 18" x 18"
3. DRAPERIES .... 16" x 16"
4. CEILING .... 14" x 14"
5. COUCH, ETC. .... 12" x 14"
6. WOODWORK .... 10" x 14"
7. LARGE CHAIR .... 8" x 8"
8. LARGE CHAIR .... 6" x 8"
9. SMALL CHAIR .... 6" x 7"
10. ACCESSORIES .... 6" x 7"
11. ACCENTS .... 5" x 6"
12. TRIMMINGS .... 5" x 6"

VARIED as used here means choice of light, dark, or medium tones, clear or grayed colors.

POINTS TO REMEMBER IN MATCHING SAMPLES FOR COLOR

1. Use larger samples if possible, especially in patterned materials, but keep approximate proportions of chart. Sizes are determined according to area and interest. Ceiling and floor areas, for example, are equal—but floor interest is greater, hence the larger sample. If several items are the same color add them to make one sample.

2. Make allowance for texture. Soft rough surface in paint, paper, or fabric makes colors appear darker. Hard glossy surfaces appear lighter.

3. Make allowance for distance. Colors look brighter when they are close; farther away they seem softer, grayed by atmosphere. Colors which match exactly 1 ft. away may seem quite different at 15 ft. This is important in a large high-ceilinged room.

4. Make allowance for proximity. When side by side: Complementary colors brighten each other; related colors, when both light or both dark, deaden each other; neutral colors brighten clear colors, but pure strong primary colors deaden neutrals such as grays, browns, etc.; light and dark tones brighten each other, especially white for dark colors and black for light tones; one color may seem to change another's hue as when a strong clear color gives a tinge of its complementary to a neutral —red, for example, may give a greenish cast to gray unless a little red has been mixed with the gray.

5. Make allowance for proportion. The larger the area the darker the color will appear. Choose a wall color slightly lighter than you really want it. Don't decide exact shade of a painted wall until all other materials have been chosen. It is easier to match paint to fabric and paper than the other way around.

(Bar chart labels: 1 WALLS MEDIUM TO LIGHT, 2 FLOORS DARK TO MEDIUM, 3 DRAPERY VARIED, 4 CEILING LIGHT, 5 LARGE COUCH BED SOFA VARIED, 6 WOODWORK VARIED, 7 LARGE CHAIR VARIED, 8 LARGE CHAIR, 9 SMALL CHAIR, 10 ACCESSORIES BRIGHT, 11 ACCENTS, 12 TRIMMINGS BRIGHT)

COLOR COMBINATION CHARTS

S = SECONDARY ..... T = TERTIARY

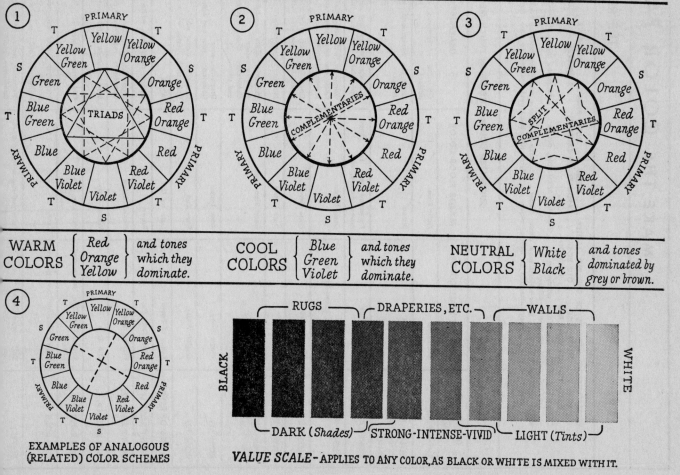

WARM COLORS { Red Orange Yellow } and tones which they dominate.

COOL COLORS { Blue Green Violet } and tones which they dominate.

NEUTRAL COLORS { White Black } and tones dominated by grey or brown.

(Chart 1: TRIADS; Chart 2: COMPLEMENTARIES; Chart 3: SPLIT COMPLEMENTARIES; Chart 4: EXAMPLES OF ANALOGOUS (RELATED) COLOR SCHEMES)

Color wheel labels: PRIMARY, Yellow, Yellow Green, Yellow Orange, Green, Orange, Blue Green, Red Orange, Blue, Red, Blue Violet, Red Violet, Violet

RUGS — DRAPERIES, ETC. — WALLS

BLACK — WHITE

DARK (Shades) — STRONG-INTENSE-VIVID — LIGHT (Tints)

VALUE SCALE - APPLIES TO ANY COLOR, AS BLACK OR WHITE IS MIXED WITH IT.

MAKE THE COLOR FAMILIES WORK FOR YOU

THE RED FAMILY

REPRESENTATIVE MEMBERS OF THE RED FAMILY . . . FLESH . . . DUSTY-PINK . . . SHELL-PINK . . . ROSE . . . DUSTY ROSE . . . OLD ROSE . . . CARDINAL OR CRIMSON . . . RASPBERRY . . . RED-BURGUNDY OR WINE RED . . . MAROON . . . ETC.

CHARACTERISTICS . . . Warm, advancing . . . Cheerful, hospitable, active . . . In strong tones, stimulating, bold, vital, dramatic, exciting.

WHAT THEY CAN DO . . . Make objects seem closer, larger . . . Make room seem smaller by bringing background closer . . . Focus attention on wall or object . . . Bring life, brightness, warmth, to drab, dark or too-cool rooms.

CORRECT USES . . . In light tints, charming background for fairly light, large rooms . . . In bright tones, highly decorative when used for comparatively small areas, as in accessories, accents, etc. . . . In darker shades, rich and warm for draperies, carpets, upholstery, especially in large rooms with heavy furniture.

CAUTION . . . Do not use too much red—especially in clear, bright tones, and in light rooms . . . Safer to soften a little by "graying," except when used for accent . . . Do not use the Red Family for background of a room that is small or crowded . . . Do not use bright red for large objects, unless you want to call attention to them . . . Do not forget when using the Red Family to include cool colors in your color schemes . . . It takes two cool colors, or a large area of one cool color, to balance red.

SUGGESTED COLOR SCHEMES IN WHICH MEMBERS OF RED FAMILY PLAY A DOMINANT ROLE

DOMINANT COLOR	MAJOR WALL COLOR	MAJOR FLOOR COLOR	DRAPERIES AND UPHOLSTERY	ACCENT COLORS	REMARKS
SHELL-PINK	Shell-pink	Light Blue	Off-white background, powder-blue and shell-pink in pattern	Italian Red	Charming for bedroom. In slightly darker tones of same colors, could be adapted to living rooms. Feminine feeling
MELON PINK (like Pompeiian terra cotta)	Melon Pink	Brown	Light tan background, melon-pink with green olive in design	Green Olive	Good for living or dining room with mahogany or walnut furniture
VENETIAN PINK	Venetian Pink	Patterned rug, soft tones, green, mauve, red	Draperies, yellow and white stripes / Upholstery, green and dull pink stripes	Red	Good for living room with 18th Century furniture
DUSTY PINK	Dusty Pink Woodwork, cocoa brown	Deep Brown	Draperies, pale aquamarine (dusty pink curtains) / Chair and bed covers, cocoa and pink stripes with cocoa brown trimming	White	Interesting for modern bedroom with furniture in cocoa tones
BOIS DE ROSE	Bois de Rose	Sage Green	Draperies, pearl gray, trimmed with bois de rose / Upholstery, pale gray with sulphur yellow	Green and Sulphur yellow	Living room color scheme with feminine feeling
DAWN ROSE	Dawn Rose	Dark Green	Neutral background, dawn rose and leaf-green in pattern	Wet Leaf-green	Attractive for bedroom
LIGHT ROSE	Light Rose	Deep Blue-green	Draperies, dusty rose background, blue-green and foliage tones in design / Upholstery, blue, blue-green and green, plain, pattern and stripes	Blue	Suitable for fairly large room with average light
ROSE (1)	Warm Gray	Rose Taupe	Draperies, rose / Upholstery, rose and cream stripes	Blue or Green	Appropriate for almost any living or bedroom
ROSE (2)	Oyster White	Rose Red	Draperies, oyster white / Upholstery, oyster white with reds, blues and soft green	Red	Charming for bedroom or woman's living room
ASHES OF ROSES	Ashes of Roses	Cafe au lait	White	Strong Blue	Adaptable to bedroom or living room
DUSTY ROSE (1)	Deep dusty Rose	Brown	Lighter dusty rose, white and brown	Silver	Good color scheme for living room or dining room
DUSTY ROSE (2)	Pickled wood	Pinkish Beige	Draperies, dusty rose / Upholstery, foam green and natural	Pale Green	Adaptable to living room, traditional or modern
OLD ROSE (1)	Old Rose	Warm Gray	Blue and pale yellow, with touch of old rose	Jade Green	This color scheme is charming and delicate, suitable for bedrooms and dressing rooms
OLD ROSE (2)	Paper, Old Rose, cream and gray	Mulberry	Old rose and gray	Blue and Silver	With woodwork painted warm gray, this scheme would be attractive for bedroom or dressing room
OLD ROSE (3)	Paper, Blue and rose pattern	Ivory	Draperies, ivory background, rose, blue and green in pattern / Upholstery, old rose, and drapery fabric	Green	Attractive for formal living room
RED (1)	Soft grayed Green	Patterned rug with red background	Draperies, pale gray background, red in pattern / Upholstery, plain green, red and green stripes	Blue and Orange	Suitable living room or dining room

Color		Patterned rug, red predominating	Chintz, red predominating in pattern	Green and Pewter	Good for Early American room, with pine or maple
RED (2)	Paper, granite flecked with red	Hooked rugs / Floors, painted blue	Draperies, textured beige / Upholstery, textured beige trimmed with red	Blue (chairs painted blue)	Colonial type living room or library
RED (3)	Paper, red toile design; woodwork, white	Red rug	Red and white brocade	Green	Living room in period feeling with walnut furniture
RED (4)	Old white / Woodwork, dark green	Red rug	Red	Green	
RED (5)	Paper, light background, red with green and brown in pattern	Dark blue	Red	Blue	Early American dining room, with pine and maple
SOFT RED (1)	Neutral	Soft Red	Draperies, blue-green background, deep red in design / Upholstery, blue-green	Yellow	Nice for living room
SOFT RED (2)	White	Rug, blue, red and white pattern	Draperies, linen color with red in pattern / Upholstery, chair seats, blue	Silver	18th Century dining room
CRIMSON (1)	Bone white	Crimson	White background, floral design in red and soft green	White	Mahogany furniture of very nice design would be lovely with white walls
CRIMSON (2)	Soft Gray	Crimson	Draperies, white, gray and crimson / Upholstery, white, trimmed with crimson	Black	A smart sophisticated color scheme
CRIMSON (3)	Slate Gray	Soft Crimson	Draperies, bluish white, trimmed with soft crimson / Upholstery, bluish white	Gold	Adaptable to modern styles
CHINESE RED	Grayed soft Green	Chinese Red	Draperies, grayed soft green / Upholstery, deep beige	Light Beige	Good for living room or dining room
LACQUER RED (1)	Gray	Brown	Gray and lacquer red	Green	Colorful living room with some red lacquer furniture
LACQUER RED (2)	Paneling, Red Lacquer, silver trim	Black	Silver gray, with red and black in design	Silver	Modern library
ITALIAN RED	Yellow	Floor, stained dark / Patterned rug in old reds and dark blues, red predominating	Draperies, Italian red damask. Upholstery, red damask, yellow, glazed chintz with white ground and red in design	Gold	Living room English in feeling; also good for Federal American
CRANBERRY RED	Paper with light ground and cranberry pattern / Paneled fireplace end painted blue	Deep soft red	Draperies, rose / Upholstery, blue, and chintz-like wallpaper pattern	Green	Cheerful living room color scheme
WINE RED (1)	Green	Wine Red	Draperies, wine red / Upholstery, grayed green and off white	Crystal	Attractive for living room with cool North or East light
WINE RED (2)	Soft grayed Blue	Deep Gray	Draperies, wine red / Upholstery, wine red, grayed white and blue	Silver	For fairly formal living room, average size
WINE RED (3)	Paper in yellow, pale gray and white	Dark Wine Red	Ruby taffeta / Upholstery, glazed maroon chintz with yellow flowers / Chair seats, bright yellow leather	Gold	Specially appropriate for Victorian dining room
AMERICAN BEAUTY	Linen color	Fawn	Draperies, fawn and American beauty / Upholstery, American beauty, fawn, blue and gray	Blue	Dramatic color scheme for fairly large living room
RED DAHLIA	Gray	Red Dahlia	Draperies, light neutral background with dahlia and melon green in pattern / Upholstery, melon green	Larkspur Blue	Adaptable to various types of living rooms
OLD RED	Soft light shade / Old Red	Deep Old Red	Draperies, old red, beige and white stripes / Upholstery, light tan	Copper	Warm, colorful plan for a room inclined to be cold
BURGUNDY (1)	Pale clear yellow	Burgundy	Draperies, white, valance and trimming / Upholstery, burgundy and white	Gold	Rich color scheme for formal room
BURGUNDY (2)	Burgundy	Darker Burgundy	Burgundy and natural	Chartreuse	For large room, living room or library
BURGUNDY (3)	Warm Gray with pinkish cast	Burgundy	Draperies, primrose yellow / Upholstery, pale grayed blue and white	White	Good for any room not too small or too sunny
BURGUNDY (4)	Beige with pinkish cast	Burgundy	Draperies, beige background, shell pink and burgundy in pattern / Upholstery, shell pink	Grayed White	Same as above

407

THE YELLOW FAMILY

REPRESENTATIVE MEMBERS OF THE YELLOW FAMILY . . . CREAM . . . BUFF . . . STRAW . . . CANARY . . . GOLD . . . TAN . . . BROWN.

CHARACTERISTICS . . . Warm, somewhat advancing . . . The sunlight color—gay, happy, bright, cheerful . . . In light tones, luminous, radiant.

WHAT THEY CAN DO . . . Diffuse and increase light by reflection, making dark rooms seem lighter and brighter . . . In pale tints, yellow lights up a small room without making it seem smaller because reflective radiance of yellow balances its advancing quality as a warm color.

CORRECT USES . . . Excellent background for all average rooms . . . In light tints, best wall-background for poorly lighted rooms . . . In clear, bright tones, safe accent color almost everywhere.

CAUTION . . . Do not use yellow without testing under artificial light, and providing lamp shades to offset color changes . . . Don't use in wide expanses in a very sunny room . . . Don't use bright tones without restful combination color.

SUGGESTED COLOR SCHEMES IN WHICH MEMBERS OF YELLOW FAMILY PLAY A DOMINANT ROLE

DOMINANT COLOR	MAJOR WALL COLOR	MAJOR FLOOR COLOR	DRAPERIES AND UPHOLSTERY	ACCENT COLORS	REMARKS
CREAM	Cream Woodwork, cream	Patterned rug, mulberry, green and cream	Draperies, green, cream trimming / Upholstery, green and green yellow	Mulberry	Appropriate for bedroom, especially in Directoire feeling with cream and gold furniture
BUFF	Buff	Buff	Copenhagen blue and burgundy	Orange, Tete de Negre	Glowing color scheme for living room or man's bedroom
PALE YELLOW (1)	Pale Yellow	Soft Beige	Draperies, light yellow background, soft reds, greens and blue in pattern / Upholstery, soft blue, chintz of draperies	Green and Red	Good color scheme for medium-sized dark room
PALE YELLOW (2)	Pale Yellow	Pale Yellow	Turquoise	Coral	Colorful for bedroom or small sitting room
BRIGHT LEMON (1)	Bright Lemon	Beige	Draperies, beige background, yellow green and lavender / Seat covers, wet leaf green	Wet Leaf Green	This color scheme will brighten up a dark dining room
PALE LEMON (2)	Pale Lemon Yellow Woodwork, white	Tobacco Brown	Draperies, white with yellow trimming / Upholstery, emerald green; some pieces white, yellow, dull orange	Orange	Suitable for living room with north light
JONQUIL YELLOW (1)	Jonquil Yellow	Gray	Draperies, white, trimmed with Chinese red / Upholstery, warm gray and white	Chinese Red	Charming for living room, modern or traditional
JONQUIL YELLOW (2)	Jonquil Yellow	Soft Blue-Green	Draperies, white and yellow / Upholstery, soft blue, green and white	White	Good for any room without too much light
YELLOW (1)	Yellow	Brown	Blue and apple green	Black	Good for room with cold light
YELLOW (2)	Yellow	Brown	Dutch blue and white	Bright Red	Attractive for informal living room
YELLOW (3)	Marbleized yellow paper Woodwork, deep green	Deep Green	Draperies, green, yellow trimming / Chair seat upholstery, yellow	Blue	Charming for dining room, especially in Directoire feeling
YELLOW (4)	Paper in Yellow and Ivory stripes, divided by narrow plum lines	Yellow Tan	Draperies, gray background, yellow, plum and rose in pattern / Upholstery, blue and light tan	Old Gold	Good combination for dark maple woodwork
GRAYED YELLOW	Grayed Yellow	Brown	Draperies, brown and beige stripes / Upholstery, yellow, beige, moss green	White	Pleasant for living room or man's bedroom
SOFT YELLOW	Soft Yellow	Deep Brown	Draperies, yellow / Upholstery, yellow, cinnamon brown	Chartreuse	Attractive and restful for library or living room
EMPIRE YELLOW	Slate Gray	Lime Green	Draperies, Empire yellow / Upholstery, Strong clear yellow	Silver	Suitable for living room or dining room
CITRON YELLOW	Citron Yellow	Citron Yellow	Coral	Silver	Modern or traditional living room
LEMON YELLOW	Lemon Yellow	Tete de Negre	Brown and henna	Orange	Distinctive for modern living room
SULPHUR YELLOW	Sulphur Yellow	Olive Green	Shades of green and sulphur	Coral	Colorful modern living room

DEEP YELLOW	Deep Yellow	Red	Draperies, gold damask — Upholstery, plum, wine red, gold with red, blue, lavender in pattern	Gold	Suitable for period room with Queen Anne, Sheraton, and other Georgian style furniture
MUTED GOLD	Caramel	Bleached wood, rubbed with gold and waxed	Draperies, soft caramel taffeta, trimmed with brown — Upholstery, brown and yellow	Ebony	Unusual modern living room scheme where there is plenty of light
GOLD (1)	Yellow, flat finish Woodwork, Olive Green	Old gold carpet	Draperies, old gold, trimmed with green — Upholstery, olive green and paprika	Light Green	Charming for modern living room with blond wood
GOLD (2)	Gray and pale Yellow paper	Harvest Gold and Gray	Draperies, oyster white, trimmed with multi-color fringe — Upholstery, rust-shot silk	Brass	Traditional or modern dining room
TAN (1)	Neutral Tan	Dark Tan	Draperies, burnt orange — Upholstery, brown and burnt orange	Rich Chocolate	Good with natural wood tones
TAN (2)	Tan linen color	Light and dark Tan	Draperies, tan and rose stripes — Upholstery, linen color with rose, tan, gray and blue in pattern	Rose	Attractive for living room or library with walnut woodwork and furniture
TAN (3)	Tan	Brown Taupe	Dark green and vermilion	Brown	Rich, warm color scheme for living room or library, especially with walnut furniture and paintings
TAN (4)	Brownish Tan	Floor, Oak Multi-colored scatter rugs	Draperies, brown with red, yellow and blue pattern — Upholstery, old red and yellow chintz	Blue	Suitable for bedroom with oak furniture in Early English feeling
BROWN (1)	Brown paneled	Deep Brown	Beige background with brilliant gold, scarlet and orange tones of fall foliage	Blue	Attractive for living room with plenty of light
BROWN (2)	Pine paneled	Pine	Old chintz in blue and brown	Silver and Pewter	Dining room in French Provincial style
BROWN (3)	Warm Beige with brown cast	Brown	Draperies, brown, beige and dusty pink — Upholstery, brown and off-white	White	Appropriate for modern living room
BROWN (4)	Pine paneled	Pine	Yellow, copper and blue chintz	Green	Suitable Early American living room with maple furniture
BROWN (5)	Chalk White	Brown	Turquoise	Peach	Charming bedroom color scheme
SABLE BROWN (1)	Sable Brown	Off-white	Draperies, off-white with turquoise — Upholstery, shell pink and off-white	Turquoise	Distinctive modern living room
SABLE BROWN (2)	Sable Brown	Deep warm Beige	Draperies, bright yellow — Upholstery, plain chartreuse with white pattern	Earth Brown	Same as above
CHESTNUT BROWN	Fawn	Chestnut Brown	Champagne background, beaver, turquoise and apricot in pattern and trimming	Turquoise	Appropriate for living or dining room
TAWNY BROWN	Tawny Brown Pine	Light beige and taupe	Blue on light ground	Yellow	Good for dining room in French period feeling
GOLDEN BROWN	Knotty Pine	Golden Brown Navajo rug	Draperies, colorful hunting print — Upholstery, red leather	Blue and Green	Library or Den
NUT BROWN	Nut Brown Pine	Moss Green	Draperies, dark linen — Upholstery, green, brown and white	Yellow	Restful living room color scheme
TOBACCO BROWN	Tobacco Brown	Beige	Clear yellow chintz with beige and dark brown in design	White	Suitable modern dining room with much sunlight
CHOCOLATE BROWN	Chocolate Brown	Eggshell	Draperies, white — Upholstery, chartreuse, brown and eggshell	Chartreuse	Interesting modern color scheme for living room or dining room
DARK BROWN (1)	Deep Beige	Dark Brown	Draperies, pale, clear blue — Upholstery, cinnamon brown	Pale Clear Blue	Good for dining room or living room
DARK BROWN (2)	Light Chartreuse	Dark Brown	Light tan and brown	White	Good for modern living room
BROWNS	Light Brown	Deep Brown	Draperies, off-white — Upholstery, Wedgwood green and off-white	Gold	Suitable for living or dining room

THE GREEN FAMILY

REPRESENTATIVE MEMBERS OF THE GREEN FAMILY . . . NILE . . . LETTUCE . . . PEA . . . GRASS . . . fion to room.
SEA . . . OLIVE . . . BOTTLE . . . ETC.   CORRECT USES . . . One of best background colors for average rooms, especially where restfulness is impor-

CHARACTERISTICS . . . Cool, receding—except when mixed with a warm color . . . Most restful color . . .   tant . . . Great corrective value for rooms too small or too warm . . . Suitable in proper tones for
Friendly with all other colors, refreshing, versatile . . . Endless variety of tones and combinations.   background in any part of room—floor, walls, ceiling.

WHAT THEY CAN DO . . . In light, soft tints, makes rooms seem larger because the wall seems farther   CAUTION . . . Do not use in quantity in cold, dark or overlarge rooms—choose warm, advancing colors for
away . . . Makes objects seem farther away, therefore smaller . . . Brings atmosphere of rest and relaxa-   backgrounds, keeping green for smaller areas.

SUGGESTED COLOR SCHEMES IN WHICH MEMBERS OF GREEN FAMILY PLAY A DOMINANT ROLE

DOMINANT COLOR	MAJOR WALL COLOR	MAJOR FLOOR COLOR	DRAPERIES AND UPHOLSTERY	ACCENT COLORS	REMARKS
PALE GREEN (1)	Pale Green	Dark Green	Draperies, off-white background, with pale blues, greens, and mauve in pattern Upholstery, darker blue	Mauve and Violet	Appropriate for average living room and bedroom
PALE GREEN (2)	Pale Green	Plum	Draperies, natural linen color, with flowered plum and green in design Upholstery, plum, gold, green	Gold	Especially good for traditional living room
LIGHT GREEN (1)	White	Light Green	Draperies, white with dark green pattern Upholstery, dark green and white	Yellow	Pleasant color scheme for modern room
LIGHT GREEN (2)	Pickled Pine	Light Green	Draperies, off-white and light green Upholstery, light green	Brown	Attractive for living room or library
LIGHT GREEN (3)	Off-white	Soft Light Green	Shell-pink, green and off-white	Crystal	Charming and cool for small living room or sitting room
APPLE GREEN (1)	Apple Green	Plum	Draperies, apple green Upholstery, gold, yellow and ivory	Gold	Good for small living room
APPLE GREEN (2)	Apple Green	Yellow Green	Gray, blue, and touches of light yellow	Light Yellow	This combination makes cool room
APPLE GREEN (3)	Pale Apple Green	Floor, brown walnut Rug, blue and tan	Draperies, royal blue background, with rose and green leaves in pattern Upholstery, same drapery chintz, also rose, antique salmon, apple green and cream stripes	Black, gold, white and ruby	Early American living room with maple or cherry furniture
SOFT GREEN (1)	Soft Green	Deeper Green	Draperies, plum background with beige and green in pattern Upholstery, plum, beige and green	Orange	Restful Color Scheme
SOFT GREEN (2)	Soft Grayed Green	Deeper Green	Draperies, corn yellow Upholstery, grayed green and off-white	Pine Green	Adaptable to living room, dining room or bedroom
SOFT GREEN (3)	Pale Soft Grayed Green	Ivy Green	Draperies, soft grayed green Upholstery, golden yellow and white	Lacquer Red	Excellent to add feeling of space to small room
FOAM GREEN	Slate Gray	Foam Green	Draperies, lemon yellow and white Upholstery, lemon yellow and gray	Gold	Good modern color scheme
IVY GREEN	Clear Beige	Ivy Green	Draperies, beige with light and dark green floral design Upholstery, same chintz and some clear beige	Black	Appropriate for living room
DEEP LIME	Deep Lime		White, green and melon pink	White	Dramatic modern scheme, especially good with blond wood

			Green	Crystal	
NILE GREEN	Nile Green	Glazed chintz with green background and white in design, red lining and trimming			Cool, airy bedroom
MINT GREEN	Pure White Woodwork, white	Turquoise, yellow and mint green	Painted Mint Green, spotter-dashed with turquoise and yellow	White	Adaptable for informal living room, dining room or bedroom
JADE GREEN	Pale Jade	Draperies, blue / Upholstery, blue and jade green	Dark Blue	Silver	Attractive for modern living room
SAGE	Slate Gray	Gray and blue with green touches	Soft Deep Sage	Silver	Excellent color to make small sunny room seem larger and cooler
BOTTLE GREEN	Pale Apricot	Green, apricot and topaz	Bottle Green	Topaz	Good for living room or dining room
CHARTREUSE GREEN	Chartreuse Green	Draperies, chartreuse green / Upholstery, shades of heliotrope	Shades of Tete de Negre	Silver	Modern bedroom. Good with furniture painted chartreuse
CHARTREUSE GREEN	Gray	Chartreuse and bright blue	Chartreuse	Silver	Adaptable to any modern room
TURQUOISE	Light Turquoise	Draperies, turquoise, green and rose stripes / Upholstery, turquoise	Patterned rug, Green with Moss Rose	Rose	Attractive for bedroom with mahogany furniture
BLUE GREEN (1)	Deep Cream	Apple green, greenish blue, touch of burnt orange	Blue Green	Burnt Orange	Versatile color scheme for average room
BLUE GREEN (2)	Blue Green	Draperies, light grayish tan background, turquoise, rose and green in pattern / Upholstery, same print and some soft rose	Blue Green	Green	Very restful for living room or bedroom
BLUE GREEN (3)	Dull Blue Green	Draperies, white / Upholstery, red violet	Rug, light field, red violet and green leaves in pattern	Dark Green	Dining room in period feeling with walnut furniture
WET LEAF GREEN	Deep Lime	White background, wet leaf green, dawn rose and bright lemon in pattern	Bronze	Rose	Sophisticated modern color scheme
DEEP GREEN (1)	Deep Green	Draperies, sky blue chintz with rose and green pattern / Upholstery, emerald green and gray	Gray	Gold and Rose	Suitable for living room or man's bedroom
DEEP GREEN (2)	Gray and White paper, Block pattern	Draperies, yellow / Upholstery, yellow flowers and pale green leaves on gray background	Deep Green	White and Green	Modern living room or dining room
DEEP GREEN (3)	Green, lighter than carpet	Draperies, off-white / Upholstery, off-white and Wedgwood green	Deep Soft Green	Yellow	Very cool and fresh
DEEP GREEN (4)	Greenish Gray	Draperies, apple green / Upholstery, grayed greens and white	Deep Green	Salmon	Good combination to make small room seem larger
DEEP GREEN (5)	Deep Soft Green	Golden yellow and white	Light Brown	White	Modern or traditional setting
GEORGIAN GREEN	Deep Georgian Green	Draperies, soft golden yellow / Upholstery, golden yellow and deep green	Deep Green	Gold	Very cool and restful for period living room or library
DARK GREEN (1)	Ivory Green	Draperies, white with dark green pattern / Upholstery, off-red, off-white and dark green	Dark Green	Black	Subtle color combination. Good for living room or dining room
DARK GREEN (2)	Warm Gray	Draperies, dark green or gray background / Upholstery, light green	Dark Green	Yellow	Cool and restful for living room
DARK GREEN (3)	Dark Green	Draperies, chintz in blue-green and soft red / Upholstery, same chintz, also some soft red	Tan	Copper	Charming for sunny living room
GREEN OLIVE	Green Olive	Lime green, red-coral, antique white	Red-Coral	Coral and White	Daring modern color scheme. Good with traditional or modern furniture in light finish

411

THE BLUE FAMILY

REPRESENTATIVE MEMBERS OF THE BLUE FAMILY . . . PALE . . . BABY . . . SKY . . . POWDER . . . NAVY . . . MIDNIGHT . . . ETC.
CHARACTERISTICS . . Coldest, most receding, unless mixed with warm colors . . . Serene, quiet, "spacious" . . . Much-loved hue . . . Too much of it in dull tones may be depressing.
WHAT THEY CAN DO . . . Make room seem larger, cooler, more airy and spacious . . . Make objects look smaller because they seem more distant . . . In dark tones, make lighter contrast colors more luminous.
CORRECT USES . . . In light tones, excellent background for small, dark, warm rooms . . . Good combining color, especially in soft tones . . . Effective background for many other colors.
CAUTION . . . Do not use in quantity in cold or dark or over-large rooms . . . Do not use too much in dull shades . . . Do not use without some warm bright accent color.

SUGGESTED COLOR SCHEMES IN WHICH MEMBERS OF BLUE FAMILY PLAY A DOMINANT ROLE

DOMINANT COLOR	MAJOR WALL COLOR	MAJOR FLOOR COLOR	DRAPERIES AND UPHOLSTERY	ACCENT COLORS	REMARKS
PALE BLUE (1)	Pale Blue	Dark Blue	Tan draperies and upholstery	Silver	Modern color scheme for bedroom with furniture in lemon color
SKY BLUE	Garden Sky Blue	Champagne	Champagne, sky blue and orchid	Orchid	Modern color scheme, good with light natural finish woods
POWDER BLUE (1)	Powder Blue	Delft Blue	Draperies, canary yellow Upholstery, yellow and powder blue	Off-white	Cool and fresh for bedroom
POWDER BLUE (2)	Powder Blue	Powder Blue	White draperies and upholstery	Peach	Dainty feminine bedroom
LARKSPUR BLUE (1)	Larkspur Blue	Pale Gray	Draperies, wine, trimmed with white Upholstery, deep blue and white	Deep Blue and Wine	Good modern living room combination
LARKSPUR BLUE (2)	Larkspur Blue	Blue	Neutral background, blue and pink in pattern	Red Dahlia	Any period room with enough light
BLUE (1)	Pale Blue, deep Rose and Ivory paper	Blue	Blue, gold and rose with touches of black—in stripes or plain	Black	Attractive for traditional living room
BLUE (2)	Faded Blue (middle value)	Floor, dark Brown Carpet, Gray and Yellow	Draperies, old yellow Upholstery, yellow, old yellow, and touch of Venetian red, also some blue	Blue	Bedroom with Directoire feeling and walnut furniture
BLUE (3)	Striped wallpaper in tones of light and medium blue and White	Dark Blue	Draperies, blue with white in pattern and trimming Upholstery, lemon yellow	Dark Blue	Good for small, low-ceilinged but light room
HYDRANGEA BLUE (1)	Pale Hydrangea Blue	Eggplant	Draperies, peach background with white, copper, gold and hydrangea blue in design Upholstery, some chintz, also old blue	Old Blue	Good for room with strong light, especially with 18th Century furniture
HYDRANGEA BLUE (2)	Hydrangea Blue	Deeper Blue	Draperies, salmon pink Chair seats, black and gold	Gold	Dining room with Directoire feeling
COPENHAGEN BLUE	Copenhagen Blue	Burgundy	Gray with blue and burgundy	Rose and Silver	Attractive for traditional living room
PENCIL BLUE	Lemon Yellow	Pencil Blue	Blue background with yellow in pattern and trim	Silver	Setting for dining room with modern furniture

Name	Walls / Woodwork	Floor / Rug	Draperies / Upholstery	Accent Color	Use
MEDIUM BLUE (1)	Blue	Mulberry ground	Draperies, cherry red. Upholstery, chintz in blue, rose and mauve, some pieces in cherry red and gold	Gold	Good for living room, especially in 18th Century French feeling
MEDIUM BLUE (2)	Blue	Mole	Lavender, gray, and some rose	Rose	Adaptable for lady's bedroom in lighter blues, also to living room in darker shades of duller blues
MEDIUM BLUE (3)	Cream	Blue	French Blue	Jade Green	Good for south living room or bedroom
DUSTY BLUE	Dusty Blue	Dark Burgundy	Draperies, gray, trimmed with soft blue. Upholstery, soft blue and gray	Crystal	Restful for living room or dining room
SOFT DULL BLUE	Ivory	Soft Dull Blue	Ivory background with blue, rose and green in design, some pieces in old rose	Green	Bedroom or informal living room
OLD BLUE	Old Blue	Deeper Blue	Faded Pink, or chintz with blue, green and pink	Green	Charming for living room or bedroom
GRAYED BLUE	Gray Blue	Deeper grayed Blue	Yellow, white, and gold	Red	Dining room in Directoire feeling with mahogany
TURQUOISE BLUE	Pale Turquoise Blue	Turquoise	Draperies, golden yellow. Upholstery, golden yellow and white	White	Any room not too large or too dark
TURQUOISE BLUE	Grayed Turquoise	Grayed Turquoise	Wine and ivory	Polished Brass	Dignified but friendly living room
GREEN BLUE	Green Blue	Plum rug, flowered pattern	Draperies, peach. Upholstery, green-blue with some plum	Peach	Simple living room in French Provincial feeling
ROYAL BLUE (1)	Walls, Silver. Woodwork, Royal Blue	Floor, painted Gray. Rug, Blue	Draperies, blue, trimmed with silver. Upholstery (chairs), silver and blue leather	Silver and Black	Distinctive modern dining room
ROYAL BLUE (2)	Old White	Royal Blue	Clear yellow	Silver	Modern living or dining room
ROYAL BLUE (3)	Dull White	Rug, Deep Blue ground with honey-yellow in pattern	Draperies, royal blue. Chair Seats, royal blue Morocco	Silver	Attractive for modern dining room, especially with lemon wood furniture
DEEP BLUE (1)	Pale Amethyst	Deep Blue	Deep blue, trimmed with gold	Amethyst and Gold	Cool and charming for living room not too dark
DEEP BLUE (2)	Deep Blue Woodwork, Ivory	Dark Blue rug with Tan and Rose in pattern	Draperies, dull ivory. Upholstery (chairs), ivory or rosy red leather	Red	Colorful for dining room with plenty of light
DEEP BLUE (3)	Deep Blue	Deep Blue	Draperies, deep sea blue. Upholstery, canary yellow	White	Modern living room or dining room
DEEP BLUE (4)	Pale Yellow	Natural	Draperies, deep sea blue (gold gauze glass curtains). Upholstery, deep blue	White	Good when blue is dominant color in a dark room
DEEP BLUE (5)	Creamy White	Blue	Draperies, deep blue. Upholstery, yellow with dash of white	Gold, Rose-Pink and Blue	Good for bedroom, furniture painted blue with flower decorations, and some smaller oyster white pieces
GARDEN POOL BLUE	Ivory	Garden Pool Blue	Draperies, garden pool blue. Chair Seats, red leather	White and Silver	Dramatic modern living room with furniture in rich mahogany or walnut tones
DARK BLUE	Cream and beige paper	Dark Blue rug with rose and tan in pattern	Draperies, linen color with blues, greens and rosy reds in pattern. Chair Seats, dark blue	Blue and Silver	Good for dining room where light is needed

THE ORANGE FAMILY

REPRESENTATIVE MEMBERS OF THE ORANGE FAMILY . . . IVORY . . . PEACH . . . CORAL . . . BEIGE . . . RUST . . . TERRA COTTA . . . WARM BROWN.

CHARACTERISTICS . . . Always warm, advancing . . . Cheerful, welcoming, gay, vibrant, glowing . . . In strong tones, akin to red . . . In softer tones, a good mixer.

WHAT THEY CAN DO . . . In slightly less degree, Orange repeats the activities of the Red Family . . . Effec-

five for "toning" up a room in too dull or quiet colors, or warming a cold room.

CORRECT USES . . . Best in off shades, except for accent . . . In softened background color for dark or cold rooms . . . Wonderful accent color in proper combinations.

CAUTION . . . Do not use too much of the clear color . . . In large areas it has the disturbing quality of red . . . Do not use for background of small room unless you want it to be very "cozy."

SUGGESTED COLOR SCHEMES IN WHICH MEMBERS OF ORANGE FAMILY PLAY A DOMINANT ROLE

DOMINANT COLOR	MAJOR WALL COLOR	MAJOR FLOOR COLOR	DRAPERIES AND UPHOLSTERY	ACCENT COLORS	REMARKS
IVORY	Ivory Woodwork, Ivory	Floor, painted ivory Rug, Jade Green	Ivory background, rose and blue green in pattern	Rose and Jade Green	Charming for bedroom or lady's sitting room with ivory painted furniture
PEACH (1)	Peach	Peach	Apple green	Bittergreen	Attractive for bedroom, modern or traditional
PEACH (2)	Peach	Old Green	Draperies and upholstery, peach, with old blue	Old Blue	For a room that needs warming up, with cool touches
PEACH (3)	Peach	Warm Brown	Draperies, brown and coral stripes Upholstery, brown background, with coral, beige and tan	Copper	Modern color scheme appropriate for living room or library
PEACH (4)	Paper, shades of yellow, through peach to brown	Brown	Draperies, brown Upholstery, light and dark peach	Yellow	Good modern living room color scheme
PEACH (5)	Floral pattern paper, white ground, peach and green	Rust	Draperies, peach Upholstery (chair seats), green	Green	Very good for late Colonial dining room with Duncan Phyfe style furniture
PEACH (6)	Yellowish Pink	Eggplant	Draperies, peach background, blue in design Upholstery, peach and blue	Coral and yellow	Good color scheme to lighten dark bedroom
APRICOT	Apricot	Rose and Cream	Draperies, old rose Bed and furniture covering, apricot, trimmed with black	Orchid	Charming for young girl's room
CORAL (1)	Paper, silver ground, coral-rose design; Woodwork, coral	Aquamarine	Aquamarine	Aquamarine and Silver	Charming for woman's bedroom
CORAL (2)	Coral Woodwork, soft Blue	Gray Blue	Draperies, off-white background rose and green in design, Coral valance; Bed and furniture covering, copper rose and same chintz used for hangings	Off-white	Attractive for bedroom with furniture painted blue
WARM BEIGE (1)	Warm Beige	Warm Beige	Brown and Copper	Bright Green	Modern living room or library
WARM BEIGE (2)	Pink and Beige wallpaper	Warm Beige	Draperies, old white and beige Upholstery, dusty pink and pale olive green	Terra Cotta	Restful living room color scheme
WARM BEIGE (3)	Warm Beige	Warm Beige	Draperies, burgundy background, white and beige in design; Upholstery, burgundy and natural	White	Good for living room, library, or man's bedroom
WARM BEIGE (4)	Warm Beige	Dark Taupe	Draperies, russet (beige glass curtains) Upholstery, brown with tan cushions	Tan	Restful, chromatic color scheme
WARM BEIGE (5)	Beige with pink cast	Light warm beige	Brown, beige and white stripes or checks	Sky Blue	Appropriate for informal living room or boy's room
HENNA (1)	Grass cloth, tan and gold	Henna and black	Henna, green and gray	Gold	Living room or man's bedroom
HENNA (2)	Mint Green Woodwork, Cream	Henna	Henna with valance of bedspread material Bedspread, henna, light and dark green and tan stripes Upholstery, same combination in patterned material	White	Man's bedroom
TERRA COTTA	Pink Terra Cotta	Eggplant	Draperies, pinkish yellow, trimmed with terra cotta Upholstery, bois de rose	Pale Green	Charming for dining room in Directoire feeling with furniture painted yellow and gold
COPPER (1)	Pine paneled	Floor, Pine Rugs (hooked) in tones of orange, yellow, green	Draperies, copper toned background with orange, yellow and green in pattern	Blue and copper	Appropriate for living room in Early American feeling with Early American style furniture
COPPER (2)	Rough plaster with oak paneling	Oak plank floor Patterned rug, tones of brown, green, copper	Draperies, copper colored, coarsely woven material Upholstery, neutral green, trimmed with brown and copper	Green	Good color scheme for large, formal, English-style living room, with furniture in natural oak and walnut
BURNT ORANGE	Neutral Woodwork, walnut	Rug, greenish background, with burnt orange and henna	Burnt orange and henna	Blue	Good for dining room with walnut furniture
WARM BROWN (1)	Tobacco Brown	Warm Beige	Chintz in clear yellow, beige and warm brown in design	White	Modern living room
WARM BROWN (2)	Tan	Warm Brown	Draperies, copper and topaz; Upholstery, warm browns	Orange, French Blue	Appropriate for boy's room
WARM BROWN (3)	Yellow Brown	Orange Brown	Burnt orange and apple green	Greenish Blue	Restful, cheerful color scheme for library
WARM BROW (4)	Pale Yellow	Orange Brown	Shades of warm browns and orange	Silver	Attractive for modern living room or dining room

THE VIOLET (OR PURPLE) FAMILY

REPRESENTATIVE MEMBERS OF THE VIOLET FAMILY . . . ORCHID . . . LAVENDER . . . MAUVE . . . . . . Create restful, quiet atmosphere when used in soft tones.
VIOLET . . . PLUM . . . PURPLE.   CORRECT USES . . . In light, soft tints, excellent wall and ceiling background for an average room . . .
CHARACTERISTICS . . . Cool when mixed with blue, warm when mixed with red . . . In pure form, cold   Strong shades good for accent . . . In deep, soft tones, attractive for carpets, upholstery, draperies.
and formal . . . In purple tones, rich and dignified but not friendly . . . May be depressing.   CAUTION . . . Do not use blue tones of violet in cold, dark, over-large rooms . . . Be careful when using
WHAT THEY CAN DO . . . Add to impression of room size and coolness, especially when mixed with blue   strong shades for dominant color . . . Do not use without some warm contrast.

SUGGESTED COLOR SCHEMES IN WHICH MEMBERS OF VIOLET FAMILY PLAY A DOMINANT ROLE

DOMINANT COLOR	MAJOR WALL COLOR	MAJOR FLOOR COLOR	DRAPERIES AND UPHOLSTERY	ACCENT COLORS	REMARKS
ORCHID (1)	Orchid	Blue	Champagne, orchid and blue	Black and Silver	Attractive for living room
ORCHID (2)	Paneled paper in Orchid and Pale Yellow	Mulberry	Green, yellow and orchid chintz	Green	Cool, airy bedroom
LAVENDER (1)	Lavender	Lavender with mauve border	Gray, light blue and touches of jade green	Jade Green	Good for sunny room
LAVENDER (2)	Lavender, Blue and White paper	Plum	Lavender	Rose	Feminine bedroom
LAVENDER (3)	Pale Lavender	Rose	Pink, lavender and white	Lavender	Bedroom with warm light
HELIOTROPE (1)	Gray	Beige	Heliotrope draperies and upholstery	Violet and Silver	Lovely color scheme for woman with gray hair
MAUVE (1)	Gray	Mauve	Light blue, Nile green, some rose	Rose	Good for sunny bedroom
MAUVE (2)	Paneled wall painted Pale Mauve	Deep Violet	Mauve and yellow	Crystal and Sepia	Especially attractive for Louis XVI style bedroom with walnut furniture
HELIOTROPE (2)	Pearl Gray	Heliotrope	Draperies, heliotrope trimmed with silver Upholstery, Tarragon green, gray and heliotrope	Green	Cool and restful living room
VIOLET	Dove Gray	Black and White	Draperies, violet Upholstery, coral and old gold	Silver and Black	Attractive with silver gray painted woodwork and violet lines, also white and gold furniture
MULBERRY (1)	Dusty Mulberry	Mahogany	Draperies, clear blue chintz with mulberry and brown in pattern Upholstery, clear blue	White	Very good for traditional living room or dining room
MULBERRY (2)	Dusty Mulberry	Ebony	Draperies, creamy peach chintz with gray, old rose and ebony design Upholstery, creamy peach	Black	Good for sunny living room or dining room
MULBERRY (3)	Scenic paper Woodwork, walnut	Deep Mulberry	Mulberry	Orange	Traditional dining room
PURPLE	Paper in Gray and soft Purple stripes	Gray	Purple, with blue, green and gray	Burnt Orange	Hall or living room

BASIC TYPES OF DESIGN

TYPE	CHARACTERISTICS	USES
SPOT MOTIFS 	**MAY BE . . .** Single dots, small clusters, leaves, flowers, any small figure. . . . **ALWAYS . . .** Small motifs, identically related at regular intervals over the paper. . . . **SOMETIMES . . .** Close together, sometimes wide apart.	**APPROPRIATE . . .** In small rooms only. . . . **IF . . .** Light, receding background color is chosen, spot motifs provide wall interest without decreasing size of room. . . . **DON'T . . .** Use in a large room; wide wall-spaces make small figures disappear. . . .
DETACHED MOTIFS 	**MAY BE . . .** Floral, conventional, geometrical; bouquets, feathers, fruit; figures of many kinds. . . . **ALWAYS . . .** Larger than the ''spots,'' but repeated in the same regular way over the paper. . . . **SOMETIMES . . .** Very large, but may be found in all sizes, styles, types—also combined with stripes or in stripe effect.	**APPROPRIATE . . .** In any room-size or type, in a harmonizing design. . . . **IF . . .** It is chosen in right style and scale for type, period, and size of room, is versatile and adaptable. . . . **DON'T . . .** Use large motifs with sharp contrast colors anywhere, except in large room, hall, or dining room. . . .
ALL-OVER . . . CONVENTIONAL 	**MAY BE . . .** Self-toned, unobtrusive, like texture-patterned cloth or bold in pattern and color like printed linen or chintz. . . . **ALWAYS . . .** In conventional, set designs, with continuous pattern lines. Often modeled after rich brocades and damasks. . . . **SOMETIMES . . .** Large in scale, which makes it very formal in effect.	**APPROPRIATE . . .** In harmonizing period rooms, rooms with some formality and dignity. . . . **IF . . .** Patterns are small and colors soft, these have charm in any average room. . . . **DON'T . . .** Use large or boldly colored designs except in large, important, dignified rooms. . . .
ALL-OVER . . . NATURAL 	**MAY BE . . .** Vines trailing, leaves or flowers branching, any gracefully flowing subject from nature. . . . **ALWAYS . . .** Repeated over the paper, but in continuous, meandering lines, so that ''repeat'' is not noticed. . . . **SOMETIMES . . .** Up-and-down in effect; sometimes open and rambling with feeling of width.	**APPROPRIATE . . .** In any not-too-formal room; very gay in light, bright, warm colors specially good for bedrooms. . . . **IF . . .** Colors are warm and light, it brightens up a dark room. . . . **DON'T . . .** Use small, dainty feminine patterns in large room; large sprawling patterns in small rooms—unless they are in soft colors and open vistas. . . .
STRIPES UP-AND-DOWN . . . OR . . . ACROSS . . . 	**MAY BE . . .** Large or small; well defined or ''shadowed''; pin-striped or panel-like; self or contrast colors; combined with another type—as floral motifs. . . . **ALWAYS . . .** Add height, formality, dignity to wall when vertical; restfulness and width when horizontal. . . . **SOMETIMES . . .** Stripe effect is in arrangement of motifs without straight lines.	**APPROPRIATE . . .** In some form in almost any room, because of great variety in pattern, scale, type, colors; modern favorite. . . . **IF . . .** Stripes are bold, use carefully; the bolder they are, the greater their effect on room proportions. . . . **DON'T . . .** Use vertical in too-high room; horizontal in too-low room. . . .
STRIPES CROSSING DIAGONAL . . . OR . . . PLAID . . . 	**MAY BE . . .** Geometrical, as in many modern designs; stylized; or combined with one of the other basic types—as, ''Detached Motif.'' . . . **ALWAYS . . .** Plaids affect size only in strong contrast colors—vertical lines offset horizontal; small diagonals seem to draw in walls—large, open spaces may seem to extend them. . . . **SOMETIMES . . .** Diagonal effect is only in motif arrangement, without lines.	**APPROPRIATE . . .** In some form in any not-too-formal room; in contemporary patterns, specially suited to modern rooms. . . . **IF . . .** This type seems too ''positive,'' combine it with plain paper or painted walls. . . . **DON'T . . .** Use in large, formal rooms. . . .
PICTORIAL MOTIFS 	**MAY BE . . .** Small scenes, repeated like detached motifs; or pictures of any size—panels or all-over designs. . . . **ALWAYS . . .** Reproductions of painted ''scenes''; small, close motifs make room seem smaller, while large open ''vistas'' make it seem larger. . . . **SOMETIMES . . .** Used as all-over pattern, sometimes in panels or friezes.	**APPROPRIATE . . .** For period or regional rooms in harmonizing style; also, large formal rooms. . . . **IF . . .** Scale and type are right for background and use of room, these are possible in almost any style of room. . . . **DON'T . . .** Use without careful study of effect you want, architecture, and style of room. See illustrations and text. . . .

HOME-DECORATING FABRIC CHART
(See Chapter XVIII)

In the chart below are listed the fabrics usually classified as primarily decorating materials. In addition to these, practically all dress materials may be used, and are often woven in extra widths for this purpose. Among these are: light weight cottons such as cambric, challis, chambray, gingham, muslin, percale, poplin, seersucker, silkaline all used for informal draperies, bed coverings, dressing tables, etc.; stiff fabrics such as buckram and crinoline for interlining curtain tops, valances, etc.; cottons such as Canton flannel used for interlinings, and sateen for linings; heavy utility cottons such as crash, denim, drill, gabardine, pique, all suited to certain types of draperies, couch covers, etc.; sheer cottons such as cheesecloth, dimity, plain and dotted Swiss, lace, lawn, organdy, voile, all used for glass curtains, bed coverings, etc.; pile fabrics such as corduroy, panne velet, velour, velvet, velveteen, all excellent for upholstery, draperies, etc.; silk fabrics such as faille, moire (watered silk), pongee and shantung, satin, taffeta, all used for draperies, bed coverings, slipcovers, sometimes upholstery; sheer silks such as chiffon for glass curtains, lamp shades, etc.

FABRIC	DESCRIPTION	SUITABLE FOR
ARMURE	Ribbed silk, cotton, rayon (sometimes wool), fabric with small design on the surface.	Draperies. Medium-weight upholstery.
ARTIFICIAL LEATHER	Available under many trade names. A woven cotton fabric, coated with nitrocellulose preparation and stamped surface to simulate different kinds of leather.	Medium-weight upholstery. Panels. Other decorative uses.
BATIK	Javanese process of coloring fabrics by blocking out various parts of the pattern with wax before dyeing.	Curtains and panels. Other decorative effects.
BOBBINET	Net with hexagonal openings. Originally handmade with a bobbin.	Glass curtains. Dressing table skirts, etc.
BROCADE	Rich, colorful fabric with embroidery effects on taffeta, twill, satin or damask weave background. Gold or silver metal threads sometimes introduced in the figures. Brocade is also the name designating a certain type of Jacquard weave.	Draperies. Medium-weight upholstery. Especially good for rooms of Queen Anne, Chippendale, Hepplewhite or Sheraton furnishings of 18th Century.
BROCATELLE	A heavy fabric with general characteristics of damask, but figures more raised and velvety in quality giving embossed effect.	Draperies on very large studio-size windows. Heavy-weight upholstery.
BROCHE	Brocade with small floral pattern.	Lined or unlined draperies. Medium-weight upholstery.
BURLAP	Coarse, plain-weave fabric made of jute or hemp. Comes in variety of colors and widths. Inexpensive.	Drapery or upholstery purposes.
CALICO	Light-weight cotton fabric in plain weave. May be printed, plain or patterned, in deep colors. Designs usually small. (Also for dresses.)	Curtains, draperies, bedspreads, comfortables. Excellent with Early American or French Provincial furnishings.
CANDLEWICK	Cotton yarn used for hand tufting on muslin sheeting. Yarn may be white or in color and design simple or elaborate.	Bedspreads, draperies, and other decorative purposes.
CANVAS	A coarse, firm cotton or linen material, rough finish, plain weave. May be bleached, unbleached, starched, dyed, or printed.	Awnings, couch covers, etc.; also used for stiff interlining as at top of draperies.
CASEMENT CLOTH	Light, plain, and usually neutral in color. Made in cotton, linen, mohair, silk, wool or rayon. Sometimes comes in small figures.	Fine for draw-curtains; also glass curtains in sheer textures.
CELLOPHANE	Glossy, transparent synthetic product woven on warp threads of cotton. Often woven in with other materials and used for many novelty effects.	Draperies in modern interiors. Trimmings, etc.
CHENILLE	Various types of fabrics woven with chenille yarn of silk, wool, mercerized cotton, or rayon.	Draperies. Yarn used for tufting, fringes, etc.
CHEVRON CLOTH	Fabric with broken twill weave forming chevron pattern.	Draperies, etc.
CHINTZ	A firm plain weave cotton fabric usually printed in gay pattern, but may be had in plain colors. May be semi-glazed or fully glazed. Some chintz has special finish so that it will retain glaze after washing. Glazed chintz is more resistant to dirt, while its shiny surface and stiff texture adds to its charm. There are many grades of chintz, and many have soil-resistant special finish.	May be formal or informal in pattern. Suitable to any room according to pattern, quality and treatment. Used for draperies, upholstery, slip covers, lamp shades, etc.
CRETONNE	Cotton or linen fabric named for French town of Creton, with plain, rep or damask weave background printed in large designs. Does not muss easily and can be washed often.	Draperies, upholstery, slip covers, bed covers, etc. Often more formal than chintz.
CREWEL EMBROIDERY	A type of wool embroidery worked on unbleached cotton or linen ground in large floral, bird, or tree designs.	Draperies and upholstery. Used extensively during Jacobean period.
DAMASK	The name originated with the beautiful silks woven in Damascus during the 12th Century. Damasks are now made of linen, cotton, wool, or any of the synthetic fibers, or combinations of the two. In taffeta weave on satin ground, this fabric in flat woven pattern is usually reversible. Damask is also the name given to a kind of Jacquard weave.	In silk or cotton it is used for draperies and upholstery. Appropriate for Queen Anne, Chippendale, Hepplewhite or Sheraton furnishings of 18th Century.
DRUID'S CLOTH	A fabric of loosely twisted cotton yarn, or cotton mixed with jute, in basket weave. Something like monk's cloth but not as rough in texture.	Draperies. Couch covers.
DUCK	Heavy plain weave cotton fabric.	Outdoor cushions, etc.
FELT	A material made by matting together, under heat or pressure, woolen fibers, mohair, cowhair, or mixed fibers.	Upholstery and couch covers. Rugs.

HOME-DECORATING FABRIC CHART CONTINUED

FABRIC	DESCRIPTION	SUITABLE FOR
FILET NET	Cotton or linen net with square mesh. Hand netted filet has a knot at each corner of square mesh.	Curtains, tablecloths, scarves, etc.
FORTUNY PRINTS	Fabrics produced in Venice by a secret printing process which gives cotton cloth the effect of antique brocades and damasks. Comes in beautiful color combinations.	Draperies. Wall hangings, screens, etc.
FRIAR'S CLOTH	Like druid's cloth but with finer basket weave.	Same as druid's cloth.
FRISE	Uncut pile fabric of wool, mohair, cotton or linen. Patterns may be printed or produced by using yarns of different colors, or by cutting some of the loops to give sculptured effect. Very durable.	Upholstery.
GAUZE	Thin, sheer transparent fabric of plain weave, sometimes printed. May be all silk, or cotton, linen, wool, mohair, synthetic fibers, or combinations.	Glass curtains.
HAIR CLOTH	A fabric with warp of cotton, worsted, or linen, and horsehair weft, woven plain, striped or patterned. May now be obtained in colors and variety of woven designs.	Upholstery. Used extensively in England and America during middle of 19th Century.
HOMESPUN	Coarse hand-woven woolen, cotton or linen fabrics. Also trade name given to imitations made on power looms.	Curtains and upholstery in informal rooms. Bedspreads in cotton.
INDIA PRINTS	Printed cotton cloth with clear colors and characteristic designs of India or Persia. Handprinted with many colors on white or natural background.	Draperies. Wall hangings. Bed coverings, etc.
JASPE	Fabrics having warp threads of different colors giving material streaked or mottled effect, resembling jasper.	Draperies and other decorative effects.
LAME	A fabric with silk and metal threads in plain weave or with a woven pattern.	Drapery. Panels.
LAMPAS	A fabric similar to damask in appearance and brocatelle in weave. Generally all silk with multi-colored pattern on plain background, often classic in design.	Used as damask is used.
MARQUISETTE	Sheer cloth in gauze weave of cotton, silk, rayon, often with woven figure. It comes in wide range of colors, and may be dyed or printed.	Excellent for glass curtains. Fluffy, dainty, tailored spreads.
METALASSE	Fabric with brocaded pattern in raised, padded or blistered effect.	Draperies.
MOHAIR	Various types of fabrics made from the fleece of the Angora goat. Most durable of all textiles. Now woven in combination with cotton, linen, silk or wool into many types of plain, twill or pile fabrics.	Very durable and widely used for upholstery.
MONK'S CLOTH	Heavy cotton fabric of coarse basket weave.	Drapery material.
MOQUETTE	Pile fabric resembling frise, woven on Jacquard loom with small set pattern in different colors.	Used for upholstery in mohair, wool, or heavy cotton.
NINON	A semi-transparent fabric of silk or rayon.	Glass curtains.
PLUSH	High pile fabric resembling fur, made of silk, wool, cotton or any synthetic fiber. Pile may be cut or uncut.	Upholstery.
REP	Plain weave fabric of heavy rib made of silk, cotton or wool, or synthetic fibers. Unpatterned and reversible.	Draperies. Upholstery.
SAIL CLOTH	Stout, firm, plain weave cotton material similar to canvas in construction but lighter. Has a stiff, hard texture and is printed in gay, bright colors.	Draperies. Slip covers. Bedspreads, etc.
SLIPPER SATIN	Sleek, smooth very heavy satin in rayon or silk; may be slightly stiff because of thickness.	Drapery and upholstery, bed coverings, etc. Suitable in formal and period rooms for draperies.
SCRIM	Fabric of coarse two-ply yarns in plain, open weave. Often mercerized.	Curtains, bedspreads, etc.
STRIE	Term used to designate fabric with uneven streaked effect. This process gives two-toned appearance to taffeta, satin, etc.	According to fabric.
TERRY CLOTH	Light cotton fabric similar to bath toweling. Woven with uncut loops. May be dyed or printed, in designs of one or two colors. Rich texture and reversible.	Draperies. Draw-curtains.
THEATRICAL GAUZE	Loosely woven, transparent plain-weave fabric of cotton or linen. Obtainable in brilliant as well as soft colors. Inexpensive.	Glass curtains.
TOILES DE JOUY	Printed cotton material with repeat designs showing landscapes, or historical scenes. Reproductions of famous printed fabric woven at Jouy, near Paris, France. Designs and figure groups usually in colors on white or cream background.	Draperies, wall hangings, upholstery, bed coverings. Excellent for French, English and American period rooms of late 18th Century and early 19th Century; also French Provincial.
TWEED WEAVES	Term applied to a large group of woolen goods made from worsted yarns, woven in plain, twill, or herringbone twill weaves in homespun type.	Draperies and upholstery. Very good for modern or masculine rooms.
VELOUR	Really a French word for velvet. Through common usage, a short-pile velvet.	Same as velvet.

CONCEALED LIGHTING PROVIDES
A TOUCH OF DRAMA

The dramatic treatment above is completely modern with its straight lines and square corners. The fluorescent lighting set in above the shelf behind the couch is modern, too, with a plain dark wall and cotton string rug providing an appropriate background. But notice the greater charm given this room by mingling in traditional and graceful curves in mirrored coffee table and accessories on the book shelf. The upholstery of the sofa is yellow cotton chenille, the wall is soft dark green. Cushions are in the same green and white prints used for slip covers and draperies in another section of the room (not shown here). The wall section behind the shelf is pale soft yellow.

CHAPTER THIRTY-SEVEN

Points on Home Lighting

CORRECT HOME LIGHTING is very easily reduced to a few simple principles, none of them difficult to apply in the average home. Often they do not involve a great deal of expense. Attractive lamps may be made from an astonishing variety of discarded articles or from almost any kind of vase. (See page 423.)

LIGHTING FIXTURES

Most rooms need an overhead light which can be switched on at entrance doors even if it is seldom used at any other time. All living or working rooms need enough lamps with correct size lamp bulbs to provide adequate light without glare on the one hand, or confusion from too many small lamps on the other. For opposite positions—as at two ends of a sofa—lamps are best in pairs. Wall sconces are a matter of taste. If you like them be sure that they are evenly balanced, in scale and harmony with the room, and placed where they will not break up major wall spaces and interfere with effective decoration. They are as a rule for additional general lighting only and should be fitted with small bulbs. They should always be shaded all the way around, not by shields which create a spot of glare on the wall behind them. Handy pin-up lamps (see page 374) often solve a problem when direct light is needed but there is no room for a table or floor lamp.

Lamps and Shades: Styles in lamps and shades are continually changing but in recent years they have been more and more adapted to suitability as well as decorative effect. For period rooms, lamps and other fixtures should be reproductions of original fixtures, combining modern light sources with traditional design. Vases or ornaments in the feeling of the period can easily be made into adequate and attractive lamps. Elaborate chandeliers should be confined to large dining rooms or formal rooms with high ceilings. Avoid over-decoration in lamps and shades; and keep shades in harmony and scale with the base as well as with other furnishings in the room.

Modern rooms have very distinctive types of lighting fixtures even when they do not use fluorescent lighting. Contemporary styles call in general for taller lamps on low, sturdy tables rather than high tables with low lamps. This allows for larger shades and bulbs suitable for all practical purposes while reducing the number of lamps needed in the room. Whether you have many or few, be sure that they are well balanced and well distributed around the room for light-effectiveness and appearance.

Utility Lighting: Correct lighting boils down to three essentials: (1) Adequate light for quick seeing without unnecessary strain, the amount needed varying with the task—for example, more for sewing than for reading. (2) Freedom from glare which is both unpleasant and definitely injurious to the eyes and is usually caused by unshaded or wrongly shaded bulbs. (3) Elimination of shadows which interfere with work or reading, and deep shadows which require too rapid adjustment of eyes to sharp contrasts between light and dark areas.

Service from Lamp Bulbs: Adequate light depends partly upon location of lamps and size of bulbs. Each spot in a room where such activities as reading, sewing, studying or game playing will be carried on should be lighted according to the demands of those pursuits. A 100-watt bulb—which is the *minimum* size recommended for reading—gives 50% more light than four 25-watt bulbs, uses the same amount of current, and costs *less than half* as much as the four small bulbs.

Avoiding Glare: The raw quality of light resulting from a lamp with a shade too thin to conceal the outline of the lighted bulb, too shallow to cover it, or without any shade at all, is very bad for the eyes. So also are sharp contrasts between light and shadows. The best way to eliminate both of these evils is to use as many floor and table lamps as possible with a glass or plastic reflector under the shade. This reflector sifts the light downward, yet throws some of it toward the ceiling and walls to be reflected throughout the room. This is called *semi-indirect lighting* and creates a soft restful dispersal of light throughout the room.

Direct light is that emanating from lamps or fixtures which direct more than 90% of the light downward, such as desk lamps with metal shades and the old-style bridge lamps. The spot-lighting which results from this type should be used in combination with the other types of lighting.

Indirect light results when ceiling fixtures throw light upward against the ceiling and walls from where it is reflected downward; when floor lamps are fitted with the same kind of indirect reflector they produce indirect lighting; when lighting is built in at a ceiling line behind a cove or some other architectural or finishing feature to operate entirely by reflection against ceiling and walls. This latter type is more often used with the new fluorescent lighting fixtures.

FLUORESCENT LIGHTING

The use of fluorescent lighting in the home is increasing daily. This relative newcomer into the home-lighting field is a mercury-vapor arc lamp with a cooler light and a different color quality from that of the incandescent bulb. It is a tubular-shaped bulb and costs less to operate than the incandescent lamp but requires special auxiliary equipment. It is particularly useful for work requiring approximately daylight quality, or wherever concentrated light is needed without undue heat, or for effective use of colored lights in decoration. Illustrations in this chapter will show characteristic installations and special uses.

One of the features of fluorescent lighting is that it has an entirely different effect on colors from that which ordinary artificial light usually imparts. Much closer to daylight, fluorescent lighting has a white, cold quality which must be taken into consideration in choosing colors. Contrary to general impression fluorescent light installed for indirect lighting mingles attractively with light from incandescent bulbs in lamps and other fixtures.

LAMP SHADES

Lamp shades should always cover the bulbs and mechanical lighting sections. They are made from many types of fabric, with silk or rayon and parchment-effect paper most widely used. There are opaque shades made of tinsel, painted tin or other metals, and translucent shades made of plastics, specially prepared glass, glazed papers which imitate leather, shell, suede cloth and even wood veneer. Hand-painted shades with historical scenes are charming specially in period rooms. Antique maps, silhouettes and other applied designs provide decoration as well as conversation themes. All the shades in the room should be keyed to each other but for the sake of variety they should not all be alike.

Lamp-shade sizes are measured by the width of the bottom diameter. The general rule for correct

TRADITIONAL LIGHTING VERSUS MODERN SPOT LIGHT EFFECTS

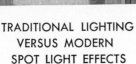

A traditional living room is shown at upper right, combining with period furnishings several modern notes. Eighteenth Century furniture and a Chinese Chippendale steel grate in the fireplace, a fine Adam gilt mirror over the mantel and a display of rare English china in the wall cupboards help create an atmosphere of charm and dignity in the period manner. The plain background of soft warm gray painted plaster has a modern feeling of spaciousness which harmonizes with the indirect lighting installed in wall sconces and above the cabinets. This architectural lighting eliminates need for any lamps in the room. Rich brocade and tapestry upholstery on sofa and chairs give pattern to the room, in combination with the soft over-all design of the Oriental rug. The three furniture groupings below illustrate fluorescent and other lighting installed according to modern ideas of comfort and convenience. Straight fluorescent tubes lend themselves to built-in applications as they are easily concealed and spread the lighting evenly over extended areas such as book shelves, desk tops, etc. Novelty lighting like that in the glass-topped table with the drumlike base can be worked out with either circular fluorescent lamps or incandescent bulbs. Long straight fluorescent tubes provide light which is not only dramatic and striking, but also ideal for practical purposes when used behind window valances and ceiling-line coves, or for illuminating book shelves—all illustrated here. At upper left, a hallway niche is turned into a charming lamp substitute by fluorescent tubes at the sides, lighting up the gold of wheat in a graceful bowl.

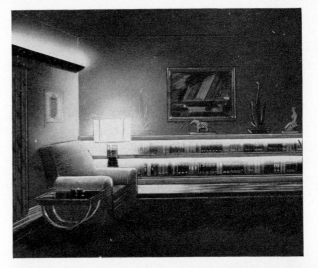

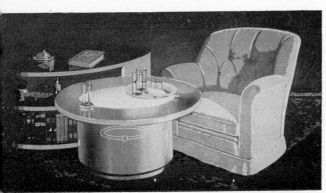

CANDLE LIGHT FOR GRACIOUS DINING

Dining rooms should be cheerful and pleasant, bright without glare. The glow from lighting fixtures should be soft and becoming as well as adequate for comfort. A central fixture is usually preferred, supplemented by wall lights or better still one of the modern types of indirect fixtures. In the room above, Federal-type furniture harmonizes with a crystal chandelier fitted for electric candles. Additional lights on the console in front of the window and candles on the sideboard, all with silk shades, provide light on the table to enhance the sparkle of crystal and the attractiveness of linen, china and silver. Notice the eagle-topped period mirror and the unusual draperies made from rows and rows of deep fringe sewed to a foundation curtain. Another interesting note is the wallpaper decoration applied at strategic points to plain painted walls. The room below illustrates the undying charm of candle-lighting even in this era of modern miracle lights. In this simple dining alcove of a living room wooden brackets with paper doilies behind them support groups of tall slender candles. An arrangement of candle brackets like this would be appropriate in any dining room, traditional or modern.

size follows in this scale: (1) For side lights and chandeliers use four-inch candle shades for each light. (2) For boudoir, pin-up and novelty lamps, eight- and ten-inch shades are usually correct. (3) For the average bridge lamp use a twelve-inch shade. (4) Table lamps usually require shades fourteen or sixteen inches across. (5) Indirect floor lamps are usually fitted with eighteen- or twenty-inch shades. (6) If your lamp is an odd size you will have to try out a shade to be sure you have it right.

Care of Shades and Bulbs: Clean parchment shades by frequent dusting. If they are good quality remove soil by wiping with a damp sudsy cloth followed by a clean cloth dampened with clear water, then wipe quickly until dry. Or, rub gently with a cloth dipped in milk. Remove reflectors and wash in soap and water (not hot), rinse, and dry thoroughly. Remove bulbs and wipe (when cool) with damp soapy cloth. Wipe away suds with clear water and damp cloth, then dry. Submerging a lamp bulb may loosen the cement around its base.

Dust pleated silk shades with a small pastry brush or a man's shaving brush. Clean silk or rayon shades with cleaning fluid on a soft cloth. Silk shades that are put together by glue, trimmed with painting or applied decoration, made of fabric which might shrink, should be dry-cleaned.

When a silk shade is *stitched* to the frame and made of washable material it can be successfully washed. Brush dust out, then plunge shade into a deep bath of lukewarm suds, dousing repeatedly. For stubborn dirt brush gently with any soft brush and downward strokes. Dip up and down in several baths of clear lukewarm water to remove soap. Dry very fast to avoid rust but not in sunlight nor *on* the radiator. Suspend outdoors in the shade if it is warm drying weather. In cold weather, suspend *above* the radiator or in a current of air from an electric fan.

If you have an old shade which cannot be restored, try making a "skirt" which can be snapped to a tape at the top of the shade. This is an easy way to brighten up a lamp without expense. You can use leftover fabrics for the shade, as suggested elsewhere in the book.

Care of Lamp Bases: Wax wood and metal bases for longer wear—unless they are chrome metal. Dust with a soft cloth, cover with a thin coat of wax and polish when dry. Wash bases of glass, marble, onyx and plastic. Make sure bases are weighted and wide enough to prevent easy tipping over.

MAKING NEW LAMPS FROM ODDS AND ENDS

The collection of "junk" shown directly below is the foundation for the entire assortment of lamps illustrated in the other three photographs. You can easily trace the relationship between the various objects in their "before" and "after" stages. Some of the lamps are sufficiently formal and beautiful to grace your living room. Others would be attractive in playrooms, children's rooms or other informal spots in your home. None of them requires much in the way of expense and some of them have real distinction—such as the one with the period effect created by draping heavy fringe over the shade. One advantage of making lamps out of odds and ends like this is that you can enamel, lacquer or otherwise finish them to harmonize with any decorating scheme you may have. Making over old shades, or reconditioning them is not difficult. Use up scraps of fabric, or find a piece of translucent plastic. In renovating a parchment shade, where the outside is good but the inside has become drab or discolored, you can refresh it by giving it a coat of white paint. If the surface is not oily you can apply one or two coats of flat white paint directly to the inner surface. If the finish is oily use one coat of clear shellac and let it dry before putting on the paint. This treatment will not only give new life to your shade but the white coating will provide much better lighting from your lamp.

Lamps shown above, ranging through styles inspired by ancient Chinese themes down to the most modern plastic designs, illustrate several fundamental principles in selecting lamps. You will notice that these are all fitted with substantial bases; shades harmonize both in shape and decoration with the bases; they are in scale with the size of the lamp.

The photograph at the top of the page shows a box spring and mattress in specially built frame, with construction details given in the small drawings. After the framework was finished, panels of composition board were cut to fit the inner back and the outer front. These panels were uphol-

stered—first, cotton padding, then muslin stretched and nailed firmly, then the green twill top. The effect of tufting was given by wooden buttons stitched on the twill, the twine drawn through the padding, to come out through small holes made in the wood itself. These tufted panels were nailed

CHAPTER THIRTY-EIGHT

Remodeling Furniture

WITHIN EASY MEMORY, when an old piece of furniture was remodeled it was either because there was no money for a new piece or because someone in the family liked to putter with tools. And almost never was the remodeling done thoughtfully or well. It generally resulted in something that was relegated to a dark corner of the upstairs hall, or otherwise kept out of sight until a new piece could be bought. It was frankly a makeshift.

But all that is changed now. We have discovered the pleasure and profit in remodeling our own discarded pieces of furniture or those we find in second-hand shops. This new interest has brought forth a great deal of ingenuity, and we have become very clever and expert at our renovating and making over.

It appeals specially to people with taste and foresight in the furnishing of their homes—people who see in the outmoded Victorian piece, not just the gingerbread on it, but also the fundamentally simple lines beneath the gingerbread; the lovely wood and the sound construction which can make it an attractive and functional piece in a home of today.

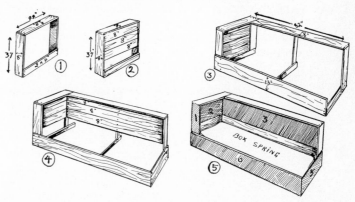

HOME CRAFTSMAN

firmly to the bed frame by lifting aside the buttons and nailing through to the frame under them, then pushing the buttons back into place. The mattress was given a removable slip cover of yellow corduroy; the box cushions are also yellow—but of the twill.

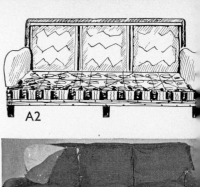

A2

B

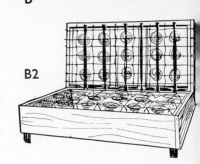

B2

A

A sofa and love seat will fit the average room where two full-sized sofas would not, or if they did, would look over-crowded and heavy. In the two pieces above needed contrast is obtained both in size and covering, and there is a complete lack of monotony in the group. The basic corduroy on both, however, makes them into matching pieces suitable for grouping together.

TRANSFORMING A DISCARDED SOFA—ALSO ONE STILL USABLE BUT BADLY WORN

A couch can be sagging and sunk, but if the original construction was sturdy and the wood of the frame is good, it should be well worth all the time and trouble and new fabric you plan to put into remodeling it. You should be able to start it on another "lifetime" of service. If it is your own couch you plan to re-do, then you know all about it; but if you buy a second-hand piece for remodeling, be sure to inspect the wood in it. You do not need experience to re-model a couch, if you will watch carefully while removing every bit of fabric, padding and webbing. Make mental or pencil notes about them and where they belong so that your new materials can replace them exactly. The two old couches on this page, above, were re-done into the sofa and love seat in the photograph. A originally had been a good piece, but it was fifteen years old and needed a complete interior overhauling. Sketch A-2 shows it stripped, with its springs retied and the front edge of the wire frame strengthened with webbing. The back and seat cushions, which had looked so crushed and shapeless, expanded and fluffed back to their original size once the old fabric was removed and they were allowed to air in their muslin cases. The couch was recovered in pink corduroy, and eleven yards of it were used. The extra padding, some webbing and other necessary

sundries cost very little. B was a regular 72″ sofa, in sturdy condition so that it would stand the cutting down to a 48″ love seat which was planned. If you are considering something similar in the way of a transformation be sure that you work with a sofa whose wood is good, otherwise it may fall apart under the saw. To make this change, all upholstery, filling and even the springs must first be removed. Next, the two arms are removed, and the third step is to cut off 24″ from one end of the bare frame, sawing through it, back and seat. The back and seat, from the piece cut off, are discarded, but the assembly—including the legs—is nailed to the 48″ frame to finish its cut edge. To even up and reinforce both ends, nail over the old frame two new end boards to correspond with the front board. To square off the back, saw off the rounded front ends and reinforce those, too, with new boards cut to match, so that you will have a straight edge all the way around for upholstery. Sketch B-2 shows these changes, with the seat webbed and the springs tied in. Padding, muslin and upholstery followed step by step, and the cushion was remade in box style. The main upholstery was the pink corduroy, but the face of the back, and the top and bottom of the box cushion, are full chintz panels—chrysanthemums on a chartreuse tone.

#1

#2

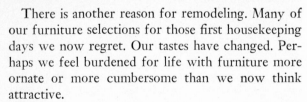

MODERNIZING OVER-LARGE AND CLUMSY UPHOLSTERED CHAIRS

The old chairs on this page represent two of the reasons, we feel certain, that upholstered furniture used to be called "overstuffed" furniture. Of good construction, they needed only to lose some of their bulky curves to be sleek and up-to-the-minute, with not one bit of their comfort sacrificed. Chair #1 had to be stripped to its bare frame to make the structural changes; the small drawings above show the frame as it was, and as it was altered. Alterations consisted of removing the wings, cutting off the top of the back and replacing it with straight wood pieces, then squaring off the legs a bit so they would not interfere with the new skirt. Chair #2 also needed to be stripped to its frame, and the little drawings show it "before" and "after." The back of this one was squared off too, and replaced with a straight wood top. The arms were taken off entirely, and to make up for the strength lost by this an angle iron was attached at the outside joinings of the seat and back. The legs also were pared off a bit.

There is another reason for remodeling. Many of our furniture selections for those first housekeeping days we now regret. Our tastes have changed. Perhaps we feel burdened for life with furniture more ornate or more cumbersome than we now think attractive.

In this case you will find there is a great deal which can be done to improve it. Careful consideration will show you that much of the ornateness can be removed; that the cumbersome effect can be lessened by such tricks as lowering the legs, or removing heavy top railings and galleries, or bleaching the wood.

Remodeling furniture is fun. It brings out the creative strain in us. Women who have learned to wield an efficient tool at home take in their stride such small repairs as tightening a bolt, regluing a drawer, or whittling a new rung for a kitchen chair. And this facility is increasing their interest in changing furniture of good wood into modern and useful pieces.

Hunting in the second-hand shops is fun too—you can now make it profitable. There may even be the joy of finding a good piece, of excellent lines and construction, which will need no remodeling at all. You will only have to wash off the strange fingerprints.

BUREAU INTO CHEST

A sturdy unneeded pine bureau can be turned into two low chests. At the foot of twin beds they are most convenient to have in a bedroom, for they can hold anything from blankets to boots. They also make lovely twin fireside pieces since they are sturdy enough to be used as seats and can hold all sorts of paraphernalia. In a family with two small daughters, each child could have her own bureau, later they would be hope chests. To make these chests, a bureau like the one shown is sawed in two—leaving the base of the second drawer on the top half. A new top goes on the bottom half, and a new base on the top two drawers. Use lumber the thickness of that in the bureau, and stain to match.

DOUBLE DUTY FROM A SHABBY OTTOMAN

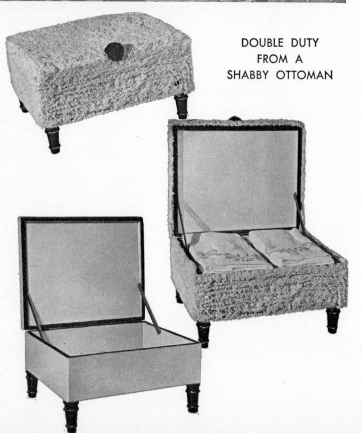

The dismal-looking ottoman shown directly above had only a sturdy, hardwood frame to recommend it—the inside upholstery was as hopeless as its cover had predicted. This is how it was remodeled to remain an ottoman—but an ottoman with a double purpose in life. Hollowed out, as illustrated, it provides ample and convenient storage space. Its entire filling was scooped out and a wooden bottom nailed on. A cover was made for it and hinged on, and the whole frame (legs excepted) was given two coats of white paint. The inside edges of both the cover and the "box" were painted burgundy to match the cover's supporting tape and the tassel. The upholstery was made from a large, white shaggy bath mat. The piece for the top was cut out first, then the balance of the mat was cut in eight-inch strips and these were sewn together to make a band nearly eight feet long, for the sides. Every cut edge was promptly bound with inch-wide white cotton tape to prevent raveling and to provide a lasting edge for tacking and retacking. Since no padding is required under it, the cover can be easily whipped off and on for the occasional washings it will need. This piece, covered with a more formal material—perhaps a plain quilted chintz—would be smart and useful in any room in the house.

AN OUT-DATED WASHSTAND BECOMES A SMART CABINET

An old and no-longer-needed washstand—shorn of its rails and towel bars, its heavy coat of varnish or paint removed—can be a quite charming addition to your home today. It can become a desk, a bookcase or a radio cabinet—and can well be the conversation piece of the room. The mahogany washstand shown above required relatively little remodeling. The lower left corner got a new dowel to steady and firm it like new; its hanging door was removed altogether. For its misfit marble top an inch molding all around the top four sides was substituted. The whole piece was scrubbed with strong soap suds. The top was stained to match and an all-over waxing job was done on it. One drawer pull had lost a brass plaque—so all were taken off to make the finished effect uniform.

DESK MADE FROM A CHEST OF DRAWERS

A chest-desk in any room is a useful piece of furniture, but it is something special in a small guest room where it provides drawer space as well as a writing spot. The steps needed to insert the writing shelf in the bureau are clear in the photographs. After removing the top, put wood strips around the back and two sides of the top of the frame, to provide space for the sliding shelf. Cut slots in the sides of the bureau for the pull-out supports of the shelf, and attach a small top to the back of each to keep it from coming out altogether. Do the same to prevent the writing shelf from coming out completely—that is, screw a metal knob on each side of the back end. Select a bureau which will give you a writing height of from 28½″ to 30″, which is about average. Almost any bureau can be adjusted to get this writing height by lowering the base, cutting down the legs, or taking them off altogether--or, in reverse, adding base or legs.

Traditional Decorating Terms

Apron. Wood strip, used below seat or top to connect furniture legs, or as facing below window sill.

Arcaded Panel. Decorated by two small columns supporting each form.

Armoire. (Fr.) Wardrobe (clothes cupboard).

Aubusson. Fine French tapestries; later, tapestry-weave rugs.

Axminster. Pile carpet-weave, originating Axminster, England.

Ball Foot. Globular in form, attached to leg by slender ankle.

Baluster (Banister). Turned or square upright support for rail of balustrade; furniture splat with outlines of baluster.

Banding. Narrow trimming inlay, contrasting in color or grain.

Baroque. Italian style following Renaissance; used as adjective to mean sweeping curves, theatrical effect, bold detail.

Beading. Small molding with beadlike design.

Beauvais. Fine tapestries made in Beauvais, France, from 1662.

Biscuit Ware. Pottery with thin glaze (or none), only one firing.

Block-Front. 18th century treatment of desks, etc., with central front section like a panel sunk between slightly projecting sections.

Bolection. Series of projecting moldings; projecting panel.

Bracket Foot. Cabinet support (not for chairs); corner edge straight, inner edge curved (in French styles both edges curved).

Broken Pediment. Triangular pediment over doors, windows, cabinets, etc., with peak cut away and lines at each side straight, or curved in swan-neck or deep scrolls (*see* PEDIMENTS)

Bulbous Form. Renaissance melon-shaped turning on legs.

Bun Foot. Slightly flattened ball, frequent in William and Mary styles.

Cabriole. Conventionalized furniture leg resembling animal's leg; knee, plain or carved; foot, usually claw-and-ball, club, etc.

Chinoiseries. (Fr.) Occidental designs based on Chinese subjects, used for decorative motifs in mid-18th century styles.

Claw-and-Ball Foot. Ball, grasped by bird's claw, from Chinese dragon's claw grasping great pearl; used with cabriole leg.

Club Foot. Round, flat pad shape curving out from ankle.

Console. (Fr.) Narrow table against wall, or shelf with supports.

Dado. Lower part of wall when marked off by panel, moldings or chair-rail, or otherwise treated differently from upper section.

Domino Wallpaper. Early type of paper grained to imitate marble.

Drake Foot. Carved conventionalized foot, like ribbed foot.

Drum Table. Round table, small drawers set in solid band below top.

Dutch Foot. Same as pad.

Fiddle-back. Having splats shaped like violin or "fiddle."

Fret. Interlaced ornamental work, carved on flat surfaces or pierced for galleries, chairbacks or aprons.

Frieze. Decorative strip at top of wall, wider than cornice or border.

Gallery. Ornamental railing along edge of table, desk, etc.

Galloon. Narrow, closely woven braid for fabric trimming.

Gimp. Flat, narrow fabric trimming, usually with wire or cord.

Girandole. (Fr.) Elaborate wall candle-holder, with branching brackets, often combined with mirror; popular 18th century France.

Gobelins. French tapestries famous for elaborate patterns.

Hoof Foot. Carved foot of doe (or deer), used with cabriole leg.

Japanning. 18th century finish for wood and metalwork, using colored shellac with raised decoration painted in gold and colors.

Klismos. Type of Greek chair with flaring, curved legs, and concave curved back rail.

Ladder-back. Chairback with horizontal rails, ladder effect.

Linenfold. Gothic panel decoration design like folds in linen.

Lowboy. Low chest of drawers mounted on four legs.

Lozenge. Another name for conventional diamond-shaped motif.

Medallion. Decorative frame, oval in circle, surrounding motif.

Neo-classic. Designating revival of classic taste in art; usually applied to revival following 18th century discovery of Pompeii.

Oriel (Window). Window built out from wall, on bracket support.

Pad Foot. End of cabriole leg flaring into flat pad shape.

Panel. Limited surface area set off by frame or some difference in appearance from background.

Parcel-Gilding. Details of carvings picked out in gold.

Pargework (Pargetry). Relief decoration of stucco or ornamental plaster applied to flat surface.

Parquet (Parquetry). Flooring of narrow wood strips laid in geometric or similar patterns, sometimes in colors.

Patina. Mellow surface appearance assumed by wood or other materials as result of long exposure or polishing.

Paw Foot. Carved paw of animal (dog, lion, etc.) with cabriole leg.

Pediment. Flat triangular space between roof lines at end of building; now often applied to over-doors, cabinet tops, etc.

Pewter. Dull gray alloy of tin with some other metal.

Plaque. Small decorated applied panel of metal, pottery, etc.

Porcelain. Pottery with translucent body, transparent glaze.

Rococo. Decorative style developed from and following Baroque; extreme of this style means over-ornamentation.

Savonnerie. French hand-woven rugs of fine wool, high pile.

Scallop Shell. Decorative motif; concave shell, semicircular, with ridges radiating from small ornamental base.

Scroll. Spiral line used in decorative forms—*Flemish, S-Scroll, C-Scroll;* sometimes roll of parchment as decorative motif.

Serpentine Curve. Undulating line in furniture fronts; bow-shaped in chair tops, with ends straight or Cupid's bow shape.

Singeries. (Fr.) Louis XV decorative motif—monkeys at play.

Snake. (Serpent) Foot. End of cabriole, flaring into snake's head.

Spade Foot. Square tapering foot used with straight legs, slight projection to mark separation-point between foot and leg.

Spindle. Long thin rod, plain as in Windsor chairback or with ornamental turned moldings or baluster shapes.

Spiral Leg. Leg or other support with rope-like twisted carving forming groove or fluting winding down its length.

Splat. Broad, flat upright support in middle of chairback.

Splay (Splayed). Spread outward obliquely.

Split Spindle. Long slim rod, turned and molded, then split down center, with flat side of each piece applied to furniture.

Squab. Thickly stuffed loose cushion, especially one used for seat of sofa, couch, chair, or stool.

Strapwork. Decorative design of narrow fillet or band with crossed, folded, or interlaced carved ornament.

Swag. Cloth draped in looped shape of garland; wood or metal decoration resembling such cloth festoons.

Tambour (Fr.) Word for *drum*, applied to drumlike furniture form.

Tester. Flat Canopy above furniture, as with four-post bed.

Term-shaped. Often refers to ornate leg or other furniture support shaped like small four-sided pillar, tapering toward bottom.

Toile-de-Jouy. (Fr.) Cotton cloth made in Jouy, France, by hand-block process; repeat motifs in colors on white ground.

Tôle. (Fr.) Painted tin used for accessories in informal styles.

Trumpet Leg. Popular William and Mary shape; sometimes pear-bulb, or combined with inverted-cup decoration and bun foot.

Tudor Arch. Slightly pointed curved arch of early Renaissance, especially characteristic of Tudor English designs.

Valance. Horizontal decorative trimming over top of draperies.

Wainscot Chair. Early chair in England and America, with straight carved wood back like a wall panel.

Wilton. Fine woolen carpet, originating 1700 in Wilton, England.

Index

Page numbers in bold face type indicate the main entry for a subject.

434